THE LOEB CLASSICAL LIBRARY

EDITED BY

E. CAPPS, Ph.D., LL.D.   T. E. PAGE, Litt.D.   W. H. D. ROUSE, Litt.D.

PLUTARCH'S LIVES

V

PLUTARCH'S LIVES.

PLUTARCH'S LIVES

WITH AN ENGLISH TRANSLATION BY
BERNADOTTE PERRIN

IN ELEVEN VOLUMES

V

AGESILAUS AND POMPEY
PELOPIDAS AND MARCELLUS

LONDON : WILLIAM HEINEMANN
NEW YORK : G. P. PUTNAM'S SONS

MCMXVII

PREFATORY NOTE

As in the preceding volumes of this series, agreement between the Sintenis (Teubner, 1873–1875) and Bekker (Tauchnitz, 1855–1857) editions of the *Parallel Lives* has been taken as the basis for the text. Any preference of one to the other, and any departure from both, have been indicated. An abridged account of the manuscripts of Plutarch may be found in the Introduction to the first volume. Of the *Lives* presented in this volume, the *Agesilaüs* and *Pompey* are contained in the Codex Sangermanensis (S^g) and the Codex Seitenstettensis (S), and in a few instances weight has been given to readings from the Codex Matritensis (M^a), on the authority of the collations of Charles Graux, as published in *Bursians Jahresbericht* (1884). No attempt has been made, naturally, to furnish either a diplomatic text or a full critical apparatus. For these, the reader must still be referred to the major edition of Sintenis (Leipzig, 1839–1846, 4 voll., 8vo). The reading which follows the colon in the critical notes is that of the Teubner Sintenis, and also, unless

PREFATORY NOTE

otherwise stated in the note, of the Tauchnitz Bekker.

All the standard translations of the *Lives* have been carefully compared and utilized, including that of the *Pompey* by Professor Long.

B. PERRIN.

NEW HAVEN, CONNECTICUT, U.S.A.
March, 1917.

CONTENTS

ORDER OF THE PARALLEL LIVES IN THIS EDITION IN THE CHRONOLOGICAL SEQUENCE OF THE GREEK LIVES.

THE TRADITIONAL ORDER OF THE PARALLEL LIVES.

(1) Theseus and Romulus.

(2) Lycurgus and Numa.

(3) Solon and Publicola.

(4) Themistocles and Camillus.

(5) Pericles and Fabius Maximus.

(6) Alcibiades and Coriolanus.

(7) Timoleon and Aemilius Paulus.

(8) Pelopidas and Marcellus.

(9) Aristides and Cato the Elder.

(10) Philopoemen and Flamininus.

(11) Pyrrhus and Caius Marius.

(12) Lysander and Sulla.

(13) Cimon and Lucullus.

(14) Nicias and Crassus.

(15) Sertorius and Eumenes.

(16) Agesilaüs and Pompey.

(17) Alexander and Julius Caesar.

(18) Phocion and Cato the Younger.

(19) Agis and Cleomenes, and Tiberius and Caius Gracchus.

(20) Demosthenes and Cicero.

(21) Demetrius and Antony.

(22) Dion and Brutus.

. . . .

(23) Aratus.

(24) Artaxerxes.

(25) Galba.

(26) Otho.

AGESILAUS

I. ARCHIDAMUS, the son of Zeuxidamas, after an illustrious reign over the Lacedaemonians, left behind him a son, Agis, by Lampido, a woman of honourable family; and a much younger son, Agesilaüs, by Eupolia, the daughter of Melesippidas. The kingdom belonged to Agis by law, and it was thought that Agesilaüs would pass his life in a private station. He was therefore given the so-called "agoge," or course of public training in Sparta, which, although austere in its mode of life and full of hardships, educated the youth to obedience. For this reason it was, we are told, that Simonides gave Sparta the epithet of "man-subduing," since more than in any other state her customs made her citizens obedient to the laws and tractable, like horses that are broken in while yet they are colts. From this compulsory training the law exempts the heirs-apparent to the throne. But Agesilaüs was singular in this also, that he had been educated to obey before he came to command. For this reason he was much more in harmony with his subjects than any of the kings; to the commanding and kingly traits which were his by nature there had been added by his public training those of popularity and kindliness.

II. While he was among the so-called "bands" of boys who were reared together, he had as his

3

ἐκπλαγέντα μάλιστα τῷ κοσμίῳ τῆς φύσεως
αὐτοῦ. φιλονεικότατος γὰρ ὢν καὶ θυμοειδέ-
στατος ἐν τοῖς νέοις καὶ πάντα πρωτεύειν βουλόμενος, καὶ τὸ σφοδρὸν ἔχων καὶ ῥαγδαῖον ἄμαχον
καὶ δυσεκβίαστον, εὐπειθείᾳ πάλιν αὖ καὶ πρᾳό-
τητι τοιοῦτος ἦν οἷος φόβῳ μηδέν, αἰσχύνῃ δὲ
πάντα ποιεῖν τὰ προσταττόμενα, καὶ τοῖς ψόγοις
ἀλγύνεσθαι μᾶλλον ἢ τοὺς πόνους βαρύνεσθαι·
2 τὴν δὲ τοῦ σκέλους πήρωσιν ἥ τε ὥρα τοῦ σώματος ἀνθοῦντος ἐπέκρυπτε, καὶ τὸ ῥᾳδίως φέρειν
καὶ ἱλαρῶς τὸ τοιοῦτο, παίζοντα καὶ σκώπτοντα
πρῶτον ἑαυτόν, οὐ μικρὸν ἦν ἐπανόρθωμα τοῦ
πάθους, ἀλλὰ καὶ τὴν φιλοτιμίαν ἐκδηλοτέραν
ἐποίει, πρὸς μηδένα πόνον μηδὲ πρᾶξιν ἀπαγορεύοντος αὐτοῦ διὰ τὴν χωλότητα. τῆς δὲ
μορφῆς εἰκόνα μὲν οὐκ ἔχομεν (αὐτὸς γὰρ οὐκ
ἠθέλησεν, ἀλλὰ καὶ ἀποθνήσκων ἀπεῖπε " μήτε
πλαστὰν μήτε μιμηλὰν " τινα ποιήσασθαι τοῦ
σώματος εἰκόνα), λέγεται δὲ μικρός τε γενέσθαι
3 καὶ τὴν ὄψιν εὐκαταφρόνητος· ἡ δὲ ἱλαρότης καὶ
τὸ εὔθυμον ἐν ἅπαντι καιρῷ καὶ παιγνιῶδες,
ἀχθεινὸν δὲ καὶ τραχὺ μηδέποτε μήτε φωνῇ μήτε
ὄψει, τῶν καλῶν καὶ ὡραίων ἐρασμιώτερον αὐτὸν
ἄχρι γήρως παρεῖχεν. ὡς δὲ Θεόφραστος ἱστορεῖ,
τὸν Ἀρχίδαμον ἐζημίωσαν οἱ ἔφοροι γήμαντα
γυναῖκα μικράν· " Οὐ γὰρ βασιλεῖς," ἔφασαν,
" ἄμμιν, ἀλλὰ βασιλείδια γεννάσει."

III. Βασιλεύοντος δὲ Ἄγιδος ἧκεν Ἀλκιβιάδης
ἐκ Σικελίας φυγὰς εἰς Λακεδαίμονα· καὶ χρόνον
οὔπω πολὺν ἐν τῇ πόλει διάγων, αἰτίαν ἔσχε τῇ

59

lover Lysander,[1] who was smitten particularly with his
native decorum. For although he was contentious
and high-spirited beyond his fellows, wishing to be
first in all things, and having a vehemence and fury
which none could contend with or overwhelm, on the
other hand he had such a readiness to obey and such
gentleness, that he did whatever was enjoined
upon him, not at all from a sense of fear, but always
from a sense of honour, and was more distressed
by censure than he was oppressed by hardships. As
for his deformity, the beauty of his person in its
youthful prime covered this from sight, while the
ease and gaiety with which he bore such a
misfortune, being first to jest and joke about himself,
went far towards rectifying it. Indeed, his lameness
brought his ambition into clearer light, since it led
him to decline no hardship and no enterprise
whatever. We have no likeness of him (for he
himself would not consent to one, and even when he
lay dying forbade the making of "either statue or
picture" of his person), but he is said to have been
a little man of unimposing presence. And yet his
gaiety and good spirits in every crisis, and his
raillery, which was never offensive or harsh either in
word or look, made him more lovable, down to his
old age, than the young and beautiful. But
according to Theophrastus, Archidamus was fined
by the ephors for marrying a little woman, "For
she will bear us," they said, "not kings, but
kinglets."

III. It was during the reign of Agis that
Alcibiades came from Sicily as an exile to Sparta,
and he had not been long in the city when he
incurred the charge of illicit intercourse with Timaea,

---

[1] Cf. *Lycurgus*, xvii. 1 ; *Lysander*, xxii. 3.

γυναικὶ τοῦ βασιλέως, Τιμαίᾳ, συνεῖναι. καὶ τὸ
γεννηθὲν ἐξ αὐτῆς παιδάριον οὐκ ἔφη γινώσκειν
ὁ Ἆγις, ἀλλ' ἐξ Ἀλκιβιάδου γεγονέναι. τοῦτο
δὲ οὐ πάνυ δυσκόλως τὴν Τιμαίαν ἐνεγκεῖν φησι
Δοῦρις, ἀλλὰ καὶ ψιθυρίζουσαν οἴκοι πρὸς τὰς
εἰλωτίδας Ἀλκιβιάδην τὸ παιδίον, οὐ Λεωτυχί-
2 δην, καλεῖν· καὶ μέντοι καὶ τὸν Ἀλκιβιάδην
αὐτὸν οὐ πρὸς ὕβριν τῇ Τιμαίᾳ φάναι πλησιάζειν,
ἀλλὰ φιλοτιμούμενον βασιλεύεσθαι Σπαρτιάτας
ὑπὸ τῶν ἐξ ἑαυτοῦ γεγονότων. διὰ ταῦτα μὲν
τῆς Λακεδαίμονος Ἀλκιβιάδης ὑπεξῆλθε, φοβηθεὶς τὸν Ἆγιν· ὁ δὲ παῖς τὸν μὲν ἄλλον χρόνον
ὕποπτος ἦν τῷ Ἄγιδι, καὶ γνησίου τιμὴν οὐκ
εἶχε παρ' αὐτῷ, νοσοῦντι δὲ προσπεσὼν καὶ
δακρύων ἔπεισεν υἱὸν ἀποφῆναι πολλῶν ἐναντίον.

3 Οὐ μὴν ἀλλὰ τελευτήσαντος τοῦ Ἄγιδος ὁ
Λύσανδρος, ἤδη κατανεναυμαχηκὼς Ἀθηναίους
καὶ μέγιστον ἐν Σπάρτῃ δυνάμενος, τὸν Ἀγησίλαον ἐπὶ τὴν βασιλείαν προῆγεν, ὡς οὐ προσή-
κουσαν ὄντι νόθῳ τῷ Λεωτυχίδῃ. πολλοὶ δὲ
καὶ τῶν ἄλλων πολιτῶν, διὰ τὴν ἀρετὴν[1] τοῦ
Ἀγησιλάου καὶ τὸ συντετράφθαι καὶ μετεσχη-
κέναι τῆς ἀγωγῆς, ἐφιλοτιμοῦντο καὶ συνέπραττον
αὐτῷ προθύμως. ἦν δὲ Διοπείθης ἀνὴρ χρησμολό-
γος ἐν Σπάρτῃ, μαντειῶν τε παλαιῶν ὑπόπλεως
καὶ δοκῶν περὶ τὰ θεῖα σοφὸς εἶναι καὶ περιττός.
4 οὗτος οὐκ ἔφη θεμιτὸν εἶναι χωλὸν γενέσθαι τῆς
Λακεδαίμονος βασιλέα, καὶ χρησμὸν ἐν τῇ δίκῃ
τοιοῦτον ἀνεγίνωσκε·

Φράζεο δή, Σπάρτη, καίπερ μεγάλαυχος ἐοῦσα,
μὴ σέθεν ἀρτίποδος βλάστῃ χωλὴ βασιλεία·

[1] διὰ τὴν ἀρετὴν Coraës and Bekker, after Bryan : τὴν
ἀρετήν.

6

the wife of the king. The child, too, that was born
of her, Agis refused to recognize as his own,
declaring that Alcibiades was its father. Duris says
that Timaea was not very much disturbed at this,
but in whispers to her Helot maids at home
actually called the child Alcibiades, not Leotychides;
moreover, that Alcibiades himself also declared that
he had not approached Timaea out of wanton passion,
but because he was ambitious to have the Spartans
reigned over by his descendants.[1] On this account
Alcibiades withdrew from Sparta, being in fear of
Agis; and the boy was always an object of suspicion
to Agis, and was not honoured by him as legitimate.
But when the king lay sick, the supplications and
tears of Leotychides prevailed upon him to declare
him his son in the presence of many witnesses.

Notwithstanding this, after the death of Agis,[2]
Lysander, who by this time had subdued the
Athenians at sea and was a man of the greatest
influence in Sparta, tried to advance Agesilaüs to the
throne, on the plea that Leotychides was a bastard
and had no claim upon it. Many of the other citizens
also, owing to the excellence of Agesilaüs and the fact
that he had been reared with them under the common
restraints of the public training, warmly espoused
the plan of Lysander and co-operated with him. But
there was a diviner in Sparta, named Diopeithes, who
was well supplied with ancient prophecies, and was
thought to be eminently wise in religious matters.
This man declared it contrary to the will of Heaven
that a lame man should be king of Sparta, and cited
at the trial of the case the following oracle:—

"Bethink thee now, O Sparta, though thou art
very glorious, lest from thee, sound of foot, there

[1] Cf. *Alcibiades*, xxiii. 7 f.   [2] In 398 B.C.

δηρὸν γὰρ νοῦσοί σε κατασχήσουσιν ἄελπτοι
φθισιβρότου τ᾽ ἐπὶ κῦμα κυλινδόμενον πολέ-
μοιο.

5 πρὸς ταῦτα Λύσανδρος ἔλεγεν ὡς, εἰ πάνυ φο-
βοῖντο τὸν χρησμὸν οἱ Σπαρτιᾶται, φυλακτέον
αὐτοῖς εἴη τὸν Λεωτυχίδην· οὐ γὰρ εἰ προσ-
πταίσας τις τὸν πόδα βασιλεύοι, τῷ θεῷ διαφέρειν, ἀλλ᾽ εἰ μὴ γνήσιος ὢν μηδὲ Ἡρακλείδης,
τοῦτο τὴν χωλὴν εἶναι βασιλείαν. ὁ δὲ Ἀγησίλαος ἔφη καὶ τὸν Ποσειδῶ καταμαρτυρεῖν τοῦ
Λεωτυχίδου τὴν νοθείαν, ἐκβαλόντα σεισμῷ τοῦ
θαλάμου τὸν Ἀγιν· ἀπ᾽ ἐκείνου δὲ πλέον ἢ δέκα
μηνῶν διελθόντων γενέσθαι τὸν Λεωτυχίδην.

IV. Οὕτω δὲ καὶ διὰ ταῦτα βασιλεὺς ἀποδειχθεὶς ὁ Ἀγησίλαος εὐθὺς εἶχε καὶ τὰ χρήματα τοῦ Ἄγιδος, ὡς νόθον ἀπελάσας τὸν Λεωτυχίδην. ὁρῶν δὲ τοὺς ἀπὸ μητρὸς οἰκείους
ἐπιεικεῖς μὲν ὄντας, ἰσχυρῶς δὲ πενομένους, ἀπέ-
νειμεν αὐτοῖς τὰ ἡμίσεα τῶν χρημάτων, εὔνοιαν
ἑαυτῷ καὶ δόξαν ἀντὶ φθόνου καὶ δυσμενείας
ἐπὶ τῇ κληρονομίᾳ κατασκευαζόμενος. ὃ δὲ
φησιν ὁ Ξενοφῶν, ὅτι πάντα τῇ πατρίδι πειθό-
μενος ἴσχυε πλεῖστον, ὥστε ποιεῖν ὃ βούλοιτο,
2 τοιοῦτόν ἐστι. τῶν ἐφόρων ἦν τότε καὶ τῶν
γερόντων τὸ μέγιστον ἐν τῇ πολιτείᾳ κράτος,
ὧν οἱ μὲν ἐνιαυτὸν ἄρχουσι μόνον, οἱ δὲ γέροντες
διὰ βίου ταύτην ἔχουσι τὴν τιμήν, ἐπὶ τῷ μὴ
πάντα τοῖς βασιλεῦσιν ἐξεῖναι συνταχθέντες,

spring a maimed royalty; for long will unexpected
toils oppress thee, and onward-rolling billows of
man-destroying war."

To this Lysander answered that, in case the
Spartans stood in great fear of the oracle, they must
be on their guard against Leotychides; for it
mattered not to the god that one who halted in his
gait should be king, but if one who was not lawfully
begotten, nor even a descendant of Heracles, should
be king, this was what the god meant by the
"maimed royalty." And Agesilaüs declared that
Poseidon also had borne witness to the bastardy of
Leotychides, for he had cast Agis forth from his bed-
chamber by an earthquake, and after this more than
ten months elapsed before Leotychides was born.[1]

IV. In this way, and for these reasons, Agesilaüs
was appointed king, and straightway enjoyed
possession of the estates of Agis as well as his throne,
after expelling Leotychides as a bastard. But seeing
that his kinsmen on his mother's side, though worthy
folk, were excessively poor, he distributed among
them the half of his estates, thereby making his
inheritance yield him good-will and reputation
instead of envy and hatred. As for Xenophon's
statement [2] that by obeying his country in everything he won very great power, so that he did what
he pleased, the case is as follows. At that time the
ephors and the senators had the greatest power in
the state, of whom the former hold office for a year
only, while the senators enjoy their dignity for life,
their offices having been instituted to restrain the
power of the kings, as I have said in my Life of

---

[1] Cf. *Alcibiades*, xxiii. 8; *Lysander*, xxii. 3 ff.; Xenophon,
Hellenica, iii. 3, 2.   [2] Xenophon's *Agesilaüs*, vi. 4.

ὡς ἐν τοῖς περὶ Λυκούργου γέγραπται. διὸ καὶ
πατρικήν τινα πρὸς αὐτοὺς ἀπὸ τοῦ παλαιοῦ
διετέλουν εὐθὺς οἱ βασιλεῖς φιλονεικίαν καὶ δια-
3 φορὰν παραλαμβάνοντες. ὁ δὲ Ἀγησίλαος ἐπὶ
τὴν ἐναντίαν ὁδὸν ἦλθε, καὶ τὸ πολεμεῖν καὶ
τὸ προσκρούειν αὐτοῖς ἐάσας ἐθεράπευε, πάσης
μὲν ἀπ' ἐκείνων πράξεως ἀρχόμενος, εἰ δὲ κλη-
θείη, θᾶττον ἢ βάδην ἐπειγόμενος, ὁσάκις δὲ
τύχοι καθήμενος ἐν τῷ βασιλικῷ θώκῳ καὶ χρη-
ματίζων, ἐπιοῦσι τοῖς ἐφόροις ὑπεξανίστατο, τῶν
δ' εἰς τὴν γερουσίαν ἀεὶ καταταττομένων ἑκάστῳ 598
4 χλαῖναν ἔπεμπε καὶ βοῦν ἀριστεῖον. ἐκ δὲ
τούτων τιμᾶν δοκῶν καὶ μεγαλύνειν τὸ ἀξίωμα
τῆς ἐκείνων ἀρχῆς, ἐλάνθανεν αὔξων τὴν ἑαυτοῦ δύναμιν καὶ τῇ βασιλείᾳ προστιθέμενος
μέγεθος ἐκ τῆς πρὸς αὐτὸν εὐνοίας συγχωρού-
μενον.

V. Ἐν δὲ ταῖς πρὸς τοὺς ἄλλους πολίτας
ὁμιλίαις ἐχθρὸς ἦν ἀμεμπτότερος ἢ φίλος. τοὺς
μὲν γὰρ ἐχθροὺς ἀδίκως οὐκ ἔβλαπτε, τοῖς δὲ
φίλοις καὶ τὰ μὴ δίκαια συνέπραττε. καὶ τοὺς
μὲν ἐχθροὺς ᾐσχύνετο μὴ τιμᾶν κατορθοῦντας,
τοὺς δὲ φίλους οὐκ ἐδύνατο ψέγειν ἁμαρτάνον-
τας, ἀλλὰ καὶ βοηθῶν ἠγάλλετο καὶ συνεξα-
μαρτάνων αὐτοῖς· οὐδὲν γὰρ ᾤετο τῶν φιλικῶν
2 ὑπουργημάτων αἰσχρὸν εἶναι. τοῖς δ' αὖ δια-
φόροις πταίσασι πρῶτος συναχθόμενος καὶ δεηθεῖσι συμπράττων προθύμως ἐδημαγώγει καὶ
προσήγετο πάντας. ὁρῶντες οὖν οἱ ἔφοροι ταῦτα
καὶ φοβούμενοι τὴν δύναμιν ἐζημίωσαν αὐτόν,
αἰτίαν ὑπειπόντες ὅτι τοὺς κοινοὺς πολίτας ἰδίους
κτᾶται.

Lycurgus.[1] Therefore from the outset, and from
generation to generation, the kings were traditionally
at feud and variance with them.   But Agesilaüs took
the opposite course.   Instead of colliding and fighting
with them, he courted their favour, winning their
support before setting out on any undertaking; and
whenever he was invited to meet them, hastening to
them on the run.   If ever the ephors visited him
when he was seated in his royal chair and administer-
ing justice, he rose in their honour; and as men
were from time to time made members of the senate,
he would send each one a cloak and an ox as a mark
of honour.   Consequently, while he was thought to
be honouring and exalting the dignity of their office,
he was unawares increasing his own influence and
adding to the power of the king a greatness which
was conceded out of good-will towards him.

V. In his dealings with the rest of the citizens he
was less blame-worthy as an enemy than as a friend;
for he would not injure his enemies without just
cause, but joined his friends even in their unjust
practices.   And whereas he was ashamed not to
honour his enemies when they did well, he could not
bring himself to censure his friends when they did
amiss, but actually prided himself on aiding them and
sharing in their misdeeds.   For he thought no aid
disgraceful that was given to a friend.   But if, on the
other hand, his adversaries stumbled and fell, he was
first to sympathize with them and give them zealous
aid if they desired it, and so won the hearts and
the allegiance of all.   The ephors, accordingly, seeing
this, and fearing his power, laid a fine upon him,
alleging as a reason that he made the citizens his own,
who should be the common property of the state.

[1] Chapters v. 6 f.; vii. 1 f.

3   Καθάπερ γὰρ οἱ φυσικοὶ τὸ νεῖκος οἴονται
καὶ τὴν ἔριν, εἰ τῶν ὅλων ἐξαιρεθείη, στῆναι
μὲν ἂν τὰ οὐράνια, παύσασθαι δὲ πάντων[1] τὴν
γένεσιν καὶ κίνησιν ὑπὸ τῆς πρὸς πάντα πάντων
ἁρμονίας, οὕτως ἔοικεν ὁ Λακωνικὸς νομοθέτης
ὑπέκκαυμα τῆς ἀρετῆς ἐμβαλεῖν εἰς τὴν πολιτείαν τὸ φιλότιμον καὶ φιλόνεικον, ἀεί τινα τοῖς
ἀγαθοῖς διαφορὰν καὶ ἅμιλλαν εἶναι πρὸς ἀλλήλους βουλόμενος, τὴν δὲ ἀνθυπείκουσαν τῷ
ἀνελέγκτῳ χάριν ἀργὴν καὶ ἀναγώνιστον οὖσαν
4   οὐκ ὀρθῶς ὁμόνοιαν λέγεσθαι. τοῦτο δὲ ἀμέλει
συνεωρακέναι καὶ τὸν Ὅμηρον οἴονταί τινες· οὐ
γὰρ ἂν τὸν Ἀγαμέμνονα ποιῆσαι χαίροντα τοῦ
Ὀδυσσέως καὶ τοῦ Ἀχιλλέως εἰς λοιδορίαν
προαχθέντων "ἐκπάγλοις ἐπέεσσιν," εἰ μὴ μέγα
τοῖς κοινοῖς ἀγαθὸν ἐνόμιζεν εἶναι τὸν πρὸς ἀλλήλους ζῆλον καὶ τὴν διαφορὰν τῶν ἀρίστων.
ταῦτα μὲν οὖν οὐκ ἂν οὕτως τις ἁπλῶς συγχω-
ρήσειεν· αἱ γὰρ ὑπερβολαὶ τῶν φιλονεικιῶν χαλε-
παὶ ταῖς πόλεσι καὶ μεγάλους κινδύνους ἔχουσι.

VI. Τοῦ δὲ Ἀγησιλάου τὴν βασιλείαν νεωστὶ
παρειληφότος, ἀπήγγελλόν τινες ἐξ Ἀσίας ἥκον-
τες ὡς ὁ Περσῶν βασιλεὺς παρασκευάζοιτο
μεγάλῳ στόλῳ Λακεδαιμονίους ἐκβαλεῖν τῆς
θαλάσσης. ὁ δὲ Λύσανδρος ἐπιθυμῶν αὖθις
εἰς Ἀσίαν ἀποσταλῆναι καὶ βοηθῆσαι τοῖς
φίλοις, οὓς αὐτὸς μὲν ἄρχοντας καὶ κυρίους
τῶν πόλεων ἀπέλιπε, κακῶς δὲ χρώμενοι καὶ
βιαίως τοῖς πράγμασιν ἐξέπιπτον ὑπὸ τῶν πολιτῶν καὶ ἀπέθνησκον, ἀνέπεισε τὸν Ἀγησίλαον
ἐπιθέσθαι τῇ στρατείᾳ καὶ προπολεμῆσαι τῆς

---

[1] πάντων Coraës and Bekker have πάντως (*utterly*), an
early, anonymous correction.

Natural philosophers are of the opinion that, if strife and discord should be banished from the universe, the heavenly bodies would stand still, and all generation and motion would cease in consequence of the general harmony. And so the Spartan law-giver seems to have introduced the spirit of ambition and contention into his civil polity as an incentive to virtue, desiring that good citizens should always be somewhat at variance and in conflict with one another, and deeming that complaisance which weakly yields without debate, which knows no effort and no struggle, to be wrongly called concord. And some think that Homer also was clearly of this mind; for he would not have represented Agamemnon as pleased when Odysseus and Achilles were carried away into abuse of one another with " frightful words," [1] if he had not thought the general interests likely to profit by the mutual rivalry and quarrelling of the chieftains. This principle, however, must not be accepted without some reservations; for excessive rivalries are injurious to states, and productive of great perils.

VI. Agesilaüs had but recently come to the throne, when tidings were brought from Asia that the Persian king was preparing a great armament with which to drive the Lacedaemonians from the sea. Now, Lysander was eager to be sent again into Asia, and to aid his friends there. These he had left governors and masters of the cities, but owing to their unjust and violent conduct of affairs, they were being driven out by the citizens, and even put to death. He therefore persuaded Agesilaüs to undertake the expedition and make war in behalf of

---

[1] *Odyssey*, viii. 75 ff.

Ἑλλάδος, ἀπωτάτω διαβάντα καὶ φθάσαντα τὴν
2 τοῦ βαρβάρου παρασκευήν. ἅμα δὲ τοῖς ἐν
Ἀσίᾳ φίλοις ἐπέστελλε πέμπειν εἰς Λακεδαίμονα
καὶ στρατηγὸν Ἀγησίλαον αἰτεῖσθαι. παρελθὼν οὖν εἰς τὸ πλῆθος Ἀγησίλαος ἀνεδέξατο
τὸν πόλεμον, εἰ δοῖεν αὐτῷ τριάκοντα μὲν ἡγεμόνας καὶ συμβούλους Σπαρτιάτας, νεοδαμώδεις
δὲ λογάδας δισχιλίους, τὴν δὲ συμμαχικὴν εἰς
3 ἑξακισχιλίους δύναμιν. συμπράττοντος δὲ τοῦ
Λυσάνδρου πάντα προθύμως ἐψηφίσαντο, καὶ
τὸν Ἀγησίλαον ἐξέπεμπον εὐθὺς [1] ἔχοντα τοὺς
τριάκοντα Σπαρτιάτας, ὧν ὁ Λύσανδρος ἦν πρῶτος,[2] οὐ διὰ τὴν ἑαυτοῦ δόξαν καὶ δύναμιν μόνον,
ἀλλὰ καὶ διὰ τὴν Ἀγησιλάου φιλίαν, ᾧ μεῖζον
ἐδόκει τῆς βασιλείας ἀγαθὸν διαπεπρᾶχθαι τὴν
στρατηγίαν ἐκείνην.

4 Ἀθροιζομένης δὲ τῆς δυνάμεως εἰς Γεραιστόν,
αὐτὸς εἰς Αὐλίδα κατελθὼν μετὰ τῶν φίλων
καὶ νυκτερεύσας ἔδοξε κατὰ τοὺς ὕπνους εἰπεῖν
τινα πρὸς αὐτόν· "Ὦ βασιλεῦ Λακεδαιμονίων,   599
ὅτι μὲν οὐδεὶς τῆς Ἑλλάδος ὁμοῦ συμπάσης ἀπεδείχθη στρατηγὸς ἢ πρότερον Ἀγαμέμνων καὶ σὺ
νῦν μετ' ἐκεῖνον, ἐννοεῖς δήπουθεν· ἐπεὶ δὲ τῶν μὲν
αὐτῶν ἄρχεις ἐκείνῳ, τοῖς δὲ αὐτοῖς πολεμεῖς, ἀπὸ
δὲ τῶν αὐτῶν τόπων ὁρμᾷς ἐπὶ τὸν πόλεμον, εἰκός
ἐστι καὶ θῦσαί σε τῇ θεῷ θυσίαν ἣν ἐκεῖνος ἐν-
5 ταῦθα θύσας ἐξέπλευσεν." ἅμα δέ πως ὑπῆλθε
τὸν Ἀγησίλαον ὁ τῆς κόρης σφαγιασμός, ἣν ὁ
πατὴρ ἔσφαξε πεισθεὶς τοῖς μάντεσιν. οὐ μὴν

___

[1] ἐξέπεμπον εὐθὺς MSS.: ἐξέπεμπον after Reiske.
[2] πρῶτος S : εὐθὺς πρῶτος.

14

Hellas, proceeding to the farthest point across the sea, and thus anticipating the preparations of the Barbarian. At the same time he wrote to his friends in Asia urging them to send messengers to Sparta and demand Agesilaüs as their commander. Accordingly, Agesilaüs went before the assembly of the people and agreed to undertake the war if they would grant him thirty Spartans as captains and counsellors, a select corps of two thousand enfranchised Helots, and a force of allies amounting to six thousand. They readily voted everything, owing to the co-operation of Lysander, and sent Agesilaüs forth at once with the thirty Spartans. Of these Lysander was first and foremost, not only because of his own reputation and influence, but also because of the friendship of Agesilaüs, in whose eyes his procuring him this command was a greater boon than his raising him to the throne.

While his forces were assembling at Geraestus,[1] Agesilaüs himself went to Aulis with his friends and spent the night. As he slept, he thought a voice came to him, saying : " King of the Lacedaemonians, thou art surely aware that no one has ever been appointed general of all Hellas together except Agamemnon, in former times, and now thyself, after him. And since thou commandest the same hosts that he did, and wagest war on the same foes, and settest out for the war from the same place, it is meet that thou shouldst sacrifice also to the goddess the sacrifice which he made there before he set sail." Almost at once Agesilaüs remembered the sacrifice of his own daughter[2] which Agamemnon had there made in obedience to the soothsayers. He was not disturbed,

---

[1] In the spring of 396 B.C.
[2] Iphigeneia. Cf. Euripides, *Iph. Aul.*, 1540 ff. (Kirchhoff).

διετάραξεν αὐτόν, ἀλλ' ἀναστὰς καὶ διηγησά-
μενος τοῖς φίλοις τὰ φανέντα τὴν μὲν θεὸν ἔφη
τιμήσειν οἷς εἰκός ἐστι χαίρειν θεὸν οὖσαν, οὐ
μιμήσεσθαι δὲ τὴν ἀπάθειαν[1] τοῦ τότε στρατηγοῦ. καὶ καταστέψας ἔλαφον ἐκέλευσεν ἀπάρξα-
σθαι τὸν ἑαυτοῦ μάντιν, οὐχ ὥσπερ εἰώθει τοῦτο
6 ποιεῖν ὁ ὑπὸ τῶν Βοιωτῶν τεταγμένος. ἀκούσαντες
οὖν οἱ βοιώταρχαι πρὸς ὀργὴν κινηθέντες ἔπεμψαν ὑπηρέτας, ἀπαγορεύοντες τῷ Ἀγησιλάῳ μὴ
θύειν παρὰ τοὺς νόμους καὶ τὰ πάτρια Βοιωτῶν.
οἱ δὲ καὶ ταῦτα ἀπήγγειλαν καὶ τὰ μηρία διέρριψαν ἀπὸ τοῦ βωμοῦ. χαλεπῶς οὖν ἔχων ὁ
Ἀγησίλαος ἀπέπλει, τοῖς τε Θηβαίοις διωργισ-
μένος καὶ γεγονὼς δύσελπις διὰ τὸν οἰωνόν, ὡς
ἀτελῶν αὐτῷ τῶν πράξεων γενησομένων καὶ τῆς
στρατείας ἐπὶ τὸ προσῆκον οὐκ ἀφιξομένης.

VII. Ἐπεὶ δὲ ἧκεν εἰς Ἔφεσον, εὐθὺς ἀξίωμα
μέγα καὶ δύναμις ἦν ἐπαχθὴς καὶ βαρεῖα περὶ τὸν
Λύσανδρον, ὄχλου φοιτῶντος ἐπὶ τὰς θύρας ἑκάστοτε καὶ πάντων παρακολουθούντων καὶ θερα-
πευόντων ἐκεῖνον, ὡς ὄνομα μὲν καὶ σχῆμα τῆς
στρατηγίας τὸν Ἀγησίλαον ἔχοντα,[2] διὰ τὸν
νόμον, ἔργῳ δὲ κύριον ὄντα[3] ἁπάντων καὶ δυνάμενον καὶ πράττοντα πάντα τὸν Λύσανδρον.
2 οὐδεὶς γὰρ δεινότερος οὐδὲ φοβερώτερος ἐκείνου
τῶν εἰς τὴν Ἀσίαν ἀποσταλέντων ἐγένετο στρατηγῶν, οὐδὲ μείζονα τοὺς φίλους ἀνὴρ ἄλλος
εὐεργέτησεν οὐδὲ κακὰ τηλικαῦτα τοὺς ἐχθροὺς
ἐποίησεν. ὧν ἔτι προσφάτων ὄντων οἱ ἄνθρωποι

---

[1] ἀπάθειαν S and Amyot: ἀμαθίαν (stupidity).
[2] ἔχοντα Coraës, after Reiske: ὄντα.
[3] κύριον ὄντα Reiske: κύριον.

however, but after rising up and imparting his vision
to his friends, declared that he would honour the
goddess with a sacrifice in which she could fitly take
pleasure, being a goddess, and would not imitate the
cruel insensibility of his predecessor. So he caused
a hind to be wreathed with chaplets, and ordered
his own seer to perform the sacrifice, instead of the
one customarily appointed to this office by the
Boeotians. Accordingly, when the Boeotian magistrates heard of this, they were moved to anger, and
sent their officers, forbidding Agesilaüs to sacrifice
contrary to the laws and customs of the Boeotians.
These officers not only delivered their message, but
also snatched the thigh-pieces of the victim from the
altar.[1] Agesilaüs therefore sailed away in great
distress of mind ; he was not only highly incensed at
the Thebans, but also full of ill-boding on account of
the omen. He was convinced that his undertakings
would be incomplete, and that his expedition would
have no fitting issue.

VII. As soon as he came to Ephesus, the great
dignity and influence which Lysander enjoyed were
burdensome and grievous to him. The doors of
Lysander were always beset with a throng, and all
followed in his train and paid him court, as though
Agesilaüs had the command in name and outward
appearance, to comply with the law, while in fact
Lysander was master of all, had all power, and did
everything.[2] In fact, none of the generals sent out
to Asia ever had more power or inspired more fear
than he ; none other conferred greater favours on his
friends, or inflicted such great injuries upon his
enemies. All this was still fresh in men's minds, and

---

[1] Cf. Xenophon, *Hell*. iii. 4, 3 f.
[2] Cf. Xenophon, *Hell*. iii. 4, 7.

μνημονεύοντες, ἄλλως δὲ τὸν μὲν Ἀγησίλαον
ἀφελῆ καὶ λιτὸν ἐν ταῖς ὁμιλίαις καὶ δημοτικὸν
ὁρῶντες, ἐκείνῳ δὲ τὴν αὐτὴν ὁμοίως σφοδρότητα
καὶ τραχύτητα καὶ βραχυλογίαν παροῦσαν,
ὑπέπιπτον αὐτῷ παντάπασι καὶ μόνῳ προσεῖχον.
3 ἐκ δὲ τούτου πρῶτον μὲν οἱ λοιποὶ Σπαρτιᾶται
χαλεπῶς ἔφερον ὑπηρέται Λυσάνδρου μᾶλλον ἢ
σύμβουλοι βασιλέως ὄντες· ἔπειτα δ' αὐτὸς ὁ
Ἀγησίλαος, εἰ καὶ μὴ φθονερὸς ἦν μηδὲ ἤχθετο
τοῖς τιμωμένοις, ἀλλὰ φιλότιμος ὢν σφόδρα καὶ
φιλόνεικος, ἐφοβεῖτο μή, κἂν ἐνέγκωσί τι λαμπρὸν
αἱ πράξεις, τοῦτο Λυσάνδρου γένηται διὰ τὴν
δόξαν. οὕτως οὖν ἐποίει.

4   Πρῶτον ἀντέκρουε ταῖς συμβουλίαις αὐτοῦ,
καὶ πρὸς ἃς ἐκεῖνος ἐσπουδάκει μάλιστα πράξεις
ἐῶν χαίρειν καὶ παραμελῶν, ἕτερα πρὸ ἐκείνων
ἔπραττεν· ἔπειτα τῶν ἐντυγχανόντων καὶ δεομένων οὓς αἴσθοιτο Λυσάνδρῳ μάλιστα πεποιθ-
ότας, ἀπράκτους ἀπέπεμπε· καὶ περὶ τὰς κρίσεις
ὁμοίως οἷς ἐκεῖνος ἐπηρεάζοι, τούτους ἔδει πλέον
ἔχοντας ἀπελθεῖν, καὶ τοὐναντίον οὓς φανερὸς
γένοιτο προθυμούμενος ὠφελεῖν, χαλεπὸν ἦν μὴ
5 καὶ ζημιωθῆναι. γινομένων δὲ τούτων οὐ κατὰ
τύχην, ἀλλ' οἷον ἐκ παρασκευῆς καὶ ὁμαλῶς,
αἰσθόμενος τὴν αἰτίαν ὁ Λύσανδρος οὐκ ἀπε-
κρύπτετο πρὸς τοὺς φίλους, ἀλλ' ἔλεγεν ὡς δι'
αὐτὸν ἀτιμάζοιντο, καὶ παρεκάλει θεραπεύειν
ἰόντας τὸν βασιλέα καὶ τοὺς μᾶλλον αὐτοῦ
δυναμένους.

VIII. Ὡς οὖν ταῦτα πράττειν καὶ λέγειν
ἐδόκει φθόνον ἐκείνῳ μηχανώμενος, ἔτι μᾶλλον
αὐτοῦ καθάψασθαι βουλόμενος Ἀγησίλαος ἀπέ-

besides, when they saw the simple, plain, and familiar
manners of Agesilaüs, while Lysander retained the
same vehemence and harshness, and the same brevity
of speech as before, they yielded to the latter's influence altogether, and attached themselves to him
alone. As a consequence of this, in the first place,
the rest of the Spartans were displeased to find themselves assistants of Lysander rather than counsellors
of the king; and, in the second place, Agesilaüs himself, though he was not an envious man, nor displeased
that others should be honoured, but exceedingly ambitious and high-spirited, began to fear that any brilliant
success which he might achieve in his undertakings
would be attributed to Lysander, owing to popular
opinion. He went to work, therefore, in this way.

To begin with, he resisted the counsels of Lysander,
and whatever enterprises were most earnestly favoured
by him, these he ignored and neglected, and did other
things in their stead; again, of those who came to
solicit favours from him, he sent away empty-handed
all who put their chief confidence in Lysander; and
in judicial cases likewise, all those against whom
Lysander inveighed were sure to come off victorious,
while, on the contrary, those whom he was manifestly
eager to help had hard work even to escape being
fined. These things happened, not casually, but as
if of set purpose, and uniformly. At last Lysander
perceived the reason, and did not hide it from his
friends, but told them it was on his account that they
were slighted, and advised them to go and pay their
court to the king, and to those more influential with
him than himself.

VIII. Accordingly, since his words and acts
seemed contrived to bring odium upon the king,
Agesilaüs, wishing to despite him still more,

19

c 2

δεῖξε κρεοδαίτην καὶ προσεῖπεν, ὡς λέγεται,
πολλῶν ἀκουόντων· "Νῦν οὖν θεραπευέτωσαν
2 οὗτοι ἀπιόντες τὸν ἐμὸν κρεοδαίτην." ἀχθόμενος
οὖν ὁ Λύσανδρος λέγει πρὸς αὐτόν· "Ἤιδεις ἄρα
σαφῶς, Ἀγησίλαε, φίλους ἐλαττοῦν." "Νὴ Δί',"[1] 600
ἔφη, "τοὺς ἐμοῦ μεῖζον δύνασθαι βουλομένους."
καὶ ὁ Λύσανδρος, "Ἀλλ' ἴσως," ἔφη, "ταῦτα
σοὶ λέλεκται βέλτιον ἢ ἐμοὶ πέπρακται. δὸς δέ
μοι τινὰ τάξιν καὶ χώραν ἔνθα μὴ λυπῶν ἔσομαί
3 σοι χρήσιμος." ἐκ τούτου πέμπεται μὲν ἐφ'
Ἑλλήσποντον, καὶ Σπιθριδάτην, ἄνδρα Πέρσην,
ἀπὸ τῆς Φαρναβάζου χώρας μετὰ χρημάτων
συχνῶν καὶ διακοσίων ἱππέων ἤγαγε πρὸς τὸν
Ἀγησίλαον, οὐκ ἔληγε δὲ τῆς ὀργῆς, ἀλλὰ βαρέως φέρων ἤδη τὸν λοιπὸν χρόνον ἐβούλευεν
ὅπως τῶν δυεῖν οἴκων τὴν βασιλείαν ἀφελόμενος
εἰς μέσον ἅπασιν ἀποδοίη Σπαρτιάταις. καὶ
ἐδόκει μεγάλην ἂν ἀπεργάσασθαι κίνησιν ἐκ
ταύτης τῆς διαφορᾶς, εἰ μὴ πρότερον ἐτελεύ-
4 τησεν εἰς Βοιωτίαν στρατεύσας. οὕτως αἱ φιλό-
τιμοι φύσεις ἐν ταῖς πολιτείαις, τὸ ἄγαν μὴ
φυλαξάμεναι, τοῦ ἀγαθοῦ μεῖζον τὸ κακὸν ἔχουσι.
καὶ γὰρ εἰ Λύσανδρος ἦν φορτικός, ὥσπερ ἦν,
ὑπερβάλλων τῇ φιλοτιμίᾳ τὸν καιρόν, οὐκ ἠγνόει
δήπουθεν Ἀγησίλαος ἑτέραν ἀμεμπτοτέραν ἐπαν-
όρθωσιν οὖσαν ἀνδρὸς ἐνδόξου καὶ φιλοτίμου
πλημμελοῦντος. ἀλλ' ἔοικε ταῦτῷ πάθει μήτε
ἐκεῖνος ἄρχοντος ἐξουσίαν γνῶναι μήτε οὗτος
ἄγνοιαν ἐνεγκεῖν συνήθους.

IX. Ἐπεὶ δὲ Τισαφέρνης ἐν ἀρχῇ μὲν φοβη-

---

[1] Νὴ Δί' Cobet, comparing Xenophon, *Hell*. iii. 4, 9:
Ἠιδειν (*I know how to humble*).

appointed him his carver of meats, and once said, we are told, in the hearing of many : "Now then, let these suppliants go off to my carver of meats and pay their court to him." Lysander, then, deeply pained, said to him : "I see, Agesilaüs, that thou knowest very well how to humble thy friends." "Yes indeed," said the king, "those who wish to be more powerful than I am." Then Lysander said : "Well, perhaps these words of thine are fairer than my deeds. Give me, however, some post and place where I shall be of service to thee, without vexing thee." [1] Upon this he was sent to the Hellespont, and brought over to Agesilaüs from the country of Pharnabazus, Spithridates, a Persian, with much money and two hundred horsemen. He did not, however, lay aside his wrath, but continued his resentment, and from this time on planned how he might wrest the kingdom from the two royal families, and make all Spartans once more eligible to it. And it was thought that he would have brought about a great disturbance in consequence of this quarrel, had not death overtaken him on his expedition into Boeotia.[2] Thus ambitious natures in a commonwealth, if they do not observe due bounds, work greater harm than good. For even though Lysander was troublesome, as he was, in gratifying his ambition unseasonably, still, Agesilaüs must surely have known another and more blameless way of correcting a man of high repute and ambition when he erred. As it was, it seems to have been due to the same passion that the one would not recognize the authority of his superior, nor the other put up with the folly of his friend and comrade.

IX. At first Tisaphernes was afraid of Agesilaüs,

[1] Cf. *Lysander*, xxiii. 9.   [2] Cf. *Lysander*, xxiv.–xxviii.

21

θεὶς τὸν Ἀγησίλαον ἐποιήσατο σπονδάς, ὡς τὰς
πόλεις αὐτῷ τὰς Ἑλληνίδας ἀφήσοντος αὐτονόμους βασιλέως, ὕστερον δὲ πεισθεὶς ἔχειν
δύναμιν ἱκανὴν ἐξήνεγκε τὸν πόλεμον, ἄσμενος ὁ
2 Ἀγησίλαος ἐδέξατο. προσδοκία γὰρ ἦν μεγάλη
τῆς στρατείας· καὶ δεινὸν ἡγεῖτο τοὺς μὲν σὺν
Ξενοφῶντι μυρίους ἥκειν ἐπὶ θάλατταν, ὁσάκις
ἐβουλήθησαν αὐτοὶ τοσαυτάκις βασιλέα νενικηκότας, αὐτοῦ δὲ Λακεδαιμονίων ἄρχοντος ἡγουμένων γῆς καὶ θαλάσσης μηδὲν ἔργον ἄξιον
μνήμης φανῆναι πρὸς τοὺς Ἕλληνας. εὐθὺς
οὖν ἀμυνόμενος ἀπάτῃ δικαίᾳ τὴν Τισαφέρνους
ἐπιορκίαν, ἐπέδειξεν ὡς ἐπὶ Καρίαν προάξων,
ἐκεῖ δὲ τὴν δύναμιν τοῦ βαρβάρου συναθροί-
3 σαντος ἄρας εἰς Φρυγίαν ἐνέβαλε. καὶ πόλεις
μὲν εἷλε συχνὰς καὶ χρημάτων ἀφθόνων ἐκυ-
ρίευσεν, ἐπιδεικνύμενος τοῖς φίλοις ὅτι τὸ μὲν
σπεισάμενον ἀδικεῖν τῶν θεῶν ἔστι καταφρονεῖν,
ἐν δὲ τῷ παραλογίζεσθαι τοὺς πολεμίους οὐ
μόνον τὸ δίκαιον, ἀλλὰ καὶ δόξα πολλὴ καὶ τὸ
μεθ' ἡδονῆς κερδαίνειν ἔνεστι. τοῖς δὲ ἱππεῦσιν
ἐλαττωθεὶς καὶ τῶν ἱερῶν ἀλόβων φανέντων,
ἀναχωρήσας εἰς Ἔφεσον ἱππικὸν συνῆγε, τοῖς
εὐπόροις προειπών, εἰ μὴ βούλονται στρατεύεσθαι,
παρασχεῖν ἕκαστον ἵππον ἀνθ' ἑαυτοῦ καὶ ἄνδρα.
4 πολλοὶ δ' ἦσαν οὗτοι, καὶ συνέβαινε τῷ Ἀγησιλάῳ ταχὺ πολλοὺς καὶ πολεμικοὺς ἔχειν ἱππεῖς
ἀντὶ δειλῶν ὁπλιτῶν. ἐμισθοῦντο γὰρ οἱ μὴ
βουλόμενοι στρατεύεσθαι τοὺς βουλομένους στρα-

and made a treaty in which he promised him to
make the Greek cities free and independent of the
King. Afterwards, however, when he was convinced
that he had a sufficient force, he declared war, and
Agesilaüs gladly accepted it. For he had great expectations from his expedition, and he thought it
would be a disgraceful thing if, whereas Xenophon
and his Ten Thousand had penetrated to the sea,
and vanquished the King just as often as they
themselves desired, he, in command of the Lacedaemonians, who had the supremacy on sea and
land, should perform no deed worthy of remem-
brance in the eyes of the Hellenes. At once,
then, requiting the perjury of Tisaphernes with a
righteous deception, he gave out word that he was
going to lead his troops against Caria ; but when the
Barbarian had assembled his forces there, he set out
and made an incursion into Phrygia. He captured
many cities and made himself master of boundless
treasure, thus shewing plainly to his friends that the
violation of a treaty is contempt for the gods, but
that in outwitting one's enemies there is not only
justice, but also great glory, and profit mixed with
pleasure. However, since he was inferior in cavalry
and his sacrifices were unpropitious, he retired to
Ephesus and began to get together a force of horsemen, commanding the well-to-do, in case they did
not wish to perform military service themselves, to
furnish instead every man a horse and rider. There
were many who chose this course, and so it came
to pass that Agesilaüs quickly had a large force
of warlike horsemen instead of worthless men-at-
arms.[1] For those who did not wish to do military
service hired those who did, and those who did not

[1] Cf. Xenophon, *Hell.* iii. 4, 15.

23

τεύεσθαι, οἱ δὲ μὴ βουλόμενοι ἱππεύειν τοὺς
βουλομένους ἱππεύειν.¹ καὶ γὰρ τὸν Ἀγαμέμνονα
ποιῆσαι καλῶς ὅτι θήλειαν ἵππον ἀγαθὴν λαβὼν
κακὸν ἄνδρα καὶ πλούσιον ἀπήλλαξε τῆς στρα-
5 τείας. ἐπεὶ δὲ κελεύσαντος αὐτοῦ τοὺς αἰχμαλώτους ἀποδύοντες ἐπίπρασκον οἱ λαφυροπῶλαι,
καὶ τῆς μὲν ἐσθῆτος ἦσαν ὠνηταὶ πολλοί, τῶν δὲ
σωμάτων λευκῶν καὶ ἁπαλῶν παντάπασι διὰ τὰς
σκιατραφίας γυμνουμένων κατεγέλων ὡς ἀχρή-
στων καὶ μηδενὸς ἀξίων, ἐπιστὰς ὁ Ἀγησίλαος,
"Οὗτοι μέν," εἶπεν, "οἷς μάχεσθε, ταῦτα δὲ
ὑπὲρ ὧν μάχεσθε."

X. Καιροῦ δὲ ὄντος αὖθις ἐμβαλεῖν εἰς τὴν
πολεμίαν προεῖπεν εἰς Λυδίαν ἀπάξειν, οὐκέτι
ψευδόμενος ἐνταῦθα τὸν Τισαφέρνην· ἀλλ' ἐκεῖνος
ἑαυτὸν ἐξηπάτησε, διὰ τὴν ἔμπροσθεν ἀπάτην
ἀπιστῶν τῷ Ἀγησιλάῳ, καὶ νῦν γοῦν αὐτὸν
ἅψεσθαι τῆς Καρίας νομίζων οὔσης δυσίππου   601
2 πολὺ τῷ ἱππικῷ λειπόμενον. ἐπεὶ δέ, ὡς προεῖπεν, ὁ Ἀγησίλαος ἧκεν εἰς τὸ περὶ Σάρδεις πεδίον,
ἠναγκάζετο κατὰ σπουδὴν ἐκεῖθεν αὖ βοηθεῖν ὁ
Τισαφέρνης· καὶ τῇ ἵππῳ διεξελαύνων διέφθειρε
πολλοὺς τῶν ἀτάκτως τὸ πεδίον πορθούντων.
ἐννοήσας οὖν ὁ Ἀγησίλαος ὅτι τοῖς πολεμίοις
οὔπω πάρεστι τὸ πεζόν, αὐτῷ δὲ τῆς δυνάμεως
3 οὐδὲν ἄπεστιν, ἔσπευσε διαγωνίσασθαι. καὶ τοῖς
μὲν ἱππεῦσιν ἀναμίξας τὸ πελταστικόν, ἐλαύνειν
ἐκέλευσεν ὡς τάχιστα καὶ προσβάλλειν τοῖς
ἐναντίοις, αὐτὸς δὲ εὐθὺς τοὺς ὁπλίτας ἐπῆγε.
γενομένης δὲ τροπῆς τῶν βαρβάρων ἐπακολουθή-

---

¹ ἐμισθοῦντο . . . ἱππεύειν bracketed by Sintenis² and Cobet.
The sentence is wanting in *Apophtheg. Lacon.* 12 (*Morals*,
p. 209 b).

wish to serve as horsemen hired those who did. Indeed, Agesilaüs thought Agamemnon had done well in accepting a good mare and freeing a cowardly rich man from military service.[1] And once when, by his orders, his prisoners of war were stripped of their clothing and offered for sale by the venders of booty, their clothing found many purchasers, but their naked bodies, which were utterly white and delicate, owing to their effeminate habits, were ridiculed as useless and worthless. Then Agesilaüs, noticing, said: "These are the men with whom you fight, and these the things for which you fight."

X. When the season again favoured an incursion into the enemy's country,[2] Agesilaüs gave out that he would march into Lydia, and this time he was not trying to deceive Tisaphernes. That satrap, however, utterly deluded himself, in that he disbelieved Agesilaüs because of his former trick, and thought that now, at any rate, the king would attack Caria, although it was ill-suited for cavalry, and he was far inferior in that arm of the service. But Agesilaüs, as he had given out that he would do, marched into the plain of Sardis, and then Tisaphernes was forced to hasten thither from Caria with aid and relief; and riding through the plain with his cavalry, he cut off many straggling plunderers there. Agesilaüs, accordingly, reflecting that the enemy's infantry had not yet come up, while his own forces were complete, made haste to give battle. He mingled his light-armed infantry with his horsemen, and ordered them to charge at full speed and assault the enemy, while he himself at once led up his men-at-arms. The Barbarians were put to flight, and the Greeks,

---

[1] *Iliad*, xxiii. 296 ff.
[2] In the spring of 395 B.C.; cf. Xenophon, *Hell.* iii. 4, 16 ff.

σαντες οἱ Ἕλληνες ἔλαβον τὸ στρατόπεδον καὶ
πολλοὺς ἀνεῖλον. ἐκ ταύτης τῆς μάχης οὐ μόνον
ὑπῆρξεν αὐτοῖς ἄγειν καὶ φέρειν ἀδεῶς τὴν βασιλέως χώραν, ἀλλὰ καὶ δίκην ἐπιδεῖν Τισαφέρνην
διδόντα, μοχθηρὸν ἄνδρα καὶ τῷ γένει τῶν Ἑλλή-
4 νων ἀπεχθέστατον. ἔπεμψε γὰρ εὐθέως ὁ βασιλεὺς Τιθραύστην ἐπ' αὐτόν, ὃς ἐκείνου μὲν τὴν
κεφαλὴν ἀπέτεμε, τὸν δὲ Ἀγησίλαον ἠξίου δια-
λυσάμενον ἀποπλεῖν οἴκαδε, καὶ χρήματα διδοὺς
αὐτῷ προσέπεμψεν. ὁ δὲ τῆς μὲν εἰρήνης ἔφη
τὴν πόλιν εἶναι κυρίαν, αὐτὸς δὲ πλουτίζων τοὺς
στρατιώτας ἥδεσθαι μᾶλλον ἢ πλουτῶν αὐτός·
καὶ ἄλλως γε μέντοι νομίζειν Ἕλληνας καλὸν οὐ
δῶρα λαμβάνειν, ἀλλὰ λάφυρα παρὰ τῶν πολε-
5 μίων. ὅμως δὲ τῷ Τιθραύστῃ χαρίζεσθαι βουλόμενος, ὅτι τὸν κοινὸν ἐχθρὸν Ἑλλήνων ἐτετι-
μώρητο Τισαφέρνην, ἀπήγαγεν εἰς Φρυγίαν τὸ
στράτευμα, λαβὼν ἐφόδιον παρ' αὐτοῦ τριάκοντα
τάλαντα.

Καὶ καθ' ὁδὸν ὢν σκυτάλην δέχεται παρὰ τῶν
οἴκοι τελῶν κελεύουσαν αὐτὸν ἄρχειν ἅμα καὶ
τοῦ ναυτικοῦ. τοῦτο μόνῳ πάντων ὑπῆρξεν
Ἀγησιλάῳ. καὶ μέγιστος μὲν ἦν ὁμολογουμένως
καὶ τῶν τότε ζώντων ἐπιφανέστατος, ὡς εἴρηκέ
που καὶ Θεόπομπος, ἑαυτῷ γε μὴν ἐδίδου δι' ἀρε-
6 τὴν φρονεῖν μεῖζον ἢ διὰ τὴν ἡγεμονίαν. τότε δὲ
τοῦ ναυτικοῦ καταστήσας ἄρχοντα Πείσανδρον
ἁμαρτεῖν ἔδοξεν, ὅτι πρεσβυτέρων καὶ φρονιμω-
τέρων παρόντων οὐ σκεψάμενος τὸ τῆς πατρίδος,
ἀλλὰ τὴν οἰκειότητα τιμῶν καὶ τῇ γυναικὶ χαριζόμενος, ἧς ἀδελφὸς ἦν ὁ Πείσανδρος, ἐκείνῳ
παρέδωκε τὴν ναυαρχίαν.

26

following close upon them, took their camp and slew many of them. As a result of this battle, the Greeks could not only harry the country of the King without fear, but had the satisfaction of seeing due punishment inflicted upon Tisaphernes, an abominable man, and most hateful to the Greek race. For the King at once sent Tithraustes after him, who cut off his head, and asked Agesilaüs to make terms and sail back home, offering him money at the hands of envoys. But Agesilaüs answered that it was for his city to make peace, and that for his own part, he took more pleasure in enriching his soldiers than in getting rich himself; moreover, the Greeks, he said, thought it honourable to take, not gifts, but spoils, from their enemies. Nevertheless, desiring to gratify Tithraustes, because he had punished Tisaphernes, that common enemy of the Greeks, he led his army back into Phrygia, taking thirty talents from the viceroy to cover the expenses of the march.

On the road he received a dispatch-roll from the magistrates at home, which bade him assume control of the navy as well as of the army.[1] This was an honour which no one ever received but Agesilaüs. And he was confessedly the greatest and most illustrious man of his time, as Theopompus also has somewhere said, although he prided himself more on his virtues than on his high command. But in putting Peisander in charge of the navy at this time, he was thought to have made a mistake; for there were older and more competent men to be had, and yet he gave the admiralty to him, not out of regard for the public good, but in recognition of the claims of relationship and to gratify his wife, who was a sister of Peisander.

[1] Cf. Xenophon, *Hell.* iii. 4, 27 ff.

XI. Αὐτὸς δὲ τὸν στρατὸν καταστήσας εἰς τὴν ὑπὸ Φαρναβάζῳ τεταγμένην χώραν οὐ μόνον ἐν ἀφθόνοις διῆγε πᾶσιν, ἀλλὰ καὶ χρήματα συνῆγε πολλά· καὶ προελθὼν ἄχρι Παφλαγονίας προσηγάγετο τὸν βασιλέα τῶν Παφλαγόνων, Κότυν, ἐπιθυμήσαντα τῆς φιλίας αὐτοῦ δι' ἀρετὴν καὶ

2 πίστιν. ὁ δὲ Σπιθριδάτης, ὡς ἀποστὰς τοῦ Φαρναβάζου τὸ πρῶτον ἦλθε πρὸς τὸν Ἀγησίλαον, ἀεὶ συναπεδήμει καὶ συνεστράτευεν αὐτῷ, κάλλιστον υἱὸν μὲν ἔχων, Μεγαβάτην, οὗ παιδὸς ὄντος ἤρα σφοδρῶς Ἀγησίλαος, καλὴν δὲ καὶ θυγατέρα παρθένον ἐν ἡλικίᾳ γάμου. ταύτην

3 ἔπεισε γῆμαι τὸν Κότυν ὁ Ἀγησίλαος· καὶ λαβὼν παρ' αὐτοῦ χιλίους ἱππεῖς καὶ δισχιλίους πελταστὰς αὖθις ἀνεχώρησεν εἰς Φρυγίαν, καὶ κακῶς ἐποίει τὴν Φαρναβάζου χώραν οὐχ ὑπομένοντος οὐδὲ πιστεύοντος τοῖς ἐρύμασιν, ἀλλὰ ἔχων ἀεὶ τὰ πλεῖστα σὺν ἑαυτῷ τῶν τιμίων καὶ ἀγαπητῶν ἐξεχώρει καὶ ὑπέφευγεν ἄλλοτε ἀλλαχόσε τῆς χώρας μεθιδρυόμενος, μέχρι οὗ παραφυλάξας αὐτὸν ὁ Σπιθριδάτης καὶ παραλαβὼν Ἡριππίδαν τὸν Σπαρτιάτην ἔλαβε τὸ στρατόπεδον καὶ τῶν

4 χρημάτων ἁπάντων ἐκράτησεν. ἔνθα δὴ πικρὸς ὢν ὁ Ἡριππίδας ἐξεταστὴς τῶν κλαπέντων, καὶ τοὺς βαρβάρους ἀναγκάζων ἀποτίθεσθαι, καὶ πάντα ἐφορῶν καὶ διερευνώμενος, παρώξυνε τὸν Σπιθριδάτην, ὥστε ἀπελθεῖν εὐθὺς εἰς Σάρδεις μετὰ τῶν Παφλαγόνων.

Τοῦτο λέγεται τῷ Ἀγησιλάῳ γενέσθαι πάντων 602

28

XI. As for himself, he stationed his army in the province of Pharnabazus,[1] where he not only lived in universal plenty, but also accumulated much money. He also advanced to the confines of Paphlagonia and brought Cotys, the king of the Paphlagonians, into alliance with him, for his virtues, and the confidence which he inspired, inclined the king to desire his friendship. Spithridates also, from the time when he abandoned Pharnabazus and came to Agesilaüs, always accompanied him in his journeys and expeditions. Spithridates had a son, a very beautiful boy, named Megabates, of whom Agesilaüs was ardently enamoured, and a beautiful daughter also, a maiden of marriageable age. This daughter Agesilaüs persuaded Cotys to marry, and then receiving from him a thousand horsemen and two thousand targeteers, he retired again into Phrygia, and harassed the country of Pharnabazus, who did not stand his ground nor trust in his defences, but always kept most of his valued and precious things with him, and withdrew or fled from one part of the country to another, having no abiding place. At last Spithridates, who had narrowly watched him, in conjunction with Herippidas the Spartan,[2] seized his camp and made himself master of all his treasures. Here, however, Herippidas, who had too sharp an eye to the booty that was stolen, and forced the Barbarians to restore it, watching over and enquiring into everything, exasperated Spithridates, so that he marched off at once to Sardis with the Paphlagonians.

This is said to have annoyed Agesilaüs beyond all

[1] In the fall of 395 B.C.; cf. Xenophon, *Hell.* iv. 1, 1 ff.
[2] The leader of the second company of thirty Spartan counsellors sent out in the spring of 395 B.C. Cf. Xenophon, *Hell.* iii. 4, 20.

ἀνιαρότατον. ἤχθετο μὲν γὰρ ἄνδρα γενναῖον
ἀποβεβληκὼς τὸν Σπιθριδάτην καὶ σὺν αὐτῷ
δύναμιν οὐκ ὀλίγην, ᾐσχύνετο δὲ τῇ διαβολῇ τῆς
μικρολογίας καὶ ἀνελευθερίας, ἧς οὐ μόνον αὑτόν,
ἀλλὰ καὶ τὴν πατρίδα καθαρεύουσαν ἀεὶ παρέ-
5 χειν ἐφιλοτιμεῖτο. χωρὶς δὲ τῶν ἐμφανῶν τούτων ἔκνιζεν αὐτὸν οὐ μετρίως ὁ τοῦ παιδὸς
ἔρως ἐνεσταγμένος, εἰ καὶ πάνυ παρόντος αὐτοῦ
τῷ φιλονείκῳ χρώμενος ἐπειρᾶτο νεανικῶς ἀπο-
μάχεσθαι πρὸς τὴν ἐπιθυμίαν. καί ποτε τοῦ
Μεγαβάτου προσιόντος ὡς ἀσπασομένου καὶ
6 φιλήσοντος ἐξέκλινεν. ἐπεὶ δὲ ἐκεῖνος αἰσχυν-
θεὶς ἐπαύσατο καὶ τὸ λοιπὸν ἄπωθεν ἤδη προση-
γόρευεν, ἀχθόμενος αὖ πάλιν καὶ μεταμελόμενος
τῇ φυγῇ τοῦ φιλήματος, ὁ Ἀγησίλαος προσεποιεῖτο θαυμάζειν ὅ τι δὴ παθὼν αὐτὸν ὁ Μεγα-
βάτης ἀπὸ στόματος οὐ φιλοφρονοῖτο. "Σὺ γὰρ
αἴτιος," οἱ συνήθεις ἔφασαν, "οὐχ ὑποστάς,
ἀλλὰ τρέσας τὸ φίλημα τοῦ καλοῦ καὶ φοβηθείς·
ἐπεὶ καὶ νῦν ἂν ἔλθοι σοι πεισθεὶς ·ἐκεῖνος ἐντὸς
φιλήματος· ἀλλ' ὅπως αὖθις οὐκ ἀποδειλιάσεις."
7 χρόνον οὖν τινα πρὸς ἑαυτῷ γενόμενος ὁ Ἀγησίλαος καὶ διασιωπήσας, "Οὐδέν," ἔφη, "δεινὸν[1]
πείθειν ὑμᾶς ἐκεῖνον· ἐγὼ γάρ μοι δοκῶ τήναν
τὰν μάχαν τὰν περὶ τοῦ φιλάματος ἅδιον ἂν
μάχεσθαι πάλιν ἢ πάντα ὅσα τεθέαμαι χρυσία
μοι γενέσθαι." τοιοῦτος μὲν ἦν τοῦ Μεγαβάτου
παρόντος, ἀπελθόντος γε μὴν οὕτω περικαῶς
ἔσχεν ὡς χαλεπὸν εἰπεῖν εἰ πάλιν αὖ μεταβαλο-
μένου καὶ φανέντος ἐνεκαρτέρησε μὴ φιληθῆναι.

---

[1] δεινὸν Reiske's correction of the δεῖν of the MSS., adopted
by both Sintenis and Bekker ; Stephanus read δεῖ (*there is
no need*).

else. For he was pained at the loss of a gallant man in Spithridates, and with him of a considerable force, and was ashamed to labour under the charge of pettiness and illiberality, from which he was always ambitious to keep not only himself, but also his country, pure and free. And apart from these manifest reasons, he was irritated beyond measure by his love for the boy, which was now instilled into his heart, although when the boy was present he would summon all his resolution and strive mightily to battle against his desires. Indeed, when Megabates once came up and offered to embrace and kiss him, he declined his caresses. The boy was mortified at this, and desisted, and afterwards kept his distance when addressing him, whereupon Agesilaüs, distressed now and repentant for having avoided his kiss, pretended to wonder what ailed Megabates that he did not greet him with a kiss. "It is thy fault," the king's companions said; "thou didst not accept, but didst decline the fair one's kiss in fear and trembling; yet even now he might be persuaded to come within range of thy lips; but see that thou dost not again play the coward." Then, after some time spent in silent reflection, Agesilaüs said: "There is no harm in your persuading him; for I think I would more gladly fight that battle of the kiss over again than to have all that my eyes behold turn into gold." Of such a mind was he while Megabates was with him, though when the boy was gone, he was so on fire with love for him that it were hard to say whether, had the boy come back into his presence, he would have had the strength to refuse his kisses.[1]

---

[1] Cf. Xenophon's *Agesilaüs*, v. 4–7.

XII. Μετὰ ταῦτα Φαρνάβαζος εἰς λόγους
αὐτῷ συνελθεῖν ἠθέλησε, καὶ συνῆγεν ἀμφοτέρους
ὧν ξένος ὁ Κυζικηνὸς Ἀπολλοφάνης. πρότερος
δὲ μετὰ τῶν φίλων ὁ Ἀγησίλαος ἐλθὼν εἰς τὸ
χωρίον, ὑπὸ σκιᾷ τινι πόας οὔσης βαθείας καταβαλὼν ἑαυτόν, ἐνταῦθα περιέμενε τὸν Φαρνά-
2 βαζον. ὁ δὲ ὡς ἐπῆλθεν, ὑποβεβλημένων αὐτῷ
κωδίων τε μαλακῶν καὶ ποικίλων δαπίδων, αἰδεσθεὶς τὸν Ἀγησίλαον οὕτω κατακείμενον κατε-
κλίνη καὶ αὐτός, ὡς ἔτυχεν, ἐπὶ τῆς πόας χαμᾶζε,
καίπερ ἐσθῆτα θαυμαστὴν λεπτότητι καὶ βαφαῖς
ἐνδεδυκώς. ἀσπασάμενοι δὲ ἀλλήλους ὁ μὲν
Φαρνάβαζος οὐκ ἠπόρει λόγων δικαίων, ἅτε δὴ
πολλὰ καὶ μεγάλα Λακεδαιμονίοις χρήσιμος
γεγονὼς ἐν τῷ πρὸς Ἀθηναίους πολέμῳ, νῦν δὲ
3 πορθούμενος ὑπ' αὐτῶν· ὁ δὲ Ἀγησίλαος, ὁρῶν
τοὺς σὺν αὐτῷ Σπαρτιάτας ὑπ' αἰσχύνης κύπτον-
τας εἰς τὴν γῆν καὶ διαπορῦντας (ἀδικούμενον
γὰρ ἑώρων τὸν Φαρνάβαζον), "Ἡμεῖς," εἶπεν,
"ὦ Φαρνάβαζε, καὶ φίλοι ὄντες πρότερον βασιλέως ἐχρώμεθα τοῖς ἐκείνου πράγμασι φιλικῶς
καὶ νῦν πολέμιοι γεγονότες πολεμικῶς. ἐν οὖν
καὶ σὲ τῶν βασιλέως κτημάτων ὁρῶντες εἶναι
βουλόμενοι, εἰκότως διὰ σοῦ βλάπτομεν ἐκεῖνον.
4 ἀφ' ἧς δ' ἂν ἡμέρας σεαυτὸν ἀξιώσῃς Ἑλλήνων
φίλον καὶ σύμμαχον μᾶλλον ἢ δοῦλον λέγεσθαι
βασιλέως, ταύτην νόμιζε τὴν φάλαγγα καὶ τὰ
ὅπλα καὶ τὰς ναῦς καὶ πάντας ἡμᾶς τῶν σῶν
κτημάτων φύλακας εἶναι καὶ τῆς ἐλευθερίας, ἧς
ἄνευ καλὸν ἀνθρώποις οὐδὲν οὐδὲ ζηλωτόν ἐστιν."
5 ἐκ τούτου λέγει πρὸς αὐτὸν ὁ Φαρνάβαζος ἣν
εἶχε διάνοιαν. "Ἐγὼ γάρ," εἶπεν, "ἐὰν μὲν
ἄλλον ἐκπέμψῃ βασιλεὺς στρατηγόν, ἔσομαι

XII. After this, Pharnabazus desired to have a conference with him, and Apollophanes of Cyzicus, who
was a guest-friend of both, brought the two together.
Agesilaüs, with his friends, came first to the appointed
place, and throwing himself down in a shady place
where the grass was deep, there awaited Pharnabazus.
And when Pharnabazus came, although soft cushions
and broidered rugs had been spread for him, he was
ashamed to see Agesilaüs reclining as he was, and
threw himself down likewise, without further ceremony, on the grassy ground, although he was clad in
raiment of wonderful delicacy and dyes.   After
mutual salutations, Pharnabazus had plenty of just
complaints to make, since, although he had rendered
the Lacedaemonians many great services in their
war against, the Athenians, his territory was now
being ravaged by them.   But Agesilaüs, seeing the
Spartans with him bowed to the earth with shame
and at a loss for words (for they saw that Pharnabazus was a wronged man), said : "We, O Pharnabazus, during our former friendship with the King,
treated what belongs to him in a friendly way, and
now that we have become his enemies, we treat it in
a hostile way.   Accordingly, seeing that thou also
desirest to be one of the King's chattels, we naturally
injure him through thee.   But from the day when
thou shalt deem thyself worthy to be called a friend
and ally of the Greeks instead of a slave of the King,
consider this army, these arms and ships, and all of
us, to be guardians of thy possessions and of thy
liberty, without which nothing in the world is
honourable or even worthy to be desired."   Upon
this, Pharnabazus declared to him his purposes.
"As for me, indeed," he said, "if the King shall
send out another general in my stead, I will be on

μεθ' ὑμῶν, ἐὰν δ' ἐμοὶ παραδῷ τὴν ἡγεμονίαν,
οὐδὲν ἐλλείψω προθυμίας ἀμυνόμενος ὑμᾶς καὶ
κακῶς ποιῶν ὑπὲρ ἐκείνου." ταῦτα δ' ἀκούσας ὁ
Ἀγησίλαος ἤσθη, καὶ τῆς δεξιᾶς αὐτοῦ λαβόμενος καὶ συνεξαναστάς, "Εἴθε," εἶπεν, "ὦ
Φαρνάβαζε, τοιοῦτος ὢν φίλος ἡμῖν γένοιο μᾶλλον
ἢ πολέμιος."

XIII. Ἀπιόντος δὲ τοῦ Φαρναβάζου μετὰ
τῶν φίλων, ὁ υἱὸς ὑπολειφθεὶς προσέδραμε τῷ
Ἀγησιλάῳ καὶ μειδιῶν εἶπεν· "Ἐγώ σε ξένον,
ὦ Ἀγησίλαε, ποιοῦμαι·" καὶ παλτὸν ἔχων ἐν   603
τῇ χειρὶ δίδωσιν αὐτῷ. δεξάμενος οὖν ὁ Ἀγησίλαος καὶ ἡσθεὶς τῇ τε ὄψει καὶ τῇ φιλοφροσύνῃ
τοῦ παιδός, ἐπεσκόπει τοὺς παρόντας, εἴ τις ἔχοι
τι τοιοῦτον οἷον ἀντιδοῦναι καλῷ καὶ γενναίῳ
2 δῶρον. ἰδὼν δὲ ἵππον Ἰδαίου [1] τοῦ γραφέως
κεκοσμημένον φαλάροις, ταχὺ ταῦτα περισπάσας
τῷ μειρακίῳ δίδωσι. καὶ τὸ λοιπὸν οὐκ ἐπαύετο
μεμνημένος, ἀλλὰ καὶ χρόνῳ περιϊόντι τὸν οἶκον
ἀποστερηθέντος αὐτοῦ καὶ φυγόντος ὑπὸ τῶν
ἀδελφῶν εἰς Πελοπόννησον, ἰσχυρῶς ἐπεμελεῖτο.
3 καί τι καὶ τῶν ἐρωτικῶν αὐτῷ συνέπραξεν. ἠράσθη γὰρ ἀθλητοῦ παιδὸς ἐξ Ἀθηνῶν· ἐπεὶ δὲ
μέγας ὢν καὶ σκληρὸς Ὀλυμπίασιν ἐκινδύνευσεν
ἐκκριθῆναι, κατέφευγε πρὸς τὸν Ἀγησίλαον
ὁ Πέρσης δεόμενος ὑπὲρ τοῦ παιδός· ὁ δὲ καὶ
τοῦτο βουλόμενος αὐτῷ χαρίζεσθαι, μάλα μόλις
διεπράξατο σὺν πολλῇ πραγματείᾳ.

Τἆλλα μὲν γὰρ ἦν ἀκριβὴς καὶ νόμιμος, ἐν

---

[1] Ἰδαίου with S and Xenophon (Hell. iv. 1, 39): Ἀδαίου.

your side; but if he entrusts me with the command, I will spare no efforts to punish and injure you in his behalf." On hearing this, Agesilaüs was delighted, and said, as he seized his hand and rose up with him, " O Pharnabazus, I would that such a man as thou might be our friend rather than our enemy."[1]

XIII. As Pharnabazus and his friends were going away, his son, who was left behind, ran up to Agesilaüs and said with a smile : " I make thee my guest-friend, Agesilaüs," and offered him a javelin which he held in his hand. Agesilaüs accepted it, and being delighted with the fair looks and kindly bearing of the boy, looked round upon his companions to see if any one of them had anything that would do for a return-gift to a fair and gallant friend ; and seeing that the horse of Idaeus, his secretary, had a decorated head-gear, he quickly took this off and gave it to the youth. Nor afterwards did he cease to remember him, but when, as time went on, the youth was robbed of his home by his brothers and driven into exile in Peloponnesus, he paid him much attention. He even gave him some assistance in his love affairs. For the Persian was enamoured of an Athenian boy, an athlete, who, owing to his stature and strength, was in danger of being ruled out of the lists at Olympia. He therefore had recourse to Agesilaüs with entreaties to help the boy, and Agesilaüs, wishing to gratify him in this matter also, with very great difficulty and with much trouble effected his desires.[2]

Indeed, although in other matters he was exact and

---

[1] Cf. Xenophon, *Hell*. iv. 1, 28–38, where Agesilaüs adds a promise to respect, in future, the property of Pharnabazus, even in case of war.

[2] Cf. Xenophon, *Hell*. iv. 1, 39 f.

δὲ τοῖς φιλικοῖς πρόφασιν ἐνόμιζεν εἶναι τὸ λίαν
4 δίκαιον. φέρεται γοῦν ἐπιστόλιον αὐτοῦ πρὸς
Ἰδριέα τὸν Κᾶρα τοιοῦτο· "Νικίας εἰ μὲν μὴ
ἀδικεῖ, ἄφες· εἰ δὲ ἀδικεῖ, ἡμῖν ἄφες· πάντως
δὲ ἄφες." ἐν μὲν οὖν τοῖς πλείστοις τοιοῦτος
ὑπὲρ τῶν φίλων ὁ Ἀγησίλαος· ἔστι δὲ ὅπου
πρὸς τὸ συμφέρον ἐχρῆτο τῷ καιρῷ μᾶλλον, ὡς
ἐδήλωσεν, ἀναζυγῆς αὐτῷ θορυβωδεστέρας γενομένης, ἀσθενοῦντα καταλιπὼν τὸν ἐρώμενον. ἐκείνου γὰρ δεομένου καὶ καλοῦντος αὐτὸν ἀπιόντα,
μεταστραφεὶς εἶπεν ὡς χαλεπὸν ἐλεεῖν ἅμα καὶ
φρονεῖν. τουτὶ μὲν Ἱερώνυμος ὁ φιλόσοφος ἱστό-
ρηκεν.

XIV. Ἤδη δὲ περιϊόντος ἐνιαυτοῦ δευτέρου
τῇ στρατηγίᾳ πολὺς ἄνω λόγος ἐχώρει τοῦ Ἀγησιλάου, καὶ δόξα θαυμαστὴ κατεῖχε τῆς τε
σωφροσύνης αὐτοῦ καὶ εὐτελείας καὶ μετριότητος.
ἐσκήνου μὲν γὰρ ἀποδημῶν καθ' αὑτὸν ἐν τοῖς
ἁγιωτάτοις ἱεροῖς, ἃ μὴ πολλοὶ καθορῶσιν ἄνθρωποι πράττοντας ἡμᾶς, τούτων τοὺς θεοὺς ποιούμενος ἐπόπτας καὶ μάρτυρας· ἐν δὲ χιλιάσι
στρατιωτῶν τοσαύταις οὐ ῥᾳδίως ἄν τις εἶδε
2 φαυλοτέραν στιβάδα τῆς Ἀγησιλάου. πρός τε
θάλπος οὕτω καὶ ψῦχος εἶχεν ὥσπερ μόνος ἀεὶ
χρῆσθαι ταῖς ὑπὸ τοῦ θεοῦ κεκραμέναις ὥραις
πεφυκώς. ἥδιστον δὲ θέαμα τοῖς κατοικοῦσι τὴν
Ἀσίαν Ἕλλησιν ἦσαν οἱ πάλαι βαρεῖς καὶ ἀφό-
ρητοι καὶ διαρρέοντες ὑπὸ πλούτου καὶ τρυφῆς
ὕπαρχοι καὶ στρατηγοὶ δεδιότες καὶ θεραπεύοντες

law-abiding, in matters of friendship he thought that rigid justice was a mere pretext. At any rate, there is in circulation a letter of his to Hidrieus the Carian, which runs as follows : "As for Nicias, if he is innocent, acquit him ; if he is guilty, acquit him for my sake ; but in any case acquit him." Such, then, was Agesilaüs in most cases where the interests of his friends were concerned ; but sometimes he used a critical situation rather for his own advantage. Of this he gave an instance when, as he was decamping in some haste and confusion, he left his favourite behind him sick. The sick one besought him loudly as he was departing, but he merely turned and said that it was hard to be compassionate and at the same time prudent. This story is related by Hieronymus the philosopher.

XIV. Agesilaüs had now been nearly two years in the field, and much was said about him in the interior parts of Asia, and a wonderful opinion of his self-restraint, of his simplicity of life, and of his moderation, everywhere prevailed. For when he made a journey, he would take up his quarters in the most sacred precincts by himself,[1] thus making the gods overseers and witnesses of those acts which few men are permitted to see us perform ; and among so many thousands of soldiers, one could hardly find a meaner couch than that of Agesilaüs ; while to heat and cold he was as indifferent as if nature had given him alone the power to adapt himself to the seasons as God has tempered them. And it was most pleasing to the Greeks who dwelt in Asia to see the Persian viceroys and generals, who had long been insufferably cruel, and had revelled in wealth and luxury, now fearful and obsequious before a man who went about

[1] Cf. Xenophon's *Agesilaüs*, v. 7.

ἄνθρωπον ἐν τρίβωνι περιϊόντα λιτῷ, καὶ πρὸς ἓν
ῥῆμα βραχὺ καὶ Λακωνικὸν ἁρμόζοντες ἑαυτοὺς
καὶ μετασχηματίζοντες, ὥστε πολλοῖς ἐπῄει τὰ
τοῦ Τιμοθέου λέγειν,

Ἄρης τύραννος· χρυσὸν δὲ Ἑλλὰς οὐ δέδοικε.

XV. Κινουμένης δὲ τῆς Ἀσίας καὶ πολλαχοῦ πρὸς ἀπόστασιν ὑπεικούσης, ἁρμοσάμενος
τὰς αὐτόθι πόλεις, καὶ ταῖς πολιτείαις δίχα
φόνου καὶ φυγῆς ἀνθρώπων ἀποδοὺς τὸν προσή-
κοντα κόσμον, ἐγνώκει πρόσω χωρεῖν, καὶ τὸν
πόλεμον διάρας ἀπὸ τῆς Ἑλληνικῆς θαλάττης,
περὶ τοῦ σώματος βασιλεῖ καὶ τῆς ἐν Ἐκβα-
τάνοις καὶ Σούσοις εὐδαιμονίας διαμάχεσθαι, καὶ
περισπάσαι πρῶτον αὐτοῦ τὴν σχολήν, ὡς μὴ
καθέζοιτο τοὺς πολέμους βραβεύων τοῖς Ἕλλησι
2 καὶ διαφθείρων τοὺς δημαγωγούς. ἐν τούτῳ δὲ
ἀφικνεῖται πρὸς αὐτὸν Ἐπικυδίδας ὁ Σπαρτιάτης, ἀπαγγέλλων ὅτι πολὺς περιέστηκε τὴν Σπάρτην πόλεμος Ἑλληνικός, καὶ καλοῦσιν ἐκεῖνον οἱ
ἔφοροι καὶ κελεύουσι τοῖς οἴκοι βοηθεῖν.

Ὦ βάρβαρ' ἐξευρόντες Ἕλληνες κακά·

τί γὰρ ἄν τις ἄλλο τὸν φθόνον ἐκεῖνον προσείποι
καὶ τὴν τότε σύστασιν καὶ σύνταξιν ἐφ' ἑαυτοὺς
τῶν Ἑλλήνων; οἳ τῆς τύχης ἄνω φερομένης ἐπε-
λάβοντο, καὶ τὰ ὅπλα πρὸς τοὺς βαρβάρους
βλέποντα καὶ τὸν πόλεμον ἤδη τῆς Ἑλλάδος   604
3 ἐξῳκισμένον αὖθις εἰς ἑαυτοὺς ἔτρεψαν. οὐ γὰρ
ἔγωγε συμφέρομαι τῷ Κορινθίῳ Δημαράτῳ μεγάλης ἡδονῆς ἀπολελεῖφθαι φήσαντι τοὺς μὴ θεα-
σαμένους Ἕλληνας Ἀλέξανδρον ἐν τῷ Δαρείου
θρόνῳ καθήμενον, ἀλλ' εἰκότως ἂν οἶμαι δακρῦ-

38

in a paltry cloak, and at one brief and laconic speech from him conforming themselves to his ways and changing their dress and mien, insomuch that many were moved to cite the words of Timotheus :—

" Ares is Lord ; of gold Greece hath no fear." [1]

XV. Asia being now unsettled and in many quarters inclining to revolt, Agesilaüs set the cities there in order, and restored to their governments, without killing or banishing any one, the proper form. Then he determined to go farther afield, to transfer the war from the Greek sea, to fight for the person of the King and the wealth of Ecbatana and Susa, and above all things to rob that monarch of the power to sit at leisure on his throne, playing the umpire for the Greeks in their wars, and corrupting their popular leaders. But at this point Epicydidas the Spartan came to him with tidings that Sparta was involved in a great war with other Greeks, and that the ephors called upon him and ordered him to come to the aid of his countrymen.

" O barbarous ills devised by Greeks !" [2]

How else can one speak of that jealousy which now leagued and arrayed the Greeks against one another ? They laid violent hands on Fortune in her lofty flight, and turned the weapons which threatened the Barbarians, and War, which had at last been banished from Greece, back again upon themselves. I certainly cannot agree with Demaratus the Corinthian, who said that those Greeks had missed a great pleasure who did not behold Alexander seated on the throne of Dareius, nay, I think that such might well have

---

[1] Cf. Bergk, *Poet. Lyr. Graeci*, iii.[4] p. 622.
[2] Euripides, *Troades*, 766 (Kirchhoff).

σαι, συννοήσαντας ὅτι ταῦτ' Ἀλεξάνδρῳ καὶ
Μακεδόσιν ἀπέλιπον οἱ τότε τοὺς τῶν Ἑλλήνων
στρατηγοὺς περὶ Λεῦκτρα καὶ Κορώνειαν καὶ
Κόρινθον καὶ Ἀρκαδίαν κατανήλωσαν.

4   Ἀγησιλάῳ μέντοι οὐδὲν κρεῖσσον ἢ μεῖζόν ἐστι
τῆς ἀναχωρήσεως ἐκείνης διαπεπραγμένον, οὐδὲ
γέγονε παράδειγμα πειθαρχίας καὶ δικαιοσύνης
ἕτερον κάλλιον. ὅπου γὰρ Ἀννίβας ἤδη κακῶς
πράττων καὶ περιωθούμενος ἐκ τῆς Ἰταλίας
μάλα μόλις ὑπήκουσε τοῖς ἐπὶ τὸν οἴκοι πόλεμον
καλοῦσιν, Ἀλέξανδρος δὲ καὶ προσεπέσκωψε
πυθόμενος τὴν πρὸς Ἆγιν Ἀντιπάτρου μάχην,
εἰπών· "Ἔοικεν, ὦ ἄνδρες, ὅτε Δαρεῖον ἡμεῖς
ἐνικῶμεν ἐνταῦθα, ἐκεῖ τις ἐν Ἀρκαδίᾳ γεγονέναι
5   μυομαχία·" πῶς οὐκ ἦν ἄξιον τὴν Σπάρτην μακα-
ρίσαι τῆς Ἀγησιλάου τιμῆς πρὸς ταύτην καὶ
πρὸς τοὺς νόμους τῆς εὐλαβείας; ὃς ἅμα τῷ
τὴν σκυτάλην ἐλθεῖν εὐτυχίαν τοσαύτην καὶ
δύναμιν παροῦσαν καὶ τηλικαύτας ἐλπίδας ὑφη-
γουμένας ἀφεὶς καὶ προέμενος εὐθὺς ἀπέπλευσεν
"ἀτελευτήτῳ ἐπὶ ἔργῳ," πολὺν ἑαυτοῦ πόθον
τοῖς συμμάχοις ἀπολιπών, καὶ μάλιστα δὴ τὸν
Ἐρασιστράτου τοῦ Φαίακος ἐλέγξας λόγον, εἰπόντος ὡς εἰσὶ δημοσίᾳ μὲν Λακεδαιμόνιοι βελτίονες,
6   ἰδίᾳ δὲ Ἀθηναῖοι. βασιλέα γὰρ ἑαυτὸν καὶ
στρατηγὸν ἄριστον ἐπιδειξάμενος, ἔτι βελτίονα
καὶ ἡδίονα τοῖς χρωμένοις ἰδίᾳ φίλον καὶ συνήθη
παρέσχε. τοῦ δὲ Περσικοῦ νομίσματος χάραγμα

---

[1] At Megalopolis, in Arcadia, 331 B.C., Agis fell fighting,
and the Spartan rebellion at once collapsed. Alexander

shed tears when they reflected that this triumph was
left for Alexander and Macedonians by those who now
squandered the lives of Greek generals on the fields
of Leuctra, Coroneia, and Corinth, and in Arcadia.

Agesilaüs, however, never performed a nobler or
a greater deed than in returning home as he now
did, nor was there ever a fairer example of righteous
obedience to authority. For Hannibal, though he
was already in an evil plight and on the point of
being driven out of Italy, could with the greatest
difficulty bring himself to obey his summons to the
war at home; and Alexander actually went so far as
to jest when he heard of Antipater's battle with
Agis,[1] saying : "It would seem, my men, that while
we were conquering Dareius here, there has been a
battle of mice there in Arcadia." Why, then, should
we not call Sparta happy in the honour paid to her
by Agesilaüs, and in his deference to her laws? No
sooner had the dispatch-roll come to him than he
renounced and abandoned the great good fortune
and power already in his grasp, and the great hopes
which beckoned him on, and at once sailed off, "with
task all unfulfilled," [2] leaving behind a great yearning
for him among his allies, and giving the strongest
confutation to the saying of Erasistratus the son of
Phaeax, who declared that the Lacedaemonians were
better men in public life, but the Athenians in
private. For while approving himself a most excellent king and general, he shewed himself a still
better and more agreeable friend and companion to
those who enjoyed his intimacy. Persian coins were
stamped with the figure of an archer, and Agesilaüs

---

had not the slightest thought of returning home to help
Antipater.

[2] *Iliad*, iv. 175.

τοξότην ἔχοντος, ἀναζευγνύων ἔφη μυρίοις τοξό-
ταις ὑπὸ βασιλέως ἐξελαύνεσθαι τῆς Ἀσίας·
τοσούτων γὰρ εἰς Ἀθήνας καὶ Θήβας κομισθέν-
των καὶ διαδοθέντων τοῖς δημαγωγοῖς, ἐξεπολε-
μώθησαν οἱ δῆμοι πρὸς τοὺς Σπαρτιάτας.

XVI. Ὡς δὲ διαβὰς τὸν Ἑλλήσποντον ἐβάδιζε διὰ τῆς Θρᾴκης, ἐδεήθη μὲν οὐδενὸς τῶν
βαρβάρων, πέμπων δὲ πρὸς ἑκάστους ἐπυνθάνετο
πότερον ὡς φιλίαν ἢ ὡς πολεμίαν διαπορεύηται
τὴν χώραν. οἱ μὲν οὖν ἄλλοι πάντες φιλικῶς
ἐδέχοντο καὶ παρέπεμπον, ὡς ἕκαστος δυνάμεως
εἶχεν· οἱ δὲ καλούμενοι Τράλλεις, οἷς καὶ Ξέρξης
ἔδωκεν, ὡς λέγεται, δῶρα, τῆς διόδου μισθὸν
ᾔτουν τὸν Ἀγησίλαον ἑκατὸν ἀργυρίου τάλαντα
2 καὶ τοσαύτας γυναῖκας. ὁ δὲ κατειρωνευσάμενος
αὐτοὺς καὶ φήσας· "Τί οὖν οὐκ εὐθὺς ἦλθον
ληψόμενοι;" προῆγε, καὶ συμβαλὼν αὐτοῖς παρα-
τεταγμένοις ἐτρέψατο καὶ διέφθειρε πολλούς. τὸ
δ' αὐτὸ καὶ τῷ βασιλεῖ τῶν Μακεδόνων ἐρώτημα
προσέπεμψε· φήσαντος δὲ βουλεύσεσθαι, "Βου-
λευέσθω τοίνυν ἐκεῖνος," εἶπεν, "ἡμεῖς δὲ δὴ
πορευόμεθα." Θαυμάσας οὖν τὴν τόλμαν αὐτοῦ
καὶ δείσας ὁ βασιλεὺς ἐκέλευσεν ὡς φίλον προά-
3 γειν. τῶν δὲ Θετταλῶν τοῖς πολεμίοις συμμα-
χούντων ἐπόρθει τὴν χώραν. εἰς δὲ Λάρισσαν
ἔπεμψε Ξενοκλέα καὶ Σκύθην περὶ φιλίας· συλ-
ληφθέντων δὲ τούτων καὶ παραφυλασσομένων
οἱ μὲν ἄλλοι βαρέως φέροντες ᾤοντο δεῖν τὸν
Ἀγησίλαον περιστρατοπεδεύσαντα πολιορκεῖν

---

[1] According to Xenophon (*Hell.* iii. 5, 1 ff.), Persian money
was distributed in Thebes, Corinth, and Argos. "The
Athenians, though they took no share of the gold, were none
the less eager for war."

said, as he was breaking camp, that the King was driving him out of Asia with ten thousand " archers "; for so much money had been sent to Athens and Thebes and distributed among the popular leaders there, and as a consequence those peoples made war upon the Spartans.[1]

XVI. And when he had crossed the Hellespont and was marching through Thrace,[2] he made no requests of any of the Barbarians, but sent envoys to each people asking whether he should traverse their country as a friend or as a foe. All the rest, accordingly, received him as a friend and assisted him on his way, as they were severally able ; but the people called Trallians, to whom even Xerxes gave gifts, as we are told, demanded of Agesilaüs as a price for his passage a hundred talents of silver and as many women. But he answered them with scorn, asking why, then, they did not come at once to get their price ; and marched forward, and finding them drawn up for battle, engaged them, routed them, and slew many of them. He sent his usual enquiry forward to the king of the Macedonians also, who answered that he would deliberate upon it. " Let him deliberate, then," said Agesilaüs, " but we will march on." In amazement therefore at his boldness, and in fear, the Macedonian king gave orders to let him pass as a friend. Since the Thessalians were in alliance with his enemies, he ravaged their country. But to the city of Larissa he sent Xenocles and Scythes, hoping to secure its friendship. His ambassadors, however, were arrested and kept in close custody, whereupon the rest of his command were indignant, and thought that Agesilaüs ought to

[2] Agesilaüs followed " the very route taken by the Great King when he invaded Hellas " (Xenophon, *Hell.* iv. 2, 8).

τὴν Λάρισσαν, ὁ δὲ φήσας οὐκ ἂν ἐθελῆσαι Θεσσαλίαν ὅλην λαβεῖν ἀπολέσας τῶν ἀνδρῶν τὸν
4 ἕτερον, ὑποσπόνδους αὐτοὺς ἀπέλαβε. καὶ τοῦτ'
ἴσως ἐπ' Ἀγησιλάῳ θαυμαστὸν οὐκ ἦν, ὃς πυθόμενος μάχην μεγάλην γεγονέναι περὶ Κόρινθον,
καὶ ἄνδρας[1] τῶν πάνυ ἐνδόξων ὡς ἔνι μάλιστα
αἰφνίδιον ἀπολωλέναι, καὶ[1] Σπαρτιατῶν μὲν
ὀλίγους παντάπασι τεθνηκέναι, παμπόλλους δὲ
τῶν πολεμίων, οὐκ ὤφθη περιχαρὴς οὐδὲ ἐπηρ-
μένος, ἀλλὰ καὶ πάνυ βαρὺ στενάξας, "Φεῦ
τῆς Ἑλλάδος," ἔφη, "τοσούτους ἄνδρας ἀπολω-
λεκυίας ὑφ' αὑτῆς, ὅσοι ζῶντες ἐδύναντο νικᾶν
5 ὁμοῦ σύμπαντας τοὺς βαρβάρους μαχόμενοι." τῶν
δὲ Φαρσαλίων προσκειμένων αὐτῷ καὶ κακούντων
τὸ στράτευμα, πεντακοσίοις ἱππεῦσιν ἐμβαλεῖν
κελεύσας σὺν αὐτῷ καὶ τρεψάμενος ἔστησε τρόπαιον ὑπὸ τῷ Ναρθακίῳ. καὶ τὴν νίκην ὑπερη-
γάπησεν ἐκείνην, ὅτι συστησάμενος ἱππικὸν αὐτὸς
δι' ἑαυτοῦ τούτῳ μόνῳ τοὺς μέγιστον ἐφ' ἱππικῇ
φρονοῦντας ἐκράτησεν.

XVII. Ἐνταῦθα Διφρίδας οἴκοθεν ἔφορος ὢν
ἀπήντησεν αὐτῷ κελεύων εὐθὺς ἐμβαλεῖν εἰς τὴν
Βοιωτίαν. ὁ δέ, καίπερ ἀπὸ μείζονος παρασκευῆς
ὕστερον τοῦτο ποιῆσαι διανοούμενος, οὐδὲν ᾤετο
δεῖν ἀπειθεῖν τοῖς ἄρχουσιν, ἀλλὰ τοῖς τε μεθ'
ἑαυτοῦ προεῖπεν ἐγγὺς εἶναι τὴν ἡμέραν ἐφ' ἣν ἐξ
Ἀσίας ἥκουσι, καὶ δύο μόρας μετεπέμψατο τῶν
2 περὶ Κόρινθον στρατευομένων. οἱ δὲ ἐν τῇ πόλει
Λακεδαιμόνιοι τιμῶντες αὐτὸν ἐκήρυξαν τῶν
νέων ἀπογράφεσθαι τὸν βουλόμενον τῷ βασιλεῖ

605

---

[1] ἄνδρας . . . καὶ rejected by Sintenis and Bekker, and
questioned by Coraës, after Schaefer; the words are wanting
in *Apophth. Lacon.* 45 (*Morals*, p. 211 e).

encamp about Larissa and lay siege to it. But he
declared that the capture of all Thessaly would not
compensate him for the loss of either one of his men,
and made terms with the enemy in order to get them
back. And perhaps we need not wonder at such
conduct in Agesilaüs, since when he learned that a
great battle had been fought near Corinth,[1] and that
men of the highest repute had suddenly been taken
off, and that although few Spartans altogether had
been killed, the loss of their enemies was very heavy,
he was not seen to be rejoiced or elated, but fetched
a deep groan and said: " Alas for Hellas, which has
by her own hands destroyed so many brave men!
Had they lived, they could have conquered in battle
all the Barbarians in the world." However, when
the Pharsalians annoyed him and harassed his army,
he ordered five hundred horsemen which he led in
person to attack them, routed them, and set up a
trophy at the foot of mount Narthacium. This
victory gave him special pleasure, because with
horsemen of his own mustering and training, and
with no other force, he had conquered those whose
chief pride was placed in their cavalry.[2]

XVII. Here Diphridas, an ephor from Sparta, met
him, with orders to invade Boeotia immediately.
Therefore, although he was purposing to do this
later with a larger armament, he thought it did not
behoove him to disobey the magistrates, but said to
those who were with him that the day was near for
which they had come from Asia. He also sent for
two divisions of the army at Corinth. Then the
Lacedaemonians at home, wishing to do him honour,
made proclamation that any young man who wished

---

[1] 394 B.C. Cf. Xenophon, *Hell*. iv. 2, 18—3, 1 f.
[2] Cf. Xenophon, *Hell*. iv. 3, 9.

βοηθεῖν. ἀπογραψαμένων δὲ πάντων προθύμως, οἱ ἄρχοντες πεντήκοντα τοὺς ἀκμαιοτάτους καὶ ῥωμαλεωτάτους ἐκλέξαντες ἀπέστειλαν.

Ὁ δὲ Ἀγησίλαος εἴσω Πυλῶν παρελθὼν καὶ διοδεύσας τὴν Φωκίδα φίλην οὖσαν, ἐπεὶ τῆς Βοιωτίας πρῶτον ἐπέβη καὶ περὶ τὴν Χαιρώνειαν κατεστρατοπέδευσεν, ἅμα μὲν τὸν ἥλιον ἐκλεί-ποντα καὶ γινόμενον μηνοειδῆ κατεῖδεν, ἅμα δὲ ἤκουσε τεθνάναι Πείσανδρον ἡττημένον ναυμαχίᾳ περὶ Κνίδον ὑπὸ Φαρναβάζου καὶ Κόνωνος. 3 ἠχθέσθη μὲν οὖν, ὡς εἰκός, ἐπὶ τούτοις καὶ διὰ τὸν ἄνδρα καὶ διὰ τὴν πόλιν, ὅπως δὲ μὴ τοῖς στρατιώταις ἐπὶ μάχην βαδίζουσιν ἀθυμία καὶ φόβος ἐμπέσῃ, τἀναντία λέγειν ἐκέλευσε τοὺς ἀπὸ θαλάττης ἥκοντας, ὅτι νικῶσι τῇ ναυμαχίᾳ· καὶ προελθὼν αὐτὸς ἐστεφανωμένος ἔθυσεν εὐαγ-γέλια καὶ διέπεμπε μερίδας τοῖς φίλοις ἀπὸ τῶν τεθυμένων.

XVIII. Ἐπεὶ δὲ προϊὼν καὶ γενόμενος ἐν Κορωνείᾳ κατεῖδε τοὺς πολεμίους καὶ κατώφθη, παρετάξατο δοὺς Ὀρχομενίοις τὸ εὐώνυμον κέρας, αὐτὸς δὲ τὸ δεξιὸν ἐπῆγεν. οἱ δὲ Θηβαῖοι τὸ μὲν δεξιὸν εἶχον αὐτοί, τὸ δὲ εὐώνυμον Ἀργεῖοι. λέγει δὲ τὴν μάχην ὁ Ξενοφῶν ἐκείνην οἵαν οὐκ ἄλλην τῶν πώποτε γενέσθαι· καὶ παρῆν αὐτὸς τῷ Ἀγησιλάῳ συναγωνιζόμενος, ἐξ Ἀσίας διαβε-2 βηκώς. ἡ μὲν οὖν πρώτη σύρραξις οὐκ ἔσχεν ὠθισμὸν οὐδὲ ἀγῶνα πολύν, ἀλλὰ οἵ τε Θηβαῖοι

---

[1] August, 394 B.C.
[2] The soldiers of Agesilaüs were consequently victorious in a skirmish with the enemy, according to Xenophon (*Hell.* iv. 3, 14).

might enlist in aid of the king. All enlisted eagerly, and the magistrates chose out the most mature and vigorous of them to the number of fifty, and sent them off.

Agesilaüs now marched through the pass of Thermopylae, traversed Phocis, which was friendly to Sparta, entered Boeotia, and encamped near Chaeroneia. Here a partial eclipse of the sun occurred, and at the same time[1] news came to him of the death of Peisander, who was defeated in a naval battle off Cnidus by Pharnabazus and Conon. Agesilaüs was naturally much distressed at these tidings, both because of the man thus lost, and of the city which had lost him; but nevertheless, that his soldiers might not be visited with dejection and fear as they were going into battle, he ordered the messengers from the sea to reverse their tidings and say that the Spartans were victorious in the naval battle. He himself also came forth publicly with a garland on his head, offered sacrifices for glad tidings, and sent portions of the sacrificial victims to his friends.[2]

XVIII. After advancing as far as Coroneia and coming within sight of the enemy, he drew up his army in battle array, giving the left wing to the Orchomenians, while he himself led forward the right. On the other side, the Thebans held the right wing themselves, and the Argives the left. Xenophon says that this battle was unlike any ever fought,[3] and he was present himself and fought on the side of Agesilaüs, having crossed over with him from Asia.[4] The first impact, it is true, did not meet with much resistance, nor was it long contested, but the

[3] *Hellenica*, iv. 3, 16.
[4] Cf. Xenophon's *Anabasis*, v. 3, 6.

ταχὺ τοὺς Ὀρχομενίους ἐτρέψαντο καὶ τοὺς
Ἀργείους ὁ Ἀγησίλαος· ἐπεὶ δὲ ἀκούσαντες
ἀμφότεροι τὰ εὐώνυμα πιέζεσθαι καὶ φεύγειν
ἀνέστρεψαν, ἐνταῦθα τῆς νίκης ἀκινδύνου παρούσης, εἰ τῆς κατὰ στόμα μάχης ὑφέσθαι .τοῖς
Θηβαίοις ἠθέλησε καὶ παίειν ἑπόμενος παραλλά-
ξαντας, ὑπὸ θυμοῦ καὶ φιλονεικίας ἐναντίος
ἐχώρει τοῖς ἀνδράσιν, ὤσασθαι κατὰ κράτος
3 βουλόμενος. οἱ δὲ οὐχ ἧττον ἐρρωμένως ἐδέξαντο, καὶ μάχη γίνεται δι' ὅλου μὲν ἰσχυρὰ τοῦ
στρατεύματος, ἰσχυροτάτη δὲ κατ' ἐκεῖνον αὐτὸν
ἐν τοῖς πεντήκοντα τεταγμένον, ὧν εἰς καιρὸν
ἔοικεν ἡ φιλοτιμία τῷ βασιλεῖ γενέσθαι καὶ
σωτήριος. ἀγωνιζόμενοι γὰρ ἐκθύμως καὶ προ-
κινδυνεύοντες ἄτρωτον μὲν αὐτὸν οὐκ ἐδυνήθησαν
φυλάξαι, πολλὰς δὲ διὰ τῶν ὅπλων δεξάμενον εἰς
τὸ σῶμα πληγὰς δόρασι καὶ ξίφεσι μόλις ἀνήρ-
πασαν ζῶντα, καὶ συμφράξαντες πρὸ αὐτοῦ
4 πολλοὺς μὲν ἀνήρουν, πολλοὶ δὲ ἔπιπτον. ὡς
δὲ μέγα ἔργον ἦν ὤσασθαι προτροπάδην τοὺς
Θηβαίους, ἠναγκάσθησαν ὅπερ ἐξ ἀρχῆς οὐκ
ἐβούλοντο ποιῆσαι. διέστησαν γὰρ αὐτοῖς τὴν
φάλαγγα καὶ διέσχον, εἶτα ἀτακτότερον ἤδη
πορευομένους, ὡς διεξέπεσον, ἀκολουθοῦντες καὶ
παραθέοντες ἐκ πλαγίων ἔπαιον. οὐ μὴν ἐτρέ-
ψαντό γε, ἀλλ' ἀπεχώρησαν οἱ Θηβαῖοι πρὸς τὸν
Ἑλικῶνα, μέγα τῇ μάχῃ φρονοῦντες, ὡς ἀήττητοι
καθ' αὑτοὺς γεγονότες.

Thebans speedily routed the Orchomenians, as Agesilaüs did the Argives. Both parties, however, on
hearing that their left wings were overwhelmed and
in flight, turned back. Then, although the victory
might have been his without peril if he had been
willing to refrain from attacking the Thebans in front
and to smite them in the rear after they had passed
by, Agesilaüs was carried away by passion and the
ardour of battle and advanced directly upon them,
wishing to bear them down by sheer force. But they
received him with a vigour that matched his own,
and a battle ensued which was fierce at all points
in the line, but fiercest where the king himself
stood surrounded by his fifty volunteers,[1] whose
opportune and emulous valour seems to have saved
his life. For they fought with the utmost fury and
exposed their lives in his behalf, and though they
were not able to keep him from being wounded, but
many blows of spears and swords pierced his armour
and reached his person, they did succeed in dragging
him off alive, and standing in close array in front of
him, they slew many foes, while many of their own
number fell. But since it proved too hard a task to
break the Theban front, they were forced to do what
at the outset they were loth to do. They opened
their ranks and let the enemy pass through, and then,
when these had got clear, and were already marching
in looser array, the Spartans followed on the run and
smote them on the flanks. They could not, however,
put them to rout, but the Thebans withdrew to
Mount Helicon,[2] greatly elated over the battle, in
which, as they reasoned, their own contingent had
been undefeated.

[1] Cf. chapter xvii. 2. They are not mentioned by Xenophon.
[2] From the slopes of which they had advanced to the battle.

49

XIX. Ἀγησίλαος δέ, καίπερ ὑπὸ τραυμάτων
πολλῶν κακῶς τὸ σῶμα διακείμενος, οὐ πρότερον
ἐπὶ σκηνὴν ἀπῆλθεν ἢ φοράδην ἐνεχθῆναι πρὸς
τὴν φάλαγγα καὶ τοὺς νεκροὺς ἰδεῖν ἐντὸς τῶν
ὅπλων συγκεκομισμένους. ὅσοι μέντοι τῶν πολεμίων εἰς τὸ ἱερὸν κατέφυγον, πάντας ἐκέλευσεν
2 ἀφεθῆναι. πλησίον γὰρ ὁ νεώς ἐστιν ὁ τῆς
Ἰτωνίας Ἀθηνᾶς, καὶ πρὸ αὐτοῦ τρόπαιον ἔστη-
κεν, ὃ πάλαι Βοιωτοὶ Σπάρτωνος στρατηγοῦντος
ἐνταῦθα νικήσαντες Ἀθηναίους καὶ Τολμίδην
ἀποκτείναντες ἔστησαν. ἅμα δ᾽ ἡμέρα βουλόμενος ἐξελέγξαι τοὺς Θηβαίους ὁ Ἀγησίλαος, εἰ
διαμαχοῦνται, στεφανοῦσθαι μὲν ἐκέλευσε τοὺς
στρατιώτας, αὐλεῖν δὲ τοὺς αὐλητάς, ἱστάναι
3 δὲ καὶ κοσμεῖν τρόπαιον ὡς νενικηκότας. ὡς δὲ
ἔπεμψαν οἱ πολέμιοι νεκρῶν ἀναίρεσιν αἰτοῦντες,
ἐσπείσατο, καὶ τὴν νίκην οὕτως ἐκβεβαιωσάμενος
εἰς Δελφοὺς ἀπεκομίσθη, Πυθίων ἀγομένων, καὶ
τήν τε πομπὴν ἐπετέλει τῷ θεῷ καὶ τὴν δεκάτην
ἀπέθυε τῶν ἐκ τῆς Ἀσίας λαφύρων ἑκατὸν
ταλάντων γενομένην.

4 Ἐπεὶ δὲ ἀπενόστησεν οἴκαδε, προσφιλὴς μὲν
ἦν εὐθὺς τοῖς πολίταις καὶ περίβλεπτος ἀπὸ τοῦ
βίου καὶ τῆς διαίτης· οὐ γάρ, ὥσπερ οἱ πλεῖστοι
τῶν στρατηγῶν, καινὸς ἐπανῆλθεν ἀπὸ τῆς ξένης
καὶ κεκινημένος ὑπ᾽ ἀλλοτρίων ἐθῶν, καὶ δυσκο-
λαίνων πρὸς τὰ οἴκοι καὶ ζυγομαχῶν, ἀλλὰ
ὁμοίως τοῖς μηδεπώποτε τὸν Εὐρώταν διαβε-
βηκόσι τὰ παρόντα τιμῶν καὶ στέργων οὐ δεῖπνον

---

[1] In 447 B.C.; cf. the *Pericles*, xviii. 2 f.
[2] Cf the *Nicias*, vi. 5.

XIX. But Agesilaüs, although he was weakened
by many wounds, would not retire to his tent until
he had first been carried to his troops and seen that
the dead were collected within the encampment.
Moreover, he ordered that all of the enemy who
had taken refuge in the sanctuary should be dismissed. For the temple of Athena Itonia was near
at hand, and a trophy stood in front of it, which
the Boeotians had long ago erected, when, under
the command of Sparto, they had defeated the
Athenians there and slain Tolmides their general.[1]
Early next morning, Agesilaüs, wishing to try the
Thebans and see whether they would give him
battle, ordered his soldiers to wreath their heads
and his pipers to play their pipes, while a trophy was
set up and adorned in token of their victory. And
when the enemy sent to him and asked permission
to take up their dead, he made a truce with them,
and having thus assured to himself the victory,[2] proceeded to Delphi,[3] where the Pythian games were
in progress. There he celebrated the customary
procession in honour of the god, and offered up the
tenth of the spoils which he had brought from Asia,
amounting to a hundred talents.

Then he went back home, where his life and
conduct brought him at once the affection and admiration of his fellow-citizens. For, unlike most of
their generals, he came back from foreign parts un-
changed and unaffected by alien customs ; he showed
no dislike towards home fashions, nor was he restive
under them, but honoured and loved what he found
there just as much as those did who had never
crossed the Eurotas ; he made no change in his

[3] Leaving the army in command of Gylis the polemarch
(Xenophon, *Hell.* iv. 3, 21).

5 ἤλλαξεν, οὐ λουτρόν, οὐ θεραπείαν γυναικός, οὐχ
ὅπλων κόσμον, οὐκ οἰκίας κατασκευήν, ἀλλὰ καὶ
τὰς θύρας ἀφῆκεν οὕτως οὔσας σφόδρα παλαιάς,
ὡς δοκεῖν εἶναι, ταύτας ἐκείνας ἃς ἐπέθηκεν
Ἀριστόδημος. καὶ τὸ κάνναθρόν φησιν ὁ Ξενοφῶν οὐδέν τι σεμνότερον εἶναι τῆς ἐκείνου θυγατρὸς ἢ τῶν ἄλλων. κάνναθρα δὲ καλοῦσιν εἴδωλα
γρυπῶν ξύλινα καὶ τραγελάφων ἐν οἷς κομίζουσι
6 τὰς παῖδας ἐν ταῖς πομπαῖς. ὁ μὲν οὖν Ξενοφῶν
ὄνομα τῆς Ἀγησιλάου θυγατρὸς οὐ γέγραφε, καὶ ὁ
Δικαίαρχος ἐπηγανάκτησεν ὡς μήτε τὴν Ἀγησιλάου θυγατέρα μήτε τὴν Ἐπαμινώνδου μητέρα
γινωσκόντων ἡμῶν· ἡμεῖς δὲ εὕρομεν ἐν ταῖς
Λακωνικαῖς ἀναγραφαῖς ὀνομαζομένην γυναῖκα
μὲν Ἀγησιλάου Κλεόραν, θυγατέρας δὲ Εὐπωλίαν
καὶ Πρόαυγαν.[1] ἔστι δὲ καὶ λόγχην ἰδεῖν αὐτοῦ
κειμένην ἄχρι νῦν ἐν Λακεδαίμονι, μηδὲν τῶν
ἄλλων διαφέρουσαν.

XX. Οὐ μὴν ἀλλὰ ὁρῶν ἐνίους τῶν πολιτῶν
ἀπὸ ἱπποτροφίας δοκοῦντας εἶναί τινας καὶ μέγα[2]
φρονοῦντας, ἔπεισε τὴν ἀδελφὴν Κυνίσκαν ἅρμα
καθεῖσαν Ὀλυμπίασιν ἀγωνίσασθαι, βουλόμενος
ἐνδείξασθαι τοῖς Ἕλλησιν ὡς οὐδεμιᾶς ἐστιν
ἀρετῆς, ἀλλὰ πλούτου καὶ δαπάνης ἡ νίκη.
2 Ξενοφῶντα δὲ τὸν σοφὸν ἔχων μεθ' ἑαυτοῦ
σπουδαζόμενον ἐκέλευε τοὺς παῖδας ἐν Λακεδαίμονι τρέφειν μεταπεμψάμενον, ὡς μαθησο-
μένους τῶν μαθημάτων τὸ κάλλιστον, ἄρχεσθαι
καὶ ἄρχειν. τοῦ δὲ Λυσάνδρου τετελευτηκότος
εὑρὼν ἑταιρείαν πολλὴν συνεστῶσαν, ἣν ἐκεῖνος

---

[1] Πρόαυγαν a reading mentioned by Stephanus, and now
found in S : Προλύταν.
[2] μέγα Cobet, van Herwerden, with Fᵃ : μεγάλα.

table, or his baths, or the attendance on his wife, or the decoration of his armour, or the furniture of his house, nay, he actually let its doors remain although they were very old,—one might say they were the very doors which Aristodemus[1] had set up. His daughter's "kannathron," as Xenophon[1] tells us, was no more elaborate than that of any other maid ("kannathra" is the name they give to the wooden figures of griffins or goat-stags in which their young girls are carried at the sacred processions).[2] Xenophon, it is true, has not recorded the name of the daughter of Agesilaüs, and Dicaearchus expressed great indignation that neither her name nor that of the mother of Epaminondas was known to us; but we have found in the Lacedaemonian records that the wife of Agesilaüs was named Cleora, and his daughters Eupolia and Proauga. And one can see his spear also, which is still preserved at Sparta, and which is not at all different from that of other men.

XX. However, on seeing that some of the citizens esteemed themselves highly and were greatly lifted up because they bred racing horses, he persuaded his sister Cynisca to enter a chariot in the contests at Olympia, wishing to shew the Greeks that the victory there was not a mark of any great excellence, but simply of wealth and lavish outlay. Also, having Xenophon the philosopher in his following, and making much of him, he ordered him to send for his sons and rear them at Sparta, that they might learn that fairest of all lessons, how to obey and how to command. Again, finding after Lysander's death that a large society was in existence, which that

---

[1] The great-great-grandson of Heracles; cf. Xenophon, *Agesilaüs*, viii. 7.

[2] These figures of animals were on wheels, and served as carriages (cf. Athenaeus, p. 139 f.).

εὐθὺς ἐπανελθὼν ἀπὸ τῆς Ἀσίας συνέστησεν ἐπὶ
τὸν Ἀγησίλαον, ὥρμησεν αὐτὸν ἐξελέγχειν οἷος
3 ἦν ζῶν πολίτης· καὶ λόγον ἀναγνοὺς ἐν βιβλίῳ
ἀπολελειμμένον, ὃν ἔγραψε μὲν Κλέων ὁ Ἁλι-
καρνασσεύς, ἔμελλε δὲ λέγειν ἀναλαβὼν ὁ Λύσανδρος ἐν τῷ δήμῳ περὶ πραγμάτων καινῶν καὶ
μεταστάσεως τοῦ πολιτεύματος, ἠθέλησεν εἰς
μέσον ἐξενεγκεῖν. ἐπεὶ δέ τις τῶν γερόντων τὸν
λόγον ἀναγνοὺς καὶ φοβηθεὶς τὴν δεινότητα συνε-
βούλευσε μὴ τὸν Λύσανδρον ἀνορύττειν, ἀλλὰ
τὸν λόγον μᾶλλον αὐτῷ συγκατορύττειν, ἐπείσθη
4 καὶ καθησύχαζε. τοὺς δὲ ὑπεναντιουμένους αὐτῷ
φανερῶς μὲν οὐκ ἔβλαπτε, διαπραττόμενος δὲ
πέμπεσθαί τινας ἀεὶ στρατηγοὺς καὶ ἄρχοντας
ἐξ αὐτῶν, ἐπεδείκνυε γενομένους ἐν ταῖς ἐξουσίαις 607
πονηροὺς καὶ πλεονέκτας, εἶτα κρινομένοις πάλιν
αὖ βοηθῶν καὶ συναγωνιζόμενος, οἰκείους ἐκ
διαφόρων ἐποιεῖτο καὶ μεθίστη πρὸς αὑτόν, ὥστε
μηθένα ἀντίπαλον εἶναι.

5 Ὁ γὰρ ἕτερος βασιλεὺς Ἀγησίπολις, ἅτε δὴ
πατρὸς μὲν ὢν φυγάδος, ἡλικίᾳ δὲ παντάπασι
μειράκιον, φύσει δὲ πρᾷος καὶ κόσμιος, οὐ πολλὰ
τῶν πολιτικῶν ἔπραττεν. οὐ μὴν ἀλλὰ καὶ
τοῦτον ἐποιεῖτο χειρόηθη. συσσιτοῦσι γὰρ οἱ
βασιλεῖς εἰς τὸ αὐτὸ φοιτῶντες φιδίτιον, ὅταν
6 ἐπιδημῶσιν. εἰδὼς οὖν ἔνοχον ὄντα τοῖς ἐρω-
τικοῖς τὸν Ἀγησίπολιν, ὥσπερ ἦν αὐτός, ἀεί τινος

---

¹ Cf. the *Lysander*, chapter xxx.

commander, immediately after returning from Asia, had formed against him, Agesilaüs set out to prove what manner of citizen Lysander had been while alive. So, after reading a speech which Lysander had left behind him in book form,—a speech which Cleon of Halicarnassus had composed, but which Lysander had intended to adopt and pronounce before the people in advocacy of a revolution and change in the form of government,—Agesilaüs wished to publish it. But one of the senators, who had read the speech and feared its ability and power, advised the king not to dig Lysander up again, but rather to bury the speech with him, to which advice Agesilaüs listened and held his peace.[1] And as for those who were in opposition to him, he would do them no open injury, but would exert himself to send some of them away from time to time as generals and commanders, and would shew them up if they proved base and grasping in their exercise of authority ; then, contrariwise, when they were brought to trial, he would come to their aid and exert himself in their behalf, and so would make them friends instead of enemies, and bring them over to his side, so that no one was left to oppose him.

For Agesipolis, the other king, since he was the son of an exile,[2] in years a mere stripling, and by nature gentle and quiet, took little part in affairs of state. And yet he too was brought under the sway of Agesilaüs. For the Spartan kings eat together in the same "phiditium," or public mess,[3] whenever they are at home. Accordingly, knowing that Agesipolis was prone to love affairs, just as he was himself,

[2] Pausanias, who was impeached in 395 B.C., went into voluntary exile, and was condemned to death.

[3] Cf. the *Lycurgus*, xii. 1 f.

ὑπῆρχε λόγου περὶ τῶν ἐν ὥρᾳ· καὶ προῆγε τὸν
νεανίσκον εἰς ταὐτὸ καὶ συνήρα καὶ συνέπραττε,
τῶν Λακωνικῶν ἐρώτων οὐδὲν αἰσχρόν, αἰδῶ δὲ
πολλὴν καὶ φιλοτιμίαν καὶ ζῆλον ἀρετῆς ἐχόντων, ὡς ἐν τοῖς περὶ Λυκούργου γέγραπται.

XXI. Μέγιστον οὖν δυνάμενος ἐν τῇ πόλει δια-
πράττεται Τελευτίαν τὸν ὁμομήτριον ἀδελφὸν ἐπὶ
τοῦ ναυτικοῦ γενέσθαι. καὶ στρατευσάμενος εἰς
Κόρινθον αὐτὸς μὲν ᾔει κατὰ γῆν τὰ μακρὰ
τείχη, ταῖς δὲ ναυσὶν ὁ Τελευτίας [1] . . . . . Ἀργείων δὲ τὴν Κόρινθον ἐχόντων τότε καὶ τὰ
Ἴσθμια συντελούντων, ἐπιφανεὶς ἐκείνους μὲν
ἐξήλασεν ἄρτι τῷ θεῷ τεθυκότας, τὴν παρα-
2 σκευὴν ἅπασαν ἀπολιπόντας· ἐπεὶ δὲ τῶν Κορινθίων ὅσοι φυγάδες ἔτυχον παρόντες ἐδεήθησαν
αὐτοῦ τὸν ἀγῶνα διαθεῖναι, τοῦτο μὲν οὐκ ἐποίησεν, αὐτῶν δὲ ἐκείνων διατιθέντων καὶ συντελούντων παρέμεινε καὶ παρέσχεν ἀσφάλειαν. ὕστερον
δὲ ἀπελθόντος αὐτοῦ πάλιν ὑπ' Ἀργείων ἤχθη
τὰ Ἴσθμια, καί τινες μὲν ἐνίκησαν πάλιν, εἰσὶ δὲ
οἳ νενικηκότες πρότερον, ἡττημένοι δὲ ὕστερον,
3 ἀνεγράφησαν. ἐπὶ τούτῳ δὲ πολλὴν ἀπέφηνε
δειλίαν κατηγορεῖν ἑαυτῶν τοὺς Ἀργείους ὁ
Ἀγησίλαος, εἰ σεμνὸν οὕτω καὶ μέγα τὴν

[1] The lacuna after this name may be filled from the words
κατὰ θάλατταν τὰς ναῦς καὶ τὰ νεώρια ἥρηκε, in Xenophon,
Hell. iv. 4, 19.

[1] Chapters xvii. 1 ; xviii. 4.

Agesilaüs would always introduce some discourse about the boys who were of an age to love. He would even lead the young king's fancy toward the object of his own affections, and share with him in wooing and loving, these Spartan loves having nothing shameful in them, but being attended rather with great modesty, high ambition, and an ardent desire for excellence, as I have written in my life of Lycurgus.[1]

XXI. Having thus obtained very great influence in the city, he effected the appointment of Teleutias, his half-brother on his mother's side, as admiral. Then he led an army to Corinth, and himself, by land, captured the long walls, while Teleutias, with his fleet, seized the enemy's ships and dockyards. Then coming suddenly upon the Argives,[2] who at that time held Corinth, and were celebrating the Isthmian games, he drove them away just as they had sacrificed to the god, and made them abandon all their equipment for the festival. At this, the exiles from Corinth who were in his army begged him to hold the games. This, however, he would not do, but remained at hand while they held the games from beginning to end, and afforded them security. Afterwards, when he had departed, the Isthmian games were held afresh by the Argives, and some contestants won their victories a second time, while some were entered in the lists as victors in the first contests, but as vanquished in the second. In this matter Agesilaüs declared that the Argives had brought down upon themselves the charge of great cowardice, since they regarded the conduct of the

---

[2] Plutarch confuses the expedition of 393 B.C. (Xenophon, *Hell*. iv. 4. 19) with that of 390 B.C. (Xenophon, *Hell*. iv. 5, 1 ff.).

ἀγωνοθεσίαν ἡγούμενοι μάχεσθαι περὶ αὐτῆς
οὐκ ἐτόλμησαν. αὐτὸς δὲ πρὸς ταῦτα πάντα
μετρίως ᾤετο δεῖν ἔχειν, καὶ τοὺς μὲν οἴκοι χοροὺς
καὶ ἀγῶνας ἐπεκόσμει καὶ συμπαρῆν ἀεὶ φιλοτιμίας καὶ σπουδῆς μεστὸς ὢν καὶ οὔτε παίδων
οὔτε παρθένων ἁμίλλης ἀπολειπόμενος, ἃ δὲ τοὺς
ἄλλους ἑώρα θαυμάζοντας ἐδόκει μηδὲ γινώσκειν.
4 καὶ ποτε Καλλιππίδης ὁ τῶν τραγῳδιῶν ὑπο-
κριτής, ὄνομα καὶ δόξαν ἔχων ἐν τοῖς Ἕλλησι
καὶ σπουδαζόμενος ὑπὸ πάντων, πρῶτον μὲν
ἀπήντησεν αὐτῷ καὶ προσεῖπεν, ἔπειτα σοβαρῶς
εἰς τοὺς συμπεριπατοῦντας ἐμβαλὼν ἑαυτὸν
ἐπεδείκνυτο νομίζων ἐκεῖνον ἄρξειν τινὸς φιλο-
φροσύνης, τέλος δὲ εἶπεν· "Οὐκ ἐπιγινώσκεις με,
ὦ βασιλεῦ;" κἀκεῖνος ἀποβλέψας πρὸς αὐτὸν
εἶπεν· "'Αλλὰ οὐ σύγε ἐσσὶ Καλλιππίδας ὁ
δεικηλίκτας;" οὕτω δὲ Λακεδαιμόνιοι τοὺς μίμους
5 καλοῦσι. παρακαλούμενος δὲ πάλιν ἀκοῦσαι
τοῦ τὴν ἀηδόνα μιμουμένου, παρῃτήσατο φήσας,
"Αὐτᾶς ἄκουκα." τοῦ δὲ ἰατροῦ Μενεκράτους,
ἐπεὶ κατατυχὼν ἔν τισιν ἀπεγνωσμέναις θεραπεί-
αις Ζεὺς ἐπεκλήθη, φορτικῶς ταύτῃ χρωμένου τῇ
προσωνυμίᾳ καὶ δὴ καὶ πρὸς ἐκεῖνον ἐπιστεῖλαι
τολμήσαντος οὕτως· "Μενεκράτης Ζεὺς βασιλεῖ
'Αγησιλάῳ χαίρειν," ἀντέγραψε· "Βασιλεὺς
'Αγησίλαος Μενεκράτει ὑγιαίνειν."

XXII. Διατρίβοντος δὲ περὶ τὴν Κορινθίων
αὐτοῦ καὶ τὸ Ἡραῖον εἰληφότος καὶ τὰ αἰχμά-
λωτα τοὺς στρατιώτας ἄγοντας καὶ φέροντας
ἐπιβλέποντος, ἀφίκοντο πρέσβεις ἐκ Θηβῶν περὶ

games as so great and august a privilege, and yet
had not the courage to fight for it. He himself
thought that moderation ought to be observed in all
these matters, and sought to improve the local choirs
and games. These he always attended, full of
ambitious ardour, and was absent from no contest in
which either boys or girls competed. Those things,
however, for which he saw the rest of the world
filled with admiration, he appeared not even to
recognize. Once upon a time Callipides the tragic
actor, who had a name and fame among the Greeks and
was eagerly courted by all, first met him and addressed
him, then pompously thrust himself into his company
of attendants, showing plainly that he expected the
king to make him some friendly overtures, and finally
said : " Dost thou not recognize me, O King ? " The
king fixed his eyes upon him and said : " Yea, art
thou not Callipides the buffoon ? " And again, when
he was invited to hear the man who imitated the
nightingale, he declined, saying : " I have heard the
bird herself." [1] Again, Menecrates the physician,
who, for his success in certain desperate cases, had
received the surname of Zeus, and had the bad taste
to employ the appellation, actually dared to write
the king a letter beginning thus : " Menecrates Zeus,
to King Agesilaüs, greeting." To this Agesilaüs
replied : " King Agesilaüs, to Menecrates, health and
sanity."

XXII. While he was lingering in the territory of
Corinth, he seized the Heraeum,[2] and as he was
watching his soldiers carry off the prisoners and
booty, messengers came from Thebes to treat for

[1] Cf. the *Lycurgus*, xx. 5.
[2] The refugees in the Heraeum came out and surrendered
of their own accord (Xenophon, *Hell.* iv. 5, 5).

φιλίας. ὁ δὲ μισῶν μὲν ἀεὶ τὴν πόλιν, οἰόμενος
δὲ τότε καὶ συμφέρειν ἐνυβρίσαι, προσεποιεῖτο
μήτε ὁρᾶν αὐτοὺς μήτε ἀκούειν ἐντυγχανόντων.

2 ἔπαθε δὲ πρᾶγμα νεμεσητόν· οὔπω γὰρ ἀπηλλαγ-
μένων τῶν Θηβαίων ἧκόν τινες ἀπαγγέλλοντες
αὐτῷ τὴν μόραν ὑπὸ Ἰφικράτους κατακεκόφθαι.
καὶ πάθος τοῦτο μέγα διὰ πολλοῦ χρόνου συνέ-
πεσεν αὐτοῖς· πολλοὺς γὰρ ἄνδρας ἀγαθοὺς ἀπέ-
βαλον κρατηθέντας ὑπό τε πελταστῶν ὁπλίτας
καὶ μισθοφόρων Λακεδαιμονίους.

3 Ἀνεπήδησε μὲν οὖν εὐθὺς ὁ Ἀγησίλαος ὡς 60
βοηθήσων· ἐπεὶ δὲ ἔγνω διαπεπραγμένους, αὖθις
εἰς τὸ Ἡραῖον ἧκε, καὶ τοὺς Βοιωτοὺς τότε προσελθεῖν κελεύσας, ἐχρημάτιζεν. ὡς δὲ ἀνθυβρί-
ζοντες ἐκεῖνοι τῆς μὲν εἰρήνης οὐκ ἐμέμνηντο,
παρεθῆναι δὲ ἠξίουν εἰς Κόρινθον, ὀργισθεὶς ὁ
Ἀγησίλαος εἶπεν· "Εἴγε βούλεσθε τοὺς φίλους
ὑμῶν ἰδεῖν μέγα φρονοῦντας ἐφ' οἷς εὐτυχοῦσιν,

4 αὔριον ἀσφαλῶς ὑμῖν τοῦτο ὑπάρξει." καὶ παραλαβὼν αὐτοὺς τῇ ὑστεραίᾳ τήν τε χώραν τῶν
Κορινθίων ἔκοπτε καὶ πρὸς τὴν πόλιν αὐτὴν
προσῆλθεν. οὕτω δὲ τοὺς Κορινθίους ἐξελέγξας
ἀμύνεσθαι μὴ τολμῶντας, ἀφῆκε τὴν πρεσβείαν.
αὐτὸς δὲ τοὺς περιλελειμμένους ἄνδρας ἐκ τῆς
μόρας ἀναλαβὼν ἀπῆγεν εἰς Λακεδαίμονα, πρὸ
ἡμέρας ποιούμενος τὰς ἀναζεύξεις καὶ πάλιν
σκοταίους τὰς καταλύσεις, ὅπως οἱ μισοῦντες καὶ
βασκαίνοντες τῶν Ἀρκάδων μὴ ἐπιχαίρωσιν.

peace. But he had always hated that city, and
thinking this an advantageous time also for insulting
it, pretended neither to see nor hear its ambassadors
when they presented themselves. But his pride
soon had a fall; for the Thebans had not yet departed when messengers came to him with tidings
that the Spartan division had been cut to pieces by
Iphicrates.[1] This was the greatest disaster that
had happened to the Spartans in a long time; for
they lost many brave men, and those men were overwhelmed by targeteers and mercenaries, though they
were men-at-arms and Lacedaemonians.

At once, then, Agesilaüs sprang up to go to their
assistance, but when he learned that it was all over
with them,[2] he came back again to the Heraeum, and
ordering the Boeotians then to come before him,
gave them an audience. But they returned his
insolence by making no mention of peace, but simply
asking safe conduct into Corinth. Agesilaüs was
wroth at this, and said: "If you wish to see your
friends when they are elated at their successes, you
can do so to-morrow in all safety." And taking them
along with him on the next day, he ravaged the
territory of the Corinthians, and advanced to the
very gates of the city. After he had thus proved
that the Corinthians did not dare to resist him, he
dismissed the embassy. Then he himself, picking up
the survivors of the division that had been cut to
pieces, led them back to Sparta, always breaking
camp before it was day, and pitching the next camp
after it was dark, in order that the hateful and
malicious Arcadians might not exult over them.

[1] At Lechaeum, the port of Corinth on the Corinthian
gulf, in 390 B.C. (Xenophon, *Hell.* iv. 5, 11-18).

[2] He had marched till he was "well within the plateau of
Lechaeum" (Xenophon, *Hell.* iv. 5, 8).

5   Ἐκ τούτου χαριζόμενος τοῖς Ἀχαιοῖς διέβαινεν
εἰς Ἀκαρνανίαν στρατιᾷ μετ' αὐτῶν, καὶ πολλὴν
μὲν ἠλάσατο λείαν, μάχῃ δὲ τοὺς Ἀκαρνᾶνας
ἐνίκησε. δεομένων δὲ τῶν Ἀχαιῶν ὅπως τὸν
χειμῶνα παραμείνας ἀφέληται τὸν σπόρον τῶν
πολεμίων, τοὐναντίον ἔφη ποιήσειν· μᾶλλον γὰρ
φοβηθήσεσθαι τὸν πόλεμον αὐτούς, ἐὰν ἐσπαρ-
μένην τὴν γῆν εἰς ὥρας ἔχωσιν· ὃ καὶ συνέβη.
παραγγελλομένης γὰρ αὖθις ἐπ' αὐτοὺς στρατείας
διηλλάγησαν τοῖς Ἀχαιοῖς.

XXIII. Ἐπεὶ δὲ Κόνων καὶ Φαρνάβαζος τῷ
βασιλέως ναυτικῷ θαλαττοκρατοῦντες ἐπόρθουν
τὰ παράλια τῆς Λακωνικῆς, ἐτειχίσθη δὲ καὶ τὸ
ἄστυ τῶν Ἀθηναίων Φαρναβάζου χρήματα δόντος,
ἔδοξε τοῖς Λακεδαιμονίοις εἰρήνην ποιεῖσθαι πρὸς
βασιλέα· καὶ πέμπουσιν Ἀνταλκίδαν πρὸς Τιρί-
βαζον, αἴσχιστα καὶ παρανομώτατα τοὺς τὴν
Ἀσίαν κατοικοῦντας Ἕλληνας, ὑπὲρ ὧν ἐπολέ-
2   μησεν Ἀγησίλαος, βασιλεῖ παραδιδόντες. ὅθεν
ἥκιστα συνέβη τῆς κακοδοξίας ταύτης Ἀγησιλάῳ
μετασχεῖν. ὁ γὰρ Ἀνταλκίδας ἐχθρὸς ἦν αὐτῷ,
καὶ τὴν εἰρήνην ἐξ ἅπαντος ἔπραττεν ὡς τοῦ
πολέμου τὸν Ἀγησίλαον αὔξοντος καὶ ποιοῦντος
ἐνδοξότατον καὶ μέγιστον. οὐ μὴν ἀλλὰ καὶ
πρὸς τὸν εἰπόντα τοὺς Λακεδαιμονίους μηδίζειν
ὁ Ἀγησίλαος ἀπεκρίνατο μᾶλλον τοὺς Μήδους
3   λακωνίζειν. τοῖς δὲ μὴ βουλομένοις δέχεσθαι
τὴν εἰρήνην ἀπειλῶν καὶ καταγγέλλων πόλεμον
ἠνάγκασεν ἐμμένειν ἅπαντας οἷς ὁ Πέρσης
ἐδικαίωσε, μάλιστα διὰ τοὺς Θηβαίους, ὅπως

---

[1] In 390–389 B.C. (Xenophon, *Hell.* iv. 6, 3—7, 1).
[2] In 393 B.C. (Xenophon, *Hell.* iv. 8, 10).
[3] The Great King's satrap in Western Asia.

After this, to gratify the Achaeans, he crossed over with them on an expedition into Acarnania,[1] where he drove away much booty and conquered the Acarnanians in battle. But when the Achaeans asked him to spend the winter there in order to prevent the enemy from sowing their fields, he said he would do the opposite of this; for the enemy would dread the war more if their land was sown when summer came. And this proved true; for when a second expedition against them was announced, they came to terms with the Achaeans.

XXIII. When Conon and Pharnabazus with the Great King's fleet were masters of the sea and were ravaging the coasts of Laconia, and after the walls of Athens had been rebuilt with the money which Pharnabazus furnished,[2] the Lacedaemonians decided to make peace with the king of Persia. To that end, they sent Antalcidas to Tiribazus,[3] and in the most shameful and lawless fashion handed over to the King the Greeks resident in Asia, in whose behalf Agesilaüs had waged war. Agesilaüs, therefore, could have had no part at all in this infamy. For Antalcidas was his enemy, and put forth all his efforts to make the peace because he saw that the war enhanced to the utmost the reputation and power of Agesilaüs. Notwithstanding this, to one who remarked that the Lacedaemonians were favouring the Medes, Agesilaüs replied that the Medes were the rather favouring the Lacedaemonians. Moreover, by threatening with war the Greeks who were unwilling to accept the peace, he forced them all to abide by the terms which the Persian dictated,[4] more especially on account of the Thebans, his object being to make

[4] The peace of Antalcidas was ratified by all the Greek states except Thebes in 387 B.C. (Xenophon, *Hell.* v. 1, 29 ff.).

αὐτόνομον τὴν Βοιωτίαν ἀφέντες ἀσθενέστεροι
γένωνται. δῆλον δὲ τοῦτο τοῖς ὕστερον ἐποίησεν.
ἐπεὶ γὰρ Φοιβίδας ἔργον εἰργάσατο δεινὸν ἐν
σπονδαῖς καὶ εἰρήνῃ τὴν Καδμείαν καταλαβών,
καὶ πάντες μὲν ἠγανάκτουν οἱ Ἕλληνες, χαλεπῶς
4 δὲ ἔφερον οἱ Σπαρτιᾶται, καὶ μάλιστα οἱ διαφερόμενοι τῷ Ἀγησιλάῳ μετ' ὀργῆς ἐπυνθάνοντο
τοῦ Φοιβίδου τίνος ταῦτα κελεύσαντος ἔπραξεν,
εἰς ἐκεῖνον τὴν ὑπόνοιαν τρέποντες, οὐκ ὤκνησε
τῷ Φοιβίδᾳ βοηθῶν λέγειν ἀναφανδὸν ὅτι δεῖ τὴν
πρᾶξιν αὐτήν, εἴ τι χρήσιμον ἔχει, σκοπεῖν· τὰ
γὰρ συμφέροντα τῇ Λακεδαίμονι καλῶς ἔχειν
5 αὐτοματίζεσθαι, κἂν μηδεὶς κελεύσῃ. καίτοι τῷ
λόγῳ πανταχοῦ τὴν δικαιοσύνην ἀπέφαινε πρωτεύειν τῶν ἀρετῶν· ἀνδρείας μὲν γὰρ οὐδὲν ὄφελος
εἶναι, μὴ παρούσης δικαιοσύνης, εἰ δὲ δίκαιοι
πάντες γένοιντο, μηδὲν ἀνδρείας δεήσεσθαι. πρὸς
δὲ τοὺς λέγοντας ὅτι ταῦτα δοκεῖ τῷ μεγάλῳ
βασιλεῖ, "Τί δ' ἐκεῖνος ἐμοῦ," εἶπε, "μείζων, εἰ
μὴ καὶ δικαιότερος;" ὀρθῶς καὶ καλῶς οἰόμενος
δεῖν τῷ δικαίῳ καθάπερ μέτρῳ βασιλικῷ μετρεῖ-
6 σθαι τὴν ὑπεροχὴν τοῦ μείζονος. ἦν δὲ τῆς
εἰρήνης γενομένης ἔπεμψεν αὐτῷ περὶ ξενίας καὶ 6
φιλίας ἐπιστολὴν ὁ βασιλεύς, οὐκ ἔλαβεν, εἰπὼν
ἐξαρκεῖν τὴν κοινὴν φιλίαν, καὶ μηδὲν ἰδίας
δεήσεσθαι μενούσης ἐκείνης. ἐν δὲ τοῖς ἔργοις
οὐκέτι ταύτην διαφυλάττων τὴν δόξαν, ἀλλὰ τῇ
φιλοτιμίᾳ καὶ τῇ φιλονεικίᾳ πολλαχοῦ συνεκ-
7 φερόμενος, καὶ μάλιστα τῇ πρὸς Θηβαίους, οὐ
μόνον ἔσωσε τὸν Φοιβίδαν, ἀλλὰ καὶ τὴν πόλιν

them weaker by leaving Boeotia independent of
the King. This he made clear by his subsequent
behaviour. For when Phoebidas committed the foul
deed of seizing the Cadmeia [1] in a time of perfect
peace, and all the Greeks were indignant and the
Spartans displeased at the act, and when especially
those who were at variance with Agesilaüs angrily
asked Phoebidas by whose command he had done
this thing, thereby turning suspicion upon Agesilaüs,
he did not scruple to come to the help of Phoebidas,
and to say openly that they must consider whether
the act itself was serviceable or not ; for that which
was advantageous to Sparta might well be done independently, even if no one ordered it. And yet in
his discourse he was always declaring that justice
was the first of the virtues ; for valour was of no use
unless justice attended it, and if all men should be
just, there would be no need of valour. And to
those who said, "This is the pleasure of the Great
King," he would say, "How is he greater than I
unless he is also more just ?", rightly and nobly
thinking that justice must be the measure wherewith
the relative greatness of kings is measured. And
when, after the peace was concluded, the Great King
sent him a letter proposing guest-friendship, he
would not accept it, saying that the public friendship
was enough, and that while that lasted there would
be no need of a private one. Yet in his acts he no
longer observed these opinions, but was often carried
away by ambition and contentiousness, and particularly in his treatment of the Thebans. For he
not only rescued Phoebidas from punishment, but

---

[1] The citadel of Thebes. It was seized by Phoebidas in
383 B.C. (Xenophon, *Hell.* v. 2, 26 ff.).

ἔπεισεν εἰς αὑτὴν ἀναδέξασθαι τὸ ἀδίκημα καὶ
κατέχειν τὴν Καδμείαν δι' ἑαυτῆς, τῶν δὲ πραγμάτων καὶ τῆς πολιτείας Ἀρχίαν καὶ Λεοντίδαν
ἀποδεῖξαι κυρίους, δι' ὧν ὁ Φοιβίδας εἰσῆλθε καὶ
κατέλαβε τὴν ἀκρόπολιν.

XXIV. Ἦν μὲν οὖν εὐθὺς ἐκ τούτων ὑπόνοια
Φοιβίδου μὲν ἔργον εἶναι, βούλευμα δὲ Ἀγησιλάου τὸ πεπραγμένον· αἱ δὲ ὕστερον πράξεις
ὁμολογουμένην ἐποίησαν τὴν αἰτίαν. ὡς γὰρ
ἐξέβαλον οἱ Θηβαῖοι τὴν φρουρὰν καὶ τὴν πόλιν
ἠλευθέρωσαν, ἐγκαλῶν αὐτοῖς ὅτι τὸν Ἀρχίαν
καὶ τὸν Λεοντίδαν ἀπεκτόνεσαν, ἔργῳ μὲν τυράννους, λόγῳ δὲ πολεμάρχους ὄντας, ἐξήνεγκε
2 πόλεμον πρὸς αὐτούς. καὶ Κλεόμβροτος ἤδη
βασιλεύων Ἀγησιπόλιδος τεθνηκότος, εἰς Βοιωτίαν ἐπέμφθη μετὰ δυνάμεως· ὁ γὰρ Ἀγησίλαος,
ὡς ἔτη τεσσαράκοντα γεγονὼς ἀφ' ἥβης καὶ
στρατείας ἔχων ἄφεσιν ὑπὸ τῶν νόμων, ἔφυγε τὴν
στρατηγίαν[1] ἐκείνην, αἰσχυνόμενος εἰ Φλιασίοις
ὀλίγον ἔμπροσθεν ὑπὲρ φυγάδων πεπολεμηκώς,
αὖθις ὀφθήσεται Θηβαίους κακῶς ποιῶν διὰ τοὺς
τυράννους.

3 Ἦν δέ τις Λάκων Σφοδρίας ἐκ τῆς ὑπεναντίας
στάσεως τῷ Ἀγησιλάῳ τεταγμένος ἐν Θεσπιαῖς
ἁρμοστής, οὐκ ἄτολμος μὲν οὐδ' ἀφιλότιμος ἀνήρ,
ἀεὶ δ' ἐλπίδων μᾶλλον ἢ φρενῶν ἀγαθῶν μεστός.
οὗτος ἐπιθυμῶν ὀνόματος μεγάλου, καὶ τὸν Φοιβίδαν νομίζων ἔνδοξον γεγονέναι καὶ περιβόητον
ἀπὸ τοῦ περὶ Θήβας τολμήματος, ἐπείσθη πολὺ
κάλλιον εἶναι καὶ λαμπρότερον εἰ τὸν Πειραιᾶ
καταλάβοι δι' ἑαυτοῦ καὶ τῶν Ἀθηναίων ἀφέ-

---

[1] στρατηγίαν with Stephanus, Coraës, and S : στρατείαν.

actually persuaded Sparta to assume responsibility
for his iniquity and occupy the Cadmeia on its own
account, besides putting the administration of Thebes
into the hands of Archias and Leontidas, by whose
aid Phoebidas had entered and seized the acropolis.

XXIV. Of course this gave rise at once to a
suspicion that while Phoebidas had done the deed,
Agesilaüs had counselled it ; and his subsequent acts
brought the charge into general belief. For when
the Thebans expelled the Spartan garrison and
liberated their city,[1] he charged them with the
murder of Archias and Leontidas, who were really
tyrants, though polemarchs in name, and levied war
upon them. And Cleombrotus, who was king now
that Agesipolis was dead, was sent into Boeotia with
an army ; for Agesilaüs, who had now borne arms for
forty years, and was therefore exempt by law from
military service, declined this command. He was
ashamed, after having recently made war upon the
Phliasians in behalf of their exiles,[2] to be seen now
harrying the Thebans in the interests of their
tyrants.[3]

Now, there was a certain Lacedaemonian named
Sphodrias, of the party opposed to Agesilaüs, who
had been appointed harmost at Thespiae. He lacked
neither boldness nor ambition, but always abounded
in hopes rather than in good judgement. This man,
coveting a great name, and considering that Phoebidas had made himself famous far and near by his
bold deed at Thebes, was persuaded that it would
be a far more honourable and brilliant exploit for him
to seize the Peiraeus on his own account and rob the

[1] In 379 B.C., with the help of the Athenians (Xenophon,
Hell. v. 4, 2–12). Cf. the *Pelopidas*, ix.–xiii.
[2] In 380–379 B.C. (Xenophon, *Hell.* v. 3, 13–25).
[3] Cf. Xenophon, *Hell.* v. 4, 13.

λοιτο τὴν θάλασσαν, ἐκ γῆς ἀπροσδοκήτως
4 ἐπελθών. λέγουσι δὲ τοῦτο μηχάνημα γενέσθαι
τῶν περὶ Πελοπίδαν καὶ Μέλωνα βοιωταρχῶν.
ὑπέπεμψαν γὰρ ἀνθρώπους λακωνίζειν προσ-
ποιουμένους, οἳ τὸν Σφοδρίαν ἐπαινοῦντες καὶ
μεγαλύνοντες ὡς ἔργου τηλικούτου μόνον ἄξιον,
ἐπῆραν καὶ παρώρμησεν ἀνελέσθαι πρᾶξιν ἄδικον
μὲν ὁμοίως ἐκείνῃ καὶ παράνομον, τόλμης δὲ καὶ
5 τύχης ἐνδεᾶ γενομένην. ἡμέρα γὰρ αὐτὸν ἐν τῷ
Θριασίῳ πεδίῳ κατέλαβε καὶ κατέλαμψεν ἐλ-
πίσαντα νυκτὸς προσμίξειν τῷ Πειραιεῖ· καὶ φῶς
ἀφ' ἱερῶν τινων Ἐλευσινόθεν ἰδόντας λέγουσι
φρῖξαι καὶ περιφόβους γενέσθαι τοὺς στρατιώτας.
αὐτὸς δὲ τοῦ θράσους ἐξέπεσεν, ὡς οὐκέτι λαθεῖν
ἦν, καί τινα βραχεῖαν ἁρπαγὴν θέμενος αἰσχρῶς
6 ἀνεχώρησε καὶ ἀδόξως εἰς τὰς Θεσπιάς. ἐκ δὲ
τούτου κατήγοροι μὲν ἐπέμφθησαν εἰς Σπάρτην ἐξ
Ἀθηνῶν, εὖρον δὲ κατηγορίας[1] μηδὲν ἐπὶ τὸν
Σφοδρίαν δεομένους τοὺς ἄρχοντας, ἀλλὰ θανάτου
κρίσιν αὐτῷ προειρηκότας, ἣν ἐκεῖνος ὑπομένειν
ἀπέγνω, φοβούμενος τὴν ὀργὴν τῶν πολιτῶν
αἰσχυνομένων τοὺς Ἀθηναίους καὶ βουλομένων
συναδικεῖσθαι δοκεῖν, ἵνα μὴ συναδικεῖν δοκῶσιν.

XXV. Εἶχεν οὖν υἱὸν ὁ Σφοδρίας Κλεώνυμον,
οὗ παιδὸς ὄντος ἔτι καὶ καλοῦ τὴν ὄψιν Ἀρχίδαμος ὁ Ἀγησιλάου τοῦ βασιλέως υἱὸς ἤρα. καὶ
τότε συνηγωνία μὲν ὡς εἰκὸς αὐτῷ[2] κινδυνεύοντι

---

[1] κατηγορίας with S : κατηγόρων.
[2] ὡς εἰκὸς αὐτῷ with S ; other MSS. ὡς εἰκὸς ἦν : αὐτῷ.

Athenians of access to the sea, attacking them unexpectedly by land. It is said, too, that the scheme was devised by Pelopidas and Melo, chief magistrates at Thebes.[1] They privily sent men to him who pretended to be Spartan sympathizers, and they, by praising and exalting Sphodrias as the only man worthy to undertake so great a task, urged and incited him into an act which was no less lawless and unjust than the seizure of the Cadmeia, though it was essayed without courage or good fortune. For full daylight overtook him while he was yet in the Thriasian plain, although he had hoped to attack the Peiraeus by night. It is said also that his soldiers saw a light streaming from certain sanctuaries at Eleusis, and were filled with shuddering fear. Their commander himself lost all his courage, since concealment was no longer possible, and after ravaging the country a little, retired disgracefully and ingloriously to Thespiae. Hereupon men were sent from Athens to Sparta to denounce Sphodrias. They found, however, that the magistrates there had no need of their denunciation, but had already indicted Sphodrias on a capital charge. This charge he determined not to meet, fearing the wrath of his countrymen, who were ashamed in the presence of the Athenians, and wished to be thought wronged with them, that they might not be thought wrongdoers with Sphodrias.

XXV. Now Sphodrias had a son, Cleonymus, who was still a boy and fair to look upon, and of whom Archidamus, the son of King Agesilaüs, was enamoured. In this crisis Archidamus naturally sympathized with his favourite because of the peril in

[1] Their object was to embroil Athens and Sparta (Xenophon, *Hell.* v. 4, 20–24).

περὶ τοῦ πατρός, συμπράττειν δὲ φανερῶς καὶ
βοηθεῖν οὐκ εἶχεν· ἦν γὰρ ὁ Σφοδρίας ἐκ τῶν
2 διαφόρων τοῦ Ἀγησιλάου. τοῦ δὲ Κλεωνύμου
προσελθόντος αὐτῷ καὶ μετὰ δεήσεως καὶ δακρύων
ἐντυχόντος, ὅπως τὸν Ἀγησίλαον εὔνουν παρά- 610
σχῃ, μάλιστα γὰρ ἐκεῖνον αὐτοῖς φοβερὸν εἶναι,
τρεῖς μὲν ἢ τέσσαρας ἡμέρας αἰδούμενος τὸν
πατέρα καὶ δεδιὼς σιωπῇ παρηκολούθει· τέλος
δὲ τῆς κρίσεως ἐγγὺς οὔσης ἐτόλμησεν εἰπεῖν
πρὸς τὸν Ἀγησίλαον ὅτι Κλεώνυμος αὐτοῦ
3 δεηθείη περὶ τοῦ πατρός. ὁ δὲ Ἀγησίλαος εἰδὼς
ἐρῶντα τὸν Ἀρχίδαμον οὐκ ἔπαυσεν· ἦν γὰρ ὁ
Κλεώνυμος εὐθὺς ἐκ παίδων ἐπίδοξος, εἴ τις καὶ
ἄλλος, ἀνὴρ ἔσεσθαι σπουδαῖος. οὐ μὴν ἐνέδωκέ
τι τότε χρηστὸν ἢ φιλάνθρωπον ἐλπίσαι δεομένῳ
τῷ παιδί, σκέψεσθαι δὲ φήσας ὅ τι καλῶς ἔχοι
4 καὶ πρεπόντως, ἀπῆλθεν. αἰδούμενος οὖν ὁ
Ἀρχίδαμος ἐξέλειπε τὸ προσιέναι τῷ Κλεωνύμῳ,
καίπερ εἰωθὼς πολλάκις τοῦτο τῆς ἡμέρας ποιεῖν
πρότερον. ἐκ δὲ τούτου κἀκεῖνοι τὰ κατὰ τὸν
Σφοδρίαν μᾶλλον ἀπέγνωσαν, ἄχρι οὗ τῶν
Ἀγησιλάου φίλων Ἐτυμοκλῆς ἔν τινι κοινολογίᾳ
πρὸς αὐτοὺς ἀπεγύμνωσε τὴν γνώμην τοῦ Ἀγησι-
λάου· τὸ μὲν γὰρ ἔργον ὡς ἔνι μάλιστα ψέγειν
αὐτόν, ἄλλως γε μὴν ἄνδρα τὸν Σφοδρίαν ἀγαθὸν
ἡγεῖσθαι καὶ τὴν πόλιν ὁρᾶν τοιούτων στρα-
5 τιωτῶν δεομένην. τούτους γὰρ ὁ Ἀγησίλαος
ἑκάστοτε τοὺς λόγους ἐποιεῖτο περὶ τῆς δίκης, τῷ
παιδὶ χαρίζεσθαι βουλόμενος, ὥστε καὶ τὸν
Κλεώνυμον εὐθὺς αἰσθάνεσθαι τὴν σπουδὴν τοῦ
Ἀρχιδάμου καὶ τοὺς φίλους τοὺς τοῦ Σφοδρίου
θαρροῦντας ἤδη βοηθεῖν. ἦν δὲ καὶ φιλότεκνος
ὁ Ἀγησίλαος διαφερόντως· καὶ περὶ ἐκείνου τὸ

which his father stood, but he was unable to aid and assist him openly, since Sphodrias was one of the opponents of Agesilaüs. But when Cleonymus came to him in tears and begged him to mollify Agesilaüs, from whom he and his father had most to fear, for three or four days he was restrained by awe and fear from saying anything to Agesilaüs as he followed him about; but finally, when the trial was near at hand, he plucked up courage to tell him that Cleonymus had begged him to intercede for his father. Now Agesilaüs, although he knew of the love of Archidamus, had not put a stop to it, since Cleonymus, from his early boyhood, had given special promise of becoming an earnest and worthy man. At this time, however, he did not permit his son to expect any advantage or kindness in answer to his prayer; he merely said, as he went away, that he would consider what was the honourable and fitting course in the matter. Archidamus was therefore mortified, and ceased to visit Cleonymus, although before this he had done so many times a day. As a consequence, the friends of Sphodrias also were more in despair of his case, until Etymocles, one of the friends of Agesilaüs, conferred with them and disclosed the mind of the king, namely, that he blamed to the utmost what Sphodrias had done, but yet thought him a brave man, and saw that the city needed just such soldiers. For this was the way in which Agesilaüs always spoke about the trial, in his desire to gratify his son, so that Cleonymus was at once aware of the zealous efforts of Archidamus in his behalf, and the friends of Sphodrias had courage at last to come to his help. It is a fact also that Agesilaüs was excessively fond of his children, and a story is told of his joining in their childish play. Once,

τῆς παιδιᾶς λέγουσιν, ὅτι μικροῖς τοῖς παιδίοις
οὖσι κάλαμον περιβεβηκὼς ὥσπερ ἵππον οἴκοι
συνέπαιζεν, ὀφθεὶς δὲ ὑπό τινος τῶν φίλων παρεκάλει μηδενὶ φράσαι, πρὶν ἂν καὶ αὐτὸς πατὴρ
παίδων γένηται.

XXVI. Ἀπολυθέντος δὲ τοῦ Σφοδρίου, καὶ
τῶν Ἀθηναίων, ὡς ἐπύθοντο, πρὸς πόλεμον τραπομένων, σφόδρα κακῶς ὁ Ἀγησίλαος ἤκουσε,
δι' ἐπιθυμίαν ἄτοπον καὶ παιδαριώδη δοκῶν
ἐμποδὼν γεγονέναι κρίσει δικαίᾳ, καὶ τὴν πόλιν
παραίτιον ἀπειργάσθαι παρανομημάτων τηλι-
2 κούτων εἰς τοὺς Ἕλληνας. ἐπεὶ δὲ τὸν Κλεόμβροτον οὐχ ἑώρα πρόθυμον ὄντα πολεμεῖν τοῖς
Θηβαίοις, οὕτω δὴ χαίρειν τὸν νόμον ἐάσας ᾧ
πρόσθεν ἐχρῆτο περὶ τῆς στρατείας, αὐτὸς εἰς
Βοιωτίαν ἐνέβαλεν ἤδη καὶ κακῶς ἐποίει τοὺς
Θηβαίους καὶ πάλιν ἀντέπασχεν, ὥστε καὶ τρω-
θέντος αὐτοῦ ποτε τὸν Ἀνταλκίδαν εἰπεῖν
"Ἦ καλὰ τὰ διδασκάλια παρὰ Θηβαίων ἀπολαμβάνεις, μὴ βουλομένους μηδὲ ἐπισταμένους
3 μάχεσθαι διδάξας." τῷ γὰρ ὄντι Θηβαίους
αὐτοὺς ἑαυτῶν πολεμικωτάτους τότε γενέσθαι
φασί, ταῖς πολλαῖς στρατείαις τῶν Λακεδαιμονίων ἐπ' αὐτοὺς ὥσπερ ἐγγυμνασαμένους. διὸ
καὶ Λυκοῦργος ὁ παλαιὸς ἐν ταῖς καλουμέναις
τρισὶ ῥήτραις ἀπεῖπε μὴ πολλάκις ἐπὶ τοὺς
αὐτοὺς στρατεύειν, ὅπως μὴ πολεμεῖν μανθά-
νωσιν.

Ἦν δὲ καὶ τοῖς συμμάχοις τῶν Λακεδαιμονίων

when they were very small, he bestrode a stick, and was playing horse with them in the house, and when he was spied doing this by one of his friends, he entreated him not to tell any one, until he himself should be a father of children.

XXVI. But after Sphodrias was acquitted,[1] and the Athenians, on learning of it, were inclined to go to war, Agesilaüs was very harshly criticized. It was thought that, to gratify an absurd and childish desire, he had opposed the course of justice in a trial, and made the city accessory to great crimes against the Greeks. Besides, when he saw that his colleague Cleombrotus was little inclined to make war upon the Thebans, he waived the exemption by law which he had formerly claimed in the matter of the expedition, and presently led an incursion into Boeotia himself,[2] where he inflicted damage upon the Thebans, and in his turn met with reverses, so that one day when he was wounded, Antalcidas said to him : " Indeed, this is a fine tuition-fee which thou art getting from the Thebans, for teaching them how to fight when they did not wish to do it, and did not even know how." For the Thebans are said to have been really more war-like at this time than ever before, owing to the many expeditions which the Lacedaemonians made against them, by which they were virtually schooled in arms. And Lycurgus of old, in one of his three so-called " rhetras," forbade his people to make frequent expeditions against the same foes, in order that those foes might not learn how to make war.[3]

Moreover, the allies of the Lacedaemonians were

---

[1] Cf. Xenophon, *Hell.* v. 4, 24–34.

[2] According to Xenophon (*Hell.* v. 4, 35), he was asked to do so by the Lacedaemonians, who preferred him to Cleombrotus as a leader.   This was in 378 B.C.

[3] Cf. the *Lycurgus*, xiii. 6.

ἐπαχθὴς ὁ Ἀγησίλαος, ὡς δι' οὐδὲν ἔγκλημα
δημόσιον, ἀλλὰ θυμῷ τινι καὶ φιλονεικίᾳ τοὺς
4 Θηβαίους ἀπολέσαι ζητῶν. οὐδὲν οὖν ἔλεγον
δεόμενοι φθείρεσθαι δεῦρο κἀκεῖσε καθ' ἕκαστον
ἐνιαυτόν, ὀλίγοις τοσοῦτοι συνακολουθοῦντες.
ἔνθα δὲ δὴ λέγεται τὸν Ἀγησίλαον, ἐξελέγξαι
βουλόμενος αὐτῶν τὸ πλῆθος, τόδε μηχανήσα-
σθαι. πάντας ἐκέλευσε καθίσαι τοὺς συμμάχους
μετ' ἀλλήλων ἀναμεμιγμένους, ἰδίᾳ δὲ τοὺς Λακε-
5 δαιμονίους ἐφ' ἑαυτῶν. εἶτα ἐκήρυττε τοὺς κερα-
μεῖς ἀνίστασθαι πρῶτον· ὡς δὲ ἀνέστησαν οὗτοι,
δεύτερον ἐκήρυττε τοὺς χαλκεῖς, εἶτα τέκτονας
ἐφεξῆς καὶ οἰκοδόμους καὶ τῶν ἄλλων τεχνῶν
ἑκάστην. πάντες οὖν ὀλίγου δεῖν ἀνέστησαν οἱ
σύμμαχοι, τῶν δὲ Λακεδαιμονίων οὐδείς· ἀπεί-
ρητο γὰρ αὐτοῖς τέχνην ἐργάζεσθαι καὶ μανθάνειν
βάναυσον. οὕτω δὴ γελάσας ὁ Ἀγησίλαος,
"Ὁρᾶτε," εἶπεν, "ὦ ἄνδρες, ὅσῳ πλείονας ὑμῶν
στρατιώτας ἐκπέμπομεν ἡμεῖς."

XXVII. Ἐν δὲ Μεγάροις, ὅτε τὴν στρατιὰν
ἀπῆγεν ἐκ Θηβῶν, ἀναβαίνοντος αὐτοῦ πρὸς τὸ
ἀρχεῖον εἰς τὴν ἀκρόπολιν, σπάσμα καὶ πόνον
ἰσχυρὸν ἔλαβε τὸ ὑγιὲς σκέλος· ἐκ δὲ τούτου
διογκωθὲν μεστὸν αἵματος ἔδοξε γεγονέναι, καὶ
2 φλεγμονὴν ὑπερβάλλουσαν παρεῖχεν. ἰατροῦ δέ
τινος Συρακουσίου τὴν ὑπὸ τῷ σφυρῷ φλέβα
σχάσαντος, αἱ μὲν ἀλγηδόνες ἔληξαν, αἵματος
δὲ πολλοῦ φερομένου καὶ ῥέοντος ἀνεπισχέτως
λιποψυχία πολλὴ καὶ κίνδυνος ὀξὺς ἀπ' αὐτῆς
περιέστη τὸν Ἀγησίλαον. οὐ μὴν ἀλλὰ τότε γε
τὴν φορὰν τοῦ αἵματος ἔπαυσε· καὶ κομισθεὶς εἰς

---

[1] Cf. the *Lycurgus*, xxiv. 2.

offended at Agesilaüs, because, as they said, it was
not upon any public ground of complaint, but by
reason of some passionate resentment of his own,
that he sought to destroy the Thebans. Accordingly,
they said they had no wish to be dragged hither and
thither to destruction every year, they themselves so
many, and the Lacedaemonians, with whom they
followed, so few. It was at this time, we are told,
that Agesilaüs, wishing to refute their argument from
numbers, devised the following scheme. He ordered
all the allies to sit down by themselves promiscuously,
and the Lacedaemonians apart by themselves. Then
his herald called upon the potters to stand up first,
and after them the smiths, next, the carpenters in
their turn, and the builders, and so on through all the
handicrafts. In response, almost all the allies rose
up, but not a man of the Lacedaemonians ; for they
were forbidden to learn or practise a manual art.[1]
Then Agesilaüs said with a laugh : "You see, O men,
how many more soldiers than you we are sending
out."

XXVII. But in Megara, when he was leading his
army back from Thebes,[2] as he was going up to the
senate-house in the acropolis, he was seized with a
cramp and violent pain in his sound leg, which then
swelled up, appeared to be congested, and showed
signs of excessive inflammation. As soon as a certain
Syracusan physician had opened a vein below the
ankle, the pains relaxed, but much blood flowed and
could not be checked, so that Agesilaüs was very
faint from its loss, and in dire peril of his life. At
last, however, the flow of blood was stopped, and
Agesilaüs was carried to Sparta, where he remained

[2] From a second incursion into Boeotia, made in 377 B.C.
(Xenophon, *Hell.* v. 4, 47–55 ; 58).

Λακεδαίμονα πολὺν χρόνον ἔσχεν ἀρρώστως καὶ
πρὸς τὰς στρατείας ἀδυνάτως.

3 Ἐν δὲ τῷ χρόνῳ τούτῳ πολλὰ συνέβη πταίσ-
ματα τοῖς Σπαρτιάταις καὶ κατὰ γῆν καὶ κατὰ
θάλατταν· ὧν ἦν τὸ περὶ Τεγύρας μέγιστον, ὅπου
πρῶτον ἐκ παρατάξεως κρατηθέντες ὑπὸ Θηβαίων ἡττήθησαν. ἔδοξεν οὖν πᾶσι θέσθαι πρὸς
πάντας εἰρήνην· καὶ συνῆλθον ἀπὸ τῆς Ἑλλάδος
πρέσβεις εἰς Λακεδαίμονα ποιησόμενοι τὰς δια-
4 λύσεις. ὧν εἷς ἦν Ἐπαμεινώνδας, ἀνὴρ ἔνδοξος
ἐπὶ παιδείᾳ καὶ φιλοσοφίᾳ, στρατηγίας δὲ πεῖραν
οὔπω δεδωκώς. οὗτος ὁρῶν τοὺς ἄλλους ἅπαντας
ὑποκατακλινομένους τῷ Ἀγησιλάῳ, μόνος ἐχρήσατο φρονήματι παρρησίαν ἔχοντι, καὶ διεξῆλθε
λόγον, οὐχ ὑπὲρ Θηβαίων, ἀλλὰ ὑπὲρ τῆς
Ἑλλάδος ὁμοῦ κοινόν, τὸν μὲν πόλεμον ἀποδει-
κνύων αὔξοντα τὴν Σπάρτην ἐξ ὧν ἅπαντες οἱ
λοιποὶ κακῶς πάσχουσι, τὴν δὲ εἰρήνην ἰσότητι
καὶ τῷ δικαίῳ κτᾶσθαι κελεύων· οὕτω γὰρ αὐτὴν
διαμενεῖν, ἴσων ἁπάντων γενομένων.

XXVIII. Ὁρῶν οὖν ὁ Ἀγησίλαος ὑπερφυῶς
ἀγαμένους καὶ προσέχοντας αὐτῷ τοὺς Ἕλληνας,
ἠρώτησεν εἰ νομίζει δίκαιον εἶναι καὶ ἴσον αὐτονομεῖσθαι τὴν Βοιωτίαν. ἀντερωτήσαντος δὲ
τοῦ Ἐπαμεινώνδου ταχὺ καὶ τεθαρρηκότως εἰ
κἀκεῖνος οἴεται δίκαιον αὐτονομεῖσθαι τὴν Λακωνικήν, ἀναπηδήσας ὁ Ἀγησίλαος μετ᾽ ὀργῆς ἐκέλευσε λέγειν σαφῶς αὐτὸν εἰ τὴν Βοιωτίαν ἀφίη-
2 σιν αὐτόνομον. τὸ δὲ αὐτὸ τοῦτο πάλιν τοῦ
Ἐπαμεινώνδου φήσαντος, εἰ τὴν Λακωνικὴν ἀφίη-

---

[1] This battle, fought in 375 B.C., is not mentioned by
Xenophon, but is described by Plutarch in the *Pelopidas*,

for a long time in a weak condition and unable to take the field.

During this time the Spartans met with many reverses both by land and sea, the greatest of which was at Tegyra, where for the first time they were overpowered by the Thebans in a pitched battle.[1] There was, accordingly, a general sentiment in favour of a general peace, and ambassadors from all Hellas came together at Sparta to settle its terms.[2] One of these ambassadors was Epaminondas, a man of repute for culture and philosophy, although he had not yet given proof of capacity as a general. This man, seeing the rest all cringing before Agesilaüs, alone had the courage of his convictions, and made a speech, not in behalf of Thebes, his native city, but of all Greece in common, declaring that war made Sparta great at the expense of the sufferings of all the other states, and urging that peace be made on terms of equality and justice, for it would endure only when all parties to it were made equal.

XXVIII. Agesilaüs, accordingly, seeing that the Greeks all listened to Epaminondas with the greatest attention and admiration, asked him whether he considered it justice and equality that the cities of Boeotia should be independent of Thebes. Then when Epaminondas promptly and boldly asked him in reply whether he too thought it justice for the cities of Laconia to be independent of Sparta, Agesilaüs sprang from his seat and wrathfully bade him say plainly whether he intended to make the cities of Boeotia independent. And when Epaminondas answered again in the same way by asking whether

chapters xvi. and xvii., doubtless on the authority of Ephorus (cf. Diodorus, xv. 81, 2).

[2] In 371 B.C. (Xenophon, *Hell.* vi. 3, 3–20).

σιν αὐτόνομον, οὕτω τραχέως ἔσχεν ὁ Ἀγησίλαος
καὶ τὴν πρόφασιν ἠγάπησεν ὡς εὐθὺς ἐξαλεῖψαι
τὸ τῶν Θηβαίων ὄνομα τῆς εἰρήνης καὶ προειπεῖν
πόλεμον αὐτοῖς· τοὺς δὲ ἄλλους Ἕλληνας διαλ-
λαγέντας ἐκέλευσεν ἀπιέναι, τὰ μὲν ἀκεστὰ τῆς
εἰρήνης, τὰ δὲ ἀνήκεστα τοῦ πολέμου ποιοῦντας.
ἔργον γὰρ ἦν πάσας ἐκκαθᾶραι καὶ διαλῦσαι τὰς
ἀμφιλογίας.

3   Ἔτυχε δὲ κατ' ἐκεῖνον τὸν χρόνον ἐν Φωκεῦσιν
ὢν ὁ Κλεόμβροτος μετὰ δυνάμεως. εὐθὺς οὖν
ἔπεμπον οἱ ἔφοροι κελεύοντες αὐτὸν ἐπὶ Θηβαίους ἄγειν τὸ στράτευμα· καὶ τοὺς συμμάχους
περιπέμποντες ἤθροιζον, ἀπροθύμους μὲν ὄντας
καὶ βαρυνομένους τὸν πόλεμον, οὔπω δὲ θαρροῦντας ἀντιλέγειν οὐδὲ ἀπειθεῖν τοῖς Λακεδαι-
4 μονίοις.   πολλῶν δὲ σημείων μοχθηρῶν γενομένων, ὡς ἐν τῷ περὶ Ἐπαμεινώνδου γέγραπται,
καὶ Προθόου τοῦ Λάκωνος ἐναντιουμένου πρὸς
τὴν στρατείαν, οὐκ ἀνῆκεν ὁ Ἀγησίλαος, ἀλλ'
ἐξέπραξε τὸν πόλεμον, ἐλπίζων αὐτοῖς μὲν τῆς
Ἑλλάδος ὅλης ὑπαρχούσης, ἐκσπόνδων δὲ τῶν
Θηβαίων γενομένων, καιρὸν εἶναι δίκην λαβεῖν
5 παρ' αὐτῶν.   δηλοῖ δὲ τὸ σὺν ὀργῇ μᾶλλον ἢ
λογισμῷ γενέσθαι τὴν στρατείαν ἐκείνην ὁ και-
ρός.   τῇ γὰρ τετράδι ἐπὶ δέκα τοῦ Σκιροφο-
ριῶνος μηνὸς ἐποιήσαντο τὰς σπονδὰς ἐν Λακε- 6
δαίμονι, τῇ δὲ πέμπτῃ τοῦ Ἑκατομβαιῶνος ἡττήθησαν ἐν Λεύκτροις ἡμερῶν εἴκοσι διαγενομένων.
ἀπέθανον δὲ χίλιοι Λακεδαιμονίων καὶ Κλεόμβροτος ὁ βασιλεὺς καὶ περὶ αὐτὸν οἱ κράτιστοι

---

[1] According to Xenophon (*loc. cit.*), who makes no mention
of Epaminondas, the Thebans had signed as Thebans, but on

he intended to make the cities of Laconia independent, Agesilaüs became violent and was glad of the pretext for at once erasing the name of the Thebans from the treaty of peace and declaring war upon them.[1] The rest of the Greeks, however, he ordered to depart, now that they were reconciled with each other, leaving differences which could be healed to the terms of peace, and those which could not, to war, since it was a hard task to settle and remove all their disputes.

At this time Cleombrotus was in Phocis with an army. The ephors therefore immediately sent him orders to lead his forces against Thebes. They also sent round a summons for an assembly of their allies, who were without zeal for the war and thought it a great burden, but were not yet bold enough to oppose or disobey the Lacedaemonians. And although many baleful signs appeared, as I have written in my Life of Epaminondas,[2] and though Prothoüs the Laconian made opposition to the expedition, Agesilaüs would not give in, but brought the war to pass. He thought that since all Hellas was on their side, and the Thebans had been excluded from the treaty, it was a favourable time for the Spartans to take vengeance on them. But the time chosen for it proves that this expedition was made from anger more than from careful calculation. For the treaty of peace was made at Lacedaemon on the fourteenth of the month Scirophorion, and on the fifth of Hecatombaeon the Lacedaemonians were defeated at Leuctra,—an interval of twenty days. In that battle a thousand Lacedaemonians fell, besides Cleombrotus the king, and

the next day wished to substitute Boeotians for Thebans. This Agesilaüs refused to permit. It would have recognized the supremacy of Thebes in Boeotia. [2] Not extant.

6 τῶν Σπαρτιατῶν. ἐν οἷς καὶ Κλεώνυμόν φασι
τὸν Σφοδρίου τὸν καλὸν τρὶς πεσόντα πρὸ τοῦ
βασιλέως καὶ τοσαυτάκις ἐξαναστάντα καὶ μαχόμενον τοῖς Θηβαίοις ἀποθανεῖν.

XXIX. Συμβάντος δὲ τοῖς τε Λακεδαιμονίοις
πταίσματος ἀπροσδοκήτου καὶ τοῖς Θηβαίοις
παρὰ δόξαν εὐτυχήματος οἷον οὐ γέγονεν ἄλλοις
Ἕλλησι πρὸς Ἕλληνας ἀγωνισαμένοις, οὐδὲν ἄν
τις ἧττον ἐζήλωσε τῆς ἀρετῆς καὶ ἠγάσθη τὴν
2 ἡττημένην πόλιν ἢ τὴν νικῶσαν. ὁ μὲν γὰρ
Ξενοφῶν φησι τῶν ἀγαθῶν ἀνδρῶν ἔχειν τι καὶ
τὰς ἐν οἴνῳ καὶ παιδιᾷ φωνὰς καὶ διατριβὰς
ἀξιομνημόνευτον, ὀρθῶς λέγων· ἔστι δὲ οὐχ ἧττον, ἀλλὰ καὶ μᾶλλον ἄξιον κατανοεῖν καὶ θεᾶ-
σθαι τῶν ἀγαθῶν ἃ παρὰ τὰς τύχας πράττουσι
καὶ λέγουσι διευσχημονοῦντες. ἔτυχε μὲν γὰρ ἡ
πόλις ἑορτὴν ἄγουσα καὶ ξένων οὖσα μεστὴ·
γυμνοπαιδίαι γὰρ ἦσαν ἀγωνιζομένων χορῶν ἐν
τῷ θεάτρῳ· παρῆσαν δ' ἀπὸ Λεύκτρων οἱ τὴν
3 συμφορὰν ἀπαγγέλλοντες. οἱ δὲ ἔφοροι, καίπερ
εὐθὺς ὄντος καταφανοῦς ὅτι διέφθαρται τὰ πράγματα καὶ τὴν ἀρχὴν ἀπολωλέκασιν, οὔτε χορὸν
ἐξελθεῖν εἴασαν οὔτε τὸ σχῆμα τῆς ἑορτῆς μετα-
βαλεῖν τὴν πόλιν, ἀλλὰ κατ' οἰκίαν τῶν τεθνεώτων τοῖς προσήκουσι τὰ ὀνόματα πέμψαντες,
αὐτοὶ τὰ περὶ τὴν θέαν καὶ τὸν ἀγῶνα τῶν χορῶν
4 ἔπραττον. ἅμα δὲ ἡμέρᾳ φανερῶν ἤδη γεγονότων
πᾶσι τῶν τε σωζομένων καὶ τῶν τεθνεώτων, οἱ
μὲν τῶν τεθνεώτων πατέρες καὶ κηδεσταὶ καὶ
οἰκεῖοι καταβαίνοντες εἰς ἀγορὰν ἀλλήλους ἐδε-
ξιοῦντο λιπαροὶ τὰ πρόσωπα, φρονήματος μεστοὶ
καὶ γήθους, οἱ δὲ τῶν σωζομένων, ὥσπερ ἐπὶ

around him the mightiest of the Spartans. Among these, they say, was Cleonymus, the beautiful son of Sphodrias,[1] who was thrice struck down in front of his king, as many times rose again to his feet, and died there, fighting the Thebans.

XXIX. Now that the Lacedaemonians had met with an unexpected reverse, and the Thebans with an unlooked-for success surpassing that of any other Hellenes at strife with Hellenes, the high conduct of the defeated city was no less to be envied and admired than that of the victorious city. Xenophon says [2] that in the case of noble men, there is much that is worth recording even in what they say and do at their wine and in their sports, and he is right; and it is no less, but even more, worth while to observe carefully the decorum with which noble men speak and act in the midst of adversity. The city was holding a festival and was full of strangers; for the "gymnopaediae" were in progress and choirs of boys were competing with one another in the theatre; then came the messengers of calamity from Leuctra. But the ephors, although it was at once apparent that their cause was ruined and their supremacy lost, would not allow a choral performance to be omitted, nor the fashion of the festival to be changed by the city, but after sending the names of the slain warriors to the homes of their kindred, they themselves conducted the spectacle and the choral contests to a close. On the next morning also, now that everyone knew who had survived the battle and who had been slain, the fathers and kindred and friends of the slain went down into the market-place and greeted one another with bright faces, full of pride and exultation; while the friends of the survivors, as if

---

[1] Cf. chapter xxv. 1.   [2] *Symposium*, i. 1.

πένθει, μετὰ τῶν γυναικῶν οἴκοι διέτριβον, εἰ δέ
τις ὑπ' ἀνάγκης προέλθοι, καὶ σχήματι καὶ φωνῇ
καὶ βλέμματι ταπεινὸς ἐφαίνετο καὶ συνεσταλ-
5 μένος. ἔτι δὲ μᾶλλον τῶν γυναικῶν ἰδεῖν ἦν καὶ
πυθέσθαι τὴν μὲν ζῶντα προσδεχομένην υἱὸν ἀπὸ
τῆς μάχης κατηφῆ καὶ σιωπηλήν, τὰς δὲ τῶν
πεπτωκέναι λεγομένων ἔν τε τοῖς ἱεροῖς εὐθὺς
ἀναστρεφομένας, καὶ πρὸς ἀλλήλας ἱλαρῶς καὶ
φιλοτίμως βαδιζούσας.

XXX. Οὐ μὴν ἀλλὰ τοῖς πολλοῖς, ὡς ἀφί-
σταντο μὲν οἱ σύμμαχοι, προσεδοκᾶτο δὲ νενικηκὼς Ἐπαμεινώνδας καὶ μεγαλοφρονῶν ἐμβαλεῖν
εἰς Πελοπόννησον, ἔννοια τῶν χρησμῶν ἐνέπεσε
τότε, πρὸς τὴν χωλότητα τοῦ Ἀγησιλάου, καὶ
δυσθυμία πολλὴ καὶ πτοία πρὸς τὸ θεῖον, ὡς
διὰ τοῦτο πραττούσης κακῶς τῆς πόλεως, ὅτι
τὸν ἀρτίποδα τῆς βασιλείας ἐκβαλόντες εἵλοντο
χωλὸν καὶ πεπηρωμένον· ὃ παντὸς μᾶλλον αὐτοὺς ἐδίδασκε φράζεσθαι καὶ φυλάττεσθαι τὸ
2 δαιμόνιον. διὰ δὲ τὴν ἄλλην δύναμιν αὐτοῦ καὶ
ἀρετὴν καὶ δόξαν οὐ μόνον ἐχρῶντο βασιλεῖ καὶ
στρατηγῷ τῶν κατὰ πόλεμον, ἀλλὰ καὶ τῶν πολιτικῶν ἀποριῶν ἰατρῷ καὶ διαιτητῇ, τοῖς ἐν τῇ
μάχῃ καταδειλιάσασιν, οὓς αὐτοὶ τρέσαντας
ὀνομάζουσιν, ὀκνοῦντες τὰς ἐκ τῶν νόμων ἀτιμίας
προσάγειν, πολλοῖς οὖσι καὶ δυνατοῖς, φοβού-
3 μενοι νεωτερισμὸν ἀπ' αὐτῶν. οὐ γὰρ μόνον
ἀρχῆς ἀπείργονται πάσης, ἀλλὰ καὶ δοῦναί τινι
τούτων γυναῖκα καὶ λαβεῖν ἄδοξόν ἐστι· παίει
δὲ ὁ βουλόμενος αὐτοὺς τῶν ἐντυγχανόντων. οἱ

in mourning, tarried at home with the women, and
if one of them was obliged to appear in public, his
garb and speech and looks betokened his humiliation
and abasement.[1]   And a still greater difference was
to be seen (or heard about) in the women; she who
expected her son back from the battle alive was
dejected and silent, but the mothers of those reported to have fallen immediately frequented the
temples, and visited one another with an air of
gladness and pride.

XXX. The greater number, however, when their
allies were falling away from them and it was expected that Epaminondas, in all the pride of a
conqueror, would invade Peloponnesus, fell to
thinking of the oracles,[2] in view of the lameness of
Agesilaüs, and were full of dejection and consternation in respect to the divine powers, believing
that their city was in an evil plight because they had
dethroned the sound-footed king and chosen instead
a lame and halting one,—the very thing which the
deity was trying to teach them carefully to avoid.
And yet otherwise he had such power and valour and
fame that they not only continued to employ him as
king and general in matters pertaining to war, but
also as physician and arbiter in their civil perplexities.
For instance, upon those who had shewn cowardice
in the battle, whom they themselves call " tresantes,"
or *run-aways*, they hesitated to inflict the disabilities
required by the laws, since the men were numerous
and powerful, for fear that they might stir up a
revolution.   For such men are not only debarred
from every office, but intermarriage with any of them
is a disgrace, and any one who meets them may
strike them if he pleases.   Moreover, they are

[1] Cf. Xenophon, *Hell.* vi. 4, 16.   [2] Cf. chapter iii. 4 f.

δὲ καρτεροῦσι περιϊόντες αὐχμηροὶ καὶ ταπεινοί,
τρίβωνάς τε προσερραμμένους χρώματος βαπτοῦ
φοροῦσι, καὶ ξυρῶνται μέρος τῆς ὑπήνης, μέρος δὲ
4 τρέφουσι. δεινὸν οὖν ἦν τοιούτους ἐν τῇ πόλει
περιορᾶν πολλοὺς οὐκ ὀλίγων δεομένῃ στρατιωτῶν. καὶ νομοθέτην αἱροῦνται τὸν Ἀγησίλαον.
ὁ δὲ μήτε προσθεὶς τι μήτε ἀφελὼν μήτε μετα-
γράψας εἰσῆλθεν εἰς τὸ πλῆθος τῶν Λακεδαι-
μονίων· καὶ φήσας ὅτι τοὺς νόμους δεῖ σήμερον 61
ἐᾶν καθεύδειν, ἐκ δὲ τῆς σήμερον ἡμέρας κυρίους
εἶναι πρὸς τὸ λοιπόν, ἅμα τούς τε νόμους τῇ
5 πόλει καὶ τοὺς ἄνδρας ἐπιτίμους ἐφύλαξε. βουλόμενος δὲ τὴν παροῦσαν ἀθυμίαν καὶ κατήφειαν ἀφελεῖν τῶν νέων ἐνέβαλεν εἰς Ἀρκαδίαν,
καὶ μάχην μὲν ἰσχυρῶς ἐφυλάξατο συνάψαι τοῖς
ἐναντίοις, ἑλὼν δὲ πολίχνην τινὰ τῶν Μαντινέων
καὶ τὴν χώραν ἐπιδραμών, ἐλαφροτέραν ἐποίησε
ταῖς ἐλπίσι καὶ ἡδίω τὴν πόλιν, ὡς οὐ παντάπασιν ἀπεγνωσμένην.

XXXI. Ἐκ δὲ τούτου παρῆν εἰς τὴν Λακωνικὴν ὁ Ἐπαμεινώνδας μετὰ τῶν συμμάχων, οὐκ
ἐλάττονας ἔχων τετρακισμυρίων ὁπλιτῶν. πολλοὶ δὲ καὶ ψιλοὶ καὶ ἄνοπλοι πρὸς ἁρπαγὴν
συνηκολούθουν, ὥστε μυριάδας ἑπτὰ τοῦ σύμ-
παντος ὄχλου συνεισβαλεῖν εἰς τὴν Λακωνικήν.
2 ἦν μὲν δὴ χρόνος οὐκ ἐλάττων ἐτῶν ἑξακοσίων
ἀφ' οὗ κατῴκουν τὴν Λακεδαίμονα Δωριεῖς· ἐν δὲ
τούτῳ παντὶ τότε πρῶτον ὤφθησαν ἐν τῇ χώρᾳ
πολέμιοι, πρότερον δὲ οὐδεὶς ἐτόλμησεν· ἀλλὰ
ἀδῄωτον καὶ ἄθικτον οὖσαν ἐμβαλόντες ἐπυρ-
πόλουν καὶ διήρπαζον ἄχρι τοῦ ποταμοῦ καὶ τῆς
3 πόλεως, μηδενὸς ἐπεξιόντος. ὁ γὰρ Ἀγησίλαος

obliged to go about unkempt and squalid, wearing
cloaks that are patched with dyed stuffs, half of
their beards shaven, and half left to grow. It was a
serious matter, therefore, to allow many such men
in the city, when she lacked not a few soldiers. So
they chose Agesilaüs as a law-giver for the occasion.
And he, without adding to or subtracting from or
changing the laws in any way, came into the assembly
of the Lacedaemonians and said that the laws must
be allowed to sleep for that day, but from that day
on must be in sovereign force. By this means he at
once saved the laws for the city and the men from
infamy. Then, wishing to remove the discouragement and dejection which prevailed among the young
men, he made an incursion into Arcadia,[1] and though
he studiously avoided joining battle with the
enemy, he took a small town of the Mantineans
and overran their territory, and thus lightened and
gladdened the expectations of his city, which felt
that its case was not wholly desperate.

XXXI. After this,[2] Epaminondas entered Laconia
with his allies, having no fewer than forty thousand
men-at-arms. Many light armed and unarmed troops
also followed him for the sake of plunder, so that a
horde of seventy thousand, all told, made this incursion into Laconia. For a period of no less than
six hundred years the Dorians had been living in
Lacedaemon, and this was the first time in all that
period that enemies had been seen in the country ;
before this, none had ventured there. But now
they burst into an unravaged and inviolate land, and
burned and plundered as far as the river and the city,
and no one came out against them. For Agesilaüs

[1] In 370 B.C. (Xenophon, *Hell.* vi. 5, 10–21).
[2] In the same year, after Agesilaüs had returned and
disbanded his forces.

85

οὐκ εἴα πρὸς τοσοῦτον, ὥς φησι Θεόπομπος,
"ῥεῦμα καὶ κλύδωνα πολέμου" μάχεσθαι τοὺς
Λακεδαιμονίους, ἀλλὰ τῆς πόλεως τὰ μέσα καὶ
κυριώτατα τοῖς ὁπλίταις περιεσπειραμένος ἐκαρ-
τέρει τὰς ἀπειλὰς καὶ τὰς μεγαλαυχίας τῶν
Θηβαίων, προκαλουμένων ἐκεῖνον ὀνομαστὶ καὶ
διαμάχεσθαι περὶ τῆς χώρας κελευόντων, ὃς τῶν
4 κακῶν αἴτιός ἐστιν ἐκκαύσας τὸν πόλεμον. οὐχ
ἧττον δὲ τούτων ἐλύπουν τὸν Ἀγησίλαον οἱ κατὰ
τὴν πόλιν θόρυβοι καὶ κραυγαὶ καὶ διαδρομαὶ
τῶν τε πρεσβυτέρων δυσανασχετούντων τὰ γινόμενα καὶ τῶν γυναικῶν οὐ δυναμένων ἡσυχάζειν,
ἀλλὰ παντάπασιν ἐκφρόνων οὐσῶν πρός τε τὴν
5 κραυγὴν καὶ τὸ πῦρ τῶν πολεμίων. ἠνία δὲ καὶ
τὸ τῆς δόξης αὐτόν, ὅτι τὴν πόλιν μεγίστην
παραλαβὼν καὶ δυνατωτάτην, ἑώρα συνεσταλμένον αὐτῆς τὸ ἀξίωμα καὶ τὸ αὔχημα κεκολου-
μένον, ᾧ καὶ αὐτὸς ἐχρήσατο πολλάκις, εἰπὼν
ὅτι γυνὴ Λάκαινα καπνὸν οὐχ ἑώρακε πολέμιον.
λέγεται δὲ καὶ Ἀνταλκίδας, Ἀθηναίου τινὸς
ἀμφισβητοῦντος ὑπὲρ ἀνδρείας πρὸς αὐτὸν καὶ
εἰπόντος, "Ἡμεῖς μέντοι πολλάκις ὑμᾶς ἀπὸ τοῦ
Κηφισοῦ ἐδιώξαμεν," ὑποτυχεῖν· "Ἀλλ' ἡμεῖς
6 γε οὐδέποτε ὑμᾶς ἀπὸ τοῦ Εὐρώτα." παραπλησίως δὲ καὶ πρὸς τὸν Ἀργεῖον ἀπεκρίνατο τῶν
ἀσημοτέρων τις Σπαρτιατῶν· ὁ μὲν γὰρ εἶπε·
"Πολλοὶ ὑμῶν ἐν τῇ Ἀργολίδι κεῖνται," ὁ δὲ
ἀπήντησεν· "Ὑμῶν δέ γε οὐδεὶς ἐν τῇ Λα-
κωνικῇ."

XXXII. Τότε μέντοι τὸν Ἀνταλκίδαν φασὶν
ἔφορον ὄντα τοὺς παῖδας εἰς Κύθηρα ὑπεκθέσθαι,
περίφοβον γενόμενον. ὁ δὲ Ἀγησίλαος, ἐπι-

would not suffer the Lacedaemonians to fight against such a " billowy torrent of war," to use the words of Theopompus, but surrounded the central and most commanding parts of the city with his men-at-arms, while he endured the boastful threats of the Thebans, who called upon him by name and bade him come out and fight for his country, since he had caused her misfortunes by lighting up the flames of war. But this was not the worst. Agesilaüs was still more harassed by the tumults and shrieks and running about throughout the city, where the elder men were enraged at the state of affairs, and the women were unable to keep quiet, but were utterly beside themselves when they heard the shouts and saw the fires of the enemy.[1] He was also distressed at the thought of what his fame would be, because he had taken command of the city when she was greatest and most powerful, and now saw her reputation lowered, and her proud boast made empty, which boast he himself also had often made, saying that no Spartan woman had ever seen the smoke of an enemy's fires. It is said also that Antalcidas, when an Athenian was disputing with him over the valour of the two peoples and said, " Yet we have often driven you away from the Cephisus," replied : " But we have never driven you away from the Eurotas." And a similar retort was made by a Spartan of lesser note to the Argive who said, " Many of you lie buried in the lands of Argos " ; the Spartan answered : " But not a man of you in the lands of Laconia."

XXXII. Now, however, they say that Antalcidas, who was an ephor, secretly sent his children away to Cythera, so full of fear was he. But Agesilaüs, when

---

[1] " The women could not endure even the sight of the smoke, since they had never set eyes upon an enemy " (Xenophon, *Hell.* vi. 5, 28).

χειρούντων διαβαίνειν τὸν ποταμὸν τῶν πολεμίων
καὶ βιάζεσθαι πρὸς τὴν πόλιν, ἐκλιπὼν τὰ λοιπὰ
2 παρετάξατο πρὸ τῶν μέσων καὶ ὑψηλῶν. ἐρρύη
δὲ πλεῖστος ἑαυτοῦ καὶ μέγιστος τότε ὁ Εὐρώτας, χιόνων γενομένων, καὶ τὸ ῥεῦμα μᾶλλον ὑπὸ
ψυχρότητος ἢ τραχύτητος ἐγένετο σκληρὸν καὶ
χαλεπὸν τοῖς Θηβαίοις. πορευόμενον δὲ πρῶτον
τῆς φάλαγγος τὸν Ἐπαμεινώνδαν ἐδείκνυσάν τινες
τῷ Ἀγησιλάῳ· κἀκεῖνος, ὡς λέγεται, πολὺν
χρόνον ἐμβλέψας αὐτῷ καὶ συμπαραπέμψας τὴν
ὄψιν οὐδὲν ἢ τοσοῦτον μόνον εἶπεν· "Ὦ τοῦ
3 μεγαλοπράγμονος ἀνθρώπου." ἐπεὶ δὲ φιλοτι-
μούμενος ὁ Ἐπαμεινώνδας ἐν τῇ πόλει μάχην
συνάψαι καὶ στῆσαι τρόπαιον οὐκ ἴσχυσεν
ἐξαγαγεῖν οὐδὲ προκαλέσασθαι τὸν Ἀγησίλαον,
ἐκεῖνος μὲν ἀναζεύξας πάλιν ἐπόρθει τὴν χώραν,
ἐν δὲ Λακεδαίμονι τῶν πάλαι τινὲς ὑπούλων καὶ
πονηρῶν ὡς διακόσιοι συστραφέντες κατελάβοντο
τὸ Ἰσσώριον, οὗ τὸ τῆς Ἀρτέμιδος ἱερόν ἐστιν,   614
4 εὐερκῆ καὶ δυσεκβίαστον τόπον. ἐφ' οὓς βουλομένων εὐθὺς ὠθεῖσθαι τῶν Λακεδαιμονίων, φοβηθεὶς τὸν νεωτερισμὸν ὁ Ἀγησίλαος ἐκέλευσε τοὺς
μὲν ἄλλους ἡσυχίαν ἄγειν, αὐτὸς δὲ ἐν ἱματίῳ
καὶ μεθ' ἑνὸς οἰκέτου προσῄει, βοῶν ἄλλως
ἀκηκοέναι τοῦ προστάγματος αὐτούς· οὐ γὰρ
ἐνταῦθα κελεῦσαι συνελθεῖν οὐδὲ πάντας, ἀλλὰ
τοὺς μὲν ἐκεῖ (δείξας ἕτερον τόπον), τοὺς δὲ
5 ἀλλαχόσε τῆς πόλεως. οἱ δὲ ἀκούσαντες ἥσθη-
σαν οἰόμενοι λανθάνειν, καὶ διαστάντες ἐπὶ
τοὺς τόπους οὓς ἐκεῖνος ἐκέλευσεν ἀπεχώρουν.
ὁ δὲ τὸ μὲν Ἰσσώριον εὐθὺς μεταπεμψάμενος
ἑτέρους κατέσχε, τῶν δὲ συστάντων ἐκείνων περὶ

the enemy tried to cross the Eurotas and force their
way to the city, abandoned the rest of it and drew
up his forces in front of its central and lofty precincts.
Now, the Eurotas at this time was flowing at its
fullest and deepest, since snows had fallen, and its
current, even more from its coldness than its violence,
was very troublesome to the Thebans. As Epaminondas was fording it at the head of his phalanx,
certain ones pointed him out to Agesilaüs, and he,
we are told, after fixing his gaze upon him and
watching him for a long time, said but these words :
" O adventurous man !" Epaminondas was ambitious
to join battle in the city and set up a trophy of
victory there, but since he could neither force nor
tempt Agesilaüs out of his positions, he withdrew
and began to ravage the country. Meanwhile, about
two hundred of the Lacedaemonians who had long
been disaffected and mutinous banded together and
seized the Issorium, where the temple of Artemis
stands, a well-walled and inaccessible spot. The
Lacedaemonians wished to make a dash upon them
at once, but Agesilaüs, fearing their insurrection,
ordered the rest to keep quiet, while he himself,
wearing his cloak and attended by a single servant,
went towards them, crying out that they had mis-
understood his orders ; for he had not commanded
them to assemble in that place, nor in a body, but
some yonder (pointing to another spot), and some in
another part of the city. They were delighted to
hear this, supposing that their design was undis-
covered, and, breaking up, went off to the places
which he ordered them to occupy. Then Agesilaüs
at once summoned other troops and took possession
of the Issorium, after which he arrested about fifteen of the conspirators who had been gathered there,

πεντεκαίδεκά τινας συλλαβὼν νυκτὸς ἀπέκτεινεν.
6 ἄλλη δὲ μείζων ἐμηνύθη συνωμοσία καὶ σύνοδος
ἀνδρῶν Σπαρτιατῶν ἐπὶ πράγμασι νεωτέροις εἰς
οἰκίαν κρύφα συνερχομένων, οὓς καὶ κρίνειν
ἄπορον ἦν ἐν ταραχῇ τοσαύτῃ καὶ περιορᾶν
ἐπιβουλεύοντας. ἀπέκτεινεν οὖν καὶ τούτους
μετὰ τῶν ἐφόρων βουλευσάμενος ὁ Ἀγησίλαος
ἀκρίτους, οὐδενὸς δίχα δίκης τεθανατωμένου
7 πρότερον Σπαρτιατῶν. ἐπεὶ δὲ πολλοὶ τῶν συντεταγμένων [1] εἰς τὰ ὅπλα περιοίκων καὶ εἰλώτων
ἀπεδίδρασκον ἐκ τῆς πόλεως πρὸς τοὺς πολεμίους,
καὶ τοῦτο πλείστην ἀθυμίαν παρεῖχεν, ἐδίδαξε
τοὺς ὑπηρέτας περὶ ὄρθρον ἐπιφοιτᾶν ταῖς
στιβάσι καὶ τὰ ὅπλα τῶν ἀποκεχωρηκότων
λαμβάνειν καὶ ἀποκρύπτειν, ὅπως ἀγνοῆται τὸ
πλῆθος.
8 Ἀναχωρῆσαι δὲ τοὺς Θηβαίους ἐκ τῆς Λακωνικῆς οἱ μὲν ἄλλοι λέγουσι χειμώνων γενομένων
καὶ τῶν Ἀρκάδων ἀρξαμένων ἀπιέναι καὶ διαρρεῖν
ἀτάκτως, οἱ δὲ τρεῖς μῆνας ἐμμεμενηκότας ὅλους
καὶ τὰ πλεῖστα τῆς χώρας διαπεπορθηκότας·
Θεόπομπος δέ φησιν, ἤδη τῶν βοιωταρχῶν ἐγνω-
κότων ἀπαίρειν, ἀφικέσθαι πρὸς αὐτοὺς Φρίξον,
ἄνδρα Σπαρτιάτην, παρὰ Ἀγησιλάου δέκα
τάλαντα κομίζοντα τῆς ἀναχωρήσεως μισθόν,
ὥστε τὰ πάλαι δεδογμένα πράττουσιν αὐτοῖς
ἐφόδιον παρὰ τῶν πολεμίων προσπεριγενέσθαι.

XXXIII. Τοῦτο μὲν οὖν οὐκ οἶδα ὅπως ἠγνό-
ησαν οἱ ἄλλοι, μόνος δὲ Θεόπομπος ᾔσθετο. τοῦ
δὲ σωθῆναι τὴν Σπάρτην τότε πάντες αἴτιον
ὁμολογοῦσι γενέσθαι τὸν Ἀγησίλαον, ὅτι τῶν

----

[1] συντεταγμένων with S : τεταγμένων.

and put them to death in the night. He was also informed of another and a larger conspiracy of Spartans, who met secretly in a house and there plotted revolution. It was impracticable either to bring these men to trial in a time of so much confusion, or to overlook their plots. Accordingly, Agesilaüs conferred with the ephors, and then put these men also to death without process of law, although no Spartan had ever before met with such a death. At this time, also, many of the provincials and Helots who had been enrolled in the army ran away from the city and joined the enemy, and this caused very deep discouragement. Agesilaüs therefore instructed his servants to go every morning before it was light to the barracks and take the arms of the deserters and hide them, that their numbers might not be known.

As for the reason why the Thebans withdrew from Laconia, most writers say that it was because winter storms came on and the Arcadians began to melt away and disband; others, because they had remained there three entire months and thoroughly ravaged most of the country;[1] but Theopompus says that when the Theban chief magistrates had already determined to take their army back, Phrixus, a Spartan, came to them, bringing ten talents from Agesilaüs to pay for their withdrawal, so that they were only doing what they had long ago decided to do, and had their expenses paid by their enemies besides.

XXXIII. This story may be true, although I know not how all other writers could be ignorant of it, while Theopompus alone heard it; but, at any rate, all agree that the salvation of Sparta at this time was

---

[1] All three reasons are given by Xenophon (*Hell.* vi. 5. 50).

ἐμφύτων αὐτῷ παθῶν, φιλονεικίας καὶ φιλοτιμίας,
ἀποστάς, ἐχρήσατο τοῖς πράγμασιν ἀσφαλῶς.
2 οὐ μέντοι τήν γε δύναμιν καὶ τὴν δόξαν ἐδυνήθη
τῆς πόλεως ἀναλαβεῖν ἐκ τοῦ πταίσματος, ἀλλ'
ὥσπερ σώματος ὑγιεινοῦ, λίαν δὲ ἀκριβεῖ καὶ
κατησκημένῃ κεχρημένου διαίτῃ παρὰ πάντα τὸν
χρόνον, ἁμαρτία μία καὶ ῥοπὴ τὴν πᾶσαν ἔκλινεν
εὐτυχίαν τῆς πόλεως· οὐκ ἀλόγως. πρὸς γὰρ
εἰρήνην καὶ ἀρετὴν καὶ ὁμόνοιαν ἄριστα συν-
τεταγμένῳ πολιτεύματι προσαγαγόντες ἀρχὰς
καὶ δυναστείας βιαίους, ὧν οὐδενὸς ἡγεῖτο δεῖσθαι
πόλιν εὐδαιμόνως βιωσομένην ὁ Λυκοῦργος, ἐσφά-
λησαν.

3   Αὐτὸς μὲν οὖν ὁ Ἀγησίλαος ἤδη πρὸς τὰς
στρατείας ἀπειρήκει διὰ τὸ γῆρας, Ἀρχίδαμος δὲ
ὁ υἱὸς αὐτοῦ, τὴν ἐκ Σικελίας ἥκουσαν παρὰ τοῦ
τυράννου βοήθειαν ἔχων, ἐνίκησεν Ἀρκάδας τὴν
λεγομένην ἄδακρυν μάχην· οὐδεὶς γὰρ ἔπεσε τῶν
μετ' αὐτοῦ, συχνοὺς δὲ τῶν ἐναντίων ἀνεῖλεν.
αὕτη μάλιστα τὴν ἀσθένειαν ἤλεγξεν ἡ νίκη τῆς
4 πόλεως. πρότερον μὲν γὰρ οὕτω σύνηθες ἡγοῦντο
καὶ προσῆκον ἔργον αὐτοῖς εἶναι τὸ νικᾶν τοὺς πολεμίους, ὥστε μήτε θύειν τοῖς θεοῖς πλὴν ἀλεκτρυόνα νικητήριον ἐν τῇ πόλει, μήτε μεγαληγορεῖν
τοὺς ἀγωνισαμένους, μήτε ὑπερχαίρειν τοὺς πυν-
θανομένους, ἀλλὰ καὶ τῆς ἐν Μαντινείᾳ μάχης
γενομένης, ἣν Θουκυδίδης γέγραφε, τῷ πρώτῳ
φράσαντι τὴν νίκην οἱ ἄρχοντες ἐκ φιδιτίου κρέας 61
5 ἔπεμψαν εὐαγγέλιον, ἄλλο δὲ οὐδέν· τότε δὲ τῆς
μάχης ἀγγελθείσης καὶ τοῦ Ἀρχιδάμου προσ-

---

[1] Dionysius the Elder.
[2] In 368 B.C. (Xenophon, *Hell*. vii. 1, 28–32).

due to Agesilaüs, because he renounced his inherent
passions of contentiousness and ambition, and adopted
a policy of safety. He could not, however, restore
the power and reputation of his city after its fall, for
it was like a human body that is sound, indeed, but
has followed all the while too strict and severe a
regimen; a single error turned the scale and
brought down the entire prosperity of the city. Nor
was this strange. For to a civil polity best arranged
for peace and virtue and unanimity they had attached
empires and sovereignties won by force, not one of
which Lycurgus thought needful for a city that was
to live in happiness; and therefore they fell.

Agesilaüs himself now declined military service on
account of his years, but Archidamus his son, with
assistance which came from the tyrant of Sicily,[1]
conquered the Arcadians in the so-called "tearless
battle," where not one of his own men fell, and he
slew great numbers of the enemy.[2] This victory,
more than anything else, showed the weakness of
the city. For up to this time they were wont to
think the conquest of their enemies so customary and
natural a thing for them to achieve, that no sacrifice
for victory was offered in the city to the gods, beyond
that of a cock, neither did the winners of the contest
exult, nor those who heard of their victory show
great joy. Nay, even after the battle at Mantinea,[3]
which Thucydides has described, the one who first
announced the victory had no other reward for his
glad tidings than a piece of meat sent by the magistrates from the public mess. But now, at the news
of the Arcadian victory and at the approach of

[3] In 418 B.C., when the Lacedaemonians defeated an allied
force of Mantineans, Argives, and Athenians (Thucydides,
v. 64–75).

ἰόντος οὐδεὶς ἐκαρτέρησεν, ἀλλὰ πρῶτος ὁ
πατὴρ ἀπήντα δακρύων ὑπὸ χαρᾶς καὶ μετ'
ἐκεῖνον τὰ ἀρχεῖα, τῶν δὲ πρεσβυτέρων καὶ τῶν
γυναικῶν τὸ πλῆθος ἐπὶ τὸν ποταμὸν κατήει, τάς
τε χεῖρας ὀρεγόντων καὶ θεοκλυτούντων, ὥσπερ
ἀπεωσμένης τὰ παρ' ἀξίαν ὀνείδη τῆς Σπάρτης
καὶ λαμπρὸν αὖθις ἐξ ἀρχῆς τὸ φῶς ὁρώσης· ἐπεὶ
πρότερόν γέ φασιν οὐδὲ ταῖς γυναιξὶν ἀντιβλέπειν
τοὺς ἄνδρας αἰσχυνομένους ἐφ' οἷς ἔπταισαν.

XXXIV. Οἰκιζομένης δὲ Μεσσήνης ὑπὸ τῶν
περὶ τὸν Ἐπαμεινώνδαν, καὶ τῶν ἀρχαίων πολιτῶν πανταχόθεν εἰς αὐτὴν συμπορευομένων, διαμάχεσθαι μὲν οὐκ ἐτόλμων οὐδὲ κωλύειν ἐδύναντο, χαλεπῶς δὲ καὶ βαρέως πρὸς τὸν Ἀγησίλαον εἶχον, ὅτι χώραν οὔτε πλήθει τῆς Λακωνικῆς
ἐλάττονα καὶ πρωτεύουσαν ἀρετῇ τῆς Ἑλληνικῆς
ἔχοντες καὶ καρπούμενοι χρόνον τοσοῦτον ἐπὶ
2 τῆς ἐκείνου βασιλείας ἀπολωλέκασι. διὸ καὶ
προτεινομένην ὑπὸ τῶν Θηβαίων τὴν εἰρήνην ὁ
Ἀγησίλαος οὐκ ἐδέξατο. μὴ βουλόμενος δὲ τῷ
λόγῳ προέσθαι τοῖς ἔργῳ κρατοῦσι τὴν χώραν,
ἀλλὰ φιλονεικῶν, ἐκείνην μὲν οὐκ ἀπέλαβε, μικροῦ δὲ τὴν Σπάρτην προσαπέβαλε καταστρα-
3 τηγηθείς. ἐπεὶ γὰρ οἱ Μαντινεῖς αὖθις ἀπέστησαν τῶν Θηβαίων καὶ μετεπέμποντο τοὺς Λακεδαιμονίους, αἰσθόμενος ὁ Ἐπαμεινώνδας τὸν
Ἀγησίλαον ἐξεστρατευμένον μετὰ τῆς δυνάμεως
καὶ προσιόντα, λαθὼν τοὺς Μαντινεῖς ἀνέζευξε
νυκτὸς ἐκ Τεγέας ἄγων ἐπ' αὐτὴν τὴν Λακεδαίμονα τὸ στράτευμα, καὶ μικρὸν ἐδέησε παραλ-

Archidamus, no one could restrain himself, but first
his father went to meet him, weeping for joy, and
after him the chief magistrates, while the elderly
men and the women went down in a throng to the
river, lifting their hands to heaven and blessing the
gods, as if Sparta had wiped away her unmerited
disgraces and now saw the light shine bright again
as of old ; for before this, we are told, her men could
not so much as look their wives in the face, out of
shame at their disasters.

XXXIV. But when Messene was built by Epaminondas, and its former citizens flocked into it from
all quarters,[1] the Spartans had not the courage to
contest the issue nor the ability to hinder it, but
cherished the deepest resentment against Agesilaüs,
because a country which was not of less extent than
their own, which stood first among Hellenic lands
for its fertility, the possession and fruits of which
they had enjoyed for so long a time, had been lost
by them during his reign. For this reason, too,
Agesilaüs would not accept the peace which was
proffered by the Thebans. He was not willing to
give up to them formally the country which was
actually in their power, and persisted in his opposition. As a consequence, he not only did not recover Messenia, but almost lost Sparta besides, after
being outgeneralled. For when the Mantineans
changed their allegiance,[2] revolted from Thebes,
and called in the Lacedaemonians to help them,
Epaminondas, learning that Agesilaüs had marched
out from Sparta with his forces and was approaching, set out by night from Tegea, without the knowledge of the Mantineans, and led his army against
Sparta itself. He passed by Agesilaüs, and came

[1] In 369 B.C.   [2] In 362 B.C.

λάξας τὸν Ἀγησίλαον ἔρημον ἐξαίφνης κατα-
4 λαβεῖν τὴν πόλιν. Εὐθύνου δὲ Θεσπιέως, ὡς
Καλλισθένης φησίν, ὡς δὲ Ξενοφῶν, Κρητός
τινος, ἐξαγγείλαντος τῷ Ἀγησιλάῳ, ταχὺ προπέμψας ἱππέα τοῖς ἐν τῇ πόλει φράσοντα, μετ᾽
οὐ πολὺ καὶ αὐτὸς παρῆλθεν εἰς τὴν Σπάρτην.
ὀλίγῳ δὲ ὕστερον οἱ Θηβαῖοι διέβαινον τὸν Εὐρώταν καὶ προσέβαλλον τῇ πόλει, μάλα ἐρρωμένως τοῦ Ἀγησιλάου καὶ παρ᾽ ἡλικίαν ἐπαμύ-
5 νοντος. οὐ γάρ, ὡς πρότερον, ἀσφαλείας ἑώρα
τὸν καιρὸν ὄντα καὶ φυλακῆς, ἀλλὰ μᾶλλον
ἀπονοίας καὶ τόλμης, οἷς τὸν ἄλλον χρόνον
οὐδέποτε πιστεύσας οὐδὲ χρησάμενος, τότε μόνοις
ἀπεώσατο τὸν κίνδυνον, ἐκ τῶν χειρῶν τοῦ Ἐπαμεινώνδου τὴν πόλιν ἐξαρπάσας, καὶ στήσας
τρόπαιον, καὶ τοῖς παισὶ καὶ ταῖς γυναιξὶν ἐπι-
δείξας τὰ κάλλιστα τροφεῖα τῇ πατρίδι τοὺς
6 Λακεδαιμονίους ἀποδιδόντας, ἐν δὲ πρώτοις τὸν
Ἀρχίδαμον ἀγωνιζόμενον ὑπερηφάνως τῇ τε
ῥώμῃ τῆς ψυχῆς καὶ τῇ κουφότητι τοῦ σώματος,
ὀξέως ἐπὶ τὰ θλιβόμενα τῆς μάχης διαθέοντα
διὰ τῶν στενωπῶν καὶ πανταχοῦ μετ᾽ ὀλίγων
ἀντερείδοντα τοῖς πολεμίοις· Ἰσίδαν δὲ δοκῶ,
τὸν Φοιβίδου υἱόν, οὐ τοῖς πολίταις μόνον, ἀλλὰ
καὶ τοῖς πολεμίοις θέαμα φανῆναι καινὸν[1] καὶ
7 ἀγαστόν. ἦν μὲν γὰρ ἐκπρεπὴς τὸ εἶδος καὶ
τὸ μέγεθος τοῦ σώματος, ὥραν δὲ ἐν ᾗ τὸ ἥδιστον ἀνθοῦσιν ἄνθρωποι παριόντες εἰς ἄνδρας
ἐκ παίδων εἶχε, γυμνὸς δὲ καὶ ὅπλων τῶν σκεπόν-

---

[1] καινὸν with Amyot and S : καλὸν (noble).

96

within a little of suddenly seizing the city in a defenceless state.[1]   But Euthynus, a Thespian, as Callisthenes says, or, according to Xenophon,[2] a certain Cretan, brought word to Agesilaüs, who quickly sent on a horseman to warn the people in Sparta, and not long after he himself also entered the city.   Soon after his arrival the Thebans were crossing the Eurotas and attacking the city, while Agesilaüs defended it right vigorously and in a manner not to be expected of his years.   For he did not think, as on a former occasion, that the crisis demanded safe and cautious measures, but rather deeds of desperate daring.   In these he had never put confidence before, nor had he employed them, but then it was only by their aid that he repelled the danger, snatching the city out of the grasp of Epaminondas, erecting a trophy of victory, and showing their wives and children that the Lacedaemonians were making the fairest of all returns to their country for its rearing of them.   Archidamus, too, fought among the foremost, conspicuous for his impetuous courage and for his agility, running swiftly through the narrow streets to the endangered points in the battle, and everywhere pressing hard upon the enemy with his few followers.[3]   But I think that Isidas, the son of Phoebidas, must have been a strange and marvellous sight, not only to his fellow-citizens, but also to his enemies.   He was of conspicuous beauty and stature, and at an age when the human flower has the greatest charm, as the boy merges into the man.   Naked as he was, without either defensive

---

[1]   " Like a nest of young birds utterly bereft of its natural defenders " (Xenophon, *Hell.* vii. 5, 10).

[2]   *Loc. cit.*   Cf. also Diodorus, xv, 82, 6.

[3]   Cf. Xenophon, *Hell.* vii. 5, 12–14.

τῶν καὶ ἱματίων, λίπα χρισάμενος τὸ σῶμα, καὶ
τῇ μὲν ἔχων χειρὶ λόγχην, τῇ δὲ ξίφος, ἐξήλατο
τῆς οἰκίας, καὶ διὰ μέσων τῶν μαχομένων ὠσάμενος ἐν τοῖς πολεμίοις ἀνεστρέφετο, παίων τὸν
8 προστυχόντα καὶ καταβάλλων. ἐτρώθη δὲ ὑπ᾽
οὐδενός, εἴτε θεοῦ δι᾽ ἀρετὴν φυλάττοντος αὐτόν,
εἴτε μεῖζόν τι καὶ κρεῖττον ἀνθρώπου φανεὶς τοῖς
ἐναντίοις. ἐπὶ τούτῳ δὲ λέγεται τοὺς ἐφόρους
στεφανώσαντας αὐτὸν εἶτα χιλίων δραχμῶν ἐπι-
βαλεῖν ζημίαν, ὅτι χωρὶς ὅπλων διακινδυνεύειν
ἐτόλμησεν.

XXXV. Ὀλίγαις δὲ ὕστερον ἡμέραις περὶ τὴν
Μαντίνειαν ἐμαχέσαντο, καὶ τὸν Ἐπαμεινώνδαν
ἤδη κρατοῦντα τῶν πρώτων, ἔτι δὲ ἐγκείμενον 61
καὶ κατασπεύδοντα τὴν δίωξιν, Ἀντικράτης
Λάκων ὑποστὰς ἔπαισε δόρατι μέν, ὡς Διοσκου-
ρίδης ἱστόρηκε, Λακεδαιμόνιοι δὲ Μαχαιρίωνας
ἔτι νῦν τοὺς ἀπογόνους τοῦ Ἀντικράτους καλοῦ-
2 σιν, ὡς μαχαίρᾳ πατάξαντος. οὕτω γὰρ ἐθαύμασαν καὶ ὑπερηγάπησαν αὐτὸν φόβῳ τοῦ
Ἐπαμεινώνδου ζῶντος, ὥστε τιμὰς μὲν ἐκείνῳ
καὶ δωρεὰς ψηφίσασθαι, γένει δ᾽ ἀτέλειαν, ἣν ἔτι
καὶ καθ᾽ ἡμᾶς ἔχει Καλλικράτης, εἷς τῶν Ἀντικράτους ἀπογόνων.

Μετὰ δὲ τὴν μάχην καὶ τὸν θάνατον[1] τοῦ
Ἐπαμεινώνδου γενομένης εἰρήνης τοῖς Ἕλλησι
πρὸς αὐτούς, ἀπήλαυνον οἱ περὶ τὸν Ἀγησίλαον
τοῦ ὅρκου τοὺς Μεσσηνίους, ὡς πόλιν οὐκ ἔχον-
3 τας. ἐπεὶ δὲ οἱ λοιποὶ πάντες ἐδέχοντο καὶ τοὺς

---

[1] τὸν θάνατον with S : θάνατον.

armour or clothing,—for he had just anointed his
body with oil,—he took a spear in one hand, and a
sword in the other, leaped forth from his house, and
after pushing his way through the midst of the combatants, ranged up and down among the enemy,
smiting and laying low all who encountered him.
And no man gave him a wound, whether it was that
a god shielded him on account of his valour, or that
the enemy thought him taller and mightier than a
mere man could be. For this exploit it is said that
the ephors put a garland on his head, and then fined
him a thousand drachmas, because he had dared to
hazard his life in battle without armour.

XXXV. A few days afterwards a battle was fought
near Mantinea, in which Epaminondas had already
routed the van of the Lacedaemonians, and was still
eagerly pressing on in pursuit of them,[1] when Anticrates, a Spartan, faced him and smote him with a
spear, as Dioscorides tells the story; but the Lacedaemonians to this day call the descendants of Anticrates "machaeriones," or *swordsmen*, because he used
a sword for the blow. For the Lacedaemonians were
filled with such admiring love for him because of the
fear in which they held Epaminondas while living,
that they voted honours and gifts to Anticrates himself, and to his posterity exemption from taxes, an
immunity which in my own day also is enjoyed by
Callicrates, one of the descendants of Anticrates.

After the battle and the death of Epaminondas,
when the Greeks concluded peace among themselves, Agesilaüs and his partisans tried to exclude
the Messenians from the oath of ratification, on the
ground that they had no city. And when all the
rest admitted the Messenians and accepted their

[1] Cf. Xenophon, *Hell.* vii. 5, 22–24.

99

ὅρκους ἐλάμβανον παρ' αὐτῶν, ἀπέστησαν οἱ
Λακεδαιμόνιοι, καὶ μόνοις αὐτοῖς πόλεμος ἦν
ἐλπίζουσιν ἀναλήψεσθαι τὴν Μεσσηνίαν. βίαιος
οὖν ἐδόκει καὶ ἀτενὴς καὶ πολέμων ἄπληστος
ὁ Ἀγησίλαος εἶναι, τὰς μὲν κοινὰς διαλύσεις
πάντα τρόπον ὑπορύττων καὶ ἀναβάλλων, πάλιν
δὲ ὑπὸ χρημάτων ἀπορίας ἀναγκαζόμενος ἐνοχλεῖν τοῖς κατὰ πόλιν φίλοις καὶ δανείζεσθαι καὶ
4 συνερανίζεσθαι, δέον ἀπηλλάχθαι κακῶν εἰς τοῦτο
περιήκοντι τῷ καιρῷ, καὶ μὴ τὴν ἅπασαν ἀρχὴν
τοσαύτην γενομένην ἀφεικότα καὶ πόλεις καὶ γῆν
καὶ θάλατταν, ὑπὲρ τῶν ἐν Μεσσήνῃ κτημάτων
καὶ προσόδων σφαδάζειν.

XXXVI. Ἔτι δὲ μᾶλλον ἠδόξησε Τάχῳ τῷ
Αἰγυπτίῳ στρατηγὸν ἐπιδοὺς ἑαυτόν. οὐ γὰρ
ἠξίουν ἄνδρα τῆς Ἑλλάδος ἄριστον κεκριμένον
καὶ δόξης ἐμπεπληκότα τὴν οἰκουμένην, ἀπο-
στάτῃ βασιλέως, ἀνθρώπῳ βαρβάρῳ, χρῆσαι τὸ
σῶμα καὶ τοὔνομα καὶ τὴν δόξαν ἀποδόσθαι χρημάτων, ἔργα μισθοφόρου καὶ ξεναγοῦ διαπρατ-
2 τόμενον. κεἰ γὰρ ὑπὲρ ὀγδοήκοντα γεγονὼς ἔτη
καὶ πᾶν ὑπὸ τραυμάτων τὸ σῶμα κατακεκομ-
μένος ἐκείνην αὖθις ἀνεδέξατο τὴν καλὴν καὶ
περίβλεπτον ἡγεμονίαν ὑπὲρ τῆς τῶν Ἑλλήνων
ἐλευθερίας, οὐ πάμπαν ἄμεμπτον εἶναι τὴν φιλο-
τιμίαν· τοῦ γὰρ καλοῦ καιρὸν οἰκεῖον εἶναι καὶ
ὥραν, μᾶλλον δὲ ὅλως τὰ καλὰ τῶν αἰσχρῶν τῷ
3 μετρίῳ διαφέρειν. οὐ μὴν ἐφρόντιζε τούτων ὁ

---

[1] Cf. Diodorus, xv. 89, 1 f.

oaths, the Lacedaemonians held aloof from the peace, and they alone remained at war in the hope of recovering Messenia.[1] Agesilaüs was therefore deemed a headstrong and stubborn man, and insatiable of war, since he did all in his power to undermine and postpone the general peace, and again since his lack of resources compelled him to lay burdens on his friends in the city and to take loans and contributions from them. And yet it was his duty to put an end to their evils, now that opportunity offered, and not, after having lost Sparta's whole empire, vast as it was, with its cities and its supremacy on land and sea, then to carry on a petty struggle for the goods and revenues of Messene.

XXXVI. He lost still more reputation by offering to take a command under Tachos the Egyptian. For it was thought unworthy that a man who had been judged noblest and best in Hellas, and who had filled the world with his fame, should furnish a rebel against the Great King, a mere Barbarian, with his person, his name, and his fame, and take money for him, rendering the service of a hired captain of mercenaries.[1] For even if, now that he was past eighty years of age and his whole body was disfigured with wounds, he had taken up again his noble and conspicuous leadership in behalf of the freedom of the Hellenes, his ambition would not have been altogether blameless, as men thought. For honourable action has its fitting time and season ; nay, rather, it is the observance of due bounds that constitutes an utter difference between honourable and base actions. Agesilaüs, however, paid no heed

[1] Xenophon (*Agesilaüs*, ii. 28-31) has Agesilaüs take this step in order to punish the Great King and liberate again the Greeks of Asia.

᾿Αγησίλαος, οὐδὲ ᾤετο παρ᾽ ἀξίαν εἶναι λει-
τούργημα δημόσιον οὐδέν, ἀλλὰ μᾶλλον ἀνάξιον
ἑαυτοῦ τὸ ζῆν ἄπρακτον ἐν τῇ πόλει καὶ καθῆσθαι περιμένοντα τὸν θάνατον. ὅθεν ἀθροίσας [1]
μισθοφόρους ἀφ᾽ ὧν ὁ Τάχως αὐτῷ χρημάτων
ἔπεμψε, καὶ πλοῖα πληρώσας, ἀνήχθη, τριάκοντα
συμβούλους ἔχων μεθ᾽ ἑαυτοῦ Σπαρτιάτας, ὡς
πρότερον.

4   ᾿Επεὶ δὲ κατέπλευσεν εἰς τὴν Αἴγυπτον, εὐθὺς
οἱ πρῶτοι τῶν βασιλικῶν ἡγεμόνων καὶ διοικητῶν
ἐβάδιζον ἐπὶ ναῦν θεραπεύοντες αὐτόν. ἦν δὲ
καὶ τῶν ἄλλων Αἰγυπτίων σπουδή τε μεγάλη
καὶ προσδοκία διὰ τοὔνομα καὶ τὴν δόξαν τοῦ
᾿Αγησιλάου, καὶ συνετρόχαζον ἅπαντες ἐπὶ τὴν
5 θέαν. ὡς δὲ ἑώρων λαμπρότητα μὲν καὶ κατα-
σκευὴν οὐδεμίαν, ἄνθρωπον δὲ πρεσβύτην κατακείμενον ἔν τινι πόᾳ παρὰ τὴν θάλασσαν, εὐτελῆ
καὶ μικρὸν τὸ σῶμα, τραχὺ καὶ φαῦλον ἱμάτιον
ἀμπεχόμενον, σκώπτειν αὐτοῖς καὶ γελωτοποιεῖν
ἐπῄει, καὶ λέγειν ὅτι τοῦτο ἦν τὸ μυθολογού-
6 μενον ὠδίνειν ὄρος, εἶτα μῦν ἀποτεκεῖν. ἔτι δὲ
μᾶλλον αὐτοῦ τὴν ἀτοπίαν ἐθαύμασαν, ὅτε ξενίων
προσκομισθέντων καὶ προσαχθέντων ἄλευρα μὲν
καὶ μόσχους καὶ χῆνας ἔλαβε, τραγήματα δὲ
καὶ πέμματα καὶ μύρα διωθεῖτο, καὶ βιαζομένων
λαβεῖν καὶ λιπαρούντων ἐκέλευσε τοῖς εἵλωσι
διδόναι κομίζοντας. τῇ μέντοι στεφανωτρίδι
βύβλῳ φησὶν αὐτὸν ἡσθέντα Θεόφραστος διὰ 61
τὴν λιτότητα καὶ καθαριότητα τῶν στεφάνων
αἰτήσασθαι καὶ λαβεῖν, ὅτε ἀπέπλει, παρὰ τοῦ
βασιλέως.

---

[1] ἀθροίσας with Coraës and S : ἤθροισε.

to these considerations, nor did he think any public
service beneath his dignity; it was more unworthy
of him, in his opinion, to live an idle life in the
city, and to sit down and wait for death. Therefore
he collected mercenaries with the money which
Tachos sent him, embarked them on transports, and
put to sea, accompanied by thirty Spartan counsellors,
as formerly.[1]

As soon as he landed in Egypt,[2] the chief captains
and governors of the king came down to meet him
and pay him honour. There was great eagerness
and expectation on the part of the other Egyptians
also, owing to the name and fame of Agesilaüs, and
all ran together to behold him. But when they saw
no brilliant array whatever, but an old man lying
in some grass by the sea, his body small and contemptible, covered with a cloak that was coarse and
mean, they were moved to laughter and jesting,
saying that here was an illustration of the fable, " a
mountain is in travail, and then a mouse is born."[3]
They were still more surprised, too, at his eccen-
tricity. When all manner of hospitable gifts were
brought to him, he accepted the flour, the calves,
and the geese, but rejected the sweetmeats, the
pastries, and the perfumes, and when he was urged
and besought to take them, ordered them to be
carried and given to his Helots. He was pleased,
however, as Theophrastus tells us, with the papyrus
used in chaplets, because the chaplets were so neat
and simple, and when he left Egypt, asked and
received some from the king.

---

[1] Cf. chapter vi. 2.　　[2] 361 B.C.

[3] In Athenaeus, p. 616 d, it is Tachos himself who makes
this jest upon Agesilaüs, who replies in anger : "Someday
you will think me a lion."

XXXVII. Τότε δὲ συμμίξας τῷ Τάχῳ παρα-
σκευαζομένῳ πρὸς τὴν στρατείαν, οὐχ, ὥσπερ
ἤλπιζεν, ἁπάσης στρατηγὸς ἀπεδείχθη τῆς δυνάμεως, ἀλλὰ τῶν μισθοφόρων μόνων, τοῦ δὲ ναυτικοῦ Χαβρίας ὁ Ἀθηναῖος· ἡγεμὼν δὲ συμπάν-
2 των αὐτὸς ἦν ὁ Τάχως. καὶ τοῦτο πρῶτον
ἠνίασε τὸν Ἀγησίλαον· ἔπειτα τὴν ἄλλην ἀλα-
ζονείαν καὶ κενοφροσύνην τοῦ Αἰγυπτίου βαρυνόμενος ἠναγκάζετο φέρειν· καὶ συνεξέπλευσεν ἐπὶ
τοὺς Φοίνικας αὐτῷ, παρὰ τὴν ἀξίαν τὴν ἑαυτοῦ
καὶ τὴν φύσιν ὑπείκων καὶ καρτερῶν, ἄχρι οὗ
καιρὸν ἔλαβε.
3 Νεκτάναβις γὰρ ἀνεψιὸς ὢν τοῦ Τάχω καὶ
μέρος ἔχων ὑφ' ἑαυτῷ τῆς δυνάμεως ἀπέστη· καὶ
βασιλεὺς ὑπὸ τῶν Αἰγυπτίων ἀναγορευθεὶς διε-
πέμπετο πρὸς τὸν Ἀγησίλαον ἀξιῶν αὐτῷ βοη-
θεῖν· τὰ δ' αὐτὰ καὶ τὸν Χαβρίαν παρεκάλει,
4 μεγάλας ὑπισχνούμενος ἀμφοτέροις δωρεάς. αἰσθομένου δὲ ταῦτα τοῦ Τάχω καὶ τραπομένου
πρὸς δέησιν αὐτῶν, ὁ μὲν Χαβρίας ἐπειρᾶτο καὶ
τὸν Ἀγησίλαον ἐν τῇ φιλίᾳ τοῦ Τάχω πείθων
καὶ παραμυθούμενος κατέχειν, ὁ δὲ Ἀγησίλαος
εἶπεν ὅτι "Σοὶ μέν, ὦ Χαβρία, κατὰ σεαυτὸν
ἀφιγμένῳ χρῆσθαι τοῖς ἑαυτοῦ λογισμοῖς ἔξεστιν,
ἐγὼ δὲ ὑπὸ τῆς πατρίδος ἐδόθην Αἰγυπτίοις
στρατηγός. οὐκ οὖν ἂν ἔχοι μοι καλῶς οἷς
ἐπέμφθην σύμμαχος πολεμεῖν, ἐὰν μὴ πάλιν ἡ
5 πατρὶς κελεύσῃ." ταῦτα δὲ εἰπὼν ἔπεμψεν εἰς
Σπάρτην ἄνδρας, οἳ τοῦ μὲν Τάχω κατηγορήσειν,
ἐπαινέσεσθαι δὲ τὸν Νεκτάναβιν ἔμελλον. ἔπεμψαν δὲ κἀκεῖνοι δεόμενοι τῶν Λακεδαιμονίων,
ὁ μὲν ὡς πάλαι σύμμαχος γεγονὼς καὶ φίλος,

XXXVII. But now, on joining Tachos, who was making preparations for his expedition, he was not, as he expected, appointed commander of all the forces, but only of the mercenaries, while Chabrias the Athenian had charge of the fleet, and Tachos himself was commander-in-chief.[1] This was the first thing that vexed Agesilaüs; then, though he was indignant at the vain pretensions of the king in other matters, he was compelled to endure them. He even sailed with him against the Phoenicians, forcing himself into a subservience which was beneath his dignity and contrary to his nature, until he found his opportunity.

For Nectanabis, who was a cousin of Tachos and had a part of the forces under his command, revolted from him, and having been proclaimed king by the Egyptians, sent to Agesilaüs asking for his aid and assistance. He made the same appeal to Chabrias also, promising large gifts to both. When Tachos learned of this and resorted to entreaties for their allegiance, Chabrias tried to persuade and encourage Agesilaüs to continue with him in the friendship of Tachos. But Agesilaüs said: "You, Chabrias, who came here on your own account, can decide your own case; but I was given by my country to the Egyptians as a general. It would therefore be dishonourable for me to make war on those to whom I was sent as an ally, unless my country gives me a new command to do so." After these words, he sent men to Sparta who were to denounce Tachos, and commend Nectanabis. Tachos and Nectanabis also sent and besought the support of the Lacedaemonians, the former on the ground that he had long been their ally and friend, the latter on the plea that he would

[1] Cf. Diodorus, xv. 92, 2 f.

ὁ δὲ ὡς εὔνους καὶ προθυμότερος περὶ τὴν πολιν
ἐσόμενος. ἀκούσαντες οὖν οἱ Λακεδαιμόνιοι τοῖς
μὲν Αἰγυπτίοις ἀπεκρίναντο φανερῶς Ἀγησιλάῳ
περὶ τούτων μελήσειν, ἐκείνῳ δὲ ἐπέστειλαν ὁρᾶν
κελεύοντες ὅπως πράξει τὸ τῇ Σπάρτῃ συμφέρον.
6 οὕτω δὴ λαβὼν τοὺς μισθοφόρους ὁ Ἀγησίλαος
ἀπὸ τοῦ Τάχω μετέστη πρὸς τὸν Νεκτάναβιν,
ἀτόπου καὶ ἀλλοκότου πράγματος παρακαλύμ-
ματι τῷ συμφέροντι τῆς πατρίδος χρησάμενος·
ἐπεὶ ταύτης γε τῆς προφάσεως ἀφαιρεθείσης τὸ
δικαιότατον ὄνομα τῆς πράξεως ἦν προδοσία.
Λακεδαιμόνιοι δὲ τὴν πρώτην τοῦ καλοῦ μερίδα
τῷ τῆς πατρίδος συμφέροντι διδόντες οὔτε μανθά-
νουσιν οὔτε ἐπίστανται δίκαιον ἄλλο πλὴν ὃ τὴν
Σπάρτην αὔξειν νομίζουσιν.

XXXVIII. Ὁ μὲν οὖν Τάχως ἐρημωθεὶς τῶν
μισθοφόρων ἔφυγεν, ἐκ δὲ Μένδητος ἕτερος ἐπανί-
σταται τῷ Νεκταναβίδι βασιλεὺς ἀναγορευθείς·
καὶ συναγαγὼν δέκα μυριάδας ἀνθρώπων ἐπῄει.
θαρσύνοντος δὲ τοῦ Νεκτανάβιδος τὸν Ἀγησίλαον, καὶ λέγοντος ὅτι πολλοὶ μέν εἰσιν οἱ πολέμιοι, μιγάδες δὲ καὶ βάναυσοι καὶ δι᾽ ἀπειρίαν
2 εὐκαταφρόνητοι, "Καὶ μὴν οὐ τὸ πλῆθος αὐτῶν,"
ὁ Ἀγησίλαος εἶπεν, "ἀλλὰ τὴν ἀπειρίαν φοβοῦ-
μαι καὶ τὴν ἀμαθίαν ὡς δυσεξαπάτητον. αἱ γὰρ
ἀπάται τὸ παράδοξον ἐπάγουσι τοῖς πρὸς ἄμυναν
ὑπονοοῦσι καὶ προσδοκῶσι τρεπομένοις, ὁ δὲ μὴ
προσδοκῶν μηδὲ ὑπονοῶν μηδὲν οὐ δίδωσι τῷ

---

[1] Xenophon, who can see no fault in Agesilaüs, says
(*Agesilaüs*, ii. 31) : " Accordingly, he chose between the two

be well disposed to their city and more eager to promote her interests. The Lacedaemonians, accordingly, after hearing the messengers, made public answer to the Egyptians that Agesilaüs would attend to these matters; but to Agesilaüs they wrote privately bidding him see to it that the interests of Sparta should not suffer. So Agesilaüs took his mercenaries and went over from Tachos to Nectanabis, making the interests of his country serve as a veil for a strange and unnatural proceeding, since when this pretext was removed, the most fitting name for his act was treachery.[1] But the Lacedaemonians assign the chief place in their ideas of honour to the interests of their country, and neither learn nor understand any other justice than that which they think will enhance the glory of Sparta.

XXXVIII. Tachos, accordingly, thus deserted by his mercenaries, took to flight. But in Mendes another rival rose up against Nectanabis and was proclaimed king, and after collecting a hundred thousand men advanced against him. Then Nectanabis sought to encourage Agesilaüs by saying that although the enemy were numerous, they were a mixed rabble of artisans whose inexperience in war made them contemptible. " Indeed," said Agesilaüs, " it is not their numbers that I fear, but the inexperience and ignorance of which you speak, which it is hard to overcome by stratagems. For stratagems array unexpected difficulties against men who try to defend themselves against them, if they suspect and await them; but he who does not await nor even suspect any stratagem gives no hold to the opponent

that one who seemed to be the truer partisan of Hellas, and with him marched against the enemy of Hellas and conquered him in battle.'

παραλογιζομένῳ λαβήν, ὥσπερ οὐδὲ τῷ παλαί-
οντι ῥοπὴν ὁ μὴ κινούμενος." ἐκ τούτου καὶ ὁ
3 Μενδήσιος ἔπεμπε πειρῶν τὸν Ἀγησίλαον. ἔδεισεν οὖν ὁ Νεκτάναβις, καὶ κελεύοντος αὐτοῦ
διαμάχεσθαι τὴν ταχίστην καὶ μὴ χρόνῳ πολεμεῖν πρὸς ἀνθρώπους ἀπείρους ἀγῶνος, πολυχειρίᾳ
δὲ περιελθεῖν καὶ περιταφρεῦσαι καὶ φθάσαι
πολλὰ καὶ προλαβεῖν δυναμένους, ἔτι μᾶλλον ἐν
ὑποψίᾳ καὶ φόβῳ γενόμενος πρὸς αὐτὸν ἀπε-
χώρησεν εἰς πόλιν εὐερκῆ καὶ μέγαν ἔχουσαν
4 περίβολον. ὁ δὲ Ἀγησίλαος ἠγανάκτει μὲν 61
ἀπιστούμενος καὶ βαρέως ἔφερεν, αἰσχυνόμενος
δὲ καὶ πάλιν μεταστῆναι πρὸς τὸν ἕτερον καὶ
τελέως ἀπελθεῖν ἄπρακτος, ἠκολούθησε καὶ συν-
εισῆλθεν εἰς τὸ τεῖχος.

XXXIX. Ἐπελθόντων δὲ τῶν πολεμίων καὶ
περιταφρευόντων τὴν πόλιν, αὖθις αὖ δείσας τὴν
πολιορκίαν ὁ Αἰγύπτιος ἐβούλετο μάχεσθαι καὶ
τοὺς Ἕλληνας μάλα συμπροθυμουμένους εἶχεν·
οὐ γὰρ ἦν ἐν τῷ χωρίῳ σῖτος. ὁ δὲ Ἀγησίλαος
οὐκ ἐῶν, ἀλλὰ κωλύων ἤκουε μὲν ἔτι μᾶλλον
κακῶς ἢ πρότερον ὑπὸ τῶν Αἰγυπτίων καὶ προδό-
της ἀπεκαλεῖτο τοῦ βασιλέως, ἔφερε δὲ πρᾳότερον
ἤδη τὰς διαβολὰς καὶ προσεῖχε τῷ καιρῷ τοῦ
στρατηγήματος.
2 Ἦν δὲ τοιόνδε. τάφρον ἔξωθεν ἦγον οἱ πολέμιοι περὶ τὸ τεῖχος βαθεῖαν ὡς παντάπασιν
ἀποκλείσοντες αὐτούς. ὡς οὖν ἐγγὺς ἦσαν αἱ
τελευταὶ τοῦ ὀρύγματος ἀπαντῶντος αὐτῷ καὶ
περιιόντος ἐν κύκλῳ τὴν πόλιν, ἑσπέραν ἀναμεί-
νας γενέσθαι καὶ κελεύσας ἐξοπλίζεσθαι τοὺς
Ἕλληνας ἔλεγεν ἐλθὼν πρὸς τὸν Αἰγύπτιον "Ὁ

who is trying to outwit him, just as, in a wrestling bout, he who does not stir gives no advantage to his antagonist." After this, the Mendesian also sent and tried to win over Agesilaüs. Nectanabis was therefore alarmed, and when Agesilaüs urged him to fight the issue out as speedily as possible, and not to wage a war of delays against men who were inexperienced in fighting, but were numerous enough to surround him and hedge him in and anticipate and get the start of him in many ways, he grew still more suspicious and fearful of him, and retired into a city which was well fortified and had a large compass. Agesilaüs was incensed at this lack of confidence, and full of indignation, but since he was ashamed to change sides again and finally go back home without accomplishing any thing, he accompanied Nectanabis and entered the city with him.

XXXIX. But when the enemy came up and began to surround the city with a trench, then the Egyptian changed his mind, grew fearful of the siege, and wished to give battle, for which the Greeks also were very eager, since there were no provisions in the place. Agesilaüs, however, would not permit it, but opposed it, and was therefore maligned by the Egyptians even more bitterly than before, and called a betrayer of the king. But he bore their calumnies more patiently now, and sought to find the fitting moment for his stratagem.

This was as follows. The enemy were digging a deep trench outside around the city, in order to shut its occupants up completely. Accordingly, when the trench had been carried almost around the city, and its ends were near one another, after waiting for evening to come and ordering the Greeks to arm themselves, Agesilaüs went to the Egyptian and said:

μὲν τῆς σωτηρίας, ὦ νεανία, καιρὸς οὗτός ἐστιν,
ὃν ἐγὼ διαφθεῖραι φοβούμενος οὐκ ἔφραζον πρὶν
3 ἐλθεῖν. ἐπεὶ δὲ ἡμῖν οἱ πολέμιοι τὴν ἀσφάλειαν
αὐτοὶ διὰ τῶν χειρῶν παρεσκευάκασι, τοσαύτην
ὀρυξάμενοι τάφρον, ἧς τὸ μὲν ἐξειργασμένον ἐκείνοις ἐμποδών ἐστι τοῦ πλήθους, τὸ δὲ διαλεῖπον
ἡμῖν δίδωσιν ἴσῳ καὶ δικαίῳ μέτρῳ διαμάχεσθαι
πρὸς αὐτούς, φέρε νῦν, προθυμηθεὶς ἀνὴρ ἀγαθὸς
γενέσθαι καὶ μεθ' ἡμῶν ἐπισπόμενος δρόμῳ σῷζε
4 σεαυτὸν ἅμα καὶ τὴν στρατιάν. ἡμᾶς γὰρ οἱ μὲν
κατὰ στόμα τῶν πολεμίων οὐχ ὑπομενοῦσιν, οἱ δὲ
ἄλλοι διὰ τὴν τάφρον οὐ βλάψουσιν." ἐθαύμασεν
οὖν ὁ Νεκτάναβις τοῦ Ἀγησιλάου τὴν δεινότητα,
καὶ δοὺς ἑαυτὸν εἰς μέσα τὰ τῶν Ἑλλήνων ὅπλα
καὶ προσπεσὼν ἐτρέψατο ῥᾳδίως τοὺς ἀντιστάν-
τας. ὡς δὲ ἅπαξ ἔλαβε πειθόμενον αὐτῷ τὸν
Νεκτάναβιν ὁ Ἀγησίλαος, αὖθις ἐπῆγε τὸ αὐτὸ
στρατήγημα καθάπερ πάλαισμα τοῖς πολεμίοις.
5 τὰ μὲν γὰρ ὑποφεύγων καὶ ὑπάγων, τὰ δὲ ἀντι-
περιχωρῶν, ἐμβάλλει τὸ πλῆθος αὐτῶν εἰς τόπον
ἔχοντα διώρυχα βαθεῖαν ἐξ ἑκατέρας πλευρᾶς
παραρρέουσαν, ὧν τὸ μέσον ἐμφράξας καὶ καταλαβὼν τῷ μετώπῳ τῆς φάλαγγος ἐξίσωσε πρὸς
τοὺς μαχομένους τῶν πολεμίων τὸ πλῆθος, οὐκ
ἔχοντας περιδρομὴν καὶ κύκλωσιν. ὅθεν οὐ
πολὺν χρόνον ἀντιστάντες ἐτράποντο· καὶ πολλοὶ
μὲν ἀνηρέθησαν, οἱ δὲ φεύγοντες ἐσκεδάσθησαν
καὶ διερρύησαν.

XL. Ἐκ δὲ τούτου καλῶς μὲν εἶχε τὰ πράγματα καὶ βεβαίως τῷ Αἰγυπτίῳ πρὸς ἀσφάλειαν·
ἀγαπῶν δὲ καὶ φιλοφρονούμενος ἐδεῖτο μεῖναι καὶ
συνδιαχειμάσαι μετ' αὐτοῦ τὸν Ἀγησίλαον. ὁ δὲ
ὥρμητο πρὸς τὸν οἴκοι πόλεμον, εἰδὼς χρημάτων

"Now is the time, young man, for us to save ourselves, and I would not speak of it until it came, for fear of vitiating it. The enemy have now worked out our safety with their own hands. They have dug their trench so far that the part which is finished hinders them from attacking us in great numbers, and the space between the ends gives us room to fight them on fair and equal terms. Come, then, be eager to shew yourself a brave man; follow with us as we charge, and save yourself and your army too. For the enemy in our front will not withstand us, and the rest will not harm us because of the trench." Nectanabis, then, was filled with admiration for the sagacity of Agesilaüs, and putting himself in the centre of the Greek array, charged forwards and easily routed his opponents. And now that Agesilaüs had won back the confidence of Nectanabis, he brought the same stratagem to bear again upon the enemy, like a trick in wrestling. By sometimes pretending to retreat and fly, and sometimes attacking them on the flanks, he drove their whole multitude into a tract which had a deep canal full of water on either side. The space between these he occupied and stopped up with the head of his column, and so made his numbers equal to those of the enemy who could fight with him, since they were unable to surround and enclose him. Therefore after a short resistance they were routed; many were slain, and the fugitives were dispersed and melted away.[1]

XL. After this, the Egyptian succeeded in establishing himself firmly and securely in power, and showed his friendliness and affection by begging Agesilaüs to remain and spend the winter with him. But Agesilaüs was eager to return to the war at

[1] The account of this Egyptian campaign in Diodorus, xv. 93, differs in many details.

δεομένην τὴν πόλιν καὶ ξενοτροφοῦσαν. προὔ-
πεμψεν οὖν αὐτὸν ἐντίμως καὶ μεγαλοπρεπῶς,
ἄλλας τε λαβόντα τιμὰς καὶ δωρεὰς καὶ πρὸς τὸν
πόλεμον ἀργυρίου διακόσια καὶ τριάκοντα τά-
2 λαντα. χειμῶνος δὲ ὄντος ἤδη τῆς γῆς ἐχόμενος
ταῖς ναυσὶ καὶ παρὰ τὴν Λιβύην εἰς χωρίον
ἔρημον κομισθείς, ὃ καλοῦσι Μενελάου λιμένα,
θνήσκει, βιώσας μὲν ὀγδοήκοντα καὶ τέσσαρα
ἔτη, βασιλεύσας δὲ τῆς Σπάρτης ἑνὶ τῶν τεσσαράκοντα πλέον, καὶ τούτων ὑπὲρ τριάκοντα
πάντων μέγιστος καὶ δυνατώτατος γενόμενος καὶ
σχεδὸν ὅλης τῆς Ἑλλάδος ἡγεμὼν καὶ βασιλεὺς
νομισθεὶς ἄχρι τῆς ἐν Λεύκτροις μάχης.

3 Ἔθους δὲ ὄντος Λακωνικοῦ τῶν μὲν ἄλλων ἐπὶ
ξένης ἀποθανόντων αὐτοῦ τὰ σώματα κηδεύειν
καὶ ἀπολείπειν, τὰ δὲ τῶν βασιλέων οἴκαδε κομίζειν, οἱ παρόντες Σπαρτιᾶται κηρὸν ἐπιτήξαντες
τῷ νεκρῷ, μέλιτος οὐ παρόντος, ἀπῆγον εἰς Λακεδαίμονα. τὴν δὲ βασιλείαν Ἀρχίδαμος ὁ υἱὸς 61
αὐτοῦ παρέλαβε, καὶ διέμεινε τῷ γένει μέχρις
Ἄγιδος, ὃν ἐπιχειροῦντα τὴν πάτριον ἀναλαβεῖν πολιτείαν ἀπέκτεινε Λεωνίδας πέμπτον ἀπ'
Ἀγησιλάου γεγονότα.

home, knowing that his city needed money and was hiring mercenaries. He was therefore dismissed with great honour and ceremony, taking with him, besides other honours and gifts, two hundred and thirty talents of silver for the war at home. But since it was now winter, he kept close to shore with his ships, and was borne along the coast of Libya to an uninhabited spot called the Harbour of Menelaüs. Here he died, at the age of eighty-four years. He had been king of Sparta forty-one years, and for more than thirty of these he was the greatest and most influential of all Hellenes, having been looked upon as leader and king of almost all Hellas, down to the battle of Leuctra.

It was Spartan custom, when men of ordinary rank died in a foreign country, to give their bodies funeral rites and burial there, but to carry the bodies of their kings home. So the Spartans who were with Agesilaüs enclosed his dead body in melted wax, since they had no honey, and carried it back to Lacedaemon. The kingdom devolved upon Archidamus his son, and remained in his family down to Agis, who was slain by Leonidas [1] for attempting to restore the ancient constitution, being the fifth in descent from Agesilaüs.

---

[1] In 240 B.C. See the *Agis*, chapters xix., xx.

POMPEY

ΠΟΜΠΗΙΟΣ

I. Πρὸς Πομπήϊον ἔοικε τοῦτο παθεῖν ὁ Ῥωμαίων δῆμος εὐθὺς ἐξ ἀρχῆς, ὅπερ ὁ Αἰσχύλου
Προμηθεὺς πρὸς τὸν Ἡρακλέα σωθεὶς ὑπ᾿ αὐτοῦ
καὶ λέγων·

Ἐχθροῦ πατρός μοι τοῦτο φίλτατον τέκνον.

οὔτε γὰρ μῖσος οὕτως ἰσχυρὸν καὶ ἄγριον ἐπεδείξαντο Ῥωμαῖοι πρὸς ἕτερον στρατηγὸν ὡς τὸν
Πομπηΐου πατέρα Στράβωνα, ζῶντος μὲν αὐτοῦ
φοβούμενοι τὴν ἐν τοῖς ὅπλοις δύναμιν (ἦν γὰρ
2 ἀνὴρ πολεμικώτατος), ἐπεὶ δὲ ἀπέθανε κεραυ-
νωθείς, ἐκκομιζόμενον τὸ σῶμα κατασπάσαντες
ἀπὸ τοῦ λέχους καὶ καθυβρίσαντες, οὔτε μὴν
εὔνοιαν αὖ πάλιν σφοδροτέραν ἢ θᾶσσον ἀρξαμέ-
νην ἢ μᾶλλον εὐτυχοῦντι συνακμάσασαν ἢ πταί-
σαντι παραμείνασαν βεβαιότερον ἄλλος ἔσχε
3 Ῥωμαίων ἢ Πομπήϊος. αἰτία δὲ τοῦ μὲν μίσους
ἐκείνῳ μία, χρημάτων ἄπληστος ἐπιθυμία, τούτῳ
δὲ πολλαὶ τοῦ ἀγαπᾶσθαι, σωφροσύνη περὶ
δίαιταν, ἄσκησις ἐν ὅπλοις, πιθανότης λόγου,
πίστις ἤθους, εὐαρμοστία πρὸς ἔντευξιν, ὡς μη-

---

¹ A fragment of the *Prometheus Loosed* (Nauck, *Trag.
Graec. Frag.*² p. 68). Prometheus was fastened to a cliff in

POMPEY

I. Towards Pompey the Roman people must have had, from the very beginning, the feeling which the Prometheus of Aeschylus has towards Heracles, when, having been saved by him, he says :—

" I hate the sire, but dearly love this child of his." [1]

For never have the Romans manifested so strong and fierce a hatred towards a general as they did towards Strabo, the father of Pompey; while he lived, indeed, they feared his talent as a soldier, for he was a very warlike man, but when he was killed by a thunderbolt,[2] and his body was on its way to the funeral pyre, they dragged it from its bier and heaped insults upon it. On the other hand, no Roman ever enjoyed a heartier goodwill on the part of his countrymen, or one which began sooner, or reached a greater height in his prosperity, or remained more constant in his adversity, than Pompey did. And whereas there was one sole reason for the hatred felt towards Strabo, namely, his insatiable desire for money, there were many reasons for the love bestowed on Pompey; his modest and temperate way of living, his training in the arts of war, his persuasive speech, his trustworthy character, and his tact in meeting people, so that no man asked a

Scythia by Zeus, whose eagle preyed upon the prisoner. Heracles slew the eagle and released the sufferer.

[2] In 87 B.C.

δενὸς ἀλυπότερον δεηθῆναι μηδὲ ἥδιον ὑπουργῆσαι δεομένῳ. προσῆν γὰρ αὐτοῦ ταῖς χάρισι καὶ τὸ ἀνεπαχθὲς διδόντος καὶ τὸ σεμνὸν λαμβάνοντος.

II. Ἐν ἀρχῇ δὲ καὶ τὴν ὄψιν ἔσχεν οὐ μετρίως συνδημαγωγοῦσαν καὶ προεντυγχάνουσαν αὐτοῦ τῆς φωνῆς. τὸ γὰρ ἐράσμιον ἀξιωματικὸν ἦν φιλανθρώπως, καὶ ἐν τῷ νεαρῷ καὶ ἀνθοῦντι διέφαινεν εὐθὺς ἡ ἀκμὴ τὸ γεραρὸν καὶ τὸ βασιλικὸν τοῦ ἤθους. ἦν δέ τις καὶ ἀναστολὴ τῆς κόμης ἀτρέμα καὶ τῶν περὶ τὰ ὄμματα ῥυθμῶν ὑγρότης τοῦ προσώπου, ποιοῦσα μᾶλλον λεγομένην ἢ φαινομένην ὁμοιότητα πρὸς τὰς Ἀλεξάν- 2 δρου τοῦ βασιλέως εἰκόνας. ᾗ καὶ τοὔνομα πολ- λῶν ἐν ἀρχῇ συνεπιφερόντων οὐκ ἔφευγεν ὁ Πομ- πήϊος, ὥστε καὶ χλευάζοντας αὐτὸν ἐνίους ἤδη καλεῖν Ἀλέξανδρον. διὸ καὶ Λεύκιος Φίλιππος, ἀνὴρ ὑπατικός, συνηγορῶν αὐτῷ, μηδὲν ἔφη ποιεῖν παράλογον εἰ Φίλιππος ὢν φιλαλέξανδρός ἐστιν.

Φλώραν δὲ τὴν ἑταίραν ἔφασαν ἤδη πρεσ- βυτέραν οὖσαν ἐπιεικῶς ἀεὶ μνημονεύειν τῆς γενομένης αὐτῇ πρὸς Πομπήϊον ὁμιλίας, λέ- γουσαν ὡς οὐκ ἦν ἐκείνῳ συναναπαυσαμένην 3 ἀδήκτως ἀπελθεῖν. πρὸς δὲ τούτοις διηγεῖσθαι τὴν Φλώραν ἐπιθυμῆσαί τινα τῶν Πομπηΐου συνήθων αὐτῆς Γεμίνιον, καὶ πράγματα πολλὰ παρέχειν πειρῶντα· αὐτῆς δὲ φαμένης οὐκ ἂν ἐθελῆσαι διὰ Πομπήϊον, ἐκείνῳ τὸν Γεμίνιον διαλέγεσθαι· τὸν οὖν Πομπήϊον ἐπιτρέψαι μὲν τῷ Γεμινίῳ, μηκέτι δὲ αὐτὸν ἅψασθαι τὸ παρά- παν μηδὲ ἐντυχεῖν αὐτῇ, καίπερ ἐρᾶν δοκοῦντα·

favour with less offence, or bestowed one with a better mien. For, in addition to his other graces, he had the art of giving without arrogance, and of receiving without loss of dignity.

II. At the outset, too, he had a countenance which helped him in no small degree to win the favour of the people, and which pleaded for him before he spoke. For even his boyish loveliness had a gentle dignity about it, and in the prime and flower of his youthful beauty there was at once manifest the majesty and kingliness of his nature. His hair was inclined to lift itself slightly from his forehead, and this, with a graceful contour of face about the eyes, produced a resemblance, more talked about than actually apparent, to the portrait statues of King Alexander. Wherefore, since many also applied the name to him in his earlier years, Pompey did not decline it, so that presently some called him Alexander in derision. Hence, too, Lucius Philippus, a man of consular rank, when pleading in his behalf, said that he was doing nothing strange if, being Philip, he loved Alexander.

We are told that Flora the courtesan, when she was now quite old, always took delight in telling about her former intimacy with Pompey, saying that she never left his embraces without bearing the marks of his teeth. Furthermore, Flora would tell how Geminius, one of Pompey's companions, fell in love with her and annoyed her greatly by his attentions; and when she declared that she could not consent to his wishes because of Pompey, Geminius laid the matter before Pompey. Pompey, accordingly, turned her over to Geminius, but never afterwards had any thing at all to do with her himself, although he was thought to be enamoured of her; and she

τοῦτο δὲ αὐτὴν οὐχ ἑταιρικῶς ἐνεγκεῖν, ἀλλὰ
πολὺν ὑπὸ λύπης καὶ πόθου χρόνον νοσῆσαι.
4 καίτοι τὴν Φλώραν οὕτω λέγουσιν ἀνθῆσαι καὶ
γενέσθαι περιβόητον ὥστε Κεκίλιον Μέτελλον
ἀνδριάσι καὶ γραφαῖς κοσμοῦντα τὸν νεὼν τῶν
Διοσκούρων, κἀκείνης εἰκόνα γραψάμενον ἀνα-
θεῖναι διὰ τὸ κάλλος. Πομπήιος δὲ καὶ τῇ 62
Δημητρίου τοῦ ἀπελευθέρου γυναικί, πλεῖστον
ἰσχύσαντος παρ' αὐτῷ καὶ τετρακισχιλίων ταλάντων ἀπολιπόντος οὐσίαν, ἐχρῆτο παρὰ τὸν
αὑτοῦ τρόπον οὐκ ἐπιεικῶς οὐδὲ ἐλευθερίως, φοβηθεὶς τὴν εὐμορφίαν αὐτῆς ἄμαχόν τινα καὶ
περιβόητον οὖσαν, ὡς μὴ φανείη κεκρατημένος.
5 οὕτω δὲ πάνυ πόρρωθεν εὐλαβὴς ὢν πρὸς τὰ
τοιαῦτα καὶ πεφυλαγμένος, ὅμως οὐ διέφυγε τῶν
ἐχθρῶν τὸν ἐπὶ τούτῳ ψόγον, ἀλλ' ἐπὶ ταῖς
γαμεταῖς ἐσυκοφαντεῖτο πολλὰ τῶν κοινῶν παρ-
ιδεῖν καὶ προέσθαι χαριζόμενος ἐκείναις.

Τῆς δὲ περὶ τὴν δίαιταν εὐκολίας καὶ λιτό-
τητος καὶ ἀπομνημόνευμα λέγεται τοιοῦτον.
6 ἰατρὸς αὐτῷ νοσοῦντι καὶ κακῶς ἔχοντι πρὸς τὰ
σιτία κίχλην προσέταξε λαβεῖν. ὡς δὲ ζητοῦντες
οὐχ εὗρον ὤνιον (ἦν γὰρ παρ' ὥραν), ἔφη δέ τις
εὑρεθήσεσθαι παρὰ Λευκόλλῳ δι' ἔτους τρεφομέ-
νας, "Εἶτα," εἶπεν, "εἰ μὴ Λεύκολλος ἐτρύφα,
Πομπήιος οὐκ ἂν ἔζησε;" καὶ χαίρειν ἐάσας τὸν
ἰατρὸν ἔλαβέ τι τῶν εὐπορίστων. ταῦτα μὲν
οὖν ὕστερον.

III. Ἔτι δὲ μειράκιον ὢν παντάπασι καὶ τῷ
πατρὶ συστρατευόμενος ἀντιτεταγμένῳ πρὸς Κίν-

herself did not take this treatment as a mere courtesan would, but was sick for a long time with grief and longing. And yet Flora is said to have flowered into such beauty, and to have been so famous for it, that when Caecilius Metellus was decorating the temple of Castor and Pollux with paintings and statues, he gave her portrait also a place among his dedications. Moreover, Pompey also treated the wife of Demetrius his freedman (who had the greatest influence with him and left an estate of four thousand talents) with a lack of courtesy and generosity unusual in him, fearing lest men should think him conquered by her beauty, which was irresistible and far-famed. But though he was so extremely cautious in such matters and on his guard, still he could not escape the censures of his enemies on this head, but was accused of illicit relations with married women, to gratify whom, it was said, he neglected and betrayed many public interests.

As regards his simplicity and indifference in matters pertaining to the table, a story is told as follows. Once when he was sick and loathed his food, a physician prescribed a thrush for him. But when, on enquiry, his servants could not find one for sale (for it was past the season for them), and some-one said they could be found at Lucullus's, where they were kept the year round, "What then," said he, "if Lucullus were not luxurious must Pompey have died?" and paying no regard to the physician he took something that could easily be procured.[1] This, however, was at a later time.

III. While he was still quite a stripling and was on a campaign with his father, who was arrayed against

---

[1] Cf. the *Lucullus*, xl. 2.

ναν, Λευκιόν τινα Τερέντιον εἶχεν ἑταῖρον καὶ
σύσκηνον. οὗτος ὑπὸ Κίννα πεισθεὶς χρήμασιν
αὐτὸς μὲν ἔμελλε Πομπήϊον ἀποκτενεῖν, ἕτεροι δὲ
2 τὴν σκηνὴν ἐμπρήσειν τοῦ στρατηγοῦ. μηνύσεως
δὲ τῷ Πομπηΐῳ περὶ δεῖπνον ὄντι προσπεσούσης,
οὐδὲν διαταραχθείς, ἀλλὰ καὶ πιὼν προθυμότερον
καὶ φιλοφρονησάμενος τὸν Τερέντιον, ἅμα τῷ
τραπέσθαι πρὸς ἀνάπαυσιν ὑπεκρυεὶς τῆς σκηνῆς ἔλαθε, καὶ τῷ πατρὶ φρουρὰν περιστήσας
ἡσύχαζεν. ὁ δὲ Τερέντιος, ὡς ἐνόμιζε καιρὸν
εἶναι, σπασάμενος τὸ ξίφος ἀνέστη καὶ τῇ στιβάδι
τοῦ Πομπηΐου προσελθὼν ὡς κατακειμένου πολ-
3 λὰς ἐνεφόρει πληγὰς τοῖς στρώμασιν. ἐκ δὲ
τούτου γίνεται μέγα κίνημα μίσει τοῦ στρατηγοῦ,
καὶ πρὸς ἀπόστασιν ὁρμὴ τῶν στρατιωτῶν, τάς
τε σκηνὰς ἀνασπώντων καὶ τὰ ὅπλα λαμβανόν-
των. ὁ μὲν οὖν στρατηγὸς οὐ προῄει δεδιὼς τὸν
θόρυβον, ὁ δὲ Πομπήϊος ἐν μέσοις ἀναστρεφό-
μενος καὶ δακρύων ἱκέτευε, τέλος δὲ ῥίψας ἑαυτὸν
ἐπὶ στόμα πρὸ τῆς πύλης τοῦ χάρακος ἐμποδὼν
ἔκειτο κλαίων καὶ πατεῖν κελεύων τοὺς ἐξιόντας,
ὥστε ἕκαστον ἀναχωρεῖν ὑπ' αἰδοῦς καὶ πάντας
οὕτω πλὴν ὀκτακοσίων μεταβαλέσθαι καὶ διαλ-
λαγῆναι πρὸς τὸν στρατηγόν.

    IV. Ἅμα δὲ τῷ τελευτῆσαι τὸν Στράβωνα,
δίκην κλοπῆς ἔσχεν ὑπὲρ αὐτοῦ δημοσίων χρημάτων ὁ Πομπήϊος. καὶ τὰ μὲν πλεῖστα φωρά-
σας ἕνα τῶν ἀπελευθέρων ὁ Πομπήϊος νενοσφισ-
μένον Ἀλέξανδρον, ἀπέδειξε τοῖς ἄρχουσιν, αὐτὸς
δὲ λίνα θηρατικὰ καὶ βιβλία τῶν ἐν Ἄσκλῳ
ληφθέντων ἔχειν κατηγορεῖτο. ταῦτα δὲ ἔλαβε
μὲν παρὰ τοῦ πατρὸς ἑλόντος τὸ Ἄσκλον, ἀπώ-

Cinna,[1] he had a certain Lucius Terentius as tentmate
and companion. This man was bribed by Cinna, and
was himself to kill Pompey, while others were to set
fire to the tent of the commander. But Pompey got
information of the plot while he was at supper. He
was not at all disturbed, but after drinking more
freely even than usual and treating Terentius with
kindness, as soon as he retired to rest stole out of
the tent unperceived, set a guard about his father,
and quietly awaited the event. Terentius, when he
thought the proper time was come, arose, and approaching the couch of Pompey with drawn sword,
stabbed the bed-clothing many times, supposing him
to be lying there. After this there was a great
commotion, owing to the hatred felt towards the
general, and a rush to revolt on the part of the
soldiers, who tore down their tents and seized their
arms. The general did not venture forth for fear of
the tumult, but Pompey went up and down among
the soldiers beseeching them with tears, and finally
threw himself on his face in front of the gate of the
camp and lay there in the way, weeping and bidding
those who were going out to trample on him. As a
consequence, everyone drew back out of shame, and
all except eight hundred changed their minds and
were reconciled to their general.

IV. As soon as Strabo was dead, Pompey, as his
heir, was put on trial for theft of public property. And
although Pompey discovered that most of the thefts
were committed by Alexander, one of his father's
freedmen, and proved it to the magistrates, still he
himself was accused of having in his possession
hunting nets and books from the booty of Asculum.
Now, he did receive these things from his father

[1] In 87 B.C.

λεσε δὲ τῶν Κίννα δορυφόρων, ὅτε κατῆλθεν,
ὠσαμένων εἰς τὴν οἰκίαν αὐτοῦ καὶ διαρπασάν-
2 των. ἐγίνοντο δὲ τῆς δίκης αὐτῷ προαγῶνες οὐκ
ὀλίγοι πρὸς τὸν κατήγορον. ἐν οἷς ὀξὺς ἅμα καὶ
παρ' ἡλικίαν εὐσταθὴς φαινόμενος δόξαν ἔσχε
μεγάλην καὶ χάριν, ὥστε Ἀντίστιον στρατη-
γοῦντα καὶ βραβεύοντα τὴν δίκην ἐκείνην ἐρα-
σθῆναι τοῦ Πομπηίου καὶ γυναῖκα διδόναι τὴν
ἑαυτοῦ θυγατέρα καὶ περὶ τούτου τοῖς φίλοις
3 διαλέγεσθαι. δεξαμένου δὲ Πομπηίου καὶ γενομένων ἐν αὐτοῖς ἀπορρήτων ὁμολογιῶν, ὅμως οὐκ
ἔλαθε τοὺς πολλοὺς τὸ πρᾶγμα διὰ τὴν τοῦ
Ἀντιστίου σπουδήν. τέλος δὲ τὴν γνώμην ἀνα-
γορεύσαντος αὐτοῦ τῶν δικαστῶν ἀπολύουσαν,
ὥσπερ ἐκ παραγγέλματος ὁ δῆμος ἐπεφώνησε
τοῦτο δὴ τὸ τοῖς γαμοῦσιν ἐπιφωνούμενον ἐξ
ἔθους παλαιοῦ, Ταλασίῳ.

4   Τὸ δὲ ἔθος ἀρχὴν λαβεῖν φασι τοιαύτην. ὅτε
τὰς θυγατέρας τῶν Σαβίνων ἐπὶ θέαν ἀγῶνος εἰς
Ῥώμην παραγενομένας οἱ πρωτεύοντες ἀρετῇ
Ῥωμαίων ἥρπαζον ἑαυτοῖς γυναῖκας, ἄδοξοί τινες
πελάται καὶ βοτῆρες ἀράμενοι κόρην καλὴν καὶ
μεγάλην ἐκόμιζον. ὅπως οὖν μὴ προστυχών τις
ἀφέληται τῶν κρειττόνων, ἐβόων θέοντες ἅμα
Ταλασίῳ (τῶν δὲ χαριέντων καὶ γνωρίμων τις ἦν
ὁ Ταλάσιος), ὥστε τοὺς ἀκούσαντας τοὔνομα
κροτεῖν καὶ βοᾶν οἷον συνηδομένους καὶ συνεπ-
5 αινοῦντας. ἐκ τούτου φασὶ (καὶ γὰρ εὐτυχὴς ὁ
γάμος ἀπέβη τῷ Ταλασίῳ) ταύτην τὴν ἐπιφώ-

when he took Asculum,[1] but he lost them when
Cinna's guards, on that general's return to Rome,
broke into his house and ransacked it. He had
many preliminary bouts in the case with his accuser,
and since in these he showed an acumen and poise
beyond his years, he won great reputation and favour,
insomuch that Antistius, the praetor and judge in the
case, took a great liking to him and offered him his
own daughter in marriage, and conferred with his
friends about the matter. Pompey accepted the
offer and a secret agreement was made between
them, but nevertheless the people got wind of the
matter, owing to the pains which Antistius took to
favour Pompey. And finally, when Antistius pro-
nounced the verdict of the judges in acquittal, the
people, as if upon a signal given, broke out in
the ancient and customary marriage acclamation,
" Talasio."

The origin of the custom is said to have been this.
At the time when the daughters of the Sabines, who
had come to Rome to see a spectacle of games, were
haled away by the most distinguished Romans to be
their wives, certain hirelings and herdsmen of the
meaner sort seized a fair and stately maiden and
were carrying her off. In order, therefore, that no
one of their betters, on meeting them, might rob
them of their prize, they shouted with one voice as
they ran, " *For Talasius,*" Talasius being a well-known
and popular personage. Consequently, those who
heard the name clapped their hands and shouted
it themselves, as if rejoicing with the others and
approving what they did. From this circumstance,
they say,—and indeed the marriage proved a happy
one for Talasius,—this acclamation is used in mirth-

---

[1] In 89 B.C.

νησιν μετὰ παιδιᾶς γενέσθαι τοῖς γαμοῦσιν.
οὗτος ὁ λόγος πιθανώτατός ἐστι τῶν περὶ τοῦ
Ταλασίου λεγομένων. ὀλίγαις δ᾽ οὖν ὕστερον
ἡμέραις ὁ Πομπήϊος ἠγάγετο τὴν Ἀντιστίαν.

V. Ἐπεὶ δὲ πρὸς Κίνναν εἰς τὸ στρατόπεδον
πορευθεὶς ἐξ αἰτίας τινὸς καὶ διαβολῆς ἔδεισε καὶ
ταχὺ λαθὼν ἐκποδὼν ἐποίησεν ἑαυτόν, οὐκ ὄντος
ἐμφανοῦς αὐτοῦ θροῦς διῆλθεν ἐν τῷ στρατοπέδῳ
καὶ λόγος ὡς ἀνῃρήκοι τὸν νεανίσκον ὁ Κίννας·
ἐκ δὲ τούτου οἱ πάλαι βαρυνόμενοι καὶ μισοῦντες
ὥρμησαν ἐπ᾽ αὐτόν. ὁ δὲ φεύγων καὶ καταλαμ-
βανόμενος ὑπό τινος τῶν λοχαγῶν γυμνῷ τῷ
ξίφει διώκοντος προσέπεσε τοῖς γόνασι καὶ τὴν
2 σφραγῖδα προὔτεινε πολύτιμον οὖσαν. ὁ δὲ καὶ
μάλα ὑβριστικῶς εἰπών, "Ἀλλ᾽ οὐκ ἐγγύην
ἔρχομαι σφραγιούμενος, ἀλλὰ ἀνόσιον καὶ παράνομον τιμωρησόμενος τύραννον," ἀπέκτεινεν αὐτόν. οὕτω δὲ τοῦ Κίννα τελευτήσαντος ἐδέξατο
μὲν τὰ πράγματα καὶ συνεῖχε Κάρβων ἐμπληκ-
τότερος ἐκείνου τύραννος, ἐπῄει δὲ Σύλλας τοῖς
πλείστοις ποθεινός, ὑπὸ τῶν παρόντων κακῶν
οὐδὲ δεσπότου μεταβολὴν μικρὸν ἡγουμένοις ἀγαθόν. εἰς τοῦτο προήγαγον αἱ συμφοραὶ τὴν πόλιν,
ὡς δουλείαν ἐπιεικεστέραν ζητεῖν ἀπογνώσει τῆς
ἐλευθερίας.

VI. Τότε οὖν ὁ Πομπήϊος ἐν τῇ Πικηνίδι τῆς
Ἰταλίας διέτριβεν, ἔχων μὲν αὐτόθι καὶ χωρία,
τὸ δὲ πλέον ταῖς πόλεσιν ἡδόμενος οἰκείως καὶ
φιλικῶς πατρόθεν ἐχούσαις πρὸς αὐτόν. ὁρῶν δὲ
τοὺς ἐπιφανεστάτους καὶ βελτίστους τῶν πολιτῶν ἀπολείποντας τὰ οἰκεῖα καὶ πανταχόθεν εἰς
τὸ Σύλλα στρατόπεδον ὥσπερ εἰς λιμένα κατα-

ful greeting of the newly wedded. This is the most credible of the stories told about Talasius.[1] But be it true or not, a few days afterwards Pompey married Antistia.

V. Then he betook himself to Cinna's camp, but because of some calumnious accusation grew fearful and quickly withdrew unnoticed. On his disappearance, there went a rumour through the camp which said that Cinna had slain the young man, and in consequence of this those who had long hated Cinna and felt oppressed by him made an onslaught upon him. Cinna, as he fled, was seized by one of the centurions who pursued him with drawn sword, and fell upon his knees and held out his seal-ring, which was of great price. But the centurion, with great insolence, said : " Indeed, I am not come to seal a surety, but to punish a lawless and wicked tyrant," and slew him. When Cinna had come to such an end,[2] Carbo, a tyrant more capricious than he, received and exercised the chief authority. But Sulla was approaching, to the great delight of most men, who were led by their present evils to think even a change of masters no slight good. To such a pass had her calamities brought the city that, in despair of freedom, she sought a more tolerable servitude.

VI. At this time, then, Pompey was tarrying in the Italian province of Picenum, partly because he had estates there, but more because he had a liking for its cities, which were dutifully and kindly disposed towards him as his father's son. And when he saw the best and most prominent citizens forsaking their homes and hastening from all quarters to the camp of Sulla as to a haven of refuge, he

---

[1] Cf. the *Romulus*, chapter xv.   [2] In 84 B.C.

θέοντας, αὐτὸς οὐκ ἠξίωσεν ἀποδρὰς οὐδὲ ἀσύμ-
βολος οὐδὲ χρῄζων βοηθείας, ἀλλὰ ὑπάρξας τινὸς
χάριτος ἐνδόξως καὶ μετὰ δυνάμεως ἐλθεῖν πρὸς
2 αὐτόν.   ὅθεν ἐκίνει τοὺς Πικηνοὺς ἀποπειρώ-
μενος.   οἱ δὲ ὑπήκουον αὐτῷ προθύμως καὶ τοῖς
παρὰ Κάρβωνος ἥκουσιν οὐ προσεῖχον.   Οὐηδίου
δέ τινος εἰπόντος ὅτι δημαγωγὸς αὐτοῖς ἐκ παι-
δαγωγείου παραπεπήδηκεν ὁ Πομπήϊος, οὕτως
ἠγανάκτησαν ὥστε εὐθὺς ἀνελεῖν προσπεσόντες
τὸν Οὐήδιον.

3   Ἐκ τούτου Πομπήϊος ἔτη μὲν τρία καὶ εἴκοσι
γεγονώς, ὑπ᾽ οὐδενὸς δὲ ἀνθρώπων ἀποδεδειγμένος στρατηγός, αὐτὸς ἑαυτῷ δοὺς τὸ ἄρχειν, ἐν
Αὐξίμῳ, πόλει μεγάλῃ, βῆμα θεὶς ἐν ἀγορᾷ, καὶ
τοὺς πρωτεύοντας αὐτῶν ἀδελφοὺς δύο Οὐεντι-
δίους ὑπὲρ Κάρβωνος ἀντιπράττοντας διατάγ-
ματι μεταστῆναι τῆς πόλεως κελεύσας, στρατιώτας κατέλεγε, καὶ λοχαγοὺς καὶ ταξιάρχους κατὰ
κόσμον ἀποδείξας ἑκάστοις τὰς κύκλῳ πόλεις
4 ἐπῄει τὸ αὐτὸ ποιῶν.   ἐξανισταμένων δὲ καὶ
ὑποχωρούντων ὅσοι τὰ Κάρβωνος ἐφρόνουν, τῶν
δὲ ἄλλων ἀσμένως ἐπιδιδόντων αὐτούς, οὕτω
κατανείμας ἐν ὀλίγῳ χρόνῳ τρία τάγματα τέλεια,
καὶ τροφὴν πορίσας καὶ σκευαγωγὰ καὶ ἁμάξας
καὶ τὴν ἄλλην πᾶσαν παρασκευήν, ἦγε πρὸς Σύλλαν, οὐκ ἐπειγόμενος οὐδὲ τὸ λαθεῖν ἀγαπῶν,
ἀλλὰ διατρίβων καθ᾽ ὁδὸν ἐν τῷ κακῶς ποιεῖν
τοὺς πολεμίους, καὶ πᾶν ὅσον ἐπῄει τῆς Ἰταλίας
πειρώμενος ἀφιστάναι τοῦ Κάρβωνος.

VII. Ἀνέστησαν οὖν ἐπ᾽ αὐτὸν τρεῖς ἅμα
στρατηγοὶ πολέμιοι, Καρίνας καὶ Κλοίλιος καὶ
Βροῦτος, οὐκ ἐναντίοι πάντες οὐδὲ ὁμόθεν, ἀλλὰ

himself would not deign to go to him as a fugitive, nor empty-handed, nor with requests for help, but only after conferring some favour first, in a way that would gain him honour, and with an armed force. Wherefore he tried to rouse up the people of Picenum and made test of their allegiance. They readily listened to him and paid no heed to the emissaries of Carbo. Indeed, when a certain Vedius remarked that Pompey had run away from pedagogues to be a demagogue among them, they were so incensed that they fell upon Vedius at once and killed him.

After this, Pompey, who was only twenty-three years old, and who had not been appointed general by anybody whomsoever, conferred the command upon himself, and setting up a tribunal in the market-place of Auximum, a large city, issued an edict ordering the chief men there, two brothers named Ventidius, who were acting against him in Carbo's interest, to leave the city. Then he proceeded to levy soldiers, and after appointing centurions and commanders for them all in due form, made a circuit of the other cities, doing the same thing. All the partisans of Carbo withdrew and gave place to him, and the rest gladly offered their services to him, so that in a short time he had mustered three complete legions, and provided them with food, baggage-waggons, carriages, and other needful equipment. Then he led his forces towards Sulla, not in haste, nor even with a desire to escape observation, but tarrying on the march as he harried the enemy, and endeavouring to detach from Carbo's interest all that part of Italy through which he passed.

VII. There came up against him, accordingly, three hostile generals at once, Carinas, Cloelius, and Brutus,[1] not all in front of him, nor from any one

---

[1] All belonging to the Marian party.

κύκλῳ τρισὶ στρατοπέδοις περιχωροῦντες ὡς
ἀναρπασόμενοι. ὁ δὲ οὐκ ἔδεισεν, ἀλλὰ πᾶσαν
εἰς ταὐτὸ τὴν δύναμιν συναγαγὼν ὥρμησεν ἐφ᾽
ἓν τὸ τοῦ Βρούτου στράτευμα, τοὺς ἱππεῖς, ἐν οἷς
2 ἦν αὐτός, προτάξας. ἐπεὶ δὲ καὶ παρὰ τῶν
πολεμίων ἀντεξίππευσαν οἱ Κελτοί, τὸν πρῶτον
αὐτῶν[1] καὶ ῥωμαλεώτατον φθάνει παίσας ἐκ
χειρὸς δόρατι καὶ καταβαλών. οἱ δὲ ἄλλοι
τραπόμενοι καὶ τὸ πεζὸν συνετάραξαν, ὥστε
φυγὴν γενέσθαι πάντων. ἐκ δὲ τούτου στασιά-
σαντες οἱ στρατηγοὶ πρὸς ἀλλήλους ἀνεχώρησαν,
ὡς ἕκαστος ἔτυχε, Πομπηΐῳ δὲ προσεχώρουν αἱ
πόλεις, ὡς διὰ φόβον ἐσκεδασμένων τῶν πολε-
3 μίων. αὖθις δὲ Σκηπίωνος ἐπιόντος αὐτῷ τοῦ
ὑπάτου, πρὶν ἐν ἐμβολαῖς ὑσσῶν γενέσθαι τὰς
φάλαγγας, οἱ Σκηπίωνος ἀσπασάμενοι τοὺς Πομπηΐου μετεβάλοντο, Σκηπίων δὲ ἔφυγε. τέλος δὲ
Κάρβωνος αὐτοῦ περὶ τὸν Ἄρσιν ποταμὸν ἱππέων συχνὰς ἴλας ἐφέντος, εὐρώστως ὑποστὰς
καὶ τρεψάμενος εἰς χαλεπὰ καὶ ἄφιππα χωρία
πάντας ἐμβάλλει διώκων· οἱ δὲ τὴν σωτηρίαν
ἀνέλπιστον ὁρῶντες ἐνεχείρισαν αὑτοὺς μετὰ τῶν
ὅπλων καὶ τῶν ἵππων.

VIII. Οὔπω δὲ ταῦτα Σύλλας ἐπέπυστο,
πρὸς δὲ τὰς πρώτας ἀγγελίας καὶ φήμας ὑπὲρ
αὐτοῦ δεδοικὼς ἐν τοσούτοις καὶ τηλικούτοις
ἀναστρεφομένου στρατηγοῖς πολεμίοις, ἐδίωκε
βοηθήσων. γνοὺς δὲ ὁ Πομπήϊος ἐγγὺς ὄντα
προσέταξε τοῖς ἡγεμόσιν ἐξοπλίζειν καὶ διακοσ-

---

[1] τὸν πρῶτον αὐτῶν with CMS and Coraës : τὸν πρῶτον.

direction, but encompassing him round with three
armies, in order to annihilate him. Pompey, however, was not alarmed, but collected all his forces
into one body and hastened to attack one of the
hostile armies, that of Brutus, putting his cavalry,
among whom he himself rode, in the van. And
when from the enemy's side also the Celtic horsemen rode out against him, he promptly closed with
the foremost and sturdiest of them, smote him with
his spear, and brought him down. Then the rest
turned and fled and threw their infantry also into
confusion, so that there was a general rout. After
this the opposing generals fell out with one another
and retired, as each best could, and the cities came
over to Pompey's side, arguing that fear had scattered
his enemies. Next, Scipio the consul came up against
him, but before the lines of battle were within reach
of each other's javelins, Scipio's soldiers saluted
Pompey's and came over to their side, and Scipio
took to flight.[1] Finally, when Carbo himself sent
many troops of cavalry against him by the river
Arsis, he met their onset vigorously, routed them,
and in his pursuit forced them all upon difficult
ground impracticable for horse; there, seeing no
hope of escape, they surrendered themselves to him,
with their armour and horses.

VIII. Sulla had not yet learned of these results,
but at the first tidings and reports about Pompey had
feared for his safety, thus engaged with so many and
such able generals of the enemy, and was hastening
to his assistance. But when Pompey learned that
he was near, he ordered his officers to have the forces

---

[1] Plutarch seems to have transferred this exploit from
Sulla to Pompey. See the *Sulla*, xxviii. 1–3, and cf. Appian,
Bell. Civ. i. 85.

μεῖν τὴν δύναμιν, ὡς καλλίστη τῷ αὐτοκράτορι
καὶ λαμπροτάτη φανείη· μεγάλας γὰρ ἤλπιζε
2 παρ' αὐτοῦ τιμάς, ἔτυχε δὲ μειζόνων. ὡς γὰρ
εἶδεν αὐτὸν ὁ Σύλλας προσιόντα καὶ τὴν στρατιὰν παρεστῶσαν εὐανδρίᾳ τε θαυμαστὴν καὶ διὰ
τὰς κατορθώσεις ἐπηρμένην καὶ ἱλαράν, ἀποπηδήσας τοῦ ἵππου καὶ προσαγορευθείς, ὡς εἰκός,
αὐτοκράτωρ ἀντιπροσηγόρευσεν αὐτοκράτορα τὸν
Πομπήιον, οὐδενὸς ἂν προσδοκήσαντος ἀνδρὶ νέῳ
καὶ μηδέπω βουλῆς μετέχοντι κοινώσασθαι τοὔνομα τοῦτο Σύλλαν, περὶ οὗ Σκηπίωσι καὶ
3 Μαρίοις ἐπολέμει. καὶ τἆλλα δὲ ἦν ὁμολο-
γοῦντα ταῖς πρώταις φιλοφροσύναις, ὑπεξανι-
σταμένου τε προσιόντι τῷ Πομπηΐῳ καὶ τῆς
κεφαλῆς ἀπάγοντος τὸ ἱμάτιον, ἃ πρὸς ἄλλον οὐ
ῥᾳδίως ἑωρᾶτο ποιῶν, καίπερ ὄντων πολλῶν καὶ
ἀγαθῶν περὶ αὐτόν.
4 Οὐ μὴν ἐκουφίσθη γε τούτοις ὁ Πομπήιος,
ἀλλ' εὐθὺς εἰς τὴν Κελτικὴν ὑπ' αὐτοῦ πεμπό-
μενος, ἣν ἔχων ὁ Μέτελλος ἐδόκει μηδὲν ἄξιον
πράττειν τῆς παρασκευῆς, οὐ καλῶς ἔφη ἔχειν
πρεσβύτερον καὶ προὔχοντα δόξῃ στρατηγίας
ἀφαιρεῖσθαι, βουλομένῳ μέντοι τῷ Μετέλλῳ καὶ
κελεύοντι συμπολεμεῖν καὶ βοηθεῖν ἕτοιμος εἶναι.
5 δεξαμένου δὲ τοῦ Μετέλλου καὶ γράψαντος ἥκειν,
ἐμβαλὼν εἰς τὴν Κελτικὴν αὐτός τε καθ' ἑαυτὸν
ἔργα θαυμαστὰ διεπράττετο, καὶ τοῦ Μετέλλου
τὸ μάχιμον καὶ θαρσαλέον ἤδη σβεννύμενον ὑπὸ
γήρως αὖθις ἐξερρίπιζε καὶ συνεξεθέρμαινεν,
ὥσπερ ὁ ῥέων καὶ πεπυρωμένος χαλκὸς τῷ πεπη-
γότι καὶ ψυχρῷ περιχυθεὶς λέγεται τοῦ πυρὸς
6 μᾶλλον ἀνυγραίνειν καὶ συνανατήκειν. ἀλλὰ

fully armed and in complete array, that they might present a very fine and brilliant appearance to the imperator; for he expected great honours from him, and he received even greater. For when Sulla saw him advancing with an admirable army of young and vigorous soldiers elated and in high spirits because of their successes, he alighted from off his horse, and after being saluted, as was his due, with the title of Imperator, he saluted Pompey in return as Imperator. And yet no one could have expected that a young man, and one who was not yet a senator, would receive from Sulla this title, to win which Sulla was at war with such men as Scipio and Marius. And the rest of his behaviour to Pompey was consonant with his first tokens of friendliness; he would rise to his feet when Pompey approached, and uncover his head before him, things which he was rarely seen to do for any one else, although there were many about him who were of high rank.

Pompey, however, was not made vain by these things, but when Sulla would have sent him forthwith into Gaul, where, as it was thought, Metellus was doing nothing worthy of the armament at his disposal, he said it was not right for him to take the command away from a man of great reputation who was his senior, but that if Metellus wished and bade him do so, he was ready to assist him in carrying on the war. And when Metellus accepted the proposal and wrote him to come, he hurried into Gaul, and not only performed wonderful exploits himself, but also fanned into fresh heat and flame the bold and warlike spirit of Metellus which old age was now quenching, just as molten and glowing bronze, when poured round that which is cold and rigid, is said to soften it more than fire does, and to melt it also

γάρ, ὥσπερ ἀθλητοῦ πρωτεύσαντος ἐν ἀνδράσι
καὶ τοὺς πανταχοῦ καθελόντος ἐνδόξως ἀγῶνας
εἰς οὐδένα λόγον τὰς παιδικὰς τίθενται νίκας οὐδ'
ἀναγράφουσιν, οὕτως ἃς ἔπραξε τότε πράξεις ὁ
Πομπήιος, αὐτὰς καθ' ἑαυτὰς ὑπερφυεῖς οὔσας,
πλήθει δὲ καὶ μεγέθει τῶν ὑστέρων ἀγώνων καὶ
πολέμων κατακεχωσμένας, ἐδεδίειν κινεῖν, μὴ
περὶ τὰ πρῶτα πολλῆς διατριβῆς γενομένης τῶν
μεγίστων καὶ μάλιστα δηλούντων τὸ ἦθος ἔργων
καὶ παθημάτων τοῦ ἀνδρὸς ἀπολειφθῶμεν.

IX. Ἐπεὶ τοίνυν ἐκράτησε τῆς Ἰταλίας ὁ
Σύλλας καὶ δικτάτωρ ἀνηγορεύθη, τοὺς μὲν ἄλλους ἡγεμόνας καὶ στρατηγοὺς ἠμείβετο πλουσίους ποιῶν καὶ προάγων ἐπὶ ἀρχὰς καὶ χαριζόμενος ἀφθόνως καὶ προθύμως ὧν ἕκαστος ἐδεῖτο,
Πομπήιον δὲ θαυμάζων δι' ἀρετὴν καὶ μέγα
νομίζων ὄφελος εἶναι τοῖς ἑαυτοῦ πράγμασιν,
ἐσπούδασεν ἀμῶς γέ πως οἰκειότητι προσθέσθαι.
2 συμβουλομένης δὲ τῆς γυναικὸς αὐτοῦ τῆς Μετέλλης, πείθουσι τὸν Πομπήιον ἀπαλλαγέντα
τῆς Ἀντιστίας λαβεῖν γυναῖκα τὴν Σύλλα πρό-
γονον Αἰμιλίαν, ἐκ Μετέλλης καὶ Σκαύρου γεγενημένην, ἀνδρὶ δὲ συνοικοῦσαν ἤδη καὶ κύουσαν
τότε.

Ἦν οὖν τυραννικὰ τὰ τοῦ γάμου καὶ τοῖς
Σύλλα καιροῖς μᾶλλον ἢ τοῖς Πομπηίου τρόποις
πρέποντα, τῆς μὲν Αἰμιλίας ἀγομένης ἐγκύμονος
3 παρ' ἑτέρου πρὸς αὐτόν, ἐξελαυνομένης δὲ τῆς

down.   However, just as athletes who have won the
primacy among men and borne away glorious prizes
everywhere, make no account of their boyish victories
and even leave them unrecorded, so it is with the
deeds which Pompey performed at this time; they
were extraordinary in themselves, but were buried
away by the multitude and magnitude of his later
wars and contests, and I am afraid to revive them,
lest by lingering too long upon his first essays, I
should leave myself no room for those achievements
and experiences of the man which were greatest, and
most illustrative of his character.

IX. So then, when Sulla had made himself master
of Italy and had been proclaimed dictator, he sought
to reward the rest of his officers and generals by
making them rich and advancing them to office and
gratifying without reserve or stint their several
requests; but since he admired Pompey for his high
qualities and thought him a great help in his administration of affairs, he was anxious to attach him
to himself by some sort of a marriage alliance.   His
wife Metella shared his wishes, and together they
persuaded Pompey to divorce Antistia and marry
Aemilia, the step-daughter of Sulla, whom Metella
had borne to Scaurus, and who was living with a
husband already and was with child by him at this
time.[1]

This marriage was therefore characteristic of a
tyranny, and befitted the needs of Sulla rather than
the nature and habits of Pompey, Aemilia being
given to him in marriage when she was with child by
another man, and Antistia being driven away from

---

[1] Cf. the *Sulla*, xxxiii. 3.   This was in 82 B.C.   With a
similar purpose Sulla tried to make Julius Caesar part with
his wife, but Caesar refused (cf. Plutarch's *Caesar*, i. 1).

Ἀντιστίας ἀτίμως καὶ οἰκτρῶς, ἅτε δὴ καὶ τοῦ
πατρὸς ἔναγχος ἐστερημένης διὰ τὸν ἄνδρα·
κατεσφάγη γὰρ ὁ Ἀντίστιος ἐν τῷ βουλευτηρίῳ
δοκῶν τὰ Σύλλα φρονεῖν διὰ Πομπήϊον· ἡ δὲ
μήτηρ αὐτῆς ἐπιδοῦσα ταῦτα προήκατο τὸν βίον
ἑκουσίως, ὥστε καὶ τοῦτο τὸ πάθος τῇ περὶ τὸν
γάμον ἐκεῖνον τραγῳδίᾳ προσγενέσθαι καὶ νὴ
Δία τὸ τὴν Αἰμιλίαν εὐθὺς διαφθαρῆναι παρὰ
τῷ Πομπηΐῳ τίκτουσαν.

X. Ἐκ τούτου Σικελίαν ἠγγέλλετο Περπέννας
αὐτῷ κρατύνεσθαι καὶ τοῖς περιοῦσιν ἔτι τῆς
ἐναντίας στάσεως ὁρμητήριον παρέχειν τὴν νῆσον,
αἰωρουμένου καὶ Κάρβωνος αὐτόθι ναυτικῷ καὶ
Δομετίου Λιβύῃ προσπεπτωκότος, ἄλλων τε
πολλῶν ἐπέκεινα μεγάλων ὠθουμένων φυγάδων,
ὅσοι τὰς προγραφὰς ἔφθησαν ἀποδράντες. ἐπὶ
τούτους Πομπήϊος ἀπεστάλη μετὰ πολλῆς δυνά-
2 μεως. καὶ Περπέννας μὲν εὐθὺς αὐτῷ Σικελίας
ἐξέστη, τὰς δὲ πόλεις ἀνελάμβανε τετρυχωμένας
καὶ φιλανθρώπως πάσαις ἐχρῆτο πλὴν Μαμερτί-
νων τῶν ἐν Μεσσήνῃ. παραιτουμένων γὰρ αὐτοῦ
τὸ βῆμα καὶ τὴν δικαιοδοσίαν ὡς νόμῳ παλαιῷ
Ῥωμαίων ἀπειρημένα, "Οὐ παύσεσθε," εἶπεν,
"ἡμῖν ὑπεζωσμένοις ξίφη νόμους ἀναγινώσκον-
3 τες;" ἔδοξε δὲ καὶ ταῖς Κάρβωνος οὐκ ἀνθρω-
πίνως ἐνυβρίσαι συμφοραῖς. εἰ γὰρ ἦν ἀναγκαῖον
αὐτόν, ὥσπερ ἦν ἴσως, ἀνελεῖν, εὐθὺς ἔδει
λαβόντα, καὶ τοῦ κελεύσαντος ἂν ἦν τὸ ἔργον.

him in dishonour, and in piteous plight too, since she had lately been deprived of her father because of her husband (for Antistius had been killed in the senate-house [1] because he was thought to be a partisan of Sulla for Pompey's sake), and her mother, on beholding these indignities, had taken her own life. This calamity was added to the tragedy of that second marriage, and it was not the only one, indeed, since Aemilia had scarcely entered Pompey's house before she succumbed to the pains of childbirth.

X. After this, word was brought to Sulla that Perpenna was making himself master of Sicily and furnishing a refuge in that island for the survivors of the opposite faction,[2] that Carbo was hovering in those waters with a fleet, that Domitius had forced an entry into Africa, and that many other exiled men of note were thronging to those parts, all, in fact, who had succeeded in escaping his proscriptions. Against these men Pompey was sent with a large force. Perpenna at once abandoned Sicily to him, and he recovered the cities there. They had been harshly used by Perpenna, but Pompey treated them all with kindness except the Mamertines in Messana. These declined his tribunal and jurisdiction on the plea that they were forbidden by an ancient law of the Romans, at which Pompey said : "Cease quoting laws to us that have swords girt about us!" Moreover, he was thought to have treated Carbo in his misfortunes with an unnatural insolence. For if it was necessary, as perhaps it was, to put the man to death, this ought to have been done as soon as he was seized, and the deed would have been his who

---

[1] Earlier in the same year, 82 B.C., by order of the younger Marius, one of the consuls (Appian, *Bell. Civ.* i. 88).
[2] The Marian party.

ὁ δὲ δέσμιον προαγαγὼν ἄνδρα Ῥωμαῖον τρὶς
ὑπατεύσαντα καὶ πρὸ τοῦ · βήματος στήσας
καθεζόμενος αὐτὸς ἀνέκρινεν, ἀχθομένων καὶ
βαρυνομένων τῶν παρόντων· εἶτα ἐκέλευσεν
4 ἀπαγαγόντας ἀνελεῖν. ἀπαχθέντα μέντοι φασὶν
αὐτόν, ὡς εἶδεν ἑλκόμενον ἤδη τὸ ξίφος, δεῖσθαι
τόπον αὐτῷ καὶ χρόνον βραχύν, ὡς ὑπὸ κοιλίας
ἐνοχλουμένῳ, παρασχεῖν. Γάϊος δὲ Ὄππιος ὁ
Καίσαρος ἑταῖρος ἀπανθρώπως φησὶ καὶ Κοΐντῳ
Οὐαλλερίῳ χρήσασθαι τὸν Πομπήϊον. ἐπιστά-
μενον γὰρ ὡς ἔστι φιλόλογος ἀνὴρ καὶ φιλομαθὴς
ἐν ὀλίγοις ὁ Οὐαλλέριος, ὡς ἤχθη πρὸς αὐτόν,
ἐπισπασάμενον καὶ συμπεριπατήσαντα καὶ πυθό-
μενον ὧν ἔχρῃζε καὶ μαθόντα, προστάξαι τοῖς
ὑπηρέταις εὐθὺς ἀνελεῖν ἀπαγαγόντας.

5 Ἀλλ᾽ Ὀππίῳ μέν, ὅταν περὶ τῶν Καίσαρος
πολεμίων ἢ φίλων διαλέγηται, σφόδρα δεῖ
πιστεύειν μετὰ εὐλαβείας· Πομπήϊος δὲ τοὺς
μὲν ἐν δόξῃ μάλιστα τῶν Σύλλα πολεμίων καὶ
φανερῶς ἁλισκομένους ἀναγκαίως ἐκόλαζε, τῶν
δ᾽ ἄλλων ὅσους ἐξῆν περιεώρα λανθάνοντας,
6 ἐνίους δὲ καὶ συνεξέπεμπε. τὴν δ᾽ Ἱμεραίων
πόλιν ἐγνωκότος αὐτοῦ κολάζειν γενομένην μετὰ
τῶν πολεμίων, Σθένις ὁ δημαγωγὸς αἰτησάμενος
λόγον οὐκ ἔφη δίκαια ποιήσειν τὸν Πομπήϊον,
ἐὰν τὸν αἴτιον ἀφεὶς ἀπολέσῃ τοὺς μηδὲν ἀδικοῦντας. ἐρομένου δὲ ἐκείνου τίνα λέγει τὸν
αἴτιον, ἑαυτὸν ὁ Σθένις ἔφη, τοὺς μὲν φίλους
πείσαντα τῶν πολιτῶν, τοὺς δ᾽ ἐχθροὺς βιασά-

ordered it. But as it was, Pompey caused a Roman who had thrice been consul to be brought in fetters and set before the tribunal where he himself was sitting, and examined him closely there, to the distress and vexation of the audience. Then he ordered him to be led away and put to death. They say, moreover, that after Carbo had been led away to execution, when he saw the sword already drawn, he begged that a short respite and a convenient place might be afforded him, since his bowels distressed him. Furthermore, Caius Oppius, the friend of Caesar, says that Pompey treated Quintus Valerius also with unnatural cruelty. For, understanding that Valerius was a man of rare scholarship and learning, when he was brought to him, Oppius says, Pompey took him aside, walked up and down with him, asked and learned what he wished from him, and then ordered his attendants to lead him away and put him to death at once.

But when Oppius discourses about the enemies or friends of Caesar, one must be very cautious about believing him. Pompey was compelled to punish those enemies of Sulla who were most eminent, and whose capture was notorious; but as to the rest, he suffered as many as possible to escape detection, and even helped to send some out of the country. Again, when he had made up his mind to chastise the city of Himera because it had sided with the enemy, Sthenis, the popular leader there, requested audience of him, and told him that he would commit an injustice if he should let the real culprit go and destroy those who had done no wrong. And when Pompey asked him whom he meant by the real culprit, Sthenis said he meant himself, since he had persuaded his friends among the citizens, and forced

139

7 μενον. ἀγασθεὶς οὖν τὴν παρρησίαν καὶ τὸ
φρόνημα τοῦ ἀνδρὸς ὁ Πομπήιος ἀφῆκε τῆς
αἰτίας πρῶτον ἐκεῖνον, εἶτα τοὺς ἄλλους ἅπαντας.
ἀκούων δὲ τοὺς στρατιώτας ἐν ταῖς ὁδοιπορίαις
ἀτακτεῖν, σφραγῖδα ταῖς μαχαίραις αὐτῶν ἐπέ-
βαλεν, ἣν ὁ μὴ φυλάξας ἐκολάζετο.

XI. Ταῦτα πράττων ἐν Σικελίᾳ καὶ πολιτευό-
μενος ἐδέξατο δόγμα συγκλήτου καὶ γράμματα
Σύλλα κελεύοντα εἰς Λιβύην πλεῖν καὶ πολεμεῖν
Δομετίῳ κατὰ κράτος, ἠθροικότι πολλαπλασίαν
δύναμιν ἧς ἔχων Μάριος οὐ πάλαι διεπέρασεν ἐκ
Λιβύης εἰς Ἰταλίαν καὶ συνέχει τὰ Ῥωμαίων
πράγματα, τύραννος ἐκ φυγάδος καταστάς.
2 ὀξέως οὖν ἅπαντα παρασκευασάμενος ὁ Πομπήιος Σικελίας μὲν ἄρχοντα Μέμμιον κατέλιπε
τὸν ἄνδρα τῆς ἀδελφῆς, αὐτὸς δὲ ἀνήγετο ναυσὶ
μὲν μακραῖς ἑκατὸν εἴκοσι, φορτηγοῖς δὲ σῖτον
καὶ βέλη καὶ χρήματα καὶ μηχανὰς κομιζούσαις
ὀκτακοσίαις. κατασχόντι δὲ αὐτῷ ταῖς μὲν εἰς
Ἰτύκην ναυσί, ταῖς δὲ εἰς Καρχηδόνα, τῶν πολεμίων ἀποστάντες ἑπτακισχίλιοι προσεχώρησαν,
αὐτὸς δὲ ἦγεν ἐξ ἐντελῆ τάγματα.
3 Συμβῆναι δὲ αὐτῷ πρᾶγμα γελοῖον ἱστοροῦσι.
στρατιῶται γάρ τινες, ὡς ἔοικε, θησαυρῷ περι-
πεσόντες ἔλαβον συχνὰ χρήματα. τοῦ δὲ πράγματος γενομένου φανεροῦ δόξα τοῖς ἄλλοις
παρέστη πᾶσι χρημάτων μεστὸν εἶναι τὸν τόπον
ἐν ταῖς ποτε τύχαις τῶν Καρχηδονίων ἀποτε-
4 θειμένων. οὐδὲν οὖν ὁ Πομπήιος εἶχε χρῆσθαι
τοῖς στρατιώταις ἐπὶ πολλὰς ἡμέρας θησαυροὺς
ζητοῦσιν, ἀλλὰ περιῄει γελῶν καὶ θεώμενος ὁμοῦ
μυριάδας τοσαύτας ὀρυσσούσας καὶ στρεφούσας

his enemies, into their course. Pompey, then, admiring the man's frank speech and noble spirit, pardoned him first, and then all the rest. And again, on hearing that his soldiers were disorderly in their journeys, he put a seal upon their swords, and whosoever broke the seal was punished.

XI. While he was thus engaged in settling the affairs of Sicily, he received a decree of the senate and a letter from Sulla ordering him to sail to Africa and wage war with all his might against Domitius. For Domitius had assembled there a much larger force than that with which Marius, no long time ago,[1] had crossed from Africa into Italy and confounded the Roman state, making himself tyrant instead of exile. Accordingly, after making all his preparations with great speed, Pompey left Memmius, his sister's husband, as governor of Sicily, while he himself put out to sea with a hundred and twenty galleys, and eight hundred transports conveying provisions, ammunition, money, and engines of war. No sooner had he landed with part of his ships at Utica,[2] and with part at Carthage, than seven thousand of the enemy deserted and came over to him; and his own army contained six complete legions.

Here, we are told, a ludicrous thing happened to him. Some soldiers, it would seem, stumbled upon a treasure and got considerable amounts of money. When the matter became public, the rest of the army all fancied that the place was full of money which the Carthaginians had hidden away in some time of calamity. Accordingly, Pompey could do nothing with his soldiers for many days because they were hunting treasures, but he went about laughing at the spectacle of so many myriads of men digging and stirring up

[1] In 87 B.C.   [2] In 81 B.C.

τὸ πεδίον, ἕως ἀπειπόντες ἐκέλευον αὐτοὺς ἄγειν
ὅπῃ βούλεται τὸν Πομπήϊον, ὡς δίκην ἱκανὴν
τῆς ἀβελτερίας δεδωκότας.

XII. Ἀντιτεταγμένου δὲ τοῦ Δομετίου καὶ
χαράδραν τινὰ προβεβλημένου χαλεπὴν περᾶσαι
καὶ τραχεῖαν, ὄμβρος ἅμα πνεύματι πολὺς ἔωθεν
ἀρξάμενος κατεῖχεν, ὥστε ἀπογνόντα τῆς ἡμέρας
ἐκείνης μαχέσασθαι τὸν Δομέτιον ἀναζυγὴν
παραγγεῖλαι. Πομπήϊος δὲ τοῦτον αὑτοῦ ποιούμενος τὸν καιρὸν ὀξέως ἐπῄει καὶ διέβαινε τὴν
2 χαράδραν. οἱ δὲ ἀτάκτως καὶ θορυβούμενοι καὶ
οὐ πάντες οὐδὲ ὁμαλῶς ὑφίσταντο, καὶ τὸ πνεῦμα
περιῄει τὴν ζάλην αὐτοῖς προσβάλλον ἐναντίαν.
οὐ μὴν ἀλλὰ καὶ τοὺς Ῥωμαίους ὁ χειμὼν ἐτάρα-
ξεν οὐ καθορῶντας ἀλλήλους ἀκριβῶς, αὐτός
τε Πομπήϊος ἐκινδύνευσεν ἀγνοηθεὶς ἀποθανεῖν,
ἐρωτῶντι στρατιώτῃ τὸ σύνθημα βράδιον ἀπο-
κρινάμενος.

3 Ὠσάμενοι δὲ πολλῷ φόνῳ τοὺς πολεμίους
(λέγονται γὰρ ἀπὸ δισμυρίων τρισχίλιοι διαφυγεῖν) αὐτοκράτορα τὸν Πομπήϊον ἠσπάσαντο.
φήσαντος δὲ ἐκείνου μὴ δέχεσθαι τὴν τιμὴν ἕως
ὀρθὸν ἕστηκε τὸ στρατόπεδον τῶν πολεμίων, εἰ
δὲ αὐτὸν ἀξιοῦσι ταύτης τῆς προσηγορίας, ἐκεῖνο
χρῆναι πρότερον καταβαλεῖν, ὥρμησαν εὐθὺς ἐπὶ
τὸν χάρακα· καὶ Πομπήϊος ἄνευ κράνους ἠγωνί-
4 ζετο δεδοικὼς τὸ πρότερον πάθος. ἁλίσκεται δὴ
τὸ στρατόπεδον καὶ ἀποθνήσκει Δομέτιος. τῶν
δὲ πόλεων αἱ μὲν εὐθὺς ὑπήκουον, αἱ δὲ κατὰ
κράτος ἐλήφθησαν. εἷλε δὲ καὶ τῶν βασιλέων

the ground. At last they grew weary of the search and bade Pompey lead them where he pleased, assuring him that they had been sufficiently punished for their folly.

XII. Domitius now drew up his army against Pompey, with a ravine in front of him which was rough and difficult to cross; but a violent storm of wind and rain began in the morning and continued to rage, so that he gave up the idea of fighting that day and ordered a retreat. But Pompey, taking advantage of this opportunity, advanced swiftly to the attack, and crossed the ravine. The enemy met his attack in a disorderly and tumultuous fashion, not all of them indeed, nor with any uniformity; besides, the wind veered round and drove the rain into their faces. However, the Romans also were troubled by the storm, since they could not see one another clearly, and Pompey himself narrowly escaped death by not being recognized, when a soldier demanded the countersign from him and he gave it rather slowly.

Nevertheless, they routed the enemy with great slaughter (it is said that out of twenty thousand only three thousand escaped), and hailed Pompey as Imperator. And when he said he would not accept the honour as long as the camp of the enemy was intact, but that if they thought him worthy of the appellation, they must first destroy that, his soldiers immediately made an assault upon the ramparts; and Pompey fought without his helmet, for fear of a peril like the one he had just escaped. The camp was soon taken, and Domitius was slain. Then some of the cities submitted at once to Pompey, and others were taken by storm. King Iarbas also, the con-

Ἰάρφαν τὸν συμμαχήσαντα Δομετίῳ, τὴν δὲ
βασιλείαν Ἰάμψᾳ παρέδωκε. χρώμενος δὲ τῇ
τύχῃ καὶ τῇ ῥύμῃ τοῦ στρατεύματος εἰς τὴν
Νομαδικὴν ἐνέβαλε· καὶ πολλῶν ὁδὸν ἡμερῶν
5 ἐλάσας καὶ πάντων κρατήσας οἷς ἐνέτυχε, καὶ
τὸ πρὸς Ῥωμαίους δέος ἤδη τῶν βαρβάρων
ἐξερρυηκὸς αὖθις ἰσχυρὸν καὶ φοβερὸν ἐγκατα-
στήσας, οὐδὲ τὰ θηρία δεῖν ἔφη τὰ τὴν Λιβύην
κατοικοῦντα τῆς τῶν Ῥωμαίων ἄπειρα ῥώμης καὶ
τόλμης ἀπολείπειν. ὅθεν ἐν θήραις λεόντων καὶ 62
ἐλεφάντων ἡμέρας διέτριψεν οὐ πολλάς· ταῖς δὲ
πάσαις, ὥς φασι, τεσσαράκοντα τοὺς πολεμίους
συνεῖλε καὶ Λιβύην ἐχειρώσατο καὶ διῄτησε τὰ
τῶν βασιλέων, ἔτος ἄγων ἐκεῖνο τέταρτον καὶ
εἰκοστόν.

XIII. Ἐπανελθόντι δὲ εἰς Ἰτύκην αὐτῷ γράμματα κομίζεται Σύλλα προστάττοντος ἀφιέναι
μὲν τὴν ἄλλην στρατιάν, αὐτὸν δὲ μεθ᾽ ἑνὸς
τάγματος περιμένειν αὐτόθι τὸν διαδεξόμενον
στρατηγόν. ἐπὶ τούτοις ἀδήλως μὲν αὐτὸς
ἤχθετο καὶ βαρέως ἔφερεν, ἐμφανῶς δὲ ὁ στρατὸς
ἠγανάκτει· καὶ δεηθέντος τοῦ Πομπηίου προ-
ελθεῖν, τόν τε Σύλλαν κακῶς ἔλεγον, κἀκεῖνον
οὐκ ἔφασαν προήσεσθαι χωρὶς αὐτῶν, οὐδὲ εἴων
2 πιστεύειν τῷ τυράννῳ. τὸ μὲν οὖν πρῶτον ὁ
Πομπήιος ἐπειρᾶτο πραΰνειν καὶ παρηγορεῖν
αὐτούς· ὡς δ᾽ οὐκ ἔπειθε, καταβὰς ἀπὸ τοῦ
βήματος ἐπὶ τὴν σκηνὴν ἀπῄει δεδακρυμένος.
οἱ δὲ συλλαβόντες αὐτὸν αὖθις ἐπὶ τοῦ βήματος
κατέστησαν· καὶ πολὺ μέρος τῆς ἡμέρας ἀνη-
λώθη, τῶν μὲν μένειν καὶ ἄρχειν κελευόντων, τοῦ
δὲ πείθεσθαι δεομένου καὶ μὴ στασιάζειν, ἄχρι

federate of Domitius, was captured, and his kingdom given to Hiempsal. Taking advantage of the good fortune and momentum of his army, Pompey now invaded Numidia. He marched through the country for many days, conquered all who came in his way, and made potent and terrible again the Barbarians' fear of the Romans, which had reached a low ebb. Nay, he declared that even the wild beasts in African lairs must not be left without experience of the courage and strength of the Romans, and therefore spent a few days in hunting lions and elephants. It took him only forty days all told, they say, to bring his enemies to naught, get Africa into his power, and adjust the relations of its kings, though he was but twenty-four years of age.

XIII. On his return to Utica, a letter from Sulla was brought to him, in which he was commanded to send home the rest of his army, but to remain there himself with one legion, awaiting the arrival of the general who was to succeed him. Pompey himself gave no sign of the deep distress which these orders caused him, but his soldiers made their indignation manifest. When Pompey asked them to go home before him, they began to revile Sulla, declared they would not forsake their general, and insisted that he should not trust the tyrant. At first, then, Pompey tried what words could do to appease and mollify them; but when he was unable to persuade them, he came down from his tribunal and withdrew to his tent in tears. Then his soldiers seized him and set him again upon his tribunal, and a great part of the day was consumed in this way, they urging him to remain and keep his command, and he begging them to obey and not to raise a sedition. At last, when their clamours and entreaties increased, he swore

οὐ προσλιπαρούντων καὶ καταβοώντων ὤμοσεν
ἀναιρήσειν ἑαυτὸν εἰ βιάζοιντο, καὶ μόλις οὕτως
ἐπαύσαντο.

3   Τῷ δὲ Σύλλᾳ πρώτη μὲν ἦλθεν ἀγγελία τὸν
Πομπήϊον ἀφεστάναι, καὶ πρὸς τοὺς φίλους εἶπεν
ὡς ἄρα πεπρωμένον ἦν αὐτῷ γενομένῳ γέροντι
παίδων ἀγῶνας ἀγωνίζεσθαι, διὰ τὸ καὶ Μάριον
αὐτῷ νέον ὄντα κομιδῇ πλεῖστα πράγματα παρασχεῖν καὶ εἰς τοὺς ἐσχάτους περιστῆσαι κινδύ-
4   νους, πυθόμενος δὲ τἀληθῆ, καὶ πάντας ἀνθρώπους αἰσθανόμενος δέχεσθαι καὶ παραπέμπειν
τὸν Πομπήϊον ὡρμημένους μετ᾽ εὐνοίας, ἔσπευδεν
ὑπερβαλέσθαι· καὶ προελθὼν ἀπήντησεν αὐτῷ,
καὶ δεξιωσάμενος ὡς ἐνῆν προθυμότατα μεγάλῃ
φωνῇ Μάγνον ἠσπάσατο, καὶ τοὺς παρόντας
5   οὕτως ἐκέλευσε προσαγορεῦσαι. σημαίνει δὲ τὸν
μέγαν ὁ Μάγνος. ἕτεροι δέ φασιν ἐν Λιβύῃ
πρῶτον ἀναφώνημα τοῦτο τοῦ στρατοῦ παντὸς
γενέσθαι, κράτος δὲ λαβεῖν καὶ δύναμιν ὑπὸ
Σύλλα βεβαιωθέν. αὐτὸς μέντοι πάντων ὕστα-
τος καὶ μετὰ πολὺν χρόνον εἰς Ἰβηρίαν ἀνθύπατος ἐκπεμφθεὶς ἐπὶ Σερτώριον ἤρξατο γράφειν
ἑαυτὸν ἐν ταῖς ἐπιστολαῖς καὶ τοῖς διατάγμασι
Μάγνον Πομπήϊον· οὐκέτι γὰρ ἦν ἐπίφθονον
τοὔνομα σύνηθες γενόμενον.

6   Ὅθεν εἰκότως ἀγασθείη καὶ θαυμάσειεν ἄν τις
τοὺς πάλαι Ῥωμαίους, οἳ ταῖς τοιαύταις ἐπι-
κλήσεσι καὶ προσωνυμίαις οὐ τὰς πολεμικὰς
ἠμείβοντο καὶ στρατιωτικὰς κατορθώσεις μόνον,
ἀλλὰ καὶ τὰς πολιτικὰς πράξεις καὶ ἀρετὰς
7   ἐκόσμουν. δύο γοῦν Μαξίμους, ὅπερ ἐστὶ μεγίστους, ἀνηγόρευσεν ὁ δῆμος· Οὐαλλέριον μὲν
ἐπὶ τῷ διαλλάξαι στασιάζουσαν αὐτῷ τὴν σύγ-

with an oath that he would kill himself if they used force with him, and even then they would hardly stop.

Sulla's first tidings of the affair were that Pompey was in revolt, and he told his friends that it was evidently his fate, now that he was an old man, to have his contests with boys. This he said because Marius also, who was quite a young man, had given him very great trouble and involved him in the most extreme perils. But when he learned the truth, and perceived that everybody was sallying forth to welcome Pompey and accompany him home with marks of goodwill, he was eager to outdo them. So he went out and met him, and after giving him the warmest welcome, saluted him in a loud voice as "Magnus," or *The Great*, and ordered those who were by to give him this surname. Others, however, say that this title was first given him in Africa by the whole army, but received authority and weight when thus confirmed by Sulla. Pompey himself, however, was last of all to use it, and it was only after a long time, when he was sent as pro-consul to Spain against Sertorius, that he began to subscribe himself in his letters and ordinances " Pompeius Magnus " ; for the name had become familiar and was no longer invidious.

And herein we may fittingly respect and admire the ancient Romans ; they did not bestow such titles and surnames as a reward for successes in war and military command alone, but also adorned with them the high qualities and achievements of their statesmen. At any rate, in two such cases the people bestowed the title of " Maximus," which signifies *the Greatest* : upon Valerius, for reconciling them with the senate when it was at variance with them ;[1] and

[1] After the famous secession of the plebs, in 494 B.C.

κλητον, Φάβιον δὲ Ῥοῦλλον, ὅτι πλουσίους τινὰς
ἐξ ἀπελευθέρων γεγονότας καὶ καταλελεγμένους
εἰς τὴν σύγκλητον ἐξέβαλεν.

XIV. Ἐκ τούτου θρίαμβον ᾔτει Πομπήιος,
ἀντέλεγε δὲ Σύλλας. ὑπάτῳ γὰρ ἢ στρατηγῷ
μόνον, ἄλλῳ δὲ οὐδενὶ δίδωσιν ὁ νόμος. διὸ καὶ
Σκηπίων ὁ πρῶτος ἀπὸ μειζόνων καὶ κρειττόνων
ἀγώνων ἐν Ἰβηρίᾳ Καρχηδονίων κρατήσας οὐκ
ᾔτησε θρίαμβον· ὕπατος γὰρ οὐκ ἦν οὐδὲ στρα-
2 τηγός. εἰ δὲ Πομπήιος οὔπω πάνυ γενειῶν
εἰσελᾷ θριαμβεύων εἰς τὴν πόλιν, ᾧ βουλῆς διὰ
τὴν ἡλικίαν οὐ μέτεστι, παντάπασιν ἐπίφθονον
ἔσεσθαι καὶ τὴν ἀρχὴν ἑαυτῷ καὶ τὴν τιμὴν
ἐκείνῳ. ταῦτα πρὸς Πομπήιον ὁ Σύλλας ἔλεγεν,
ὡς οὐκ ἐάσων, ἀλλὰ ἐνστησόμενος αὐτῷ καὶ
κωλύσων τὸ φιλόνεικον ἀπειθοῦντος.

3 Ὁ δὲ Πομπήιος οὐχ ὑπέπτηξεν, ἀλλ' ἐννοεῖν
ἐκέλευσε τὸν Σύλλαν ὅτι τὸν ἥλιον ἀνατέλλοντα
πλείονες ἢ δυόμενον προσκυνοῦσιν, ὡς αὐτῷ μὲν 62
αὐξανομένης, μειουμένης δὲ καὶ μαραινομένης
ἐκείνῳ τῆς δυνάμεως. ταῦτα ὁ Σύλλας οὐκ ἀκριβῶς ἐξακούσας, ὁρῶν δὲ τοὺς ἀκούσαντας ἀπὸ
τοῦ προσώπου καὶ τοῦ σχήματος ἐν θαύματι
ποιουμένους, ἤρετο τί τὸ λεχθὲν εἴη. πυθόμενος
δὲ καὶ καταπλαγεὶς τοῦ Πομπηΐου τὴν τόλμαν
4 ἀνεβόησε δὶς ἐφεξῆς, " Θριαμβευσάτω." πολλῶν
δὲ δυσχεραινόντων καὶ ἀγανακτούντων, ἔτι μᾶλλον αὐτούς, ὥς φασι, βουλόμενος ἀνιᾶν ὁ Πομπήιος, ἐπεχείρησεν ἐλεφάντων ἅρματι τεττάρων
ἐπιβὰς εἰσελαύνειν· ἤγαγε γὰρ ἐκ Λιβύης τῶν

upon Fabius Rullus,[1] because he expelled from the senate certain descendants of freedmen who had been enrolled in it on account of their wealth.

XIV. After this, Pompey asked for a triumph, but Sulla opposed his request. The law, he said, permitted only a consul or a praetor to celebrate a triumph, but no one else. Therefore the first Scipio, after conquering the Carthaginians in Spain in far greater conflicts, did not ask for a triumph; for he was not consul, nor even praetor. And if Pompey, who had scarcely grown a beard as yet, and who was too young to be a senator, should ride into the city in a triumph, it would not only make Sulla's government altogether odious, but also Pompey's honour. This was what Sulla said to Pompey, declaring that he would not allow his request, but would oppose him and thwart his ambition if he refused to listen to him.

Pompey, however, was not cowed, but bade Sulla reflect that more worshipped the rising than the setting sun, intimating that his own power was on the increase, while that of Sulla was on the wane and fading away. Sulla did not hear the words distinctly, but seeing, from their looks and gestures, that those who did hear them were amazed, he asked what it was that had been said. When he learned what it was, he was astounded at the boldness of Pompey, and cried out twice in succession: " Let him triumph! " Further, when many showed displeasure and indignation at his project, Pompey, we are told, was all the more desirous of annoying them, and tried to ride into the city on a chariot drawn by four elephants; for he had brought many

[1] Cf. the *Fabius Maximus*, i. 2. It was in the capacity of censor, 304 B.C., that Rullus thus purified the senate.

βασιλικῶν συχνοὺς αἰχμαλώτους· ἀλλὰ τῆς πύλης
στενωτέρας οὔσης ἀπέστη καὶ μετῆλθεν ἐπὶ τοὺς
5 ἵππους. ἐπεὶ δὲ οἱ στρατιῶται μὴ τυχόντες
ἡλίκων προσεδόκησαν ἐνοχλεῖν ἐβούλοντο καὶ
θορυβεῖν, οὐδὲν ἔφη φροντίζειν, ἀλλὰ μᾶλλον
ἀφήσειν τὸν θρίαμβον ἢ κολακεύσειν ἐκείνους.
ὅτε δὴ καὶ Σερουίλιος, ἀνὴρ ἐπιφανὴς καὶ μάλιστα
πρὸς τὸν θρίαμβον ἐνστὰς τοῦ Πομπηίου, νῦν
ἔφη τὸν Πομπήιον ὁρᾶν καὶ μέγαν ἀληθῶς καὶ
6 ἄξιον τοῦ θριάμβου. δῆλον δ' ἐστὶν ὅτι καὶ
βουλῆς ἂν ἐθελήσας τότε ῥαδίως ἔτυχεν. ἀλλ'
οὐκ ἐσπούδασεν, ὡς λέγουσι, τὸ ἔνδοξον ἐκ τοῦ
παραδόξου θηρώμενος. οὐ γὰρ ἦν θαυμαστὸν εἰ
πρὸ ἡλικίας ἐβούλευε Πομπήιος, ἀλλ' ὑπέρλαμ-
προν ὅτι μηδέπω βουλεύων ἐθριάμβευε. τοῦτο
δὲ αὐτῷ καὶ πρὸς εὔνοιαν ὑπῆρχε τῶν πολλῶν
οὐ μικρόν· ἔχαιρε γὰρ ὁ δῆμος αὐτῷ μετὰ θρίαμβον ἐν τοῖς ἱππικοῖς ἐξεταζομένῳ.

XV. Σύλλας δὲ ἠνιᾶτο μὲν ὁρῶν εἰς ὅσον
δόξης πρόεισι καὶ δυνάμεως, αἰσχυνόμενος δὲ
κωλύειν ἡσυχίαν ἦγε· πλήν, ὅτε βίᾳ καὶ ἄκοντος
αὐτοῦ Λέπιδον εἰς ὑπατείαν κατέστησε, συναρχ-
αιρεσιάσας καὶ τὸν δῆμον εὐνοίᾳ τῇ πρὸς ἑαυτὸν
ἐκείνῳ σπουδάζοντα παρασχών, θεασάμενος αὐτὸν
ἀπιόντα μετὰ πλήθους δι' ἀγορᾶς ὁ Σύλλας,
2 " Ὁρῶ σε," εἶπεν, " ὦ νεανία, χαίροντα τῇ νίκῃ·
πῶς γὰρ οὐχὶ γενναῖα ταῦτα καὶ καλά, Κάτλου
τοῦ πάντων ἀρίστου Λέπιδον τὸν πάντων κά-

from Africa which he had captured from its kings. But the gate of the city was too narrow, and he therefore gave up the attempt and changed over to his horses. Moreover, when his soldiers, who had not got as much as they expected, were inclined to raise a tumult and impede the triumph, he said he did not care at all, but would rather give up his triumph than truckle to them. Then Servilius, a man of distinction, and one who had been most opposed to Pompey's triumph, said he now saw that Pompey was really great, and worthy of the honour. And it is clear that he might also have been easily made a senator at that time, had he wished it; but he was not eager for this, as they say, since he was in the chase for reputation of a surprising sort. And indeed it would have been nothing wonderful for Pompey to be a senator before he was of age for it; but it was a dazzling honour for him to celebrate a triumph before he was a senator. And this contributed not a little to win him the favour of the multitude; for the people were delighted to have him still classed among the knights after a triumph.

XV. Sulla, however, was annoyed at seeing to what a height of reputation and power Pompey was advancing, but being ashamed to obstruct his career, he kept quiet. Only, when in spite of him and against his wishes Pompey made Lepidus consul,[1] by canvassing for him and making the people zealously support him through their goodwill towards himself, seeing Pompey going off through the forum with a throng, Sulla said: "I see, young man, that you rejoice in your victory; and surely it was a generous and noble thing for Lepidus, the worst of men, to be proclaimed consul by a larger vote than Catulus, the

[1] In 79 B.C.

κιστον ἀποδειχθῆναι πρότερον ὕπατον, σοῦ τὸν
δῆμον οὕτω παρασκευάσαντος; ὥρα μέντοι σοι
μὴ καθεύδειν, ἀλλὰ προσέχειν τοῖς πράγμασιν·
ἰσχυρότερον γὰρ τὸν ἀνταγωνιστὴν σεαυτῷ κατεσκεύακας."[1] ἐδήλωσε δὲ μάλιστα Σύλλας ὅτι
πρὸς Πομπήϊον οὐκ εὐμενῶς εἶχε ταῖς διαθήκαις
3 ἃς ἔγραψεν. ἑτέροις γὰρ φίλοις δωρεὰς ἀπολιπών, καὶ τοῦ παιδὸς ἀποδείξας ἐπιτρόπους, τὸν
Πομπήϊον ὅλως παρῆλθεν. ἤνεγκε μέντοι τοῦτο
μετρίως πάνυ καὶ πολιτικῶς ἐκεῖνος, ὥστε Λεπί-
δου καί τινων ἄλλων ἐνισταμένων μὴ ταφῆναι τὸν
νεκρὸν ἐν τῷ πεδίῳ, μηδὲ δημοσίᾳ τὴν ἐκφορὰν
γενέσθαι, βοηθῆσαι καὶ παρασχεῖν δόξαν ἅμα
ταῖς ταφαῖς καὶ ἀσφάλειαν.

XVI. Ἐπεὶ δὲ ταχὺ τοῦ Σύλλα τελευτήσαντος
εἰς φῶς παρήει τὰ μαντεύματα, καὶ Λέπιδος
εἰσποιῶν ἑαυτὸν εἰς τὴν ἐκείνου δύναμιν οὐ κύκλῳ
περιϊὼν οὐδὲ μετὰ σχήματος, ἀλλὰ εὐθὺς ἐν τοῖς
ὅπλοις ἦν, τὰ πάλαι νοσοῦντα καὶ διαφυγόντα
τὸν Σύλλαν ὑπολείμματα τῶν στάσεων αὖθις
ἀνακινῶν καὶ περιβαλλόμενος, ὁ δὲ συνάρχων
αὐτοῦ Κάτλος, ᾧ τὸ καθαρὸν καὶ ὑγιαῖνον μάλιστα τῆς βουλῆς καὶ τοῦ δήμου προσεῖχεν, ἦν
μὲν ἐν ἀξιώματι σωφροσύνης καὶ δικαιοσύνης
2 μέγιστος τῶν τότε Ῥωμαίων, ἐδόκει δὲ πολιτικῆς
ἡγεμονίας μᾶλλον ἢ στρατιωτικῆς οἰκεῖος εἶναι,
τῶν πραγμάτων αὐτῶν ποθούντων τὸν Πομπήϊον
οὐ διεμέλλησεν ὅπη τράπηται, προσθεὶς δὲ τοῖς
ἀρίστοις ἑαυτὸν ἀπεδείχθη στρατεύματος ἡγεμὼν
ἐπὶ τὸν Λέπιδον ἤδη πολλὰ τῆς Ἰταλίας κεκινη-
κότα καὶ τὴν ἐντὸς Ἄλπεων Γαλατίαν κατέχοντα
διὰ Βρούτου στρατεύματι.

[1] κατεσκεύακας with Bekker and S : παρεσκεύακας.

best of men, because you influenced the people to take this course. Now, however, it is time for you to be wide awake and watchful of your interests; you have made your adversary stronger than yourself." But Sulla showed most clearly that he was not well-disposed to Pompey by the will which he wrote. For whereas he bequeathed gifts to other friends, and made some of them guardians of his son, he omitted all mention of Pompey. And yet Pompey bore this with great composure, and loyally, insomuch that when Lepidus and sundry others tried to prevent the body of Sulla from being buried in the Campus Martius, or even from receiving public burial honours, he came to the rescue, and gave to the interment alike honour and security.[1]

XVI. Soon after the death of Sulla,[2] his prophecies were fulfilled, and Lepidus tried to assume Sulla's powers. He took no circuitous route and used no pretence, but appeared at once in arms, stirring up anew and gathering about himself the remnants of faction, long enfeebled, which had escaped the hand of Sulla. His colleague, Catulus, to whom the incorrupt and sounder element in the senate and people attached themselves, was the greatest Roman of the time in the estimate set upon his wisdom and justice, but was thought better adapted for political than military leadership. The situation itself, therefore demanded Pompey, who was not long in deciding what course to take. He took the side of the nobility, and was appointed commander of an army against Lepidus, who had already stirred up a large part of Italy and was employing Brutus to hold Cisalpine Gaul with an army.

[1] Cf. the *Sulla*, chapter xxxviii.
[2] 78 B.C.

3   Τῶν μὲν οὖν ἄλλων ἐκράτησε ῥᾳδίως ἐπελθὼν
ὁ Πομπήϊος· ἐν δὲ Μουτίνῃ τῆς Γαλατίας ἀντε-
κάθητο τῷ Βρούτῳ συχνὸν χρόνον· ἐν ᾧ Λέπιδος
ἐπὶ τὴν Ῥώμην ῥυεὶς καὶ προσκαθήμενος ἔξωθεν
ὑπατείαν ᾔτει δευτέραν, ὄχλῳ πολλῷ δεδιττό-
4 μενος τοὺς ἔνδον. ἔλυσε δὲ τὸν φόβον ἐπιστολὴ
παρὰ Πομπηΐου κομισθεῖσα κατωρθωκότος ἄνευ
μάχης τὸν πόλεμον. ὁ γὰρ Βροῦτος, εἴτε παραδοὺς τὴν δύναμιν αὐτός, εἴτε προδοθεὶς μετα-
βαλομένης ἐκείνης, ἐνεχείρισε τῷ Πομπηΐῳ τὸ
σῶμα, καὶ λαβὼν ἱππεῖς προπομποὺς ἀπεχώ-
ρησεν εἰς πολίχνιόν τι τῶν περὶ τὸν Πάδον, ὅπου
μεθ' ἡμέραν μίαν, ἐπιπέμψαντος αὐτῷ τοῦ Πομ-
5 πηΐου Γεμίνιον, ἀνῃρέθη· καὶ πολλὴν ἔσχεν ἀπὸ
τούτου Πομπήϊος αἰτίαν. γεγραφὼς γὰρ εὐθὺς
ἐν ἀρχῇ τῆς μεταβολῆς πρὸς τὴν σύγκλητον ὡς
ἑκὼν αὐτῷ πρόσθοιτο Βροῦτος, ἑτέρας αὖθις
ἔπεμψεν ἐπιστολὰς ἀνῃρημένου τοῦ ἀνθρώπου
κατηγορούσας. τούτου Βροῦτος ὁ υἱὸς ὁ Καίσαρα σὺν Κασσίῳ κτείνας, ἀνὴρ ὁμοίως τῷ πατρὶ
μήτε πολεμήσας μήτε ἀποθανών, ὡς ἐν τοῖς περὶ
6 ἐκείνου γέγραπται. Λέπιδος μὲν οὖν εὐθὺς
ἐκπεσὼν τῆς Ἰταλίας ἀπεπέρασεν εἰς Σαρδόνα·
κἀκεῖ νοσήσας ἐτελεύτησε δι' ἀθυμίαν, οὐ τῶν
πραγμάτων, ὥς φασιν, ἀλλὰ γραμματίῳ περι-
πεσὼν ἐξ οὗ μοιχείαν τινὰ τῆς γυναικὸς ἐφώρασε.

XVII. Λεπίδῳ δὲ οὐδὲν ὅμοιος στρατηγὸς
Ἰβηρίαν κατέχων Σερτώριος ἐπηωρεῖτο Ῥωμαίοις
φοβερός, ὥσπερ ἐπ' ἔσχατον¹ νόσημα τῶν ἐμ-
φυλίων πολέμων εἰς τοῦτον τὸν ἄνδρα συνερ-
ρυηκότων, πολλοὺς μὲν ἤδη τῶν ἐλαττόνων στρα-

---

¹ ἐπ' ἔσχατον Stephanus, Coraës, and S : ἔσχατον.

Other opponents against whom Pompey came were easily mastered by him, but at Mutina, in Gaul, he lay a long while besieging Brutus. Meanwhile, Lepidus had made a hasty rush upon Rome, and sitting down before it, was demanding a second consulship, and terrifying the citizens with a vast throng of followers. But their fear was dissipated by a letter brought from Pompey, announcing that he had brought the war to a close without a battle. For Brutus, whether he himself betrayed his army, or whether his army changed sides and betrayed him, put himself in the hands of Pompey, and receiving an escort of horsemen, retired to a little town upon the Po. Here, after a single day had passed, he was slain by Geminius, who was sent by Pompey to do the deed. And Pompey was much blamed for this. For as soon as the army of Brutus changed sides, he wrote to the senate that Brutus had surrendered to him of his own accord ; then he sent another letter denouncing the man after he had been put to death. The Brutus who, with Cassius, killed Caesar, was a son of this Brutus, a man who was like his father neither in his wars nor in his death, as is written in his Life. As for Lepidus, moreover, as soon as he was expelled from Italy, he made his way over to Sardinia. There he fell sick and died of despondency, which was due, as we are told, not to the loss of his cause, but to his coming accidentally upon a writing from which he discovered that his wife was an adulteress.

XVII. But a general quite unlike Lepidus, namely Sertorius, was in possession of Spain, and was threatening the Romans like a formidable cloud. As if for a final disease of the state, the civil wars had poured all their venom into this man. He had

τηγῶν ἀνῃρηκότα, Μετέλλῳ δὲ Πίῳ τότε συμ-
2 πεπλεγμένον, ἀνδρὶ λαμπρῷ μὲν καὶ πολεμικῷ,
δοκοῦντι δὲ ἀργότερον ὑπὸ γήρως ἕπεσθαι τοῖς
καιροῖς τοῦ πολέμου, καὶ ἀπολείπεσθαι τῶν
πραγμάτων ἁρπαζομένων ὀξύτητι καὶ τάχει, τοῦ
Σερτωρίου παραβόλως καὶ λῃστρικώτερον αὐτῷ
προσφερομένου, καὶ ταράττοντος ἐνέδραις καὶ
περιδρομαῖς ἄνδρα νομίμων ἀθλητὴν ἀγώνων καὶ
3 δυνάμεως στασίμου καὶ βαρείας ἡγεμόνα. πρὸς
ταῦτα Πομπήϊος ἔχων τὴν στρατιὰν ὑφ' ἑαυτῷ
διεπράττετο Μετέλλῳ πεμφθῆναι βοηθός· καὶ
Κάτλου κελεύοντος οὐ διέλυεν, ἀλλ' ἐν τοῖς
ὅπλοις ἦν περὶ τὴν πόλιν, ἀεί τινας ποιούμενος
προφάσεις, ἕως ἔδωκαν αὐτῷ τὴν ἀρχὴν Λευκίου
4 Φιλίππου γνώμην εἰπόντος. ὅτε καί φασιν ἐν
συγκλήτῳ πυθομένου τινὸς καὶ θαυμάζοντος εἰ
Πομπήϊον ἀνθύπατον οἴεται δεῖν ἐκπεμφθῆναι
Φίλιππος· "Οὐκ ἔγωγε," φάναι τὸν Φίλιππον,
"ἀλλ' ἀνθ' ὑπάτων," ὡς ἀμφοτέρους τοὺς τότε
ὑπατεύοντας οὐδενὸς ἀξίους ὄντας.

XVIII. Ἐπεὶ δὲ τῆς Ἰβηρίας ἁψάμενος ὁ
Πομπήϊος, οἷα φιλεῖ πρὸς νέου δόξαν ἡγεμόνος,
ἑτέρους ταῖς ἐλπίσιν ἐποίησε τοὺς ἀνθρώπους καὶ
τὰ μὴ πάνυ βεβαίως τῷ Σερτωρίῳ συνεστῶτα
τῶν ἐθνῶν ἐκινεῖτο καὶ μετεβάλλετο, λόγους
ὑπερηφάνους ὁ Σερτώριος κατὰ τοῦ Πομπηίου
διέσπειρε, καὶ σκώπτων ἔλεγε νάρθηκος ἂν αὐτῷ
δεῆσαι καὶ σκύτους ἐπὶ τὸν παῖδα τοῦτον, εἰ μὴ
τὴν γραῦν ἐκείνην ἐφοβεῖτο, λέγων τὸν Μέτελ-
2 λον. ἔργῳ μέντοι φυλαττόμενος σφόδρα καὶ

already slain many of the inferior commanders, and was now engaged with Metellus Pius, an illustrious man and a good soldier, but, as men thought, too slow by reason of his years in following up the opportunities of war, and outdistanced when events swept along at high speed. For Sertorius attacked him recklessly and in robber fashion, and by his ambuscades and flanking movements confounded a man who was practised in regular contests only, and commanded immobile and heavy-armed troops.[1] Pompey, therefore, who kept his army under his command, tried to get himself sent out to reinforce Metellus, and although Catulus ordered him to disband his soldiers, he would not do so, but remained under arms near the city, ever making some excuse or other, until the senate gave him the command, on motion of Lucius Philippus. On this occasion, too, they say that a certain senator asked with amazement if Philippus thought it necessary to send Pompey out as proconsul. "No indeed!" said Philippus, "but as pro-consuls," implying that both the consuls of that year were good for nothing.

XVIII. When Pompey arrived in Spain,[2] the reputation of a new commander produced the usual results; he transformed the men of Metellus with fresh hopes, and those nations which were not very firmly leagued with Sertorius began to be restless and change sides. Thereupon Sertorius disseminated haughty speeches against Pompey, and scoffingly said he should have needed but a cane and whip for this boy, were he not in fear of that old woman, meaning Metellus.[3] In fact, however, he kept very close watch on Pompey, and was afraid of him, and

---

[1] Cf. the *Sertorius*, xii. 5.   [2] In 76 B.C.
[3] Cf. the *Sertorius*, xix. 6.

δεδοικὼς τὸν Πομπήϊον ἀσφαλέστερον ἐστρατή-
γει. καὶ γὰρ ὁ Μέτελλος, ὅπερ οὐκ ἄν τις ᾠήθη,
διετέθρυπτο τῷ βίῳ κομιδῇ πρὸς τὰς ἡδονὰς
ἐνδεδωκώς, καὶ μεγάλη τις εἰς ὄγκον καὶ πολυ-
τέλειαν ἐξαίφνης ἐγεγόνει μεταβολὴ περὶ αὐτόν,
ὥστε τῷ Πομπηΐῳ καὶ τοῦτο θαυμαστὴν εὔνοιαν
ἅμα δόξῃ φέρειν, ἐπιτείνοντι τὴν εὐτέλειαν τῆς
διαίτης οὐ πολλῆς ἐπιτηδεύσεως δεομένην· φύσει
γὰρ ἦν σώφρων καὶ τεταγμένος ἐν ταῖς ἐπιθυμίαις.

3   Τοῦ δὲ πολέμου πολλὰς ἰδέας ἔχοντος, ἠνίασε
μάλιστα τὸν Πομπήϊον ἡ Λαύρωνος ἅλωσις ὑπὸ 6
Σερτωρίου. κυκλοῦσθαι γὰρ αὐτὸν οἰηθεὶς καί
τι μεγαληγορήσας, αὐτὸς ἐξαίφνης ἀνεφάνη περι-
εχόμενος κύκλῳ· καὶ διὰ τοῦτο κινεῖσθαι δεδιὼς
ἐπεῖδε καταπιμπραμένην τὴν πόλιν αὐτοῦ παρόντος. Ἑρέννιον δὲ καὶ Περπένναν, ἄνδρας ἡγε-
μονικοὺς τῶν πρὸς Σερτώριον καταπεφευγότων
καὶ στρατηγούντων ἐκείνῳ, νικήσας περὶ Οὐαλεν-
τίαν ὑπὲρ μυρίους ἀπέκτεινεν.

XIX. Ἐπαρθεὶς δὲ τῇ πράξει καὶ μέγα φρονῶν ἐπ᾽ αὐτὸν ἔσπευδε Σερτώριον, ὡς μὴ μετά-
σχοι τῆς νίκης Μέτελλος. περὶ δὲ Σούκρωνι
ποταμῷ τῆς ἡμέρας ἤδη τελευτώσης συνέβαλον
τὰς δυνάμεις, δεδιότες ἐπελθεῖν τὸν Μέτελλον,
2 ὁ μὲν ὡς μόνος, ὁ δὲ ὡς μόνῳ διαγωνίσαιτο. τὸ
μὲν οὖν τέλος ἀμφίδοξον ἔσχεν ὁ ἀγών· ἑκατέρου
γὰρ θάτερον κέρας ἐνίκησε· τῶν δὲ στρατηγῶν
πλέον ἠνέγκατο Σερτώριος· ἐτρέψατο γὰρ τὸ

therefore conducted his campaign with more caution. For Metellus, contrary to all expectation, had become luxurious in his way of living and had given himself up completely to his pleasures; in fact, there had been all at once a great change in him towards pomp and extravagance,[1] so that this circumstance also brought Pompey an astonishing goodwill, and enhanced his reputation, since he always maintained that simplicity in his habits which cost him no great effort; for he was naturally temperate and orderly in his desires.

The war had many phases, but what most vexed Pompey was the capture of Lauron by Sertorius. For when he supposed that his enemy was surrounded, and had made some boasts about it, all of a sudden it turned out that he was himself completely enveloped. He was therefore afraid to stir, and had to look on while the city was burned before his eyes.[2] However, near Valentia he conquered Herennius and Perpenna, men of military experience among the refugees with Sertorius, and generals under him, and slew more than ten thousand of their men.

XIX. Elated by this achievement and full of pride, he made all haste to attack Sertorius himself, that Metellus might not share in the victory. By the river Sucro, though it was now late in the day, they joined battle, both fearing the arrival of Metellus; the one wished to fight alone, the other wished to have only one antagonist. Well, then, the struggle had a doubtful issue, for one wing on each side was victorious; but of the generals, Sertorius bore away the more honour, for he put to

---

[1] Cf. the *Sertorius*, xiii. 1 f.
[2] Cf. the *Sertorius*, chapter xviii.

καθ᾽ αὑτὸν ἐκεῖνος ἀντιταχθείς. Πομπηΐῳ δὲ
ἀνὴρ μέγας ἱππότῃ πεζὸς ἐφώρμησε· συμπεσόντων δ᾽ εἰς τὸ αὐτὸ καὶ γενομένων ἐν λαβαῖς ἀπέ-
σκηψαν αἱ πληγαὶ τῶν ξιφῶν εἰς τὰς χεῖρας
ἀμφοῖν, οὐχ ὁμοίως· ἐτρώθη μὲν γὰρ ὁ Πομπήϊος
3 μόνον, ἐκείνου δὲ ἀπέκοψε τὴν χεῖρα. πλειόνων
δὲ συνδραμόντων ἐπ᾽ αὐτόν, ἤδη τῆς τροπῆς γε-
γενημένης, ἀνελπίστως διέφυγε, προέμενος τὸν
ἵππον τοῖς πολεμίοις φάλαρα χρυσᾶ καὶ κόσμον
ἄξιον πολλοῦ περικείμενον. ταῦτα γὰρ διανεμό-
μενοι καὶ περὶ τούτων μαχόμενοι πρὸς ἀλλήλους
4 ἀπελείφθησαν. ἅμα δὲ ἡμέρᾳ παρετάξαντο μὲν
ἀμφότεροι πάλιν ἐκβεβαιούμενοι τὸ νίκημα, Μετέλλου δὲ προσιόντος ἀνεχώρησεν ὁ Σερτώριος
σκεδασθέντι τῷ στρατῷ. τοιαῦται γὰρ ἦσαν αἱ
διαλύσεις καὶ πάλιν συνδρομαὶ τῶν ἀνθρώπων
ὥστε πολλάκις μόνον πλανᾶσθαι τὸν Σερτώριον,
πολλάκις δὲ αὖθις ἐπιέναι μυριάσι πεντεκαίδεκα
στρατιᾶς, ὥσπερ χειμάρρουν ἐξαίφνης πιμπλά-
μενον.
5   Ὁ δ᾽ οὖν Πομπήϊος, ἐπεὶ μετὰ τὴν μάχην
ἀπήντα τῷ Μετέλλῳ καὶ πλησίον ἀλλήλων
ἦσαν, ἐκέλευσεν ὑφεῖναι τὰς ῥάβδους, θεραπεύων
ὡς προὔχοντα τιμῇ τὸν Μέτελλον. ὁ δὲ καὶ
τοῦτο διεκώλυσε καὶ τἆλλα χρηστὸς ἦν ἀνὴρ
περὶ αὐτόν, οὐδὲν ὡς ὑπατικῷ καὶ πρεσβυτέρῳ
νέμων ἑαυτῷ πλέον, ἀλλ᾽ ἢ τὸ σύνθημα κοινῇ
στρατοπεδευόντων εἰς ἅπαντας ἐξεπέμπετο παρὰ
Μετέλλου· τὰ πολλὰ δὲ χωρὶς ἐστρατοπεδεύοντο.
6 διέκοπτε γὰρ αὐτοὺς καὶ διΐστη ποικίλος ὢν ὁ

flight the enemy in front of his position. But
Pompey, who was on horseback, was attacked by a
tall man who fought on foot; when they came to
close quarters and were at grips, the strokes of their
swords fell upon each other's hands, but not with
like result, for Pompey was merely wounded, whereas he lopped off the hand of his opponent. Then,
when more foes rushed upon him together, his troops
being now routed, he made his escape, contrary to
all expectation, by abandoning to the enemy his
horse, which had golden head-gear and ornamented
trappings of great value. They fought with one
another over the division of these spoils, and so
were left behind in the pursuit.[1] At break of day,
however, both generals drew up their forces again
to make the victory assured, but on the approach of
Metellus, Sertorius retired and his army dispersed.
His men were accustomed to scatter in this way, and
then to come together again, so that often Sertorius
wandered about alone, and often took the field again
with an army of a hundred and fifty thousand men,
like a winter torrent suddenly swollen.

Pompey, then, when he went to meet Metellus
after the battle and they were near each other,
ordered his lictors to lower their fasces, out of
deference to Metellus as his superior in rank. But
Metellus would not allow this, and in all other ways
was considerate of him, not assuming any superiority
as a man of consular rank and the elder, except that
when they shared the same camp the watchword was
given out to all from the tent of Metellus; but for
the most part they encamped apart. For their
versatile enemy used to cut off their communications

---

[1] Cf. the *Sertorius*, xix. 4.

πολέμιος καὶ δεινὸς ἐν βραχεῖ πολλαχοῦ περι-
φανῆναι καὶ μεταγαγεῖν ἀπ' ἄλλων εἰς ἄλλους
ἀγῶνας. τέλος δὲ περικόπτων μὲν ἀγοράς, λη-
ζόμενος δὲ τὴν χώραν, ἐπικρατῶν δὲ τῆς θαλάσσης, ἐξέβαλεν ἀμφοτέρους τῆς ὑφ' ἑαυτὸν Ἰβηρίας, ἀναγκασθέντας εἰς ἀλλοτρίας καταφυγεῖν
ἐπαρχίας ἀπορίᾳ τῶν ἐπιτηδείων.

XX. Πομπήϊος δὲ τὰ πλεῖστα τῶν ἰδίων
ἐξανηλωκὼς καὶ κατακεχρημένος εἰς τὸν πόλεμον,
ᾔτει χρήματα τὴν σύγκλητον, ὡς ἀφιξόμενος εἰς
Ἰταλίαν μετὰ τῆς δυνάμεως εἰ μὴ πέμποιεν.
ὑπατεύων δὲ Λεύκολλος τότε καὶ Πομπηΐῳ μὲν
ὢν διάφορος, μνώμενος δ' ἑαυτῷ τὸν Μιθριδατικὸν
πόλεμον, ἔσπευσεν ἀποσταλῆναι τὰ χρήματα,
φοβούμενος αἰτίαν Πομπηΐῳ παρασχεῖν δεομένῳ
Σερτώριον ἀφεῖναι καὶ πρὸς Μιθριδάτην τραπέσθαι, λαμπρὸν μὲν εἰς δόξαν, εὐμεταχείριστον δὲ
2 φαινόμενον ἀνταγωνιστήν. ἐν τούτῳ δὲ θνήσκει
Σερτώριος ὑπὸ τῶν φίλων δολοφονηθείς· ὧν Περπέννας ὁ κορυφαιότατος ἐπεχείρησεν ἐκείνῳ τὰ
αὐτὰ ποιεῖν, ἀπὸ τῶν αὐτῶν μὲν ὁρμώμενος δυνάμεων καὶ παρασκευῶν, τὸν δὲ χρώμενον αὐταῖς
ὁμοίως οὐκ ἔχων λογισμόν. εὐθὺς οὖν ὁ Πομπήϊος ἐπεξελθὼν καὶ ῥεμβόμενον ἐν τοῖς πράγμασι τὸν Περπένναν καταμαθών, δέλεαρ αὐτῷ 62
δέκα σπείρας ὑφῆκεν, εἰς τὸ πεδίον διασπαρῆναι
3 κελεύσας. τραπομένου δὲ πρὸς ταύτας ἐκείνου
καὶ διώκοντος, ἄθρους ἐπιφανεὶς καὶ συνάψας
μάχην ἐκράτησε πάντων. καὶ διεφθάρησαν οἱ

and separate them, and showed great skill in appearing in many places within a short time, and in drawing them from one contest into another. And finally, by cutting off their supplies, plundering the country, and getting control of the sea, he drove both of them out of that part of Spain which was under him, and forced them to take refuge in other provinces for lack of provisions.[1]

XX. When Pompey had exhausted most of his private resources and spent them on the war, he asked money of the senate, threatening to come back to Italy with his army if they did not send it. Lucullus was consul at this time, and was not on good terms with Pompey, but since he was soliciting the conduct of the Mithridatic war for himself, made great efforts to have the money sent,[2] for fear of furthering Pompey's desire to let Sertorius go, and march against Mithridates, an antagonist whose subjection, as it was thought, would bring great glory and involve little difficulty. But in the meantime Sertorius was treacherously killed by his friends,[3] and Perpenna, the ringleader among them, attempted to carry on his work. He had indeed the same forces and equipment, but lacked equal judgement in the use of them. Accordingly, Pompey took the field against him at once, and perceiving that he had no fixed plan of campaign, sent out ten cohorts as a decoy for him, giving them orders to scatter at random over the plain. Perpenna attacked these cohorts, and was engaged in their pursuit, when Pompey appeared in force, joined battle, and won a complete victory. Most of Perpenna's officers

[1] Cf. the *Sertorius*, chapter xxi.
[2] Cf. the *Lucullus*, v. 2 f.
[3] In 72 B.C., two years after Lucullus had set out against Mithridates.

πλεῖστοι τῶν ἡγεμόνων ἐν τῇ μάχῃ· τὸν δὲ Περπένναν ἀχθέντα πρὸς αὐτὸν ἀπέκτεινεν, οὐκ
ἀχάριστος οὐδ' ἀμνήμων γενόμενος τῶν περὶ
Σικελίαν, ὡς ἐγκαλοῦσιν ἔνιοι, μεγάλῃ δὲ διανοίᾳ
4 καὶ σωτηρίῳ τῶν ὅλων γνώμῃ χρησάμενος. ὁ
γὰρ Περπέννας τῶν Σερτωρίου γραμμάτων γεγονὼς κύριος ἐδείκνυεν ἐπιστολὰς τῶν ἐν Ῥώμῃ
δυνατωτάτων ἀνδρῶν, οἳ τὰ παρόντα κινῆσαι
βουλόμενοι πράγματα καὶ μεταστῆσαι τὴν πολιτείαν ἐκάλουν τὸν Σερτώριον εἰς τὴν Ἰταλίαν.
φοβηθεὶς οὖν ὁ Πομπήϊος ταῦτα, μὴ μείζονας
ἀναστήσῃ τῶν πεπαυμένων πολέμων, τόν τε Περπένναν ἀνεῖλε καὶ τὰς ἐπιστολὰς οὐδ' ἀναγνοὺς
κατέκαυσεν.

XXI. Ἐκ δὲ τούτου παραμείνας χρόνον ὅσον
τὰς μεγίστας κατασβέσαι ταραχὰς καὶ τὰ
φλεγμαίνοντα μάλιστα καταστῆσαι καὶ διαλῦσαι
τῶν πραγμάτων, ἀπῆγεν εἰς Ἰταλίαν τὸν στρατόν, ἀκμάζοντι τῷ δουλικῷ πολέμῳ κατὰ τύχην
φερόμενος. διὸ καὶ Κράσσος ὁ στρατηγὸς ἤπειξε
παραβόλως τὴν μάχην, καὶ κατευτύχησε, δισχι-
2 λίους τριακοσίους ἐπὶ μυρίοις κτείνας. οὐ μὴν
ἀλλὰ καὶ τούτῳ τὸν Πομπήϊον εἰσποιούσης
ἁμῶς γέ πως τῷ κατορθώματι τῆς τύχης, πεντακισχίλιοι φεύγοντες ἐκ τῆς μάχης ἐνέπεσον εἰς
αὐτόν, οὓς ἅπαντας διαφθείρας, ἔγραψε πρὸς τὴν
σύγκλητον ὑποφθάσας ὡς Κράσσος μὲν ἐκ παρατάξεως νενίκηκε τοὺς μονομάχους, αὐτὸς δὲ τὸν
πόλεμον ἐκ ῥιζῶν παντάπασιν ἀνῄρηκε. καὶ

perished in the battle, but Perpenna himself was brought before Pompey, who ordered him to be put to death. In this he did not show ingratitude, nor that he was unmindful of what had happened in Sicily,[1] as some allege against him, but exercised great forethought and salutary judgement for the commonwealth. For Perpenna, who had come into possession of the papers of Sertorius, offered to produce letters from the chief men at Rome, who had desired to subvert the existing order and change the form of government, and had therefore invited Sertorius into Italy. Pompey, therefore, fearing that this might stir up greater wars than those now ended, put Perpenna to death and burned the letters without even reading them.

XXI. After this, he remained in Spain long enough to quell the greatest disorders and compose and settle such affairs as were in the most inflammatory state ; then he led his army back to Italy, where, as chance would have it, he found the servile war at its height. For this reason, too, Crassus, who had the command in that war, precipitated the battle at great hazard, and was successful, killing twelve thousand three hundred of the enemy. Even in this success, however, fortune somehow or other included Pompey, since five thousand fugitives from the battle fell in his way, all of whom he slew, and then stole a march on Crassus by writing to the senate that Crassus had conquered the gladiators in a pitched battle, but that he himself had extirpated the war entirely.[2]

---

[1] Cf. chapter x. 2, where there is nothing to imply that Perpenna put Pompey under obligations to him, except that he made no resistance.

[2] Cf. the *Crassus*, xi. 7.

ταῦτα βουλομένοις ἦν δι' εὔνοιαν ἀκροᾶσθαι καὶ
λέγειν τοῖς Ῥωμαίοις. Ἰβηρίαν δὲ καὶ Σερτώριον
οὐδὲ παίζων ἄν τις εἶπεν ἑτέρου καὶ μὴ Πομπηΐου
τὸ πᾶν ἔργον εἶναι.

3 Ἐν τοσαύτῃ δὲ τιμῇ καὶ προσδοκίᾳ τοῦ ἀνδρὸς
ὅμως ἐνῆν καὶ ὑποψία τις καὶ δέος, ὡς οὐ προ-
ησομένου τὸ στράτευμα, βαδιουμένου δὲ δι'
ὅπλων καὶ μοναρχίας ἄντικρυς ἐπὶ τὴν Σύλλα
πολιτείαν. ὅθεν οὐκ ἐλάττονες ἦσαν τῶν δι'
εὔνοιαν τρεχόντων καὶ φιλοφρονουμένων καθ'
4 ὁδὸν οἱ φόβῳ ταῦτα ποιοῦντες. ἐπεὶ δὲ καὶ
ταύτην ἀνεῖλε τὴν ὑπόνοιαν ὁ Πομπήϊος προειπὼν
ἀφήσειν τὸ στράτευμα μετὰ τὸν θρίαμβον, ἓν
αἰτιᾶσθαι τοῖς βασκαίνουσι περιῆν ὑπόλοιπον,
ὅτι τῷ δήμῳ προσνέμει μᾶλλον ἑαυτὸν ἢ τῇ
βουλῇ, καὶ τὸ τῆς δημαρχίας ἀξίωμα, Σύλλα
καταβαλόντος, ἔγνωκεν ἀνιστάναι καὶ χαρίζεσθαι
5 τοῖς πολλοῖς, ὅπερ ἦν ἀληθές. οὐ γὰρ ἔστιν
οὗτινος ἐμμανέστερον ὁ Ῥωμαίων ἠράσθη δῆμος
καὶ μᾶλλον ἐπόθησεν ἢ τὴν ἀρχὴν αὖθις ἐπιδεῖν
ἐκείνην, ὥστε καὶ Πομπήϊον εὐτύχημα ποιεῖσθαι
μέγα τὸν τοῦ πολιτεύματος καιρόν, ὡς οὐκ ἂν
εὑρόντα χάριν ἄλλην ἢ τὴν εὔνοιαν ἀμείψεται
τῶν πολιτῶν, εἰ ταύτην ἕτερος προέλαβε.

XXII. Ψηφισθέντος οὖν αὐτῷ δευτέρου θριάμβου καὶ ὑπατείας οὐ διὰ ταῦτα θαυμαστὸς ἐδόκει

And it was agreeable to the Romans to hear this said and to repeat it, so kindly did they feel towards him; while as for Spain and Sertorius, there was no one who would have said, even in jest, that the entire work of their subjugation was performed by any one else than Pompey.

Nevertheless, mingled with the great honour shown the man and the great expectations cherished of him, there was also considerable suspicion and fear; men said he would not disband his army, but would make his way by force of arms and absolute power straight to the polity of Sulla. Wherefore those who ran out and greeted him on his way, out of their goodwill, were no more numerous than those who did it out of fear. But Pompey soon removed this suspicion also by declaring that he would disband his army after his triumph. Then there remained but one accusation for envious tongues to make, namely, that he devoted himself more to the people than to the senate, and had determined to restore the authority of the tribunate, which Sulla had overthrown, and to court the favour of the many; which was true. For there was nothing on which the Roman people had more frantically set their affections, or for which they had a greater yearning, than to behold that office again. Pompey therefore regarded it as a great good fortune that he had the opportunity for this political measure, since he could have found no other favour with which to repay the goodwill of his fellow-citizens, if another had anticipated him in this.

XXII. Accordingly, a second triumph was decreed him,[1] and the consulship. It was not on this account, however, that men thought him admirable

---

[1] In 71 B.C.

καὶ μέγας, ἀλλ' ἐκεῖνο τεκμήριον ἐποιοῦντο τῆς
λαμπρότητος, ὅτι Κράσσος, ἀνὴρ τῶν τότε πολι-
τευομένων πλουσιώτατος καὶ δεινότατος εἰπεῖν
καὶ μέγιστος, αὐτόν τε Πομπήϊον ὑπερφρονῶν
καὶ τοὺς ἄλλους ἅπαντας, οὐκ ἐθάρρησεν ὑπατείαν μετιέναι πρότερον ἢ Πομπηΐου δεηθῆναι.

2 καὶ μέντοι Πομπήϊος ἠγάπησε, πάλαι δεόμενος
χρείας τινὸς ὑπάρξαι καὶ φιλανθρωπίας πρὸς
αὐτόν· ὥστε καὶ δεξιοῦσθαι προθύμως καὶ παρα-
καλεῖν τὸν δῆμον, ἐπαγγελλόμενος χάριν ἕξειν
οὐκ ἐλάττονα τοῦ συνάρχοντος ἢ τῆς ἀρχῆς.

3 οὐ μὴν ἀλλ' ἀποδειχθέντες ὕπατοι διεφέροντο
πάντα καὶ προσέκρουον ἀλλήλοις· καὶ ἐν μὲν 63
τῇ βουλῇ μᾶλλον ἴσχυεν ὁ Κράσσος, ἐν δὲ τῷ
δήμῳ μέγα τὸ Πομπηΐου κράτος ἦν. καὶ γὰρ
ἀπέδωκε τὴν δημαρχίαν αὐτῷ, καὶ τὰς δίκας
περιεῖδεν αὖθις εἰς τοὺς ἱππέας νόμῳ μεταφερο-
μένας. ἥδιστον δὲ θέαμα τῷ δήμῳ παρέσχεν
αὐτὸς ἑαυτὸν τὴν στρατείαν παραιτούμενος.

4 Ἔθος γάρ ἐστι Ῥωμαίων τοῖς ἱππεῦσιν, ὅταν
στρατεύσωνται τὸν νόμιμον χρόνον, ἄγειν εἰς
ἀγορὰν τὸν ἵππον ἐπὶ τοὺς δύο ἄνδρας οὓς τιμητὰς
καλοῦσι, καὶ καταριθμησαμένους τῶν στρατηγῶν
καὶ αὐτοκρατόρων ἕκαστον ὑφ' οἷς ἐστρατεύσαντο,
καὶ δόντας εὐθύνας τῆς στρατείας ἀφίεσθαι.
νέμεται δὲ καὶ τιμὴ καὶ ἀτιμία προσήκουσα τοῖς
βίοις ἑκάστων.

5 Τότε δὴ προεκάθηντο μὲν οἱ τιμηταὶ Γέλλιος
καὶ Λέντλος ἐν κόσμῳ, καὶ πάροδος ἦν τῶν

and great, nay, they considered this circumstance a proof of his splendid distinction, that Crassus, the richest statesman of his time, the ablest speaker, and the greatest man, who looked down on Pompey himself and everybody else, had not the courage to sue for the consulship until he had asked the support of Pompey. Pompey, moreover, was delighted, since he had long wanted an opportunity of doing him some service and kindness, and therefore granted his request readily and solicited the people in his behalf, announcing that he should be no less grateful to them for such a colleague than for the consulship. Notwithstanding, after they had been elected consuls, they differed on all points, and were constantly in collision.[1] In the senate, Crassus had more weight; but among the people the power of Pompey was great. For he gave them back their tribunate, and suffered the courts of justice to be transferred again to the knights by law.[2] But the most agreeable of all spectacles was that which he afforded the people when he appeared in person and solicited his discharge from military service.

It is customary for a Roman knight, when he has served for the time fixed by law, to lead his horse into the forum before the two men who are called censors, and after enumerating all the generals and imperators under whom he has served, and rendering an account of his service in the field, to receive his discharge. Honours and penalties are also awarded, according to the career of each.

At this time, then, the censors Gellius and Lentulus were sitting in state, and the knights were

---

[1] Cf. the *Crassus*, xii. 1 f.
[2] By a law passed in the time of Sulla, only senators were eligible as judges.

ἱππέων ἐξεταζομένων, ὤφθη δὲ Πομπήϊος ἄνωθεν
ἐπ' ἀγορὰν κατερχόμενος, τὰ μὲν ἄλλα παράσημα
τῆς ἀρχῆς ἔχων, αὐτὸς δὲ διὰ χειρὸς ἄγων τὸν
ἵππον. ὡς δ' ἐγγὺς ἦν καὶ καταφανὴς ἐγεγόνει,
κελεύσας διασχεῖν τοὺς ῥαβδοφόρους τῷ βήματι
6 προσήγαγε τὸν ἵππον. ἦν δὲ τῷ δήμῳ θαῦμα
καὶ σιωπὴ πᾶσα, τούς τε ἄρχοντας αἰδὼς ἅμα
καὶ χαρὰ πρὸς τὴν ὄψιν ἔσχεν. εἶτα ὁ μὲν
πρεσβύτερος ἠρώτησε· "Πυνθάνομαί σου, ὦ
Πομπήϊε Μάγνε, εἰ πάσας ἐστράτευσαι τὰς κατὰ
νόμον στρατείας;" Πομπήϊος δὲ μεγάλῃ φωνῇ,
"Πάσας," εἶπεν, "ἐστράτευμαι, καὶ πάσας ὑπ'
ἐμαυτῷ αὐτοκράτορι." τοῦτο ἀκούσας ὁ δῆμος
ἐξέκραγε, καὶ κατασχεῖν οὐκέτι τὴν βοὴν ὑπὸ
χαρᾶς ἦν, ἀλλ' ἀναστάντες οἱ τιμηταὶ προέπεμ-
πον αὐτὸν οἴκαδε, χαριζόμενοι τοῖς πολίταις
ἑπομένοις καὶ κροτοῦσιν.

XXIII. Ἤδη δὲ τῆς ἀρχῆς περαινομένης τῷ
Πομπηΐῳ, τῆς δὲ πρὸς Κράσσον αὐξομένης διαφορᾶς, Γάϊός τις Αὐρήλιος, ἀξίωμα μὲν ἱππικὸν
ἔχων, βίῳ δὲ ἀπράγμονι κεχρημένος, ἐκκλησίας
οὔσης ἀναβὰς ἐπὶ τὸ βῆμα καὶ προσελθὼν ἔφη
κατὰ τοὺς ὕπνους αὐτῷ τὸν Δία φανῆναι, κελεύοντα τοῖς ὑπάτοις φράσαι μὴ πρότερον ἀποθέσθαι
2 τὴν ἀρχὴν ἢ φίλους ἀλλήλοις γενέσθαι. ῥηθέντων δὲ τούτων ὁ μὲν Πομπήϊος ἡσυχίαν ἦγεν
ἑστώς, ὁ δὲ Κράσσος ἀρξάμενος δεξιοῦσθαι καὶ
προσαγορεύειν αὐτόν, "Οὐδέν," εἶπεν, "οἶμαι
ποιεῖν ἀγεννὲς οὐδὲ ταπεινόν, ὦ πολῖται, Πομπηΐῳ πρότερος ἐνδιδούς, ὃν ὑμεῖς μήπω μὲν
γενειῶντα Μέγαν ἠξιώσατε καλεῖν, μήπω δὲ
μετέχοντι βουλῆς ἐψηφίσασθε δύο θριάμβους."
ἐκ τούτου διαλλαγέντες ἀπέθεντο τὴν ἀρχήν.

passing in review before them, when Pompey was seen coming down the descent into the forum, otherwise marked by the insignia of his office, but leading his horse with his own hand. When he was near and could be plainly seen, he ordered his lictors to make way for him, and led his horse up to the tribunal. The people were astonished and kept perfect silence, and the magistrates were awed and delighted at the sight. Then the senior censor put the question: "Pompeius Magnus, I ask thee whether thou hast performed all the military services required by law?" Then Pompey said with a loud voice: "I have performed them all, and all under myself as imperator." On hearing this, the people gave a loud shout, and it was no longer possible to check their cries of joy, but the censors rose up and accompanied Pompey to his home, thus gratifying the citizens, who followed with applause.

XXIII. When Pompey's term of office was now about to expire, and his differences with Crassus were increasing, a certain Caius Aurelius, who, though belonging to the equestrian order, had never meddled in public affairs, ascended the rostra at an assembly of the people, and came forward to say that Jupiter had appeared to him in his sleep, bidding him tell the consuls not to lay down their office before they had become friends. After these words had been said, Pompey stood motionless, but Crassus took the initiative, clasped his hand and greeted him, and then said: "I think I do nothing ignoble or mean, my fellow-citizens, in yielding first to Pompey, whom you were pleased to call Magnus when he was still beardless, and to whom you decreed two triumphs before he was a senator." Upon this, they were reconciled, and afterwards laid down their office.[1]

[1] Cf. the *Crassus*, xii. 3 f.

3 Καὶ Κράσσος μὲν ὅνπερ ἐξ ἀρχῆς εἵλετο
τρόπον τοῦ βίου διεφύλαττε, Πομπήϊος δὲ τάς
τε πολλὰς ἀνεδύετο συνηγορίας καὶ τὴν ἀγορὰν
κατὰ μικρὸν ἀπέλειπε καὶ προῄει σπανίως εἰς τὸ
δημόσιον, ἀεὶ δὲ μετὰ πλήθους. οὐ γὰρ ἦν ἔτι
ῥᾴδιον ὄχλου χωρὶς ἐντυχεῖν οὐδ᾽ ἰδεῖν αὐτόν,
ἀλλ᾽ ἥδιστος ὁμοῦ πολλοῖς καὶ ἀθρόοις ἐφαίνετο,
σεμνότητα περιβαλλόμενος ἐκ τούτου τῇ ὄψει
καὶ ὄγκον, ταῖς δὲ τῶν πολλῶν ἐντεύξεσι καὶ
συνηθείαις ἄθικτον οἰόμενος δεῖν τὸ ἀξίωμα δια-
4 τηρεῖν. ὁ γὰρ ἐν ἱματίῳ βίος ἐπισφαλής ἐστι
πρὸς ἀδοξίαν τοῖς ἐκ τῶν ὅπλων μεγάλοις καὶ
πρὸς ἰσότητα δημοτικὴν ἀσυμμέτροις· αὐτοὶ μὲν
γὰρ καὶ ἐνταῦθα πρωτεύειν, ὡς ἐκεῖ, δικαιοῦσι,
τοῖς δὲ ἐκεῖ φερομένοις ἔλαττον ἐνταῦθα γοῦν
μὴ πλέον ἔχειν οὐκ ἀνεκτόν ἐστι. διὸ τὸν ἐν
στρατοπέδοις καὶ θριάμβοις λαμπρόν, ὅταν ἐν
ἀγορᾷ λάβωσιν, ὑπὸ χεῖρα ποιοῦνται καὶ κατα-
βάλλουσι, τῷ δὲ ἀπολεγομένῳ καὶ ὑποχωροῦντι
τὴν ἐκεῖ τιμὴν καὶ δύναμιν ἀνεπίφθονον φυλάττουσιν. ἐδήλωσε δὲ αὐτὰ τὰ πράγματα μετ᾽ ὀλίγον
χρόνον.

XXIV. Ἡ γὰρ πειρατικὴ δύναμις ὡρμήθη μὲν
ἐκ Κιλικίας τὸ πρῶτον, ἀρχὴν παράβολον λαβοῦσα καὶ λανθάνουσαν, φρόνημα δὲ καὶ τόλμαν
ἔσχεν ἐν τῷ Μιθριδατικῷ πολέμῳ, χρήσασα ταῖς
2 βασιλικαῖς ὑπηρεσίαις ἑαυτήν. εἶτα Ῥωμαίων 63
ἐν τοῖς ἐμφυλίοις πολέμοις περὶ θύρας τῆς Ῥώμης
συμπεσόντων, ἔρημος οὖσα φρουρᾶς ἡ θάλασσα
κατὰ μικρὸν αὐτοὺς ἐφείλκετο καὶ προῆγεν,

Now, Crassus continued the manner of life which he had chosen at the outset; but Pompey ceased his frequent appearances as an advocate, gradually forsook the forum, rarely shewed himself in public, and when he did, it was always with a retinue of followers. In fact, it was no longer easy to meet him or even to see him without a throng around him, but he took the greatest pleasure in making his appearance attended by large crowds, encompassing his presence thus with majesty and pomp, and thinking that he must keep his dignity free from contact and familiar association with the multitude. For life in the robes of peace has a dangerous tendency to diminish the reputation of those whom war has made great and ill suited for democratic equality. Such men claim that precedence in the city also which they have in the field, while those who achieve less distinction in the field feel it to be intolerable if in the city at any rate they have no advantage. Therefore when the people find a man active in the forum who has shone in camps and triumphs, they depress and humiliate him, but when he renounces and withdraws from such activity, they leave his military reputation and power untouched by their envy. How true this is, events themselves soon showed.

XXIV. The power of the pirates had its seat in Cilicia at first, and at the outset it was venturesome and elusive; but it took on confidence and boldness during the Mithridatic war,[1] because it lent itself to the king's service. Then, while the Romans were embroiled in civil wars at the gates of Rome, the sea was left unguarded, and gradually drew and enticed them on until they no longer attacked navi-

------

[1] 88–85, 83–81, 74 B.C.

οὐκέτι τοῖς πλέουσι μόνον ἐπιτιθεμένους, ἀλλὰ
καὶ νήσους καὶ πόλεις παραλίους ἐκκόπτοντας.
ἤδη δὲ καὶ χρήμασι δυνατοὶ καὶ γένεσι λαμπροὶ
καὶ τὸ [1] φρονεῖν ἀξιούμενοι διαφέρειν ἄνδρες
ἐνέβαινον εἰς τὰ ληστρικὰ καὶ μετεῖχον, ὡς καὶ
δόξαν τινὰ καὶ φιλοτιμίαν τοῦ ἔργου φέροντος.
3 ἦν δὲ καὶ ναύσταθμα πολλαχόθι πειρατικὰ καὶ
φρυκτώρια τετειχισμένα, καὶ στόλοι προσέπιπτον
οὐ πληρωμάτων μόνον εὐανδρίαις οὐδὲ τέχναις
κυβερνητῶν οὐδὲ τάχεσι νεῶν καὶ κουφότησιν
ἐξησκημένοι πρὸς τὸ οἰκεῖον ἔργον, ἀλλὰ τοῦ
φοβεροῦ μᾶλλον αὐτῶν τὸ ἐπίφθονον ἐλύπει καὶ
ὑπερήφανον, στυλίσι χρυσαῖς καὶ παραπετάσμα-
σιν ἁλουργοῖς καὶ πλάταις ἐπαργύροις, ὥσπερ
ἐντρυφώντων τῷ κακουργεῖν καὶ καλλωπιζομένων.
4 αὐλοὶ δὲ καὶ ψαλμοὶ καὶ μέθαι παρὰ πᾶσαν
ἀκτὴν καὶ σωμάτων ἡγεμονικῶν ἁρπαγαὶ καὶ
πόλεων αἰχμαλώτων ἀπολυτρώσεις ὄνειδος ἦσαν
τῆς Ῥωμαίων ἡγεμονίας. ἐγένοντο δ' οὖν αἱ μὲν
ληστρίδες νῆες ὑπὲρ χιλίας, αἱ δὲ ἁλοῦσαι πόλεις
5 ὑπ' αὐτῶν τετρακόσιαι. τῶν δὲ ἀσύλων καὶ
ἀβάτων πρότερον ἱερῶν ἐξέκοψαν ἐπιόντες τὸ
Κλάριον, τὸ Διδυμαῖον, τὸ Σαμοθράκιον, τὸν ἐν
Ἑρμιόνῃ τῆς Χθονίας νεὼν καὶ τὸν ἐν Ἐπιδαύρῳ
τοῦ Ἀσκληπιοῦ καὶ τὸν Ἰσθμοῖ καὶ Ταινάρῳ καὶ
Καλαυρίᾳ τοῦ Ποσειδῶνος, τοῦ δὲ Ἀπόλλωνος
τὸν ἐν Ἀκτίῳ καὶ Λευκάδι, τῆς δὲ Ἥρας τὸν ἐν
Σάμῳ, τὸν ἐν Ἄργει, τὸν ἐπὶ Λακινίῳ. ξένας δὲ
θυσίας ἔθυον αὐτοὶ τὰς ἐν Ὀλύμπῳ, καὶ τελετάς
τινας ἀπορρήτους ἐτέλουν, ὧν ἡ τοῦ Μίθρου καὶ
μέχρι δεῦρο διασώζεται καταδειχθεῖσα πρῶτον
ὑπ' ἐκείνων.

[1]. τὸ Sintenis, with SgA ; Bekker, with inferior MSS., τῷ.

gators only, but also laid waste islands and maritime cities. And presently men whose wealth gave them power, and those whose lineage was illustrious, and those who laid claim to superior intelligence, began to embark on piratical craft and share their enterprises, feeling that the occupation brought them a certain reputation and distinction. There were also fortified roadsteads and signal-stations for piratical craft in many places, and fleets put in here which were not merely furnished for their peculiar work with sturdy crews, skilful pilots, and light and speedy ships; nay, more annoying than the fear which they inspired was the odious extravagance of their equipment, with their gilded sails, and purple awnings, and silvered oars, as if they rioted in their iniquity and plumed themselves upon it. Their flutes and stringed instruments and drinking bouts along every coast, their seizures of persons in high command, and their ransomings of captured cities, were a disgrace to the Roman supremacy. For, you see, the ships of the pirates numbered more than a thousand, and the cities captured by them four hundred. Besides, they attacked and plundered places of refuge and sanctuaries hitherto inviolate, such as those of Claros, Didyma, and Samothrace; the temple of Chthonian Earth at Hermione; that of Asclepias in Epidaurus; those of Poseidon at the Isthmus, at Taenarum, and at Calauria; those of Apollo at Actium and Leucas; and those of Hera at Samos, at Argos, and at Lacinium. They also offered strange sacrifices of their own at Olympus,[1] and celebrated there certain secret rites, among which those of Mithras continue to the present time, having been first instituted by them.

[1] A town in southern Asia Minor, one of the strongholds of the pirates.

6 Πλεῖστα δὲ Ῥωμαίοις ἐνυβρίσαντες, ἔτι καὶ
τὰς ὁδοὺς αὐτῶν ἀναβαίνοντες ἀπὸ θαλάσσης
ἐληΐζοντο καὶ τὰς ἐγγὺς ἐπαύλεις ἐξέκοπτον.
ἥρπασαν δέ ποτε καὶ στρατηγοὺς δύο Σεξτίλιον
καὶ Βελλῖνον ἐν ταῖς περιπορφύροις, καὶ τοὺς
ὑπηρέτας ἅμα καὶ ῥαβδοφόρους ᾤχοντο σὺν
αὐτοῖς ἐκείνοις ἔχοντες. ἥλω δὲ καὶ θυγάτηρ Ἀντωνίου, θριαμβικοῦ ἀνδρός, εἰς ἀγρὸν
βαδίζουσα, καὶ πολλῶν χρημάτων ἀπελυτρώθη.
7 ἐκεῖνο δὲ ἦν ὑβριστικώτατον. ὁπότε γάρ τις
ἑαλωκὼς ἀναβοήσειε Ῥωμαῖος εἶναι καὶ τοὔνομα
φράσειεν, ἐκπεπλῆχθαι προσποιούμενοι καὶ δεδιέναι τούς τε μηροὺς ἐπαίοντο καὶ προσέπιπτον
αὐτῷ, συγγνώμην ἔχειν ἀντιβολοῦντες· ὁ δὲ
ἐπείθετο ταπεινοὺς ὁρῶν καὶ δεομένους. ἐκ τούτου δὲ οἱ μὲν ὑπέδουν τοῖς καλκίοις αὐτόν, οἱ δὲ
τήβεννον περιέβαλλον, ὡς δὴ μὴ πάλιν ἀγνοηθείη.
8 πολὺν δὲ χρόνον οὕτω κατειρωνευσάμενοι καὶ
ἀπολαύσαντες τοῦ ἀνθρώπου, τέλος ἐν μέσῳ πελάγει κλίμακα προσβαλόντες ἐκέλευον ἐκβαίνειν
καὶ ἀπιέναι χαίροντα, τὸν δὲ μὴ βουλόμενον
ὠθοῦντες αὐτοὶ κατέδυον.

XXV. Ἐπενείματο δὲ ἡ δύναμις αὕτη πᾶσαν
ὁμοῦ τι τὴν καθ' ἡμᾶς θάλασσαν, ὥστε ἄπλουν
καὶ ἄβατον ἐμπορίᾳ πάσῃ γενέσθαι. τοῦτο δὴ
μάλιστα Ῥωμαίους ἐπέστρεψε, θλιβομένους τῇ
ἀγορᾷ καὶ σπάνιν μεγάλην προσδοκῶντας, ἐκ-
πέμψαι Πομπήϊον ἀφαιρησόμενον τῶν πειρατῶν
2 τὴν θάλασσαν. ἔγραψε δὲ Γαβίνιος, εἷς τῶν
Πομπηΐου συνήθων, νόμον οὐ ναυαρχίαν, ἄντικρυς
δὲ μοναρχίαν αὐτῷ διδόντα καὶ δύναμιν ἐπὶ
πάντας ἀνθρώπους ἀνυπεύθυνον. ἐδίδου γὰρ

But they heaped most insults upon the Romans, even going up from the sea along their roads and plundering there, and sacking the neighbouring villas. Once, too, they seized two praetors, Sextilius and Bellinus, in their purple-edged robes, and carried them away, together with their attendants and lictors. They also captured a daughter of Antonius, a man who had celebrated a triumph, as she was going into the country, and exacted a large ransom for her. But their crowning insolence was this. Whenever a captive cried out that he was a Roman and gave his name, they would pretend to be frightened out of their senses, and would smite their thighs, and fall down before him entreating him to pardon them; and he would be convinced of their sincerity, seeing them so humbly suppliant. Then some would put Roman boots on his feet, and others would throw a toga round him, in order, forsooth, that there might be no mistake about him again. And after thus mocking the man for a long time and getting their fill of amusement from him, at last they would let down a ladder in mid ocean and bid him disembark and go on his way rejoicing; and if he did not wish to go, they would push him overboard themselves and drown him.

XXV. This power extended its operations over the whole of our Mediterranean Sea, making it unnavigable and closed to all commerce. This was what most of all inclined the Romans, who were hard put to it to get provisions and expected a great scarcity, to send out Pompey with a commission to take the sea away from the pirates. Gabinius, one of Pompey's intimates, drew up a law which gave him, not an admiralty, but an out-and-out monarchy and irresponsible power over all men. For the law

ἄρχειν ὁ νόμος αὐτῷ τῆς ἐντὸς Ἡρακλείων
στηλῶν θαλάσσης, ἠπείρου δὲ πάσης ἐπὶ στα-
δίους τετρακοσίους ἀπὸ θαλάσσης. τοῦτο δὲ οὐ
πάνυ πολλὰ χωρία τῆς ὑπὸ Ῥωμαίων οἰκουμένης
τὸ μέτρον ἐξέφυγεν, ἀλλὰ τὰ μέγιστα τῶν ἐθνῶν
καὶ τῶν βασιλέων οἱ δυνατώτατοι περιελαμβά-
3 νοντο. πρὸς δὲ τούτοις ἐλέσθαι πεντεκαίδεκα 6
πρεσβευτὰς αὐτὸν ἐκ βουλῆς ἐπὶ τὰς κατὰ μέρος
ἡγεμονίας, χρήματα δὲ λαμβάνειν ἐκ τῶν τα-
μιείων καὶ παρὰ τῶν τελωνῶν ὅσα βούλοιτο καὶ
ναῦς διακοσίας, κύριον ὄντα πλήθους καὶ κατα-
λόγου στρατιᾶς καὶ πληρωμάτων ἐρετικῶν.

Ἀναγνωσθέντων δὲ τούτων ὁ μὲν δῆμος ὑπερφυῶς ἐδέξατο, τῆς δὲ συγκλήτου τοῖς μεγίστοις
καὶ δυνατωτάτοις ἔδοξε μεῖζον μὲν φθόνου, φόβου
δὲ ἄξιον εἶναι τὸ τῆς ἐξουσίας ἀπερίληπτον καὶ
4 ἀόριστον. ὅθεν ἐνίσταντο τῷ νόμῳ, πλὴν Καί-
σαρος· οὗτος δὲ συνηγόρει τῷ νόμῳ, Πομπηΐου
μὲν ἐλάχιστα φροντίζων, ὑποδυόμενος δὲ τὸν
δῆμον ἐξ ἀρχῆς ἑαυτῷ καὶ κτώμενος. οἱ δὲ ἄλλοι
τοῦ Πομπηΐου σφοδρῶς καθήπτοντο. καὶ τῶν
μὲν ὑπάτων ἅτερος, εἰπὼν πρὸς αὐτὸν ὅτι Ῥω-
μύλον ζηλῶν οὐ φεύξεται ταὐτὸν ἐκείνῳ τέλος,
ἐκινδύνευσεν ὑπὸ τοῦ πλήθους διαφθαρῆναι·
5 Κάτλου δὲ κατὰ τοῦ νόμου προσελθόντος, πολλὴν
μὲν αἰδούμενος ὁ δῆμος ἡσυχίαν παρεῖχεν, ἐπεὶ
δὲ πολλὰ μετὰ τιμῆς ἀνεπιφθόνως ὑπὲρ τοῦ
Πομπηΐου διελθὼν συνεβούλευε φείδεσθαι καὶ
μὴ προβάλλειν τοιοῦτον ἄνδρα κινδύνοις ἐπαλ-

gave him dominion over the sea this side of the pillars of Hercules, and over all the mainland to the distance of four hundred furlongs from the sea. These limits included almost all places in the Roman world, and the greatest nations and most powerful kings were comprised within them. Besides this, he was empowered to choose fifteen legates from the senate for the several principalities, and to take from the public treasuries and the tax-collectors as much money as he wished, and to have two hundred ships, with full power over the number and levying of soldiers and oarsmen.

When these provisions of the law were read in the assembly,[1] the people received them with excessive pleasure, but the chief and most influential men of the senate thought that such unlimited and absolute power, while it was beyond the reach of envy, was yet a thing to be feared. Therefore they all opposed the law, with the exception of Caesar; he advocated the law, not because he cared in the least for Pompey, but because from the outset he sought to ingratiate himself with the people and win their support. The rest vehemently attacked Pompey. And when one of the consuls told him that if he emulated Romulus he would not escape the fate of Romulus,[2] he was near being torn in pieces by the multitude. Moreover, when Catulus came forward to speak against the law the people had regard enough for him to be quiet for some time; but after he had spoken at length in Pompey's praise and without any disparagement of him, and then counselled the people to spare such a man and

---

[1] In 67 B.C., Pompey being then thirty-nine years old.
[2] That is, he would be mysteriously put out of the way. Cf. the *Romulus*, chapter xxvii.

λήλοις καὶ πολέμοις, "Ἦ τίνα," εἶπεν, "ἕξετε
ἄλλον, ἂν ἀπολέσητε τοῦτον;" ἐκ μιᾶς γνώμης
6 ὑπεφώνησαν ἅπαντες, "Σὲ αὐτόν." ὁ μὲν οὖν
Κάτλος, ὡς οὐκ ἔπειθεν, ἀπέστη· Ῥωσκίου δὲ
προσελθόντος οὐδεὶς ἤκουσεν· ὁ δὲ τοῖς δακτύλοις
διεσήμαινε μὴ μόνον, ἀλλὰ δεύτερον αἱρεῖσθαι
Πομπήϊον. ἐπὶ τούτῳ λέγεται δυσχεράναντα
τὸν δῆμον τηλικοῦτον ἀνακραγεῖν ὥστε ὑπερπετό-
μενον κόρακα τῆς ἀγορᾶς τυφωθῆναι καὶ κατα-
7 πεσεῖν εἰς τὸν ὄχλον. ὅθεν οὐ δοκεῖ ῥήξει τοῦ
ἀέρος καὶ διασπασμῷ κενὸν πολὺ λαμβάνοντος
ἐνολισθαίνειν τὰ πίπτοντα τῶν ὀρνέων, ἀλλὰ
τυπτόμενα τῇ πληγῇ τῆς φωνῆς, ὅταν ἐν τῷ
ἀέρι σάλον καὶ κῦμα ποιήσῃ πολλὴ καὶ ἰσχυρὰ
φερομένη.

XXVI. Τότε μὲν οὖν διελύθησαν· ᾗ δὲ ἡμέρᾳ
τὴν ψῆφον ἐποίσειν ἔμελλον, ὑπεξῆλθεν ὁ Πομπήϊος εἰς ἀγρόν. ἀκούσας δὲ κεκυρῶσθαι τὸν
νόμον εἰσῆλθε νύκτωρ εἰς τὴν πόλιν, ὡς ἐπιφθό-
νου τῆς πρὸς αὐτὸν ἀπαντήσεως καὶ συνδρομῆς
ἐσομένης. ἅμα δὲ ἡμέρᾳ προελθὼν ἔθυσε· καὶ
γενομένης ἐκκλησίας αὐτῷ, διεπράξατο προσλαβεῖν ἕτερα πολλὰ τοῖς ἐψηφισμένοις ἤδη,
2 μικροῦ διπλασιάσας τὴν παρασκευήν. πεντα-
κόσιαι μὲν γὰρ αὐτῷ νῆες ἐπληρώθησαν, ὁπλιτῶν δὲ μυριάδες δώδεκα καὶ πεντακισχίλιοι
ἱππεῖς ἠθροίσθησαν. ἡγεμονικοὶ δὲ καὶ στρα-
τηγικοὶ κατελέγησαν ἀπὸ βουλῆς ἄνδρες εἰκο-
σιτέσσαρες ὑπ᾽ αὐτοῦ, δύο δὲ ταμίαι παρῆσαν.
αἱ δὲ τιμαὶ τῶν ὠνίων εὐθὺς πεσοῦσαι λόγον

not expose him to successive wars and perils, asking, " Whom else will you have if you lose him ? " all with one accord replied, " Thyself." Catulus, accordingly, since he could not persuade them, retired ; but when Roscius came forward to speak, no one would listen to him. He therefore made signs with his fingers that they should not choose Pompey alone to this command, but give him a colleague. At this, we are told, the people were incensed and gave forth such a shout that a raven flying over the forum was stunned by it and fell down into the throng. From this it appears that such falling of birds is not due to a rupture and division of the air wherein a great vacuum is produced, but that they are struck by the blow of the voice, which raises a surge and billow in the air when it is borne aloft loud and strong.

XXVI. For the time being, then, the assembly was dissolved ; but when the day came for the vote upon the law, Pompey withdrew privately into the country. On hearing, however, that the law had been passed, he entered the city by night, feeling that he was sure to awaken envy if the people thronged to meet him. But when day came, he appeared in public and offered sacrifice, and at an assembly held for him he managed to get many other things besides those already voted, and almost doubled his armament. For five hundred ships were manned for him, and a hundred and twenty thousand men-at-arms and five thousand horsemen were raised. Twenty-four men who had held command or served as praetors were chosen from the senate by him, and he had two quaestors. And since the prices of provisions immediately fell, the people

ἡδομένῳ τῷ δήμῳ παρεῖχον, ὡς αὐτὸ τοὔνομα τοῦ
Πομπηΐου λέλυκε τὸν πόλεμον.

3 Οὐ μὴν ἀλλὰ διελὼν τὰ πελάγη καὶ τὸ διάστημα τῆς ἐντὸς θαλάσσης εἰς μέρη τρισκαίδεκα,
καὶ νεῶν ἀριθμὸν ἐφ' ἑκάστῳ καὶ ἄρχοντα τάξας,
ἅμα πανταχοῦ τῇ δυνάμει σκεδασθείσῃ τὰ μὲν
ἐμπίπτοντα τῶν πειρατικῶν ἀθρόα περιλαμβάνων
εὐθὺς ἐξεθηρᾶτο καὶ κατῆγεν· οἱ δὲ φθάσαντες
διαλυθῆναι καὶ διεκπεσόντες ὥσπερ εἰς σμῆνος
ἐδύοντο πανταχόθεν καταφερόμενοι τὴν Κιλικίαν,
ἐφ' οὓς αὐτὸς ἐστέλλετο ναῦς ἔχων ἑξήκοντα τὰς
4 ἀρίστας. οὐ μὴν πρότερον ἐπ' ἐκείνους ἐξέπλευσεν ἢ παντάπασι καθῆραι τῶν αὐτόθι
λῃστηρίων τὸ Τυρρηνικὸν πέλαγος, τὸ Λιβυκόν,
τὸ περὶ Σαρδόνα καὶ Κύρνον καὶ Σικελίαν,
ἡμέραις τεσσαράκοντα ταῖς πάσαις, αὐτῷ τε
χρώμενος ἀτρύτῳ καὶ τοῖς στρατηγοῖς προθύμοις.

XXVII. Ἐν δὲ Ῥώμῃ τοῦ ὑπάτου Πείσωνος
ὀργῇ καὶ φθόνῳ λυμαινομένου τὴν παρασκευὴν
καὶ διαλύοντος τὰ πληρώματα, τὸ μὲν ναυτικὸν
εἰς Βρεντέσιον περιέπεμψεν, αὐτὸς δὲ διὰ Τυρ-
ρηνίας εἰς Ῥώμην ἀνέβαινεν. αἰσθόμενοι δὲ
πάντες ἐξεχύθησαν εἰς τὴν ὁδόν, ὥσπερ οὐ πρὸ
2 ἡμερῶν ὀλίγων ἐκπέμψαντες αὐτόν. ἐποίει δὲ
τὴν χαρὰν τὸ παρ' ἐλπίδα τῆς μεταβολῆς τάχος,
ὑπερβάλλουσαν ἀφθονίαν τῆς ἀγορᾶς ἐχούσης.
ὅθεν ὁ Πείσων ἐκινδύνευσε τὴν ὑπατείαν ἀφαι-
ρεθῆναι, Γαβινίου νόμον ἔχοντος ἤδη συγγεγραμ-
μένον. ἀλλὰ καὶ τοῦτο διεκώλυσεν ὁ Πομπήιος,
καὶ τἆλλα χρηματίσας ἐπιεικῶς καὶ διαπραξά-

were moved to say in their joy that the very name
of Pompey had put an end to the war.

However, he divided the waters and the adjacent
coasts[1] of the Mediterranean Sea into thirteen
districts, and assigned to each a certain number of
ships with a commander, and with his forces thus
scattered in all quarters he encompassed whole fleets
of piratical ships that fell in his way, and straightway hunted them down and brought them into port;
others succeeded in dispersing and escaping, and
sought their hive, as it were, hurrying from all
quarters into Cilicia. Against these Pompey intended to proceed in person with his sixty best
ships. He did not, however, sail against them until
he had entirely cleared of their pirates the Tyrr-
henian Sea, the Libyan Sea, and the sea about
Sardinia, Corsica, and Sicily, in forty days all told.
This was owing to his own tireless energy and the
zeal of his lieutenants.

XXVII. But the consul Piso at Rome, out of
wrath and envy, was interfering with Pompey's
equipment and discharging his crews; Pompey
therefore sent his fleet round to Brundisium, while
he himself went up by way of Tuscany to Rome. On
learning of this, the citizens all streamed out into
the road, just as if they had not escorted him forth
only a few days before. What caused their joy was
the unhoped for rapidity of the change, the market
being now filled to overflowing with provisions.
As a consequence Piso came near being deprived of
his consulship, and Gabinius had the requisite law
already written out. But Pompey prevented this,
as well as other hostile acts, and after arranging
everything else in a reasonable manner and getting

[1] Cf. chapter xxv. 2

μενος ὧν ἐδεῖτο, καταβὰς εἰς Βρεντέσιον ἐξέ-
3 πλευσεν. ἐπειγόμενος δὲ τῷ καιρῷ καὶ παρα-
πλέων τὰς πόλεις ὑπὸ σπουδῆς, ὅμως οὐ παρῆλθε
τὰς Ἀθήνας, ἀναβὰς δὲ καὶ θύσας τοῖς θεοῖς καὶ
προσαγορεύσας τὸν δῆμον εὐθὺς ἀπιὼν ἀνεγίνωσκεν εἰς αὐτὸν ἐπιγεγραμμένα μονόστιχα, τὸ
μὲν ἐντὸς τῆς πύλης·

Ἐφ' ὅσον ὢν ἄνθρωπος οἶδας, ἐπὶ τοσοῦτον εἶ
θεός·

τὸ δ' ἐκτός·

Προσεδοκῶμεν, προσεκυνοῦμεν, εἴδομεν, προ-
πέμπομεν.

4 ἐπεὶ δὲ τῶν συνεστώτων ἔτι καὶ πλανωμένων ἔξω
πειρατηρίων ἐνίοις δεηθεῖσιν ἐπιεικῶς ἐχρήσατο
καὶ παραλαβὼν τὰ πλοῖα καὶ τὰ σώματα κακὸν
οὐδὲν ἐποίησεν, ἐπ' ἐλπίδος χρηστῆς οἱ λοιποὶ
γενόμενοι τοὺς μὲν ἄλλους διέφευγον ἡγεμόνας,
Πομπηΐῳ δὲ φέροντες ἑαυτοὺς μετὰ τέκνων καὶ
γυναικῶν ἐνεχείριζον. ὁ δὲ πάντων ἐφείδετο,
καὶ μάλιστα διὰ τούτων τοὺς ἔτι λανθάνοντας
ἐξιχνεύων καὶ λαμβάνων ἐκόλαζεν ὡς αὐτοὺς
ἑαυτοῖς ἀνήκεστα συνειδότας.

XXVIII. Οἱ δὲ πλεῖστοι καὶ δυνατώτατοι
γενεὰς μὲν αὐτῶν καὶ χρήματα καὶ τὸν ἄχρηστον
ὄχλον ἐν φρουρίοις καὶ πολίσμασι καρτεροῖς
περὶ τὸν Ταῦρον εἶχον ἀποκείμενα, τὰς δὲ ναῦς
πληρώσαντες αὐτοὶ περὶ τὸ Κορακήσιον τῆς
Κιλικίας ἐπιπλέοντα τὸν Πομπήϊον ἐδέξαντο·
καὶ μάχης γενομένης νικηθέντες ἐπολιορκοῦντο.
τέλος δὲ πέμψαντες ἱκετηρίας παρέδωκαν ἑαυτοὺς
καὶ πόλεις καὶ νήσους ὧν ἐπεκράτουν ἐντειχι-

what he wanted, went down to Brundisium and set sail. But though his immediate business was urgent and he sailed past other cities in his haste, still, he could not pass Athens by, but went up into the city, sacrificed to the gods, and addressed the people. Just as he was leaving the city, he read two inscriptions, each of a single verse, addressed to him, one inside the gate :—

" As thou knowest thou art mortal, in so far thou art a god;"

and the other outside :—

" We awaited, we saluted, we have seen, and now conduct thee forth."

Some of the pirate bands that were still roving at large begged for mercy, and since he treated them humanely, and after seizing their ships and persons did them no further harm, the rest became hopeful of mercy too, and made their escape from the other commanders, betook themselves to Pompey with their wives and children, and surrendered to him. All these he spared, and it was chiefly by their aid that he tracked down, seized, and punished those who were still lurking in concealment because conscious of unpardonable crimes.

XXVIII. But the most numerous and powerful had bestowed their families and treasures and useless folk in forts and strong citadels near the Taurus mountains, while they themselves manned their ships and awaited Pompey's attack near the promontory of Coracesium in Cilicia; here they were defeated in a battle and then besieged. At last, however, they sent suppliant messages and surrendered themselves, together with the cities and islands of which they were in control; these they

σάμενοι, χαλεπὰς βιασθῆναι καὶ δυσπροσπελά-
2 στους. κατελύθη μὲν οὖν ὁ πόλεμος καὶ τὰ
πανταχοῦ λῃστήρια τῆς θαλάσσης ἐξέπεσεν οὐκ
ἐν πλείονι χρόνῳ τριῶν μηνῶν, ναῦς δὲ πολλὰς
μὲν ἄλλας, ἐνενήκοντα δὲ χαλκεμβόλους παρέ-
λαβεν. αὐτοὺς δὲ δισμυρίων πλείονας γενομένους
ἀνελεῖν μὲν οὐδὲ ἐβουλεύσατο, μεθεῖναι δὲ καὶ
περιϊδεῖν σκεδασθέντας ἢ συστάντας αὖθις,
ἀπόρους καὶ πολεμικοὺς καὶ πολλοὺς [1] ὄντας, οὐκ
3 ᾤετο καλῶς ἔχειν. ἐννοήσας οὖν ὅτι φύσει μὲν
ἄνθρωπος οὔτε γέγονεν οὔτ' ἔστιν ἀνήμερον ζῷον
οὐδ' ἄμικτον, ἀλλ' ἐξίσταται τῇ κακίᾳ παρὰ
φύσιν χρώμενος, ἔθεσι δὲ καὶ τόπων καὶ βίων
μεταβολαῖς ἐξημεροῦται, καὶ θηρία δὲ [2] διαίτης
κοινωνοῦντα πραοτέρας ἐκδύεται τὸ ἄγριον καὶ
χαλεπόν, ἔγνω τοὺς ἄνδρας εἰς γῆν μεταφέρειν
ἐκ τῆς θαλάσσης καὶ βίου γεύειν ἐπιεικοῦς, συν-
4 εθισθέντας ἐν πόλεσιν οἰκεῖν καὶ γεωργεῖν. ἐνίοις
μὲν οὖν αἱ μικραὶ καὶ ὑπέρημοι τῶν Κιλίκων
πόλεις ἐδέξαντο καὶ κατέμιξαν ἑαυταῖς χώραν
προσλαβοῦσαι, τὴν δὲ Σολίων ἠρημωμένην ἔναγχος ὑπὸ Τιγράνου τοῦ Ἀρμενίων βασιλέως
ἀναλαβὼν ἵδρυσε πολλοὺς ἐν αὐτῇ. τοῖς δὲ
πολλοῖς οἰκητήριον ἔδωκε Δύμην τὴν Ἀχαΐδα,
χηρεύουσαν ἀνδρῶν τότε, γῆν δὲ πολλὴν καὶ
ἀγαθὴν ἔχουσαν.

XXIX. Ταῦτα μὲν οὖν οἱ βασκαίνοντες ἔψεγον·
τοῖς δὲ περὶ Κρήτην πραχθεῖσι πρὸς Μέτελλον
οὐδ' οἱ πάνυ φιλοῦντες αὐτὸν ἔχαιρον. ὁ γὰρ

---

[1] καὶ πολλοὺς Coraës and Bekker, with Sg : τοὺς πολλοὺς
after Stephanus (most of them being, etc.).
[2] δὲ supplied, after Emperius ; Bekker has ὅπου καὶ θηρία,
after Coraës.

had fortified, making them hard to get at and difficult to take by storm. The war was therefore
brought to an end and all piracy driven from the
sea in less than three months, and besides many
other ships, Pompey received in surrender ninety
which had brazen beaks. The men themselves, who
were more than twenty thousand in number, he did
not once think of putting to death; and yet to let
them go and suffer them to disperse or band together
again, poor, warlike, and numerous as they were, he
thought was not well. Reflecting, therefore, that
by nature man neither is nor becomes a wild or an
unsocial creature, but is transformed by the unnatural
practice of vice, whereas he may be softened by
new customs and a change of place and life; also
that even wild beasts put off their fierce and savage
ways when they partake of a gentler mode of life, he
determined to transfer the men from the sea to land,
and let them have a taste of gentle life by being
accustomed to dwell in cities and to till the ground.
Some of them, therefore, were received and incor-
porated into the small and half-deserted cities of
Cilicia, which acquired additional territory; and
after restoring the city of Soli, which had lately
been devastated by Tigranes, the king of Armenia,
Pompey settled many there. To most of them,
however, he gave as a residence Dyme in Achaea,
which was then bereft of men and had much good
land.

XXIX. Well, then, his maligners found fault with
these measures, and even his best friends were not
pleased with his treatment of Metellus in Crete.

Μέτελλος, οἰκεῖος ὢν ἐκείνου τοῦ συνάρξαντος
ἐν Ἰβηρίᾳ τῷ Πομπηΐῳ, στρατηγὸς εἰς Κρήτην
ἐπέμφθη πρότερον ἢ τὸν Πομπήϊον αἱρεθῆναι·
δευτέρα γάρ τις ἦν αὕτη τῶν πειρατηρίων πηγή
μετὰ τὴν ἐν Κιλικίᾳ· καὶ πολλοὺς ἐγκαταλαβὼν
2 ὁ Μέτελλος ἐξῄρει καὶ διέφθειρεν. οἱ δὲ περιόντες   63
ἔτι καὶ πολιορκούμενοι πέμψαντες ἱκετηρίαν
ἐπεκαλοῦντο τὸν Πομπήϊον εἰς τὴν νῆσον, ὡς
τῆς ἐκείνου μέρος οὖσαν ἀρχῆς καὶ πανταχόθεν
ἐμπίπτουσαν εἰς τὸ μέτρον τὸ ἀπὸ θαλάσσης.
ὁ δὲ δεξάμενος ἔγραφε τῷ Μετέλλῳ κωλύων τὸν
πόλεμον. ἔγραφε δὲ καὶ ταῖς πόλεσι μὴ προσέχειν Μετέλλῳ, καὶ στρατηγὸν ἔπεμψε τῶν ὑφ'
3 ἑαυτὸν ἀρχόντων ἕνα Λεύκιον Ὀκταούϊον, ὃς
συνεισελθὼν εἰς τὰ τείχη τοῖς πολιορκουμένοις
καὶ μαχόμενος μετ' αὐτῶν, οὐ μόνον ἐπαχθῆ καὶ
βαρύν, ἀλλὰ καὶ καταγέλαστον ἐποίει τὸν Πομπήϊον, ἀνθρώποις ἀνοσίοις καὶ ἀθέοις τοὔνομα
κιχράντα καὶ περιάπτοντα τὴν αὑτοῦ δόξαν
ὥσπερ ἀλεξιφάρμακον ὑπὸ φθόνου καὶ φιλοτιμίας
4 τῆς πρὸς τὸν Μέτελλον. οὐδὲ γὰρ τὸν Ἀχιλλέα
ποιεῖν ἀνδρὸς ἔργον, ἀλλὰ μειρακίου παντάπασιν
ἐμπλήκτου καὶ σεσοβημένου πρὸς δόξαν, ἀνα-
νεύοντα τοῖς ἄλλοις καὶ διακωλύοντα βάλλειν
Ἕκτορα,

Μή τις κῦδος ἄροιτο βαλών, ὁ δὲ δεύτερος ἔλθοι·

5 Πομπήϊον δὲ καὶ σῴζειν ὑπερμαχοῦντα τῶν
κοινῶν πολεμίων ἐπὶ τῷ τὸν θρίαμβον ἀφελέσθαι
στρατηγοῦ πολλὰ πεπονηκότος. οὐ μὴν ἐνέδω-

POMPEY

Metellus, a kinsman of the Metellus who was a colleague of Pompey in Spain, had been sent as general to Crete before Pompey was chosen to his command; for Crete was a kind of second source for pirates, next to Cilicia. Metellus hemmed in many of them and was killing and destroying them. But those who still survived and were besieged sent suppliant messages to Pompey and invited him into the island, alleging that it was a part of his government, and that all parts of it were within the limit to be measured from the sea.[1] Pompey accepted the invitation and wrote to Metellus putting a stop to his war. He also wrote the cities not to pay any attention to Metellus, and sent them one of his own officers as general, namely, Lucius Octavius, who entered the strongholds of the besieged pirates and fought on their side, thus making Pompey not only odious and oppressive, but actually ridiculous, since he lent his name to godless miscreants, and threw around them the mantle of his reputation to serve like a charm against evil, through envy and jealousy of Metellus. For not even Achilles played the part of a man, men said, but that of a youth wholly crazed and frantic in his quest of glory, when he made a sign to the rest which prevented them from smiting Hector,

"Lest some one else win honour by the blow, and he come only second";[2]

whereas Pompey actually fought in behalf of the common enemy and saved their lives, that he might rob of his triumph a general who had toiled hard to win it. Metellus, however, would not give in,

---

[1] Cf. chapter xxv. 2.   [2] *Iliad*, xxii. 207.

κεν ὁ Μέτελλος, ἀλλὰ τούς τε πειρατὰς ἐξελὼν
ἐτιμωρήσατο, καὶ τὸν Ὀκταούϊον ἐν τῷ στρατοπέδῳ καθυβρίσας καὶ λοιδορήσας ἀφῆκεν.

XXX. Ἀπαγγελθέντος δὲ εἰς Ῥώμην πέρας
ἔχειν τὸν πειρατικὸν πόλεμον καὶ σχολὴν ἄγοντα
τὸν Πομπήϊον ἐπέρχεσθαι τὰς πόλεις, γράφει
νόμον εἷς τῶν δημάρχων Μάλλιος, ὅσης Λεύκολλος ἄρχει χώρας καὶ δυνάμεως, Πομπήϊον
παραλαβόντα πᾶσαν, προσλαβόντα δὲ καὶ Βιθυ-
νίαν, ἣν ἔχει Γλαβρίων, πολεμεῖν Μιθριδάτῃ καὶ
Τιγράνῃ τοῖς βασιλεῦσιν, ἔχοντα καὶ τὴν ναυτι-
κὴν δύναμιν καὶ τὸ κράτος τῆς θαλάσσης ἐφ'
2 οἷς ἔλαβεν ἐξ ἀρχῆς. τοῦτο δ' ἦν ἐφ' ἑνὶ
συλλήβδην γενέσθαι τὴν Ῥωμαίων ἡγεμονίαν·
ὧν γὰρ ἐδόκει μόνων ἐπαρχιῶν μὴ ἐφικνεῖσθαι
τῷ προτέρῳ νόμῳ, Φρυγίας, Λυκαονίας, Γαλατίας,
Καππαδοκίας, Κιλικίας, τῆς ἄνω Κολχίδος, Ἀρμενίας, αὗται προσετίθεντο μετὰ στρατοπέδων
καὶ δυνάμεως αἷς Λεύκολλος κατεπολέμησε
3 Μιθριδάτην καὶ Τιγράνην. ἀλλὰ Λευκόλλου
μὲν ἀποστερουμένου τὴν δόξαν ὧν κατειργάσατο
καὶ θριάμβου μᾶλλον ἢ πολέμου διαδοχὴν λαμβάνοντος, ἥττων λόγος ἦν τοῖς ἀριστοκρατικοῖς,
καίπερ οἰομένοις ἄδικα καὶ ἀχάριστα πάσχειν
τὸν ἄνδρα, τὴν δὲ δύναμιν τοῦ Πομπηΐου βαρέως
φέροντες ὡς τυραννίδα καθισταμένην, ἰδίᾳ παρε-
κάλουν καὶ παρεθάρρυνον αὐτοὺς ἐπιλαβέσθαι
τοῦ νόμου καὶ μὴ προέσθαι τὴν ἐλευθερίαν.

but captured the pirates and punished them, and then sent Octavius away after insulting and abusing him before the army.

XXX. When word was brought to Rome that the war against the pirates was at an end, and that Pompey, now at leisure, was visiting the cities, Manlius,[1] one of the popular tribunes, proposed a law giving Pompey all the country and forces which Lucullus commanded, with the addition, too, of Bithynia, which Glabrio[2] had, and the commission to wage war upon Mithridates and Tigranes, the kings, retaining also his naval force and his dominion over the sea as he had originally received them. But this meant the placing of the Roman supremacy entirely in the hands of one man; for the only provinces which were held to be excluded from his sway by the former law, namely, Phrygia, Lycaonia, Galatia, Cappadocia, Cilicia, Upper Colchis, and Armenia, these were now added to it, together with the military forces which Lucullus had used in his conquest of Mithridates and Tigranes. But though Lucullus was thus robbed of the glory of his achievements, and was receiving a successor who would enjoy his triumph rather than prosecute the war,[3] this was of less concern to the aristocratic party, although they did think that the man was unjustly and thanklessly treated; they were, however, displeased at the power given to Pompey, which they regarded as establishing a tyranny, and privately exhorted and encouraged one another to attack the law, and not to surrender their freedom. But when

---

[1] More correctly, Manilius. The Manilian law was passed in 66 B.C. Cf. the oration of Cicero *Pro Lege Manilia*.

[2] Glabrio, consul in 67 B.C., had been sent out to supersede Lucullus.

[3] Cf. the *Lucullus*, xxxv. 7.

4 ἐνστάντος δὲ τοῦ καιροῦ, τὸν δῆμον φοβηθέντες
ἐξέλιπον καὶ κατεσιώπησαν οἱ λοιποί, Κάτλος
δὲ τοῦ νόμου πολλὰ κατηγορήσας καὶ τοῦ δη-
μάρχου, μηδένα δὲ πείθων, ἐκέλευε τὴν βουλὴν
ἀπὸ τοῦ βήματος κεκραγὼς πολλάκις ὄρος ζητεῖν,
ὥσπερ οἱ πρόγονοι, καὶ κρημνόν, ὅπου κατα-
5 φυγοῦσα διασώσει τὴν ἐλευθερίαν. ἐκυρώθη δ'
οὖν ὁ νόμος, ὡς λέγουσι, πάσαις ταῖς φυλαῖς, καὶ
κύριος ἀποδέδεικτο μὴ παρὼν ὁ Πομπήϊος ἁπάντων σχεδὸν ὧν ὁ Σύλλας ὅπλοις καὶ πολέμῳ τῆς
πόλεως κρατήσας. αὐτὸς δὲ δεξάμενος τὰ γράμματα καὶ πυθόμενος τὰ δεδογμένα, τῶν φίλων
παρόντων καὶ συνηδομένων, τὰς ὀφρῦς λέγεται
συναγαγεῖν καὶ τὸν μηρὸν πατάξαι καὶ εἰπεῖν
ὡς ἂν βαρυνόμενος ἤδη καὶ δυσχεραίνων τὸ ἄρ-
6 χειν· "Φεῦ τῶν ἀνηνύτων ἄθλων, ὡς ἄρα κρεῖττον
ἦν ἕνα τῶν ἀδόξων γενέσθαι, εἰ μηδέποτε παύ-
σομαι στρατευόμενος μηδὲ τὸν φθόνον τοῦτον
ἐκδὺς ἐν ἀγρῷ διαιτήσομαι μετὰ τῆς γυναικός."
ἐφ' οἷς λεγομένοις οὐδ' οἱ πάνυ συνήθεις ἔφερον
αὐτοῦ τὴν εἰρωνείαν, γινώσκοντες ὅτι τῆς ἐμφύτου
φιλοτιμίας καὶ φιλαρχίας ὑπέκκαυμα τὴν πρὸς
Λεύκολλον ἔχων διαφορὰν μειζόνως ἔχαιρεν.

XXXI. Ἀμέλει δὲ καὶ τὰ ἔργα ταχέως αὐτὸν
ἀπεκάλυπτε. πανταχοῦ γὰρ ἐκτιθεὶς διαγράμματα τοὺς στρατιώτας ἀνεκαλεῖτο καὶ μετεπέμπετο τοὺς ὑπηκόους δυνάστας καὶ βασιλεῖς ὡς
ἑαυτόν. ἐπιών τε τὴν χώραν οὐδὲν ἀκίνητον εἴα
τῶν ὑπὸ τοῦ Λευκόλλου γεγονότων, ἀλλὰ καὶ

63

the time came, their hearts failed them through fear
of the people, and all held their peace except Catulus;
he denounced the law at great length and the tribune
who proposed it, and when none of the people would
listen to him, he called out in loud tones from the
rostra urging the senate again and again to seek out
a mountain, as their forefathers had done,[1] or a lofty
rock, whither they might fly for refuge and preserve
their freedom. But still the law was passed by
all the tribes, as we are told, and Pompey, in his
absence, was proclaimed master of almost all the
powers which Sulla had exercised after subduing the
city in armed warfare. Pompey himself, however, on
receiving his letters and learning what had been
decreed, while his friends surrounded him with their
congratulations, frowned, we are told, smote his thigh,
and said, in the tone of one who was already oppressed and burdened with command : " Alas for
my endless tasks ! How much better it were to be
an unknown man, if I am never to cease from military
service, and cannot lay aside this load of envy and
spend my time in the country with my wife ! " As
he said this, even his intimate friends could not
abide his dissimulation ; they knew that his enmity
towards Lucullus gave fuel to his innate ambition
and love of power, and made him all the more
delighted.

XXXI. And certainly his actions soon unmasked
him. For he sent out edicts in all directions calling
the soldiers to his standard, and summoned the
subject potentates and kings into his presence.
Moreover, as he traversed the country, he left
nothing undisturbed that Lucullus had done, but

---

[1] In reference to the secession of the plebs to Mons Sacer.
See the *Coriolanus*, chapter vi.

κολάσεις ἀνῆκε πολλοῖς καὶ δωρεὰς ἀφείλετο καὶ
πάντα ὅλως ἔπραττεν ἐπιδεῖξαι τὸν ἄνδρα φιλονεικῶν τοῖς θαυμάζουσιν οὐδενὸς ὄντα κύριον.
2 ἐγκαλοῦντος δ' ἐκείνου διὰ τῶν φίλων, ἔδοξε
συνελθεῖν εἰς ταὐτό· καὶ συνῆλθον περὶ τὴν
Γαλατίαν. οἷα δὲ μεγίστων στρατηγῶν καὶ
μέγιστα κατωρθωκότων δάφναις ἀνεστεμμένας
ἔχοντες ὁμοῦ καὶ τὰς ῥάβδους οἱ ὑπηρέται
ἀπήντων· ἀλλὰ Λεύκολλος μὲν ἐκ τόπων χλοερῶν
καὶ κατασκίων προσῄει, Πομπήϊος δὲ πολλὴν
ἄδενδρον καὶ κατεψυγμένην ἔτυχε διεληλυθώς.
3 ἰδόντες οὖν οἱ τοῦ Λευκόλλου ῥαβδοφόροι τοῦ
Πομπηΐου τὰς δάφνας ἀθαλλεῖς καὶ μεμαραμ-
μένας παντάπασιν, ἐκ τῶν ἰδίων προσφάτων
οὐσῶν μεταδιδόντες ἐπεκόσμησαν καὶ κατέστεψαν
τὰς ἐκείνου ῥάβδους. ὃ σημεῖον ἔδοξεν εἶναι
τοῦ τὰ Λευκόλλου νικητήρια καὶ τὴν δόξαν οἰσό-
4 μενον ἔρχεσθαι Πομπήϊον. ἦν δὲ Λεύκολλος
μὲν ἐν ὑπατείας τε τάξει καὶ καθ' ἡλικίαν πρεσβύτερος, τὸ δὲ τοῦ Πομπηΐου μεῖζον ἀξίωμα τοῖς
δυσὶ θριάμβοις. οὐ μὴν ἀλλὰ τὴν πρώτην ἔντευξιν ὡς ἐνῆν μάλιστα πολιτικῶς καὶ φιλοφρόνως ἐποιήσαντο, μεγαλύνοντες ἀλλήλων τὰ
ἔργα καὶ συνηδόμενοι τοῖς κατορθώμασιν· ἐν δὲ
τοῖς λόγοις πρὸς οὐδὲν ἐπιεικὲς οὐδὲ μέτριον
συμβάντες, ἀλλὰ καὶ λοιδορήσαντες, ὁ μὲν εἰς
φιλαργυρίαν τὸν Λεύκολλον, ὁ δὲ εἰς φιλαρχίαν
ἐκεῖνον, ὑπὸ τῶν φίλων μόλις διελύθησαν.
5   Καὶ Λεύκολλος μὲν ἐν Γαλατίᾳ διέγραψε χώρας τῆς αἰχμαλώτου καὶ δωρεὰς ἄλλας οἷς ἐβούλετο, Πομπήϊος δὲ μικρὸν ἀπωτέρω στρατοπεδεύ-
σας ἐκώλυε προσέχειν αὐτῷ, καὶ τοὺς στρατιώτας

remitted punishments in many cases, and took away rewards, and did everything, in a word, with an eager desire to shew the admirers of that general that he was wholly without power. Lucullus expostulated through his friends, and it was decided that they should have a meeting; they met, therefore, in Galatia. And since both were very great and very successful generals, their lictors had their rods alike wreathed with laurel when they met; but Lucullus was advancing from green and shady regions, while Pompey chanced to have made a long march through a parched and treeless country. Accordingly, when the lictors of Lucullus saw that Pompey's laurels were withered and altogether faded, they took some of their own, which were fresh, and with them wreathed and decorated his rods. This was held to be a sign that Pompey was coming to rob Lucullus of the fruits of his victories and of his glory. Now, Lucullus had been consul before Pompey, and was older than he; but Pompey's two triumphs gave him a greater dignity. At first, however, their interview was conducted with all possible civility and friendliness, each magnifying the other's exploits and congratulating him on his successes; but in the conferences which followed they could come to no fair or reasonable agreement, nay, they actually abused each other, Pompey charging Lucullus with love of money, and Lucullus charging Pompey with love of power, and they were with difficulty separated by their friends.

Furthermore, Lucullus, remaining in Galatia, assigned parts of the conquered territory and made other gifts to whom he pleased; while Pompey, encamped at a little distance from him, tried to prevent any attention to his commands, and took away all

ἅπαντας ἀφείλετο πλὴν χιλίων ἑξακοσίων, οὓς
ἐνόμιζεν ὑπ᾽ αὐθαδείας ἀχρήστους μὲν ἑαυτῷ, τῷ
6 Λευκόλλῳ δὲ δυσμενεῖς εἶναι. πρὸς δὲ τούτοις
διασύρων τὰ ἔργα ἐμφανῶς ἔλεγε τραγῳδίαις
καὶ σκιαγραφίαις πεπολεμηκέναι βασιλικαῖς τὸν
Λεύκολλον, αὐτῷ δὲ πρὸς ἀληθινὴν καὶ σεσωφρο-
νισμένην τὸν ἀγῶνα λείπεσθαι δύναμιν, εἰς θυ-
ρεοὺς καὶ ξίφη καὶ ἵππους Μιθριδάτου κατα-
φεύγοντος. ἀμυνόμενος δὲ ὁ Λεύκολλος εἰδώλῳ
καὶ σκιᾷ πολέμου τὸν Πομπήϊον ἔφη μαχούμενον
βαδίζειν, εἰθισμένον ἀλλοτρίοις νεκροῖς, ὥσπερ
ὄρνιν ἀργόν, ἐπικαταίρειν καὶ λείψανα πολέμων
7 σπαράσσειν. οὕτω γὰρ αὐτὸν ἐπιγράψαι Σερτωρίῳ, Λεπίδῳ, τοῖς Σπαρτακείοις, τὰ μὲν Κράσσου, τὰ δὲ Μετέλλου, τὰ δὲ Κάτλου κατορθω-
κότος. ὅθεν οὐ θαυμάζειν εἰ τῶν Ἀρμενιακῶν
καὶ Ποντικῶν πολέμων ὑποβάλλεται τὴν δόξαν,
ἄνθρωπος ἑαυτὸν εἰς δραπετικὸν θρίαμβον ἁμῶς
γέ πως ἐμβαλεῖν μηχανησάμενος.

XXXII. Ἐκ τούτου Λεύκολλος μὲν ἀπῆρε,
Πομπήϊος δὲ τῷ στόλῳ παντὶ τὴν μεταξὺ Φοινί-
κης καὶ Βοσπόρου θάλασσαν ἐπὶ φρουρᾷ δια-
λαβών, αὐτὸς ἐβάδιζεν ἐπὶ Μιθριδάτην, ἔχοντα
τρισμυρίους πεζοὺς ἐν φάλαγγι καὶ δισχιλίους
2 ἱππεῖς, μάχεσθαι δὲ μὴ θαρροῦντα. καὶ πρῶτον
μὲν αὐτοῦ καρτερὸν ὄρος καὶ δύσμαχον, ἐν ᾧ
στρατοπεδεύων ἔτυχεν, ὡς ἄνυδρον ἐκλιπόντος,
αὐτὸ τοῦτο κατασχὼν ὁ Πομπήϊος, καὶ τῇ φύσει
τῶν βλαστανόντων καὶ ταῖς συγκλινίαις τῶν
τόπων τεκμαιρόμενος ἔχειν πηγὰς τὸ χωρίον,

his soldiers from him, except sixteen hundred, whose mutinous spirit made them, as he thought, useless to himself and hostile to Lucullus.[1] Besides this, he would belittle the achievements of Lucullus, declaring that he had waged war against mimic and shadowy kings only, while to himself there was now left the struggle against a real military force, and one disciplined by defeat, since Mithridates had now betaken himself to shields, swords, and horses. To this Lucullus retorted that Pompey was going forth to fight an image and shadow of war, following his custom of alighting, like a lazy carrion-bird, on bodies that others had killed, and tearing to pieces the scattered remnants of wars. For it was in this way that he had appropriated to himself the victories over Sertorius, Lepidus, and the followers of Spartacus, although they had actually been won by Metellus, Catulus, and Crassus. Therefore it was no wonder that he was trying to usurp the glory of the Pontic and Armenian wars, a man who had contrived to thrust himself in some way or other into the honour of a triumph for defeating runaway slaves.[2]

XXXII. After this, Lucullus withdrew from those parts, and Pompey, having distributed his whole fleet so as to guard the sea between Phoenicia and the Bosporus, himself marched against Mithridates, who had a fighting force of thirty thousand foot and two thousand horse, but did not dare to offer battle. To begin with, the king was strongly encamped on a mountain which was difficult of assault, but abandoned it, supposing that it had no water. Pompey took possession of this very mountain, and judging by the nature of the vegetation and by the channels in the slopes that the place had springs, ordered his men to

---

[1] Cf. the *Lucullus*, xvi. 1-4.   [2] Cf. chapter xxi. 2.

ἐκέλευσεν ἐκβαλεῖν πανταχοῦ φρέατα. καὶ μεστὸν ἦν εὐθὺς ὕδατος ἀφθόνου τὸ στρατόπεδον,
ὥστε θαυμάζειν εἰ τῷ παντὶ χρόνῳ τοῦτο Μιθρι-
3 δάτης ἠγνόησεν. ἔπειτα περιστρατοπεδεύσας 63
περιετείχιζεν αὐτόν. ὁ δὲ πέντε καὶ τετταράκοντα πολιορκηθεὶς ἡμέρας ἔλαθεν ἀποδρὰς μετὰ
τῆς ἐρρωμενεστάτης δυνάμεως, κτείνας τοὺς ἀχρήστους καὶ νοσοῦντας. εἶτα μέντοι περὶ τὸν
Εὐφράτην καταλαβὼν αὐτὸν ὁ Πομπήϊος παρε-
στρατοπέδευσε· καὶ δεδιὼς μὴ φθάσῃ περάσας
τὸν Εὐφράτην, ἐκ μέσων νυκτῶν ἐπῆγεν ὡπλι-
4 σμένην τὴν στρατιάν· καθ' ὃν χρόνον λέγεται
τὸν Μιθριδάτην ὄψιν ἐν ὕπνοις ἰδεῖν τὰ μέλλοντα προδηλοῦσαν. ἐδόκει γὰρ οὐρίῳ πνεύματι
πλέων τὸ Ποντικὸν πέλαγος ἤδη Βόσπορον
καθορᾶν καὶ φιλοφρονεῖσθαι τοὺς συμπλέοντας,
ὡς ἄν τις ἐπὶ σωτηρίᾳ σαφεῖ καὶ βεβαίῳ χαίρων·
ἄφνω δὲ ἀναφανῆναι πάντων ἔρημος ἐπὶ λεπτοῦ
ναυαγίου διαφερόμενος. ἐν τοιούτοις δὲ αὐτὸν
ὄντα πάθεσι καὶ φάσμασιν ἐπιστάντες ἀνέστη-
5 σαν οἱ φίλοι, φράζοντες ἐπιέναι Πομπήϊον. ἦν
οὖν ἐξ ἀνάγκης μαχητέον ὑπὲρ τοῦ χάρακος, καὶ
προαγαγόντες οἱ στρατηγοὶ τὴν δύναμιν ἔταξαν.
αἰσθόμενος δὲ τὴν παρασκευὴν αὐτῶν ὁ Πομπήϊος ὤκνει κατὰ σκότος εἰς κίνδυνον ἐλθεῖν,
καὶ κύκλῳ μόνον ᾤετο δεῖν περιελαύνειν, ὅπως
μὴ φεύγοιεν, ἡμέρας δὲ κρείττους ὄντας ἐπιχειρεῖν. οἱ δὲ πρεσβύτατοι τῶν ταξιαρχῶν δεόμενοι καὶ παρακαλοῦντες ἐξώρμησαν αὐτόν· οὐδὲ
γὰρ σκότος ἦν παντάπασιν, ἀλλὰ ἡ σελήνη

sink wells everywhere. At once, then, his camp was abundantly supplied with water, and men wondered that in all the time of his encampment there Mithridates had been ignorant of this possibility. Next, he invested the king's camp and walled him in. But after enduring a siege of forty-five days, Mithridates succeeded in stealing off with his most effective troops; the sick and unserviceable he killed. Then, however, Pompey overtook him near the Euphrates river, and encamped close by; and fearing lest the king should get the advantage of him by crossing the Euphrates, he put his army in battle array and led it against him at midnight. At this time Mithridates is said to have seen a vision in his sleep, revealing what should come to pass. He dreamed that he was sailing the Pontic Sea with a fair wind, and was already in sight of the Bosporus, and was greeting pleasantly his fellow-voyagers, as a man would do in his joy over a manifest and sure deliverance; but suddenly he saw himself bereft of all his companions and tossed about on a small piece of wreckage. As he dreamed of such distress, his friends came to his couch and roused him with the news that Pompey was advancing to the attack. He was therefore compelled to give battle in defence of his camp, and his generals led out their troops and put them in array. But when Pompey perceived their preparations to meet him, he hesitated to hazard matters in the dark, and thought it necessary merely to surround them, in order to prevent their escape, and then to attack them when it was day, since they were superior in numbers. But his oldest officers, by their entreaties and exhortations, prevailed upon him to attack at once; for it was not wholly dark, but the moon, which was setting, made it still possible

καταφερομένη παρεῖχεν ἔτι τῶν σωμάτων ἱκανὴν
ἔποψιν. καὶ τοῦτο μάλιστα τοὺς βασιλικοὺς
6 ἔσφηλεν. ἐπήεσαν μὲν γὰρ οἱ Ῥωμαῖοι κατὰ
νώτου τὴν σελήνην ἔχοντες· πεπιεσμένου δὲ περὶ
τὰς δύσεις τοῦ φωτός, αἱ σκιαὶ πολὺ τῶν σωμάτων ἔμπροσθεν προϊοῦσαι τοῖς πολεμίοις ἐπέ-
βαλλον, οὐ δυναμένοις τὸ διάστημα συνιδεῖν
ἀκριβῶς· ἀλλ᾽ ὡς ἐν χερσὶν ἤδη γεγονότων
τοὺς ὑσσοὺς ἀφέντες μάτην οὐδενὸς ἐφίκοντο.
7 τοῦτο συνιδόντες οἱ Ῥωμαῖοι μετὰ κραυγῆς ἐπέ-
δραμον, καὶ μηκέτι μένειν τολμῶντας, ἀλλ᾽ ἐκπε-
πληγμένους καὶ φεύγοντας ἔκτεινον, ὥστε πολὺ
πλείονας μυρίων ἀποθανεῖν, ἁλῶναι δὲ τὸ στρατόπεδον.

Αὐτὸς δὲ Μιθριδάτης ἐν ἀρχῇ μὲν ὀκτακοσίοις
ἱππεῦσι διέκοψε καὶ διεξήλασε τοὺς Ῥωμαίους,
ταχὺ δὲ τῶν ἄλλων σκεδασθέντων ἀπελείφθη
8 μετὰ τριῶν. ἐν οἷς ἦν Ὑψικράτεια παλλακίς,
ἀεὶ μὲν ἀνδρώδης τις οὖσα καὶ παράτολμος·
Ὑψικράτην γοῦν αὐτὴν ὁ βασιλεὺς ἐκάλει· τότε
δὲ ἀνδρὸς ἔχουσα Πέρσου στολὴν καὶ ἵππον οὔτε
τῷ σώματι πρὸς τὰ μήκη τῶν δρόμων ἀπηγό-
ρευσεν οὔτε θεραπεύουσα τοῦ βασιλέως τὸ σῶμα
καὶ τὸν ἵππον ἐξέκαμεν, ἄχρι ἧκον εἰς χωρίον
Σίνωρα χρημάτων καὶ κειμηλίων βασιλικῶν
9 μεστόν. ἐξ οὗ λαβὼν ὁ Μιθριδάτης ἐσθῆτας
πολυτελεῖς διένειμε τοῖς συνδεδραμηκόσι πρὸς
αὑτὸν ἐκ τῆς φυγῆς. ἔδωκε δὲ καὶ τῶν φίλων
ἑκάστῳ φορεῖν θανάσιμον φάρμακον, ὅπως ἄκων
μηδεὶς ὑποχείριος γένοιτο τοῖς πολεμίοις. ἐν-

to distinguish persons clearly enough; indeed, it was this circumstance that brought most harm to the king's troops. For the Romans came to the attack with the moon at their backs, and since her light was close to the horizon, the shadows made by their bodies were thrown far in advance and fell upon the enemy, who were thus unable to estimate correctly the distance between themselves and their foes, but supposing that they were already at close quarters, they hurled their javelins to no purpose and hit nobody. The Romans, seeing this, charged upon them with loud cries, and when the enemy no longer ventured to stand their ground, but fled in panic fear, they cut them down, so that many more than ten thousand of them were slain, and their camp was captured.

Mithridates himself, however, at the outset, cut and charged his way through the Romans with eight hundred horsemen; but the rest were soon dispersed and he was left with three companions. One of these was Hypsicrateia, a concubine, who always displayed a right manly spirit and extravagant daring (for which reason the king was wont to call her Hypsicrates), and at this time, mounted and accoutred like a Persian, she was neither exhausted by the long journeys, nor did she weary of caring for the king's person and for his horse, until they came to a place called Sinora, which was full of the king's money and treasures. Thence Mithridates took costly raiment and distributed it to those who had flocked to him in his flight. He also gave each of his friends a deadly poison to carry with them, that no one of them might fall into the hands of the enemy against his will. From thence he set out

τεῦθεν ὥρμητο μὲν ἐπ᾽ Ἀρμενίας πρὸς Τιγράνην,
ἐκείνου δὲ ἀπαγορεύοντος καὶ τάλαντα ἑκατὸν
ἐπικηρύξαντος αὐτῷ, παραμειψάμενος τὰς πηγὰς
τοῦ Εὐφράτου διὰ τῆς Κολχίδος ἔφευγε.

XXXIII. Πομπήϊος δὲ εἰς Ἀρμενίαν ἐνέβαλε
τοῦ νέου Τιγράνου καλοῦντος αὐτόν· ἤδη γὰρ
ἀφειστήκει τοῦ πατρός, καὶ συνήντησε τῷ Πομπηΐῳ περὶ τὸν Ἀράξην ποταμόν, ὃς ἀνίσχει μὲν
ἐκ τῶν αὐτῶν τῷ Εὐφράτῃ τόπων, ἀποτρεπόμενος
δὲ πρὸς τὰς ἀνατολὰς εἰς τὸ Κάσπιον ἐμβάλλει
2 πέλαγος. οὗτοι μὲν οὖν προῆγον ἅμα τὰς πόλεις
παραλαμβάνοντες· ὁ δὲ βασιλεὺς Τιγράνης ἔναγχος μὲν ὑπὸ Λευκόλλου συντετριμμένος, ἥμερον
δέ τινα τῷ τρόπῳ καὶ πρᾷον πυθόμενος εἶναι τὸν
Πομπήϊον, ἐδέξατο μὲν εἰς τὰ βασίλεια φρουράν,
ἀναλαβὼν δὲ τοὺς φίλους καὶ συγγενεῖς αὐτὸς
3 ἐπορεύετο παραδώσων ἑαυτόν. ὡς δὲ ἦλθεν ἱπ-
πότης ἐπὶ τὸν χάρακα, ῥαβδοῦχοι δύο τοῦ Πομπηΐου προσελθόντες ἐκέλευσαν ἀποβῆναι τοῦ
ἵππου καὶ πεζὸν ἐλθεῖν· οὐδένα γὰρ ἀνθρώπων
ἐφ᾽ ἵππου καθεζόμενον ἐν Ῥωμαϊκῷ στρατοπέδῳ
πώποτε ὀφθῆναι. καὶ ταῦτα οὖν ὁ Τιγράνης
ἐπείθετο καὶ τὸ ξίφος αὐτοῖς ἀπολυσάμενος
παρεδίδου· καὶ τέλος, ὡς πρὸς αὐτὸν ἦλθε τὸν
Πομπήϊον, ἀφελόμενος τὴν κίταριν ὥρμησε πρὸ
τῶν ποδῶν θεῖναι, καὶ καταβαλὼν ἑαυτόν, αἴσχιστα δὴ πάντων, προσπεσεῖν αὐτοῦ τοῖς γόνασιν.
4 ἀλλ᾽ ὁ Πομπήϊος ἔφθη τῆς δεξιᾶς αὐτοῦ λαβόμενος προσαγαγέσθαι· καὶ πλησίον ἱδρυσάμενος
ἑαυτοῦ, τὸν δὲ υἱὸν ἐπὶ θάτερα, τῶν μὲν ἄλλων
ἔφησε δεῖν αἰτιᾶσθαι Λεύκολλον, ὑπ᾽ ἐκείνου γὰρ
ἀφῃρῆσθαι Συρίαν, Φοινίκην, Κιλικίαν, Γαλατίαν, Σωφηνήν, ἃ δὲ ἄχρι ἑαυτοῦ διατετήρηκεν,

towards Armenia on his way to Tigranes; but that monarch forbade his coming and proclaimed a reward of a hundred talents for his person; he therefore passed by the sources of the Euphrates and continued his flight through Colchis.

XXXIII. Pompey then invaded Armenia on the invitation of young Tigranes, who was now in revolt from his father, and who met Pompey near the river Araxes, which takes its rise in the same regions as the Euphrates, but turns towards the east and empties into the Caspian Sea. These two, then, marched forward together, receiving the submission of the cities as they passed; King Tigranes, however, who had recently been crushed by Lucullus, but now learned that Pompey was rather mild and gentle in his disposition, received a Roman garrison into his palace, and taking with him his friends and kindred, set out of his own accord to surrender himself. When he rode up to the Roman camp, two of Pompey's lictors came to him and bade him dismount from his horse and go on foot; for no man mounted on horseback had ever been seen in a Roman camp. Tigranes, accordingly, not only obeyed them in this, but also unloosed his sword and gave it to them; and finally, when he came into the presence of Pompey himself, he took off his royal tiara and made as if to lay it at his feet, and what was most humiliating of all, would have thrown himself down and clasped his knees in supplication. But before he could do this, Pompey caught him by the hand and drew him forward, and after giving him a seat near himself, and putting his son on the other side, told him that he must lay the rest of his losses to Lucullus, who had robbed him of Syria, Phoenicia, Cilicia, Galatia, and Sophene; but that

ἕξειν ἐκτίσαντα ποινὴν ἑξακισχίλια τάλαντα
Ῥωμαίοις τῆς ἀδικίας, Σωφηνῆς δὲ βασιλεύσειν
5 τὸν υἱόν. ἐπὶ τούτοις ὁ μὲν Τιγράνης ἠγάπησε,
καὶ τῶν Ῥωμαίων ἀσπασαμένων αὐτὸν βασιλέα
περιχαρὴς γενόμενος ἐπηγγείλατο στρατιώτῃ μὲν
ἡμιμναῖον ἀργυρίου δώσειν, ἑκατοντάρχῃ δὲ μνᾶς
δέκα, χιλιάρχῳ δὲ τάλαντον· ὁ δ' υἱὸς ἐδυσφόρει,
καὶ κληθεὶς ἐπὶ δεῖπνον οὐκ ἔφη Πομπηΐου δεῖσθαι τοιαῦτα τιμῶντος· καὶ γὰρ αὐτὸς ἄλλον
εὑρήσειν Ῥωμαίων. ἐκ τούτου δεθεὶς εἰς τὸν
6 θρίαμβον ἐφυλάττετο. καὶ μετ' οὐ πολὺν χρόνον
ἔπεμψε Φραάτης ὁ Πάρθος ἀπαιτῶν μὲν τὸν
νεανίσκον, ὡς αὑτοῦ γαμβρόν, ἀξιῶν δὲ τῶν ἡγε-
μονιῶν ὅρῳ χρῆσθαι τῷ Εὐφράτῃ. Πομπήϊος δὲ
ἀπεκρίνατο τὸν μὲν Τιγράνην τῷ πατρὶ μᾶλλον
ἢ τῷ πενθερῷ προσήκειν, ὅρῳ δὲ χρήσεσθαι τῷ
δικαίῳ.

XXXIV. Καταλιπὼν δὲ φρουρὸν Ἀρμενίας
Ἀφράνιον αὐτὸς ἐβάδιζε διὰ τῶν περιοικούντων τὸν
Καύκασον ἐθνῶν ἀναγκαίως ἐπὶ Μιθριδάτην. μέγιστα δὲ αὐτῶν ἐστιν ἔθνη[1] Ἀλβανοὶ καὶ Ἴβηρες,
Ἴβηρες μὲν ἐπὶ τὰ Μοσχικὰ ὄρη καὶ τὸν Πόντον
καθήκοντες, Ἀλβανοὶ δὲ ἐπὶ τὴν ἕω καὶ τὴν
2 Κασπίαν κεκλιμένοι θάλασσαν. οὗτοι πρῶτον
μὲν αἰτοῦντι Πομπηΐῳ δίοδον ἔδοσαν· χειμῶνος
δὲ τὴν στρατιὰν ἐν τῇ χώρᾳ καταλαβόντος καὶ
τῆς Κρονικῆς ἑορτῆς τοῖς Ῥωμαίοις καθηκούσης,

---

[1] ἔθνη bracketed by Sintenis.

what he had kept up to the present time he should continue to hold if he paid six thousand talents to the Romans as a penalty for his wrongdoing; and that his son should be king of Sophene. With these terms Tigranes was well pleased, and when the Romans hailed him as King, he was overjoyed, and promised to give each soldier half a mina of silver, to each centurion ten minas, and to each tribune a talent. But his son was dissatisfied, and when he was invited to supper, said that he was not dependent on Pompey for such honours, for he himself could find another Roman to bestow them. Upon this, he was put in chains and reserved for the triumph. Not long after this, Phraates the Parthian sent a demand for the young man, on the plea that he was his son-in-law, and a proposition that the Euphrates be adopted as a boundary between his empire and that of the Romans. Pompey replied that as for Tigranes, he belonged to his father more than to his father-in-law; and as for a boundary, the just one would be adopted.

XXXIV. Then leaving Afranius in charge of Armenia, Pompey himself proceeded against Mithridates,[1] and of necessity passed through the peoples dwelling about the Caucasus mountains. The greatest of these peoples are the Albanians and the Iberians, of whom the Iberians extend to the Moschian mountains and the Euxine Sea, while the Albanians lie to the eastward as far as the Caspian Sea. These latter at first granted Pompey's request for a free passage; but when winter had overtaken his army in their country and it was occupied in celebrating the Roman festival of the Saturnalia, they mustered no less than forty

[1] In 65 B.C.

γενόμενοι τετρακισμυρίων οὐκ ἐλάττους ἐπεχεί-
ρησαν αὐτοῖς, διαβάντες τὸν Κύρνον ποταμόν, ὃς
ἐκ τῶν Ἰβηρικῶν ὀρῶν ἀνιστάμενος καὶ δεχόμενος
κατιόντα τὸν Ἀράξην ἀπ' Ἀρμενίας ἐξίησι δώ-
3 δεκα στόμασιν εἰς τὸ Κάσπιον. οἱ δὲ οὔ φασι
τούτῳ συμφέρεσθαι τὸν Ἀράξην, ἀλλὰ καθ'
ἑαυτόν, ἐγγὺς δὲ ποιεῖσθαι τὴν ἐκβολὴν εἰς ταὐτὸ
πέλαγος. Πομπήϊος δέ, καίπερ ἐνστῆναι δυνάμενος πρὸς τὴν διάβασιν τοῖς πολεμίοις, περιεῖδε
διαβάντας καθ' ἡσυχίαν· εἶτα ἐπαγαγὼν ἐτρέ-
4 ψατο καὶ διέφθειρε παμπληθεῖς. τῷ δὲ βασιλεῖ
δεηθέντι καὶ πέμψαντι πρέσβεις ἀφεὶς τὴν ἀδικίαν καὶ σπεισάμενος, ἐπὶ τοὺς Ἴβηρας ἐβάδιζε,
πλήθει μὲν οὐκ ἐλάττονας, μαχιμωτέρους δὲ τῶν
ἑτέρων ὄντας, ἰσχυρῶς δὲ βουλομένους τῷ Μιθριδάτῃ χαρίζεσθαι καὶ διωθεῖσθαι τὸν Πομπήϊον.
5 οὔτε γὰρ Μήδοις οὔτε Πέρσαις ὑπήκουσαν
Ἴβηρες, διέφυγον δὲ καὶ τὴν Μακεδόνων ἀρχήν,
Ἀλεξάνδρου διὰ ταχέων ἐκ τῆς Ὑρκανίας ἀπά-
ραντος. οὐ μὴν ἀλλὰ καὶ τούτους μάχῃ μεγάλῃ
τρεψάμενος ὁ Πομπήϊος, ὥστε ἀποθανεῖν μὲν
ἐνακισχιλίους, ἁλῶναι δὲ πλείους μυρίων, εἰς τὴν
Κολχικὴν ἐνέβαλε· καὶ πρὸς τὸν Φᾶσιν αὐτῷ
Σερουΐλιος ἀπήντησε, τὰς ναῦς ἔχων αἷς ἐφρούρει
τὸν Πόντον.

XXXV. Ἡ μὲν οὖν Μιθριδάτου δίωξις ἐνδεδυ-
κότος εἰς τὰ περὶ Βόσπορον ἔθνη καὶ τὴν Μαιῶτιν
ἀπορίας εἶχε μεγάλας· Ἀλβανοὶ δὲ αὖθις ἀφε-
στῶτες αὐτῷ προσηγγέλθησαν. πρὸς οὓς ὑπ' 6
ὀργῆς καὶ φιλονεικίας ἐπιστρέψας τόν τε Κύρνον
μόλις καὶ παραβόλως πάλιν διεπέρασεν ἐπὶ
πολὺ σταυροῖς ὑπὸ τῶν βαρβάρων ἀποκεχαρα-

thousand men and made an attack upon it. To
do this, they crossed the river Cyrnus, which rises
in the Iberian mountains, and receiving the Araxes
as it issues from Armenia, empties itself by twelve
mouths into the Caspian. Others say that the
Araxes makes no junction with this stream, but
takes a course of its own, and empties itself close
by into the same sea. Although Pompey could
have opposed the enemy's passage of the river,
he suffered them to cross undisturbed; then he attacked them, routed them, and slew great numbers
of them. When, however, their king sent envoys
and begged for mercy, Pompey condoned his wrongdoing and made a treaty with him; then he marched
against the Iberians, who were not less numerous
than the others and more warlike, and had a strong
desire to gratify Mithridates by repulsing Pompey.
For the Iberians had not been subject either to the
Medes or the Persians, and they escaped the
Macedonian dominion also, since Alexander departed
from Hyrcania in haste. Notwithstanding, Pompey
routed this people also in a great battle, in which
nine thousand of them were slain and more than
ten thousand taken prisoners; then he invaded
Colchis, where, at the river Phasis, Servilius met
him, at the head of the fleet with which he was
guarding the Euxine.

XXXV. Now, the pursuit of Mithridates, who had
thrown himself among the peoples about the Bosporus and the Maeotic Sea, was attended with great
difficulties; besides, word was brought to Pompey
that the Albanians had again revolted. Turning back
against these in resentment and wrath, he crossed
the Cyrnus again with great difficulty and hazard,
since the Barbarians had fenced off its banks with

2 κωμένον, καὶ μακρᾶς αὐτὸν ἐκδεχομένης ἀνύδρου
καὶ ἀργαλέας ὁδοῦ, μυρίους ἀσκοὺς ὕδατος ἐμ-
πλησάμενος ἤλαυνεν ἐπὶ τοὺς πολεμίους, καὶ κατέλαβε πρὸς Ἄβαντι ποταμῷ παρατεταγμένους
ἑξακισμυρίους πεζοὺς καὶ δισχιλίους ἱππεῖς ἐπὶ
μυρίοις, ὡπλισμένους δὲ φαύλως καὶ δέρμασι
θηρίων τοὺς πολλούς. ἡγεῖτο δὲ αὐτῶν βασιλέως
3 ἀδελφὸς ὄνομα Κῶσις. οὗτος ἐν χερσὶ τῆς μάχης
γενομένης ἐπὶ τὸν Πομπήϊον ὁρμήσας αὐτὸν
ἔβαλεν ἐπὶ τὴν τοῦ θώρακος ἐπιπτυχὴν ἀκοντί-
σματι, Πομπήϊος δὲ ἐκεῖνον ἐκ χειρὸς διελάσας
ἀνεῖλεν.

Ἐν ταύτῃ τῇ μάχῃ λέγονται καὶ Ἀμαζόνες
συναγωνίσασθαι τοῖς βαρβάροις, ἀπὸ τῶν περὶ
τὸν Θερμώδοντα ποταμὸν ὀρῶν καταβᾶσαι. μετὰ
γὰρ τὴν μάχην σκυλεύοντες οἱ Ῥωμαῖοι τοὺς
βαρβάρους πέλταις Ἀμαζονικαῖς καὶ κοθόρνοις
ἐνετύγχανον, σῶμα δὲ οὐδὲν ὤφθη γυναικεῖον.
4 νέμονται δὲ τοῦ Καυκάσου τὰ καθήκοντα πρὸς
τὴν Ὑρκανίαν θάλασσαν, οὐχ ὁμοροῦσαι τοῖς
Ἀλβανοῖς, ἀλλὰ Γέλαι καὶ Λῆγες οἰκοῦσι διὰ
μέσου· καὶ τούτοις ἔτους ἑκάστου δύο μῆνας εἰς
ταὐτὸ φοιτῶσαι περὶ τὸν Θερμώδοντα ποταμὸν
ὁμιλοῦσιν, εἶτα καθ᾽ αὑτὰς ἀπαλλαγεῖσαι βιο-
τεύουσιν.

XXXVI. Ὁρμήσας δὲ μετὰ τὴν μάχην ὁ Πομπήϊος ἐλαύνειν ἐπὶ τὴν Ὑρκανίαν καὶ Κασπίαν
θάλασσαν, ὑπὸ πλήθους ἑρπετῶν θανασίμων
ἀπετράπη τριῶν ὁδὸν ἡμερῶν ἀποσχών, εἰς δὲ τὴν
2 μικρὰν Ἀρμενίαν ἀνεχώρησε. καὶ τῷ μὲν Ἐλυ-
μαίων καὶ Μήδων βασιλεῖ πέμψασι πρέσβεις
ἀντέγραψε φιλικῶς, τὸν δὲ Πάρθον, εἰς τὴν
Γορδυηνὴν ἐμβεβληκότα καὶ περικόπτοντα τοὺς

long stretches of palisades; then, since he must make a long march through a waterless and difficult country, he ordered ten thousand skins to be filled with water, and with this provision advanced upon the enemy. He found them drawn up on the river Abas, sixty thousand foot and twelve thousand horse, but wretchedly armed, and clad for the most part in the skins of wild beasts. They were led by a brother of the king, named Cosis, who, as soon as the fighting was at close quarters, rushed upon Pompey himself and smote him with a javelin on the fold of his breastplate; but Pompey ran him through the body and killed him.

In this battle it is said that there were also Amazons fighting on the side of the Barbarians, and that they came down from the mountains about the river Thermodon. For when the Romans were despoiling the Barbarians after the battle, they came upon Amazonian shields and buskins; but no body of a woman was seen. The Amazons inhabit the parts of the Caucasus mountains that reach down to the Hyrcanian Sea, and they do not border on the Albani, but Gelae and Leges dwell between. With these peoples, who meet them by the river Thermodon, they consort for two months every year; then they go away and live by themselves.

XXXVI. After the battle, Pompey set out to march to the Hyrcanian and Caspian Sea, but was turned back by a multitude of deadly reptiles when he was only three days march distant, and withdrew into Lesser Armenia. Here the kings of the Ely-maeans and the Medes sent ambassadors to him, and he wrote them a friendly answer; but against the Parthian king, who had burst into Gordyene and was plundering the subjects of Tigranes, he sent

209

ὑπὸ Τιγράνῃ, πέμψας μετὰ Ἀφρανίου δύναμιν
ἐξήλασε διωχθέντα μέχρι τῆς Ἀρβηλίτιδος.

Ὅσαι δὲ τῶν Μιθριδάτου παλλακίδων ἀνή-
χθησαν, οὐδεμίαν ἔγνω, πάσας δὲ τοῖς γονεῦσι
καὶ οἰκείοις ἀνέπεμπεν. ἦσαν γὰρ αἱ πολλαὶ
θυγατέρες καὶ γυναῖκες στρατηγῶν καὶ δυναστῶν.
3 Στρατονίκη δέ, ἣ μέγιστον εἶχεν ἀξίωμα καὶ τὸ
πολυχρυσότατον τῶν φρουρίων ἐφύλαττεν, ἦν
μέν, ὡς ἔοικε, ψάλτου τινὸς οὐχ εὐτυχοῦς τἆλλα,
πρεσβύτου δὲ θυγάτηρ, οὕτω δὲ εὐθὺς εἷλε παρὰ
πότον ψήλασα τὸν Μιθριδάτην, ὥστε ἐκείνην μὲν
ἔχων ἀνεπαύετο, τὸν δὲ πρεσβύτην ἀπέπεμψε
δυσφοροῦντα τῷ μηδὲ προσρήσεως τυχεῖν ἐπι-
4 εικοῦς. ὡς μέντοι περὶ ὄρθρον ἐγερθεὶς εἶδεν
ἔνδον ἐκπωμάτων μὲν ἀργυρῶν καὶ χρυσῶν τρα-
πέζας, ὄχλον δὲ θεραπείας πολύν, εὐνούχους δὲ
καὶ παῖδας ἱμάτια τῶν πολυτελῶν προσφέροντας
αὐτῷ, καὶ πρὸ τῆς θύρας ἵππον ἑστῶτα κεκοσμημένον ὥσπερ οἱ τῶν φίλων τοῦ βασιλέως, χλευα-
σμὸν εἶναι τὸ χρῆμα καὶ παιδιὰν ἡγούμενος
5 ὥρμησε φεύγειν διὰ θυρῶν. τῶν δὲ θεραπόντων
ἀντιλαμβανομένων, καὶ λεγόντων ὅτι πλουσίου
τεθνηκότος ἔναγχος οἶκον αὐτῷ μέγαν ὁ βασιλεὺς
δεδώρηται, καὶ ταῦτα μικραί τινες ἀπαρχαὶ καὶ
δείγματα τῶν ἄλλων χρημάτων καὶ κτημάτων
εἰσίν, οὕτω πιστεύσας μόλις καὶ τὴν πορ-
φύραν ἀναλαβὼν καὶ ἀναπηδήσας ἐπὶ τὸν ἵππον
ἤλαυνε διὰ τῆς πόλεως βοῶν· "Ἐμὰ ταῦτα
6 πάντα ἐστί." πρὸς δὲ τοὺς καταγελῶντας οὐ
τοῦτο ἔλεγεν εἶναι θαυμαστόν, ἀλλ' ὅτι μὴ λίθοις
βάλλει τοὺς ἀπαντῶντας ὑφ' ἡδονῆς μαινόμενος.
ταύτης μὲν ἦν καὶ γενεᾶς καὶ αἵματος ἡ Στρατο-

an armed force under Afranius, which drove him out
of the country and pursued him as far as the district
of Arbela.

Of all the concubines of Mithridates that were
brought to Pompey, he used not one, but restored
them all to their parents and kindred; for most of
them were daughters and wives of generals and
princes. But Stratonice, who was held in highest
esteem by the king and had the custody of the
richest of his fortresses, was, it would seem, the
daughter of a humble harpist, an old man, and poor
besides; but she made such a swift conquest of
Mithridates as she once played for him at his wine,
that he took her with him to his bed, but sent the
old man away in great displeasure at not getting so
much as a kindly greeting. In the morning, however,
when the old man rose and saw in his house tables
loaded with gold and silver beakers, a large retinue
of servants, and eunuchs and pages bringing costly
garments to him, and a horse standing before his
door caparisoned like those of the king's friends, he
thought the thing a mockery and a joke, and tried
to run out of doors. But the servants laid hold of him
and told him that the king had bestowed on him
the large estate of a rich man who had recently
died, and that these things were only small fore-
tastes and specimens of the goods and chattels still
remaining. In this way he was with difficulty persuaded, and putting on his purple robes and leaping
upon his horse, he rode through the city, crying:
" All this is mine." To those who laughed at him
he said that what he was doing was no wonder;
the wonder was that he did not throw stones at
those who met him, for he was mad with joy. Of
such a stock and lineage was Stratonice. But she

νίκη. τῷ δὲ Πομπηΐῳ καὶ τὸ χωρίον παρε-
δίδου τοῦτο καὶ δῶρα πολλὰ προσήνεγκεν, ὧν
ἐκεῖνος ὅσα κόσμον ἱεροῖς καὶ λαμπρότητα τῷ
θριάμβῳ παρέξειν ἐφαίνετο λαβὼν μόνα, τὰ
λοιπὰ τὴν Στρατονίκην ἐκέλευε κεκτῆσθαι χαί-
7 ρουσαν. ὁμοίως δὲ καὶ τοῦ βασιλέως τῶν Ἰβήρων
κλίνην τε καὶ τράπεζαν καὶ θρόνον, ἅπαντα   63
χρυσᾶ, πέμψαντος αὐτῷ καὶ δεηθέντος λαβεῖν,
καὶ ταῦτα τοῖς ταμίαις παρέδωκεν εἰς τὸ δημόσιον.

XXXVII. Ἐν δὲ τῷ Καινῷ φρουρίῳ καὶ γράμμασιν ἀπορρήτοις ὁ Πομπήϊος ἐνέτυχε τοῦ Μιθριδάτου, καὶ διῆλθεν οὐκ ἀηδῶς αὐτὰ πολλὴν
ἔχοντα τοῦ ἤθους κατανόησιν. ὑπομνήματα γὰρ
ἦν, ἐξ ὧν ἐφωράθη φαρμάκοις ἄλλους τε πολλοὺς
καὶ τὸν υἱὸν Ἀριαράθην ἀνῃρηκὼς καὶ τὸν
Σαρδιανὸν Ἀλκαῖον, ὅτι παρευδοκίμησεν αὐτὸν
2 ἵππους ἀγωνιστὰς ἐλαύνων. ἦσαν δὲ ἀναγεγραμ-
μέναι καὶ κρίσεις ἐνυπνίων, ὧν τὰ μὲν αὐτὸς
ἑωράκει, τὰ δὲ ἔνιαι τῶν γυναικῶν, ἐπιστολαί τε
Μονίμης πρὸς αὐτὸν ἀκόλαστοι καὶ πάλιν ἐκείνου
πρὸς αὐτήν. Θεοφάνης δὲ καὶ Ῥουτιλίου λόγον
εὑρεθῆναί φησι παροξυντικὸν ἐπὶ τὴν ἀναίρεσιν
3 τῶν ἐν Ἀσίᾳ Ῥωμαίων. ὃ καλῶς εἰκάζουσιν
οἱ πλεῖστοι κακοήθευμα τοῦ Θεοφάνους εἶναι,
τάχα μὲν οὐδὲν αὐτῷ τὸν Ῥουτίλιον ἐοικότα
μισοῦντος, εἰκὸς δὲ καὶ διὰ Πομπήϊον, οὗ τὸν
πατέρα παμπόνηρον ἀπέδειξεν ὁ Ῥουτίλιος ἐν
ταῖς ἱστορίαις.

XXXVIII. Ἐντεῦθεν εἰς Ἀμισὸν ἐλθὼν ὁ
Πομπήϊος πάθος νεμεσητὸν ὑπὸ φιλοτιμίας
ἔπαθε. πολλὰ γὰρ τὸν Λεύκολλον ἐπικερτο-
μήσας, ὅτι τοῦ πολεμίου ζῶντος ἔγραφε διατάξεις

surrendered this stronghold to Pompey, and brought
him many gifts, of which he accepted only those
which were likely to adorn the temples at Rome
and add splendour to his triumph; the rest he
bade Stratonice keep and welcome. In like manner,
too, when the king of the Iberians sent him a couch,
a table, and a throne, all of gold, and begged him to
accept them, he delivered these also to the quaestors,
for the public treasury.

XXXVII. In the fortress of Caenum Pompey
found also private documents belonging to Mithridates, and read them with no little satisfaction, since
they shed much light upon the king's character. For
there were memoranda among them from which it
was discovered that, besides many others, he had
poisoned to death his son Ariarathes, and also
Alcaeus of Sardis, because he had surpassed him in
driving race-horses. Among the writings were also in-
terpretations of dreams, some of which he himself
had dreamed, and others, some of his wives. There
were also letters from Monime to him, of a lascivious
nature, and answering letters from him to her.
Moreover, Theophanes says there was found here an
address of Rutilius, which incited the king to the
massacre of the Romans in Asia. But most people
rightly conjecture that this was a malicious in-
vention on the part of Theophanes, perhaps because
he hated Rutilius, who was wholly unlike himself,
but probably also to please Pompey, whose father had
been represented as an utter wretch by Rutilius in
his histories.

XXXVIII. From Caenum Pompey went to Amisus,
where his ambition led him into obnoxious courses.
For whereas he had roundly abused Lucullus because, while his enemy was still alive, he would

καὶ δωρεὰς ἔνεμε καὶ τιμάς, ἃ συνηρημένου πολέμου καὶ πέρας ἔχοντος εἰώθασι ποιεῖν οἱ νενικηκότες, αὐτὸς ἐν Βοσπόρῳ Μιθριδάτου κρατοῦντος
καὶ συνειλοχότος ἀξιόμαχον δύναμιν, ὡς δὴ
2 συντετελεσμένων ἁπάντων, ἔπραττε ταῦτά, διακοσμῶν τὰς ἐπαρχίας καὶ διανέμων δωρεάς,
πολλῶν μὲν ἡγεμόνων καὶ δυναστῶν, βασιλέων
δὲ δώδεκα βαρβάρων ἀφιγμένων πρὸς αὐτόν.
ὅθεν οὐδὲ ἠξίωσε τὸν Πάρθον ἀντιγράφων, ὥσπερ
οἱ λοιποί, βασιλέα βασιλέων προσαγορεῦσαι,
τοῖς ἄλλοις χαριζόμενος. αὐτὸν δέ τις ἔρως καὶ
ζῆλος εἶχε Συρίαν ἀναλαβεῖν καὶ διὰ τῆς Ἀρα-
βίας ἐπὶ τὴν ἐρυθρὰν ἐλάσαι θάλασσαν, ὡς τῷ
περιϊόντι τὴν οἰκουμένην πανταχόθεν Ὠκεανῷ
3 προσμίξειε νικῶν· καὶ γὰρ ἐν Λιβύῃ πρῶτος
ἄχρι τῆς ἐκτὸς θαλάσσης κρατῶν προῆλθε, καὶ
τὴν ἐν Ἰβηρίᾳ πάλιν ἀρχὴν ὡρίσατο Ῥωμαίοις
τῷ Ἀτλαντικῷ πελάγει, καὶ τρίτον ἔναγχος
Ἀλβανοὺς διώκων ὀλίγον ἐδέησεν ἐμβαλεῖν εἰς
τὴν Ὑρκανίαν θάλασσαν. ὡς οὖν συνάψων τῇ
ἐρυθρᾷ τὴν περίοδον τῆς στρατείας ἀνίστατο.
καὶ γὰρ ἄλλως τὸν Μιθριδάτην ἑώρα δυσθήρατον
ὄντα τοῖς ὅπλοις καὶ φεύγοντα χαλεπώτερον ἢ
μαχόμενον.

XXXIX. Διὸ τούτῳ μὲν εἰπὼν ἰσχυρότερον
ἑαυτοῦ πολέμιον τὸν λιμὸν ἀπολείψειν, ἐπέστησε
φυλακὰς τῶν νεῶν ἐπὶ τοὺς πλέοντας εἰς Βόσπορον ἐμπόρους· καὶ θάνατος ἦν ἡ ζημία τοῖς
ἁλισκομένοις. ἀναλαβὼν δὲ τῆς στρατιᾶς τὴν

issue edicts and distribute gifts and honours,—things which victors are wont to do only when a war has been brought to an end and finished,—yet he himself, while Mithridates was supreme in Bosporus and had collected a formidable force, just as though the whole struggle was ended, took the same course, regulating the provinces and distributing gifts; for many leaders and princes and twelve barbarian kings had come to him. Wherefore, to gratify these other kings, he would not deign, in answering a letter from the king of Parthia, to address him as King of Kings, which was his usual title. Moreover, a great and eager passion possessed him to recover Syria, and march through Arabia to the Red Sea,[1] in order that he might bring his victorious career into touch with the Ocean which surrounds the world on all sides; for in Africa he had been the first to carry his conquests as far as the Outer Sea, and again in Spain he had made the Atlantic Ocean the boundary of the Roman dominion, and thirdly, in his recent pursuit of the Albani, he had narrowly missed reaching the Hyrcanian Sea. In order, therefore, that he might connect the circuit of his military expeditions with the Red Sea, he put his army in motion. And, besides, he saw that it was difficult to hunt Mithridates down with an armed force, and that he was harder to deal with when he fled than when he gave battle.

XXXIX. Wherefore, remarking that he would leave behind him for this fugitive a mightier enemy than himself, to wit, famine, he stationed ships to keep guard against the merchants sailing to Bosporus; and death was the penalty for such as were caught. Then taking the great mass of his army,

---

[1] *i.e.* the Persian Gulf.

πληθὺν συχνὴν προῆγε· καὶ τῶν μετὰ Τριαρίου
πρὸς Μιθριδάτην ἀτυχῶς ἀγωνισαμένων καὶ
πεσόντων ἐντυχὼν ἀτάφοις ἔτι τοῖς νεκροῖς,
ἔθαψε λαμπρῶς καὶ φιλοτίμως ἅπαντας, ὃ δοκεῖ
παραλειφθὲν οὐχ ἥκιστα Λευκόλλῳ μίσους
2 αἴτιον γενέσθαι. χειρωσάμενος δὲ δι' Ἀφρανίου τοὺς περὶ Ἀμανὸν Ἄραβας καὶ καταβὰς
αὐτὸς εἰς Συρίαν, ταύτην μὲν ὡς οὐκ ἔχουσαν
γνησίους βασιλεῖς ἐπαρχίαν ἀπέφηνε καὶ κτῆμα
τοῦ δήμου Ῥωμαίων, τὴν δὲ Ἰουδαίαν κατε-
στρέψατο, καὶ συνέλαβεν Ἀριστόβουλον τὸν
βασιλέα. πόλεις δὲ τὰς μὲν ἔκτιζε, τὰς δὲ
ἠλευθέρου κολάζων τοὺς ἐν αὐταῖς τυράννους.
3 τὴν δὲ πλείστην διατριβὴν ἐν τῷ δικάζειν
ἐποιεῖτο, πόλεων καὶ βασιλέων ἀμφισβητήματα
διαιτῶν, ἐφ' ἃ δὲ αὐτὸς οὐκ ἐξικνεῖτο, πέμπων
τοὺς φίλους, ὥσπερ Ἀρμενίοις καὶ Πάρθοις περὶ
ἧς διεφέροντο χώρας τὴν κρίσιν ποιησαμένοις
ἐπ' αὐτῷ τρεῖς ἀπέστειλε κριτὰς καὶ διαλλακτάς.
4 μέγα μὲν γὰρ ἦν ὄνομα τῆς δυνάμεως, οὐκ ἔλαττον   64
δὲ τῆς ἀρετῆς καὶ πραότητος· ᾧ καὶ τὰ πλεῖστα
τῶν περὶ αὐτὸν ἁμαρτήματα φίλων καὶ συνήθων
ἀπέκρυπτε, κωλύειν μὲν ἢ κολάζειν τοὺς πονη-
ρευομένους οὐ πεφυκώς, αὐτὸν δὲ παρέχων τοῖς
ἐντυγχάνουσι τοιοῦτον ὥστε καὶ τὰς ἐκείνων
πλεονεξίας καὶ βαρύτητας εὐκόλως ὑπομένειν.

XL. Ὁ δὲ μέγιστον δυνάμενος παρ' αὐτῷ
Δημήτριος ἦν ἀπελεύθερος, οὐκ ἄφρων εἰς τἆλλα
νεανίας, ἄγαν δὲ τῇ τύχῃ χρώμενος· περὶ οὗ καὶ
τοιόνδε τι λέγεται. Κάτων ὁ φιλόσοφος ἔτι μὲν

216

he set out on his march, and when he came upon the
still unburied bodies of those who, led by Triarius,
had fallen in an unsuccessful combat with Mithridates,[1] he gave them all an honourable and splendid
burial. The neglect of this is thought to have been
the chief reason why Lucullus was hated by his
soldiers. After his legate Afranius had subdued for
him the Arabians about Amanus, he himself went
down into Syria,[2] and since this country had no
legitimate kings, he declared it to be a province and
possession of the Roman people; he also subdued
Judaea, and made a prisoner of Aristobulus the
king. Some cities he built up, others he set free,
chastising their tyrants. But most of his time he
spent in judicial business, settling the disputes of
cities and kings, and for those to which he himself
could not attend, sending his friends. Thus when
the Armenians and Parthians referred to him the
decision of a territorial quarrel, he sent them three
arbiters and judges. For great was the name of his
power, and not less that of his virtue and clemency.
This enabled him to hide away most of the transgressions of his friends and intimates, since he
was not fitted by nature to restrain or chastise
evil doers; but he was so helpful himself to those
who had dealings with him that they were content to endure the rapacity and severity of his
friends.

XL. The one who had most influence with him
was Demetrius, a freedman, a young man of some
intelligence otherwise, but who abused his good
fortune. The following story is told about him.
Cato the philosopher, when he was still a young man,

---

[1] Three years earlier. Cf. the *Lucullus*, xxxv. 1.
[2] In the spring of 64 B.C.

ὢν νέος, ἤδη δὲ μεγάλην ἔχων δόξαν καὶ μέγα
φρονῶν, ἀνέβαινεν εἰς Ἀντιόχειαν, οὐκ ὄντος
αὐτόθι Πομπηίου, βουλόμενος ἱστορῆσαι ˙ τὴν
2 πόλιν. αὐτὸς μὲν οὖν, ὥσπερ ἀεί, πεζὸς ἐβάδιζεν, οἱ δὲ φίλοι συνώδευον ἵπποις χρώμενοι.
κατιδὼν δὲ πρὸ τῆς πύλης ὄχλον ἀνδρῶν ἐν
ἐσθῆσι λευκαῖς καὶ παρὰ τὴν ὁδὸν ἔνθεν μὲν τοὺς
ἐφήβους, ἔνθεν δὲ τοὺς παῖδας διακεκριμένους,
ἐδυσχέραινεν οἰόμενος εἰς τιμήν τινα καὶ θεραπείαν ἑαυτοῦ μηδὲν δεομένου ταῦτα γίνεσθαι.
3 τοὺς μέντοι φίλους ἐκέλευσε καταβῆναι καὶ
πορεύεσθαι μετ' αὐτοῦ· γενομένοις δὲ πλησίον
ὁ πάντα διακοσμῶν ἐκεῖνα καὶ καθιστὰς ἔχων
στέφανον καὶ ῥάβδον ἀπήντησε, πυνθανόμενος
παρ' αὐτῶν ποῦ Δημήτριον ἀπολελοίπασι καὶ
πότε ἀφίξεται. τοὺς μὲν οὖν φίλους τοῦ Κάτωνος
γέλως ἔλαβεν, ὁ δὲ Κάτων εἰπών, "Ὢ τῆς
ἀθλίας πόλεως," παρῆλθεν, οὐδὲν ἕτερον ἀπο-
κρινάμενος.

4   Οὐ μὴν ἀλλὰ καὶ τοῖς ἄλλοις τοῦτον τὸν
Δημήτριον ἧττον ἐπίφθονον ἐποίει αὐτὸς ὁ
Πομπήιος ἐντρυφώμενος ὑπ' αὐτοῦ καὶ μὴ δυσκο-
λαίνων. λέγεται γάρ, ὅτι πολλάκις ἐν ταῖς
ὑποδοχαῖς τοῦ Πομπηίου προσμένοντος καὶ δεχο-
μένου τοὺς ἄλλους ἐκεῖνος ἤδη κατέκειτο σοβαρός,
ἔχων δι' ὤτων κατὰ τῆς κεφαλῆς τὸ ἱμάτιον.
5 οὔπω δὲ εἰς Ἰταλίαν ἐπανεληλυθὼς ἐκέκτητο
τῆς Ῥώμης τὰ ἥδιστα προάστεια καὶ τῶν ἡβη-
τηρίων τὰ κάλλιστα, καὶ κῆποι πολυτελεῖς ἦσαν
ὀνομαζόμενοι Δημητρίου· καίτοι Πομπήιος αὐτὸς
ἄχρι τοῦ τρίτου θριάμβου μετρίως καὶ ἀφελῶς
ᾤκησεν. ὕστερον δὲ Ῥωμαίοις τοῦτο δὴ τὸ καλὸν

but had already great reputation and lofty purposes, went up to Antioch,[1] at a time when Pompey was not there, wishing to inspect the city. Cato himself, the story goes, marched on foot, as always, but the friends who journeyed with him were on horseback. When he beheld before the gate of the city a throng of men in white raiment, and drawn up along the road the youths on one side, and the boys on the other, he was vexed, supposing this to be done out of deference and honour to himself, who desired nothing of the kind. However, he ordered his friends to dismount and walk with him; but when they drew near, the master of all these ceremonies met them, with a wreath on his head and a wand in his hand, and asked them where they had left Demetrius, and when he would come. The friends of Cato, accordingly, burst out laughing, but Cato said, "O the wretched city!" and passed on without any further answer.

However, Pompey himself made this Demetrius less odious to the rest by enduring his caprices without vexation. For instance, it is said that many times at his entertainments, when Pompey was awaiting and receiving his other guests, that fellow would be already reclining at table in great state, with the hood of his toga drawn down behind his ears.[2] Before his return to Italy, he had purchased the pleasantest suburbs of Rome and the most beautiful places of entertainment, and very costly gardens were called "Demetrian" after him; and yet Pompey himself, up to the time of his third triumph, had a simple and modest house. After that, it is true, when he was erecting the famous and beautiful

---

[1] Cf. *Cato the Younger*, chapter xiii.
[2] A mark of slovenliness.

καὶ περιβόητον ἀνιστὰς θέατρον, ὥσπερ ἐφόλκιόν
τι, παρετεκτήνατο λαμπροτέραν οἰκίαν ἐκείνης,
ἀνεπίφθονον δὲ καὶ ταύτην, ὥστε τὸν γενόμενον
δεσπότην αὐτῆς μετὰ Πομπήϊον εἰσελθόντα θαυμάζειν καὶ πυνθάνεσθαι ποῦ Πομπήϊος Μάγνος
ἐδείπνει. ταῦτα μὲν οὖν οὕτω λέγεται.

XLI. Τοῦ δὲ βασιλέως τῶν περὶ τὴν Πέτραν
Ἀράβων πρότερον μὲν ἐν οὐδενὶ λόγῳ τὰ Ῥωμαίων τιθεμένου, τότε δὲ δείσαντος ἰσχυρῶς
καὶ γράψαντος ὅτι πάντα πείθεσθαι καὶ ποιεῖν
ἔγνωκεν, ἐκβεβαιώσασθαι βουλόμενος αὐτοῦ τὴν
διάνοιαν ὁ Πομπήϊος ἐστράτευσεν ἐπὶ τὴν Πέτραν
οὐ πάνυ τι τοῖς πολλοῖς ἄμεμπτον στρατείαν.
2 ἀπόδρασιν γὰρ ᾤοντο τῆς Μιθριδάτου διώξεως
εἶναι, καὶ πρὸς ἐκεῖνον ἠξίουν τρέπεσθαι τὸν
ἀρχαῖον ἀνταγωνιστήν, αὖθις ἀναζωπυροῦντα
καὶ παρασκευαζόμενον, ὡς ἀπηγγέλλετο, διὰ
Σκυθῶν καὶ Παιόνων στρατὸν ἐλαύνειν ἐπὶ τὴν
Ἰταλίαν. ὁ δὲ ῥᾷον οἰόμενος αὐτοῦ καταλύσειν
τὴν δύναμιν πολεμοῦντος ἢ τὸ σῶμα λήψεσθαι
φεύγοντος, οὐκ ἐβούλετο τρίβεσθαι μάτην περὶ
τὴν δίωξιν, ἑτέρας δὲ τοῦ πολέμου παρενθήκας
ἐποιεῖτο καὶ τὸν χρόνον εἷλκεν.
3 Ἡ δὲ τύχη τὴν ἀπορίαν ἔλυσεν. οὐκέτι γὰρ
αὐτοῦ τῆς Πέτρας πολλὴν ὁδὸν ἀπέχοντος, ἤδη
δὲ τῆς ἡμέρας ἐκείνης βεβλημένου χάρακα καὶ
γυμνάζοντος ἑαυτὸν ἵππῳ παρὰ τὸ στρατόπεδον,
γραμματηφόροι προσήλαυνον ἐκ Πόντου κομί-
ζοντες εὐαγγέλια. δῆλοι δ' εὐθύς εἰσι ταῖς
αἰχμαῖς τῶν δοράτων· δάφναις γὰρ ἀναστέφονται.
τούτους ἰδόντες οἱ στρατιῶται συνετρόχαζον πρὸς 6
4 τὸν Πομπήϊον. ὁ δὲ πρῶτον μὲν ἐβούλετο τὰ

theatre which bears his name, he built close by it,
like a small boat towed behind a ship, a more splendid house than the one he had before. But even
this was not large enough to excite envy, so that
when he who succeeded Pompey as its owner entered
it, he was amazed, and inquired where Pompey the
Great used to sup. At any rate, so the story runs.

XLI. The king of the Arabians about Petra had
hitherto made no account of the Roman power, but
now he was thoroughly alarmed and wrote that he
had determined to obey and perform all commands.
Pompey, therefore, wishing to confirm him in his
purpose, marched towards Petra, an expedition
which was not a little censured by most of his
followers. For they thought it an evasion of the
pursuit of Mithridates, and demanded that he should
rather turn against that inveterate enemy, who was
again kindling the flames of war and preparing, as it
was reported, to march an army through Scythia and
Paeonia against Italy. Pompey, however, thinking
it easier to crush the king's forces when he made
war than to seize his person when he was in flight,
was not willing to wear out his own strength in a
vain pursuit, and therefore sought other employment in the interval of the war and thus protracted
the time.

But fortune resolved the difficulty. For when he
was come within a short distance of Petra, and had
already pitched his camp for that day and was
exercising himself on horseback near by, dispatch-
bearers rode up from Pontus bringing good tidings.
Such messengers are known at once by the tips of
their spears, which are wreathed with laurel. As soon
as the soldiers saw these couriers they ran in throngs
to Pompey. At first he was disposed to finish his

γυμνάσια συντελεῖν, βοώντων δὲ καὶ δεομένων
καταπηδήσας ἀπὸ τοῦ ἵππου καὶ λαβὼν τὰ
γράμματα προῄει. βήματος δὲ οὐκ ὄντος οὐδὲ
τοῦ στρατιωτικοῦ γενέσθαι φθάσαντος (ὃ ποιοῦσιν
αὐτοὶ τῆς γῆς ἐκτομὰς βαθείας λαμβάνοντες καὶ
κατ᾽ ἀλλήλων συντιθέντες), ὑπὸ τῆς τότε σπουδῆς
καὶ προθυμίας τὰ σάγματα τῶν ὑποζυγίων συμ-
5 φορήσαντες ὕψος¹ ἐξῆραν. ἐπὶ τοῦτο προβὰς
ὁ Πομπήιος ἀπήγγειλεν αὐτοῖς ὅτι Μιθριδάτης
τέθνηκε στασιάσαντος Φαρνάκου τοῦ υἱοῦ δια-
χρησάμενος αὐτόν, τὰ δὲ ἐκεῖ πάντα πράγματα
Φαρνάκης κατεκληρώσατο, καὶ ἑαυτῷ καὶ Ῥωμαίοις γέγραφε ποιούμενος.

XLII. Ἐκ τούτου τὸ μὲν στράτευμα τῇ χαρᾷ
χρώμενον, ὡς εἰκός, ἐν θυσίαις καὶ συνουσίαις
διῆγεν, ὡς ἐν τῷ Μιθριδάτου σώματι μυρίων
τεθνηκότων πολεμίων. Πομπήιος δὲ ταῖς πρά-
ξεσιν αὐτοῦ καὶ ταῖς στρατείαις κεφαλὴν ἐπιτε-
θεικὼς οὐ πάνυ ῥᾳδίως οὕτω προσδοκηθεῖσαν,
2 εὐθὺς ἀνέζευξεν ἐκ τῆς Ἀραβίας· καὶ ταχὺ τὰς
ἐν μέσῳ διεξελθὼν ἐπαρχίας εἰς Ἀμισὸν ἀφίκετο,
καὶ κατέλαβε πολλὰ μὲν δῶρα παρὰ Φαρνάκου
κεκομισμένα, πολλὰ δὲ σώματα τῶν βασιλικῶν,
αὐτὸν δὲ τὸν Μιθριδάτου νεκρὸν οὐ πάνυ γνώ-
ριμον ἀπὸ τοῦ προσώπου (τὸν γὰρ ἐγκέφαλον
ἔλαθεν ἐκτῆξαι τοὺς θεραπεύοντας)· ἀλλὰ ταῖς
οὐλαῖς ἐπεγίγνωσκον οἱ δεόμενοι τοῦ θεάματος.
3 οὐ γὰρ αὐτὸς Πομπήιος ἰδεῖν ὑπέμεινεν, ἀλλ᾽
ἀφοσιωσάμενος τὸ νεμεσητὸν εἰς Σινώπην ἀπέπεμψε. τῆς δ᾽ ἐσθῆτος, ἣν ἐφόρει, καὶ τῶν ὅπλων
τὸ μέγεθος καὶ τὴν λαμπρότητα ἐθαύμασε· καίτοι

---

¹ ὕψος Coraës and Bekker have εἰς ὕψος, after Solanus.

exercise, but at their shouts and entreaties he dismounted from his horse, took the dispatches, and led the way into camp. There was no regular tribunal, nor had there been time to erect the military substitute, which the soldiers make with their own hands by digging up large clods of earth and heaping them one upon another; but in the eager haste of the moment they piled up the pack-saddles of the beasts of burden and made an eminence of them. Pompey ascended this and announced to his soldiers that Mithridates was dead, having made away with himself because his son Pharnaces had revolted from him, and that Pharnaces had come into possession of all the power there, acting, as he wrote, in behalf ot himself and the Romans.[1]

XLII. Upon this the army, filled with joy, as was natural, gave itself up to sacrifices and entertainments, feeling that in the person of Mithridates ten thousand enemies had died. Then Pompey, having brought his achievements and expeditions to such an unexpectedly easy completion, straightway withdrew from Arabia, and passing rapidly through the intervening provinces, came to Amisus. Here he found many gifts that had been brought from Pharnaces, and many dead bodies of the royal family, and the corpse of Mithridates himself, which was not easy to recognize by the face (for the embalmers had neglected to remove the brain), but those who cared to see the body recognized it by the scars. Pompey himself could not bring himself to look upon the body, but to propitiate the divine jealousy sent it away to Sinope. He was amazed at the size and splendour of the arms and raiment which Mithridates used to wear; although the sword-belt, which

---

[1] This was in 63 B.C.

τὸν μὲν ξιφιστῆρα πεποιημένον ἀπὸ τετρακοσίων
ταλάντων Πόπλιος κλέψας ἐπώλησεν Ἀριαράθῃ,
τὴν δὲ κίταριν Γάϊος ὁ τοῦ Μιθριδάτου σύντροφος
ἔδωκε κρύφα δεηθέντι Φαύστῳ τῷ Σύλλα παιδί,
θαυμαστῆς οὖσαν ἐργασίας. ὃ τότε τὸν Πομπήϊον διέλαθε, Φαρνάκης δὲ γνοὺς ὕστερον ἐτιμωρήσατο τοὺς ὑφελομένους.

4   Διοικήσας δὲ τὰ ἐκεῖ καὶ καταστησάμενος
οὕτως ἤδη πανηγυρικώτερον ἐχρῆτο τῇ πορείᾳ.
καὶ γὰρ εἰς Μιτυλήνην ἀφικόμενος τήν τε πόλιν
ἠλευθέρωσε διὰ Θεοφάνη, καὶ τὸν ἀγῶνα τὸν
πάτριον ἐθεάσατο τῶν ποιητῶν, ὑπόθεσιν μίαν
ἔχοντα τὰς ἐκείνου πράξεις. ἡσθεὶς δὲ τῷ θεά-
τρῳ περιεγράψατο τὸ εἶδος αὐτοῦ καὶ τὸν τύπον,
ὡς ὅμοιον ἀπεργασόμενος τὸ ἐν Ῥώμῃ, μεῖζον δὲ
5   καὶ σεμνότερον. ἐν δὲ Ῥόδῳ γενόμενος πάντων
μὲν ἠκροάσατο τῶν σοφιστῶν, καὶ δωρεὰν ἑκάστῳ
τάλαντον ἔδωκε· Ποσειδώνιος δὲ καὶ τὴν ἀκρό-
ασιν ἀνέγραψεν ἣν ἔσχεν ἐπ' αὐτοῦ πρὸς Ἑρ-
μαγόραν τὸν ῥήτορα περὶ τῆς καθόλου ζητήσεως
ἀντιταξάμενος. ἐν δὲ Ἀθήναις τὰ μὲν πρὸς τοὺς
6   φιλοσόφους ὅμοια τοῦ Πομπηΐου· τῇ πόλει δὲ
ἐπιδοὺς εἰς ἐπισκευὴν πεντήκοντα τάλαντα λαμ-
πρότατος ἀνθρώπων ἤλπιζεν ἐπιβήσεσθαι τῆς
Ἰταλίας καὶ ποθῶν ὀφθήσεσθαι τοῖς οἴκοι ποθοῦ-
σιν. ᾧ δ' ἄρα πρὸς τὰ λαμπρὰ καὶ μεγάλα τῶν
ἀπὸ τῆς τύχης ἀγαθῶν ἀεί τινα κεραννύναι κακοῦ
μοῖραν ἐπιμελές ἐστι δαιμονίῳ, τοῦτο ὑποικούρει
πάλαι παρασκευάζον αὐτῷ λυπηροτέραν τὴν
7   ἐπάνοδον. ἐξύβρισε γὰρ ἡ Μουκία παρὰ τὴν

cost four hundred talents, was stolen by Publius and sold to Ariarathes, and the tiara was secretly given by Caius, the foster brother of Mithridates, to Faustus the son of Sulla, at his request; it was a piece of wonderful workmanship. All this escaped the knowledge of Pompey at the time, but Pharnaces afterwards learned of it and punished the thieves.

After arranging and settling affairs in those parts, Pompey proceeded on his journey, and now with greater pomp and ceremony. For instance, when he came to Mitylene, he gave the city its freedom, for the sake of Theophanes, and witnessed the traditional contest of the poets there, who now took as their sole theme his own exploits. And being pleased with the theatre, he had sketches and plans of it made for him, that he might build one like it in Rome, only larger and more splendid.[1] And when he was in Rhodes, he heard all the sophists there, and made each of them a present of a talent. Poseidonius has actually described the discourse which he held before him, against Hermagoras the rhetorician, on Investigation in General. At Athens, too, he not only treated the philosophers with like munificence, but also gave fifty talents to the city towards its restoration. He therefore hoped to set foot in Italy with a reputation more brilliant than that of any other man, and that his family would be as eager to see him as he was to see them. But that divine agency which always takes pains to mingle with the great and splendid gifts of fortune a certain portion of evil, had long been secretly at work preparing to make his return a very bitter one. For Mucia his wife

[1] Cf. chapter xl. 5. The theatre was opened in 55 B.C., and accommodated 40,000 persons.

ἀποδημίαν αὐτοῦ. καὶ πόρρω μὲν ὢν ὁ Πομπήϊος
κατεφρόνει τοῦ λόγου· πλησίον δὲ Ἰταλίας γενόμενος καὶ σχολάζοντι τῷ λογισμῷ μᾶλλον, ὡς
ἔοικε, τῆς αἰτίας ἁψάμενος, ἔπεμψεν αὐτῇ τὴν
ἄφεσιν, οὔτε τότε γράψας οὔθ' ὕστερον ἐφ' οἷς
ἀφῆκεν ἐξειπών· ἐν δ' ἐπιστολαῖς Κικέρωνος ἡ
αἰτία γέγραπται.

XLIII. Λόγοι δὲ παντοδαποὶ περὶ τοῦ Πομπηΐου προκατέπιπτον εἰς τὴν Ῥώμην, καὶ θόρυβος
ἦν πολύς, ὡς εὐθὺς ἄξοντος ἐπὶ τὴν πόλιν τὸ 64
στράτευμα καὶ μοναρχίας βεβαίας ἐσομένης.
Κράσσος δὲ τοὺς παῖδας καὶ τὰ χρήματα λαβὼν
ὑπεξῆλθεν, εἴτε δείσας ἀληθῶς, εἴτε μᾶλλον, ὡς
ἐδόκει, πίστιν ἀπολείπων τῇ διαβολῇ καὶ τὸν
2 φθόνον ποιῶν τραχύτερον. εὐθὺς οὖν ἐπιβὰς
Ἰταλίας ὁ Πομπήϊος καὶ συναγαγὼν εἰς ἐκκλησίαν τοὺς στρατιώτας καὶ τὰ πρέποντα
διαλεχθεὶς καὶ φιλοφρονησάμενος, ἐκέλευσε
διαλύεσθαι κατὰ πόλιν ἑκάστους καὶ τρέπεσθαι πρὸς τὰ οἰκεῖα, μεμνημένους αὖθις ἐπὶ
τὸν θρίαμβον αὐτῷ συνελθεῖν. οὕτω δὲ τῆς
στρατιᾶς σκεδασθείσης καὶ πυνθανομένων ἁπάν-
3 των πρᾶγμα συνέβη θαυμαστόν. ὁρῶσαι γὰρ
αἱ πόλεις Πομπήϊον Μάγνον ἄνοπλον καὶ μετ'
ὀλίγων τῶν συνήθων ὥσπερ ἐξ ἄλλης ἀποδημίας
διαπορευόμενον, ἐκχεόμεναι δι' εὔνοιαν καὶ προ-
πέμπουσαι μετὰ μείζονος δυνάμεως συγκατῆγον
εἰς τὴν Ῥώμην, εἴ τι κινεῖν διενοεῖτο καὶ νεωτερί-

had played the wanton during his absence. While Pompey was far away, he had treated the report of it with contempt; but when he was nearer Italy and, as it would seem, had examined the charge more at his leisure, he sent her a bill of divorce, although he neither wrote at that time, nor afterwards declared, the grounds on which he put her away; but the reason is stated in Cicero's letters.[1]

XLIII. All sorts of stories about Pompey kept travelling to Rome before him, and there was much commotion there, where it was thought that he would straightway lead his army against the city, and that a monarchy would be securely established. Crassus took his children and his money and secretly withdrew, whether it was that he was really afraid, or rather, as seemed likely, because he wished to give credibility to the calumny and make the envious hatred of Pompey more severe. Pompey, accordingly, as soon as he set foot in Italy,[2] held an assembly of his soldiers, and after he had said what fitted the occasion, and had expressed his gratitude and affection for them, he bade them disperse to their several cities and seek their homes, remembering to come together again for the celebration of his triumph. When the army had been thus disbanded and all the world had learned about it, a wonderful thing happened. When the cities saw Pompey the Great journeying along unarmed and with only a few intimate friends, as though returning from an ordinary sojourn abroad, the people streamed forth to show their good will, and escorting him on his way with a larger force, brought him with them back to Rome, where, had he purposed any revolutionary

---

[1] Not in any which are extant. In a letter to Atticus (i. 12, 3) Cicero says that Pompey's divorce of Mucia was heartily approved.   [2] In 62 B.C.

227

ζειν τότε, μηδὲν ἐκείνου δεόμενον τοῦ στρατεύματος.

XLIV. Ἐπεὶ δὲ ὁ νόμος οὐκ εἴα πρὸ τοῦ
θριάμβου παρελθεῖν εἰς τὴν πόλιν, ἔπεμψεν
ἀξιῶν εἰς τὴν βουλὴν ἀναβαλέσθαι τὰς τῶν
ὑπάτων ἀρχαιρεσίας, καὶ δοῦναι ταύτην αὐτῷ
τὴν χάριν ὅπως παρὼν Πείσωνι συναρχαιρε-
2 σιάσῃ. Κάτωνος δὲ πρὸς τὴν ἀξίωσιν ἐνστάντος
οὐκ ἔτυχε τοῦ βουλεύματος. θαυμάσας δὲ τὴν
παρρησίαν αὐτοῦ καὶ τὸν τόνον ᾧ μόνος ἐχρῆτο
φανερῶς ὑπὲρ τῶν δικαίων, ἐπεθύμησεν ἀμῶς γέ
πως κτήσασθαι τὸν ἄνδρα· καὶ δυεῖν οὐσῶν ἀδελ-
φιδῶν τῷ Κάτωνι τὴν μὲν αὐτὸς ἐβούλετο λαβεῖν
3 γυναῖκα, τὴν δὲ τῷ παιδὶ συνοικίσαι. τοῦ δὲ
Κάτωνος ὑπιδομένου τὴν πεῖραν, ὡς διαφθορὰν
οὖσαν αὐτοῦ τρόπον τινὰ δεκαζομένου διὰ τῆς
οἰκειότητος, ἥ τε ἀδελφὴ καὶ ἡ γυνὴ χαλεπῶς
ἔφερον εἰ Πομπήϊον Μάγνον ἀποτρίψεται κηδεσ-
τήν. ἐν τούτῳ δὲ βουλόμενος ὕπατον ἀποδεῖξαι
Πομπήϊος Ἀφράνιον ἀργύριον εἰς τὰς φυλὰς ἀνή-
λισκεν ὑπὲρ αὐτοῦ, καὶ τοῦτο κατιόντες εἰς τοὺς
4 Πομπηΐου κήπους ἐλάμβανον, ὥστε τὸ πρᾶγμα
περιβόητον εἶναι καὶ τὸν Πομπήϊον ἀκούειν
κακῶς, ἧς αὐτὸς ἀρχῆς ἐφ' οἷς κατώρθωσεν ὡς
μεγίστης ἔτυχε, ταύτην ὤνιον ποιοῦντα τοῖς δι'
ἀρετῆς κτήσασθαι μὴ δυναμένοις. "Τούτων
μέντοι," πρὸς τὰς γυναῖκας ὁ Κάτων ἔφησε,
"τῶν ὀνειδῶν κοινωνητέον οἰκείοις Πομπηΐου
γενομένοις." αἱ δὲ ἀκούσασαι συνέγνωσαν βέλτιον
αὐτῶν ἐκεῖνον λογίζεσθαι περὶ τοῦ πρέποντος.

changes at that time, he had no need of the army that he had disbanded.

XLIV. Now, since the law did not permit a commander to enter the city before his triumph, Pompey sent a request to the senate that they should put off the consular elections, asking them to grant him this favour in order that he might personally assist Piso in his candidacy. But Cato opposed the request, and Pompey did not get what he wished. However, Pompey admired Cato's boldness of speech and the firmness which he alone publicly displayed in defence of law and justice, and therefore set his heart on winning him over in some way or other; and since Cato had two nieces, Pompey wished to take one of them to wife himself, and to marry the other to his son. But Cato saw through the design, which he thought aimed at corrupting him and in a manner bribing him by means of marriage alliance, although his sister and his wife were displeased that he should reject Pompey the Great as a family connection. In the meantime, however, wishing to have Afranius made consul, Pompey spent money lavishly on his behalf among the tribes, and the people went down to Pompey's gardens to get it. As a consequence, the matter became notorious and Pompey was in ill repute; the office of consul was highest of all, and he himself had therefore received it as a reward for his successes, and yet he was making this office a thing to be bought by those who were unable to win it by merit. "In these reproaches, however," said Cato to the women, "we must have taken our share, if we had become allied to Pompey." And when they heard this, they agreed that his estimate of the fit and proper was better than theirs.[1]

[1] Cf. *Cato the Younger*, xxx. 1–5.

XLV. Τοῦ δὲ θριάμβου τῷ μεγέθει, καίπερ εἰς
ἡμέρας δύο μερισθέντος, ὁ χρόνος οὐκ ἐξήρκεσεν,
ἀλλὰ τῶν παρεσκευασμένων πολλὰ τῆς θέας
ἐξέπεσεν, ἑτέρας ἀποχρῶντα πομπῆς ἀξίωμα καὶ
κόσμος εἶναι. γράμμασι δὲ προηγουμένοις ἐδη-
2 λοῦτο τὰ γένη καθ᾽ ὧν ἐθριάμβευεν. ἦν δὲ τάδε·
Πόντος, Ἀρμενία, Καππαδοκία, Παφλαγονία,
Μηδία, Κολχίς, Ἴβηρες, Ἀλβανοί, Συρία, Κιλι-
κία, Μεσοποταμία, τὰ περὶ Φοινίκην καὶ Πα-
λαιστίνην, Ἰουδαία, Ἀραβία, τὸ πειρατικὸν ἅπαν
ἐν γῇ καὶ θαλάσσῃ καταπεπολεμημένον. ἐν δὲ
τούτοις φρούρια μὲν ἡλωκότα χιλίων οὐκ ἐλάττονα, πόλεις δὲ οὐ πολὺ τῶν ἐνακοσίων ἀποδέ-
ουσαι, πειρατικαὶ δὲ νῆες ὀκτακόσιαι, κατοικίαι
3 δὲ πόλεων μιᾶς δέουσαι τετταράκοντα. πρὸς δὲ
τούτοις ἔφραζε διὰ τῶν γραμμάτων ὅτι πεντακισ-
χίλιαι μὲν μυριάδες ἐκ τῶν τελῶν ὑπῆρχον, ἐκ
δὲ ὧν αὐτὸς προσεκτήσατο τῇ πόλει μυριάδας
ὀκτακισχιλίας πεντακοσίας λαμβάνουσιν, ἀνα-
φέρεται δὲ εἰς τὸ δημόσιον ταμιεῖον ἐν νομίσματι
καὶ κατασκευαῖς ἀργυρίου καὶ χρυσίου δισμύρια
τάλαντα, πάρεξ τῶν εἰς τοὺς στρατιώτας δεδο-
μένων, ὧν ὁ τοὐλάχιστον αἴρων κατὰ λόγον
4 δραχμὰς εἴληφε χιλίας πεντακοσίας. αἰχμάλωτοι δ᾽ ἐπομπεύθησαν, ἄνευ τῶν ἀρχιπειρατῶν,
υἱὸς Τιγράνου τοῦ Ἀρμενίου μετὰ γυναικὸς καὶ
θυγατρός, αὐτοῦ τε Τιγράνου τοῦ βασιλέως γυνὴ 6
Ζωσίμη, καὶ βασιλεὺς Ἰουδαίων Ἀριστόβουλος,
Μιθριδάτου δὲ ἀδελφὴ καὶ πέντε τέκνα, καὶ
Σκυθίδες γυναῖκες, Ἀλβανῶν δὲ καὶ Ἰβήρων
ὅμηροι καὶ τοῦ Κομμαγηνῶν βασιλέως, καὶ τρόπαια πάμπολλα καὶ ταῖς μάχαις ἰσάριθμα

XLV. His triumph had such a magnitude that, although it was distributed over two days, still the time would not suffice, but much of what had been prepared could not find a place in the spectacle, enough to dignify and adorn another triumphal procession. Inscriptions borne in advance of the procession indicated the nations over which he triumphed. These were: Pontus, Armenia, Cappadocia, Paphlagonia, Media, Colchis, Iberia, Albania, Syria, Cilicia, Mesopotamia, Phoenicia and Palestine, Judaea, Arabia, and all the power of the pirates by sea and land which had been overthrown. Among these peoples no less than a thousand strongholds had been captured, according to the inscriptions, and cities not much under nine hundred in number, besides eight hundred piratical ships, while thirty-nine cities had been founded. In addition to all this the inscriptions set forth that whereas the public revenues from taxes had been fifty million drachmas, they were receiving from the additions which Pompey had made to the city's power eighty-five million, and that he was bringing into the public treasury in coined money and vessels of gold and silver twenty thousand talents, apart from the money which had been given to his soldiers, of whom the one whose share was the smallest had received fifteen hundred drachmas. The captives led in triumph, besides the chief pirates, were the son of Tigranes the Armenian with his wife and daughter, Zosime, a wife of King Tigranes himself, Aristobulus, king of the Jews, a sister and five children of Mithridates, Scythian women, and hostages given by the Iberians, by the Albanians, and by the king of Commagene; there were also very many trophies, equal in number to all the battles in which Pompey

πάσαις ἃς ἢ αὐτὸς ἢ διὰ τῶν στρατηγῶν ἐνίκησε.
5 μέγιστον δὲ ὑπῆρχε πρὸς δόξαν καὶ μηδενὶ τῶν
πώποτε Ῥωμαίων γεγονός, ὅτι τὸν τρίτον θρίαμβον ἀπὸ τῆς τρίτης ἠπείρου κατήγαγεν. ἐπεὶ
τρίς γε καὶ πρότερον ἦσαν ἕτεροι τεθριαμβευκότες·
ἐκεῖνος δὲ τὸν μὲν πρῶτον ἐκ Λιβύης, τὸν δὲ δεύτερον ἐξ Εὐρώπης, τοῦτον δὲ τὸν τελευταῖον ἀπὸ
τῆς Ἀσίας εἰσαγαγὼν τρόπον τινὰ τὴν οἰκουμένην ἐδόκει τοῖς τρισὶν ὑπῆχθαι θριάμβοις.

XLVI. Ἡλικίᾳ δὲ τότε ἦν, ὡς μὲν οἱ κατὰ
πάντα τῷ Ἀλεξάνδρῳ παραβάλλοντες αὐτὸν
καὶ προσβιβάζοντες ἀξιοῦσι, νεώτερος τῶν τριάκοντα καὶ τεττάρων ἐτῶν, ἀληθείᾳ δὲ τοῖς
τετταράκοντα προσῆγεν. ὡς ὤνητό γ' ἂν ἐνταῦθα
τοῦ βίου παυσάμενος, ἄχρι οὗ τὴν Ἀλεξάνδρου
τύχην ἔσχεν· ὁ δὲ ἐπέκεινα χρόνος αὐτῷ τὰς μὲν
εὐτυχίας ἤνεγκεν ἐπιφθόνους, ἀνηκέστους δὲ τὰς
2 δυστυχίας. ἣν γὰρ ἐκ προσηκόντων αὐτὸς ἐκτή-
σατο δύναμιν ἐν τῇ πόλει, ταύτῃ χρώμενος ὑπὲρ
ἄλλων οὐ δικαίως, ὅσον ἐκείνοις ἰσχύος προσε-
τίθει τῆς ἑαυτοῦ δόξης ἀφαιρῶν, ἔλαθε ῥώμῃ
καὶ μεγέθει τῆς αὐτοῦ δυνάμεως καταλυθείς.
καὶ καθάπερ τὰ καρτερώτατα μέρη καὶ χωρία
τῶν πόλεων, ὅταν δέξηται πολεμίους, ἐκείνοις
προστίθησι τὴν αὐτῶν ἰσχύν, οὕτως διὰ τῆς
Πομπηΐου δυνάμεως Καῖσαρ ἐξαρθεὶς ἐπὶ τὴν
πόλιν, ᾧ κατὰ τῶν ἄλλων ἴσχυσε, τοῦτον ἀνέ-
τρεψε καὶ κατέβαλεν. ἐπράχθη δὲ οὕτως.
3 Λεύκολλον, ὡς ἐπανῆλθεν ἐξ Ἀσίας ὑπὸ Πομ-

had been victorious either in person or in the persons
of his lieutenants. But that which most enhanced
his glory and had never been the lot of any Roman
before, was that he celebrated his third triumph
over the third continent. For others before him
had celebrated three triumphs ; but he celebrated
his first over Libya, his second over Europe, and
this last over Asia, so that he seemed in a way
to have included the whole world in his three
triumphs.

XLVI. His age at this time, as those insist who
compare him in all points to Alexander and force
the parallel, was less than thirty-four years, though
in fact he was nearly forty.[1] How happy would it
have been for him if he had ended his life at this
point, up to which he enjoyed the good fortune of
Alexander ! For succeeding time brought him only
success that made him odious, and failure that was
irreparable. That political power which he had won
by his own legitimate efforts, this he used in the
interests of others illegally, thus weakening his own
reputation in proportion as he strengthened them,
so that before he was aware of it he was ruined by
the very vigour and magnitude of his own power.
And just as the strongest parts of a city's defences,
when they are captured by an enemy, impart to him
their own inherent strength, so it was by Pompey's
power and influence that Caesar was raised up
against the city, and Caesar overthrew and cast
down the very man by whose aid he had waxed
strong against the rest. And this was the way it
came about.

When Lucullus came back from Asia, where he

[1] In 61 B.C., when this triumph was celebrated, Pompey
was in his forty-sixth year.

πηΐου περιϋβρισμένος, αὐτίκα τε λαμπρῶς ἡ
σύγκλητος ἐδέξατο, καὶ μᾶλλον ἔτι Πομπηΐου
παραγενομένου κολούουσα τὴν δόξαν ἤγειρεν ἐπὶ
τὴν πολιτείαν. ὁ δὲ τἆλλα μὲν ἀμβλὺς ἦν ἤδη
καὶ κατέψυκτο τὸ πρακτικόν, ἡδονῇ σχολῆς καὶ
ταῖς περὶ τὸν πλοῦτον διατριβαῖς ἑαυτὸν ἐνδεδωκώς, ἐπὶ δὲ Πομπήϊον εὐθὺς ἀΐξας καὶ λαβόμενος
ἐντόνως αὐτοῦ περί τε τῶν διατάξεων ἃς ἔλυσεν
ἐκράτει, καὶ πλέον εἶχεν ἐν τῇ βουλῇ συναγωνι-
4 ζομένου Κάτωνος. ἐκπίπτων δὲ καὶ περιωθούμενος
ὁ Πομπήϊος ἠναγκάζετο δημαρχοῦσι προσφεύγειν
καὶ προσαρτᾶσθαι μειρακίοις· ὧν ὁ βδελυρώτατος
καὶ θρασύτατος Κλώδιος ἀναλαβὼν αὐτὸν ὑπέρ-
ριψε τῷ δήμῳ, καὶ παρ' ἀξίαν κυλινδούμενον ἐν
ἀγορᾷ ἔχων καὶ περιφέρων ἐχρῆτο τῶν πρὸς χάριν
ὄχλου καὶ κολακείαν γραφομένων καὶ λεγομένων
5 βεβαιωτῇ, καὶ προσέτι μισθὸν ᾔτει, ὥσπερ οὐ
καταισχύνων, ἀλλὰ εὐεργετῶν, ὃν ὕστερον ἔλαβε
παρὰ Πομπηΐου, προέσθαι Κικέρωνα, φίλον ὄντα
καὶ πλεῖστα δὴ πεπολιτευμένον ὑπὲρ αὐτοῦ.
κινδυνεύοντι γὰρ αὐτῷ καὶ δεομένῳ βοηθείας
οὐδὲ εἰς ὄψιν προῆλθεν, ἀλλὰ τοῖς ἥκουσιν
ἀποκλείσας τὴν αὔλειον ἑτέραις θύραις ᾤχετο
ἀπιών. Κικέρων δὲ φοβηθεὶς τὴν κρίσιν ὑπεξῆλθε τῆς Ῥώμης.

---

[1] Cf. chapter xxxi. 1.

had been outrageously treated by Pompey, the
senate at once gave him a splendid reception, and
after Pompey's arrival, wishing to obstruct that
leader's reputation, it urged Lucullus all the more to
take part in public life. In other matters Lucullus
was already dulled and chilled past all efficiency,
having given himself over to the pleasures of ease
and the enjoyment of his wealth; but he sprang at
once upon Pompey and by a vigorous attack won a
victory over him in the matter of those ordinances
of his own which Pompey had annulled,[1] and carried
the day in the senate with the support of Cato.
Thus worsted and hard pressed, Pompey was forced
to fly for refuge to popular tribunes and attach
himself to young adventurers. Among these the
boldest and vilest was Clodius, who took him up and
threw him down under the feet of the people, and
keeping him ignobly rolled about in the dust of the
forum, and dragging him to and fro there, he used
him for the confirmation of what was said and proposed to gratify and flatter the people. He even
went so far as to ask a reward for his services from
Pompey, as if he were helping him instead of
disgracing him, and this reward he subsequently
got in the betrayal of Cicero, who was Pompey's
friend and had done him more political favours than
any one else. For when Cicero was in danger of
condemnation and begged his aid, Pompey would
not even see him, but shut his front door upon
those who came in Cicero's behalf, and slipped away
by another. Cicero, therefore, fearing the result of
his trial, withdrew secretly from Rome.[2]

[2] Having been impeached for illegally putting Lentulus
and Cethegus to death, he went into voluntary exile in
58 B.C. See the *Cicero*, chapters xxx. and xxxi.

XLVII. Τότε δὲ Καῖσαρ ἐλθὼν ἀπὸ στρατείας ἥψατο πολιτεύματος ὃ πλείστην μὲν αὐτῷ χάριν ἐν τῷ παρόντι καὶ δύναμιν εἰσαῦθις ἤνεγκε, μέγιστα δὲ Πομπήϊον ἔβλαψε καὶ τὴν πόλιν. ὑπατείαν μὲν γὰρ μετῄει πρώτην· ὁρῶν δὲ ὅτι Κράσσου πρὸς Πομπήϊον διαφερομένου θατέρῳ προσθέμενος ἐχθρῷ χρήσεται τῷ ἑτέρῳ, τρέπεται πρὸς διαλλαγὰς ἀμφοῖν, πρᾶγμα καλὸν μὲν ἄλλως καὶ πολιτικόν, αἰτίᾳ δὲ φαύλῃ καὶ μετὰ
2 δεινότητος ὑπ' ἐκείνου συντεθὲν ἐπιβούλως. ἡ γὰρ ὥσπερ ἐν σκάφει τὰς ἀποκλίσεις ἐπανισοῦσα τῆς πόλεως ἰσχὺς εἰς ἓν συνελθοῦσα καὶ γενομένη μία τὴν πάντα πράγματα καταστασιάσασαν καὶ καταβαλοῦσαν ἀνανταγώνιστον ῥοπὴν ἐποίησεν. ὁ γοῦν Κάτων τοὺς λέγοντας ὑπὸ τῆς ὕστερον γενομένης πρὸς Καίσαρα Πομπηΐῳ διαφορᾶς ἀνατραπῆναι τὴν πόλιν ἁμαρτάνειν ἔλεγεν αἰτιω-
3 μένους τὸ τελευταῖον· οὐ γὰρ τὴν στάσιν οὐδὲ τὴν ἔχθραν, ἀλλὰ τὴν σύστασιν καὶ τὴν ὁμόνοιαν αὐτῶν τῇ πόλει κακὸν πρῶτον γενέσθαι καὶ μέγιστον. ᾑρέθη μὲν γὰρ ὕπατος Καῖσαρ· εὐθὺς δὲ θεραπεύων τὸν ἄπορον καὶ πένητα κατοικίας πόλεων καὶ νομὰς ἀγρῶν ἔγραφεν, ἐκβαίνων τὸ τῆς ἀρχῆς ἀξίωμα καὶ τρόπον τινὰ δημαρχίαν
4 τὴν ὑπατείαν καθιστάς. ἐναντιουμένου δὲ τοῦ συνάρχοντος αὐτῷ Βύβλου, καὶ Κάτωνος ἐρρω-μενέστατα τῷ Βύβλῳ παρεσκευασμένου βοηθεῖν, προαγαγὼν ὁ Καῖσαρ ἐπὶ τοῦ βήματος Πομπήϊον ἐμφανῆ καὶ προσαγορεύσας ἠρώτησεν εἰ τοὺς

XLVII. At this time Caesar had returned from his province [1] and had inaugurated a policy which brought him the greatest favour for the present and power for the future, but proved most injurious to Pompey and the city. He was a candidate for his first consulship, and seeing that, while Crassus and Pompey were at variance, if he attached himself to the one he would make an enemy of the other, he sought to reconcile them with one another, —a thing which was honourable in itself and conducive to the public good, but he undertook it for an unworthy reason and with all the cleverness of an intriguer. For those opposing forces which, as in a vessel, prevented the city from rocking to and fro, were united into one, thereby giving to faction an irresistible momentum that overpowered and overthrew everything. At all events, Cato, when men said that the state had been overturned by the quarrel which afterwards arose between Caesar and Pompey, declared that they wrongly laid the blame on what had merely happened last; for it was not their discord nor yet their enmity, but their concord and harmony which was the first and greatest evil to befall the city. Caesar was, indeed, chosen consul; but he at once paid his court to the indigent and pauper classes by proposing measures for the founding of cities and the distribution of lands, thereby lowering the dignity of his office and making the consulate a kind of tribunate. And when he was opposed by his colleague Bibulus, and Cato stood ready to support Bibulus with all his might, Caesar brought Pompey on the rostra before the people, and asked him in so many words

[1] He returned from Spain in 60 B.C. See the *Caesar*, chapters xiii. and xiv.

νόμους ἐπαινοίη· τοῦ δὲ συμφήσαντος, "Οὐκοῦν,"
εἶπεν, "ἄν τις τοὺς νόμους βιάζηται, εἰς τὸν
5 δῆμον ἀφίξῃ βοηθῶν;" "Πάνυ μὲν οὖν," ἔφη ὁ
Πομπήϊος, "ἀφίξομαι, πρὸς τοὺς ἀπειλοῦντας τὰ
ξίφη μετὰ ξίφους καὶ θυρεὸν κομίζων." τούτου
Πομπήϊος οὐδὲν οὔτε εἰπεῖν οὔτε ποιῆσαι μέχρι
τῆς ἡμέρας ἐκείνης φορτικώτερον ἔδοξεν, ὥστε
καὶ τοὺς φίλους ἀπολογεῖσθαι φάσκοντας ἐκ-
φυγεῖν αὐτὸν ἐπὶ καιροῦ τὸ ῥῆμα. τοῖς μέντοι
μετὰ ταῦτα πραττομένοις φανερὸς ἦν ἤδη παντάπασιν ἑαυτὸν τῷ Καίσαρι χρήσασθαι παραδεδω-
6 κώς. Ἰουλίαν γὰρ τὴν Καίσαρος θυγατέρα,
Καιπίωνι καθωμολογημένην καὶ γαμεῖσθαι μέλλουσαν ὀλίγων ἡμερῶν, οὐδενὸς ἂν προσδοκήσαντος ἔγημε Πομπήϊος, μείλιγμα Καιπίωνι τῆς
ὀργῆς τὴν ἑαυτοῦ θυγατέρα καταινέσας, Φαύστῳ
τῷ παιδὶ Σύλλα πρότερον ἐγγεγυημένην. αὐτὸς
δὲ Καῖσαρ ἔγημε Καλπουρνίαν τὴν Πείσωνος.

XLVIII. Ἐκ δὲ τούτου Πομπήϊος ἐμπλήσας
στρατιωτῶν τὴν πόλιν ἅπαντα τὰ πράγματα βίᾳ
κατεῖχε. Βύβλῳ τε γὰρ εἰς ἀγορὰν τῷ ὑπάτῳ
κατιόντι μετὰ Λευκόλλου καὶ Κάτωνος ἄφνω
προσπεσόντες κατέκλασαν τὰς ῥάβδους, αὐτοῦ
δέ τις κοπρίων κόφινον ἐκ κεφαλῆς τοῦ Βύβλου
κατεσκέδασε, δύο δὲ δήμαρχοι τῶν συμπροπεμ-
2 πόντων ἐτρώθησαν. οὕτω δὲ τῶν ἐνισταμένων
τὴν ἀγορὰν ἐρημώσαντες ἐπεκύρωσαν τὸν περὶ
τῆς διανομῆς τῶν χωρίων νόμον· ᾧ δελεασθεὶς ὁ
δῆμος εἰς πᾶσαν ἤδη τιθασὸς αὐτοῖς ἐγεγόνει καὶ
κατάντης πρᾶξιν, οὐδὲν πολυπραγμονῶν, ἀλλ'
ἐπιφέρων σιωπῇ τοῖς γραφομένοις τὴν ψῆφον.
3 ἐκυρώθησαν οὖν Πομπηΐῳ μὲν αἱ διατάξεις ὑπὲρ

whether he approved the proposed laws: and when Pompey said he did, "Then," said Caesar, "in case any resistance should be made to the laws, will you come to the aid of the people?" "Yes, indeed," said Pompey, "I will come, bringing, against those who threaten swords, both sword and buckler." Never up to that day had Pompey said or done anything more vulgar and arrogant, as it was thought, so that even his friends apologized for him and said the words must have escaped him on the spur of the moment. However, by his subsequent acts he made it clear that he had now wholly given himself up to do Caesar's bidding. For to everybody's surprise he married Julia, the daughter of Caesar, although she was betrothed to Caepio and was going to be married to him within a few days; and to appease the wrath of Caepio, Pompey promised him his own daughter in marriage, although she was already engaged to Faustus the son of Sulla. Caesar himself married Calpurnia, the daughter of Piso.

XLVIII. After this, Pompey filled the city with soldiers and carried everything with a high hand. As Bibulus the consul was going down into the forum with Lucullus and Cato, the crowd fell upon him and broke the fasces of his lictors, and somebody threw a basket of ordure all over the head of Bibulus himself, and two of the tribunes who were escorting him were wounded. When they had thus cleared the forum of their opponents, they passed the law concerning the distribution of lands; and the people, caught by this bait, became tame at once in their hands, and ready to support any project, not meddling at all, but silently voting for what was proposed to them. Accordingly, Pompey got those enactments of his ratified which Lucullus contested;

239

ὧν Λεύκολλος ἤριζε, Καίσαρι δὲ τὴν ἐντὸς Ἄλπεων καὶ τὴν ἐκτὸς ἔχειν Γαλατίαν καὶ Ἰλλυριοὺς
εἰς πενταετίαν καὶ τέσσαρα τάγματα τέλεια
στρατιωτῶν, ὑπάτους δὲ εἰς τὸ μέλλον εἶναι
Πείσωνα τὸν Καίσαρος πενθερὸν καὶ Γαβίνιον,
ἄνδρα τῶν Πομπηΐου κολάκων ὑπερφυέστατον.

4 Πραττομένων δὲ τούτων Βύβλος μὲν εἰς τὴν
οἰκίαν κατακλεισάμενος ὀκτὼ μηνῶν οὐ προῆλθεν
ὑπατεύων, ἀλλ᾿ ἐξέπεμπε διαγράμματα βλασφημίας ἀμφοῖν ἔχοντα καὶ κατηγορίας, Κάτων δὲ
ὥσπερ ἐπίπνους καὶ φοιβόληπτος ἐν τῇ βουλῇ
τὰ μέλλοντα τῇ πόλει καὶ τῷ Πομπηΐῳ προη-
γόρευε, Λεύκολλος δὲ ἀπειπὼν ἡσυχίαν ἦγεν ὡς
οὐκέτι πρὸς πολιτείαν ὡραῖος· ὅτε δὴ καὶ Πομπήϊος ἔφη, γέροντι τὸ τρυφᾶν ἀωρότερον εἶναι
5 τοῦ πολιτεύεσθαι. ταχὺ μέντοι καὶ αὐτὸς ἐμα-
λάσσετο τῷ τῆς κόρης ἔρωτι καὶ προσεῖχεν
ἐκείνῃ τὰ πολλὰ καὶ συνδιημέρευεν ἐν ἀγροῖς
καὶ κήποις, ἠμέλει δὲ τῶν κατ᾿ ἀγορὰν πραττομένων, ὥστε καὶ Κλώδιον αὐτοῦ καταφρονῆσαι
δημαρχοῦντα τότε καὶ θρασυτάτων ἅψασθαι
6 πραγμάτων. ἐπεὶ γὰρ ἐξέβαλε Κικέρωνα, καὶ
Κάτωνα προφάσει στρατηγίας εἰς Κύπρον ἀπέπεμψε, Καίσαρος εἰς Γαλατίαν ἐξεληλακότος,
αὐτῷ δὲ προσέχοντα τὸν δῆμον ἑώρα πάντα 64
πράττοντι καὶ πολιτευομένῳ πρὸς χάριν, εὐθὺς
ἐπεχείρει τῶν Πομπηΐου διατάξεων ἐνίας ἀναιρεῖν,
καὶ Τιγράνην τὸν αἰχμάλωτον ἀφαρπάσας εἶχε
σὺν αὑτῷ, καὶ τοῖς φίλοις δίκας ἐπῆγε, πεῖραν

Caesar received the two Gauls and Illyricum for five
years, together with four complete legions ; and it
was decided that the consuls for the ensuing year [1]
should be Piso, the father-in-law of Caesar, and
Gabinius, who was the most extravagant of Pompey's
flatterers.

While this was going on, Bibulus shut himself up
in his house and for the eight months remaining of
his consulship did not appear in public, but issued
edicts which were full of accusations and slanders
against Pompey and Caesar ; Cato, as though inspired
and possessed by a spirit of prophecy, foretold in
the senate what the future would bring to the city
and to Pompey ; while Lucullus renounced the
struggle and led a life of ease, on the plea that he
was past the age for political affairs ; whereat Pompey
remarked that for an old man luxurious living was
more unseasonable than political activity. However,
Pompey himself also soon gave way weakly to his
passion for his young wife, devoted himself for the
most part to her, spent his time with her in villas
and gardens, and neglected what was going on in
the forum, so that even Clodius, who was then a
tribune of the people, despised him and engaged in
most daring measures. For after he had driven
Cicero into banishment, and sent Cato off to Cyprus
under pretence of giving him military command,
and Caesar was gone off to Gaul, and when he saw
that the people were devoted to him because all his
political measures were undertaken to please them,
he straightway attempted to repeal some of the
arrangements which Pompey had made ; he took
away his prisoner, Tigranes, and kept him about his
own person ; and he prosecuted some of his friends,

[1] 58 B.C.

241

ἐν ἐκείνοις τῆς Πομπηΐου λαμβάνων δυνάμεως.
7 τέλος δέ, προελθόντος αὐτοῦ πρός τινα δίκην,
ἔχων ὑφ' αὑτῷ πλῆθος ἀνθρώπων ἀσελγείας καὶ
ὀλιγωρίας μεστὸν αὐτὸς μὲν εἰς ἐπιφανῆ τόπον
καταστὰς ἐρωτήματα τοιαῦτα προὔβαλλε· "Τίς
ἐστιν αὐτοκράτωρ ἀκόλαστος; τίς ἀνὴρ ἄνδρα
ζητεῖ; τίς ἑνὶ δακτύλῳ κνᾶται τὴν κεφαλήν;" οἱ
δέ, ὥσπερ χορὸς εἰς ἀμοιβαῖα συγκεκροτημένος,
ἐκείνου τὴν τήβεννον ἀνασείοντος ἐφ' ἑκάστῳ
μέγα βοῶντες ἀπεκρίναντο· "Πομπήϊος."

XLIX. Ἡνία μὲν οὖν καὶ ταῦτα Πομπήϊον
ἀήθη τοῦ κακῶς ἀκούειν ὄντα καὶ μάχης τοιαύτης
ἄπειρον· ἤχθετο δὲ μᾶλλον αἰσθανόμενος τὴν
βουλὴν ἐπιχαίρουσαν αὐτῷ προπηλακιζομένῳ καὶ
2 διδόντι δίκην τῆς Κικέρωνος προδοσίας. ἐπεὶ δὲ
καὶ πληγὰς ἐν ἀγορᾷ μέχρι τραυμάτων συνέβη
γενέσθαι, καὶ Κλωδίου τις οἰκέτης παραδιδόμενος
ἐν ὄχλῳ διὰ τῶν περιεστώτων πρὸς τὸν Πομπήϊον
ἠλέγχθη ξίφος ἔχειν, ταῦτα ποιούμενος πρόφασιν,
ἄλλως δὲ τοῦ Κλωδίου τὴν ἀσέλγειαν καὶ τὰς
βλασφημίας δεδιώς, οὐκέτι προῆλθεν εἰς ἀγορὰν
ὅσον ἐκεῖνος ἦρχε χρόνον, ἀλλ' οἰκουρῶν διετέλει
καὶ σκεπτόμενος μετὰ τῶν φίλων ὅπως ἂν ἐξα-
κέσαιτο τῆς βουλῆς καὶ τῶν ἀρίστων τὴν πρὸς
3 αὐτὸν ὀργήν. Κουλλέωνι μὲν οὖν κελεύοντι τὴν
Ἰουλίαν ἀφεῖναι καὶ μεταβαλέσθαι πρὸς τὴν
σύγκλητον ἀπὸ τῆς Καίσαρος φιλίας οὐ προσέσχε, τοῖς δὲ Κικέρωνα καταγαγεῖν ἀξιοῦσιν,
ἄνδρα καὶ Κλωδίῳ πολεμιώτατον καὶ τῇ βουλῇ
προσφιλέστατον, ἐπείσθη· καὶ προαγαγὼν τὸν

making a test of the power of Pompey by his proceedings against them. And finally, when Pompey appeared at a public trial,[1] Clodius, having at his beck and call a rabble of the lewdest and most arrogant ruffians, stationed himself in a conspicuous place and put to them such questions as these: "Who is a licentious imperator?" "What man seeks for a man?" "Who scratches his head with one finger?" And they, like a chorus trained in responsive song, as he shook his toga, would answer each question by shouting out "Pompey."

XLIX. Of course this also was annoying to Pompey, who was not accustomed to vilification and was inexperienced in this sort of warfare; but he was more distressed when he perceived that the senate was delighted to see him insulted and paying a penalty for his betrayal of Cicero. When, however, it had come to blows and even wounds in the forum, and a servant of Clodius, stealing along through the crowd of bystanders towards Pompey, was found to have a sword in his hand, Pompey made this his excuse, although he was also afraid of the insolent abuse of Clodius, and came no more into the forum as long as Clodius was tribune, but kept himself continually at home, where he was ever debating with his friends how he might appease the anger of the senate and the nobility against him. To Culleo, however, who urged him to divorce Julia and exchange the friendship of Caesar for that of the senate, he would not listen, but he yielded to the arguments of those who thought he ought to bring Cicero back, who was the greatest enemy of Clodius and most beloved in the senate, and he escorted

---

[1] The trial of Milo, in 56 B.C. Cf. Dio Cassius, xxxix. 19.

ἀδελφὸν αὐτοῦ δεόμενον σὺν χειρὶ πολλῇ, τραυμάτων ἐν ἀγορᾷ γενομένων καί τινων ἀναιρεθέν-
4 των, ἐκράτησε τοῦ Κλωδίου. καὶ νόμῳ κατελθὼν
ὁ Κικέρων τήν τε βουλὴν εὐθὺς τῷ Πομπηΐῳ
διήλλαττε, καὶ τῷ σιτικῷ νόμῳ συνηγορῶν τρόπῳ
τινὶ πάλιν γῆς καὶ θαλάττης, ὅσην ἐκέκτηντο
Ῥωμαῖοι, κύριον ἐποίει Πομπήϊον. ἐπ' αὐτῷ
γὰρ ἐγίνοντο λιμένες, ἐμπόρια, καρπῶν διαθέσεις,
ἑνὶ λόγῳ, τὰ τῶν πλεόντων πράγματα, τὰ τῶν
5 γεωργούντων. Κλώδιος δὲ ᾐτιᾶτο μὴ γεγράφθαι
τὸν νόμον διὰ τὴν σιτοδείαν, ἀλλ' ὅπως ὁ νόμος
γραφείη γεγονέναι τὴν σιτοδείαν, ὥσπερ ἐκ λιπο-
θυμίας αὐτοῦ μαραινομένην τὴν δύναμιν ἀρχῇ
νέᾳ πάλιν ἀναζωπυροῦντος καὶ ἀναλαμβάνοντος.
ἕτεροι δὲ τοῦ ὑπάτου Σπινθῆρος ἀποφαίνουσι
τοῦτο σόφισμα, κατακλείσαντος εἰς ἀρχὴν μείζονα Πομπήϊον, ὅπως αὐτὸς ἐκπεμφθῇ Πτολε-
6 μαίῳ τῷ βασιλεῖ βοηθῶν. οὐ μὴν ἀλλὰ καὶ
Κανίδιος εἰσήνεγκε δημαρχῶν νόμον, ἄνευ στρατιᾶς Πομπήϊον ἔχοντα ῥαβδούχους δύο διαλλάττειν Ἀλεξανδρεῦσι τὸν βασιλέα. καὶ Πομπήϊος
μὲν ἐδόκει τῷ νόμῳ μὴ δυσχεραίνειν, ἡ δὲ
σύγκλητος ἐξέβαλεν, εὐπρεπῶς σκηψαμένη δεδιέναι περὶ τἀνδρός. ἦν δὲ γράμμασιν ἐντυχεῖν
διερριμμένοις κατ' ἀγορὰν καὶ παρὰ τὸ βουλευτήριον ὡς δὴ Πτολεμαίου δεομένου Πομπήϊον
αὐτῷ στρατηγὸν ἀντὶ τοῦ Σπινθῆρος δοθῆναι.
7 Τιμαγένης δὲ καὶ ἄλλως τὸν Πτολεμαῖον οὐκ

---

[1] In 57 b c.

The law made Pompey *Praefectus Annonae* for five years.

Cicero's brother, who was a petitioner for his return, with a large force into the forum, where, though some were wounded and some killed, he nevertheless got the better of Clodius. And when Cicero returned to the city [1] by virtue of the law then passed, he immediately reconciled Pompey to the senate, and by his advocacy of the corn law he in a manner once more made Pompey master of all the land and sea in Roman possession. For under his direction were placed harbours, trading-places, distributions of crops,—in a word, navigation and agriculture.[2] Clodius alleged that the law had not been proposed on account of the scarcity of grain, but the scarcity of grain had arisen in order that the law might be proposed, a law whereby the power of Pompey, which was withering away, as it were, in consequence of his failing spirits, might be rekindled again and recovered in a new office. But others declare that this was a device of the consul Spinther, whose aim was to confine Pompey in a higher office, in order that he himself might be sent out to aid King Ptolemy.[3] However, Canidius, as tribune of the people, brought in a law providing that Pompey, without an army, and with two lictors only, should go out as a meditator between the king and the people of Alexandria. Pompey was thought to regard the law with no disfavour, but the senate rejected it, on the plausible pretence that it feared for his safety. Besides, writings were to be found scattered about the forum and near the senate-house, stating that it was Ptolemy's wish to have Pompey given to him as a commander instead of Spinther. And Timagenes actually says that Ptolemy left home

[3] Ptolemy had taken refuge from his dissatisfied subjects in Rome, and wished to be restored. Cf. Dio Cassius, xxxix. 12–17. He is referred to again in chapter lxxvi. 5.

οὔσης ἀνάγκης ἀπελθεῖν φησι, καὶ καταλιπεῖν
Αἴγυπτον ὑπὸ Θεοφάνους πεισθέντα πράττοντος
Πομπηΐῳ χρηματισμοὺς καὶ στρατηγίας καινῆς
ὑπόθεσιν. ἀλλὰ τοῦτο μὲν οὐχ οὕτως ἡ Θεοφάνους μοχθηρία πιθανὸν ὡς ἄπιστον ἡ Πομπηΐου
ποιεῖ φύσις, οὐκ ἔχουσα κακόηθες οὐδ' ἀνελεύθερον
οὕτω τὸ φιλότιμον.

L. Ἐπισταθεὶς δὲ τῇ περὶ τὸ σιτικὸν οἰκονομίᾳ
καὶ πραγματείᾳ, πολλαχοῦ μὲν ἀπέστειλε πρεσβευτὰς καὶ φίλους, αὐτὸς δὲ πλεύσας εἰς Σικελίαν
καὶ Σαρδόνα καὶ Λιβύην ἤθροιζε σῖτον. ἀνάγε- 64
σθαι δὲ μέλλων πνεύματος μεγάλου κατὰ θάλατταν ὄντος καὶ τῶν κυβερνητῶν ὀκνούντων, πρῶτος
ἐμβὰς καὶ κελεύσας τὴν ἄγκυραν αἴρειν ἀνεβόησε·
2 "Πλεῖν ἀνάγκη, ζῆν οὐκ ἀνάγκη." τοιαύτῃ δὲ
τόλμῃ καὶ προθυμίᾳ χρώμενος μετὰ τύχης ἀγαθῆς
ἐνέπλησε σίτου τὰ ἐμπόρια καὶ πλοίων τὴν
θάλασσαν, ὥστε καὶ τοῖς ἐκτὸς ἀνθρώποις ἐπαρ-
κέσαι τὴν περιουσίαν ἐκείνης τῆς παρασκευῆς,
καὶ γενέσθαι καθάπερ ἐκ πηγῆς ἄφθονον ἀπορ-
ροὴν εἰς πάντας.

LI. Ἐν τούτῳ δὲ τῷ χρόνῳ μέγαν ἦραν οἱ
Κελτικοὶ πόλεμοι Καίσαρα· καὶ δοκῶν πορρωτάτω τῆς Ῥώμης ἀπεῖναι καὶ συνηρτῆσθαι Βέλ-
γαις καὶ Σουήβοις καὶ Βρεττανοῖς, ἐλάνθανεν ὑπὸ
δεινότητος ἐν μέσῳ τῷ δήμῳ καὶ τοῖς κυριωτάτοις
πράγμασι καταπολιτευόμενος τὸν Πομπήϊον.
2 αὐτὸς μὲν γὰρ ὡς σῶμα τὴν στρατιωτικὴν δύναμιν περικείμενος, οὐκ ἐπὶ τοὺς βαρβάρους, ἀλλ'
ὥσπερ ἐν θήραις καὶ κυνηγεσίοις τοῖς πρὸς ἐκείνους ἀγῶσι γυμνάζων, διεπόνει, καὶ κατεσκεύαζεν
ἄμαχον καὶ φοβεράν, χρυσὸν δὲ καὶ ἄργυρον καὶ

without sufficient reason and under no necessity, and that his abandonment of Egypt was owing to the persuasions of Theophanes, who was aiming to give Pompey profitable occupation in the holding of a new command. But this is not made credible by the baseness of Theophanes as much as it is made incredible by the nature of Pompey, in which ambition was not of such a mean and base order.

L. Having thus been set over the administration and management of the grain trade, Pompey sent out his agents and friends in various directions, while he himself sailed to Sicily, Sardinia and Africa, and collected grain. When he was about to set sail with it, there was a violent storm at sea, and the ship-captains hesitated to put out; but he led the way on board and ordered them to weigh anchor, crying with a loud voice: "To sail is necessary; to live is not." By this exercise of zeal and courage attended by good fortune, he filled the sea with ships and the markets with grain, so that the excess of what he had provided sufficed also for foreign peoples, and there was an abundant overflow, as from a spring, for all.

LI. Meanwhile, his Gallic wars raised Caesar to greatness; and though he was thought to be very far removed from Rome, and to be occupied with Belgae, Suevi, and Britanni, he secretly and cleverly contrived to thwart Pompey's designs in the heart of the city and in the most important matters. For he himself, with his military force clothing him as the body does the soul, was carefully training it, not against the Barbarians merely, nay, he used its combats with these only to give it exercise, as if in hunting and the chase,—and was making it invincible and terrible; but all the while he was

τἆλλα λάφυρα καὶ τὸν ἄλλον πλοῦτον τὸν ἐκ
πολέμων τοσούτων περιγινόμενον εἰς τὴν Ῥώμην
ἀποστέλλων, καὶ διαπειρῶν ταῖς δωροδοκίαις καὶ
συγχορηγῶν ἀγορανόμοις καὶ στρατηγοῖς καὶ
ὑπάτοις καὶ γυναιξὶν αὐτῶν, ᾠκειοῦτο πολλούς·
3 ὥστε ὑπερβαλόντος αὐτοῦ τὰς Ἄλπεις καὶ δια-
χειμάζοντος ἐν Λούκῃ, τῶν μὲν ἄλλων ἀνδρῶν
καὶ γυναικῶν ἁμιλλωμένων καὶ φερομένων πολὺ
πλῆθος γενέσθαι, συγκλητικοὺς δὲ διακοσίους, ἐν
οἷς καὶ Πομπήϊος ἦν καὶ Κράσσος, ἀνθυπάτων
δὲ καὶ στρατηγῶν ἑκατὸν εἴκοσι ῥάβδους ἐπὶ
4 ταῖς Καίσαρος θύραις ὀφθῆναι. τοὺς μὲν οὖν ἄλλους ἅπαντας ἐμπλήσας ἐλπίδων καὶ χρημάτων
ἀπέστελλε, Κράσσῳ δὲ καὶ Πομπηΐῳ πρὸς αὐτὸν
ἐγένοντο συνθῆκαι, μετιέναι μὲν ὑπατείας ἐκείνους καὶ Καίσαρα συλλαμβάνειν αὐτοῖς, πέμπον-
τα τῶν στρατιωτῶν συχνοὺς ἐπὶ τὴν ψῆφον, ἐπὰν
δὲ αἱρεθῶσι τάχιστα, πράττειν μὲν ἑαυτοῖς ἐπαρχιῶν καὶ στρατοπέδων ἡγεμονίας, Καίσαρι δὲ τὰς
5 οὔσας βεβαιοῦν εἰς ἄλλην πενταετίαν. ἐπὶ τούτοις ἐξενεχθεῖσιν εἰς τοὺς πολλοὺς χαλεπῶς
ἔφερον οἱ πρῶτοι· καὶ Μαρκελλῖνος ἐν τῷ δήμῳ
καταστὰς ἀμφοῖν ἐναντίον ἠρώτησεν εἰ μετίασιν
ὑπατείαν. καὶ τῶν πολλῶν ἀποκρίνασθαι κελευόντων, πρῶτος Πομπήϊος εἶπεν ὡς τάχα μὲν ἂν
μετέλθοι, τάχα δὲ οὐκ ἂν μετέλθοι· Κράσσος δὲ
πολιτικώτερον· οὕτω γὰρ ἔφη πράξειν ὁποτέρως
6 ἂν οἴηται τῷ κοινῷ συνοίσειν. ἐπιφυομένου δὲ

sending back to Rome gold and silver and the other spoils and the rest of the wealth which came to him in abundance from his numerous wars, and by tempting people with his bribes, and contributing to the expenses of aediles, praetors, consuls, and their wives, he was winning many to his side. Therefore when he crossed the Alps and spent the winter in Luca, a great crowd of ordinary men and women gathered there in eager haste to see him, while two hundred men of senatorial rank, among whom were Pompey and Crassus, and a hundred and twenty fasces of proconsuls and praetors were seen at Caesar's door.[1] Accordingly, he filled all the rest with hopes and loaded them with money, and sent them away; but between himself, Pompey, and Crassus the following compact was made : these two were to stand for the consulship, and Caesar was to assist their candidacy by sending large numbers of his soldiers home to vote for them ; as soon as they were elected, they were to secure for themselves commands of provinces and armies, and to confirm Caesar's present provinces to him for another term of five years. When all this was publicly known, it gave displeasure to the chief men of the state, and Marcellinus rose in the assembly and asked Pompey and Crassus to their faces whether they were going to be candidates for the consulship. As the majority of the people bade them answer, Pompey did so first, and said that perhaps he would be a candidate, and perhaps he would not ; but Crassus gave a more politic answer, for he said he would take whichever course he thought would be for the advantage of the common-wealth.[2] And when Marcellinus persisted in his

---

[1] This was in 56 B.C. Cf. the *Caesar*, chapter xxi.
[2] Cf. the *Crassus*, xv. 1 f.

Πομπηΐῳ Μαρκελλίνου καὶ σφοδρῶς λέγειν δοκοῦντος, ὁ Πομπήϊος ἔφη πάντων ἀδικώτατον εἶναι τὸν Μαρκελλῖνον, ὃς χάριν οὐκ ἔχει λόγιος μὲν ἐξ ἀφώνου δι᾽ αὐτόν, ἐμετικὸς δὲ ἐκ πεινατικοῦ γενόμενος.

LII. Οὐ μὴν ἀλλὰ τῶν ἄλλων ἀποστάντων τοῦ παραγγέλλειν ὑπατείαν, Λεύκιον Δομέτιον Κάτων ἔπεισε καὶ παρεθάρρυνε μὴ ἀπειπεῖν· οὐ γὰρ ὑπὲρ ἀρχῆς, ἀλλ᾽ ὑπὲρ ἐλευθερίας εἶναι τὸν ἀγῶνα πρὸς τοὺς τυράννους. οἱ δὲ περὶ τὸν Πομπήϊον φοβηθέντες τὸν τόνον τοῦ Κάτωνος, μὴ τὴν βουλὴν ἔχων ἅπασαν ἀποσπάσῃ καὶ μεταβάλῃ τοῦ δήμου τὸ ὑγιαῖνον, οὐκ εἴασαν εἰς ἀγο-
2 ρὰν κατελθεῖν τὸν Δομέτιον, ἀλλ᾽ ἐπιπέμψαντες ἐνόπλους ἄνδρας ἀπέκτειναν μὲν τὸν προηγούμενον λυχνοφόρον, ἐτρέψαντο δὲ τοὺς ἄλλους· ἔσχατος δὲ Κάτων ἀνεχώρησε, τρωθεὶς τὸν δεξιὸν πῆχυν ἀμυνόμενος πρὸ τοῦ Δομετίου.

Τοιαύτῃ δὲ ὁδῷ παρελθόντες ἐπὶ τὴν ἀρχὴν οὐδὲ τἆλλα κοσμιώτερον ἔπραττον. ἀλλὰ πρῶτον μὲν τὸν Κάτωνα τοῦ δήμου στρατηγὸν αἱρουμένου καὶ τὴν ψῆφον ἐπιφέροντος, Πομπήϊος ἔλυσε τὴν ἐκκλησίαν οἰωνοὺς αἰτιώμενος, ἀντὶ δὲ Κάτωνος Βατίνιον ἀνηγόρευσαν, ἀργυρίῳ τὰς
3 φυλὰς διαφθείραντες. ἔπειτα νόμους διὰ Τρεβωνίου δημαρχοῦντος εἰσέφερον, Καίσαρι μέν, ὥσπερ ὡμολόγητο, δευτέραν ἐπιμετροῦντας πεντα-ετίαν, Κράσσῳ δὲ Συρίαν καὶ τὴν ἐπὶ Πάρθους στρατείαν διδόντας, αὐτῷ δὲ Πομπηΐῳ Λιβύην ἅπασαν καὶ Ἰβηρίαν ἑκατέραν καὶ τέσσαρα τάγματα στρατιωτῶν, ὧν ἐπέχρησε δύο Καίσαρι
4 δεηθέντι πρὸς τὸν ἐν Γαλατίᾳ πόλεμον. ἀλλὰ Κράσσος μὲν ἐξῆλθεν εἰς τὴν ἐπαρχίαν ἀπαλ-

attack upon Pompey and was thought to be making a strong speech, Pompey remarked that Marcellinus was of all men most unjust, since he was not grateful to him for making him eloquent instead of speechless, and full to vomiting instead of famished.

LII. However, though all the rest declined to be candidates for the consulship, Cato encouraged and persuaded Lucius Domitius not to desist, for the struggle with the tyrants, he said, was not for office, but for liberty. But Pompey and his partisans, seeing the firmness of Cato, and fearing lest, having all the senate with him, he should draw away and pervert the sound-minded among the people, would not suffer Domitius to go down into the forum, but sent armed men and slew the link-bearer who was leading his company, and put the rest to flight; Cato was the last to retire, after being wounded in the right arm while he was fighting to defend Domitius.

By such a path they made their way into the office they sought, nor even then did they behave more decently. But first of all, while the people were casting their votes for the election of Cato to the praetorship, Pompey dissolved the assembly, alleging an inauspicious omen, and after corrupting the tribes with money, they proclaimed Vatinius praetor instead of Cato. Then, by means of Trebonius, a tribune, they introduced laws which, according to the agreement, continued his provinces to Caesar for a second term of five years, gave Crassus Syria and the expedition against the Parthians, and to Pompey himself the whole of Africa, both Spains, and four legions; of these he lent two to Caesar, at his request, for the war in Gaul. But although Crassus went out to his province at the expiration of

λαγεὶς τῆς ὑπατείας, Πομπήιος δὲ τὸ θέατρον
ἀναδείξας ἀγῶνας ἦγε γυμνικοὺς καὶ μουσικοὺς
ἐπὶ τῇ καθιερώσει, καὶ θηρῶν ἁμίλλας ἐν οἷς
πεντακόσιοι λέοντες ἀνῃρέθησαν, ἐπὶ πᾶσι δὲ τὴν
ἐλεφαντομαχίαν, ἐκπληκτικώτατον θέαμα, παρέσχεν.

LIII. Ἐπὶ τούτοις δὲ θαυμαστωθεὶς καὶ ἀγα-
πηθείς, αὖθις οὐκ ἐλάττονα φθόνον ἔσχεν, ὅτι
πρεσβευταῖς φίλοις παραδοὺς τὰ στρατεύματα
καὶ τὰς ἐπαρχίας, αὐτὸς ἐν τοῖς περὶ τὴν Ἰταλίαν
ἡβητηρίοις, μετιὼν ἄλλοτε ἀλλαχόσε, μετὰ τῆς
γυναικὸς διῆγεν, εἴτε ἐρῶν αὐτῆς, εἴτε ἐρῶσαν
οὐχ ὑπομένων ἀπολιπεῖν· καὶ γὰρ καὶ τοῦτο
2 λέγεται. καὶ περιβόητον ἦν τῆς κόρης τὸ φίλαν-
δρον, οὐ καθ᾽ ὥραν ποθούσης τὸν Πομπήιον, ἀλλ᾽
αἴτιον ἔοικεν ἥ τε σωφροσύνη τοῦ ἀνδρὸς εἶναι
μόνην γινώσκοντος τὴν γεγαμημένην, ἥ τε σεμ-
νότης οὐκ ἄκρατον, ἀλλ᾽ εὔχαριν ἔχουσα τὴν
ὁμιλίαν καὶ μάλιστα γυναικῶν ἀγωγόν, εἰ δεῖ
μηδὲ Φλώραν ἁλῶναι τὴν ἑταίραν ψευδομαρτυ-
3 ριῶν. ἐν δ᾽ οὖν ἀγορανομικοῖς ἀρχαιρεσίοις εἰς
χεῖράς τινων ἐλθόντων καὶ φονευθέντων περὶ
αὐτὸν οὐκ ὀλίγων ἀναπλησθεὶς αἵματος ἤλλαξε
τὰ ἱμάτια. πολλοῦ δὲ θορύβου καὶ δρόμου πρὸς
τὴν οἰκίαν γενομένου τῶν κομιζόντων τὰ ἱμάτια
θεραπόντων, ἔτυχε μὲν ἡ κόρη κύουσα, θεασαμένη
δὲ καθηγμαγμένην τὴν τήβεννον ἐξέλιπε καὶ μόλις
ἀνήνεγκεν, ἐκ δὲ τῆς ταραχῆς ἐκείνης καὶ τοῦ
4 πάθους ἀπήμβλωσεν. ὅθεν οὐδὲ οἱ μάλιστα
μεμφόμενοι τὴν πρὸς Καίσαρα Πομπηίου φιλίαν
ᾐτιῶντο τὸν ἔρωτα τῆς γυναικός. αὖθις μέντοι
κυήσασα καὶ τεκοῦσα θῆλυ παιδίον ἐκ τῶν

his consulship,[1] Pompey opened his theatre and held
gymnastic and musical contests at its dedication,
and furnished combats of wild beasts in which five
hundred lions were killed, and above all, an elephant
fight, a most terrifying spectacle.

LIII. All this won him admiration and affection;
but on the other hand he incurred a corresponding
displeasure, because he handed over his provinces
and his armies to legates who were his friends, while
he himself spent his time with his wife among the
pleasure-places of Italy, going from one to another,
either because he loved her, or because she loved
him so that he could not bear to leave her; for this
reason too is given. Indeed, the fondness of the
young woman for her husband was notorious, although the mature age of Pompey did not invite
such devotion. The reason for it, however, seems
to have lain in the chaste restraint of her husband,
who knew only his wedded wife, and in the dignity
of his manners, which were not severe, but full of
grace, and especially attractive to women, as even
Flora the courtesan may be allowed to testify. It
once happened that at an election of aediles people
came to blows, and many were killed in the vicinity
of Pompey and he was covered with their blood, so
that he changed his garments. His servants carried
these garments to his house with much confusion
and haste, and his young wife, who chanced to be
with child, at sight of the blood-stained toga, fainted
away and with difficulty regained her senses, and in
consequence of the shock and her sufferings, mis-
carried. Thus it came to pass that even those who
found most fault with Pompey's friendship for Caesar
could not blame him for the love he bore his wife.
However, she conceived again and gave birth to a

[1] In 54 B.C.

ὠδίνων ἐτελεύτησε, καὶ τὸ παιδίον οὐ πολλὰς
ἡμέρας ἐπέζησε. παρεσκευασμένου δὲ τοῦ Πομπηΐου τὸ σῶμα θάπτειν ἐν Ἀλβανῷ, βιασάμενος
ὁ δῆμος εἰς τὸ Ἄρειον πεδίον κατήνεγκεν, οἴκτῳ
τῆς κόρης μᾶλλον ἢ Πομπηΐῳ καὶ Καίσαρι
5 χαριζόμενος.   αὐτῶν δὲ ἐκείνων μεῖζον ἐδόκει
μέρος ἀπόντι Καίσαρι νέμειν ὁ δῆμος ἢ Πομπηΐῳ
παρόντι τῆς τιμῆς.   εὐθὺς γὰρ ἐκύμαινεν ἡ πόλις,
καὶ πάντα τὰ πράγματα σάλον εἶχε καὶ λόγους
διαστατικούς, ὡς ἡ πρότερον παρακαλύπτουσα
μᾶλλον ἢ κατείργουσα τῶν ἀνδρῶν τὴν φιλαρχίαν
6 οἰκειότης ἀνῄρηται. μετ' οὐ πολὺ δὲ καὶ Κράσσος
ἐν Πάρθοις ἀπολωλὼς ἠγγέλλετο· καὶ τοῦτο
κώλυμα ὂν μέγα τοῦ συμπεσεῖν τὸν ἐμφύλιον
πόλεμον ἐκποδὼν ἐγεγόνει· δεδιότες γὰρ ἐκεῖνον
ἀμφότεροι τοῖς πρὸς ἀλλήλους ἁμῶς γε πως
ἐνέμενον δικαίοις. ἐπεὶ δὲ ἀνεῖλεν ἡ τύχη τὸν
ἔφεδρον τοῦ ἀγῶνος, εὐθὺς ἦν εἰπεῖν τὸ κωμι-
κόν, ὡς

ἅτερος πρὸς τὸν ἕτερον
ὑπαλείφεται τὼ χεῖρέ θ' ὑποκονίεται.

7 οὕτως ἡ τύχη μικρόν ἐστι πρὸς τὴν φύσιν. οὐ
γὰρ ἀποπίμπλησιν αὐτῆς τὴν ἐπιθυμίαν, ὅπου
τοσοῦτον βάθος ἡγεμονίας καὶ μέγεθος εὐρυ-
χωρίας δυοῖν ἀνδροῖν οὐκ ἐπέσχεν, ἀλλ' ἀκού-
οντες καὶ ἀναγινώσκοντες ὅτι "τριχθὰ δὲ πάντα
δέδασται" τοῖς θεοῖς, "ἕκαστος δ' ἔμμορε τιμῆς,"

female child, but died from the pains of travail, and the child survived her only a few days. Pompey made preparations to bury her body at his Alban villa, but the people took it by force and carried it down to the Campus Martius for burial, more out of pity for the young woman than as a favour to Pompey and Caesar. But of these two, it was thought that the people gave a larger share of the honour to Caesar, who was absent, than to Pompey, who was present. For the city became at once a tossing sea, and everywhere surging tumult and discordant speeches prevailed, since the marriage alliance which had hitherto veiled rather than restrained the ambition of the two men was now at an end. After a short time, too, tidings came that Crassus had lost his life in Parthia, and so what had been a great hindrance to the breaking out of civil war was removed; for through fear of him both Pompey and Caesar had somehow or other continued to treat one another fairly. But when fortune had removed the third champion who waited to compete with the victor in their struggle, at once the comic poet's words were apt, and

> " each wrestler against the other
> Anoints himself with oil and smears his hands
>   with dust." [1]

So slight a thing is fortune when compared with human nature; for she cannot satisfy its desires, since all that extent of empire and magnitude of wide-stretching domain could not suffice for two men. They had heard and read that the gods [2] " divided the universe into three parts, and each got his share of power," and yet they did not think

[1] Cf. Kock, *Com. Graec. Frag.* iii. p. 484.
[2] Zeus, Poseidon, and Pluto; *Iliad*, xv. 189.

ἑαυτοῖς οὐκ ἐνόμιζον ἀρκεῖν δυσὶν οὖσι τὴν Ῥωμαίων ἀρχήν.

LIV. Καίτοι Πομπήϊος εἶπέ ποτε δημηγορῶν
ὅτι πᾶσαν ἀρχὴν λάβοι πρότερον ἢ προσεδόκησε
καὶ κατάθοιτο θᾶττον ἢ προσεδοκήθη. καὶ νὴ
Δία μαρτυρούσας εἶχεν ἀεὶ τὰς διαλύσεις τῶν
στρατοπέδων. τότε δὲ τὸν Καίσαρα δοκῶν οὐ
προήσεσθαι τὴν δύναμιν ἐζήτει ταῖς πολιτικαῖς
ἀρχαῖς ὀχυρὸς εἶναι πρὸς αὐτόν, ἄλλο δὲ οὐδὲν
ἐνεωτέριζεν, οὐδὲ ἐβούλετο δοκεῖν ἀπιστεῖν, ἀλλ᾽
2 ὑπερορᾶν μᾶλλον καὶ καταφρονεῖν. ἐπεὶ δὲ τὰς
ἀρχὰς οὐ κατὰ γνώμην ἑώρα βραβευομένας,
δεκαζομένων τῶν πολιτῶν, ἀναρχίαν ἐν τῇ πόλει
περιεῖδε γενομένην· καὶ λόγος εὐθὺς ἐχώρει πολὺς
ὑπὲρ δικτάτορος, ὃν πρῶτος εἰς μέσον ἐξενεγκεῖν
ἐτόλμησε Λουκίλλιος ὁ δήμαρχος, τῷ δήμῳ
παραινῶν ἑλέσθαι δικτάτορα Πομπήϊον. ἐπι-
λαβομένου δὲ Κάτωνος οὗτος μὲν ἐκινδύνευσε
τὴν δημαρχίαν ἀποβαλεῖν, ὑπὲρ δὲ Πομπηΐου
πολλοὶ τῶν φίλων ἀπελογοῦντο παριόντες ὡς οὐ
δεομένου τῆς ἀρχῆς ἐκείνης οὐδὲ βουλομένου.
3 Κάτωνος δὲ Πομπήϊον ἐπαινέσαντος καὶ προ-
τρεψαμένου τῆς εὐκοσμίας ἐπιμεληθῆναι, τότε
μὲν αἰδεσθεὶς ἐπεμελήθη, καὶ κατεστάθησαν
ὕπατοι Δομέτιος καὶ Μεσσάλας, ὕστερον δὲ πάλιν
ἀναρχίας γινομένης καὶ πλειόνων ἤδη τὸν περὶ
τοῦ . δικτάτορος λόγον ἐγειρόντων ἰταμώτερον,
φοβηθέντες οἱ περὶ Κάτωνα μὴ βιασθῶσιν,
ἔγνωσαν ἀρχήν τινα τῷ Πομπηΐῳ προέμενοι

the Roman dominion enough for themselves, who were but two.

LIV. Still, Pompey once said in addressing the people that he had received every office earlier than he had expected, and had laid it down more quickly than others had expected. And in truth his disbanding of his armies was a perpetual witness to the truth of his words. But at this time he thought that Caesar was not going to dismiss his forces, and therefore sought to make himself strong against him by means of magistracies in the city. Beyond this, however, he attempted no revolutionary changes, nor did he wish to be thought to distrust Caesar, but rather to neglect and despise him. But when he saw that the magistracies were not bestowed according to his wishes, because the citizens were bribed, he suffered an anarchy to arise in the city;[1] and forthwith there was prevalent much talk in favour of a dictator, which Lucilius the popular tribune first ventured to make public, when he advised the people to elect Pompey dictator. But Cato attacked him, and Lucilius came near losing his tribunate, and many of Pompey's friends came forward in defence of him, declaring that he neither asked nor desired that office. And when Cato applauded Pompey and urged him to devote himself to the cause of law and order, for the time being he did so, out of shame, and Domitius and Messala were installed in the consulship[2]; but afterwards an anarchy arose again, and more people now agitated the question of a dictatorship more boldly. Therefore Cato and his party, fearing lest they should be overborne, determined to allow Pompey a certain

---

[1] That is, no consuls were elected.
[2] In 53 B.C., seven months after the regular time.

νόμιμον ἀποτρέψαι τῆς ἀκράτου καὶ τυραννικῆς
4 ἐκείνης. καὶ Βύβλος ἐχθρὸς ὢν Πομπηΐῳ πρῶτος
ἀπεφήνατο γνώμην ἐν συγκλήτῳ Πομπήϊον μόνον
ἑλέσθαι ὕπατον· ἢ γὰρ ἀπαλλαγήσεσθαι τῆς
παρούσης τὴν πόλιν ἀκοσμίας, ἢ δουλεύσειν τῷ
κρατίστῳ. φανέντος δὲ παραδόξου τοῦ λόγου
διὰ τὸν εἰπόντα, Κάτων ἀναστὰς καὶ παρασχὼν
δόκησιν ὡς ἀντιλέξοι, γενομένης σιωπῆς εἶπε
τὴν προκειμένην γνώμην αὐτὸς μὲν οὐκ ἂν εἰσενεγκεῖν, εἰσενηνεγμένη δὲ ὑφ' ἑτέρου πείθεσθαι
κελεύειν, πᾶσαν μὲν ἀρχὴν μᾶλλον αἱρούμενος
ἀναρχίας, Πομπηΐου δὲ μηδένα βέλτιον ἄρξειν
5 ἐν ταραχαῖς τηλικαύταις νομίζων. δεξαμένης δὲ
τῆς βουλῆς, καὶ ψηφισαμένης ὅπως ὕπατος
αἱρεθεὶς ὁ Πομπήϊος ἄρχοι μόνος, εἰ δὲ αὐτὸς
συνάρχοντος δεηθείη, μὴ θᾶττον δυοῖν μηνοῖν
δοκιμάσας ἕλοιτο, κατασταθεὶς οὕτως καὶ ἀποδειχθεὶς διὰ Σουλπικίου μεσοβασιλέως ὕπατος
ἠσπάζετο φιλοφρόνως τὸν Κάτωνα, πολλὴν ὁμο-
λογῶν χάριν ἔχειν καὶ παρακαλῶν γίνεσθαι
6 σύμβουλον ἰδίᾳ τῆς ἀρχῆς. Κάτων δὲ χάριν μὲν
ἔχειν αὐτῷ τὸν Πομπήϊον οὐκ ἠξίου· δι' ἐκεῖνον
γὰρ ὧν εἶπεν οὐδὲν εἰπεῖν, διὰ δὲ τὴν πόλιν·
ἔσεσθαι δὲ σύμβουλος ἰδίᾳ παρακαλούμενος, ἐὰν
δὲ μὴ παρακαλῆται, δημοσίᾳ φράσειν τὸ φαινόμενον. τοιοῦτος μὲν οὖν Κάτων ἐν πᾶσι.

---

[1] In 52 B.C.

legalized office, and so to divert him from the un-
mixed tyranny of a dictatorship. Consequently,
Bibulus, who was an enemy of Pompey, was first to
propose in the senate that Pompey be chosen sole
consul; for thus, he said, the city would either be
set free from the prevailing disorder, or would
become the slave of its strongest man. The proposal seemed strange, considering the man who
made it; but Cato rose, leading everybody to think
that he was going to speak against it, and when
silence was made, said that he himself would not
have introduced the proposed measure, but that
since it had been introduced by another, he urged
its adoption, because he preferred any government
whatever to no government at all, and thought that
no one would govern better than Pompey in a time
of such disorder. The senate accepted the measure,
and decreed that Pompey, if elected consul, should
govern alone, but that if he himself desired a colleague, he might choose whom he thought fit after
two months had fully expired. Having in this way
been made consul [1] and so declared by Sulpicius,
the Interrex,[2] Pompey addressed himself in a
friendly manner to Cato, acknowledging that he
was much indebted to him, and inviting him to
give advice in a private capacity on the conduct of
the government. But Cato would not admit that
Pompey was indebted to him, declaring that none
of his words had been spoken in the interests of
Pompey, but in the interests of the city; and that
he would give him advice in a private capacity if he
were invited, and in case he should not be invited,
would publicly make known his opinion. Such,
indeed, was Cato in everything.

[2] One who held supreme power in the absence of regularly
elected consuls.

259

LV. Πομπήϊος δὲ παρελθὼν εἰς τὴν πόλιν
ἔγημε Κορνηλίαν θυγατέρα Μετέλλου Σκηπίωνος,
οὐ παρθένον, ἀλλὰ χήραν ἀπολελειμμένην νεωστὶ
Ποπλίου τοῦ Κράσσου παιδός, ᾧ συνῴκησεν ἐκ
παρθενίας, ἐν Πάρθοις τεθνηκότος. ἐνῆν δὲ τῇ
κόρῃ πολλὰ φίλτρα δίχα τῶν ἀφ' ὥρας. καὶ γὰρ
περὶ γράμματα καλῶς ἤσκητο καὶ περὶ λύραν
καὶ γεωμετρίαν, καὶ λόγων φιλοσόφων εἴθιστο
2 χρησίμως ἀκούειν. καὶ προσῆν τούτοις ἦθος
ἀηδίας καὶ περιεργίας καθαρόν, ἃ δὴ νέαις προσ-
τρίβεται γυναιξὶ τὰ τοιαῦτα μαθήματα· πατὴρ
δὲ καὶ γένους ἕνεκα καὶ δόξης ἄμεμπτος. ἀλλ'
ὅμως τοῦ γάμου τοῖς μὲν οὐκ ἤρεσκε τὸ μὴ καθ'
ἡλικίαν· υἱῷ γὰρ αὐτοῦ συνοικεῖν ὥραν εἶχεν ἡ
3 Κορνηλία μᾶλλον· οἱ δὲ κομψότεροι τὸ τῆς
πόλεως ἡγοῦντο παρεωρακέναι τὸν Πομπήϊον ἐν
τύχαις οὔσης, ὧν ἐκεῖνον ἰατρὸν ᾕρηται καὶ μόνῳ
παραδέδωκεν αὐτήν· ὁ δὲ στεφανοῦται καὶ θύει
γάμους, αὐτὴν τὴν ὑπατείαν ὀφείλων ἡγεῖσθαι
συμφοράν, οὐκ ἂν οὕτω παρανόμως δοθεῖσαν 6
4 εὐτυχούσης τῆς πατρίδος. ἐπεὶ δὲ ταῖς δίκαις
τῶν δωροδοκιῶν καὶ δεκασμῶν ἐπιστάς, καὶ
νόμους γράψας καθ' οὓς αἱ κρίσεις ἐγίνοντο, τὰ
μὲν ἄλλα σεμνῶς ἐβράβευε καὶ καθαρῶς, ἀσφάλειαν ἅμα καὶ κόσμον καὶ ἡσυχίαν αὐτοῦ προσ-
καθημένου μεθ' ὅπλων τοῖς δικαστηρίοις παρέχων,
Σκηπίωνος δὲ τοῦ πενθεροῦ κρινομένου, μεταπεμψάμενος οἴκαδε τοὺς ἑξήκοντα καὶ τριακοσίους
δικαστὰς ἐνέτυχε βοηθεῖν, ὁ δὲ κατήγορος ἀπέστη
τῆς δίκης ἰδὼν τὸν Σκηπίωνα προπεμπόμενον

LV. Pompey now entered the city, and married
Cornelia, a daughter of Metellus Scipio. She was
not a virgin, but had lately been left a widow by
Publius, the son of Crassus, whose virgin bride she
had been before his death in Parthia. The young
woman had many charms apart from her youthful
beauty. She was well versed in literature, in playing
the lyre, and in geometry, and had been accustomed
to listen to philosophical discourses with profit. In
addition to this, she had a nature which was free
from that unpleasant officiousness which such ac-
complishments are apt to impart to young women ;
and her father's lineage and reputation were above
reproach. Nevertheless, the marriage was displeasing
to some on account of the disparity in years ; for
Cornelia's youth made her a fitter match for a son
of Pompey. Those, too, who were more critical,
considered that Pompey was neglectful of the un-
happy condition of the city, which had chosen him
as her physician and put herself in his sole charge ;
whereas he was decking himself with garlands and
celebrating nuptials, though he ought to have regarded his very consulship as a calamity, since it
would not have been given him in such an illegal
manner had his country been prosperous. Moreover,
although he presided over the suits for corruption
and bribery, and introduced laws for the conduct
of the trials, and in all other cases acted as
arbiter with dignity and fairness, making the
court-rooms safe, orderly, and quiet by his presence
there with an armed force, still, when Scipio, his
father-in-law, was put on trial, he summoned the
three hundred and sixty jurors to his house and
solicited their support, and the prosecutor abandoned
the case when he saw Scipio conducted from the

ἐξ ἀγορᾶς ὑπὸ τῶν δικαστῶν, πάλιν οὖν ἤκουε
5 κακῶς, ἔτι δὲ μᾶλλον ὅτι λύσας νόμῳ τοὺς γινο-
μένους περὶ τῶν κρινομένων ἐπαίνους, αὐτὸς
εἰσῆλθε Πλάγκον ἐπαινεσόμενος. καὶ Κάτων
(ἔτυχε γὰρ κρίνων) ἐπισχόμενος τὰ ὦτα ταῖς
χερσὶν οὐκ ἔφη καλῶς ἔχειν αὐτῷ παρὰ τὸν
6 νόμον ἀκούειν τῶν ἐπαίνων. ὅθεν ὁ μὲν Κάτων
ἀπεβλήθη πρὸ τοῦ φέρειν τὴν ψῆφον, ἑάλω δὲ
ταῖς ἄλλαις ὁ Πλάγκος σὺν αἰσχύνῃ τοῦ Πομπηΐου. καὶ γὰρ ὀλίγαις ὕστερον ἡμέραις Ὑψαῖος,
ἀνὴρ ὑπατικός, δίκην φεύγων καὶ παραφυλάξας
τὸν Πομπήϊον ἐπὶ δεῖπνον ἀπιόντα λελουμένον,
ἱκέτευε τῶν γονάτων λαβόμενος. ὁ δὲ παρῆλθεν
ὑπεροπτικῶς εἰπὼν διαφθείρειν τὸ δεῖπνον αὐτόν,
ἄλλο δὲ μηδὲν περαίνειν. οὕτως οὖν ἄνισος εἶναι
7 δοκῶν αἰτίας εἶχε. τὰ δ' ἄλλα καλῶς ἅπαντα
κατέστησεν εἰς τάξιν, καὶ προσείλετο συνάρχοντα
τὸν πενθερὸν εἰς τοὺς ὑπολοίπους πέντε μῆνας.
ἐψηφίσθη δὲ αὐτῷ τὰς ἐπαρχίας ἔχειν εἰς ἄλλην
τετραετίαν, καὶ χίλια τάλαντα λαμβάνειν καθ᾽
ἕκαστον ἐνιαυτόν, ἀφ᾽ ὧν θρέψει καὶ διοικήσει
τὸ στρατιωτικόν.

LVI. Οἱ δὲ Καίσαρος φίλοι ταύτην ἀρχὴν
λαβόντες ἠξίουν τινὰ γενέσθαι καὶ Καίσαρος
λόγον, ἀγωνιζομένου τοσούτους ἀγῶνας ὑπὲρ τῆς
ἡγεμονίας· ἢ γὰρ ὑπατείας ἄξιον εἶναι τυχεῖν
ἑτέρας, ἢ προσλαβεῖν τῇ στρατείᾳ χρόνον, ἐν ᾧ
τῶν πεπονημένων οὐκ ἄλλος ἐπελθὼν ἀφαιρή-
σεται τὴν δόξαν, ἀλλ᾽ αὐτὸς ἄρξει καὶ τιμήσεται
2 καθ᾽ ἡσυχίαν ὁ κατεργασάμενος. οὔσης δὲ περὶ

forum by the jurors. Once more, therefore, Pompey was in ill repute, and this was still further increased because, although he had put a stop by law to encomiums on persons under trial, he himself came into court to pronounce an encomium on Plancus. Cato, who happened to be one of the jurors, clapped his hands to his ears and said it was not right for him, contrary to the law, to listen to encomiums. Cato was therefore set aside before he could cast his vote, but Plancus was convicted by the other votes, to the disgrace of Pompey. For, a few days afterwards, Hypsaeus, a man of consular dignity, who was under prosecution, lay in wait for Pompey as he was returning from his bath for supper, clasped his knees, and supplicated his favour; but Pompey passed along contemptuously, telling him that, except for spoiling his supper, he was accomplishing nothing. In this way he got the reputation of being partial, and was blamed for it. Everything else, however, he succeeded in bringing into good order, and chose his father-in-law as his colleague for the remaining five months of the year. It was also decreed that he should retain his provinces for another four years, and receive a thousand talents yearly, out of which he was to feed and maintain his soldiers.

LVI. But the friends of Caesar took occasion from this to demand that some consideration be shewn for Caesar also, who was waging so many contests in behalf of the Roman supremacy; they said he deserved either another consulship, or the prolongation of his command, so that no one else might succeed to his labours and rob him of the glory of them, but that the one who had performed them might himself continue in power and enjoy his honours undisturbed. A debate arose on these matters, during

τούτων ἁμίλλης, ὡς δὴ παραιτούμενος ὑπὲρ τοῦ
Καίσαρος ἐπ' εὐνοίᾳ τὸν φθόνον ὁ Πομπήϊος ἔφη
γράμματα Καίσαρος ἔχειν βουλομένου λαβεῖν
διάδοχον καὶ παύσασθαι τῆς στρατείας· ὑπατείας
μέντοι καὶ μὴ παρόντι καλῶς ἔχειν αἴτησιν αὐτῷ
3 δοθῆναι. πρὸς ταῦτα ἐνισταμένων τῶν περὶ
Κάτωνα καὶ κελευόντων ἰδιώτην γενόμενον καὶ
τὰ ὅπλα καταθέμενον εὑρίσκεσθαί τι παρὰ τῶν
πολιτῶν ἀγαθόν, οὐκ ἐξερίσας, ἀλλ' οἷον ἡττηθεὶς
ὁ Πομπήϊος ὕποπτος ἦν μᾶλλον ὧν ἐφρόνει περὶ
Καίσαρος. ἔπεμψε δὲ καὶ τὰς δυνάμεις ἀπαιτῶν
ἃς ἔχρησεν αὐτῷ, τὰ Παρθικὰ ποιούμενος πρόφασιν. ὁ δέ, καίπερ εἰδὼς ἐφ' οἷς ἀπῃτεῖτο τοὺς
στρατιώτας, ἀπέπεμψε καλῶς δωρησάμενος.

LVII. Ἐκ τούτου δὲ Πομπήϊος ἐν Νεαπόλει
νοσήσας ἐπισφαλῶς ἀνέρρωσε, Πραξαγόρου δὲ
πείσαντος τοὺς Νεαπολίτας ἔθυσαν ὑπὲρ αὐτοῦ
σωτήρια. μιμουμένων δὲ τούτους τῶν προσοίκων
καὶ τοῦ πράγματος οὕτω περιϊόντος τὴν Ἰταλίαν
πᾶσαν, καὶ μικρὰ καὶ μεγάλη πόλις ἐφ' ἡμέρας
2 πολλὰς ἑώρταζε. τοὺς δὲ ἀπαντῶντας πανταχόθεν οὐδεὶς ἐχώρει τόπος, ἀλλὰ ὁδοί τε κατεπίμ-
πλαντο καὶ κῶμαι καὶ λιμένες εὐωχουμένων καὶ
θυόντων. πολλοὶ δὲ καὶ στεφανηφοροῦντες ὑπὸ
λαμπάδων ἐδέχοντο καὶ παρέπεμπον ἀνθοβολού-
μενον, ὥστε τὴν κομιδὴν αὐτοῦ καὶ πορείαν
3 θέαμα κάλλιστον εἶναι καὶ λαμπρότατον. οὐδενὸς μέντοι τοῦτο λέγεται τῶν ἀπεργασαμένων

which Pompey, giving the impression that it was goodwill towards Caesar that led him to deprecate the odium in which Caesar stood, said he had letters from Caesar wherein he expressed a wish to have a successor and be relieved of his command; he thought it right, however, that he should be permitted to stand for the consulship even in his absence. Opposition to this was made by Cato and his party, who urged that Caesar must lay down his arms and become a private citizen before he could obtain any favour from his fellow-citizens; and since Pompey made no contention, but as it were accepted defeat, there was more suspicion about his sentiments towards Caesar. He also sent and asked back the troops which he had lent him,[1] making the Parthian war his pretext for doing so. And although Caesar knew the real reasons for asking back the soldiers, he sent them home with generous gifts.

LVII. After this Pompey had a dangerous illness at Naples,[2] but recovered from it, and on the advice of Praxagoras the Neapolitans offered sacrifices of thanksgiving for his preservation. Their example was followed by the neighbouring peoples, and so the thing made its way throughout all Italy, and every city, small and great, held festival for many days. No place could contain those who came to greet him from all quarters, but roads and villages and ports were filled with sacrificing and feasting throngs. Many also with garlands on their heads and lighted torches in their hands welcomed and escorted him on his way, pelting him with flowers, so that his progress and return to Rome was a most beautiful and splendid sight. And yet this is said to have done more than anything else to bring about

---

[1] Cf. chapter lii. 3.   [2] In 50 B.C.

τὸν πόλεμον αἰτίων ἔλαττον γενέσθαι. φρόνημα
γὰρ εἰσῆλθεν ὑπεραῖρον ἅμα τῷ μεγέθει τῆς
χαρᾶς τοὺς ἀπὸ τῶν πραγμάτων λογισμούς· καὶ
τὴν εἰς ἀσφαλὲς ἀεὶ τὰ εὐτυχήματα καὶ τὰς
πράξεις αὐτοῦ θεμένην εὐλάβειαν προέμενος εἰς
ἄκρατον ἐξέπεσε θράσος καὶ περιφρόνησιν τῆς
Καίσαρος δυνάμεως, ὡς οὔτε ὅπλων ἐπ᾽ αὐτὸν
οὔτε τινὸς ἐργώδους πραγματείας δεησόμενος,
ἀλλὰ πολὺ ῥᾷον καθαιρήσων ἢ πρότερον ηὔξησε
4 τὸν ἄνδρα. πρὸς δὲ τούτοις Ἄππιος ἀφίκετο
κομίζων ἐκ Γαλατίας ἣν ἔχρησε Πομπήϊος
Καίσαρι στρατιάν· καὶ πολλὰ μὲν ἐξεφλαύριζε
τὰς ἐκεῖ πράξεις καὶ λόγους ἐξέφερε βλασφήμους
περὶ Καίσαρος, αὐτὸν δὲ Πομπήϊον ἀπείρως ἔχειν
ἔλεγε τῆς αὐτοῦ δυνάμεως καὶ δόξης, ἑτέροις
ὅπλοις πρὸς Καίσαρα φραγνύμενον, ὃν αὐτοῖς
κατεργάσεται τοῖς ἐκείνου στρατεύμασιν, ὅταν
πρῶτον ὀφθῇ· τοσοῦτον καὶ μίσους πρὸς Καίσαρα
καὶ πόθου πρὸς Πομπήϊον ἐνυπάρχειν αὐτοῖς.
5 οὕτω δ᾽ οὖν ὁ Πομπήϊος ἐπήρθη, καὶ τοιαύτης
καὶ τοσαύτης ὀλιγωρίας διὰ τὸ θαρρεῖν ἐγένετο
μεστὸς ὥστε καὶ τῶν δεδιότων τὸν πόλεμον
κατεγέλα, καὶ τοὺς λέγοντας ἂν ἐλαύνῃ Καῖσαρ
ἐπὶ τὴν πόλιν, οὐχ ὁρᾶν δυνάμεις αἷς αὐτὸν ἀμυ-
νοῦνται, μειδιῶν τῷ προσώπῳ καὶ διακεχυμένος
ἀμελεῖν ἐκέλευσεν· "Ὅπου γὰρ ἄν," ἔφη, "τῆς
Ἰταλίας ἐγὼ κρούσω τῷ ποδὶ τὴν γῆν, ἀναδύ-
σονται καὶ πεζικαὶ καὶ ἱππικαὶ δυνάμεις."

LVIII. Ἤδη δὲ καὶ Καῖσαρ ἐπεφύετο τοῖς
πράγμασιν ἐρρωμενέστερον, αὐτὸς μὲν οὐκέτι
μακρὰν τῆς Ἰταλίας ἀπαίρων, εἰς δὲ τὴν πόλιν
ἀεὶ τοὺς στρατιώτας ἀποστέλλων ἀρχαιρεσιά-

the war. For while the public rejoicing was so great, a spirit of exaltation entered into the conclusions which Pompey drew from the progress of events, and, throwing to the winds that caution which had thus far always given security to his successful achievements, he indulged himself in unlimited confidence and contempt for Caesar's power, feeling that he would need neither an armed force to oppose him nor any irksome labour of preparation, but that he would pull him down much more easily than he had raised him up. Besides this, Appius came, bringing from Gaul the troops which Pompey had lent Caesar. He said much to belittle Caesar's achievements there, and gave out scandalous stories about Caesar. He also said that Pompey knew not his own power and reputation if he surrounded himself with other troops against Caesar, for he could put down Caesar with Caesar's own soldiers as soon as he appeared on the scene, so great was their hatred of Caesar and their warm affection for Pompey. In this way, then, Pompey was elated, and his confidence filled him with so great a contempt for his adversary that he mocked at those who were afraid of the war; and when some said that if Caesar should march upon the city, they did not see any forces with which to defend it from him, with a smiling countenance and calm mien he bade them be in no concern; " For," said he, " in whatever part of Italy I stamp upon the ground, there will spring up armies of foot and horse."

LVIII. And now, too, Caesar devoted himself to public affairs with greater vigour. He no longer kept himself far away from Italy, was always sending his soldiers back to the city to take part in the elections, and by means of his money was

σοντας, χρήμασι δὲ πολλοὺς ὑποικουρῶν καὶ
διαφθείρων ἄρχοντας· ὧν καὶ Παῦλος ἦν ὁ
ὕπατος ἐπὶ χιλίοις καὶ πεντακοσίοις ταλάντοις
μεταβαλόμενος, καὶ Κουρίων ὁ δήμαρχος ἀμηχά-
νων πλήθει δανείων ἐλευθερωθεὶς ὑπ' αὐτοῦ, καὶ
Μάρκος Ἀντώνιος διὰ φιλίαν Κουρίωνος ὢν
2 ὠφελεῖτο μετέχων. ἐλέχθη μὲν οὖν ὅτι τῶν
ἀφιγμένων τις ἀπὸ Καίσαρος ταξιαρχῶν ἑστὼς
παρὰ τὸ βουλευτήριον, καὶ πυθόμενος ὡς οὐ
δίδωσιν ἡ βουλὴ Καίσαρι χρόνον τῆς ἀρχῆς,
εἶπεν ἐπικρούων τῇ χειρὶ τὸ ξίφος, "Ἀλλὰ τοῦτο
δώσει." καὶ τὰ πραττόμενα καὶ τὰ παρασκευα-
ζόμενα ταύτην εἶχε τὴν διάνοιαν.

3 Αἱ μέντοι Κουρίωνος ἀξιώσεις καὶ παρακλή-
σεις ὑπὲρ Καίσαρος ἐφαίνοντο δημοτικώτεραι.
δυεῖν γὰρ ἠξίου θάτερον, ἢ καὶ Πομπήϊον ἀπαι-
τεῖν ἢ μηδὲ Καίσαρος ἀφαιρεῖσθαι τὸ στρατιω-
τικόν· ἢ γὰρ ἰδιώτας γενομένους ἐπὶ τοῖς δικαίοις
ἢ μένοντας ἀντιπάλους ἐφ' οἷς ἔχουσιν ἀτρεμή-
σειν· ὁ δὲ τὸν ἕτερον ἀσθενῆ ποιῶν ἣν φοβεῖται
4 δύναμιν διπλασιάζει. πρὸς ταῦτα Μαρκέλλου
τοῦ ὑπάτου λῃστὴν ἀποκαλοῦντος τὸν Καίσαρα,
καὶ ψηφίζεσθαι πολέμιον κελεύοντος εἰ μὴ κατα-
θήσεται τὰ ὅπλα, Κουρίων ὅμως ἴσχυσε μετὰ
Ἀντωνίου καὶ Πείσωνος ἐξελέγξαι τὴν σύγκλητον.
ἐκέλευσε γὰρ μεταστῆναι τοὺς Καίσαρα μόνον
τὰ ὅπλα καταθέσθαι κελεύοντας, Πομπήϊον δὲ
5 ἄρχειν· καὶ μετέστησαν οἱ πλείους. αὖθις δὲ
μεταστῆναι κελεύσαντος ὅσοις ἀμφοτέρους ἀρέ-

secretly working upon many of the magistrates and corrupting them. Among these was Paulus the consul, who was won over by a bribe of fifteen hundred talents; and Curio the popular tribune, whom Caesar set free from innumerable debts; and Mark Antony, whose friendship for Curio had involved him in Curio's obligations. It was said, indeed, that one of Caesar's centurions who had come back to Rome and was standing near the senate-house, when he heard that the senate would not give Caesar a prolongation of his term of office, struck his hand upon his sword and said: "But this will give it." And Caesar's intrigues and preparations had this purpose.

And yet the requests and demands which Curio made in behalf of Caesar seemed to be very popular in their character. For he demanded one of two things: either that Pompey also should be required to give up his soldiery, or else that Caesar's should not be taken away from him; for whether they became private persons on just and equal terms, or remained a match for each other with their present forces, they would make no disturbance; but he who weakened one of them doubled the power of which he stood in fear. To this Marcellus the consul replied by calling Caesar a robber, and urging that he be voted a public enemy unless he should lay down his arms; nevertheless, Curio, aided by Antony and Piso, prevailed so far as to have the opinion of the senate taken. He therefore moved that those should withdraw to one side who wished that Caesar only should lay down his arms and that Pompey should remain in command; and the majority withdrew. But when he moved again that all those should withdraw who wished both to lay down their

σκει τὰ ὅπλα καταθέσθαι καὶ μηδέτερον ἄρχειν,
Πομπηΐῳ μὲν εἴκοσι καὶ δύο μόνον, Κουρίωνι δὲ
πάντες οἱ λοιποὶ προσέθεντο. κἀκεῖνος μὲν ὡς
νενικηκὼς λαμπρὸς ὑπὸ χαρᾶς εἰς τὸν δῆμον
ἐξήλατο, κρότῳ καὶ βολαῖς στεφάνων καὶ ἀνθῶν
δεξιούμενον αὐτόν. ἐν δὲ τῇ βουλῇ Πομπήϊος οὐ
παρῆν· οἱ γὰρ ἄρχοντες στρατοπέδων εἰς τὴν
6 πόλιν οὐκ εἰσίασι. Μάρκελλος δὲ ἀναστὰς οὐκ
ἔφη λόγων ἀκροάσεσθαι καθήμενος, ἀλλ' ὁρῶν
ὑπερφαινόμενα τῶν Ἄλπεων ἤδη δέκα τάγματα
βαδίζειν, καὶ αὐτὸς ἐκπέμψειν τὸν ἀντιταξόμενον
αὐτοῖς ὑπὲρ τῆς πατρίδος.

LIX. Ἐκ τούτου τὰς ἐσθῆτας ὡς ἐπὶ πένθει
μετεβάλοντο. Μάρκελλος δὲ πρὸς Πομπήϊον δι'
ἀγορᾶς ἐβάδιζε τῆς βουλῆς ἑπομένης, καὶ καταστὰς ἐναντίος, " Κελεύω σε," εἶπεν, " ὦ Πομπήϊε, 6
βοηθεῖν τῇ πατρίδι καὶ χρῆσθαι ταῖς παρε-
σκευασμέναις δυνάμεσι καὶ καταλέγειν ἑτέρας."
τὰ δ' αὐτὰ ταῦτα καὶ Λέντλος ἔλεγε, τῶν ἀποδε-
2 δειγμένων εἰς τὸ μέλλον ὑπάτων ἅτερος. ἀρξα-
μένου δὲ τοῦ Πομπηΐου καταλέγειν οἱ μὲν οὐχ
ὑπήκουον, ὀλίγοι δὲ γλίσχρως καὶ ἀπροθύμως
συνῄεσαν, οἱ δὲ πλείους διαλύσεις ἐβόων. καὶ
γὰρ ἀνέγνω τινὰ Καίσαρος ἐπιστολὴν Ἀντώνιος
ἐν τῷ δήμῳ, βιασάμενος τὴν βουλήν, ἔχουσαν
ἐπαγωγοὺς ὄχλου προκλήσεις. ἠξίου γὰρ ἀμφοτέρους ἐκβάντας τῶν ἐπαρχιῶν καὶ τὰς στρατιωτικὰς δυνάμεις ἀφέντας ἐπὶ τῷ δήμῳ γενέσθαι
3 καὶ τῶν πεπραγμένων εὐθύνας ὑποσχεῖν. οἱ δὲ
περὶ Λέντλον ὑπατεύοντες ἤδη βουλὴν οὐ συνῆ-
γον· ἄρτι δὲ ἐκ Κιλικίας ἀφιγμένος Κικέρων
ἔπραττε διαλλαγάς, ὅπως Καῖσαρ, ἐξελθὼν

arms and neither to remain in command, only twenty-two favoured Pompey, while all the rest sided with Curio. Curio, therefore, felt that he had won the day, and with a joyful countenance rushed before the people, who clapped their hands in welcome and pelted him with garlands and flowers. Pompey was not present in the senate, since commanders of armies cannot enter the city; Marcellus, however, rose and declared that he would not sit there listening to speeches, but since he saw ten legions already looming up in their march over the Alps, he himself also would send forth a man who would oppose them in defence of his country.

LIX. Upon this, the city went into mourning, as in the presence of a public calamity; and Marcellus, followed by the senate, marched through the forum to meet Pompey, and standing before him said: "I bid thee, Pompey, to defend thy country, to employ the forces now in readiness, and to levy others." Lentulus also said the same, being one of the consuls elected for the coming year. But when Pompey began to levy recruits, some refused to obey the summons, and a few came together reluctantly and without zest, but the greater part cried out for a settlement of the controversy. For Antony, in defiance of the senate, had read before the people a letter of Caesar containing propositions which were attractive to the multitude. He asked, namely, that both Pompey and he should give up their provinces, disband their armies, put themselves in the hands of the people, and render an account of what they had done. But Lentulus, who was by this time consul, would not call the senate together; Cicero, however, who was just returned from Cilicia, tried to effect a settlement of the dispute on these terms, namely,

271

Γαλατίας καὶ τὴν ἄλλην στρατιὰν ἀφεὶς πᾶσαν,
ἐπὶ δυσὶ τάγμασι καὶ τῷ Ἰλλιρικῷ τὴν δευτέραν
4 ὑπατείαν περιμένῃ. Πομπηΐου δὲ δυσκολαί-
νοντος ἐπείσθησαν οἱ Καίσαρος φίλοι θάτερον
ἀφεῖναι· Λέντλου δὲ ἀντικρούσαντος καὶ Κάτωνος
αὖθις ἁμαρτάνειν τὸν Πομπήϊον ἐξαπατώμενον
βοῶντος οὐκ ἔσχον αἱ διαλύσεις πέρας.

LX. Ἐν τούτῳ δὲ ἀπαγγέλλεται Καῖσαρ Ἀρίμινον, πόλιν μεγάλην τῆς Ἰταλίας, κατειληφὼς
καὶ βαδίζων ἄντικρυς ἐπὶ τὴν Ῥώμην μετὰ πάσης
τῆς δυνάμεως. τοῦτο δὲ ἦν ψεῦδος. ἐβάδιζε γὰρ
οὐ πλείονας ἔχων ἱππέων τριακοσίων καὶ πεντα-
κισχιλίων ὁπλιτῶν· τὴν δὲ ἄλλην δύναμιν ἐπέκεινα τῶν Ἄλπεων οὖσαν οὐ περιέμενεν, ἐμπεσεῖν
ἄφνω τεταραγμένοις καὶ μὴ προσδοκῶσι βουλόμενος μᾶλλον ἢ χρόνον δοὺς ἐκ παρασκευῆς μάχε-
2 σθαι. καὶ γὰρ ἐπὶ τὸν Ῥουβίκωνα ποταμὸν
ἐλθών, ὃς ἀφώριζεν αὐτῷ τὴν δεδομένην ἐπαρχίαν,
ἔστη σιωπῇ καὶ διεμέλλησεν, αὐτὸς ἄρα πρὸς
ἑαυτὸν συλλογιζόμενος τὸ μέγεθος τοῦ τολμήματος. εἶτα, ὥσπερ οἱ πρὸς βάθος ἀφιέντες
ἀχανὲς ἀπὸ κρημνοῦ τινος ἑαυτούς, μύσας τῷ
λογισμῷ καὶ παρακαλυψάμενος πρὸς τὸ δεινόν,
καὶ τοσοῦτον μόνον Ἑλληνιστὶ πρὸς τοὺς παρόντας ἐκβοήσας, "Ἀνερρίφθω κύβος," διεβίβαζε
τὸν στρατόν.

3   Ὡς δὲ πρῶτον ἡ φήμη προσέπεσε καὶ κατέσχε
τὴν Ῥώμην μετὰ ἐκπλήξεως θόρυβος καὶ φόβος
οἷος οὔπω πρότερον, εὐθὺς μὲν ἡ βουλὴ φερομένη
πρὸς τὸν Πομπήϊον συνέτρεχε καὶ παρῆσαν αἱ

that Caesar should renounce Gaul and dismiss the rest of his forces, but should retain two legions and Illyricum, and wait for his second consulship. And when Pompey was dissatisfied with this, the friends of Caesar conceded that he should dismiss one of the two legions; but since Lentulus still opposed, and Cato cried out that Pompey was blundering again in allowing himself to be deceived, the settlement came to naught.

LX. And now word was brought that Caesar had seized Ariminum,[1] a large city of Italy, and was marching directly upon Rome with all his forces. But this was false. For he was marching with no more than three hundred horsemen and five thousand men-at-arms; the rest of his forces were beyond the Alps, and he did not wait for them, since he wished to fall upon his enemies suddenly, when they were in confusion and did not expect him, rather than to give them time and fight them after they were prepared. And so, when he was come to the river Rubicon, which was the boundary of the province allotted to him, he stood in silence and delayed to cross, reasoning with himself, of course, upon the magnitude of his adventure. Then, like one who casts himself from a precipice into a yawning abyss, he closed the eyes of reason and put a veil between them and his peril, and calling out in Greek to the bystanders these words only, "Let the die be cast," he set his army across.

As soon as the report of this came flying to Rome and the city was filled with tumult, consternation, and a fear that was beyond compare, the senate at once went in a body and in all haste to Pompey, and

---

[1] In January, 49 B.C. See the *Caesar*, chapter xxxii.

ἀρχαί, πυθομένου δὲ τοῦ Τύλλου περὶ στρατιᾶς
καὶ δυνάμεως καὶ τοῦ Πομπηΐου μετά τινος μελ-
λήσεως ἀθαρσῶς εἰπόντος ὅτι τοὺς παρὰ Καίσαρος
4 ἥκοντας ἑτοίμους ἔχει, νομίζει δὲ καὶ τοὺς κατει-
λεγμένους πρότερον ἐν τάχει συνάξειν τρισμυρίους
ὄντας, ὁ μὲν Τύλλος ἀναβοήσας, "'Εξηπάτηκας
ἡμᾶς, ὦ Πομπήϊε," συνεβούλευεν ὡς Καίσαρα
πρέσβεις ἀποστέλλειν, Φαώνιος δέ τις, ἀνὴρ τἆλλα μὲν οὐ πονηρός, αὐθαδείᾳ δὲ καὶ ὕβρει πολλάκις τὴν Κάτωνος οἰόμενος ἀπομιμεῖσθαι παρρησίαν, ἐκέλευε τὸν Πομπήϊον τῷ ποδὶ τύπτειν
τὴν γῆν, ἃς ὑπισχνεῖτο δυνάμεις ἀνακαλούμενος.
5 ὁ δὲ ταύτην μὲν ἤνεγκε τὴν ἀκαιρίαν πράως· τοῦ
δὲ Κάτωνος ὑπομιμνήσκοντος ὧν ἐν ἀρχῇ περὶ
Καίσαρος αὐτῷ προεῖπεν, ἀπεκρίνατο μαντικώ-
τερα μὲν εἶναι τὰ Κάτωνι λεχθέντα, φιλικώτερα
δὲ ὑπ' αὐτοῦ πεπρᾶχθαι.

LXI. Κάτων δὲ συνεβούλευεν αἱρεῖσθαι στρατηγὸν αὐτοκράτορα Πομπήϊον, ἐπειπὼν ὅτι τῶν
αὐτῶν ἐστι καὶ ποιεῖν τὰ μεγάλα κακὰ καὶ παύειν.
οὗτος μὲν οὖν εὐθὺς ἐξῆλθεν εἰς Σικελίαν (ἔλαχε
γὰρ αὐτὴν τῶν ἐπαρχιῶν) καὶ τῶν ἄλλων ἕκαστος
εἰς ἃς ἐκληρώθη. τῆς δ' Ἰταλίας σχεδὸν ὅλης
2 ἀνισταμένης ἀπορίαν εἶχε τὸ γινόμενον. οἱ μὲν
γὰρ ἔξωθεν φερόμενοι φυγῇ πανταχόθεν εἰς τὴν
Ῥώμην ἐνέπιπτον, οἱ δὲ τὴν Ῥώμην οἰκοῦντες
ἐξέπιπτον αὐτοὶ καὶ ἀπέλειπον τὴν πόλιν, ἐν
χειμῶνι καὶ ταράχῳ τοσούτῳ τὸ μὲν χρήσιμον

the magistrates came too. And when Tullus asked Pompey about an army and a military force, and Pompey, after some delay, said timidly that he had in readiness the soldiers who had come from Caesar, and thought that he could speedily assemble also those who had been previously levied, thirty thousand in number, Tullus cried aloud, "Thou hast deceived us, Pompey!" and advised sending envoys to Caesar; and a certain Favonius, a man otherwise of no bad character, but who often thought that his insolent presumption was an imitation of Cato's boldness of speech, ordered Pompey to stamp upon the ground and call up the forces which he used to promise. But Pompey bore this ill-timed raillery with meekness[1]; and when Cato reminded him of what he had said to him at the outset about Caesar, he replied that what Cato had said was more prophetic, but what he himself had done was more friendly.

LXI. Cato now advised that Pompey should be elected general with unlimited powers, adding that the very men who caused great mischief must also put an end to it. Then he set out at once for Sicily, the province which had fallen to his lot, and the other senators likewise departed for the provinces which had severally been allotted to them. But since nearly all Italy was in commotion, the course of things was perplexing. For those who dwelt outside the city came rushing in hurried flight from all quarters into Rome, and those who dwelt in Rome were rushing out of it and abandoning the city, where, in such tempestuous confusion, the better element

---

[1] In Appian, *Bell. Civ.* ii. 37, Pompey replies : " You will have them if you follow me, and do not think it a terrible thing to leave Rome, and Italy too, if it should be necessary."

PLUTARCH'S LIVES

ἀσθενὲς ἔχουσαν, τὸ δὲ ἀπειθὲς ἰσχυρὸν καὶ δυσ-
μεταχείριστον τοῖς ἄρχουσιν. οὐ γὰρ ἦν παῦσαι
τὸν φόβον, οὐδὲ εἴασέ τις χρῆσθαι τοῖς ἑαυτοῦ
λογισμοῖς Πομπήϊον, ἀλλ' ᾧ τις ἐνετύγχανε πάθει, φοβηθεὶς ἢ λυπηθεὶς ἢ διαπορήσας, τούτῳ
3 φέρων ἐκεῖνον ἀνεπίμπλη· καὶ τἀναντία τῆς αὐτῆς ἡμέρας ἐκράτει βουλεύματα, καὶ πυθέσθαι
περὶ τῶν πολεμίων οὐδὲν ἦν ἀληθὲς αὐτῷ διὰ τὸ
πολλοὺς ἀπαγγέλλειν ὅ τι τύχοιεν, εἶτα ἀπισ-
τοῦντι χαλεπαίνειν. οὕτω δὴ ψηφισάμενος ταραχὴν ὁρᾶν καὶ κελεύσας ἅπαντας ἕπεσθαι αὐτῷ
τοὺς ἀπὸ βουλῆς, καὶ προειπὼν ὅτι Καίσαρος
ἡγήσεται τὸν ἀπολειφθέντα, περὶ δείλην ὀψίαν
4 ἀπέλιπε τὴν πόλιν. οἱ δὲ ὕπατοι μηδὲ θύσαντες
ἃ νομίζεται πρὸ πολέμων ἔφυγον. ἦν δὲ καὶ παρ'
αὐτὰ τὰ δεινὰ ζηλωτὸς ἀνὴρ τῆς πρὸς αὐτὸν
εὐνοίας τῶν ἀνθρώπων, ὅτι πολλῶν τὴν στρατηγίαν μεμφομένων οὐδεὶς ἦν ὁ μισῶν τὸν στρατηγόν, ἀλλὰ πλείονας ἄν τις εὗρε τῶν διὰ τὴν
ἐλευθερίαν φευγόντων τοὺς ἀπολιπεῖν Πομπήϊον
μὴ δυναμένους.

LXII. Ὀλίγαις δὲ ὕστερον ἡμέραις Καῖσαρ
εἰσελάσας καὶ κατασχὼν τὴν Ῥώμην τοῖς μὲν
ἄλλοις ἐπιεικῶς ἐνέτυχε καὶ κατεπράϋνε, τῶν δὲ
δημάρχων ἑνὶ Μετέλλῳ κωλύοντι χρήματα λαβεῖν
αὐτὸν ἐκ τοῦ ταμιείου θάνατον ἠπείλησε, καὶ
προσέθηκε τῇ ἀπειλῇ τραχύτερον λόγον· ἔφη γὰρ
ὡς τοῦτο φῆσαι χαλεπὸν ἦν αὐτῷ μᾶλλον ἢ

276

was weak, and the insubordinate element strong and hard for the magistrates to manage. For it was impossible to check the reigning fear, nor would any one suffer Pompey to follow the dictates of his own judgement, but whatever feeling each one had, whether fear, or distress, or perplexity, he promptly infected Pompey's mind with this. Therefore opposite counsels prevailed in the same day, and it was impossible for Pompey to get any true information about the enemy, since many reported to him whatever they happened to hear, and then were vexed if he did not believe them. Under these circumstances he issued an edict in which he recognized a state of civil war, ordered all the senators to follow him, declared that he would regard as a partisan of Caesar any one who remained behind, and late in the evening left the city. The consuls also fled, without even making the sacrifices customary before a war. But even amid the actual terrors of the hour Pompey was a man to be envied for the universal good will felt towards him, because, though many blamed his generalship, there was no one who hated the general. Indeed, one would have found that those who fled the city for the sake of liberty were not so numerous as those who did so because they were unable to forsake Pompey.

LXII. A few days after this, Caesar entered and took possession of Rome. He treated everybody with kindness and calmed their fears, except that when Metellus, one of the tribunes, attempted to prevent him from taking money out of the public treasury, he threatened to kill him, and added to the threat a still harsher speech, namely, that it was easier for him to execute it than to utter it.[1] Having

---

[1] Cf. the *Caesar* xxxv. 4.

2 πρᾶξαι. τρεψάμενος δὲ τὸν Μέτελλον οὕτω, καὶ
λαβὼν ὧν ἔχρηζεν, ἐδίωκε Πομπήϊον, ἐκβαλεῖν
σπεύδων ἐκ τῆς Ἰταλίας πρὶν ἀφικέσθαι τὴν ἐξ
Ἰβηρίας αὐτῷ δύναμιν. ὁ δὲ τὸ Βρεντέσιον
κατασχὼν καὶ πλοίων εὐπορήσας τοὺς μὲν
ὑπάτους εὐθὺς ἐμβιβάσας καὶ μετ' αὐτῶν σπείρας
τριάκοντα προεξέπεμψεν εἰς Δυρράχιον, Σκηπίωνα δὲ τὸν πενθερὸν καὶ Γναῖον τὸν υἱὸν εἰς
Συρίαν ἀπέστειλε ναυτικὸν κατασκευάσοντας.
3 αὐτὸς δὲ φραξάμενος τὰς πύλας καὶ τοῖς τείχεσι
τοὺς ἐλαφροτάτους στρατιώτας ἐπιστήσας, τοὺς
δὲ Βρεντεσίνους ἀτρεμεῖν κατ' οἰκίαν κελεύσας,
ὅλην ἐντὸς τὴν πόλιν ἀνέσκαψε καὶ διετάφρευσε,
καὶ σκολόπων ἐνέπλησε τοὺς στενωποὺς πλὴν
δυεῖν, δι' ὧν ἐπὶ θάλατταν αὐτὸς κατῆλθεν.
4 ἡμέρᾳ δὲ τρίτῃ τὸν μὲν ἄλλον ὄχλον ἐν ταῖς
ναυσὶν εἶχεν ἤδη καθ' ἡσυχίαν ἐμβεβηκότα, τοῖς
δὲ τὰ τείχη φυλάττουσιν ἐξαίφνης σημεῖον ἄρας
καὶ καταδραμόντας ὀξέως ἀναλαβὼν ἀπεπέρασεν.
ὁ δὲ Καῖσαρ, ὡς εἶδεν ἐκλελειμμένα τὰ τείχη, τὴν
φυγὴν αἰσθόμενος μικροῦ μὲν ἐδέησε διώκων τοῖς
σταυροῖς καὶ τοῖς ὀρύγμασι περιπετὴς γενέσθαι,
τῶν δὲ Βρεντεσίνων φρασάντων φυλαττόμενος
τὴν πόλιν καὶ κύκλῳ περιϊὼν ἀνηγμένους εὗρε
πάντας πλὴν δυεῖν πλοίων στρατιώτας τινὰς οὐ
πολλοὺς ἔχοντων.

LXIII. Οἱ μὲν οὖν ἄλλοι τοῦ Πομπηΐου τὸν
ἀπόπλουν ἐν τοῖς ἀρίστοις τίθενται στρατηγή-
μασιν, αὐτὸς δὲ Καῖσαρ ἐθαύμαζεν ὅτι καὶ πόλιν

thus driven away Metellus, he took what he wanted,
and then set out in pursuit of Pompey, being anxious
to drive him out of Italy before his forces came back
from Spain. But Pompey, having taken possession
of Brundisium, where he found plenty of transports,
immediately embarked the consuls, and with them
thirty cohorts of soldiers, and sent them before him
to Dyrrachium; Scipio his father-in-law, however,
and Gnaeus his son, he sent to Syria to raise a fleet.
He himself, after barricading the gates and manning
the walls with his lightest-armed soldiers, ordered
the Brundisians to remain quietly in their houses,
and then dug up all the ground inside the city into
trenches, and filled the streets with sunken stakes,[1]
all except two, by which he himself finally went
down to the sea. Then on the third day, when he
had already embarked the rest of his host at his
leisure, he suddenly raised a signal for those who
were still guarding the walls to run swiftly down to
the sea, took them on board, and set them across to
Dyrrachium. Caesar, however, when he saw the
walls deserted, perceived that Pompey had fled, and
in his pursuit of him came near getting entangled in
the ditches and stakes; but since the Brundisians
told him about them, he avoided the city,[2] and
making a circuit round it, found that all the transports had put out to sea except two, which had only
a few soldiers aboard.

LXIII. Other people, now, count this sailing
away of Pompey among his best stratagems, but
Caesar himself was astonished that when he was in

---

[1] Ditches were dug across the streets, sharpened stakes
planted in the ditches, and the whole work lightly covered
so as to look undisturbed. Cf. Caesar, *Bell. Civ.* I. xxvii.

[2] He had besieged it for nine days, and had also begun to
close up the harbour (Caesar, *Bell. Civ.* I. xxv.–xxvii.).

ἔχων ὀχυρὰν καὶ προσδοκῶν τὰς ἐξ Ἰβηρίας
δυνάμεις καὶ θαλασσοκρατῶν ἐξέλιπε καὶ προήκατο τὴν Ἰταλίαν. αἰτιᾶται καὶ Κικέρων ὅτι
τὴν Θεμιστοκλέους ἐμιμήσατο στρατηγίαν μᾶλλον
ἢ τὴν Περικλέους, τῶν πραγμάτων τούτοις
2 ὁμοίων ὄντων, οὐκ ἐκείνοις. ἐδήλωσε δὲ Καῖσαρ
ἔργῳ σφόδρα φοβούμενος τὸν χρόνον. ἑλὼν γὰρ
Νουμέριον Πομπηΐου φίλον ἀπέστειλεν εἰς Βρεντέσιον ἐπὶ τοῖς ἴσοις ἀξιῶν διαλλαγῆναι· Νου-
μέριος δὲ Πομπηΐῳ συνεξέπλευσεν. ἐντεῦθεν ὁ
μὲν ἐν ἡμέραις[1] ἑξήκοντα κύριος γεγονὼς ἀναι-
μωτὶ τῆς Ἰταλίας ὅλης ἐβούλετο μὲν εὐθὺς
Πομπήϊον διώκειν, πλοίων δὲ μὴ παρόντων
ἀποστρέψας εἰς Ἰβηρίαν ἤλαυνε, τὰς ἐκεῖ δυνάμεις προσαγαγέσθαι βουλόμενος.

LXIV. Ἐν δὲ τῷ χρόνῳ τούτῳ μεγάλη συνέστη
Πομπηΐῳ δύναμις, ἡ μὲν ναυτικὴ καὶ παντελῶς
ἀνανταγώνιστος (ἦσαν γὰρ αἱ μάχιμοι πεντα-
κόσιαι, λιβυρνίδων δὲ καὶ κατασκόπων ὑπερβάλλων ἀριθμός), ἱππεῖς δέ, Ῥωμαίων καὶ
Ἰταλῶν τὸ ἀνθοῦν, ἑπτακισχίλιοι, γένεσι καὶ
πλούτῳ καὶ φρονήμασι διαφέροντες· τὴν δὲ πεζὴν
σύμμικτον οὖσαν καὶ μελέτης δεομένην ἐγύμναζεν
ἐν Βεροίᾳ καθήμενος οὐκ ἀργός, ἀλλ' ὥσπερ
ἀκμάζοντι χρώμενος αὑτῷ πρὸς τὰ γυμνάσια.
2 μεγάλη γὰρ ἦν ῥοπὴ πρὸς τὸ θαρρεῖν τοῖς ὁρῶσι
Πομπήϊον Μάγνον ἑξήκοντα μὲν ἔτη δυεῖν λεί-
ποντα γεγενημένον, ἐν δὲ τοῖς ὅπλοις ἁμιλλώμενον
πεζόν, εἶτα ἱππότην αὖθις ἑλκόμενόν τε τὸ ξίφος
ἀπραγμόνως θέοντι τῷ ἵππῳ καὶ κατακλείοντα
πάλιν εὐχερῶς, ἐν δὲ τοῖς ἀκοντισμοῖς οὐ μόνον

65

---

[1] ἐν ἡμέραις. Bekker, after Emperius: ἡμέραις.

possession of a strong city and expected his forces from Spain and was master of the sea, he gave up and abandoned Italy. Cicero also blames him [1] for imitating the generalship of Themistocles rather than that of Pericles, although he was situated like Pericles, and not like Themistocles. Moreover, Caesar had shown by what he did that he greatly feared a protraction of the war. For after capturing Numerius, a friend of Pompey, he sent him to Brundisium with a request for a reconciliation on equal terms. But Numerius sailed away with Pompey. Then Caesar, who in sixty days had become master of all Italy without bloodshed, wished to pursue Pompey at once, but since he had no transports, he turned back and marched into Spain, desiring to win over to himself the forces there.

LXIV. In the meantime a great force was gathered by Pompey. His navy was simply irresistible, since he had five hundred ships of war, while the number of his light galleys and fast cruisers was immense; his cavalry numbered seven thousand, the flower of Rome and Italy, preëminent in lineage, wealth, and courage; and his infantry, which was a mixed multitude and in need of training, he exercised at Beroea, not sitting idly by, but taking part in their exercises himself, as if he had been in the flower of his age. And indeed it was a great incentive to confidence when they saw Pompey the Great, who was now sixty years of age less two, but who nevertheless competed in full armour as a foot-soldier, and then again, as a horseman, drew his sword without trouble while his horse was at a gallop and put it back in its sheath with ease; while in hurling the javelin he not only displayed accuracy,

---

[1] *Epist. ad Att.* vii. 11.

ἀκρίβειαν, ἀλλὰ καὶ ῥώμην ἐπιδεικνύμενον εἰς
μῆκος, ὃ πολλοὶ τῶν νέων οὐχ ὑπερέβαλλον.
3 ἐπεφοίτων δὲ καὶ βασιλεῖς ἐθνῶν καὶ δυνάσται,
καὶ τῶν ἀπὸ Ῥώμης ἡγεμονικῶν ἀριθμὸς ἦν
ἐντελοῦς βουλῆς περὶ αὐτόν. ἦλθε δὲ καὶ
Λαβιηνὸς [1] ἀπολιπὼν Καίσαρα φίλος γεγονὼς
καὶ συνεστρατευμένος ἐν Γαλατίᾳ, καὶ Βροῦτος,
υἱὸς ὢν Βρούτου τοῦ περὶ Γαλατίαν σφαγέντος,
ἀνὴρ μεγαλόφρων καὶ μηδέποτε Πομπήϊον προσειπὼν μηδὲ ἀσπασάμενος πρότερον ὡς φονέα
τοῦ πατρός, τότε δὲ ὡς ἐλευθεροῦντι τὴν Ῥώμην
4 ὑπέταξεν ἑαυτόν. Κικέρων δέ, καίπερ ἄλλα
γεγραφὼς καὶ βεβουλευμένος, ὅμως κατῃδέσθη
μὴ γενέσθαι τοῦ προκινδυνεύοντος ἀριθμοῦ τῆς
πατρίδος. ἦλθε δὲ καὶ Τίδιος Σέξτιος, ἐσχα-
τόγηρως ἀνὴρ θάτερον πεπηρωμένος σκέλος, εἰς
Μακεδονίαν· ὃν τῶν ἄλλων γελώντων καὶ χλευα-
ζόντων, ὁ Πομπήϊος ἰδὼν ἐξανέστη καὶ προσέδραμε, μέγα νομίζων μαρτύριον εἶναι καὶ τοὺς
παρ' ἡλικίαν καὶ παρὰ δύναμιν αἱρουμένους τὸν
μετ' αὐτοῦ κίνδυνον ἀντὶ τῆς ἀσφαλείας.

LXV. Ἐπεὶ δὲ βουλῆς γενομένης καὶ γνώμην
Κάτωνος εἰπόντος ἐψηφίσαντο μηδένα Ῥωμαίων
ἄνευ παρατάξεως ἀναιρεῖν μηδὲ διαρπάζειν πόλιν
ὑπήκοον Ῥωμαίοις, ἔτι μᾶλλον ἡ Πομπηΐου μερὶς
ἠγαπήθη· καὶ γὰρ οἷς μηδὲν ἦν πρᾶγμα τοῦ
πολέμου πόρρω κατοικοῦσιν ἢ δι' ἀσθένειαν
ἀμελουμένοις, τῷ γε βούλεσθαι συγκατετίθεντο
καὶ τῷ λόγῳ συνεμάχουν ὑπὲρ τῶν δικαίων,

---

[1] Λαβιηνὸς with Coraës and Bekker : Λαβεών.

but also vigour in the length of his cast, which many
of the young men could not surpass. There kept
coming to him also kings of nations and potentates,
and of the leading men from Rome there were
enough about him to form a full senate. Labienus
also came, having deserted Caesar, though he had
been his friend and had served under him in Gaul;
and Brutus, a son of the Brutus who had been put to
death by Pompey in Gaul,[1] a man of lofty spirit, who
had never spoken to Pompey nor even saluted him
before, because he held him to be the murderer of
his father, but now he put himself under his command, believing him to be a deliverer of Rome.
Cicero, too, although he had advocated other
measures in his writings and his speeches in the
senate, nevertheless was ashamed not to be of the
number of those who risked all for their country.
There came also Tidius Sextius, a man of extreme
old age and lame of one leg, into Macedonia. The
rest laughed and jeered at him, but when Pompey
saw him, he rose and ran to meet him, counting it a
great testimony that men past the years and past
the power of service should choose danger with him
in preference to their safety.

LXV. When their senate convened and a decree
was passed, on motion of Cato, that no Roman
should be killed except on a field of battle, and that
no city subject to Rome should be plundered, the
party of Pompey was held in still greater favour.
For those even who took no part in the war, either
because they dwelt too far away, or were too weak
to be regarded, attached themselves to it in their
wishes at least, and, as far as their words went,
fought with it in behalf of the right, considering

---

[1] Cf. chapter xvi. 3 f.; *Brutus*, iv. 1 f.

ἡγούμενοι θεοῖς εἶναι καὶ ἀνθρώποις ἐχθρὸν ᾧ
μὴ καθ᾽ ἡδονήν ἐστι νικᾶν Πομπήϊον.

2 Οὐ μὴν ἀλλὰ καὶ Καῖσαρ εὐγνώμονα παρεῖχεν
ἑαυτὸν ἐν τῷ κρατεῖν, ὃς καὶ τὰς ἐν Ἰβηρίᾳ τοῦ
Πομπηΐου δυνάμεις ἑλὼν καὶ καταπολεμήσας
ἀφῆκε τοὺς στρατηγούς, τοῖς δὲ στρατιώταις
ἐχρῆτο. καὶ πάλιν ὑπερβαλὼν τὰς Ἄλπεις καὶ
διαδραμὼν τὴν Ἰταλίαν εἰς Βρεντέσιον ἧκεν ἐν
3 τροπαῖς ἤδη τοῦ χειμῶνος ὄντος· καὶ διαπεράσας
τὸ πέλαγος αὐτὸς μὲν εἰς Ὤρικον παρενέβαλεν,
Οὐιβούλλιον [1] δὲ τὸν Πομπηΐου φίλον αἰχμάλωτον ἔχων σὺν ἑαυτῷ πρὸς Πομπήϊον ἀνέστειλε,
προκαλούμενος εἰς ἓν συνελθόντας ἀμφοτέρους
ἡμέρᾳ τρίτῃ πάντα διαλῦσαι τὰ στρατεύματα
καὶ γενομένους φίλους καὶ ὀμόσαντας ἐπανελθεῖν
4 εἰς Ἰταλίαν. ταῦτα Πομπήϊος αὖθις ἐνέδραν
ἡγεῖτο· καὶ καταβὰς ὀξέως ἐπὶ θάλατταν κατέλαβε χωρία καὶ τόπους ἕδρας τε τοῖς πεζοῖς
στρατοπέδοις ὑπεραλκεῖς ἔχοντα, καὶ ναύλοχα
καὶ κατάρσεις ἐπιφόρους τοῖς ἐπιφοιτῶσι διὰ
θαλάττης, ὥστε πάντα πνεῖν ἄνεμον Πομπηΐῳ
σῖτον ἢ στρατιὰν ἢ χρήματα κομίζοντα, Καίσαρα
δὲ δυσχερείαις κατὰ γῆν ὁμοῦ καὶ κατὰ θάλατταν
5 περιεχόμενον ἐξ ἀνάγκης φιλομαχεῖν, καὶ προσ-
βάλλοντα τοῖς ἐρύμασι καὶ προκαλούμενον
ἑκάστοτε τὰ μὲν πλεῖστα νικᾶν καὶ κρατεῖν τοῖς
ἀκροβολισμοῖς, ἅπαξ δὲ μικροῦ συντριβῆναι καὶ
τὴν στρατιὰν ἀποβαλεῖν, τοῦ Πομπηΐου λαμπρῶς
ἀγωνισαμένου μέχρι τροπῆς ἁπάντων καὶ φόνου
δισχιλίων, βιάσασθαι δὲ καὶ συνεισπεσεῖν μὴ 6
δυνηθέντος ἢ φοβηθέντος, ὥστε εἰπεῖν Καίσαρα

---

[1] Οὐιβούλλιον after Caesar, *Bell. Civ.* iii. 10 : Ἰούβιον.

him a foe to gods and men who did not wish Pompey to be victorious.

However, it is also true that Caesar showed himself merciful as a conqueror; after defeating and capturing the forces of Pompey in Spain, he sent away their commanders, and took the soldiers into his service.[1] Then he re-crossed the Alps, marched rapidly through Italy, and came to Brundisium shortly after the winter solstice.[2] Crossing the sea there, he himself put in at Oricum, but he dispatched Vibullius, the friend of Pompey, who was his prisoner of war, to Pompey, with a proposition that they should hold a conference, disband all their armies within three days, and after renewing their friendship under oath, return to Italy. This Pompey thought to be another snare, and marching swiftly down to the sea, he took possession of the posts, regions, and sites which offered strong positions for land forces, as well as of the naval stations and landing-places which were favourable for those who came by sea, so that every wind that blew brought Pompey grain, or troops, or money; while Caesar, on the other hand, reduced to straits by sea and land, was forced to seek a battle, attacking Pompey's defences and challenging him to come out all the while. In these skirmishes Caesar was for the most part victorious and carried the day; but once he narrowly escaped being utterly crushed and losing his army, for Pompey made a brilliant fight and at last routed Caesar's whole force and killed two thousand of them. He did not, however, force his way into their camp with the fugitives, either because he could not, or because he feared to do so, and this led Caesar to say to his friends: "To-day

---

[1] See Caesar, *Bell. Civ.* I. xli.–lxxxvii. [2] Of 49 B.C.

πρὸς τοὺς φίλους ὅτι Σήμερον ἂν ἡ νίκη παρὰ
τοῖς πολεμίοις ἦν, εἰ τὸν νικῶντα εἶχον.

LXVI. Ἐπὶ τούτῳ μέγα φρονήσαντες οἱ Πομπηίου διὰ μάχης ἔσπευδον κριθῆναι. Πομπήιος
δὲ τοῖς μὲν ἔξω βασιλεῦσι καὶ στρατηγοῖς καὶ
πόλεσιν ὡς νενικηκὼς ἔγραφε, τὸν δὲ τῆς μάχης
κίνδυνον ὠρρώδει, τῷ χρόνῳ καὶ ταῖς ἀπορίαις
καταπολεμήσειν νομίζων ἄνδρας ἀμάχους μὲν ἐν
τοῖς ὅπλοις καὶ συνειθισμένους νικᾶν μετ' ἀλλή-
2 λων πολὺν ἤδη χρόνον, πρὸς δὲ τὴν ἄλλην
στρατείαν καὶ πλάνας καὶ μεταβάσεις καὶ τάφρων
ὀρύξεις καὶ τειχῶν οἰκοδομίας ἀπαγορεύοντας
ὑπὸ γήρως, καὶ διὰ τοῦτο ταῖς χερσὶν ἐμφῦναι
τάχιστα καὶ συμπλακῆναι σπεύδοντας. οὐ μὴν
ἀλλὰ πρότερον ἁμῶς γέ πως παρῆγε πείθων τοὺς
περὶ αὐτὸν ἀτρεμεῖν ὁ Πομπήιος· ἐπεὶ δὲ μετὰ
τὴν μάχην ὁ Καῖσαρ ὑπὸ τῶν ἀποριῶν ἀναστὰς
ἐβάδιζε δι' Ἀθαμάνων εἰς Θετταλίαν, οὐκέτι
3 καθεκτὸν ἦν τὸ φρόνημα τῶν ἀνδρῶν, ἀλλὰ
φεύγειν Καίσαρα βοῶντες οἱ μὲν ἀκολουθεῖν καὶ
διώκειν ἐκέλευον, οἱ δὲ διαβαίνειν εἰς Ἰταλίαν,
οἱ δὲ θεράποντας εἰς Ῥώμην καὶ φίλους ἔπεμπον
οἰκίας προκαταληψομένους ἐγγὺς ἀγορᾶς ὡς αὐτίκα μετιόντες ἀρχάς. ἐθελονταὶ δὲ πολλοὶ πρὸς
Κορνηλίαν ἔπλεον εἰς Λέσβον εὐαγγελιζόμενοι
πέρας ἔχειν τὸν πόλεμον· ἐκεῖ γὰρ αὐτὴν ὑπεξέ-
πεμψεν ὁ Πομπήιος.

4 Ἀθροισθείσης δὲ βουλῆς Ἀφράνιος μὲν ἀπε-
φαίνετο γνώμην ἔχεσθαι τῆς Ἰταλίας, ταύτην γὰρ
εἶναι τοῦ πολέμου τὸ μέγιστον ἆθλον, προστι-

victory would have been with the enemy if they
had had a victor in command."

LXVI. At this success the followers of Pompey
were so elated that they were eager to have the
issue decided by a battle. Pompey, however, although he wrote to distant kings and generals and
cities in the tone of a victor, feared the risk of such
a battle, thinking that by imposing delays and
distresses upon them he would finally subdue men
who were invincible in arms and had been accustomed to conquer together now for a long time, but
who for the other duties of a campaign, such as long
marches, changes of position, the digging of trenches,
and the building of walls, were incapacitated by old
age, and therefore eager to come to close quarters
and fight hand to hand without delay. Notwithstanding their over-confidence, Pompey had hitherto
somehow or other succeeded in inducing his followers
to keep quiet ; but when after the battle Caesar
was compelled by his lack of supplies to break
camp and march through Athamania into Thessaly,
their spirits could no longer be restrained, but, crying out that Caesar was in flight, some of them were
for following in pursuit of him, others for crossing
over into Italy, and others were sending their
attendants and friends to Rome in order to pre-
occupy houses near the forum, purposing at once to
become candidates for office. Many, too, of their
own accord sailed to Cornelia in Lesbos with the
glad tidings that the war was at an end ; for Pompey
had sent her there for safety.

A senate having been assembled, Afranius gave it
as his opinion that they should make sure of Italy,
for Italy was the greatest prize of the war, and

θέναι δὲ τοῖς κρατοῦσιν εὐθὺς Σικελίαν, Σαρδόνα,
Κύρνον, Ἰβηρίαν, Γαλατίαν ἅπασαν· ἧς τε δὴ
πλεῖστος ὁ λόγος Πομπηΐῳ πατρίδος ὀρεγούσης
χεῖρας ἐγγύθεν, οὐ καλῶς ἔχειν περιορᾶν προπη-
λακιζομένην καὶ δουλεύουσαν οἰκέταις καὶ κόλαξι
5 τυράννων. αὐτὸς δὲ Πομπήϊος οὔτε πρὸς δόξαν
ἡγεῖτο καλὸν αὑτῷ δευτέραν φυγὴν φεύγειν
Καίσαρα καὶ διώκεσθαι, τῆς τύχης διώκειν δι-
δούσης, οὔτε ὅσιον ἐγκαταλιπεῖν Σκηπίωνα καὶ
τοὺς περὶ τὴν Ἑλλάδα καὶ Θετταλίαν ἄνδρας
ὑπατικούς, εὐθὺς ὑπὸ Καίσαρι γενησομένους μετὰ
χρημάτων καὶ δυνάμεων μεγάλων, τῆς δὲ Ῥώμης
μάλιστα κήδεσθαι τὸν ἀπωτάτω πολεμοῦντα
περὶ αὐτῆς, ὅπως ἀπαθὴς κακῶν οὖσα καὶ ἀνή-
κοος περιμένῃ τὸν κρατοῦντα.

LXVII. Ταῦτα ψηφισάμενος ἐδίωκε Καίσαρα,
μάχης μὲν ἐγνωκὼς ἀπέχεσθαι, πολιορκεῖν δὲ
καὶ τρίβειν ταῖς ἀπορίαις ἐγγύθεν ἐπακολουθῶν.
καὶ γὰρ ἄλλως ταῦτα συμφέρειν ἡγεῖτο, καὶ
λόγος τις εἰς αὐτὸν ἧκεν ἐν τοῖς ἱππεῦσι φερόμενος, ὡς χρὴ τάχιστα τρεψαμένους Καίσαρα
2 συγκαταλύειν κἀκεῖνον αὐτόν. ἔνιοι δέ φασι
διὰ τοῦτο καὶ Κάτωνι μηδὲν ἄξιον σπουδῆς χρήσασθαι Πομπήϊον, ἀλλὰ καὶ πορευόμενον ἐπὶ
Καίσαρα πρὸς θαλάσσῃ καταλιπεῖν ἐπὶ τῆς
ἀποσκευῆς, φοβηθέντα μὴ Καίσαρος ἀναιρεθέν-
τος ἀναγκάσῃ κἀκεῖνον εὐθὺς ἀποθέσθαι τὴν
ἀρχήν. οὕτω δὲ παρακολουθῶν ἀτρέμα τοῖς
πολεμίοις ἐν αἰτίαις ἦν καὶ καταβοήσεσιν ὡς οὐ
Καίσαρα καταστρατηγῶν, ἀλλὰ τὴν πατρίδα καὶ

would at once put also into the hands of her masters
Sicily, Sardinia, Corsica, Spain, and all Gaul; and
since his native land, which was of the greatest
concern to Pompey, stretched out suppliant hands
to him close by, it was not right to allow her to be
enslaved and insulted by servants and flatterers of
tyrants.   Pompey himself, however, thought it
neither well for his own reputation to run away
a second time from Caesar and to be pursued by
him, when fortune made him the pursuer, nor right
before Heaven to abandon Scipio and the men of
consular rank in Thessaly and Hellas, who would
at once come into the power of Caesar together with
their moneys and large forces; but that he cared
most for Rome who fought for her at the farthest
remove, in order that she might neither suffer nor
hear about any evil, but quietly await her master.

LXVII. Having decided the matter in this way,
Pompey set out in pursuit of Caesar, determined to
avoid a battle, but to keep him under siege and
harass him with lack of supplies by following close
upon him.   He had reasons for thinking this the
best course, and besides, a saying current among the
cavalry reached his ears, to the effect that as soon as
they had routed Caesar they must put down Pompey
himself also.   And some say this was also the reason
why Pompey called upon Cato for no service of any
importance, but even when marching against Caesar
left him at the coast in charge of the baggage,
fearing lest, if Caesar should be taken off, he himself also might be forced by Cato to lay down his
command at once.   While he was thus quietly
following the enemy he was loudly denounced, and
charges were rife that he was directing his campaign,
not against Caesar, but against his country and the

289

τὴν βουλήν, ὅπως διὰ παντὸς ἄρχῃ καὶ μηδέποτε
παύσηται τοῖς ἀξιοῦσι τῆς οἰκουμένης ἄρχειν
3 χρώμενος ὑπηρέταις καὶ δορυφόροις. Δομέτιος
δὲ αὐτὸν Ἀηνόβαρβος Ἀγαμέμνονα καλῶν καὶ
βασιλέα βασιλέων ἐπίφθονον ἐποίει. καὶ Φαώνιος οὐχ ἧττον ἦν ἀηδὴς τῶν παρρησιαζομένων
ἀκαίρως ἐν τῷ σκώπτειν, "Ἄνθρωποι," βοῶν,
"οὐδὲ τῆτες ἔσται τῶν ἐν Τουσκλάνῳ σύκων
μεταλαβεῖν;" Λεύκιος δὲ Ἀφράνιος ὁ τὰς ἐν 6
Ἰβηρίᾳ δυνάμεις ἀποβαλὼν ἐν αἰτίᾳ προδοσίας
γεγονώς, τότε δὲ τὸν Πομπήϊον ὁρῶν φυγομαχ-
οῦντα, θαυμάζειν ἔλεγε τοὺς κατηγοροῦντας αὐτοῦ,
πῶς πρὸς τὸν ἔμπορον τῶν ἐπαρχιῶν οὐ μάχονται
προελθόντες.

4 Ταῦτα καὶ τὰ τοιαῦτα πολλὰ λέγοντες ἄνδρα
δόξης ἥττονα καὶ τῆς πρὸς τοὺς φίλους αἰδοῦς
τὸν Πομπήϊον ἐξεβιάσαντο καὶ συνεπεσπάσαντο
ταῖς ἑαυτῶν ἐλπίσι καὶ ὁρμαῖς ἐπακολουθῆσαι,
προέμενον τοὺς ἀρίστους λογισμούς, ὅπερ οὐδὲ
πλοίου κυβερνήτῃ, μήτιγε[1] τοσούτων ἐθνῶν καὶ
δυνάμεων αὐτοκράτορι στρατηγῷ παθεῖν ἦν προσ-
5 ῆκον. ὁ δὲ τῶν μὲν ἰατρῶν τοὺς μηδέποτε
χαριζομένους ταῖς ἐπιθυμίαις ἐπῄνεσεν, αὐτὸς δὲ
τῷ νοσοῦντι τῆς στρατιᾶς ἐνέδωκε, δείσας ἐπὶ
σωτηρίᾳ λυπηρὸς γενέσθαι. πῶς γὰρ ἄν τις
φήσειεν ὑγιαίνειν ἐκείνους τοὺς ἄνδρας, ὧν οἱ
μὲν ὑπατείας ἤδη καὶ στρατηγίας ἐν τῷ στρατοπέδῳ περινοστοῦντες ἐμνῶντο, Σπινθῆρι δὲ καὶ
Δομετίῳ καὶ Σκηπίωνι περὶ τῆς Καίσαρος ἀρχι-
ερωσύνης ἔριδες ἦσαν καὶ φιλονεικίαι καὶ
6 δεξιώσεις; ὥσπερ αὐτοῖς Τιγράνου τοῦ Ἀρμενίου

---

[1] μήτιγε Bekker reads μήτοιγε, with C.

senate, in order that he might always be in office and never cease to have for his attendants and guards men who claimed to rule the world. Domitius Ahenobarbus, too, by calling him Agamemnon, and King of Kings, made him odious. And Favonius was no less displeasing to him than those who used a bolder speech, when he bawled out his untimely jest: " O men, this year, also, shall we eat no figs of Tusculum?" And Lucius Afranius, who lay under a charge of treachery for having lost his forces in Spain,[1] on seeing Pompey now avoiding a battle with Caesar, said he was astonished that his accusers did not go forth and fight this trafficker in provinces.

With these and many similar speeches they forced Pompey from his settled purpose,—a man who was a slave to fame and loath to disappoint his friends,— and dragged him into following after their own hopes and impulses, abandoning his best laid plans, a thing which even in the master of a ship, to say nothing of a general in sole command of so many nations and armies, would have been unbecoming. Pompey himself approved of those physicians who never gratify the morbid desires of their patients, and yet he yielded to the diseased passion of his followers, for fear of offending if he tried to heal and save them. For how can one say that those men were sound and well, some of whom were already going about among the soldiers and canvassing for consul-ships and praetorships, while Spinther, Domitius, and Scipio were quarrelling, scheming, and conspir-ing over the pontificate of Caesar,[2] just as though Tigranes the Armenian were encamped over against

---

[1] He was accused of taking a bribe from Caesar for the surrender of the Spains (see the *Caesar*, xli. 2).

[2] Since 63 B.C., Caesar had been pontifex maximus. Cf. *Bell. Civ.* iii. 83.

παραστρατοπεδεύοντος ἢ τοῦ Ναβαταίων βασιλέως, ἀλλ' οὐ Καίσαρος ἐκείνου καὶ τῆς δυνάμεως ᾗ χιλίας μὲν ᾑρήκει πόλεις κατὰ κράτος,
ἔθνη δὲ πλείονα τριακοσίων ὑπῆκτο, Γερμανοῖς
δὲ καὶ Γαλάταις μεμαχημένος ἀήττητος ὅσας
οὐκ ἄν τις ἀριθμήσαι μάχας ἑκατὸν μυριάδας
αἰχμαλώτων ἔλαβεν, ἑκατὸν δὲ ἀπέκτεινε τρεψάμενος ἐκ παρατάξεως.

LXVIII. Ἀλλ' ὅμως ἐγκείμενοι καὶ θορυ-
βοῦντες, ἐπεὶ κατέβησαν εἰς τὸ Φαρσάλιον
πεδίον, ἠνάγκασαν βουλὴν προθεῖναι τὸν Πομπήϊον, ἐν ᾗ Λαβιηνὸς ὁ τῶν ἱππέων ἄρχων
πρῶτος ἀναστὰς ὤμοσε μὴ ἀναχωρήσειν ἐκ τῆς
μάχης, εἰ μὴ τρέψαιτο τοὺς πολεμίους· τὰ δὲ
2 αὐτὰ καὶ πάντες ὤμνυσαν. τῆς δὲ νυκτὸς ἔδοξε
κατὰ τοὺς ὕπνους Πομπήϊος εἰς τὸ θέατρον
εἰσιόντος αὐτοῦ κροτεῖν τὸν δῆμον, αὐτὸς δὲ
κοσμεῖν ἱερὸν Ἀφροδίτης νικηφόρου πολλοῖς
λαφύροις. καὶ τὰ μὲν ἐθάρρει, τὰ δὲ ὑπέθραττεν
αὐτὸν ἡ ὄψις, δεδοικότα μὴ τῷ γένει τῷ Καίσαρος
εἰς Ἀφροδίτην ἀνήκοντι δόξα καὶ λαμπρότης
ἀπ' αὐτοῦ γένηται· καὶ πανικοί τινες θόρυβοι
3 διάττοντες ἐξανέστησαν αὐτόν. ἑωθινῆς δὲ
φυλακῆς ὑπὲρ τοῦ Καίσαρος στρατοπέδου πολλὴν ἡσυχίαν ἄγοντος ἐξέλαμψε μέγα φῶς, ἐκ δὲ
τούτου λαμπὰς ἀρθεῖσα φλογοειδὴς ἐπὶ τὸ [1] Πομ-
πήϊου κατέσκηψε· καὶ τοῦτο ἰδεῖν φησι Καῖσαρ
αὐτὸς ἐπιὼν τὰς φυλακάς. ἅμα δὲ ἡμέρα μέλλοντος αὐτοῦ πρὸς Σκοτοῦσαν ἀναζευγνύειν καὶ
τὰς σκηνὰς τῶν στρατιωτῶν καθαιρούντων καὶ
προπεμπόντων ὑποζύγια καὶ θεράποντας, ἧκον οἱ
σκοποὶ φράζοντες ὅπλα πολλὰ καθορᾶν ἐν τῷ

---

[1] ἐπὶ τὸ Coraës and Bekker, after Reiske : ἐπί.

them, or the king of the Nabataeans, and not that Caesar, and that army, who had taken by storm a thousand cities, subdued more than three hundred nations, and fought unvanquished with Germans and Gauls in more battles than one could number, taking a hundred times ten thousand prisoners, and slaying as many, after routing them on the battle-field.

LXVIII. But notwithstanding, by their importunities and agitations, after they had gone down into the plain of Pharsalia, they forced Pompey to hold a council of war, where Labienus, the commander of the cavalry, rose first and took an oath that he would not come back from the battle unless he routed the enemy; then all likewise swore the same oath. That night Pompey dreamed that as he entered his theatre the people clapped their hands, and that he decorated a temple of Venus Victrix with many spoils. On some accounts he was encouraged, but on others depressed, by the dream; he feared lest the race of Caesar, which went back to Venus, was to receive glory and splendour through him; and certain panic tumults which went rushing through the camp roused him from sleep. Furthermore, during the morning watch a great light shone out above the camp of Caesar, which was perfectly quiet, and a flaming torch rose from it and darted down upon the camp of Pompey; Caesar himself says he saw this as he was visiting the watches.[1] At break of day, Caesar was about to decamp and move to Scotussa, and his soldiers were taking down their tents and sending on ahead the beasts of burden and servants, when the scouts came in with a report that they saw many shields moving to and fro in the

---

[1] Cf. the *Caesar*, xliii. 3. It is not mentioned in the *Commentaries*.

χάρακι τῶν πολεμίων διαφερόμενα, καὶ κίνησιν
εἶναι καὶ θόρυβον ἀνδρῶν ἐπὶ μάχην ἐξιόντων.
4 μετὰ δὲ τούτους ἕτεροι παρῆσαν εἰς τάξιν ἤδη
καθίστασθαι τοὺς πρώτους λέγοντες. ὁ μὲν οὖν
Καῖσαρ εἰπὼν τὴν προσδοκωμένην ἥκειν ἡμέραν,
ἐν ᾗ πρὸς ἄνδρας, οὐ πρὸς λιμὸν οὐδὲ πενίαν
μαχοῦνται, κατὰ τάχος πρὸ τῆς σκηνῆς ἐκέλευσε
προθεῖναι τὸν φοινικοῦν χιτῶνα· τοῦτο γὰρ
5 μάχης Ῥωμαίοις ἐστὶ σύμβολον. οἱ δὲ στρατιῶται θεασάμενοι μετὰ βοῆς καὶ χαρᾶς τὰς
σκηνὰς ἀφέντες ἐφέροντο πρὸς τὰ ὅπλα. καὶ
τῶν ταξιαρχῶν ἀγόντων εἰς ἣν ἔδει τάξιν, ἕκαστος, ὥσπερ χορός, ἄνευ θορύβου μεμελετημένως
εἰς τάξιν[1] καὶ πράως καθίστατο.

LXIX. Πομπήιος δὲ τὸ μὲν δεξιὸν αὐτὸς ἔχων
ἔμελλεν ἀνθίστασθαι πρὸς Ἀντώνιον, ἐν δὲ τῷ
μέσῳ Σκηπίωνα τὸν πενθερὸν ἀντέταξε Καλβίνῳ
Λευκίῳ, τὸ δὲ εὐώνυμον εἶχε μὲν Λεύκιος Δομέ-
2 τιος, ἐρρώσθη δὲ τῷ πλήθει τῶν ἱππέων. ἐνταῦθα
γὰρ ὀλίγου δεῖν ἅπαντες ἐρρύησαν ὡς Καίσαρα   65
βιασόμενοι καὶ τὸ δέκατον τάγμα διακόψοντες,
οὗ πλεῖστος ἦν ὁ λόγος ὡς μαχιμωτάτου, καὶ
Καῖσαρ ἐν ἐκείνῳ ταττόμενος εἰώθει μάχεσθαι.
κατιδὼν δὲ πεφραγμένον ἵππῳ τοσαύτῃ τῶν
πολεμίων τὸ εὐώνυμον, καὶ φοβηθεὶς τὴν λαμπρότητα τοῦ ὁπλισμοῦ, μετεπέμψατο σπείρας ἓξ
ἀπὸ τῶν ἐπιταγμάτων καὶ κατέστησεν ὄπισθεν
3 τοῦ δεκάτου, κελεύσας ἡσυχίαν ἄγειν ἀδήλους
τοῖς πολεμίοις ὄντας· ὅταν δὲ προσελαύνωσιν οἱ
ἱππεῖς, διὰ τῶν προμάχων ἐκδραμόντας μὴ προέσθαι τοὺς ὑσσούς, ὥσπερ εἰώθασιν οἱ κράτιστοι

---

[1] εἰς τάξιν bracketed by Bekker.

enemy's camp, and that there was a noisy movement there of men coming out to battle. After these, others came announcing that the foremost ranks were already forming in battle array. Caesar, therefore, after saying that the expected day had come, on which they would fight against men, and not against want and hunger, quickly ordered the purple tunic to be hung up in front of his tent, that being the Roman signal for battle. His soldiers, on seeing this, left their tents with shouts of joy, and hurried to arms. And when their officers led them to the proper place, each man, as if in a chorus, not tumultuously, but with the quiet ease which training gives, fell into line.

LXIX. Pompey himself, with the right wing, intended to oppose Antony; in the centre he stationed Scipio, his father-in-law, over against Lucius Calvinus; his left wing was commanded by Lucius Domitius, and was supported by the main body of the cavalry.[1] For almost all the horsemen had crowded to this point, in order to overpower Caesar and cut to pieces the tenth legion; for this was generally said to fight better than any other, and in its ranks Caesar usually stood when he fought a battle. But Caesar, observing that the left wing of the enemy was enclosed by such a large body of horsemen, and alarmed at their brilliant array, sent for six cohorts from his reserves and stationed them behind the tenth legion, with orders to keep quiet and out of the enemy's sight; but whenever the cavalry charged, they were to run out through the front ranks, and were not to hurl their javelins, as

[1] Both Plutarch (not only here, but also in his *Caesar*, xliv. 1 f.) and Appian (*Bell. Civ.* ii. 76) differ in their accounts of the order of battle from that which Caesar himself gives (*Bell. Civ.* iii. 88 f.).

σπεύδοντες ἐπὶ τὰς ξιφουλκίας, ἀλλὰ παίειν ἄνω
συντιτρώσκοντας ὄμματα καὶ πρόσωπα τῶν
πολεμίων· οὐ γὰρ μενεῖν τοὺς καλοὺς τούτους
καὶ ἀνθηροὺς πυρριχιστὰς διὰ τὸν ὡραϊσμόν,
οὐδὲ ἀντιβλέψειν πρὸς τὸν σίδηρον ἐν ὀφθαλμοῖς
γινόμενον. ἐν τούτοις μὲν οὖν ὁ Καῖσαρ ἦν.

4   Ὁ δὲ Πομπήϊος ἀφ' ἵππου τὴν παράταξιν
ἐπισκοπῶν, ὡς ἑώρα τοὺς μὲν ἀντιπάλους μεθ'
ἡσυχίας τὸν καιρὸν ἐν τάξει προσμένοντας, τῆς
δ' ὑφ' αὑτῷ στρατιᾶς τὸ πλεῖστον οὐκ ἀτρεμοῦν,
ἀλλὰ κυμαῖνον ἀπειρίᾳ καὶ θορυβούμενον, ἔδεισε
μὴ διασπασθῇ παντάπασιν ἐν ἀρχῇ τῆς μάχης,
καὶ παράγγελμα τοῖς προτεταγμένοις ἔδωκεν
ἑστῶτας ἐν προβολῇ καὶ μένοντας ἀραρότως δέ-
5 χεσθαι τοὺς πολεμίους. ὁ δὲ Καῖσαρ αἰτιᾶται
τὸ στρατήγημα τοῦτο· τῶν τε γὰρ πληγῶν τὸν
ἐξ ἐπιδρομῆς τόνον ἀμαυρῶσαι, καὶ τὴν μάλιστα
τοὺς πολλοὺς ἐν τῷ συμφέρεσθαι τοῖς πολεμίοις
πληροῦσαν ἐνθουσιασμοῦ καὶ φορᾶς ἀντεξόρμη-
σιν, ἅμα κραυγῇ καὶ δρόμῳ τὸν θυμὸν αὔξουσαν,
ἀφελόντα πῆξαι καὶ καταψῦξαι τοὺς ἄνδρας.
ἦσαν δὲ οἱ μὲν μετὰ Καίσαρος δισχίλιοι πρὸς
δισμυρίοις, οἱ δὲ μετὰ Πομπηΐου βραχεῖ πλείονες
ἢ διπλάσιοι τούτων.

LXX. Ἤδη δὲ συνθήματος διδομένου παρὰ
ἀμφοτέρων καὶ τῆς σάλπιγγος ἀρχομένης ἐγκε-

the best soldiers usually did in their eagerness to draw their swords, but to strike upwards with them and wound the faces and eyes of the enemy; for these blooming and handsome war-dancers (he said) would not stand their ground for fear of having their youthful beauty marred, nor would they face the steel when it was right at their eyes. Caesar, then, was thus engaged.

But Pompey, who was surveying on horseback the battle array, when he saw that his antagonists were standing quietly in their ranks and awaiting the moment of attack, while the greater part of his own army was not at rest, but tossing about in waves of tumult, owing to its inexperience, was afraid that his array would be completely broken up at the beginning of the battle, and therefore ordered his front ranks to stand with their spears advanced, to remain fixed in their places, and so to receive the enemy's onset. Now, Caesar finds fault with these tactics [1]; he says that Pompey thereby robbed the blows of his weapons of that impetus which a rapid charge would have given them; and as for that rushing counter-charge, which more than any thing else fills most soldiers with impetuous enthusiasm as they close with their enemies, and combines with their shouts and running to increase their courage, Pompey deprived his men of this, and so rooted them to the spot where they stood, and chilled their spirits. And yet Caesar's forces numbered twenty-two thousand, while those of Pompey were a little more than twice as many.

LXX. And now at last the signal was given on both sides and the trumpet began to call to the

---

[1] *Bell. Civ.* iii. 92. Appian (*Bell. Civ.* ii. 79) says Caesar does this in his letters.

λεύεσθαι πρὸς τὴν σύστασιν, τῶν μὲν πολλῶν
ἕκαστος ἐσκόπει τὸ καθ᾽ αὑτόν, ὀλίγοι δὲ Ῥωμαίων οἱ βέλτιστοι καί τινες Ἑλλήνων παρόντες
ἔξω τῆς μάχης, ὡς ἐγγὺς ἦν τὸ δεινόν, ἐλογίζοντο
τὴν πλεονεξίαν καὶ φιλονεικίαν, ὅπου φέρουσα
2 τὴν ἡγεμονίαν ἐξέθηκεν. ὅπλα γὰρ συγγενικὰ
καὶ τάξεις ἀδελφαὶ καὶ κοινὰ σημεῖα καὶ μιᾶς
πόλεως εὐανδρία τοσαύτη καὶ δύναμις αὐτὴ πρὸς
ἑαυτὴν συνέπιπτεν, ἐπιδεικνυμένη τὴν ἀνθρω-
πίνην φύσιν, ὡς ἐν πάθει γενομένη τυφλόν ἐστι
καὶ μανιῶδες. ἦν μὲν γὰρ ἤδη καθ᾽ ἡσυχίαν
χρῄζουσιν ἄρχειν καὶ ἀπολαύειν τῶν κατειργασ-
μένων τὸ πλεῖστον καὶ κράτιστον ἀρετῇ γῆς καὶ
θαλάσσης ὑπήκοον, ἢν δ᾽ ἔτι τροπαίων καὶ θριάμβων ἔρωτι βουλομένους χαρίζεσθαι καὶ διψῶντας
ἐμπίπλασθαι Παρθικῶν πολέμων ἢ Γερμανικῶν.
3 πολὺ δὲ καὶ Σκυθία λειπόμενον ἔργον καὶ Ἰνδοί,
καὶ πρόφασις οὐκ ἄδοξος ἐπὶ ταῦτα τῆς πλεονεξίας ἡμερῶσαι τὰ βαρβαρικά. τίς δ᾽ ἂν ἢ
Σκυθῶν ἵππος ἢ τοξεύματα Πάρθων ἢ πλοῦτος
Ἰνδῶν ἐπέσχε μυριάδας ἑπτὰ Ῥωμαίων ἐν ὅπλοις
ἐπερχομένας Πομπηΐου καὶ Καίσαρος ἡγουμένων,
ὧν ὄνομα πολὺ πρότερον ἤκουσαν ἢ τὸ Ῥωμαίων;
οὕτως ἄμικτα καὶ ποικίλα καὶ θηριώδη φῦλα
4 νικῶντες ἐπῆλθον. τότε δὲ ἀλλήλοις μαχούμενοι
συνῄεσαν, οὐδὲ τὴν δόξαν αὑτῶν, δι᾽ ἣν τῆς
πατρίδος ἠφείδουν, οἰκτείραντες, ἄχρι τῆς ἡμέρας
ἐκείνης ἀνικήτων προσαγορευομένων. ἡ μὲν γὰρ
γενομένη συγγένεια καὶ τὰ Ἰουλίας φίλτρα καὶ
γάμος ἐκεῖνος εὐθὺς ἦν ἀπατηλὰ καὶ ὕποπτα
κοινωνίας ἐπὶ χρείᾳ συνισταμένης ὁμηρεύματα,
φιλίας δ᾽ ἀληθινῆς οὐ μετέσχεν.

conflict, and of that great host every man sought to do his part; but a few Romans, the noblest, and some Greeks, men who were present without taking part in the battle, now that the dreadful crisis was near, began to reflect upon the pass to which contentiousness and greed had brought the sovereign Roman state. For with kindred arms, fraternal ranks, and common standards, the strong manhood and might of a single city in such numbers was turning its own hand against itself, showing how blind and frenzied a thing human nature is when passion reigns. For had they now been willing quietly to govern and enjoy what they had conquered, the greatest and best part of earth and sea was subject to them, and if they still desired to gratify their thirst for trophies and triumphs, they might have had their fill of wars with Parthians or Germans. Besides, a great task still remained in the subjugation of Scythia and India, and here their greed would have had no inglorious excuse in the civilization of barbarous peoples. And what Scythian horse or Parthian archery or Indian wealth could have checked seventy thousand Romans coming up in arms under the leadership of Pompey and Caesar, whose names those nations had heard of long before that of Rome, so remote and various and savage were the peoples which they had attacked and conquered. But now they were about to join battle with one another, nor were they moved even by a compassion for their own glory to spare their country, men who up to that day had been called invincible! For the family alliance which had been made between them, and the charms of Julia, and her marriage, were now seen to have been from the first suspicious and deceptive pledges of a partnership based on self-interest; there was no real friendship in it.

LXXI. Ὡς δ᾽ οὖν τὸ Φαρσάλιον πεδίον ἀνδρῶν
καὶ ἵππων καὶ ὅπλων ἀνεπέπληστο καὶ μάχης
ἤρθη παρ᾽ ἀμφοτέρων σημεῖα, πρῶτος ἐκ τῆς
Καίσαρος φάλαγγος ἐξέδραμε Γάϊος Κρασσιανός,
ἀνδρῶν ἑκατὸν εἴκοσι λοχαγῶν, μεγάλην ἀποδι-
2 δοὺς ὑπόσχεσιν Καίσαρι. πρῶτον γὰρ αὐτὸν
ἐξιὼν τοῦ χάρακος εἶδε, καὶ προσαγορεύσας ἤρετο
πῶς φρονοίη περὶ τῆς μάχης. ὁ δὲ τὴν δεξιὰν
προτείνας ἀνεβόησε· "Νικήσεις λαμπρῶς, ὦ
Καῖσαρ· ἐμὲ δὲ ἢ ζῶντα τήμερον ἢ νεκρὸν ἐπαινέ-
σεις." τούτων τῶν λόγων μεμνημένος ἐξώρμησε
καὶ συνεπεσπάσατο πολλοὺς καὶ προσέβαλε
3 κατὰ μέσους τοὺς πολεμίους. γενομένου δὲ τοῦ
ἀγῶνος εὐθὺς ἐν ξίφεσι καὶ πολλῶν φονευομένων,
βιαζόμενον πρόσω καὶ διακόπτοντα τοὺς πρώτους
ὑποστάς τις ὠθεῖ διὰ τοῦ στόματος τὸ ξίφος,
ὥστε τὴν αἰχμὴν περάσασαν ἀνασχεῖν κατὰ τὸ
ἰνίον.

Πεσόντος δὲ τοῦ Κρασσιανοῦ, κατὰ τοῦτο μὲν
ἦν ἰσόρροπος ἡ μάχη, τὸ δὲ δεξιὸν ὁ Πομπήϊος οὐ
ταχέως ἐπῆγεν, ἀλλὰ παπταίνων ἐπὶ θάτερα καὶ
4 τὸ τῶν ἱππέων ἀναμένων ἔργον ἐνδιέτριβεν. ἤδη
δὲ ἐκεῖνοι τοὺς οὐλαμοὺς ἀνῆγον ὡς κυκλωσόμενοι
τὸν Καίσαρα, καὶ τοὺς προτεταγμένους ἱππεῖς
ὀλίγους ὄντας ἐμβαλοῦντες εἰς τὴν φάλαγγα.
Καίσαρος δὲ σημεῖον ἄραντος, οἱ μὲν ἱππεῖς
ἐξανεχώρησαν, αἱ δὲ ἐπιτεταγμέναι σπεῖραι πρὸς
τὴν κύκλωσιν ἐκδραμοῦσαι, τρισχίλιοι ἄνδρες,

---

[1] The name is Crastinus in Caesar's own story of the battle
(*Bell. Civ.* iii. 91).

LXXI. So then, when the Pharsalian plain was filled with men and horses and arms and the signals for battle had been lifted on both sides, the first to rush out from Caesar's lines was Caius Crassianus,[1] a centurion in command of one hundred and twenty men, who was thus redeeming a great promise made to Caesar. For he had been the first man whom Caesar saw as he issued from the camp, and addressing him, he had asked him what he thought about the battle. The centurion stretched forth his right hand and cried with a loud voice: "Thou wilt win a splendid victory, O Caesar; and I shall have thy praise to-day, whether I live or die." Mindful now of these words of his, he rushed forward, carrying many along with him, and threw himself into the midst of the enemy. The combatants at once took to their swords and many were slain, and as the centurion was forcing his way along and cutting down the men in the front ranks, one of them confronted him and drove his sword in at his mouth with such force that its point went through to the nape of his neck.[2]

After Crassianus had fallen, the battle was evenly contested at this point; Pompey, however, did not lead up his right wing swiftly, but kept looking anxiously towards the other parts of the field, and awaited the action of his cavalry on the left, thus losing time. These at last deployed their squadrons with a view to envelop Caesar, and to hurl back upon their supporting lines the horsemen whom he had stationed in front, only a few in number. But Caesar gave a signal, his cavalry retired, and the cohorts drawn up to oppose the enveloping movement ran out, three thousand men, and confronted

[2] Cf. Caesar, *op. cit.* iii. 99, where Caesar gives Crastinus that high praise for which he was willing to die.

ὑπαντιάζουσι τοὺς πολεμίους, καὶ παριστάμενοι
καθ' ἵππων, ὡς ἐδιδάχθησαν, ὑψηλοῖς ἐχρῶντο
5 τοῖς ὑσσοῖς, ἐφιέμενοι τῶν προσώπων. οἱ δέ, ἅτε
μάχης πάσης ἄπειροι, τοιαύτην δὲ μὴ προσδοκή-
σαντες μηδὲ προμαθόντες, οὐκ ἐτόλμων οὐδὲ ἠνεί-
χοντο τὰς πληγὰς ἐν ὄμμασι καὶ στόμασιν οὔσας,
ἀλλ' ἀποστρεφόμενοι καὶ προϊσχόμενοι τῶν
ὄψεων τὰς χεῖρας ἀκλεῶς ἐτράποντο. φευγόντων δὲ τούτων ἀμελήσαντες οἱ Καίσαρος ἐχώρουν
ἐπὶ τοὺς πεζούς, ᾗ μάλιστα τῶν ἱππέων τὸ κέρας
ἐψιλωμένον περιδρομὴν ἐδίδου καὶ κύκλωσιν.
6 ἅμα δὲ τούτων ἐκ πλαγίου προσπεσόντων καὶ
κατὰ στόμα τοῦ δεκάτου προσμίξαντος οὐχ
ὑπέμειναν οὐδὲ συνέστησαν, ὁρῶντες ἐν ᾧ κυκλώ-
σεσθαι τοὺς πολεμίους ἤλπιζον αὐτοὺς τοῦτο
πάσχοντας.

LXXII. Τραπομένων δὲ τούτων, ὡς κατεῖδε
τὸν κονιορτὸν ὁ Πομπήϊος καὶ τὸ περὶ τοὺς ἱππέας πάθος εἴκασεν, ᾧ μὲν ἐχρήσατο λογισμῷ
χαλεπὸν εἰπεῖν, μάλιστα δὲ ὅμοιος παράφρονι
καὶ παραπλῆγι τὴν διάνοιαν, καὶ μηδ' ὅτι Μάγνος
ἐστὶ Πομπήϊος ἐννοοῦντι, μηδένα προσειπὼν
ἀπῄει βάδην εἰς τὸν χάρακα, πάνυ τοῖς ἔπεσι
πρέπων ἐκείνοις·

2   Ζεὺς δὲ πατὴρ Αἴανθ' ὑψίζυγος ἐν φόβον ὦρσε·
   στῆ δὲ ταφών, ὄπιθεν δὲ σάκος βάλεν ἑπτα-
      βόειον,
  τρέσσε δὲ παπτήνας ἐφ' ὁμίλου.

their enemies, and standing close by the horses, as they had been directed, they thrust their javelins upwards, aiming at the faces of the riders. These, since they were without experience in every kind of fighting, and did not expect or even know anything about such a kind as this, had neither courage nor endurance to meet the blows which were aimed at their mouths and eyes, but wheeling about and putting their hands before their faces, they ingloriously took to flight. Then Caesar's soldiers, suffering these to make their escape, advanced upon the enemy's infantry, attacking at just that point where the wing, left unprotected by the flight of the cavalry, could be surrounded and enclosed. And since this body attacked them on the flank, while at the same time the tenth legion fell upon their front, the enemy did not stand their ground nor even hold together, for they saw that while they were expecting to surround the enemy, they were themselves being surrounded.

LXXII. After his infantry was thus routed, and when, from the cloud of dust which he saw, Pompey conjectured the fate of his cavalry, what thoughts passed through his mind it were difficult to say; but he was most like a man bereft of sense and crazed, who had utterly forgotten that he was Pompey the Great, and without a word to any one, he walked slowly off to his camp, exemplifying those verses of Homer[1]:

But Zeus the father, throned on high, in Ajax
    stirred up fear;
He stood confounded, and behind him cast his
    shield of seven ox-hides,
And trembled as he peered around upon the throng.

[1] *Iliad*, xi. 544 ff., where Telamonian Ajax retires before Hector and his Trojans.

τοιοῦτος εἰς τὴν σκηνὴν παρελθὼν ἄφθογγος καθ-
ῆστο, μέχρι οὗ τοῖς φεύγουσι πολλοὶ διώκοντες
συνεισέπιπτον· τότε δὲ φωνὴν μίαν ἀφεὶς ταύτην,
" Οὐκοῦν καὶ ἐπὶ τὴν παρεμβολήν ; " ἄλλο δὲ
μηδὲν εἰπών, ἀναστὰς καὶ λαβὼν ἐσθῆτα τῇ
3 παρούσῃ τύχῃ πρέπουσαν ὑπεξῆλθεν. ἔφυγε δὲ
καὶ τὰ λοιπὰ τάγματα, καὶ φόνος ἐν τῷ στρατοπέδῳ πολὺς ἐγένετο σκηνοφυλάκων καὶ θεραπόν-
των· στρατιώτας δὲ μόνους ἑξακισχιλίους πεσεῖν
φησιν Ἀσίννιος Πολλίων, μεμαχημένος ἐκείνην
τὴν μάχην μετὰ Καίσαρος.

4   Αἱροῦντες δὲ τὸ στρατόπεδον ἐθεῶντο τὴν ἄνοιαν
καὶ κουφότητα τῶν πολεμίων. πᾶσα γὰρ σκηνὴ
μυρσίναις κατέστεπτο καὶ στρωμναῖς ἀνθιναῖς
ἤσκητο καὶ τραπέζαις ἐκπωμάτων μεσταῖς· καὶ
κρατῆρες οἴνου προὔκειντο, καὶ παρασκευὴ καὶ
κόσμος ἦν τεθυκότων καὶ πανηγυριζόντων μᾶλλον
ἢ πρὸς μάχην ἐξοπλιζομένων. οὕτω ταῖς ἐλπίσι
διεφθαρμένοι καὶ γέμοντες ἀνοήτου θράσους ἐπὶ
τὸν πόλεμον ἐχώρουν.

LXXIII. Πομπήϊος δὲ μικρὸν ἔξω τοῦ χάρακος
προελθὼν τὸν μὲν ἵππον ἀφῆκεν, ὀλίγων δὲ κομιδῇ περὶ αὐτὸν ὄντων, ὡς οὐδεὶς ἐδίωκεν, ἀπῄει
καθ' ἡσυχίαν, ἐν διαλογισμοῖς ὢν οἵους εἰκὸς
λαμβάνειν ἄνθρωπον ἔτη τέτταρα καὶ τριάκοντα
νικᾶν καὶ κρατεῖν ἁπάντων εἰθισμένον, ἥττης δὲ
καὶ φυγῆς τότε πρῶτον ἐν γήρᾳ λαμβάνοντα πεῖραν, ἐννοούμενον δὲ ἐξ ὅσων ἀγώνων καὶ πολέμων
ηὐξημένην ἀποβαλὼν ὥρᾳ μιᾷ δόξαν καὶ δύναμιν,
2 ὁ[1] πρὸ μικροῦ τοσούτοις ὅπλοις καὶ ἵπποις καὶ

---

[1] ὁ Reiske's correction of ᾗ in the MSS., which Sintenis
and Bekker delete.

In such a state of mind he went to his tent and
sat down speechless, until many pursuers burst into
the camp with the fugitives; then he merely ejacu-
lated: "What! even to my quarters?" and without
another word rose up, took clothing suitable to his
present fortune, and made his escape. The rest of
his legions also fled, and there was a great slaughter
in the camp of tent-guards and servants; but only
six thousand soldiers fell,[1] according to Asinius
Pollio, who fought in that battle on the side of
Caesar.

When Caesar's troops captured the camp, they
beheld the vanity and folly of the enemy. For
every tent was wreathed with myrtle boughs and
decked out with flowered couches and tables loaded
with beakers; bowls of wine also were laid out, and
preparation and adornment were those of men who
had sacrificed and were holding festival rather than
of men who were arming themselves for battle. With
such infatuated hopes and such a store of foolish
confidence did they go forth to war.[2]

LXXIII. But Pompey, when he had gone a little
distance from the camp, gave his horse the rein, and
with only a few followers, since no one pursued him,
went quietly away, indulging in such reflections as a
man would naturally make who for four and thirty
years had been accustomed to conquer and get the
mastery in everything, and who now for the first
time, in his old age, got experience of defeat and
flight; he thought how in a single hour he had lost
the power and glory gained in so many wars and
conflicts, he who a little while ago was guarded by

---

[1] Caesar says that fifteen thousand of Pompey's soldiers
fell, and twenty-four thousand surrendered. His own losses
he puts at two hundred soldiers and thirty centurions (*Bell.
Civ*. iii. 99).   [2] Cf. Caesar, *op. cit*. iii. 96.

στόλοις δορυφορούμενος ἀπέρχεται μικρὸς οὕτω
γεγονὼς καὶ συνεσταλμένος ὥστε λανθάνειν ζη-
τοῦντας τοὺς πολεμίους. παραμειψάμενος δὲ
Λάρισσαν, ὡς ἦλθεν ἐπὶ τὰ Τέμπη, καταβαλὼν
ἑαυτὸν ἐπὶ στόμα δεδιψηκὼς ἔπινε τοῦ ποταμοῦ,
καὶ πάλιν ἀναστὰς ἐβάδιζε διὰ τῶν Τεμπῶν, ἄχρι
3 οὗ κατῆλθεν ἐπὶ θάλατταν. ἐκεῖ δὲ τῆς νυκτὸς τὸ
λοιπὸν ἀναπαυσάμενος ἐν καλυβίῳ τινὶ σαγηνέων,
καὶ περὶ τὸν ὄρθρον ἐπιβὰς ποταμίου πλοίου, καὶ
τῶν ἑπομένων τοὺς ἐλευθέρους ἀναλαβών, τοὺς δὲ
θεράποντας ἀπιέναι πρὸς Καίσαρα κελεύσας καὶ
μὴ δεδιέναι, παρὰ γῆν κομιζόμενος εἶδεν εὐμεγέθη
φορτηγὸν ἀνάγεσθαι μέλλουσαν, ἧς ἐναυκλήρει
Ῥωμαῖος ἀνὴρ οὐ πάνυ Πομπηΐῳ συνήθης, γινώ-
σκων δὲ τὴν ὄψιν αὐτοῦ· Πετίκιος ἐπεκαλεῖτο.
4 τούτῳ συνεβεβήκει τῆς παρῳχημένης νυκτὸς ἰδεῖν
κατὰ τοὺς ὕπνους Πομπήϊον, οὐχ ὃν ἑωράκει
πολλάκις, ἀλλὰ ταπεινὸν καὶ κατηφῆ, προσδια-
λεγόμενον αὐτῷ. καὶ ταῦτα τοῖς συμπλέουσιν
ἐτύγχανε διηγούμενος, ὡς δὴ φιλεῖ περὶ πραγμάτων τηλικούτων λόγον ἔχειν ἀνθρώπους σχολὴν
5 ἄγοντας. ἐξαίφνης δέ τις τῶν ναυτῶν ἔφρασε
κατιδὼν ὅτι πλοῖον ποτάμιον ἀπὸ τῆς γῆς ἐρέ-
σεται καὶ κατασείουσί τινες ἄνθρωποι τὰ ἱμάτια
καὶ τὰς χεῖρας ὀρέγουσι πρὸς αὐτούς. ἐπιστήσας
οὖν ὁ Πετίκιος εὐθὺς ἔγνω τὸν Πομπήϊον, οἷον
ὄναρ εἶδε· καὶ πληξάμενος τὴν κεφαλὴν ἐκέλευσε
τοὺς ναύτας τὸ ἐφόλκιον παραβαλεῖν, καὶ τὴν
δεξιὰν ἐξέτεινε καὶ προσεκάλει τὸν Πομπήϊον,
ἤδη συμφρονῶν τῷ σχήματι τὴν τύχην καὶ μετα-
6 βολὴν τοῦ ἀνδρός. ὅθεν οὔτε παράκλησιν ἀνα-
μείνας οὔτε λόγον, ἀλλ᾽ ἀναλαβὼν ὅσους ἐκέλευσε
μετ᾽ αὐτοῦ (Λέντουλοι δὲ ἦσαν ἀμφότεροι καὶ

such an array of infantry and horse, but was now going away so insignificant and humbled as to escape the notice of the enemies who were in search of him. After passing by Larissa, he came to the Vale of Tempe, and there, being thirsty, he threw himself down on his face and drank of the river; then, rising up again, he went on his way through Tempe, and at last came down to the sea. There he rested for the remainder of the night in a fisherman's hut. At early dawn he went aboard a river-boat, taking with him such of his followers as were freemen, but bidding his servants to go back to Caesar and to have no fear. Then he coasted along until he saw a merchant-ship of goodly size about to put to sea, the master of which was a Roman who, though not intimately acquainted with Pompey, nevertheless knew him by sight; his name was Peticius. This man, as it happened, had dreamed the night before that Pompey, not as he had often seen him, but humble and downcast, was addressing him. He was just telling this dream to his shipmates, as men who are at leisure are wont to make much of such matters, when suddenly one of the sailors told him that he saw a river-boat rowing out from the shore, and some men in it waving their garments and stretching out their hands towards them. Peticius, accordingly, turned his attention in that direction, and at once recognised Pompey, as he had seen him in his dream; then, smiting his head, he ordered the sailors to bring the little boat alongside, and stretching out his hand, hailed Pompey, already comprehending from his garb the change of fortune which the man had suffered. Wherefore, without waiting for argument or entreaty, he took Pompey on board, and also all whom Pompei wished to have with him (these were the two Lentul

Φαώνιος) ἀνήχθη· καὶ μικρὸν ὕστερον ἰδόντες
ἀπὸ γῆς ἁμιλλώμενον Δηϊόταρον τὸν βασιλέα
προσαναλαμβάνουσιν. ἐπεὶ δὲ καιρὸς ἦν δείπνου
καὶ παρεσκεύασεν ὁ ναύκληρος ἐκ τῶν παρόντων,
ἰδὼν ὁ Φαώνιος οἰκετῶν ἀπορίᾳ τὸν Πομπήϊον
ἀρχόμενον αὐτὸν ὑπολύειν προσέδραμε καὶ ὑπέ-
7 λυσε καὶ συνήλειψε. καὶ τὸ λοιπὸν ἐκ τούτου
περιέπων καὶ θεραπεύων ὅσα δεσπότας δοῦλοι,
μέχρι νίψεως ποδῶν καὶ δείπνου παρασκευῆς,
διετέλεσεν, ὥστε τὴν ἐλευθεριότητα τῆς ὑπουργίας
ἐκείνης θεασάμενον ἄν τινα καὶ τὸ ἀφελὲς καὶ
ἄπλαστον εἰπεῖν·

Φεῦ τοῖσι γενναίοισιν ὡς ἅπαν καλόν.

LXXIV. Οὕτω δὲ παραπλεύσας ἐπ' Ἀμφι-
πόλεως ἐκεῖθεν εἰς Μιτυλήνην ἐπεραιοῦτο, βουλόμενος τὴν Κορνηλίαν ἀναλαβεῖν καὶ τὸν υἱόν.
ἐπεὶ δὲ προσέσχε τῇ νήσῳ κατ' αἰγιαλόν, ἔπεμψεν εἰς πόλιν ἄγγελον, οὐχ ὡς ἡ Κορνηλία προσ-
εδόκα τοῖς πρὸς χάριν ἀπαγγελλομένοις καὶ
γραφομένοις, ἐλπίζουσα τοῦ πολέμου κεκριμένου
περὶ Δυρράχιον ἔτι λοιπὸν ἔργον εἶναι Πομπηΐῳ
2 τὴν Καίσαρος δίωξιν. ἐν τούτοις οὖσαν αὐτὴν
καταλαβὼν ὁ ἄγγελος ἀσπάσασθαι μὲν οὐχ ὑπέμεινε, τὰ δὲ πλεῖστα καὶ μέγιστα τῶν κακῶν τοῖς
δάκρυσι μᾶλλον ἢ τῇ φωνῇ φράσας σπεύδειν
ἐκέλευσεν, εἰ βούλεταί πως Πομπήϊον ἰδεῖν ἐπὶ
νεὼς μιᾶς καὶ ἀλλοτρίας. ἡ δὲ ἀκούσασα προήκατο μὲν αὐτὴν χαμᾶζε καὶ πολὺν χρόνον
ἔκφρων καὶ ἄναυδος ἔκειτο, μόλις δέ πως ἔμφρων

and Favonius), and set sail; and shortly after, seeing
Deiotarus the king hurrying out from shore, they
took him on board also. Now, when it was time for
supper and the master of the ship had made such
provision for them as he could, Favonius, seeing that
Pompey, for lack of servants, was beginning to take
off his own shoes, ran to him and took off his shoes
for him, and helped him to anoint himself. And
from that time on he continued to give Pompey such
ministry and service as slaves give their masters, even
down to the washing of his feet and the preparation
of his meals, so that any one who beheld the courtesy and the unfeigned simplicity of that service
might have exclaimed:

"Ah, yes! to generous souls how noble every task!"[1]

LXXIV. And so, after coasting along towards
Amphipolis, he crossed over to Mitylene, desiring to
take on board Cornelia and his son. And when he
had reached the shore of the island, he sent a
messenger to the city, not such a one as Cornelia
was expecting in view of the joyful messages and
letters she had received, for she was hoping that the
war was ended at Dyrrachium, and that the only
task left for Pompey was the pursuit of Caesar.
The messenger, finding her in this mood, could not
bring himself to salute her, but indicated to her the
most and greatest of her misfortunes by his tears
rather than by his speech, and merely bade her
hasten if she had any wish to see Pompey with one
ship only, and that not his own. When she heard
this, she cast herself upon the ground and lay there
a long time bereft of sense and speech. At last,

[1] The verse is assigned to Euripides in *Morals*, p. 85a
(Nauck, *Trag. Graec. Frag*[2], p. 671).

γενομένη καὶ συννοήσασα τὸν καιρὸν οὐκ ὄντα
θρήνων καὶ δακρύων, ἐξέδραμε διὰ τῆς πόλεως
3 ἐπὶ θάλατταν. ἀπαντήσαντος δὲ τοῦ Πομπηΐου
καὶ δεξαμένου ταῖς ἀγκάλαις αὐτὴν ὑπερειπο-
μένην καὶ περιπίπτουσαν, "Ὁρῶ σε," εἶπεν,
"ἄνερ, οὐ τῆς σῆς τύχης ἔργον, ἀλλὰ τῆς ἐμῆς, 6
προσερριμμένον ἑνὶ σκάφει τὸν πρὸ τῶν Κορ-
νηλίας γάμων πεντακοσίαις ναυσὶ ταύτην περι-
πλεύσαντα τὴν θάλασσαν. τί μ' ἦλθες ἰδεῖν καὶ
οὐκ ἀπέλιπες τῷ βαρεῖ δαίμονι τὴν καὶ σὲ δυστυχίας ἀναπλήσασαν τοσαύτης; ὡς εὐτυχὴς μὲν ἂν
ἤμην γυνὴ πρὸ τοῦ Πόπλιον ἐν Πάρθοις ἀκοῦσαι
τὸν παρθένιον ἄνδρα κείμενον ἀποθανοῦσα, σώφρων δὲ καὶ μετ' ἐκεῖνον, ὥσπερ ὥρμησα, τὸν
ἐμαυτῆς προεμένη βίον· ἐσωζόμην δ' ἄρα καὶ
Πομπηΐῳ Μάγνῳ συμφορὰ γενέσθαι."

LXXV. Ταῦτα εἰπεῖν τὴν Κορνηλίαν λέγουσι,
τὸν δὲ Πομπήϊον ἀποκρίνασθαι· "Μίαν ἄρα,
Κορνηλία, τύχην ᾔδεις τὴν ἀμείνονα, ἣ καὶ σὲ
ἴσως ἐξηπάτησεν, ὅτι μοι χρόνον πλείονα τοῦ
συνήθους παρέμεινεν. ἀλλὰ καὶ ταῦτα δεῖ φέρειν γενομένους ἀνθρώπους, καὶ τῆς τύχης ἔτι
πειρατέον. οὐ γὰρ ἀνέλπιστον ἐκ τούτων ἀναλαβεῖν ἐκεῖνα τὸν ἐξ ἐκείνων ἐν τούτοις γενόμενον."

2 Ἡ μὲν οὖν γυνὴ μετεπέμπετο χρήματα καὶ
θεράποντας ἐκ πόλεως· τῶν δὲ Μιτυληναίων
τὸν Πομπήϊον ἀσπασαμένων καὶ παρακαλούντων
εἰσελθεῖν εἰς τὴν πόλιν, οὐκ ἠθέλησεν, ἀλλὰ
κἀκείνους ἐκέλευσε τῷ κρατοῦντι πείθεσθαι καὶ
θαρρεῖν· εὐγνώμονα γὰρ εἶναι Καίσαρα καὶ
3 χρηστόν. αὐτὸς δὲ πρὸς Κράτιππον τραπόμενος
τὸν φιλόσοφον (κατέβη γὰρ ἐκ τῆς πόλεως

however, and with difficulty, she regained her senses, and perceiving that the occasion was not one for tears and lamentations, she ran out through the city to the sea. Pompey met her and caught her in his arms as she tottered and was falling. " I see thee," she cried, " husband, not by thy fortune, but by mine, reduced to one small vessel, thou who before thy marriage with Cornelia didst sail this sea with five hundred ships. Why hast thou come to see me, and why didst thou not leave to her cruel destiny one who has infected thee also with an evil fortune so great ? What a happy woman I had been if I had died before hearing that Publius, whose virgin bride I was, was slain among the Parthians ! And how wise if, even after his death, as I essayed to do, I had put an end to my own life ! But I was spared, it seems, to bring ruin also upon Pompey the Great."

LXXV. So spake Cornelia, as we are told, and Pompey answered, saying : " It is true, Cornelia, thou hast known but one fortune to be mine, the better one, and this has perhaps deceived thee too, as well as me, in that it remained with me longer than is customary. But this reverse also we must bear, since we are mortals, and we must still put fortune to the test. For I can have some hope of rising again from this low estate to my former high estate, since I fell from that to this."

His wife, accordingly, sent for her goods and servants from the city; and though the Mitylenaeans gave Pompey a welcome and invited him to enter their city, he would not consent to do so, but bade them also to submit to the conqueror, and to be of good heart, for Caesar was humane and merciful. He himself, however, turning to Cratippus the philosopher, who had come down from the city to

ὀψόμενος αὐτόν), ἐμέμψατο καὶ συνδιηπόρησε
βραχέα περὶ τῆς προνοίας, ὑποκατακλινομένου τοῦ
Κρατίππου καὶ παράγοντος αὐτὸν ἐπὶ τὰς ἀμεί-
νονας ἐλπίδας, ὅπως μὴ λυπηρὸς μηδὲ ἄκαιρος
4 ἀντιλέγων εἴη. ἐπεὶ τὸ μὲν ἐρέσθαι τὸν Πομπήϊον ἦν ὑπὲρ τῆς προνοίας, τὸν δ᾽ ἀποφαίνεσθαι
ὅτι τοῖς πράγμασιν ἤδη μοναρχίας ἔδει διὰ τὴν
κακοπολιτείαν· ἐρέσθαι δέ· " Πῶς, ὦ Πομπήϊε,
καὶ τίνι τεκμηρίῳ πεισθῶμεν ὅτι βέλτιον ἂν σὺ
τῇ τύχῃ Καίσαρος ἐχρήσω κρατήσας ; " ἀλλὰ
ταῦτα μὲν ἐατέον ὥσπερ ἔχει, τὰ τῶν θεῶν.

LXXVI. Ἀναλαβὼν δὲ τὴν γυναῖκα καὶ τοὺς
φίλους ἐκομίζετο, προσίσχων ὅρμοις ἀναγκαίοις
ὕδωρ ἢ ἀγορὰν ἔχουσιν. εἰς δὲ πόλιν εἰσῆλθε
πρώτην Ἀττάλειαν τῆς Παμφυλίας. ἐνταῦθα δὲ
αὐτῷ καὶ τριήρεις τινὲς ἀπήντησαν ἐκ Κιλικίας
καὶ στρατιῶται συνελέγοντο καὶ τῶν συγκλητι-
2 κῶν πάλιν ἑξήκοντα περὶ αὐτὸν ἦσαν. ἀκούων
δὲ καὶ τὸ ναυτικὸν ἔτι συνεστάναι, καὶ Κάτωνα
πολλοὺς στρατιώτας ἀνειληφότα περαιοῦν εἰς
Λιβύην, ὠδύρετο πρὸς τοὺς φίλους, καταμεμφό-
μενος ἑαυτὸν ἐκβιασθέντα τῷ πεζῷ συμβαλεῖν,
τῇ δὲ κρείττονι ἀδηρίτως δυνάμει πρὸς μηδὲν
ἀποχρήσασθαι μηδὲ περιορμίσαι τὸ ναυτικόν,
ὅπου κατὰ γῆν σφαλεὶς εὐθὺς ἂν εἶχεν ἀντίπαλον
ἐκ θαλάττης παρεστῶσαν ἀλκὴν καὶ δύναμιν
3 τοσαύτην. οὐδὲν γὰρ ἁμάρτημα Πομπηΐου μεῖζον
οὐδὲ δεινότερον στρατήγημα Καίσαρος ἢ τὸ τὴν

see him, complained and argued briefly with him
about Providence, Cratippus yielding somewhat to
his reasoning and trying to lead him on to better
hopes, that he might not give him pain by arguing
against him at such a time. For when Pompey
raised questions about Providence, Cratippus might
have answered that the state now required a
monarchy because it was so badly administered ; and
he might have asked Pompey : " How, O Pompey,
and by what evidence, can we be persuaded that
thou wouldst have made a better use of fortune
than Caesar, hadst thou got the mastery ? " But
this matter of the divine ordering of events must be
left without further discussion.[1]

LXXVI. After taking on board his wife and his
friends, Pompey went on his way, putting in at
harbours only when he was compelled to get food or
water there. The first city that he entered was
Attaleia in Pamphylia ; there some triremes from
Cilicia met him, soldiers were assembled for him, and
he was surrounded again by senators, sixty of them.
On hearing, too, that his fleet still held together,
and that Cato had taken many soldiers aboard and
was crossing the sea to Africa, he lamented to his
friends, blaming himself for having been forced to
do battle with his land forces, while he made no use
of his navy, which was indisputably superior, and
had not even stationed it at a point where, if
defeated on land, he might have had this powerful
force close at hand by sea to make him a match for
his enemy. And, in truth, Pompey made no greater
mistake, and Caesar showed no abler generalship,

---

[1] Sintenis[2] follows Amyot in including this last sentence
with the words supposed to be spoken by Cratippus : " *But
these matters must be left to the will of the gods.*"

μάχην οὕτω μακρὰν ἀποσπάσασθαι τῆς ναυτικῆς
βοηθείας. οὐ μὴν ἀλλ᾽ ἐκ τῶν παρόντων κρίνειν
τι καὶ πράττειν ἀναγκαζόμενος, ἐπὶ τὰς πόλεις
περιέπεμπε· τὰς δ᾽ αὐτὸς περιπλέων ᾔτει χρήματα καὶ ναῦς ἐπλήρου. τὴν δ᾽ ὀξύτητα τοῦ
πολεμίου καὶ τὸ τάχος δεδοικώς, μὴ προαναρπάσῃ
τῆς παρασκευῆς αὐτὸν ἐπελθών, ἐσκόπει κατα-
4 φυγὴν ἐπὶ τῷ παρόντι καὶ ἀναχώρησιν. ἐπαρχία
μὲν οὖν οὐδεμία φύξιμος ἐφαίνετο βουλευομένοις
αὐτοῖς, τῶν δὲ βασιλειῶν αὐτὸς μὲν ἀπέφαινε
τὴν Πάρθων ἱκανωτάτην οὖσαν ἔν τε τῷ παρόντι
δέξασθαι καὶ περιβαλεῖν σφᾶς ἀσθενεῖς ὄντας,
αὖθίς τε ῥῶσαι καὶ προπέμψαι μετὰ πλείστης
5 δυνάμεως· τῶν δ᾽ ἄλλων οἱ μὲν εἰς Λιβύην καὶ
Ἰόβαν ἔτρεπον τὴν γνώμην, Θεοφάνει δὲ τῷ
Λεσβίῳ μανικὸν ἐδόκει τριῶν ἡμερῶν πλοῦν
ἀπέχουσαν Αἴγυπτον ἀπολιπόντα καὶ Πτολεμαῖον, ἡλικίαν μὲν ἀντίπαιδα, φιλίας δὲ καὶ χάριτος πατρῴας ὑπόχρεων, Πάρθοις ὑποβαλεῖν 6
ἑαυτόν, ἀπιστοτάτῳ γένει, καὶ Ῥωμαίῳ μὲν ἀνδρὶ
κηδεστῇ γενομένῳ τὰ δεύτερα λέγοντα πρῶτον
εἶναι τῶν ἄλλων μὴ θέλειν μηδὲ πειρᾶσθαι τῆς
6 ἐκείνου μετριότητος, Ἀρσάκην δὲ ποιεῖσθαι κύριον ἑαυτοῦ τὸν μηδὲ Κράσσου δυνηθέντα ζῶντος·
καὶ γυναῖκα νέαν οἴκου τοῦ Σκηπίωνος εἰς βαρβάρους κομίζειν ὕβρει καὶ ἀκολασίᾳ τὴν ἐξουσίαν
μετροῦντας, ᾗ, κἂν μὴ πάθῃ, δόξῃ δὲ παθεῖν,

---

[1] His father was Ptolemy Auletes, mentioned in chapter
xlix. 5. He had been restored to his throne in 55 B.C.
through Pompey's influence. The son, Ptolemy Dionysius,

than in removing the battle so far from naval assistance. However, since he was compelled to decide and act as best he could under the circumstances, he sent messengers round to the cities; to some also he sailed about in person, asking for money and manning ships. But fearing the quickness and speed of his enemy, who might come upon him and seize him before he was prepared, he began to look about for a temporary refuge and retreat. Accordingly, as he deliberated with his followers, there appeared to be no province to which they could safely fly, and as for the kingdoms, he himself expressed the opinion that the Parthian was best able for the present to receive and protect them in their weak condition, and later on to strengthen them and send them forth with a large force; of the rest, some turned their thoughts to Africa and Juba. But Theophanes the Lesbian thought it a crazy thing for Pompey to decide against Egypt, which was only three days' sail away, and Ptolemy, who was a mere youth and indebted to Pompey for friendship and kindness shown his father,[1] and put himself in the power of Parthians, a most treacherous race; to refuse to take the second place under a Roman who had been connected with him by marriage, and to be second to none other, nay, to refuse even to make trial of that Roman's moderation, but instead to make Arsaces his lord and master, a thing which even Crassus could not be made to do while he lived; and to carry a young wife, of the family of Scipio, among Barbarians who measure their power by their insolence and licentiousness, where, even if she suffer no harm, but

---

[1] now fifteen years of age, had been left joint ruler of Egypt with his sister, Cleopatra.

δεινόν ἐστιν ἐπὶ τοῖς ποιῆσαι δυναμένοις γενομένη. τοῦτο μόνον, ὥς φασιν, ἀπέτρεψε τῆς ἐπὶ
τὸν Εὐφράτην ὁδοῦ Πομπήιον· εἰ δή τις ἔτι Πομπηίου λογισμός, ἀλλ' οὐχὶ δαίμων ἐκείνην ὑφη-
γεῖτο τὴν ὁδόν.

LXXVII. Ὡς δ' οὖν ἐνίκα φεύγειν εἰς τὴν
Αἴγυπτον, ἀναχθεὶς ἀπὸ Κύπρου Σελευκίδι τριήρει μετὰ τῆς γυναικός (τῶν δ' ἄλλων οἱ μὲν ἐν
μακραῖς ὁμοίως ναυσίν, οἱ δὲ ἐν ὁλκάσιν ἅμα
συμπαρέπλεον), τὸ μὲν πέλαγος διεπέρασεν ἀσφαλῶς, πυθόμενος δὲ τὸν Πτολεμαῖον ἐν Πη-
λουσίῳ καθῆσθαι μετὰ στρατιᾶς, πολεμοῦντα
πρὸς τὴν ἀδελφήν, ἐκεῖ κατέσχε, προπέμψας τὸν
2 φράσοντα τῷ βασιλεῖ καὶ δεησόμενον. ὁ μὲν
οὖν Πτολεμαῖος ἦν κομιδῇ νέος· ὁ δὲ πάντα
διέπων τὰ πράγματα Ποθεινὸς ἤθροισε βουλὴν
τῶν δυνατωτάτων· ἐδύναντο δὲ μέγιστον οὓς
ἐκεῖνος ἐβούλετο· καὶ λέγειν ἐκέλευσεν ἣν ἔχει
γνώμην ἕκαστος. ἦν οὖν δεινὸν περὶ Πομπηίου
Μάγνου βουλεύεσθαι Ποθεινὸν τὸν εὐνοῦχον καὶ
Θεόδοτον τὸν Χῖον, ἐπὶ μισθῷ ῥητορικῶν λόγων
διδάσκαλον ἀνειλημμένον, καὶ τὸν Αἰγύπτιον
Ἀχιλλᾶν· κορυφαιότατοι γὰρ ἦσαν ἐν κατευνα-
σταῖς καὶ τιθηνοῖς τοῖς ἄλλοις οὗτοι σύμβουλοι.
3 καὶ τοιούτου δικαστηρίου ψῆφον Πομπήιος ἐπ'
ἀγκυρῶν πρόσω τῆς χώρας ἀποσαλεύων περιέμενεν, ὃν Καίσαρι σωτηρίας χάριν οὐκ ἦν ἄξιον
ὀφείλειν.

Τῶν μὲν οὖν ἄλλων τοσοῦτον αἱ γνῶμαι διέστησαν ὅσον οἱ μὲν ἀπελαύνειν ἐκέλευον, οἱ δὲ
4 καλεῖν καὶ δέχεσθαι τὸν ἄνδρα· Θεόδοτος δὲ
δεινότητα λόγου καὶ ῥητορείαν ἐπιδεικνύμενος

is only thought to have suffered harm, her fate is a terrible one, since she has come into the power of those who are able to do her harm. This consideration alone, as we are told, diverted Pompey from journeying to the Euphrates, if indeed it was longer any calculation of Pompey's, and not rather an evil genius, that was guiding him on this last journey.

LXXVII. So when it was decided that he should fly to Egypt, he set sail from Cyprus on a Seleucian trireme with his wife (of the rest, some sailed along with him in ships of war like his own, and others in merchant vessels), and crossed the sea in safety; but on learning that Ptolemy was posted at Pelusium with an army, making war upon his sister, he put in there, and sent on a messenger to announce his arrival to the king and to ask his aid. Now, Ptolemy was quite young; but Potheinus, who managed all his affairs, assembled a council of the most influential men (and those were most influential whom he wished to be so), and bade each one give his opinion. It was certainly a dreadful thing that the fate of Pompey the Great was to be decided by Potheinus the eunuch, and Theodotus of Chios, who was a hired teacher of rhetoric, and Achillas the Egyptian; for these were the chief counsellors of the king among the chamberlains and tutors also gathered there. And it was such a tribunal's verdict which Pompey, tossing at anchor some distance off the shore, was waiting for, a man who would not deign to be under obligations to Caesar for his life.

The opinions of the other counsellors were so far divergent that some advised to drive Pompey away, and others to invite him in and receive him. But Theodotus, making a display of his powerful speech

οὐδέτερον ἀπέφηνεν ἀσφαλές, ἀλλὰ δεξαμένους
μὲν ἕξειν Καίσαρα πολέμιον καὶ δεσπότην Πομπήϊον, ἀπωσαμένους δὲ καὶ Πομπηΐῳ τῆς ἐκβολῆς
ὑπαιτίους ἔσεσθαι καὶ Καίσαρι τῆς διώξεως·
κράτιστον οὖν εἶναι μεταπεμψαμένους ἀνελεῖν
τὸν ἄνδρα· καὶ γὰρ ἐκείνῳ χαριεῖσθαι καὶ τοῦτον
οὐ φοβήσεσθαι. προσεπεῖπε δὲ διαμειδιάσας, ὡς
φασιν, ὅτι νεκρὸς οὐ δάκνει.

LXXVIII. Ταῦτα κυρώσαντες ἐπ᾽ Ἀχιλλᾷ
ποιοῦνται τὴν πρᾶξιν. ὁ δὲ Σεπτίμιόν τινα
πάλαι γεγονότα Πομπηΐου ταξίαρχον παραλα-
βών, καὶ Σάλβιον ἕτερον ἑκατοντάρχην καὶ τρεῖς
ἢ τέτταρας ὑπηρέτας, ἀνήχθη πρὸς τὴν Πομπηΐου
ναῦν. ἔτυχον δὲ πάντες εἰς αὐτὴν οἱ δοκιμώτατοι
τῶν συμπλεόντων ἐμβεβηκότες, ὅπως εἰδεῖεν τὸ
2 πραττόμενον. ὡς οὖν εἶδον οὐ βασιλικὴν οὐδὲ
λαμπρὰν οὐδὲ ταῖς Θεοφάνους ἐλπίσιν ὁμοίαν
ὑποδοχήν, ἀλλ᾽ ἐπὶ μιᾶς ἁλιάδος προσπλέοντας
ὀλίγους ἀνθρώπους, ὑπείδοντο τὴν ὀλιγωρίαν καὶ
τῷ Πομπηΐῳ παρῄνουν εἰς πέλαγος ἀνακρούεσθαι
τὴν ναῦν, ἕως ἔξω βέλους εἰσίν. ἐν τούτῳ δὲ
πελαζούσης τῆς ἁλιάδος φθάσας ὁ Σεπτίμιος
ἐξανέστη καὶ Ῥωμαϊστὶ τὸν Πομπήϊον αὐτοκρά-
3 τορα προσηγόρευσεν. ὁ δὲ Ἀχιλλᾶς ἀσπασάμενος αὐτὸν Ἑλληνιστὶ παρεκάλει μετελθεῖν εἰς
τὴν ἁλιάδα· τέναγος γὰρ εἶναι πολύ, καὶ βάθος
οὐκ ἔχειν πλόϊμον τριήρει τὴν θάλατταν ὑπόψαμ-
μον οὖσαν. ἅμα δὲ καὶ ναῦς τινες ἑωρῶντο τῶν
βασιλικῶν πληρούμεναι, καὶ τὸν αἰγιαλὸν ὁπλῖται
κατεῖχον, ὥστ᾽ ἄφυκτα καὶ μεταβαλλομένοις ἐφαί-

and rhetorical art, set forth that neither course was
safe for them, but that if they received Pompey,
they would have Caesar for an enemy and Pompey
for a master; while if they rejected him, Pompey
would blame them for casting him off, and Caesar
for making him continue his pursuit; the best
course, therefore, was to send for the man and put
him to death, for by so doing they would gratify
Caesar and have nothing to fear from Pompey. To
this he smilingly added, we are told, "A dead man
does not bite."

LXXVIII. Having determined upon this plan,
they entrusted the execution of it to Achillas. So
he took with him a certain Septimius, who had once
been a tribune of Pompey's, and Salvius besides, a
centurion, with three or four servants, and put out
towards the ship of Pompey. Now, all the most
distinguished of Pompey's fellow-voyagers had come
aboard of her to see what was going on. Accordingly, when they saw a reception that was not royal,
nor splendid, nor in accordance with the hopes of
Theophanes, but a few men sailing up in a single
fishing-boat, they viewed this lack of respect with
suspicion, and advised Pompey to have his ship
rowed back into the open sea, while they were
beyond reach of missiles. But meanwhile the boat
drew near, and first Septimius rose up and addressed
Pompey in the Roman tongue as Imperator. Then
Achillas saluted him in Greek, and invited him to
come aboard the boat, telling him that the shallows
were extensive, and that the sea, which had a sandy
bottom, was not deep enough to float a trireme. At
the same time some of the royal ships were seen to
be taking their crews aboard, and men-at-arms were
occupying the shore, so that there seemed to be no

νετο, καὶ προσῆν τὸ διδόναι τοῖς φονεῦσι τὴν
4 ἀπιστίαν αὐτὴν τῆς ἀδικίας ἀπολογίαν. ἀσπασάμενος οὖν τὴν Κορνηλίαν προαποθρηνοῦσαν αὐτοῦ
τὸ τέλος, καὶ δύο ἑκατοντάρχας προεμβῆναι κελεύσας καὶ τῶν ἀπελευθέρων ἕνα Φίλιππον καὶ
θεράποντα Σκύθην ὄνομα, δεξιουμένων αὐτὸν ἤδη
τῶν περὶ τὸν Ἀχιλλᾶν ἐκ τῆς ἁλιάδος, μεταστραφεὶς πρὸς τὴν γυναῖκα καὶ τὸν υἱὸν εἶπε
Σοφοκλέους ἰαμβεῖα·

   Ὅστις δὲ πρὸς τύραννον ἐμπορεύεται,
   κείνου 'στὶ δοῦλος, κἂν ἐλεύθερος μόλῃ.

LXXIX. Ταῦτα δ' ἔσχατα πρὸς τοὺς ἑαυτοῦ
φθεγξάμενος ἐνέβη· καὶ συχνοῦ διαστήματος ὄντος
ἐπὶ τὴν γῆν ἀπὸ τῆς τριήρους, ὡς οὐδεὶς παρὰ τῶν
συμπλεόντων ἐγίνετο λόγος φιλάνθρωπος πρὸς
αὐτόν, ἀποβλέψας εἰς τὸν Σεπτίμιον, "Οὐ δή
πού σε," εἶπεν, "ἐγὼ γεγονότα συστρατιώτην
2 ἐμὸν ἀμφιγνοῶ ;" κἀκεῖνος ἐπένευσε τῇ κεφαλῇ
μόνον, οὐδὲν προσειπὼν οὐδὲ φιλοφρονηθείς. πολλῆς οὖν πάλιν οὔσης σιωπῆς ὁ Πομπήϊος ἔχων
ἐν βιβλίῳ μικρῷ γεγραμμένον ὑπ' αὐτοῦ λόγον
Ἑλληνικόν, ᾧ παρεσκεύαστο χρῆσθαι πρὸς τὸν
3 Πτολεμαῖον, ἀνεγίνωσκεν. ὡς δὲ τῇ γῇ προσ-
επέλαζον, ἡ μὲν Κορνηλία μετὰ τῶν φίλων ἐκ τῆς
τριήρους περιπαθὴς οὖσα τὸ μέλλον ἀπεσκοπεῖτο,
καὶ θαρρεῖν ἤρχετο πολλοὺς ὁρῶσα πρὸς τὴν
ἀπόβασιν τῶν βασιλικῶν οἷον ἐπὶ τιμῇ καὶ δεξιώ-
σει συνερχομένους. ἐν τούτῳ δὲ τὸν Πομπήϊον

escape even if they changed their minds; and
besides, this very lack of confidence might give the
murderers an excuse for their crime. Accordingly,
after embracing Cornelia, who was bewailing his
approaching death, he ordered two centurions to go
into the boat before him, besides Philip, one of his
freedmen, and a servant named Scythes, and while
Achillas was already stretching out his hand to him
from the boat, turned towards his wife and son and
repeated the verses of Sophocles :—

Whatever man unto a tyrant takes his way,
His slave he is, even though a freeman when he
  goes.[1]

LXXIX. After these last words to his friends, he
went into the boat. And since it was a long
distance from the trireme to the land, and none of
his companions in the boat had any friendly word
for him, turning his eyes upon Septimius he said :
"Surely I am not mistaken, and you are an old
comrade of mine!" Septimius nodded merely,
without saying anything to him or showing any
friendliness. So then, as there was profound silence
again, Pompey took a little roll containing a speech
written by him in Greek, which he had prepared for
his use in addressing Ptolemy, and began to read
in it. Then, as they drew near the shore, Cornelia,
together with his friends, stood on the trireme
watching with great anxiety for the outcome, and
began to take heart when she saw many of the
king's people assembling at the landing as if to give
him an honourable welcome. But at this point,

---

[1] Nauck, *Trag. Graec. Frag.*[2] p. 316. The recitation of
these verses is a feature common also to the accounts of the
tragedy in Appian (*Bell. Civ.* ii. 84) and Dio Cassius (xlii. 4).

τῆς τοῦ Φιλίππου λαμβανόμενον χειρός, ὅπως
ῥᾷον ἐξανασταίη, Σεπτίμιος ὄπισθεν τῷ ξίφει διε-
λαύνει πρῶτος, εἶτα Σάλβιος μετ' ἐκεῖνον, εἶτα
4 Ἀχιλλᾶς ἐσπάσαντο τὰς μαχαίρας. ὁ δὲ ταῖς
χερσὶν ἀμφοτέραις τὴν τήβεννον ἐφελκυσάμενος
κατὰ τοῦ προσώπου, μηδὲν εἰπὼν ἀνάξιον ἑαυτοῦ
μηδὲ ποιήσας, ἀλλὰ στενάξας μόνον, ἐνεκαρτέρησε
ταῖς πληγαῖς, ἑξήκοντα μὲν ἑνὸς δέοντα βεβιωκὼς
ἔτη, μιᾷ δ' ὕστερον ἡμέρᾳ τῆς γενεθλίου τελευ-
τήσας τὸν βίον.

LXXX. Οἱ δ' ἀπὸ τῶν νεῶν ὡς ἐθεάσαντο τὸν
φόνον, οἰμωγὴν ἐξάκουστον ἄχρι τῆς γῆς ἐκχέ-
αντες ἔφυγον, ἀράμενοι τὰς ἀγκύρας κατὰ τάχος.
καὶ πνεῦμα λαμπρὸν ἐβοήθει πελαγίοις ὑπεκθέ-
ουσιν, ὥστε βουλομένους διώκειν ἀποτραπέσθαι
τοὺς Αἰγυπτίους. τοῦ δὲ Πομπηΐου τὴν μὲν
κεφαλὴν ἀποτέμνουσι, τὸ δὲ ἄλλο σῶμα γυμνὸν
ἐκβαλόντες ἀπὸ τῆς ἁλιάδος τοῖς δεομένοις τοιού-
2 του θεάματος ἀπέλιπον. παρέμεινε δὲ αὐτῷ
Φίλιππος, ἕως ἐγένοντο μεστοὶ τῆς ὄψεως· εἶτα
περιλούσας τῇ θαλάσσῃ τὸ σῶμα καὶ χιτωνίῳ
τινὶ τῶν ἑαυτοῦ περιστείλας, ἄλλο δὲ οὐδὲν ἔχων,
ἀλλὰ περισκοπῶν τὸν αἰγιαλὸν εὗρε μικρᾶς ἁλιάδος λείψανα, παλαιὰ μέν, ἀρκοῦντα δὲ νεκρῷ
γυμνῷ καὶ οὐδὲ ὅλῳ πυρκαϊὰν ἀναγκαίαν παρα-
3 σχεῖν. ταῦτα συγκομίζοντος αὐτοῦ καὶ συντι-
θέντος ἐπιστὰς ἀνὴρ Ῥωμαῖος ἤδη γέρων, τὰς δὲ
πρώτας ἔτι νέος Πομπηΐῳ συνεστρατευμένος, "Τίς ὤν, ὦ ἄνθρωπε," ἔφη, "θάπτειν
διανοῇ Μάγνον Πομπήϊον;" ἐκείνου δὲ φήσαντος
ὡς ἀπελεύθερος, "Ἀλλ' οὐ μόνῳ σοί," ἔφη, "τοῦτο τὸ καλὸν ὑπάρξει· κἀμὲ δὲ ὥσπερ εὑρήματος

while Pompey was clasping the hand of Philip that he might rise to his feet more easily, Septimius, from behind, ran him through the body with his sword, then Salvius next, and then Achillas, drew their daggers and stabbed him.[1] And Pompey, drawing his toga down over his face with both hands, without an act or a word that was unworthy of himself, but with a groan merely, submitted to their blows, being sixty years of age less one, and ending his life only one day after his birth-day.

LXXX. When the people on the ships beheld the murder, they uttered a wailing cry that could be heard as far as the shore, and weighing anchor quickly, took to flight. And a strong wind came to their aid as they ran out to sea, so that the Egyptians, though desirous of pursuing, turned back. But they cut off Pompey's head, and threw the rest of his body unclothed out of the boat, and left it for those who craved so pitiful a sight. Philip, however, stayed by the body, until such had taken their fill of gazing; then he washed it in sea-water, wrapped it in a tunic of his own, and since he had no other supply, sought along the coast until he found the remnants of a small fishing-boat, old stuff, indeed, but sufficient to furnish a funeral pyre that would answer for an unclothed corpse, and that too not entire. As he was gathering the wood and building the pyre, there came up a Roman who was now an old man, but who in his youth had served his first campaigns with Pompey, and said: "Who art thou, my man, that thinkest to give burial rites to Pompey the Great?" And when Philip said that he was his freedman, the man said: "But thou shalt not have this honour all to thyself; let me too share in a pious privilege thus

[1] Ibi ab Achilla et Septimio interficitur (Caesar, *Bell. Civ.* iii. 104).

εὐσεβοῦς δέξαι κοινωνόν, ὡς μὴ κατὰ πάντα μέμφωμαι τὴν ἀποξένωσιν, ἀντὶ πολλῶν ἀνιαρῶν τοῦτο γοῦν εὐράμενος, ἅψασθαι καὶ περιστεῖλαι ταῖς ἐμαῖς χερσὶ τὸν μέγιστον αὐτοκράτορα Ῥω-

4 μαίων." οὕτω μὲν ἐκηδεύετο Πομπήϊος. τῇ δ' ὑστεραίᾳ Λεύκιος Λέντλος οὐκ εἰδὼς τὰ πεπραγμένα, πλέων ἀπὸ Κύπρου καὶ παρὰ γῆν κομιζόμενος, ὡς εἶδε νεκροῦ πυρὰν καὶ παρεστῶτα τὸν Φίλιππον, οὔπω καθορώμενος· "Τίς ἄρα," ἔφη, " τὸ πεπρωμένον ἐνταῦθα τελέσας ἀναπέπαυται;" καὶ μικρὸν διαλιπὼν καὶ στενάξας, "Τάχα δέ," εἶπε, " σύ, Πομπήϊε Μάγνε." καὶ μετὰ μικρὸν ἀποβὰς καὶ συλληφθεὶς ἀπέθανε.

5 Τοῦτο Πομπηΐου τέλος. οὐ πολλῷ δὲ ὕστερον Καῖσαρ ἐλθὼν εἰς Αἴγυπτον ἄγους τοσούτου καταπεπλησμένην τὸν μὲν προσφέροντα τὴν κεφαλὴν ὡς παλαμναῖον ἀπεστράφη, τὴν δὲ σφραγῖδα τοῦ Πομπηΐου δεξάμενος ἐδάκρυσεν· ἦν δὲ γλυφὴ λέων ξιφήρης. Ἀχιλλᾶν δὲ καὶ Ποθεινὸν ἀπέσφαξεν· αὐτὸς δὲ ὁ βασιλεὺς μάχῃ λειφθεὶς

6 περὶ τὸν ποταμὸν ἠφανίσθη. Θεόδοτον δὲ τὸν σοφιστὴν ἡ μὲν ἐκ Καίσαρος δίκη παρῆλθε· φυγὼν γὰρ Αἴγυπτον ἐπλανᾶτο ταπεινὰ πράττων καὶ μισούμενος· Βροῦτος δὲ Μάρκος, ὅτε Καίσαρα κτείνας ἐκράτησεν, ἐξευρὼν αὐτὸν ἐν Ἀσίᾳ καὶ πᾶσαν αἰκίαν αἰκισάμενος ἀπέκτεινεν. τὰ δὲ λείψανα τοῦ Πομπηΐου Κορνηλία δεξαμένη κομισθέντα, περὶ τὸν Ἀλβανὸν ἔθηκεν.

offered, that I may not altogether regret my sojourn
in a foreign land, if in requital for many hardships I
find this happiness at least, to touch with my hands
and array for burial the greatest of Roman imperators." Such were the obsequies of Pompey. And
on the following day Lucius Lentulus, as he came
sailing from Cyprus and coasted along the shore not
knowing what had happened, saw a funeral pyre and
Philip standing beside it, and before he had been
seen himself exclaimed : " Who, pray, rests here at
the end of his allotted days ? " Then, after a slight
pause and with a groan he said : " But perhaps it is
thou, Pompey the Great ! " And after a little he
went ashore, was seized, and put to death.

This was the end of Pompey. But not long afterwards Caesar came to Egypt, and found it filled with
this great deed of abomination. From the man who
brought him Pompey's head he turned away with
loathing, as from an assassin ; and on receiving Pompey's seal-ring, he burst into tears ; the device was a
lion holding a sword in his paws. But Achillas and
Potheinus he put to death. The king himself, moreover, was defeated in battle along the river, and dis-
appeared. Theodotus the sophist, however, escaped
the vengeance of Caesar ; for he fled out of Egypt
and wandered about in wretchedness and hated of all
men. But Marcus Brutus, after he had slain Caesar
and come into power, discovered him in Asia, and
put him to death with every possible torture. The
remains of Pompey were taken to Cornelia, who gave
them burial at his Alban villa.

ΑΓΗΣΙΛΑΟΥ ΚΑΙ ΠΟΜΠΗΙΟΥ ΣΥΓΚΡΙΣΙΣ

I. Ἐκκειμένων οὖν τῶν βίων ἐπιδράμωμεν τῷ
λόγῳ ταχέως τὰ ποιοῦντα τὰς διαφοράς, παρ᾽
ἄλληλα συνάγοντες. ἔστι δὲ ταῦτα· πρῶτον, ὅτι
Πομπήιος ἐκ τοῦ δικαιοτάτου τρόπου παρῆλθεν
εἰς δύναμιν καὶ δόξαν, αὐτὸς ὁρμηθεὶς ἀφ᾽ ἑαυτοῦ
καὶ πολλὰ καὶ μεγάλα Σύλλᾳ τὴν Ἰταλίαν ἀπὸ
τῶν τυράννων ἐλευθεροῦντι συγκατεργασάμενος,
2 Ἀγησίλαος δὲ τὴν βασιλείαν ἔδοξε λαβεῖν οὔτε
τὰ πρὸς θεοὺς ἄμεμπτος οὔτε τὰ πρὸς ἀνθρώπους,
κρίνας νοθείας Λεωτυχίδην, ὃν υἱὸν αὑτοῦ [1] ἀπέδειξεν ὁ ἀδελφὸς γνήσιον, τὸν δὲ χρησμὸν κατειρωνευσάμενος τὸν περὶ τῆς χωλότητος. δεύτερον,
ὅτι Πομπήιος Σύλλαν καὶ ζῶντα τιμῶν διετέλεσε
καὶ τεθνηκότος ἐκήδευσε βιασάμενος Λέπιδον τὸ
σῶμα, καὶ τῷ παιδὶ Φαύστῳ τὴν αὑτοῦ θυγατέρα συνῴκισεν, Ἀγησίλαος δὲ Λύσανδρον ἐκ
τῆς τυχούσης προφάσεως ὑπεξέρριψε καὶ καθύ-
3 βρισε. καίτοι Σύλλας μὲν οὐκ ἐλαττόνων ἔτυχεν
ἢ Πομπηΐῳ παρέσχεν, Ἀγησίλαον δὲ Λύσανδρος
καὶ τῆς Σπάρτης βασιλέα καὶ τῆς Ἑλλάδος
στρατηγὸν ἐποίησε. τρίτον δέ, αἱ περὶ τὰ πολι-
τικὰ τῶν δικαίων παραβάσεις Πομπηΐῳ μὲν δι᾽
οἰκειότητας ἐγένοντο· τὰ γὰρ πλεῖστα Καίσαρι
καὶ Σκηπίωνι συνεξήμαρτε κηδεσταῖς οὖσιν·
4 Ἀγησίλαος δὲ Σφοδρίαν μὲν ἐφ᾽ οἷς Ἀθηναίους
ἠδίκησεν ἀποθανεῖν ὀφείλοντα τῷ τοῦ παιδὸς
ἔρωτι χαριζόμενος ἐξήρπασε, Φοιβίδᾳ δὲ Θηβαίους

---

[1] αὑτοῦ bracketed by Sintenis[2].

COMPARISON OF AGESILAUS AND POMPEY

I. Now that their lives lie spread before us, let us briefly run over the points in which the two men differed, and bring these together side by side. They are as follows. In the first place, it was in the justest manner that Pompey came to fame and power, setting out on his career independently, and rendering many great services to Sulla when Sulla was freeing Italy from her tyrants; Agesilaüs, on the contrary, appeared to get his kingdom by sinning against both gods and men, since he brought Leotychides under condemnation for bastardy, although his brother had recognised him as his legitimate son, and made light of the oracle concerning his lameness. In the second place, Pompey not only continued to hold Sulla in honour while he lived, but also after his death gave his body funeral obsequies in despite of Lepidus, and bestowed upon his son Faustus his own daughter in marriage; whereas Agesilaüs cast out Lysander on the merest pretext, and heaped insult upon him. And yet Sulla got no less from Pompey than he gave him, while in the case of Agesilaüs, it was Lysander who made him king of Sparta and general of all Greece. And, thirdly, Pompey's transgressions of right and justice in his political life were due to his family connections, for he joined in most of the wrongdoings of Caesar and Scipio because they were his relations by marriage; but Agesilaüs snatched Sphodrias from the death which hung over him for wronging the Athenians, merely to gratify the love of his son, and when Phoebidas treacherously broke the peace with Thebes, he

παρασπονδήσαντι δῆλος ἦν δι᾿ αὐτὸ τὸ ἀδίκημα
προθύμως βοηθῶν. καθόλου δὲ ὅσα Ῥωμαίους
δι᾿ αἰδῶ Πομπήϊος ἢ ἄγνοιαν αἰτίαν ἔσχε βλάψαι,
ταῦτα θυμῷ καὶ φιλονεικίᾳ Λακεδαιμονίους
Ἀγησίλαος ἔβλαψε τὸν Βοιώτιον ἐκκαύσας πόλεμον.

II. Εἰ δὲ καὶ τύχην τινὰ τῶν ἀνδρῶν ἑκατέρου
τοῖς σφάλμασι προσοιστέον, ἀνέλπιστος μὲν ἡ
Πομπηΐου Ῥωμαίοις, Ἀγησίλαος δὲ Λακεδαιμονίους ἀκούοντας καὶ προειδότας οὐκ εἴασε φυ-
λάξασθαι τὴν χωλὴν βασιλείαν. καὶ γὰρ εἰ μυρι-
άκις ἠλέγχθη Λεωτυχίδης ἀλλότριος εἶναι καὶ
νόθος, οὐκ ἂν ἠπόρησαν Εὐρυπωντίδαι γνήσιον
καὶ ἀρτίποδα τῇ Σπάρτῃ βασιλέα παρασχεῖν, εἰ
μὴ δι᾿ Ἀγησίλαον ἐπεσκότησε τῷ χρησμῷ Λύσανδρος.

2 Οἷον μέντοι τῇ περὶ τῶν τρεσάντων ἀπορίᾳ
προσήγαγεν ὁ Ἀγησίλαος ἴαμα μετὰ τὴν ἐν
Λεύκτροις ἀτυχίαν, κελεύσας τοὺς νόμους ἐκείνην
τὴν ἡμέραν καθεύδειν, οὐ γέγονεν ἄλλο σόφισμα
πολιτικόν, οὐδ᾿ ἔχομέν τι τοῦ Πομπηΐου παρα-
πλήσιον, ἀλλὰ τοὐναντίον οὐδ᾿ οἷς αὐτὸς ἐτίθει
νόμοις ᾤετο δεῖν ἐμμένειν, τὸ δύνασθαι μέγα τοῖς
φίλοις ἐνδεικνύμενος. ὁ δὲ εἰς ἀνάγκην καταστὰς
τοῦ λῦσαι τοὺς νόμους ἐπὶ τῷ σῶσαι τοὺς πολίτας, ἐξεῦρε τρόπον ᾧ μήτε ἐκείνους βλάψουσι
3 μήτε ὅπως οὐ βλάψωσι λυθήσονται. τίθεμαι δὲ

evidently made the crime itself a reason for zealously supporting him. In a word, whatever harm Pompey was accused of bringing upon the Romans out of deference to his friends or through ignorance, Agesilaüs brought as much upon the Lacedaemonians out of obstinacy and resentment when he kindled the Boeotian war.

II. Moreover, if we must assign to any ill-fortune of the two men the disasters which overtook them, that of Pompey could not have been anticipated by the Romans; but Agesilaüs would not permit the Lacedaemonians to guard against the "lame sovereignty," although they had heard and knew beforehand about it. For even if Leotychides had been ten thousand times convicted of being bastard and alien, the family of the Eurypontidae could easily have furnished Sparta with a king who was of legitimate birth and sound of limb, had not Lysander darkened the meaning of the oracle in the interests of Agesilaüs.

On the other hand, when we consider the remedy which Agesilaüs applied to the perplexity of the state in dealing with those who had played the coward, after the disaster at Leuctra, when he urged that the laws should slumber for that day, there was never another political device like it, nor can we find anything in Pompey's career to compare with it; on the contrary, he did not even think it incumbent upon him to abide by the laws which he himself had made, if he might only display the greatness of his power to his friends. But Agesilaüs, when he confronted the necessity of abrogating the laws in order to save his fellow-citizens, devised a way by which the citizens should not be harmed by the laws, nor the laws be abrogated to avoid such

κἀκεῖνο τὸ ἀμίμητον ἔργον εἰς πολιτικὴν ἀρετὴν
τοῦ Ἀγησιλάου, τὸ δεξάμενον τὴν σκυτάλην
ἀπολιπεῖν τὰς ἐν Ἀσίᾳ πράξεις. οὐ γάρ, ὡς
Πομπήϊος, ἀφ' ὧν ἑαυτὸν ἐποίει μέγαν ὠφέλει τὸ
κοινόν, ἀλλὰ τὸ τῆς πατρίδος σκοπῶν τηλικαύτην
ἀφῆκε δύναμιν καὶ δόξαν ἡλίκην οὐδεὶς πρότερον
οὐδὲ ὕστερον πλὴν Ἀλέξανδρος ἔσχεν.

III. Ἀπ' ἄλλης τοίνυν ἀρχῆς, ἐν ταῖς στρατη-
γίαις καὶ τοῖς πολεμικοῖς, ἀριθμῷ μὲν τροπαίων
καὶ μεγέθει δυνάμεως ἃς ἐπηγάγετο Πομπήϊος,
καὶ πλήθει παρατάξεων ἃς ἐνίκησεν, οὐδ' ἂν ὁ
Ξενοφῶν μοι δοκεῖ παραβαλεῖν τὰς Ἀγησιλάου
νίκας, ᾧ διὰ τἆλλα καλὰ καθάπερ γέρας ἐξαίρετον
δέδοται καὶ γράφειν ὃ βούλοιτο καὶ λέγειν περὶ
2 τοῦ ἀνδρός. οἶμαι δὲ καὶ τῇ πρὸς τοὺς πολεμίους ἐπιεικείᾳ διαφέρειν τὸν ἄνδρα τοῦ ἀνδρός. ὁ
μὲν γὰρ ἀνδραποδίσασθαι Θήβας καὶ Μεσσήνην
ἐξοικίσασθαι βουλόμενος, ἣν μὲν ὁμόκληρον τῆς
πατρίδος, ἣν δὲ μητρόπολιν τοῦ γένους, παρ'
οὐδὲν ἦλθε τὴν Σπάρτην ἀποβαλεῖν, ἀπέβαλε δὲ
τὴν ἡγεμονίαν· ὁ δὲ καὶ τῶν πειρατῶν τοῖς μετα-
βαλομένοις πόλεις ἔδωκε, καὶ Τιγράνην τὸν
Ἀρμενίων βασιλέα γενόμενον ἐφ' ἑαυτῷ θριαμ-
βεῦσαι σύμμαχον ἐποιήσατο, φήσας ἡμέρας μιᾶς
αἰῶνα προτιμᾶν.

3 Εἰ μέντοι τοῖς μεγίστοις καὶ κυριωτάτοις εἰς
τὰ ὅπλα πράγμασι καὶ λογισμοῖς προστίθεται
πρωτεῖον ἀρετῆς ἀνδρὸς ἡγεμόνος, οὐ μικρὸν ὁ

harm. Further, I attribute also to political virtue in Agesilaüs that inimitable act of his in abandoning his career in Asia on receipt of the dispatch-roll. For he did not, like Pompey, help the commonwealth only as he made himself great, but with an eye to the welfare of his country he renounced such great fame and power as no man won before or since his day, except Alexander.

III. And now from another point of view, that of their campaigns and achievements in war, the trophies of Pompey were so many, the forces led by him so vast, and the pitched battles in which he was victorious so innumerable, that not even Xenophon, I think, would compare the victories of Agesilaüs, although that historian, by reason of his other excellent qualities, is specially privileged, as it were, to say and write whatever he pleases about the man. I think also that in merciful behaviour towards their enemies the two men were different. For Agesilaüs was so bent on enslaving Thebes and depopulating Messenia, Thebes the mother-city of his royal line, and Messenia a sister colony to his country,[1] that he nearly lost Sparta, and did lose her supremacy in Greece; whereas Pompey gave cities to such of the pirates as changed their mode of life, and when it was in his power to lead Tigranes the king of Armenia in his triumphal procession, made him an ally instead, saying that he thought more of future time than of a single day.

If, however, it is the greatest and most far-reaching decisions and acts in war that are to determine preëminence in the virtues of leadership, then the

---

[1] Thebes was the birth-place of Heracles, from whom the Spartan kings were supposed to be descended; and Messenia, like Sparta, was settled by the Heracleidae.

Λάκων τὸν Ῥωμαῖον ἀπολέλοιπε. πρῶτον μὲν
γὰρ οὐ προήκατο τὴν πόλιν οὐδ' ἐξέλιπεν ἑπτὰ
μυριάσι στρατοῦ τῶν πολεμίων ἐμβαλόντων,
ὀλίγους ἔχων ὁπλίτας καὶ προνενικημένους ἐν
4 Λεύκτροις· Πομπήϊος δέ, πεντακισχιλίοις μόνοις
καὶ τριακοσίοις μίαν Καίσαρος πόλιν Ἰταλι-
κὴν καταλαβόντος, ἐξέπεσε τῆς Ῥώμης ὑπὸ
δέους, ἢ τοσούτοις εἴξας ἀγεννῶς ἢ πλείονας
ψευδῶς εἰκάσας· καὶ συσκευασάμενος τὰ τέκνα
καὶ τὴν γυναῖκα αὐτοῦ, τὰς δὲ τῶν ἄλλων
πολιτῶν ἐρήμους ἀπολιπὼν ἔφυγε, δέον ἢ κρατεῖν
μαχόμενον ὑπὲρ τῆς πατρίδος ἢ δέχεσθαι διαλύσεις παρὰ τοῦ κρείττονος· ἦν γὰρ πολίτης καὶ
5 οἰκεῖος· νῦν δὲ ᾧ στρατηγίας χρόνον ἐπιμετρῆσαι
καὶ ὑπατείαν ψηφίσασθαι δεινὸν ἡγεῖτο, τούτῳ
παρέσχε λαβόντι τὴν πόλιν εἰπεῖν πρὸς Μέτελλον ὅτι κἀκεῖνον αἰχμάλωτον αὐτοῦ νομίζει καὶ
τοὺς ἄλλους ἅπαντας.

IV. Ὁ τοίνυν ἔργον ἐστὶν ἀγαθοῦ στρατηγοῦ
μάλιστα, κρείττονα μὲν ὄντα βιάσασθαι τοὺς
πολεμίους μάχεσθαι, λειπόμενον δὲ δυνάμει μὴ
βιασθῆναι, τοῦτο ποιῶν Ἀγησίλαος ἀεὶ διεφύλαξεν ἑαυτὸν ἀνίκητον· Πομπήϊον δὲ Καῖσαρ, οὗ
μὲν ἦν ἐλάττων, διέφυγε μὴ βλαβῆναι, καθὸ δὲ
κρείττων ἦν, ἠνάγκασεν ἀγωνισάμενον τῷ πεζῷ
περὶ πάντων σφαλῆναι, καὶ κύριος εὐθὺς ἦν χρημάτων καὶ ἀγορᾶς καὶ θαλάττης, ὑφ' ὧν διεπέ-
2 πρακτο ἂν ἄνευ μάχης ἐκείνοις προσόντων. τὸ δ'
ὑπὲρ τούτων ἀπολόγημα μέγιστόν ἐστιν ἔγκλημα

Lacedaemonian leaves the Roman far behind. For, in the first place, he did not desert nor abandon his city, though the enemy attacked it with an army of seventy thousand men, while he had only a few men-at-arms, and these had recently been vanquished at Leuctra ; but Pompey, after Caesar had occupied a single city of Italy with only fifty-three hundred men, hurried away from Rome in a panic, either yielding ignobly to so few, or conjecturing falsely that there were more ; and after conveying away with him his own wife and children, he left those of the other citizens defenceless and took to flight, when he ought either to have conquered in a battle for his country, or to have accepted terms from his conqueror, who was a fellow-citizen and a relation by marriage. But as it was, to the man for whom he thought it a terrible thing to prolong a term of military command or vote a consulship, to this man he gave the power of capturing the city and saying to Metellus that he considered him and all the rest of the citizens as his prisoners of war.

IV. Furthermore, the chief task of a good general is to force his enemies to give battle when he is superior to them, but not to be forced himself to do this when his forces are inferior, and by so doing Agesilaüs always kept himself unconquered ; whereas in Pompey's case, Caesar escaped injury at his hands when he was inferior to him, and forced him to stake the whole issue on a battle with his land forces, wherein Caesar was superior, thus defeating him and becoming at once master of treasures, provisions, and the sea,—advantages which would have brought his ruin without a battle had they remained in his enemy's control. And that which is urged as an excuse for this failure is really a very severe

στρατηγοῦ τηλικούτου. νέον μὲν γὰρ ἄρχοντα
θορύβοις καὶ καταβοήσεσιν εἰς μαλακίαν καὶ δειλίαν ἐπιταραχθέντα τῶν ἀσφαλεστάτων ἐκπεσεῖν
λογισμῶν εἰκός ἐστι καὶ συγγνωστόν· Πομπήϊον
δὲ Μάγνον, οὗ Ῥωμαῖοι τὸ μὲν στρατόπεδον
πατρίδα, σύγκλητον δὲ τὴν σκηνήν, ἀποστάτας
δὲ καὶ προδότας τοὺς ἐν Ῥώμῃ πολιτευομένους
καὶ στρατηγοῦντας καὶ ὑπατεύοντας ἐκάλουν,
3 ἀρχόμενον δὲ ὑπ' οὐδενὸς ἔγνωσαν, πάσας δὲ
αὐτοκράτορα στρατευσάμενον ἄριστα τὰς στρατείας, τίς ἂν ἀνάσχοιτο τοῖς Φαωνίου σκώμμασι
καὶ Δομετίου, καὶ ἵνα μὴ Ἀγαμέμνων λέγηται,
παρ' ἐλάχιστον ἐκβιασθέντα τὸν περὶ τῆς ἡγεμονίας καὶ ἐλευθερίας ἀναρρῖψαι κίνδυνον; ὃς εἰ
μόνον ἐσκόπει τὸ παρ' ἡμέραν ἄδοξον, ὤφειλεν
ἀντιστὰς ἐν ἀρχῇ διαγωνίσασθαι περὶ τῆς Ῥώμης, ἀλλὰ μὴ τὴν φυγὴν ἐκείνην ἀποφαίνων
στρατήγημα Θεμιστόκλειον ὕστερον ἐν αἰσχρῷ
τίθεσθαι τὴν ἐν Θετταλίᾳ πρὸ μάχης διατριβήν. 6
4 οὐ γὰρ ἐκεῖνό γε στάδιον αὐτοῖς καὶ θέατρον
ἐναγωνίσασθαι περὶ τῆς ἡγεμονίας ὁ θεὸς ἀπέδειξε τὸ Φαρσάλιον πεδίον, οὐδὲ ὑπὸ κήρυκος
ἐκαλεῖτο μάχεσθαι κατιὼν ἢ λιπεῖν ἑτέρῳ τὸν
στέφανον, ἀλλὰ πολλὰ μὲν πεδία μυρίας δὲ πόλεις καὶ γῆν ἄπλετον ἢ κατὰ θάλατταν εὐπορία
παρέσχε βουλομένῳ μιμεῖσθαι Μάξιμον καὶ
Μάριον καὶ Λεύκολλον καὶ αὐτὸν Ἀγησίλαον,
5 ὃς οὐκ ἐλάττονας μὲν ἐν Σπάρτῃ θορύβους ὑπέμεινε βουλομένων Θηβαίοις ὑπὲρ τῆς χώρας μάχεσθαι, πολλὰς δ' ἐν Αἰγύπτῳ διαβολὰς καὶ κατηγορίας καὶ ὑπονοίας τοῦ βασιλέως ἤνεγκεν ἡσυχίαν ἄγειν κελεύων, χρησάμενος δὲ τοῖς ἀρίστοις

accusation against a general like him. For that a youthful commander should be frightened by tumults and outcries into cowardly weakness and abandon his safest plans, is natural and pardonable ; but that Pompey the Great, whose camp the Romans called their country, and his tent their senate, while they gave the name of traitors and rebels to the consuls and praetors and other magistrates at Rome,—that he who was known to be under no one's command, but to have served all his campaigns most success-fully as imperator, should be almost forced by the scoffs of Favonius and Domitius, and by the fear of being called Agamemnon, to put to the hazard the supremacy and freedom of Rome, who could tolerate this ? If he had regard only for the immediate infamy involved, then he ought to have made a stand at the first and to have fought to its finish the fight for Rome, instead of calling the flight which he then made a Themistoclean stratagem and after-wards counting it a disgraceful thing to delay before fighting in Thessaly. For surely Heaven had not appointed that Pharsalian plain to be the stadium and theatre of their struggle for the supremacy, nor was he summoned by voice of herald to go down thither and do battle or leave to another the victor's wreath ; nay, there were many plains, ten thousand cities, and a whole earth which his great resources by sea afforded him had he wished to imitate Maximus, or Marius, or Lucullus, or Agesilaüs him-self, who withstood no less tumults in Sparta when its citizens wished to fight with the Thebans in de-fence of their land, and in Egypt endured many calumnies and accusations and suspicions on the part of the king when he urged him to keep quiet ; but he followed his own best counsels as he wished, and

6 ὡς ἐβούλετο λογισμοῖς, οὐ μόνον Αἰγυπτίους
ἄκοντας ἔσωσεν, οὐδὲ τὴν Σπάρτην ἐν τοσούτῳ
σεισμῷ μόνος ὀρθὴν ἀεὶ διεφύλαξεν, ἀλλὰ καὶ
τρόπαιον ἔστησε κατὰ Θηβαίων ἐν τῇ πόλει, τὸ
νικῆσαι παρασχὼν αὖθις ἐκ τοῦ τότε μὴ προαπ-
ολέσθαι βιασαμένους. ὅθεν Ἀγησίλαος μὲν ὑπὸ
τῶν βιασθέντων ὕστερον ἐπηνεῖτο σωθέντων,
Πομπήϊος δὲ δι' ἄλλους ἁμαρτών, αὐτοὺς οἷς ἐπεί-
7 σθη κατηγόρους εἶχε. καίτοι φασί τινες ὡς ὑπὸ
τοῦ πενθεροῦ Σκηπίωνος ἐξηπατήθη· τὰ γὰρ
πλεῖστα τῶν χρημάτων ὧν ἐκόμιζεν ἐξ Ἀσίας
βουλόμενον αὐτὸν νοσφίσασθαι καὶ ἀποκρύψαντα
κατεπεῖξαι τὴν μάχην, ὡς οὐκέτι χρημάτων
ὄντων. ὃ κἂν ἀληθὲς ἦν, παθεῖν οὐκ ὤφειλεν ὁ
στρατηγός, οὐδὲ ῥᾳδίως οὕτω παραλογισθεὶς
ἀποκινδυνεῦσαι περὶ τῶν μεγίστων. ἐν μὲν οὖν
τούτοις οὕτως ἑκάτερον ἀποθεωροῦμεν.

V. Εἰς Αἴγυπτον δ' ὁ μὲν ἐξ ἀνάγκης ἔπλευσε
φεύγων, ὁ δὲ οὔτε καλῶς οὔτε ἀναγκαίως ἐπὶ
χρήμασιν, ὅπως ἔχῃ τοῖς Ἕλλησι πολεμεῖν ἀφ'
ὧν τοῖς βαρβάροις ἐστρατήγησεν. εἶτα ἃ διὰ
Πομπήϊον Αἰγυπτίοις ἐγκαλοῦμεν, ταῦτα Αἰγύ-
πτιοι κατηγοροῦσιν Ἀγησιλάου. ὁ μὲν γὰρ
ἠδικήθη πιστεύσας, ὁ δὲ πιστευθεὶς ἐγκατέλιπε
καὶ μετέστη πρὸς τοὺς πολεμοῦντας οἷς ἔπλευσε
συμμαχήσων.

not only saved the Egyptians against their wills, and by his sole efforts ever kept Sparta upright in the midst of so great a convulsion, but actually set up a trophy in the city for a victory over the Thebans, which victory he put his countrymen in the way of winning later, by keeping them then from the destruction into which they would have forced their way. Wherefore Agesilaüs was afterwards commended by those whom he had forced to take the path of safety, while Pompey, whom others had led into error, found accusers in the very ones to whom he had yielded. And yet some say that he was deceived by his father-in-law Scipio, who wished to appropriate to his own uses the greater part of the treasure which he had brought from Asia, and therefore hid it away, and then hastened on the battle, on the plea that there was no longer any money. But even if this were true, a general ought not to suffer himself to be so easily deceived, nor afterwards to put his greatest interests at hazard. In these matters, then, such is the way in which we regard each of the men.

V. And as to their voyages to Egypt, one went thither of necessity and in flight; the other for no honourable reason, nor of necessity, but for money, that what he got for serving the Barbarians as commander might enable him to make war upon the Greeks. Then again, as to the charges which we bring against the Egyptians for their treatment of Pompey, these the Egyptians lay at the door of Agesilaüs for his treatment of them. For Pompey trusted them and was wronged by them; while Agesilaüs was trusted by them and yet forsook them and went over to the enemies of those whom he had sailed to assist.

PELOPIDAS

ΠΕΛΟΠΙΔΑΣ

I. Κάτων ὁ πρεσβύτερος πρός τινας ἐπαινοῦντας ἄνθρωπον ἀλογίστως παράβολον καὶ τολμηρὸν ἐν τοῖς πολεμικοῖς διαφέρειν ἔφη τὸ πολλοῦ τινα τὴν ἀρετὴν ἀξίαν καὶ τὸ μὴ πολλοῦ ἄξιον τὸ ζῆν νομίζειν· ὀρθῶς ἀποφαινόμενος. ὁ γοῦν παρ' Ἀντιγόνῳ στρατευόμενος ἰταμός, φαῦλος δὲ τὴν ἕξιν καὶ τὸ σῶμα διεφθορώς, ἐρομένου τοῦ βασιλέως τὴν αἰτίαν τῆς ὠχρότητος ὡμολόγησέ τινα
2 νόσον τῶν ἀπορρήτων· ἐπεὶ δὲ φιλοτιμηθεὶς ὁ βασιλεὺς προσέταξε τοῖς ἰατροῖς, ἐάν τις ᾖ βοήθεια, μηδὲν ἐλλιπεῖν τῆς ἄκρας ἐπιμελείας, οὕτω θεραπευθεὶς ὁ γενναῖος ἐκεῖνος οὐκέτ' ἦν φιλοκίνδυνος οὐδὲ ῥαγδαῖος ἐν τοῖς ἀγῶσιν, ὥστε καὶ τὸν Ἀντίγονον ἐγκαλεῖν καὶ θαυμάζειν τὴν μεταβολήν. οὐ μὴν ὁ ἄνθρωπος ἀπεκρύψατο τὸ αἴτιον, ἀλλ' εἶπεν· "Ὦ βασιλεῦ, σύ με πεποίηκας ἀτολμότερον, ἀπαλλάξας ἐκείνων τῶν κακῶν
3 δι' ἃ τοῦ ζῆν ὠλιγώρουν." πρὸς τοῦτο δὲ φαίνεται καὶ Συβαρίτης ἀνὴρ εἰπεῖν περὶ τῶν Σπαρτιατῶν ὡς οὐ μέγα ποιοῦσι θανατῶντες ἐν τοῖς πολέμοις ὑπὲρ τοῦ τοσούτους πόνους καὶ τοιαύτην ἀποφυγεῖν δίαιταν. ἀλλὰ Συβαρίταις μὲν ἐκτετηκόσιν ὑπὸ τρυφῆς καὶ μαλακίας διὰ τὴν πρὸς τὸ καλὸν ὁρμὴν καὶ φιλοτιμίαν εἰκότως ἐφαίνοντο μισεῖν τὸν βίον οἱ μὴ φοβούμενοι τὸν θάνατον,
4 Λακεδαιμονίοις δὲ καὶ ζῆν ἡδέως καὶ θνήσκειν

340

PELOPIDAS

I. Cato the Elder, when certain persons praised a man who was inconsiderately rash and daring in war, told them there was a difference between a man's setting a high value on valour and his setting a low value on life; and his remark was just. At any rate, there was a soldier of Antigonus who was venturesome, but had miserable health and an impaired body. When the king asked him the reason for his pallor, the man admitted that it was a secret disease, whereupon the king took compassion on him and ordered his physicians, if there was any help for him, to employ their utmost skill and care. Thus the man was cured; but then the good fellow ceased to court danger and was no longer a furious fighter, so that even Antigonus rebuked him and expressed his wonder at the change. The man, however, made no secret of the reason, but said: "O King, it is thou who hast made me less daring, by freeing me from those ills which made me set little value on life." On these grounds, too, as it would seem, a man of Sybaris said it was no great thing for the Spartans to seek death in the wars in order to escape so many hardships and such a wretched life as theirs. But to the Sybarites, who were dissolved in effeminate luxury, men whom ambition and an eager quest of honour led to have no fear of death naturally seemed to hate life; whereas the virtues of the Lacedaemonians gave them

341

ἀμφότερα ἀρετὴ παρεῖχεν, ὡς δηλοῖ τὸ ἐπική-
δειον· οἵδε γάρ φησιν ἔθανον [1]

οὐ τὸ ζῆν θέμενοι καλὸν οὐδὲ τὸ θνήσκειν,
Ἀλλὰ τὸ ταῦτα καλῶς ἀμφότερ᾿ ἐκτελέσαι.

οὔτε γὰρ φυγὴ θανάτου μεμπτόν, ἂν ὀρέγηταί τις
τοῦ βίου μὴ αἰσχρῶς, οὔτε ὑπομονὴ καλόν, εἰ
5 μετ᾿ ὀλιγωρίας γίνοιτο τοῦ ζῆν. ὅθεν Ὅμηρος
μὲν ἀεὶ τοὺς θαρραλεωτάτους καὶ μαχιμωτάτους
ἄνδρας εὖ καὶ καλῶς ὡπλισμένους ἐξάγει πρὸς
τοὺς ἀγῶνας, οἱ δὲ τῶν Ἑλλήνων νομοθέται τὸν
ῥίψασπιν κολάζουσιν, οὐ τὸν ξίφος οὐδὲ λόγχην
προέμενον, διδάσκοντες ὅτι τοῦ μὴ παθεῖν κακῶς
πρότερον ἢ τοῦ ποιῆσαι τοὺς πολεμίους ἑκάστῳ
μέλειν προσήκει, μάλιστα δὲ ἄρχοντι πόλεως ἢ
στρατεύματος.

II. Εἰ γάρ, ὡς Ἰφικράτης διῄρει, χερσὶ μὲν
ἐοίκασιν οἱ ψιλοί, ποσὶ δὲ τὸ ἱππικόν, αὐτὴ δὲ ἡ
φάλαγξ στέρνῳ καὶ θώρακι, κεφαλῇ δὲ ὁ στρατηγός, οὐχ αὑτοῦ δόξειεν ἂν ἀποκινδυνεύων παραμελεῖν καὶ θρασυνόμενος, ἀλλ᾿ ἁπάντων, οἷς ἡ
σωτηρία γίνεται δι᾿ αὐτοῦ καὶ τοὐναντίον. ὅθεν
ὁ Καλλικρατίδας, καίπερ ὢν τἄλλα μέγας, οὐκ
εὖ πρὸς τὸν μάντιν εἶπε· δεομένου γὰρ αὐτοῦ
φυλάττεσθαι θάνατον, ὡς τῶν ἱερῶν προδηλούν-
2 των, ἔφη μὴ παρ᾿ ἕνα εἶναι τὰν Σπάρταν. μαχόμενος γὰρ εἷς ἦν καὶ πλέων καὶ στρατευόμενος ὁ
Καλλικρατίδας, στρατηγῶν δὲ τὴν ἁπάντων εἶχε
συλλαβὼν ἐν αὑτῷ δύναμιν, ὥστε οὐκ ἦν εἷς ᾧ
τοσαῦτα συναπώλλυτο. βέλτιον δὲ Ἀντίγονος ὁ

---

[1] Οἱ θάνον οὐ τὸ ζῆν κτλ., attributed to Simonides (Bergk,
Poet. Lyr. Graec. iii.⁴ p. 516).

happiness alike in living or dying, as the following elegy testifies: These, it says, died,

" not deeming either life or death honourable in
    themselves,
But only the accomplishment of them both with
    honour."

For neither is a man to be blamed for shunning death, if he does not cling to life disgracefully, nor to be praised for boldly meeting death, if he does this with contempt of life. For this reason Homer always brings his boldest and most valiant heroes into battle well armed and equipped; and the Greek lawgivers punish him who casts away his shield, not him who throws down his sword or spear, thus teaching that his own defence from harm, rather than the infliction of harm upon the enemy, should be every man's first care, and particularly if he governs a city or commands an army.

II. For if, as Iphicrates analyzed the matter, the light-armed troops are like the hands, the cavalry like the feet, the line of men-at-arms itself like chest and breastplate, and the general like the head, then he, in taking undue risks, would seem to neglect not himself, but all, inasmuch as their safety depends on him, and their destruction too. Therefore Callicratidas, although otherwise he was a great man, did not make a good answer to the seer who begged him to be careful, since the sacrificial omens foretold his death; "Sparta," said he, " does not depend upon one man." For when fighting, or sailing, or marching under orders, Callicratidas was " one man "; but as general, he comprised in himself the strength and power of all, so that he was not " one man," when such numbers perished with him. Better was the speech of old Antigonus

γέρων, ὅτε ναυμαχεῖν περὶ Ἄνδρον ἔμελλεν, εἰπόντος τινὸς ὡς πολὺ πλείους αἱ τῶν πολεμίων
νῆες εἶεν, "Ἐμὲ δὲ αὐτόν," ἔφη, "πρὸς πόσας
ἀντιστήσεις; μέγα τὸ τῆς ἀρχῆς, ὥσπερ ἐστίν,
ἀξίωμα ποιῶν μετὰ ἐμπειρίας καὶ ἀρετῆς ταττό-
μενον, ἧς πρῶτον ἔργον ἐστὶ σώζειν τὸν ἅπαντα
3 τἆλλα σώζοντα.   διὸ καλῶς ὁ Τιμόθεος, ἐπιδει-
κνυμένου ποτὲ τοῖς Ἀθηναίοις τοῦ Χάρητος ὠτει-
λάς τινας ἐν τῷ σώματι καὶ τὴν ἀσπίδα λόγχῃ
διακεκομμένην, "Ἐγὼ δέ," εἶπεν, "ὡς λίαν
ᾐσχύνθην ὅτι μου πολιορκοῦντος Σάμον ἐγγὺς
ἔπεσε βέλος, ὡς μειρακιωδέστερον ἐμαυτῷ χρώμενος ἢ κατὰ στρατηγὸν καὶ ἡγεμόνα δυνάμεως
4 τοσαύτης."   ὅπου μὲν γὰρ εἰς τὰ ὅλα μεγάλην
φέρει ῥοπὴν ὁ τοῦ στρατηγοῦ κίνδυνος, ἐνταῦθα
καὶ χειρὶ καὶ σώματι χρηστέον ἀφειδῶς, χαίρειν
φράσαντα τοῖς λέγουσιν ὡς χρὴ τὸν ἀγαθὸν
στρατηγὸν μάλιστα μὲν ὑπὸ γήρως, εἰ δὲ μή,
γέροντα θνήσκειν· ὅπου δὲ μικρὸν τὸ περιγινόμενον ἐκ τοῦ κατορθώματος, τὸ δὲ πᾶν συναπόλ-
λυται σφαλέντος, οὐδεὶς ἀπαιτεῖ στρατιώτου
πρᾶξιν κινδύνῳ πραττομένην στρατηγοῦ.
5   Ταῦτα δέ μοι παρέστη προαναφωνῆσαι γρά-
φοντι τὸν Πελοπίδου βίον καὶ τὸν Μαρκέλλου,
μεγάλων ἀνδρῶν παραλόγως πεσόντων.   καὶ γὰρ
χειρὶ χρῆσθαι μαχιμώτατοι γενόμενοι, καὶ στρα-
τηγίαις ἐπιφανεστάταις κοσμήσαντες ἀμφότεροι
τὰς πατρίδας, ἔτι δὲ τῶν βαρυτάτων ἀνταγωνι-
στῶν ὁ μὲν Ἀννίβαν ἀήττητον ὄντα πρῶτος, ὡς
λέγεται, τρεψάμενος, ὁ δὲ γῆς καὶ θαλάττης ἄρχοντας Λακεδαιμονίους ἐκ παρατάξεως νικήσας, ἠφεί-
δησαν ἑαυτῶν, σὺν οὐδενὶ λογισμῷ προέμενοι τὸν
βίον ὁπηνίκα μάλιστα τοιούτων καιρὸς ἦν ἀνδρῶν

as he was about to fight a sea-fight off Andros, and
someone told him that the enemy's ships were far
more numerous than his : " But what of myself," said
he, " how many ships wilt thou count me ? " implying
that the worth of the commander is a great thing,
as it is in fact, when allied with experience and
valour, and his first duty is to save the one who
saves everything else. Therefore Timotheus was
right, when Chares was once showing the Athenians
some wounds he had received, and his shield pierced
by a spear, in saying : " But I, how greatly ashamed
I was, at the siege of Samos, because a bolt fell near
me ; I thought I was behaving more like an impetuous youth than like a general in command of
so large a force." For where the whole issue is
greatly furthered by the general's exposing himself
to danger, there he must employ hand and body
unsparingly, ignoring those who say that a good
general should die, if not of old age, at least in old
age ; but where the advantage to be derived from
his success is small, and the whole cause perishes
with him if he fails, no one demands that a general
should risk his life in fighting like a common soldier.

Such is the preface I have thought fit to make for
the Lives of Pelopidas and Marcellus, great men who
rashly fell in battle. For both were most valiant
fighters, did honour to their countries in most illustrious campaigns, and what is more, had the most
formidable adversaries, one being the first, as we
are told, to rout Hannibal, who was before invincible,
the other conquering in a pitched battle the Lacedaemonians, who were supreme on land and sea ; and
yet they were careless of their own lives, and recklessly threw them away at times when it was most
important that such men should live and hold

σωζομένων καὶ ἀρχόντων. διόπερ ἡμεῖς ἑπόμενοι
ταῖς ὁμοιότησι παραλλήλους ἀνεγράψαμεν αὐτῶν
τοὺς βίους.

III. Πελοπίδα τῷ Ἱπποκλου γένος μὲν ἦν εὐ-
δόκιμον ἐν Θήβαις ὥσπερ Ἐπαμεινώνδα, τραφεὶς
δὲ ἐν οὐσίᾳ μεγάλῃ καὶ παραλαβὼν ἔτι νέος λαμπρὸν οἶκον ὥρμησε τῶν δεομένων τοῖς ἀξίοις βοηθεῖν, ἵνα κύριος ἀληθῶς φαίνοιτο χρημάτων γεγονώς, ἀλλὰ μὴ δοῦλος. τῶν γὰρ πολλῶν, ὡς
Ἀριστοτέλης φησίν, οἱ μὲν οὐ χρῶνται τῷ πλού-
τῷ διὰ μικρολογίαν, οἱ δὲ παραχρῶνται δι' ἀσω-
τίαν, καὶ δουλεύοντες οὗτοι μὲν ἀεὶ ταῖς ἡδοναῖς,
2 ἐκεῖνοι δὲ ταῖς ἀσχολίαις, διατελοῦσιν. οἱ μὲν
οὖν ἄλλοι τῷ Πελοπίδᾳ χάριν ἔχοντες ἐχρῶντο
τῇ πρὸς αὐτοὺς ἐλευθεριότητι καὶ φιλανθρωπίᾳ,
μόνον δὲ τῶν φίλων τὸν Ἐπαμεινώνδαν οὐκ ἔπειθε
τοῦ πλούτου μεταλαμβάνειν· αὐτὸς μέντοι μετ-
εῖχε τῆς ἐκείνου πενίας, ἐσθῆτος ἀφελείᾳ καὶ
τραπέζης λιτότητι καὶ τῷ πρὸς τοὺς πόνους ἀόκνῳ
3 καὶ κατὰ στρατείας ἀδόλῳ καλλωπιζόμενος, ὥσπερ ὁ Εὐριπίδου Καπανεύς, ᾧ " βίος μὲν ἦν πολύς,
ἥκιστα δὲ δι' ὄλβον γαῦρος ἦν," αἰσχυνόμενος εἰ
φανεῖται πλείοσι χρώμενος εἰς τὸ σῶμα τοῦ τὰ
ἐλάχιστα κεκτημένου Θηβαίων. Ἐπαμεινώνδας
μὲν οὖν συνήθη καὶ πατρῴαν οὖσαν αὐτῷ τὴν
πενίαν ἔτι μᾶλλον εὔζωνον καὶ κοῦφον ἐποίησε
φιλοσοφῶν καὶ μονότροπον βίον ἀπ' ἀρχῆς ἑλό-
4 μενος· Πελοπίδα δὲ ἦν μὲν γάμος λαμπρός, ἐγένοντο δὲ καὶ παῖδες, ἀλλ' οὐδὲν ἧττον ἀμελῶν τοῦ
χρηματίζεσθαι καὶ σχολάζων τῇ πόλει τὸν ἅπαντα χρόνον ἠλάττωσε τὴν οὐσίαν. τῶν δὲ φίλων
νουθετούντων καὶ λεγόντων ὡς ἀναγκαίου πρά-

PELOPIDAS

command. These are the resemblances between them which have led me to write their lives in parallel.

III. Pelopidas the son of Hippoclus was of a highly honourable family in Thebes, as was Epaminondas, and having been reared in affluence, and having inherited in youth a splendid estate, he devoted himself to the assistance of worthy men who needed it, that he might be seen to be really master of his wealth, and not its slave. For most wealthy men, as Aristotle says,[1] either make no use of their wealth through avarice, or abuse it through prodigality, and so they are forever slaves, these to their pleasures, those to their business. The rest, accordingly, thankfully profited by the kindness and liberality of Pelopidas towards them; but Epaminondas was the only one of his friends whom he could not persuade to share his wealth. Pelopidas, however, shared the poverty of this friend, and gloried in modest attire, meagre diet, readiness to undergo hardships, and straightforward service as a soldier. Like the Capaneus of Euripides, he " had abundant wealth, but riches did not make him arrogant at all,[2] " and he was ashamed to let men think that he spent more upon his person than the poorest Theban. Now Epaminondas, whose poverty was hereditary and familiar, made it still more light and easy by philosophy, and by electing at the outset to lead a single life; Pelopidas, on the contrary, made a brilliant marriage, and had children too, but nevertheless he neglected his private interests to devote his whole time to the state, and so lessened his substance. And when his friends admonished him and told him that the possession of money, which

---

[1] Fragment 56 (Rose) ; cf. *Morals*, p. 527 a.
[2] *Supplices*, 863 f. (Kirchhoff, ἥκιστα δ' ὄλβῳ).

γματος ὀλιγωρεῖ, τοῦ χρήματα ἔχειν, "Ἀναγκαίου, νὴ Δία, Νικοδήμῳ τούτῳ," ἔφη, δείξας τινὰ
χωλὸν καὶ τυφλόν.

IV. Ἦσαν δὲ καὶ πρὸς πᾶσαν ἀρετὴν πεφυ-
κότες ὁμοίως, πλὴν ὅτι τῷ γυμνάζεσθαι μᾶλλον
ἔχαιρε Πελοπίδας, τῷ δὲ μανθάνειν Ἐπαμεινώνδας, καὶ τὰς διατριβὰς ἐν τῷ σχολάζειν ὁ μὲν περὶ
παλαίστρας καὶ κυνηγέσια, ὁ δὲ ἀκούων τι καὶ
φιλοσοφῶν ἐποιεῖτο. πολλῶν δὲ καὶ καλῶν
ὑπαρχόντων ἀμφοτέροις πρὸς δόξαν, οὐδὲν οἱ νοῦν
ἔχοντες ἡγοῦνται τηλικοῦτον ἡλίκον τὴν διὰ τοσούτων ἀγώνων καὶ στρατηγιῶν καὶ πολιτειῶν
ἀνεξέλεγκτον εὔνοιαν καὶ φιλίαν ἀπ' ἀρχῆς μέχρι
2 τέλους ἐμμείνασαν. εἰ γάρ τις ἀποβλέψας τὴν
Ἀριστείδου καὶ Θεμιστοκλέους καὶ Κίμωνος καὶ
Περικλέους καὶ Νικίου καὶ Ἀλκιβιάδου πολιτείαν,
ὅσων γέγονε μεστὴ διαφορῶν καὶ φθόνων καὶ
ζηλοτυπιῶν πρὸς ἀλλήλους, σκέψαιτο πάλιν τὴν
Πελοπίδου πρὸς Ἐπαμεινώνδαν εὐμένειαν καὶ
τιμήν, τούτους ἂν ὀρθῶς καὶ δικαίως προσαγο-
ρεύσειε συνάρχοντας καὶ συστρατήγους ἢ ἐκείνους,
οἳ μᾶλλον ἀλλήλων ἢ τῶν πολεμίων ἀγωνιζόμενοι
3 περιεῖναι διετέλεσαν. αἰτία δὲ ἀληθινὴ μὲν ἦν ἡ
ἀρετή, δι' ἣν οὐ δόξαν, οὐ πλοῦτον ἀπὸ τῶν
πράξεων μετιόντες, οἷς ὁ χαλεπὸς καὶ δύσερις
ἐμφύεται φθόνος, ἀλλ' ἔρωτα θεῖον ἀπ' ἀρχῆς
ἐρασθέντες ἀμφότεροι τοῦ τὴν πατρίδα λαμπρο-
τάτην καὶ μεγίστην ἐφ' ἑαυτῶν ἰδεῖν γενομένην,
ὥσπερ ἰδίοις ἐπὶ τούτῳ τοῖς αὐτῶν ἐχρῶντο
κατορθώμασιν.

Οὐ μὴν ἀλλ' οἵ γε πολλοὶ νομίζουσιν αὐτοῖς τὴν
σφοδρὰν φιλίαν ἀπὸ τῆς ἐν Μαντινείᾳ γενέσθαι

he scorned, was a necessary thing, "Yes indeed,"
he said, "necessary for this Nicodemus here," pointing to a man who was lame and blind.

IV. They were also fitted by nature for the
pursuit of every excellence, and in like measure, except that Pelopidas delighted more in exercising the
body, Epaminondas in storing the mind, so that the
one devoted his leisure hours to bodily exercise and
hunting, the other to lectures and philosophy. Both
had many claims upon the world's esteem, but wise
men consider none of these so great as the un-
questioned good will and friendship which subsisted
between them from first to last through all their
struggles and campaigns and civil services. For if
one regards the political careers of Themistocles and
Aristides, or of Cimon and Pericles, or of Nicias and
Alcibiades, which were so full of mutual dissensions,
envyings, and jealousies, and then turns his eyes
upon the honour and kindly favour which Pelopidas showed Epaminondas, he will rightly and
justly call these men colleagues in government and
command rather than those, who ever strove to get
the better of one another rather than of the enemy.
And the true reason for the superiority of the Thebans was their virtue, which led them not to aim in
their actions at glory or wealth, which are naturally
attended by bitter envying and strife ; on the contrary, they were both filled from the beginning with
a divine desire to see their country become most
powerful and glorious in their day and by their
efforts, and to this end they treated one another's
successes as their own.

However, most people think that their ardent
friendship dated from the campaign at Mantineia,[1]

---

[1] In 418 B.C., when Athens gave assistance to Argos, Elis,
and Mantineia against Sparta. See the *Alcibiades*, xv. 1.

στρατείας, ἣν συνεστρατεύσαντο Λακεδαιμονίοις,
ἔτι φίλοις καὶ συμμάχοις οὖσι, πεμφθείσης ἐκ
Θηβῶν βοηθείας. τεταγμένοι γὰρ ἐν τοῖς ὁπλίταις
μετ' ἀλλήλων καὶ μαχόμενοι πρὸς τοὺς Ἀρκάδας,
ὡς ἐνέδωκε τὸ κατ' αὐτοὺς κέρας τῶν Λακεδαιμονίων καὶ τροπὴ τῶν πολλῶν ἐγεγόνει, συνασπί-
5 σαντες ἠμύναντο τοὺς ἐπιφερομένους. καὶ Πελοπίδας μὲν ἑπτὰ τραύματα λαβὼν ἐναντία πολλοῖς
ἐπικατερρύη νεκροῖς ὁμοῦ φίλοις καὶ πολεμίοις,
Ἐπαμεινώνδας δέ, καίπερ ἀβιώτως ἔχειν αὐτὸν
ἡγούμενος, ὑπὲρ τοῦ σώματος καὶ τῶν ὅπλων
ἔστη προελθὼν καὶ διεκινδύνευσε πρὸς πολλοὺς
μόνος, ἐγνωκὼς ἀποθανεῖν μᾶλλον ἢ Πελοπίδαν
ἀπολιπεῖν κείμενον. ἤδη δὲ καὶ τούτου κακῶς
ἔχοντος, καὶ λόγχῃ μὲν εἰς τὸ στῆθος, ξίφει δὲ εἰς
τὸν βραχίονα τετρωμένου, προσεβοήθησεν ἀπὸ
θατέρου κέρως Ἀγησίπολις ὁ βασιλεὺς τῶν
Σπαρτιατῶν, καὶ περιεποίησεν ἀνελπίστως αὐτοὺς ἀμφοτέρους.

V. Μετὰ δὲ ταῦτα τῶν Σπαρτιατῶν λόγῳ μὲν
ὡς φίλοις καὶ συμμάχοις προσφερομένων τοῖς
Θηβαίοις, ἔργῳ δὲ τὸ φρόνημα τῆς πόλεως καὶ τὴν
δύναμιν ὑφορωμένων, καὶ μάλιστα τὴν Ἰσμηνίου
καὶ Ἀνδροκλείδου μισούντων ἑταιρείαν, ἧς μετεῖ-
χεν ὁ Πελοπίδας, φιλελεύθερον ἅμα καὶ δημοτι-
2 κὴν εἶναι δοκοῦσαν, Ἀρχίας καὶ Λεοντίδας καὶ
Φίλιππος, ἄνδρες ὀλιγαρχικοὶ καὶ πλούσιοι καὶ
μέτριον οὐδὲν φρονοῦντες, ἀναπείθουσι Φοιβίδαν
τὸν Λάκωνα μετὰ στρατιᾶς διαπορευόμενον ἐξαίφνης καταλαβεῖν τὴν Καδμείαν καὶ τοὺς ὑπεναντιουμένους αὐτοῖς ἐκβαλόντα πρὸς τὸ Λακεδαιμονίων ὑπήκοον ἁρμόσασθαι δι' ὀλίγων τὴν πολι-
3 τείαν. πεισθέντος δ' ἐκείνου καὶ μὴ προσδοκῶσι

where they fought on the side of the Lacedaemonians,
who were still their friends and allies, and who
received assistance from Thebes. For they stood
side by side among the men-at-arms and fought
against the Arcadians, and when the Lacedaemonian
wing to which they belonged gave way and was
routed for the most part, they locked their shields
together and repelled their assailants. Pelopidas,
after receiving seven wounds in front, sank down
upon a great heap of friends and enemies who
lay dead together; but Epaminondas, although he
thought him lifeless, stood forth to defend his body
and his arms, and fought desperately, single-handed
against many, determined to die rather than leave
Pelopidas lying there. And now he too was in a
sorry plight, having been wounded in the breast
with a spear and in the arm with a sword, when
Agesipolis the Spartan king came to his aid from the
other wing, and when all hope was lost, saved them
both.

V. After this the Spartans ostensibly treated the
Thebans as friends and allies, but they really looked
with suspicion on the ambitious spirit and the power
of the city, and above all they hated the party of
Ismenias and Androcleides, to which Pelopidas belonged, and which was thought to be friendly to
freedom and a popular form of government. Therefore Archias, Leontidas, and Philip, men of the
oligarchical faction who were rich and immoderately
ambitious, sought to persuade Phoebidas the Spartan,
as he was marching past with an army, to take the
Cadmeia by surprise, expel from the city the party
opposed to them, and bring the government into
subserviency to the Lacedaemonians by putting it in
the hands of a few men. Phoebidas yielded to their

τοῖς Θηβαίοις ἐπιθεμένου Θεσμοφορίων ὄντων,
καὶ τῆς ἄκρας κυριεύσαντος, Ἰσμηνίας μὲν συναρ-
πασθεὶς καὶ κομισθεὶς εἰς Λακεδαίμονα μετ' οὐ
πολὺν χρόνον ἀνηρέθη, Πελοπίδας δὲ καὶ Φερέ-
νικος καὶ Ἀνδροκλείδας μετὰ συχνῶν ἄλλων φεύγοντες ἐξεκηρύχθησαν, Ἐπαμεινώνδας δὲ κατὰ
χώραν ἔμεινε τῷ καταφρονηθῆναι διὰ μὲν φιλο-
σοφίαν ὡς ἀπράγμων, διὰ δὲ πενίαν ὡς ἀδύνατος.

VI. Ἐπεὶ δὲ Λακεδαιμόνιοι Φοιβίδαν μὲν ἀφεί-
λοντο τῆς ἀρχῆς καὶ δέκα δραχμῶν μυριάσιν
ἐζημίωσαν, τὴν δὲ Καδμείαν οὐδὲν ἧττον φρουρᾷ
κατέσχον, οἱ μὲν ἄλλοι πάντες Ἕλληνες ἐθαύμαζον τὴν ἀτοπίαν, εἰ τὸν μὲν πράξαντα κολάζουσι,
τὴν δὲ πρᾶξιν δοκιμάζουσι, τοῖς δὲ Θηβαίοις τὴν
πάτριον ἀποβεβληκόσι πολιτείαν καὶ καταδεδου-
λωμένοις ὑπὸ τῶν περὶ Ἀρχίαν καὶ Λεοντίδαν
οὐδὲ ἐλπίσαι περιῆν ἀπαλλαγήν τινα τῆς τυραν-
2 νίδος, ἣν ἑώρων τῇ Σπαρτιατῶν δορυφορουμένην
ἡγεμονίᾳ καὶ καταλυθῆναι μὴ δυναμένην, εἰ μή
τις ἄρα παύσειε κἀκείνους γῆς καὶ θαλάττης
ἄρχοντας. οὐ μὴν ἀλλ' οἱ περὶ Λεοντίδαν πυνθα-
νόμενοι τοὺς φυγάδας Ἀθήνησι διατρίβειν τῷ τε
πλήθει προσφιλεῖς ὄντας καὶ τιμὴν ἔχοντας ὑπὸ
τῶν καλῶν καὶ ἀγαθῶν, ἐπεβούλευον αὐτοῖς κρύ-
φα· καὶ πέμψαντες ἀνθρώπους ἀγνῶτας Ἀνδρο-
κλείδαν μὲν ἀποκτιννύουσι δόλῳ, τῶν δὲ ἄλλων
3 διαμαρτάνουσιν. ἧκε δὲ καὶ παρὰ Λακεδαιμονίων
γράμματα τοῖς Ἀθηναίοις προστάσσοντα μὴ δέχεσθαι μηδὲ παρακινεῖν, ἀλλ' ἐξελαύνειν τοὺς
φυγάδας ὡς κοινοὺς πολεμίους ὑπὸ τῶν συμμάχων

persuasions, made his attack upon the Thebans when they did not expect it, since it was the festival of the Thesmophoria, and got possession of the citadel.[1] Then Ismenias was arrested, carried to Sparta, and after a little while put to death; while Pelopidas, Pherenicus, Androcleides and many others took to flight and were proclaimed outlaws. Epaminondas, however, was suffered to remain in the city, because his philosophy made him to be looked down upon as a recluse, and his poverty as impotent.

VI. But when the Lacedaemonians deprived Phoebidas of his command and fined him a hundred thousand drachmas, and yet held the Cadmeia with a garrison notwithstanding, all the rest of the Greeks were amazed at their inconsistency, since they punished the wrong-doer, but approved his deed. And as for the Thebans, they had lost their ancestral form of government and were enslaved by Archias and Leontidas, nor had they hopes of any deliverance from this tyranny, which they saw was guarded by the dominant military power of the Spartans and could not be pulled down unless those Spartans should somehow be deposed from their command of land and sea. Nevertheless, Leontidas and his associates, learning that the fugitive Thebans were living at Athens, where they were not only in favour with the common people but also honoured by the nobility, secretly plotted against their lives, and sending men who were unknown, they treacherously killed Androcleides, but failed in their designs upon the rest. There came also letters from the Lacedaemonians charging the Athenians not to harbour or encourage the exiles, but to expel them as men

[1] In the winter of 382 B.C. Cf. the *Agesilaüs*, xxiii. 3–7.

4 ἀποδεδειγμένους. οἱ μὲν οὖν Ἀθηναῖοι, πρὸς τῷ
πάτριον αὐτοῖς καὶ σύμφυτον εἶναι τὸ φιλάνθρωπον, ἀμειβόμενοι τοὺς Θηβαίους μάλιστα συναι-
τίους γενομένους τῷ δήμῳ τοῦ κατελθεῖν, καὶ
ψηφισαμένους, ἐάν τις Ἀθηναίων ἐπὶ τοὺς τυράννους ὅπλα διὰ τῆς Βοιωτίας κομίζῃ, μηδένα Βοιω-
τὸν ἀκούειν μηδὲ ὁρᾶν, οὐδὲν ἠδίκησαν τοὺς
Θηβαίους.

VII. Ὁ δὲ Πελοπίδας, καίπερ ἐν τοῖς νεωτά-
τοις ὤν, ἰδίᾳ τε καθ' ἕκαστον ἐξώρμα τῶν φυγάδων, καὶ πρὸς τὸ πλῆθος ἐποιήσατο λόγους, ὡς 2
οὔτε καλὸν οὔτε ὅσιον εἴη[1] δουλεύουσαν τὴν
πατρίδα καὶ φρουρουμένην περιορᾶν, αὐτοὺς δὲ
μόνον τὸ σώζεσθαι καὶ διαζῆν ἀγαπῶντας ἐκκρέ-
μασθαι τῶν Ἀθήνησι ψηφισμάτων καὶ θεραπεύειν ὑποπεπτωκότας ἀεὶ τοῖς λέγειν δυναμένοις
2 καὶ πείθειν τὸν ὄχλον, ἀλλὰ κινδυνευτέον ὑπὲρ
τῶν μεγίστων, παράδειγμα θεμένους τὴν Θρασυ-
βούλου τόλμαν καὶ ἀρετήν, ἵνα, ὡς ἐκεῖνος ἐκ
Θηβῶν πρότερον ὁρμηθεὶς κατέλυσε τοὺς ἐν Ἀθήναις τυράννους, οὕτως αὐτοὶ πάλιν ἐξ Ἀθηνῶν
προελθόντες ἐλευθερώσωσι τὰς Θήβας. ὡς οὖν
ἔπεισε ταῦτα λέγων, πέμπουσιν εἰς Θήβας κρύφα
πρὸς τοὺς ὑπολελειμμένους τῶν φίλων τὰ δεδογ-
3 μένα φράζοντες. οἱ δὲ συνεπήνουν· καὶ Χάρων
μέν, ὥσπερ ἦν ἐπιφανέστατος, ὡμολόγησε τὴν
οἰκίαν παρέξειν, Φιλλίδας δὲ διεπράξατο τῶν
περὶ Ἀρχίαν καὶ Φίλιππον γραμματεὺς γενέσθαι
πολεμαρχούντων. Ἐπαμεινώνδας δὲ τοὺς νέους

───────

[1] εἴη Coraës and Bekker, with most MSS.: εἶναι with A.

[1] In 403 B.C., when Thrasybulus set out from Thebes on
his campaign against the Thirty Tyrants at Athens (Xenophon, *Hell.* ii. 4, 2).

declared common enemies by the allied cities. The Athenians, however, not only yielding to their traditional and natural instincts of humanity, but also making a grateful return for the kindness of the Thebans, who had been most ready to aid them in restoring their democracy,[1] and had passed a decree that if any Athenians marched through Boeotia against the tyrants in Athens, no Boeotian should see or hear them, did no harm to the Thebans in their city.

VII. But Pelopidas, although he was one of the youngest of the exiles, kept inciting each man of them privately, and when they met together pleaded before them that it was neither right nor honourable for them to suffer their native city to be garrisoned and enslaved, and, content with mere life and safety, to hang upon the decrees of the Athenians, and to be always cringing and paying court to such orators as could persuade the people; nay, they must risk their lives for the highest good, and take Thrasybulus and his bold valour for their example, in order that, as he once sallied forth from Thebes [1] and overthrew the tyrants in Athens, so they in their turn might go forth from Athens and liberate Thebes. When, therefore, they had been persuaded by his appeals, they sent secretly to the friends they had left in Thebes, and told them what they purposed. These approved their plan; and Charon, a man of the highest distinction, agreed to put his house at their disposal, while Phillidas contrived to have himself appointed secretary to Archias and Philip, the polemarchs. Epaminondas,[2] too, had long since filled

---

[2] There is no mention either of Epaminondas or Pelopidas in Xenophon's account of these matters (*Hell.* v. 4, 1–12), and his story differs in many details from that of Plutarch.

355

πάλαι φρονήματος ἦν ἐμπεπληκώς· ἐκέλευε γὰρ
ἐν τοῖς γυμνασίοις ἐπιλαμβάνεσθαι τῶν Λακεδαιμονίων καὶ παλαίειν, εἶτα ὁρῶν ἐπὶ τῷ κρατεῖν
καὶ περιεῖναι γαυρουμένους ἐπέπληττεν, ὡς
αἰσχύνεσθαι μᾶλλον αὐτοῖς προσῆκον, εἰ δουλεύ-
ουσι δι' ἀνανδρίαν ὧν τοσοῦτον ταῖς ῥώμαις
διαφέρουσιν.

VIII. Ἡμέρας δὲ πρὸς τὴν πρᾶξιν ὁρισθείσης,
ἔδοξε τοῖς φυγάσι τοὺς μὲν ἄλλους συναγαγόντα
Φερένικον ἐν τῷ Θριασίῳ περιμένειν, ὀλίγους δὲ
τῶν νεωτάτων παραβαλέσθαι προεισελθεῖν εἰς
τὴν πόλιν, ἐὰν δέ τι πάθωσιν ὑπὸ τῶν πολεμίων
οὗτοι, τοὺς ἄλλους ἐπιμελεῖσθαι πάντας ὅπως
μήτε παῖδες αὐτῶν μήτε γονεῖς ἐνδεεῖς ἔσονται
2 τῶν ἀναγκαίων. ὑφίσταται δὲ τὴν πρᾶξιν Πελοπίδας πρῶτος, εἶτα Μέλων καὶ Δαμοκλείδας καὶ
Θεόπομπος, ἄνδρες οἴκων τε πρώτων καὶ πρὸς
ἀλλήλους τὰ ἄλλα μὲν φιλικῶς καὶ πιστῶς, ὑπὲρ
δὲ δόξης καὶ ἀνδρείας ἀεὶ φιλονείκως ἔχοντες.
γενόμενοι δὲ οἱ σύμπαντες δώδεκα, καὶ τοὺς ἀπο-
λειπομένους ἀσπασάμενοι, καὶ προπέμψαντες
ἄγγελον τῷ Χάρωνι, προῆγον ἐν χλαμυδίοις,
σκύλακάς τε θηρατικὰς καὶ στάλικας ἔχοντες, ὡς
μηδὲ εἷς ὑποπτεύοι τῶν ἐντυγχανόντων καθ' ὁδόν,
ἀλλ' ἀλύοντες ἄλλως πλανᾶσθαι καὶ κυνηγεῖν
δοκοῖεν.
3 Ἐπεὶ δὲ ὁ πεμφθεὶς παρ' αὐτῶν ἄγγελος ἧκε
πρὸς τὸν Χάρωνα καὶ καθ' ὁδὸν ὄντας ἔφραζεν,
αὐτὸς μὲν ὁ Χάρων οὐδὲ ὑπὸ τοῦ δεινοῦ πλησιά-
ζοντος ἔτρεψέ τι τῆς γνώμης, ἀλλ' ἀνὴρ ἀγαθὸς
ἦν καὶ παρεῖχε τὴν οἰκίαν, Ἱπποσθενίδας δέ τις,
οὐ πονηρὸς μέν, ἀλλὰ καὶ φιλόπατρις καὶ τοῖς
φυγάσιν εὔνους ἄνθρωπος, ἐνδεὴς δὲ τόλμης

the minds of the Theban youth with high thoughts; for he kept urging them in the gymnastic schools to try the Lacedaemonians in wrestling, and when he saw them elated with victory and mastery, he would chide them, telling them they ought rather to be ashamed, since their cowardice made them the slaves of the men whom they so far surpassed in bodily powers.

VIII. A day for the enterprise having been fixed,[1] the exiles decided that Pherenicus, with the rest of the party under his command, should remain in the Thriasian plain, while a few of the youngest took the risk of going forward into the city; and if anything happened to these at the hands of their enemies, the rest should all see to it that neither their children nor their parents came to any want. Pelopidas was first to undertake the enterprise, then Melon, Damocleides, and Theopompus, men of foremost families, and of mutual fidelity and friendship, although in the race for heroic achievement and glory they were constant rivals. When their number had reached twelve, they bade farewell to those who stayed behind, sent a messenger before them to Charon, and set out in short cloaks, taking hunting dogs and nets with them, that anyone who met them on the road might not suspect their purpose, but take them for hunters beating about the country.

When their messenger came to Charon and told him they were on the way, Charon himself did not change his mind at all even though the hour of peril drew nigh, but was a man of his word and prepared his house to receive them; a certain Hipposthenidas, however, not a bad man, nay, both patriotic and well disposed towards the exiles, but lacking in that

---

[1] In the winter of 379 B.C.

τοσαύτης ὅσης ὅ τε καιρὸς ὀξὺς ὢν αἵ τε ὑποκεί-
μεναι πράξεις ἀπήτουν, ὥσπερ ἰλιγγιάσας πρὸς
τὸ μέγεθος τοῦ ἀγῶνος ἐν χερσὶ γενομένου, καὶ
4 μόλις ποτὲ τῷ λογισμῷ συμφρονήσας ὅτι τρόπον
τινὰ τὴν τῶν Λακεδαιμονίων σαλεύουσιν ἀρχὴν
καὶ τῆς ἐκεῖθεν δυνάμεως ὑποβάλλονται κατάλυσιν, πιστεύσαντες ἀπόροις καὶ φυγαδικαῖς
ἐλπίσιν, ἀπελθὼν οἴκαδε σιωπῇ πέμπει τινὰ τῶν
φίλων πρὸς Μέλωνα καὶ Πελοπίδαν, ἀναβαλέσθαι
κελεύων ἐν τῷ παρόντι καὶ περιμένειν βελτίονα
καιρὸν αὖθις ἀπαλλαγέντας εἰς Ἀθήνας. Χλίδων
ἦν ὄνομα τῷ πεμφθέντι, καὶ κατὰ σπουδὴν οἴκαδε
πρὸς αὑτὸν τραπόμενος καὶ τὸν ἵππον ἐξαγαγὼν
5 ᾔτει χαλινόν. ἀπορουμένης δὲ τῆς γυναικὸς
ὡς οὐκ εἶχε δοῦναι, καὶ χρῆσαί τινι τῶν συνήθων
λεγούσης, λοιδορίαι τὸ πρῶτον ἦσαν, εἶτα δυσφη-
μίαι, τῆς γυναικὸς ἐπαρωμένης αὐτῷ τε κακὰς
ὁδοὺς ἐκείνῳ καὶ τοῖς πέμπουσιν, ὥστε καὶ τὸν
Χλίδωνα πολὺ τῆς ἡμέρας ἀναλώσαντα πρὸς
τούτοις δι' ὀργήν, ἅμα δὲ καὶ τὸ συμβεβηκὸς
οἰωνισάμενον, ἀφεῖναι τὴν ὁδὸν ὅλως καὶ πρὸς
ἄλλο τι τραπέσθαι. παρὰ τοσοῦτον μὲν ἦλθον 28
αἱ μέγισται καὶ κάλλισται τῶν πράξεων εὐθὺς ἐν
ἀρχῇ διαφυγεῖν τὸν καιρόν.

IX. Οἱ δὲ περὶ τὸν Πελοπίδαν ἐσθῆτας γεωρ-
γῶν μεταλαβόντες καὶ διελόντες αὑτοὺς ἄλλοι
κατ' ἄλλα μέρη τῆς πόλεως παρεισῆλθον ἔτι
ἡμέρας οὔσης. ἦν δέ τι πνεῦμα καὶ νιφετὸς
ἀρχομένου τρέπεσθαι τοῦ ἀέρος, καὶ μᾶλλον
ἔλαθον καταπεφευγότων ἤδη διὰ τὸν χειμῶνα τῶν
πλείστων εἰς τὰς οἰκίας. οἷς δὲ ἦν ἐπιμελὲς τὰ
πραττόμενα γινώσκειν, ἀνελάμβανον τοὺς προσ-
ερχομένους καὶ καθίστων εὐθὺς εἰς τὴν οἰκίαν

degree of boldness which the sharp crisis and the projected enterprise demanded, was made dizzy, so to
speak, by the magnitude of the struggle now so close
at hand, and at last comprehended that, in undertaking
to overthrow the armed force in the city, they were
in a manner trying to shake the empire of the Lacedaemonians, and had placed their reliance on the hopes
of men in exile and without resources. He therefore
went quietly home, and sent one of his friends to
Melon and Pelopidas, urging them to postpone the
enterprise for the present, go back to Athens, and
await a more favourable opportunity. Chlidon was
the name of this messenger, and going to his own
home in haste, he brought out his horse and asked
for the bridle. His wife, however, was embarrassed
because she could not give it to him, and said she
had lent it to a neighbour. Words of abuse were
followed by imprecations, and his wife prayed that
the journey might prove fatal both to him and
to those that sent him. Chlidon, therefore, after
spending a great part of the day in this angry
squabble, and after making up his mind, too, that
what had happened was ominous, gave up his journey
entirely and turned his thoughts to something else.
So near can the greatest and fairest enterprises come,
at the very outset, to missing their opportunity.

IX. But Pelopidas and his companions, after putting on the dress of peasants, and separating, entered
the city at different points while it was yet day.
There was some wind and snow as the weather
began to change, and they were the more un-
observed because most people had already taken
refuge from the storm in their houses. Those, however, whose business it was to know what was going
on, received the visitors as they came, and brought

τοῦ Χάρωνος· ἐγένοντο δὲ σὺν τοῖς φυγάσι πεντήκοντα δυοῖν δέοντες.

2   Τὰ δὲ περὶ τοὺς τυράννους οὕτως εἶχε. Φιλλίδας ὁ γραμματεὺς συνέπραττε μέν, ὥσπερ εἴρηται,
πάντα καὶ συνῄδει τοῖς φυγάσιν, εἰς δὲ τὴν
ἡμέραν ἐκείνην ἐκ παλαιοῦ κατηγγελκὼς τοῖς
περὶ τὸν Ἀρχίαν πότον τινὰ καὶ συνουσίαν καὶ
γύναια τῶν ὑπάνδρων, ἔπραττεν ὅτι μάλιστα
ταῖς ἡδοναῖς ἐκλελυμένους καὶ κατοίνους μεταχει-
3   ρίσασθαι παρέξειν τοῖς ἐπιτιθεμένοις. οὔπω δὲ
πάνυ πόρρω μέθης οὖσιν αὐτοῖς προσέπεσέ τις οὐ
ψευδὴς μέν, ἀβέβαιος δὲ καὶ πολλὴν ἀσάφειαν
ἔχουσα περὶ τῶν φυγάδων μήνυσις ὡς ἐν τῇ
πόλει κρυπτομένων. τοῦ δὲ Φιλλίδου παραφέρ-
οντος τὸν λόγον, ὅμως Ἀρχίας ἔπεμψέ τινα τῶν
ὑπηρετῶν πρὸς τὸν Χάρωνα, προστάσσων εὐθὺς
ἥκειν αὐτόν. ἦν δὲ ἑσπέρα, καὶ συνέταττον ἔνδον
αὐτοὺς οἱ περὶ τὸν Πελοπίδαν, ἤδη τεθωρακι-
4   σμένοι καὶ τὰς μαχαίρας ἀνειληφότες. ἐξαίφνης
δὲ κοπτομένης τῆς θύρας προσδραμών τις, καὶ
πυθόμενος τοῦ ὑπηρέτου Χάρωνα μετιέναι παρὰ
τῶν πολεμάρχων φάσκοντος, ἀπήγγειλεν εἴσω
τεθορυβημένος, καὶ πᾶσιν εὐθὺς παρέστη τήν τε
πρᾶξιν ἐκμεμηνῦσθαι καὶ σφᾶς ἅπαντας ἀπολωλέναι, μηδὲ δράσαντάς τι τῆς ἀρετῆς ἄξιον. οὐ
μὴν ἀλλ' ἔδοξεν ὑπακοῦσαι τὸν Χάρωνα καὶ
παρασχεῖν ἑαυτὸν δεῖν ἀνυπόπτως τοῖς ἄρχουσιν,
ἄλλως μὲν ἀνδρώδη καὶ βαρὺν ὄντα τῷ θαρρεῖν
5   παρὰ τὰ δεινά, τότε δὲ δι' ἐκείνους ἐκπεπληγ-
μένον καὶ περιπαθοῦντα, μή τις ὑποψία προ-

them at once to the house of Charon; and there were, counting the exiles, forty-eight of them.

With the tyrants, matters stood as follows. Phillidas, their secretary, as I have said, was privy to the plans of the exiles and was co-operating fully with them, and some time before had proposed for that day that Archias and his friends should have a drinking-bout, at which a few married women should join them, his scheme being that when they were full of wine and completely relaxed in their pleasures, he would deliver them into the hands of their assailants. But before the party were very deep in their cups, some information was suddenly brought them, not false, indeed, but uncertain and very vague, that the exiles were concealed in the city. Although Phillidas tried to change the subject, Archias nevertheless sent one of his attendants to Charon, commanding him to come to him at once. It was evening, and Pelopidas and his companions in Charon's house were getting themselves ready for action, having already put on their breastplates and taken up their swords. Then there was a sudden knocking at the door. Someone ran to it, learned from the attendant that he was come from the polemarchs with a summons for Charon, and brought the news inside, much perturbed. All were at once convinced that their enterprise had been revealed, and that they themselves were all lost, before they had even done anything worthy of their valour. However, they decided that Charon must obey the summons and present himself boldly before the magistrates. Charon was generally an intrepid man and of a stern courage in the face of danger, but in this case he was much concerned and frightened on account of his friends, and feared that some

δοσίας ἐπ' αὐτὸν ἔλθῃ τοσούτων ἅμα καὶ τοιούτων πολιτῶν ἀπολομένων. ὡς οὖν ἔμελλεν ἀπιέναι, παραλαβὼν ἐκ τῆς γυναικωνίτιδος τὸν υἱόν,
ἔτι μὲν ὄντα παῖδα, κάλλει δὲ καὶ ῥώμῃ σώματος
πρωτεύοντα τῶν καθ' ἡλικίαν, ἐνεχείριζε τοῖς
περὶ Πελοπίδαν, εἴ τινα δόλον καὶ προδοσίαν
αὐτοῦ καταγνοῖεν, ὡς πολεμίῳ χρῆσθαι κελεύων
6 ἐκείνῳ καὶ μὴ φείδεσθαι. πολλοῖς μὲν οὖν αὐτῶν
δάκρυα πρὸς τὸ πάθος καὶ τὸ φρόνημα τοῦ Χάρωνος ἐξέπεσε, πάντες δὲ ἠγανάκτουν εἰ δειλὸν
οὕτως εἶναί τινα δοκεῖ καὶ διεφθαρμένον ὑπὸ τοῦ
παρόντος, ὥστε ὑπονοεῖν ἐκεῖνον ἢ ὅλως αἰτιᾶ-
σθαι· καὶ τὸν υἱὸν ἐδέοντο μὴ καταμιγνύειν αὐτοῖς, ἀλλ' ἐκποδὼν θέσθαι τοῦ μέλλοντος, ὅπως
αὐτός γε τῇ πόλει καὶ τοῖς φίλοις τιμωρὸς ὑπο-
τρέφοιτο περισωθεὶς καὶ διαφυγὼν τοὺς τυράν-
7 νους. ὁ δὲ Χάρων τὸν μὲν υἱὸν ἀπαλλάξειν οὐκ
ἔφη· ποῖον γὰρ αὐτῷ βίον ὁρᾶν ἢ τίνα σωτηρίαν
καλλίονα τῆς ὁμοῦ μετὰ πατρὸς καὶ φίλων τοσούτων ἀνυβρίστου τελευτῆς; ἐπευξάμενος δὲ τοῖς
θεοῖς καὶ πάντας ἀσπασάμενος καὶ παραθαρρύνας
ἀπῄει, προσέχων ἑαυτῷ καὶ ῥυθμίζων σχήματι
προσώπου καὶ τόνῳ φωνῆς ἀνομοιότατος οἷς
ἔπραττε φανῆναι.

X. Γενομένου δ' ἐπὶ ταῖς θύραις αὐτοῦ, προῆλθεν ὁ Ἀρχίας, καὶ Φιλλίδας,[1] καὶ εἶπεν· "Ὦ
Χάρων, τινὰς ἀκήκοα παρεληλυθότας ἐν τῇ πόλει
κρύπτεσθαι, καὶ συμπράττειν αὐτοῖς ἐνίους τῶν
πολιτῶν." καὶ ὁ Χάρων διαταραχθεὶς τὸ πρῶτον, εἶτα ἐρωτήσας τίνες εἰσὶν οἱ παρεληλυθότες
καὶ τίνες οἱ κρύπτοντες αὐτούς, ὡς οὐδὲν ἑώρα

---

[1] Φιλλίδας with the MSS.: Φίλιππος, Bryan's correction
(cf. *Morals*, p. 595 f.). Bekker brackets καὶ Φίλιππος.

suspicion of treachery would fall upon him if so many and such excellent citizens now lost their lives. Accordingly, as he was about to depart, he brought his son from the women's apartments, a mere boy as yet, but in beauty and bodily strength surpassing those of his years, and put him in the hands of Pelopidas, telling him that if he found any guile or treachery in the father, he must treat the son as an enemy and show him no mercy. Many were moved to tears by the noble concern which Charon showed, and all were indignant that he should think any one of them so demoralized by the present peril and so mean-spirited as to suspect him or blame him in the least. They also begged him not to involve his son with them, but to put him out of harm's way, that he might escape the tyrants and live to become an avenger of his city and his friends. Charon, however, refused to take his son away, asking if any kind of life or any safety could be more honourable for him than a decorous death with his father and all these friends. Then he addressed the gods in prayer, and after embracing and encouraging them all, went his way, striving so to compose his countenance and modulate his voice as not to betray what he was really doing.

X. When he reached the door of the house, Archias came out to him, with Phillidas, and said: "Charon, I have heard that certain men have come and hid themselves in the city, and that some of the citizens are in collusion with them." Charon was disturbed at first, but on asking who the men were that had come and who were concealing them, he saw that Archias could give no clear account of the

σαφὲς εἰπεῖν ἔχοντα τὸν Ἀρχίαν, ὑπονοήσας ἀπ'
οὐδενὸς τῶν ἐπισταμένων γεγονέναι τὴν μήνυσιν,
" Ὁρᾶτε τοίνυν," ἔφη, " μὴ κενός τις ὑμᾶς δια-
ταράττῃ λόγος. οὐ μὴν ἀλλὰ σκέψομαι· δεῖ
2 γὰρ ἴσως μηδενὸς καταφρονεῖν." ταῦτα καὶ
Φιλλίδας παρὼν ἐπήνει, καὶ τὸν Ἀρχίαν ἀπαγαγὼν αὖθις εἰς ἄκρατον πολὺν κατέβαλε, καὶ
ταῖς περὶ τῶν γυναικῶν ἐλπίσι διεπαιδαγώγει
τὸν πότον. ὡς δ' ἐπανῆλθεν ὁ Χάρων οἴκαδε
καὶ διεσκευασμένους τοὺς ἄνδρας εὗρεν οὐχ ὡς
ἄν τινα νίκην ἢ σωτηρίαν ἐλπίζοντας, ἀλλ' ὡς
ἀποθανουμένους λαμπρῶς καὶ μετὰ φόνου πολλοῦ
τῶν πολεμίων, τὸ μὲν ἀληθὲς αὐτοῖς ἔφραζε τοῖς
περὶ τὸν Πελοπίδαν, πρὸς δὲ τοὺς ἄλλους ἐψεύσατο λόγους τινὰς τοῦ Ἀρχίου περὶ πραγμάτων
ἑτέρων πλασάμενος.
3   Ἔτι δὲ τοῦ πρώτου παραφερομένου δεύτερον
ἐπῆγεν ἡ τύχη χειμῶνα τοῖς ἀνδράσιν. ἧκε γάρ
τις ἐξ Ἀθηνῶν παρὰ Ἀρχίου τοῦ ἱεροφάντου
πρὸς Ἀρχίαν τὸν ὁμώνυμον, ξένον ὄντα καὶ φίλον,
ἐπιστολὴν κομίζων οὐ κενὴν ἔχουσαν οὐδὲ πε-
πλασμένην ὑπόνοιαν, ἀλλὰ σαφῶς ἕκαστα περὶ
τῶν πρασσομένων φάσκουσαν, ὡς ὕστερον ἐπε-
4 γνώσθη. τότε δὲ μεθύοντι τῷ Ἀρχίᾳ προσ-
αχθεὶς ὁ γραμματοφόρος καὶ τὴν ἐπιστολὴν
ἐπιδούς, " Ὁ ταύτην," ἔφη, " πέμψας ἐκέλευσεν
εὐθὺς ἀναγνῶναι· περὶ σπουδαίων γάρ τινων
γεγράφθαι." καὶ ὁ Ἀρχίας μειδιάσας, " Οὐκοῦν
εἰς αὔριον," ἔφη, " τὰ σπουδαῖα." καὶ τὴν ἐπιστολὴν δεξάμενος ὑπὸ τὸ προσκεφάλαιον ὑπέθη-
κεν, αὐτὸς δὲ πάλιν τῷ Φιλλίδᾳ περὶ ὧν ἐτύγχανον
διαλεγόμενοι προσεῖχεν. ὁ μὲν οὖν λόγος οὗτος

matter, and conjectured that his information had not
come from any of those who were privy to the plot.
He therefore said : " Do not, then, suffer any empty
rumour to disturb you. However, I will look into
the matter ; for perhaps no story should be ignored."
Phillidas, too, who stood by, approved of this, and
after leading Archias back, got him to drink hard,
and tried to protract the revel with hopes of a visit
from the women. But Charon, when he got back
home, and found the men there disposed, not to
expect safety or victory at all, but to die gloriously
after a great slaughter of their enemies, told the
truth only to Pelopidas himself, while for the rest he
concocted a false tale that Archias had talked with
him about other matters.[1]

Before this first storm had yet blown over, fortune brought a second down upon the men. For
there came a messenger from Athens, from Archias
the hierophant to his namesake Archias, who was his
guest-friend, bearing a letter which contained no
empty nor false suspicion, but stated clearly all the
details of the scheme that was on foot, as was subsequently learned. At the time, however, Archias was
drunk, and the bearer of the letter was brought to
him and put it into his hands, saying : " The sender
of this bade thee read it at once ; for it is on serious
business." Then Archias answered with a smile :
" Serious business for the morrow " ; and when he
had received the letter he put it under his pillow,
and resumed his casual conversation with Phillidas.

[1] According to Plutarch's lengthy version of this affair in
his *Discourse concerning the Daemon of Socrates* (chapter 29,
Morals, p. 595 f.), Charon hid the truth from no one.

ἐν παροιμίας τάξει περιφερόμενος μέχρι νῦν
διασώζεται παρὰ τοῖς Ἕλλησι.

XI. Τῆς δὲ πράξεως δοκούσης ἔχειν ἤδη τὸν
οἰκεῖον καιρόν, ἐξώρμων δίχα διελόντες αὐτούς,
οἱ μὲν περὶ Πελοπίδαν καὶ Δαμοκλείδαν ἐπὶ
τὸν Λεοντίδαν καὶ τὸν Ὑπάτην ἐγγὺς ἀλλήλων
οἰκοῦντας, Χάρων δὲ καὶ Μέλων ἐπὶ τὸν Ἀρχίαν
καὶ Φίλιππον, ἐσθῆτας ἐπενδεδυμένοι γυναικείας
τοῖς θώραξι, καὶ δασεῖς στεφάνους ἐλάτης τε καὶ
πεύκης περικείμενοι κατασκιάζοντας τὰ πρόσ-
2 ωπα. διὸ καὶ ταῖς θύραις τοῦ συμποσίου τὸ
πρῶτον ἐπιστάντες, κρότον ἐποίησαν καὶ θόρυβον
οἰομένων ἃς πάλαι προσεδόκων γυναῖκας ἥκειν.
ἐπεὶ δὲ περιβλέψαντες ἐν κύκλῳ τὸ συμπόσιον
καὶ τῶν κατακεκλιμένων ἕκαστον ἀκριβῶς καταμαθόντες ἐσπάσαντο τὰς μαχαίρας, καὶ φερόμενοι διὰ τῶν τραπεζῶν ἐπὶ τὸν Ἀρχίαν καὶ
3 Φίλιππον ἐφάνησαν οἵπερ ἦσαν, ὀλίγους μὲν ὁ
Φιλλίδας τῶν κατακειμένων ἔπεισεν ἡσυχίαν
ἄγειν, τοὺς δὲ ἄλλους ἀμύνεσθαι μετὰ τῶν πολεμάρχων ἐπιχειροῦντας καὶ συνεξανισταμένους
διὰ τὴν μέθην οὐ πάνυ χαλεπῶς ἀπέκτειναν.

Τοῖς δὲ περὶ τὸν Πελοπίδαν ἐργωδέστερον
ἀπήντα τὸ πρᾶγμα· καὶ γὰρ ἐπὶ νήφοντα καὶ
δεινὸν ἄνδρα τὸν Λεοντίδαν ἐχώρουν, καὶ κεκλει-
σμένην τὴν οἰκίαν εὗρον ἤδη καθεύδοντος, καὶ
πολὺν χρόνον κόπτουσιν αὐτοῖς ὑπήκουεν οὐδείς·
4 μόλις δέ ποτε τοῦ θεράποντος αἰσθομένου προϊ-
όντος ἔνδοθεν καὶ τὸν μοχλὸν ἀφαιροῦντος, ἅμα
τῷ πρῶτον ἐνδοῦναι καὶ χαλάσαι τὰς θύρας
ἐμπεσόντες ἀθρόοι καὶ τὸν οἰκέτην ἀνατρέψαντες
ἐπὶ τὸν θάλαμον ὥρμησαν. ὁ δὲ Λεοντίδας αὐτῷ
τεκμαιρόμενος τῷ κτύπῳ καὶ δρόμῳ τὸ γιγνό-

Wherefore these words of his are a current proverb to this day among the Greeks.

XI. Now that the fitting time for their undertaking seemed to have come, they sallied forth in two bands; one, under the lead of Pelopidas and Damocleidas, against Leontidas and Hypates, who lived near together; the other against Archias and Philip, under Charon and Melon, who had put on women's apparel over their breastplates, and wore thick garlands of pine and fir which shaded their faces. For this reason, when they stood at the door of the banquet-room, at first the company shouted and clapped their hands, supposing that the women whom they had long been expecting were come. But then, after surveying the banquet and carefully marking each of the reclining guests, the visitors drew their swords, and rushing through the midst of the tables at Archias and Philip, revealed who they were. A few of the guests were persuaded by Phillidas to remain quiet, but the rest, who, with the polemarchs, offered resistance and tried to defend themselves, were dispatched without any trouble, since they were drunk.

Pelopidas and his party, however, were confronted with a harder task; for Leontidas, against whom they were going, was a sober and formidable man, and they found his house closed, since he had already gone to bed. For a long time no one answered their knocking, but at last the attendant heard them and came out and drew back the bolt. As soon as the door yielded and gave way, they rushed in together, overturned the servant, and hastened towards the bed-chamber. But Leontidas, conjecturing what was happening by the very noise and trampling, rose from

5 μενον, ἐσπάσατο μὲν τὸ ἐγχειρίδιον ἐξαναστάς,
ἔλαθε δὲ αὐτὸν καταβαλεῖν τὰ λύχνα καὶ διὰ
σκότους αὐτοὺς ἑαυτοῖς περιπετεῖς ποιῆσαι τοὺς
ἄνδρας. ἐν δὲ φωτὶ πολλῷ καθορώμενος, ὑπήντα
πρὸς τὰς θύρας αὐτοῖς τοῦ θαλάμου, καὶ τὸν
πρῶτον εἰσιόντα Κηφισόδωρον πατάξας κατέβαλε. πεσόντος δὲ τούτου δευτέρῳ συνεπλέκετο
τῷ Πελοπίδᾳ· καὶ τὴν μάχην χαλεπὴν ἐποίει καὶ
δύσεργον ἡ στενότης τῶν θυρῶν καὶ κείμενος
6 ἐμποδὼν ἤδη νεκρὸς ὁ Κηφισόδωρος. ἐκράτησε
δ' οὖν ὁ Πελοπίδας, καὶ κατεργασάμενος τὸν
Λεοντίδαν ἐπὶ τὸν Ὑπάτην εὐθὺς ἐχώρει μετὰ
τῶν σὺν αὐτῷ. καὶ παρεισέπεσον μὲν εἰς τὴν
οἰκίαν ὁμοίως, αἰσθόμενον δὲ ταχέως καὶ κατα-
φυγόντα πρὸς τοὺς γείτονας, ἐκ ποδῶν διώξαντες
εἷλον καὶ διέφθειραν.

XII. Διαπραξάμενοι δὲ ταῦτα καὶ τοῖς περὶ
Μέλωνα συμβαλόντες ἔπεμψαν μὲν εἰς τὴν
Ἀττικὴν ἐπὶ τοὺς ὑπολελειμμένους ἐκεῖ τῶν
φυγάδων, ἐκάλουν δὲ τοὺς πολίτας ἐπὶ τὴν ἐλευθερίαν, καὶ τοὺς προσιόντας ὥπλιζον, ἀφαιροῦντες
ἀπὸ τῶν στοῶν τὰ περικείμενα σκῦλα, καὶ τὰ
περὶ τὴν οἰκίαν ἐργαστήρια δορυξόων καὶ μαχαι-
ροποιῶν ἀναρρηγνύντες. ἧκον δὲ βοηθοῦντες
2 αὐτοῖς μετὰ τῶν ὅπλων οἱ περὶ Ἐπαμεινώνδαν
καὶ Γοργίδαν, συνειλοχότες οὐκ ὀλίγους τῶν νέων
καὶ τῶν πρεσβυτέρων τοὺς βελτίστους. ἡ δὲ
πόλις ἤδη μὲν ἀνεπτόητο πᾶσα, καὶ πολὺς θόρυβος ἦν καὶ φῶτα περὶ τὰς οἰκίας καὶ διαδρομαὶ
πρὸς ἀλλήλους, οὔπω δὲ συνειστήκει τὸ πλῆθος,
ἀλλ' ἐκπεπληγμένοι πρὸς τὰ γινόμενα καὶ σαφὲς
3 οὐδὲν εἰδότες ἡμέραν περιέμενον. ὅθεν ἁμαρτεῖν οἱ
τῶν Λακεδαιμονίων ἄρχοντες ἔδοξαν εὐθὺς οὐκ ἐπι-

bed and drew his dagger, but he forgot to overthrow the lamps and make the men fall foul of one
another in the darkness. On the contrary, exposed
to view by an abundance of light, he went to meet
them at the door of his chamber, and struck down
the first one that entered, Cephisodorus. When this
assailant had fallen, he engaged Pelopidas next ; and
their conflict was rendered troublesome and difficult
by the narrowness of the door and by Cephisodorus,
whose body, now dead, lay in their way. But at last
Pelopidas prevailed, and after dispatching Leontidas,
he and his followers went at once to attack Hypates.
They broke into his house as they had done into the
other, but he promptly perceived their design and
fled for refuge to his neighbours. Thither they
closely followed him, and caught him, and slew him.

XII. These things accomplished, they joined
Melon's party, and sent into Attica for the exiles they
had left there.[1] They also summoned the citizens to
fight for their freedom, and armed those who came,
taking from the porticos the spoils suspended there,
and breaking open the neighbouring workshops of
spear-makers and sword-makers. Epaminondas and
Gorgidas also came to their aid with an armed following, composed of many young men and the best
of the older men. And now the city was all in a
flutter of excitement, there was much noise, the
houses had lights in them, and there was running to
and fro. The people, however, did not yet assemble ;
they were terrified at what was going on, and had
no clear knowledge of it, and were waiting for day.
Wherefore the Spartan commanders were thought to
have made a mistake in not attacking and engaging

---

[1] Cf. chapter viii. 1.

δραμόντες οὐδὲ συμβαλόντες, αὐτὴ μὲν ἡ φρουρὰ
περὶ χιλίους πεντακοσίους ὄντες, ἐκ δὲ τῆς πόλεως
πρὸς αὐτοὺς πολλῶν συντρεχόντων, ἀλλὰ τὴν
βοὴν καὶ τὰ πυρὰ καὶ τὸν ὄχλον χωροῦντα [1]
πανταχόθεν πολὺν φοβηθέντες ἡσύχαζον, αὐτὴν
4 τὴν Καδμείαν κατέχοντες. ἅμα δὲ ἡμέρᾳ παρῆσαν μὲν ἐκ τῆς Ἀττικῆς οἱ φυγάδες ὡπλισμένοι,
συνήθροιστο δὲ εἰς τὴν ἐκκλησίαν ὁ δῆμος.
εἰσῆγον δὲ τοὺς περὶ Πελοπίδαν Ἐπαμεινώνδας
καὶ Γοργίδας ὑπὸ τῶν ἱερέων περιεχομένους
στέμματα προτεινόντων καὶ παρακαλούντων τοὺς
πολίτας τῇ πατρίδι καὶ τοῖς θεοῖς βοηθεῖν. ἡ δ᾽
ἐκκλησία ὀρθὴ πρὸς τὴν ὄψιν μετὰ κρότου καὶ
βοῆς ἐξανέστη, δεχομένων τοὺς ἄνδρας ὡς
εὐεργέτας καὶ σωτῆρας.

XIII. Ἐκ δὲ τούτου βοιωτάρχης αἱρεθεὶς μετὰ
Μέλωνος καὶ Χάρωνος ὁ Πελοπίδας εὐθὺς ἀπε-
τείχιζε τὴν ἀκρόπολιν καὶ προσβολὰς ἐποιεῖτο
πανταχόθεν, ἐξελεῖν σπουδάζων τοὺς Λακεδαιμονίους καὶ τὴν Καδμείαν ἐλευθερῶσαι πρὶν ἐκ
2 Σπάρτης στρατὸν ἐπελθεῖν. καὶ παρὰ τοσοῦτον
ἔφθασεν ἀφεὶς ὑποσπόνδους τοὺς ἄνδρας ὅσον
ἐν Μεγάροις οὖσιν αὐτοῖς ἀπαντῆσαι Κλεόμβροτον ἐπὶ τὰς Θήβας ἐλαύνοντα μετὰ μεγάλης
δυνάμεως. οἱ δὲ Σπαρτιᾶται, τριῶν ἁρμοστῶν
γενομένων ἐν Θήβαις, Ἡριππίδαν μὲν καὶ Ἄρ-
κισσον ἀπέκτειναν κρίναντες, ὁ δὲ τρίτος Λυσα-
νορίδας χρήμασι πολλοῖς ζημιωθεὶς αὐτὸν ἐκ τῆς
Πελοποννήσου μετέστησε.

3 Ταύτην τὴν πρᾶξιν ἀρεταῖς μὲν ἀνδρῶν καὶ
κινδύνοις καὶ ἀγῶσι παραπλησίαν τῇ Θρασυ-

[1] χωροῦντα Coraës' correction of the MSS. ἀναχωροῦντα,
adopted by Bekker.

at once, since their garrison numbered about fifteen hundred men, and many ran to join them out of the city; but the shouting, the fires, and the great throngs in motion everywhere, terrified them, and they kept quiet, holding the citadel itself in their possession. At break of day the exiles came in from Attica under arms, and a general assembly of the people was convened. Then Epaminondas and Gorgidas brought before it Pelopidas and his companions, surrounded by the priests, holding forth garlands, and calling upon the citizens to come to the aid of their country and their gods. And the assembly, at the sight, rose to its feet with shouts and clapping of hands, and welcomed the men as deliverers and benefactors.

XIII. After this, having been elected boeotarch, or governor of Boeotia, together with Melon and Charon, Pelopidas at once blockaded the acropolis and assaulted it on every side, being anxious to drive out the Lacedaemonians and free the Cadmeia before an army came up from Sparta. And he succeeded by so narrow a margin that, when the men had surrendered conditionally and had been allowed to depart, they got no further than Megara before they were met by Cleombrotus marching against Thebes with a great force. Of the three men who had been harmosts, or governors, in Thebes, the Spartans condemned and executed Herippidas and Arcissus, and the third, Lysanoridas, was heavily fined and forsook the Peloponnesus.

This exploit, so like that of Thrasybulus in the valour, the perils, and the struggles of its heroes,

βούλου γενομένην, καὶ βραβευθεῖσαν ὁμοίως ὑπὸ
τῆς τύχης, ἀδελφὴν ἐκείνης προσηγόρευον οἱ
Ἕλληνες. οὐ γὰρ ἔστι ῥᾳδίως ἑτέρους εἰπεῖν οἳ
πλειόνων ἐλάττους καὶ δυνατωτέρων ἐρημότεροι
τόλμῃ καὶ δεινότητι κρατήσαντες αἴτιοι μειζόνων
4 ἀγαθῶν ταῖς πατρίσι κατέστησαν. ἐνδοξοτέραν
δὲ ταύτην ἐποίησεν ἡ μεταβολὴ τῶν πραγμάτων.
ὁ γὰρ καταλύσας τὸ τῆς Σπάρτης ἀξίωμα καὶ
παύσας ἄρχοντας αὐτοὺς γῆς τε καὶ θαλάττης
πόλεμος ἐξ ἐκείνης ἐγένετο τῆς νυκτός, ἐν ᾗ
Πελοπίδας οὐ φρούριον, οὐ τεῖχος, οὐκ ἀκρόπολιν
καταλαβών, ἀλλ' εἰς οἰκίαν δωδέκατος κατελθών,
εἰ δεῖ μεταφορᾷ τὸ ἀληθὲς εἰπεῖν, ἔλυσε καὶ
διέκοψε τοὺς δεσμοὺς τῆς Λακεδαιμονίων ἡγεμονίας, ἀλύτους καὶ ἀρρήκτους εἶναι δοκοῦντας.

XIV. Ἐπεὶ τοίνυν στρατῷ μεγάλῳ Λακεδαιμονίων εἰς τὴν Βοιωτίαν ἐμβαλόντων οἱ
Ἀθηναῖοι περίφοβοι γενόμενοι τήν τε συμμαχίαν
ἀπείπαντο τοῖς Θηβαίοις καὶ τῶν βοιωτιαζόντων
εἰς τὸ δικαστήριον παραγαγόντες τοὺς μὲν ἀπέκτειναν, τοὺς δ' ἐφυγάδευσαν, τοὺς δὲ χρήμασιν
ἐζημίωσαν, ἐδόκει δὲ κακῶς ἔχειν τὰ τῶν Θηβαίων
πράγματα μηδενὸς αὐτοῖς βοηθοῦντος, ἔτυχε μὲν
ὁ Πελοπίδας μετὰ Γοργίδου βοιωταρχῶν, ἐπι-
βουλεύοντες δὲ συγκροῦσαι πάλιν τοὺς Ἀθηναίους τοῖς Λακεδαιμονίοις τοιόνδε τι μηχανῶνται.
2 Σφοδρίας, ἀνὴρ Σπαρτιάτης, εὐδόκιμος μὲν ἐν
τοῖς πολεμικοῖς καὶ λαμπρός, ὑπόκουφος δὲ τὴν
γνώμην καὶ κενῶν ἐλπίδων καὶ φιλοτιμίας ἀνοήτου μεστός, ἀπελείφθη περὶ Θεσπιὰς μετὰ δυνάμεως τοὺς ἀφισταμένους τῶν Θηβαίων δέχεσθαι
καὶ βοηθεῖν. πρὸς τοῦτον ὑποπέμπουσιν οἱ περὶ
τὸν Πελοπίδαν ἰδίᾳ ἔμπορόν τινα τῶν φίλων,

and, like that, crowned with success by fortune, the Greeks were wont to call a sister to it. For it is not easy to mention other cases where men so few in number and so destitute have overcome enemies so much more numerous and powerful by the exercise of courage and sagacity, and have thereby become the authors of so great blessings for their countries. And yet the subsequent change in the political situation made this exploit the more glorious. For the war which broke down the pretensions of Sparta and put an end to her supremacy by land and sea, began from that night, in which Pelopidas, not by surprising any fort or castle or citadel, but by coming back into a private house with eleven others, loosed and broke in pieces, if the truth may be expressed in a metaphor, the fetters of the Lacedaemonian supremacy, which were thought indissoluble and not to be broken.

XIV. The Lacedaemonians now invaded Boeotia with a large army, and the Athenians, having become fearful, renounced their alliance with the Thebans, and prosecuting those in their city who favoured the Boeotian cause, put some of them to death, banished others, and others still they fined, so that the Thebans seemed to be in a desperate case with none to aid them. But Pelopidas and Gorgias, who were boeotarchs, plotted to embroil the Athenians again with the Lacedaemonians, and devised the following scheme. Sphodrias, a Spartan, who had a splendid reputation as a soldier, but was rather weak in judgement and full of vain hopes and senseless ambition, had been left at Thespiae with an armed force to receive and succour the renegade Thebans. To this man Pelopidas and Gorgidas privately sent one of their friends who was a merchant, with money,

χρήματα κομίζοντα καὶ λόγους, οἳ τῶν χρημάτων
μᾶλλον ἀνέπεισαν αὐτὸν ὡς χρὴ πραγμάτων
ἅψασθαι μεγάλων καὶ τὸν Πειραιᾶ καταλαβεῖν,
ἀπροσδόκητον ἐπιπεσόντα μὴ φυλαττομένοις τοῖς
3 Ἀθηναίοις· Λακεδαιμονίοις τε γὰρ οὐδὲν οὕτως
ἔσεσθαι κεχαρισμένον ὡς λαβεῖν τὰς Ἀθήνας,
Θηβαίους τε χαλεπῶς ἔχοντας αὐτοῖς καὶ προδότας νομίζοντας οὐκ ἐπιβοηθήσειν. τέλος δὲ
συμπεισθεὶς ὁ Σφοδρίας καὶ τοὺς στρατιώτας
ἀναλαβών, νυκτὸς εἰς τὴν Ἀττικὴν ἐνέβαλε. καὶ
μέχρι μὲν Ἐλευσῖνος προῆλθεν, ἐκεῖ δὲ τῶν
στρατιωτῶν ἀποδειλιασάντων φανερὸς γενόμενος,
καὶ συνταράξας οὐ φαῦλον οὐδὲ ῥᾴδιον τοῖς
Σπαρτιάταις πόλεμον, ἀνεχώρησεν εἰς Θεσπιάς.

XV. Ἐκ τούτου πάλιν προθυμότατα Ἀθηναῖοι
τοῖς Θηβαίοις συνεμάχουν, καὶ τῆς θαλάττης
ἀντελαμβάνοντο, καὶ περιιόντες ἐδέχοντο καὶ
προσήγοντο τοὺς ἀποστατικῶς τῶν Ἑλλήνων
ἔχοντας. οἱ δὲ Θηβαῖοι καθ' αὑτοὺς ἐν τῇ
Βοιωτίᾳ συμπλεκόμενοι τοῖς Λακεδαιμονίοις ἑκάστοτε, καὶ μαχόμενοι μάχας αὐτὰς μὲν οὐ μεγάλας, μεγάλην δὲ τὴν μελέτην ἐχούσας καὶ τὴν
2 ἄσκησιν, ἐξερριπίζοντο τοῖς θυμοῖς καὶ διεπο-
νοῦντο τοῖς σώμασιν, ἐμπειρίαν ἅμα τῇ συνηθείᾳ
καὶ φρόνημα προσλαμβάνοντες ἐκ τῶν ἀγώνων.
διὸ καί φασιν Ἀνταλκίδαν τὸν Σπαρτιάτην, ὡς
Ἀγησίλαος ἐπανῆλθεν ἐκ Βοιωτίας τετρωμένος,
εἰπεῖν πρὸς αὐτόν· "Ἦ καλὰ διδασκάλια παρὰ
Θηβαίων ἀπολαμβάνεις, μὴ βουλομένους αὐτοὺς
3 πολεμεῖν καὶ μάχεσθαι διδάξας." ἦν δὲ ὡς

and, what proved more persuasive than money with
Sphodrias, this advice. He ought to put his hand
to a large enterprise and seize the Piraeus, attacking
it unexpectedly when the Athenians were off their
guard; for nothing would gratify the Lacedaemonians so much as the capture of Athens, and the
Thebans, who were now angry with the Athenians
and held them to be traitors, would give them no
aid. Sphodrias was finally persuaded, and taking his
soldiers, invaded Attica by night. He advanced as
far as Eleusis, but there the hearts of his soldiers
failed them and his design was exposed, and after
having thus stirred up a serious and difficult war
against the Spartans, he withdrew to Thespiae.[1]

XV. After this, the Athenians with the greatest
eagerness renewed their alliance with the Thebans,
and began hostile operations against Sparta by sea,
sailing about and inviting and receiving the allegiance of those Greeks who were inclined to revolt.
The Thebans, too, by always engaging singly in
Boeotia with the Lacedaemonians, and by fighting
battles which, though not important in themselves,
nevertheless afforded them much practice and training, had their spirits roused and their bodies
thoroughly inured to hardships, and gained experience and courage from their constant struggles.
For this reason Antalcidas the Spartan, we are told,
when Agesilaüs came back from Boeotia with a
wound, said to him : " Indeed, this is a fine tuition-fee
which thou art getting from the Thebans, for teaching them how to war and fight when they did not
wish to do it." [2] But, to tell the truth, it was not

[1] The attempt of Sphodrias on the Piraeus is more fully
described in the *Agesilaüs*, xxiv. 3–6.
[2] Cf. the *Agesilaüs*, xxvi. 2.

ἀληθῶς διδάσκαλος οὐκ 'Αγησίλαος, ἀλλ' οἱ σὺν
καιρῷ καὶ μετὰ λογισμοῦ τοὺς Θηβαίους ὥσπερ
σκύλακας ἐμπείρως προσβάλλοντες τοῖς πολεμίοις, εἶτα γευσαμένους νίκης καὶ φρονήματος
ἀσφαλῶς ἀπάγοντες· ὧν μεγίστην δόξαν εἶχεν
ὁ Πελοπίδας. ἀφ' ἧς γὰρ εἵλοντο πρῶτον ἡγεμόνα τῶν ὅπλων, οὐκ ἐπαύσαντο καθ' ἕκαστον
ἐνιαυτὸν ἄρχοντα χειροτονοῦντες, ἀλλ' ἢ τὸν
ἱερὸν λόχον ἄγων ἢ τὰ πλεῖστα βοιωταρχῶν
ἄχρι τῆς τελευτῆς ἔπραττεν.

4   Ἐγένοντο μὲν οὖν καὶ περὶ Πλαταιὰς καὶ
Θεσπιὰς ἧτται καὶ φυγαὶ τῶν Λακεδαιμονίων,
ὅπου καὶ Φοιβίδας ὁ τὴν Καδμείαν καταλαβὼν
ἀπέθανε, πολλοὺς δὲ καὶ πρὸς Τανάγρα τρεψάμενος αὐτῶν καὶ Πανθοίδαν τὸν ἁρμοστὴν
ἀνεῖλεν. ἀλλ' οὗτοι μὲν οἱ ἀγῶνες ὥσπερ τοὺς
κρατοῦντας εἰς φρόνημα καὶ θάρσος προῆγον,
οὕτως τῶν ἡσσωμένων οὐ παντάπασιν ἐδουλοῦντο
5 τὴν γνώμην· οὐ γὰρ ἐκ παρατάξεως ἦσαν οὐδὲ
μάχης ἐμφανῆ κατάστασιν ἐχούσης καὶ νόμιμον,
ἐκδρομὰς δὲ προσκαίρους τιθέμενοι, καὶ φυγὰς ἢ
διώξεις ἐπιχειροῦντες αὐτοῖς καὶ συμπλεκόμενοι
κατώρθουν.

XVI. Ὁ δὲ περὶ Τεγύρας τρόπον τινὰ τοῦ
Λευκτρικοῦ προάγων γενόμενος μέγαν ἦρε δόξῃ τὸν
Πελοπίδαν, οὔτε πρὸς κατόρθωμα τοῖς συστρα-
τήγοις ἀμφισβήτησιν οὔτε τῆς ἥττης πρόφασιν
τοῖς πολεμίοις ἀπολιπών. τῇ γὰρ 'Ορχομενίων   28
πόλει τὰ Σπαρτιατῶν ἑλομένῃ καὶ δύο δεδεγμένῃ
μόρας αὐτῶν ὑπὲρ ἀσφαλείας ἐπεβούλευε μὲν
2 ἀεὶ καὶ παρεφύλαττε καιρόν, ὡς δὲ ἤκουσε τοῖς
φρουροῖς εἰς τὴν Λοκρίδα γεγενῆσθαι στρατείαν

Agesilaüs who was their teacher, but those leaders of theirs who, at the right time and place, gave the Thebans, like young dogs in training, experience in attacking their enemies, and then, when they had got a taste of victory and its ardours, brought them safely off; and of these leaders Pelopidas was in greatest esteem. For after his countrymen had once chosen him their leader in arms, there was not a single year when they did not elect him to office, but either as leader of the sacred band, or, for the most part, as boeotarch, he continued active until his death.

Well, then, at Plataea the Lacedaemonians were defeated and put to flight, and at Thespiae, where, too, Phoebidas, who had seized the Cadmeia, was slain; and at Tanagra a large body of them was routed and Panthoidas the harmost was killed. But these combats, though they gave ardour and boldness to the victors, did not altogether break the spirits of the vanquished; for they were not pitched battles, nor was the fighting in open and regular array, but it was by making well-timed sallies, and by either retreating before the enemy or by pursuing and coming to close quarters with them that the Thebans won their successes.

XVI. But the conflict at Tegyra, which was a sort of prelude to that at Leuctra, raised high the reputation of Pelopidas; for it afforded his fellow commanders no rival claim in its success, and his enemies no excuse for their defeat. Against the city of Orchomenus, which had chosen the side of the Spartans and received two divisions of them for its protection, he was ever laying plans and watching his opportunity, and when he heard that its garrison had made an expedition into Locris, he hoped to find

377

ἐλπίσας ἔρημον αἱρήσειν τὸν Ὀρχομενὸν ἐστράτευσεν, ἔχων μεθ' ἑαυτοῦ τὸν ἱερὸν λόχον καὶ
τῶν ἱππέων οὐ πολλούς. ἐπεὶ δὲ πρὸς τὴν πόλιν
προσαγαγὼν εὗρεν ἥκουσαν ἐκ Σπάρτης διαδοχὴν
τῆς φρουρᾶς, ἀπῆγεν ὀπίσω τὸ στράτευμα πάλιν
διὰ Τεγυρῶν, ᾗ μόνῃ βάσιμον ἦν κύκλῳ παρὰ
3 τὴν ὑπώρειαν· τὴν γὰρ διὰ μέσου πᾶσαν ὁ Μέλας
ποταμὸς εὐθὺς ἐκ πηγῶν εἰς ἕλη πλωτὰ καὶ
λίμνας διασπειρόμενος ἄπορον ἐποίει.

Μικρὸν δὲ ὑπὸ τὰ ἕλη νεώς ἐστιν Ἀπόλλωνος
Τεγυραίου καὶ μαντεῖον ἐκλελειμμένον οὐ πάνυ
πολὺν χρόνον, ἀλλ' ἄχρι τῶν Μηδικῶν ἤκμαζε,
τὴν προφητείαν Ἐχεκράτους ἔχοντος. ἐνταῦθα
μυθολογοῦσι τὸν θεὸν γενέσθαι· καὶ τὸ μὲν πλησίον ὄρος Δῆλος καλεῖται, καὶ πρὸς αὐτὸ κατα-
4 λήγουσιν αἱ τοῦ Μέλανος διαχύσεις, ὀπίσω δὲ
τοῦ ναοῦ δύο ῥήγνυνται πηγαὶ γλυκύτητι καὶ
πλήθει καὶ ψυχρότητι θαυμαστοῦ νάματος, ὧν
τὸ μὲν Φοίνικα, τὸ δὲ Ἐλαίαν ἄχρι νῦν ὀνομά-
ζομεν, οὐ φυτῶν μεταξὺ δυεῖν, ἀλλὰ ῥείθρων τῆς
θεοῦ λοχευθείσης. καὶ γὰρ τὸ Πτῷον ἐγγύς,
ὅθεν αὐτὴν ἀναπτοηθῆναι προφανέντος ἐξαίφνης
κάπρου λέγουσι, καὶ τὰ περὶ Πύθωνα καὶ Τιτυὸν
ὡσαύτως οἱ τόποι τῇ γενέσει τοῦ θεοῦ συνοικει-
5 οῦσι. τὰ γὰρ πλεῖστα παραλείπω τῶν τεκμη-
ρίων· οὐ γὰρ ἐν τοῖς ἐκ μεταβολῆς ἀθανάτοις
γενομένοις γεννητοῖς ὁ πάτριος λόγος τὸν θεὸν
τοῦτον ἀπολείπει δαίμοσιν, ὥσπερ Ἡρακλέα καὶ

the city without defenders, and marched against it, having with him the sacred band and a few horsemen. But when, on approaching the city, he found that its garrison had been replaced with other troops from Sparta, he led his army back again through the district of Tegyra, that being the only way by which he could make a circuit along the foot of the mountains. For all the intervening plain was made impassable by the river Melas, which no sooner begins to flow than it spreads itself out into navigable marshes and lakes.

A little below the marshes stands the temple of Apollo Tegyraeus, with an oracle which had not been long abandoned, but was flourishing down to the Persian wars, when Echecrates was prophet-priest. Here, according to the story, the god was born; and the neighbouring mountain is called Delos, and at its base the river Melas ceases to be spread out, and behind the temple two springs burst forth with a wonderful flow of sweet, copious, and cool water. One of these we call Palm, the other Olive, to the present day, for it was not between two trees,[1] but between two fountains, that the goddess Leto was delivered of her children. Moreover, the Ptoüm [2] is near, from which, it is said, a boar suddenly came forth and frightened the goddess, and in like manner the stories of the Python [3] and of Tityus [3] are associated with the birth of Apollo in this locality. Most of the proofs, however, I shall pass over; for my native tradition removes this god from among those deities who were changed from mortals into im-

---

[1] As in the Delian story of the birth of Apollo and Artemis.

[2] A mountain at the south-eastern side of Lake Copaïs, on which was a celebrated sanctuary of Apollo.

[3] A dragon and a giant, who were slain by Apollo and Artemis.

Διόνυσον, ἐκ μεταβολῆς ἀρετῇ τὸ θνητὸν καὶ
παθητὸν ἀποβαλόντας, ἀλλὰ τῶν ἀϊδίων καὶ
ἀγεννήτων εἷς ἐστιν, εἰ δεῖ τοῖς ὑπὸ τῶν φρονιμω-
τάτων καὶ παλαιοτάτων λεγομένοις τεκμαίρεσθαι
περὶ τῶν τηλικούτων.

XVII. Εἰς δ᾽ οὖν Τεγύρας οἱ Θηβαῖοι κατὰ
τὸν αὐτὸν χρόνον ἐκ τῆς Ὀρχομενίας ἀπιόντες
καὶ οἱ Λακεδαιμόνιοι συνέπιπτον, ἐξ ἐναντίας
αὐτοῖς ἐκ τῆς Λοκρίδος ἀναζευγνύντες. ὡς δὲ
πρῶτον ὤφθησαν τὰ στενὰ διεκβάλλοντες, καί
τις εἶπε τῷ Πελοπίδᾳ προσδραμών· "Ἐμπεπτώ-
καμεν εἰς τοὺς πολεμίους," "Τί μᾶλλον," εἶπεν,
2 "ἢ εἰς ἡμᾶς ἐκεῖνοι;" καὶ τὴν μὲν ἵππον εὐθὺς
πᾶσαν ἐκέλευσε παρελαύνειν ἀπ᾽ οὐρᾶς ὡς προ-
εμβαλοῦσαν, αὐτὸς δὲ τοὺς ὁπλίτας τριακοσίους
ὄντας εἰς ὀλίγον συνήγαγεν, ἐλπίζων καθ᾽ ὃ
προσβάλοι μάλιστα διακόψειν ὑπερβάλλοντας
πλήθει τοὺς πολεμίους. ἦσαν δὲ δύο μόραι
Λακεδαιμονίων, τὴν δὲ μόραν Ἔφορος μὲν ἄνδρας
εἶναι πεντακοσίους φησί, Καλλισθένης δ᾽ ἑπτα-
κοσίους, ἄλλοι δέ τινες ἐνακοσίους, ὧν Πολύβιός
3 ἐστι. καὶ θαρροῦντες οἱ πολέμαρχοι τῶν Σπαρτιατῶν Γοργολέων καὶ Θεόπομπος ὥρμησαν ἐπὶ
τοὺς Θηβαίους. γενομένης δέ πως μάλιστα τῆς
ἐφόδου κατ᾽ αὐτοὺς τοὺς ἄρχοντας ἀπ᾽ ἀμφοτέρων
μετὰ θυμοῦ καὶ βίας, πρῶτον μὲν οἱ πολέμαρχοι
τῶν Λακεδαιμονίων τῷ Πελοπίδᾳ συρράξαντες
4 ἔπεσον· ἔπειτα τῶν περὶ ἐκείνους παιομένων καὶ
ἀποθνησκόντων ἅπαν εἰς φόβον κατέστη τὸ
στράτευμα, καὶ διέσχε μὲν ἐπ᾽ ἀμφότερα τοῖς
Θηβαίοις, ὡς διεκπεσεῖν εἰς τοὐμπροσθεν καὶ
διεκδῦναι βουλομένοις, ἐπεὶ δὲ τὴν δεδομένην ὁ
Πελοπίδας ἡγεῖτο πρὸς τοὺς συνεστῶτας καὶ

mortals, like Heracles and Dionysus, whose virtues enabled them to cast off mortality and suffering; but he is one of those deities who are unbegotten and eternal, if we may judge by what the most ancient and wisest men have said on such matters.

XVII. So, then, as the Thebans entered the district of Tegyra on their way back from Orchomenus, the Lacedaemonians also entered it at the same time, returning in the opposite direction from Locris, and met them. As soon as they were seen marching through the narrow pass, some one ran up to Pelopidas and said: "We have fallen into our enemies' hands!" "Why any more," said he, "than they into ours?" Then he at once ordered all his horsemen to ride up from the rear in order to charge, while he himself put his men-at-arms, three hundred in number, into close array, expecting that wherever they charged he would be most likely to cut his way through the enemy, who outnumbered him. Now, there were two divisions of the Lacedaemonians, the division consisting of five hundred men, according to Ephorus, of seven hundred, according to Callisthenes, of nine hundred, according to certain other writers, among whom is Polybius. Confident of victory, the polemarchs of the Spartans, Gorgoleon and Theopompus, advanced against the Thebans. The onset being made on both sides particularly where the commanders themselves stood, in the first place, the Lacedaemonian polemarchs clashed with Pelopidas and fell; then, when those about them were being wounded and slain, their whole army was seized with fear and opened up a lane for the Thebans, imagining that they wished to force their way through to the opposite side and get away. But Pelopidas used the path thus opened to lead his men against those of

διεξῄει φονεύων, οὕτω πάντες προτροπάδην
ἔφευγον. ἐγένετο δὲ οὐκ ἐπὶ πολὺν τόπον ἡ
δίωξις· ἐφοβοῦντο γὰρ ἐγγὺς ὄντας οἱ Θηβαῖοι
τοὺς Ὀρχομενίους καὶ τὴν διαδοχὴν τῶν Λακε-
5 δαιμονίων. ὅσον δὲ νικῆσαι κατὰ κράτος καὶ
διεξελθεῖν διὰ παντὸς ἡσσωμένου τοῦ στρατεύματος, ἐξεβιάσαντο· καὶ στήσαντες τρόπαιον
καὶ νεκροὺς σκυλεύσαντες ἀνεχώρησαν ἐπ᾽ οἴκου
μέγα φρονοῦντες. ἐν γὰρ τοσούτοις, ὡς ἔοικε,
πολέμοις Ἑλληνικοῖς καὶ βαρβαρικοῖς πρότερον
οὐδέποτε Λακεδαιμόνιοι πλείονες ὄντες ὑπ᾽ ἐλαττόνων ἐκρατήθησαν, ἀλλ᾽ οὐδὲ ἴσοι πρὸς ἴσους
6 ἐκ παρατάξεως συμβαλόντες. ὅθεν ἦσαν ἀνυ-
πόστατοι τὰ φρονήματα, καὶ τῇ δόξῃ κατα-
πληττόμενοι τοὺς ἀντιταττομένους, οὐδὲ αὐτοὺς
ἀξιοῦντας ἀπ᾽ ἴσης δυνάμεως τὸ ἴσον φέρεσθαι
Σπαρτιάταις, εἰς χεῖρας συνέστησαν. ἐκείνη δὲ
ἡ μάχη πρώτη καὶ τοὺς ἄλλους ἐδίδαξεν Ἕλληνας ὡς οὐχ ὁ Εὐρώτας οὐδ᾽ ὁ μεταξὺ Βαβύκας
καὶ Κνακιῶνος τόπος ἄνδρας ἐκφέρει μαχητὰς
καὶ πολεμικούς, ἀλλὰ παρ᾽ οἷς ἂν αἰσχύνεσθαι
τὰ αἰσχρὰ καὶ τολμᾶν ἐπὶ τοῖς καλοῖς ἐθέλοντες
ἐγγένωνται νέοι καὶ τοὺς ψόγους τῶν κινδύνων
μᾶλλον φεύγοντες, οὗτοι φοβερώτατοι τοῖς ἐναντίοις εἰσί.

XVIII. Τὸν δ᾽ ἱερὸν λόχον, ὥς φασι, συνετά-
ξατο Γοργίδας πρῶτος ἐξ ἀνδρῶν ἐπιλέκτων
τριακοσίων, οἷς ἡ πόλις ἄσκησιν καὶ δίαιταν ἐν
τῇ Καδμείᾳ στρατοπεδευομένοις παρεῖχε, καὶ διὰ
τοῦθ᾽ ὁ ἐκ πόλεως λόχος ἐκαλοῦντο· τὰς γὰρ
ἀκροπόλεις ἐπιεικῶς οἱ τότε πόλεις ὠνόμαζον.
ἔνιοι δέ φασιν ἐξ ἐραστῶν καὶ ἐρωμένων γενέσθαι
2 τὸ σύστημα τοῦτο. καὶ Παμμένους ἀπομνημο-

the enemy who still held together, and slew them as
he went along, so that finally all turned and fled.
The pursuit, however, was carried but a little way,
for the Thebans feared the Orchomenians, who were
near, and the relief force from Sparta. They had
succeeded, however, in conquering their enemy out-
right and forcing their way victoriously through his
whole army; so they erected a trophy, spoiled the
dead, and retired homewards in high spirits. For in
all their wars with Greeks and Barbarians, as it
would seem, never before had Lacedaemonians in
superior numbers been overpowered by an inferior
force, nor, indeed, in a pitched battle where the
forces were evenly matched. Hence they were of
an irresistible courage, and when they came to close
quarters their very reputation sufficed to terrify their
opponents, who also, on their part, thought themselves no match for Spartans with an equal force.
But this battle first taught the other Greeks also
that it was not the Eurotas, nor the region between
Babyce [1] and Cnacion,[1] which alone produced warlike
fighting men, but that wheresoever young men are
prone to be ashamed of baseness and courageous in
a noble cause, shunning disgrace more than danger,
these are most formidable to their foes.

XVIII. The sacred band, we are told, was first
formed by Gorgidas, of three hundred chosen men,
to whom the city furnished exercise and maintenance,
and who encamped in the Cadmeia; for which reason,
too, they were called the city band; for citadels in
those days were properly called cities. But some say
that this band was composed of lovers and beloved.
And a pleasantry of Pammenes is cited, in which

---

[1] Probably names of small tributaries of the Eurotas near
Sparta. Cf. the *Lycurgus*, vi. 1–3.

νεύεταί τι μετὰ παιδιᾶς εἰρημένον· οὐ γὰρ ἔφη
τακτικὸν εἶναι τὸν Ὁμήρου Νέστορα κελεύοντα
κατὰ φῦλα καὶ φρήτρας συλλοχίζεσθαι τοὺς
Ἕλληνας,

Ὡς φρήτρη φρήτρηφιν ἀρήγῃ, φῦλα δὲ φύλοις,

δέον ἐραστὴν παρ' ἐρώμενον τάττειν. φυλέτας
μὲν γὰρ φυλετῶν καὶ φράτορας φρατόρων οὐ
πολὺν λόγον ἔχειν ἐν τοῖς δεινοῖς, τὸ δ' ἐξ ἐρω-
τικῆς φιλίας συνηρμοσμένον στῖφος ἀδιάλυτον
εἶναι καὶ ἄρρηκτον, ὅταν οἱ μὲν ἀγαπῶντες τοὺς
ἐρωμένους, οἱ δὲ αἰσχυνόμενοι τοὺς ἐρῶντας
3 ἐμμένωσι τοῖς δεινοῖς ὑπὲρ ἀλλήλων. καὶ τοῦτο
θαυμαστὸν οὐκ ἔστιν, εἴγε δὴ καὶ μὴ παρόντας
αἰδοῦνται μᾶλλον ἑτέρων παρόντων, ὡς ἐκεῖνος
ὁ τοῦ πολεμίου κείμενον αὐτὸν ἐπισφάττειν
μέλλοντος δεόμενος καὶ ἀντιβολῶν διὰ τοῦ στέρ-
νου διεῖναι τὸ ξίφος, "Ὅπως," ἔφη, "μή με
νεκρὸν ὁ ἐρώμενος ὁρῶν κατὰ νώτου τετρωμένον
4 αἰσχυνθῇ." λέγεται δὲ καὶ τὸν Ἰόλεων τοῦ Ἡρακλέους ἐρώμενον ὄντα κοινωνεῖν τῶν ἄθλων καὶ
παρασπίζειν. Ἀριστοτέλης δὲ καὶ καθ' αὑτὸν
ἔτι φησὶν ἐπὶ τοῦ τάφου τοῦ Ἰόλεω τὰς κατα-
πιστώσεις ποιεῖσθαι τοὺς ἐρωμένους καὶ τοὺς
ἐραστάς. εἰκὸς οὖν καὶ τὸν λόχον ἱερὸν προσα-
γορεύεσθαι, καθότι καὶ Πλάτων ἔνθεον φίλον
5 τὸν ἐραστὴν προσεῖπε. λέγεται δὲ διαμεῖναι
μέχρι τῆς ἐν Χαιρωνείᾳ μάχης ἀήττητον· ὡς δὲ
μετὰ τὴν μάχην ἐφορῶν τοὺς νεκροὺς ὁ Φίλιππος

he said that Homer's Nestor was no tactician when
he urged the Greeks to form in companies by clans
and tribes,

"That clan might give assistance unto clan, and
    tribes to tribes," [1]

since he should have stationed lover by beloved.
For tribesmen and clansmen make little account of
tribesmen and clansmen in times of danger; whereas,
a band that is held together by the friendship
between lovers is indissoluble and not to be broken,
since the lovers are ashamed to play the coward
before their beloved, and the beloved before their
lovers, and both stand firm in danger to protect each
other. Nor is this a wonder, since men have more
regard for their lovers even when absent than for
others who are present, as was true of him who,
when his enemy was about to slay him where he lay,
earnestly besought him to run his sword through his
breast, "in order," as he said, "that my beloved
may not have to blush at sight of my body with
a wound in the back." It is related, too, that Iolaüs,
who shared the labours of Heracles and fought by
his side, was beloved of him. And Aristotle says [2]
that even down to his day the tomb of Iolaüs was
a place where lovers and beloved plighted mutual
faith. It was natural, then, that the band should
also be called sacred, because even Plato calls the
lover a friend "inspired of God." [3] It is said, moreover, that the band was never beaten, until the
battle of Chaeroneia; [4] and when, after the battle,
Philip was surveying the dead, and stopped at the

---

[1] *Iliad*, ii. 363. Cf. *Morals*, p. 761 b.
[2] Fragment 97 (Rose). Cf. *Morals*, p. 761 d.
[3] *Symposium*, p. 179 a.   [4] 338 B.C.

ἔστη κατὰ τοῦτο τὸ χωρίον ἐν ᾧ συνετύγχανε
κεῖσθαι τοὺς τριακοσίους, ἐναντίους ἀπηντηκότας
ταῖς σαρίσαις ἅπαντας ἐν τοῖς ὅπλοις καὶ μετ'
ἀλλήλων ἀναμεμιγμένους, θαυμάσαντα καὶ πυθό-
μενον ὡς ὁ τῶν ἐραστῶν καὶ τῶν ἐρωμένων οὗτος
εἴη λόχος, δακρῦσαι καὶ εἰπεῖν· "'Απόλοιντο
κακῶς οἱ τούτους τι ποιεῖν ἢ πάσχειν αἰσχρὸν
ὑπονοοῦντες."

XIX. Ὅλως δὲ τῆς περὶ τοὺς ἐραστὰς συνη-
θείας οὐχ, ὥσπερ οἱ ποιηταὶ λέγουσι, Θηβαίοις
τὸ Λαΐου πάθος ἀρχὴν παρέσχεν, ἀλλ' οἱ νομοθέται τὸ φύσει θυμοειδὲς αὐτῶν καὶ ἄκρατον
ἀνιέναι καὶ ἀνυγραίνειν εὐθὺς ἐκ παίδων βουλόμενοι, πολὺν μὲν ἀνεμίξαντο καὶ σπουδῇ καὶ
παιδιᾷ πάσῃ τὸν αὐλόν, εἰς τιμὴν καὶ προεδρίαν
ἄγοντες, λαμπρὸν δὲ τὸν ἔρωτα ταῖς παλαίστραις
ἐνεθρέψαντο, συγκεραννύντες τὰ ἤθη τῶν νέων.

2 ὀρθῶς δὲ πρὸς τοῦτο καὶ τὴν ἐξ Ἄρεως καὶ
Ἀφροδίτης γεγονέναι λεγομένην θεὸν τῇ πόλει
συνῳκείωσαν, ὡς, ὅπου τὸ μαχητικὸν καὶ πολε-
μικὸν μάλιστα τῷ μετέχοντι πειθοῦς καὶ χαρίτων
ὁμιλεῖ καὶ σύνεστιν, εἰς τὴν ἐμμελεστάτην καὶ
κοσμιωτάτην πολιτείαν δι' ἁρμονίας καθιστα-
μένων ἁπάντων.

3 Τὸν οὖν ἱερὸν λόχον τοῦτον ὁ μὲν Γοργίδας
διαιρῶν εἰς τὰ πρῶτα ζυγὰ καὶ παρ' ὅλην τὴν
φάλαγγα τῶν ὁπλιτῶν προβαλλόμενος ἐπίδηλον
οὐκ ἐποίει τὴν ἀρετὴν τῶν ἀνδρῶν, οὐδ' ἐχρῆτο
τῇ δυνάμει πρὸς κοινὸν ἔργον, ἅτε δὴ διαλελυ-
μένῃ καὶ πρὸς πολὺ μεμιγμένῃ τὸ φαυλότερον,
ὁ δὲ Πελοπίδας, ὡς ἐξέλαμψεν αὐτῶν ἡ ἀρετὴ
περὶ Τεγύρας, καθαρῶς καὶ περὶ αὐτὸν ἀγωνισαμένων, οὐκ ἔτι διεῖλεν οὐδὲ διέσπασεν, ἀλλ'

place where the three hundred were lying, all where they had faced the long spears of his phalanx, with their armour, and mingled one with another, he was amazed, and on learning that this was the band of lovers and beloved, burst into tears and said : "Perish miserably they who think that these men did or suffered aught disgraceful."

XIX. Speaking generally, however, it was not the passion of Laius that, as the poets say, first made this form of love customary among the Thebans ;[1] but their law-givers, wishing to relax and mollify their strong and impetuous natures in earliest boyhood, gave the flute great prominence both in their work and in their play, bringing this instrument into pre-eminence and honour, and reared them to give love a conspicuous place in the life of the palaestra, thus tempering the dispositions of the young men. And with this in view, they did well to give the goddess who was said to have been born of Ares and Aphrodite a home in their city ; for they felt that, where the force and courage of the warrior are most closely associated and united with the age which possesses grace and persuasiveness, there all the activities of civil life are brought by Harmony into the most perfect consonance and order.

Gorgidas, then, by distributing this sacred band among the front ranks of the whole phalanx of men-at-arms, made the high excellence of the men inconspicuous, and did not direct their strength upon a common object, since it was dissipated and blended with that of a large body of inferior troops ; but Pelopidas, after their valour had shone out at Tegyra, where they fought by themselves and about his own person, never afterwards divided or scattered them,

[1] Laius was enamoured of Chrysippus, a young son of Pelops (Apollodorus, iii. 5, 5, 10).

ὥσπερ σώματι χρώμενος ὅλῳ προεκινδύνευε
4 τοῖς μεγίστοις ἀγῶσιν. ὥσπερ γὰρ οἱ ἵπποι
θᾶσσον ὑπὸ τοῖς ἅρμασιν ἢ καθ' αὑτοὺς ἐλαυνό-
μενοι θέουσιν, οὐχ ὅτι μᾶλλον ἐμπίπτοντες
ἐκβιάζονται τὸν ἀέρα τῷ πλήθει ῥηγνύμενον, ἀλλ'
ὅτι συνεκκαίει τὸν θυμὸν ἡ μετ' ἀλλήλων ἅμιλλα
καὶ τὸ φιλόνεικον, οὕτως ᾤετο τοὺς ἀγαθοὺς ζῆλον
ἀλλήλοις καλῶν ἔργων ἐνιέντας ὠφελιμωτάτους
εἰς κοινὸν ἔργον εἶναι καὶ προθυμοτάτους.

XX. Ἐπεὶ δὲ Λακεδαιμόνιοι πᾶσι τοῖς Ἕλλησιν εἰρήνην συνθέμενοι πρὸς μόνους Θηβαίους
ἐξήνεγκαν τὸν πόλεμον, ἐνεβεβλήκει δὲ Κλεόμβροτος ὁ βασιλεὺς ἄγων ὁπλίτας μυρίους, ἱππεῖς
δὲ χιλίους, ὁ δὲ κίνδυνος οὐ περὶ ὧν πρότερον
ἦν Θηβαίοις, ἀλλ' ἄντικρυς ἀπειλὴ καὶ καταγ-
γελία διοικισμοῦ, καὶ φόβος οἷος οὔπω τὴν Βοιωτίαν κατεῖχεν, ἐξιὼν μὲν ἐκ τῆς οἰκίας ὁ Πελοπίδας, καὶ τῆς γυναικὸς ἐν τῷ προπέμπειν
δακρυούσης καὶ παρακαλούσης σώζειν ἑαυτόν,
2 "Ταῦτα," εἶπεν, "ὦ γύναι, τοῖς ἰδιώταις χρὴ
παραινεῖν, τοῖς δὲ ἄρχουσιν ὅπως τοὺς ἄλλους
σώζωσιν·" ἐλθὼν δὲ εἰς τὸ στρατόπεδον καὶ τοὺς
βοιωτάρχας καταλαβὼν οὐχ ὁμογνωμονοῦντας,
πρῶτος Ἐπαμεινώνδᾳ προσέθετο γνώμην ψηφι-
ζομένῳ διὰ μάχης ἰέναι τοῖς πολεμίοις, βοιωτάρχης μὲν οὐκ ἀποδεδειγμένος, ἄρχων δὲ τοῦ
ἱεροῦ λόχου, καὶ πιστευόμενος, ὡς ἦν δίκαιον
ἄνδρα τηλικαῦτα δεδωκότα τῇ πατρίδι σύμβολα
εἰς τὴν ἐλευθερίαν.

but, treating them as a unit, put them into the fore-front of the greatest conflicts. For just as horses run faster when yoked to a chariot than when men ride them singly, not because they cleave the air with more impetus owing to their united weight, but because their mutual rivalry and ambition in-flame their spirits; so he thought that brave men were most ardent and serviceable in a common cause when they inspired one another with a zeal for high achievement.

XX. But now the Lacedaemonians made peace with all the other Greeks and directed the war against the Thebans alone;[1] Cleombrotus their king invaded Boeotia with a force of two thousand men-at-arms and a thousand horse; a new peril confronted the Thebans, since they were openly threatened with downright dispersion; and an unprecedented fear reigned in Boeotia. It was at this time that Pelopidas, on leaving his house, when his wife followed him on his way in tears and begging him not to lose his life, said: "This advice, my wife, should be given to private men; but men in authority should be told not to lose the lives of others." And when he reached the camp and found that the boeotarchs were not in accord, he was first to side with Epaminondas in voting to give the enemy battle. Now Pelopidas, although he had not been appointed boeotarch, was captain of the sacred band, and highly trusted, as it was right that a man should be who had given his country such tokens of his devotion to freedom.

---

[1] In 371 B.C.

3 Ὡς οὖν ἐδέδοκτο διακινδυνεύειν καὶ περὶ τὰ
Λεῦκτρα τοῖς Λακεδαιμονίοις ἀντεστρατοπέδευον,
ὄψιν εἶδε κατὰ τοὺς ὕπνους ὁ Πελοπίδας εὖ μάλα
διαταράξασαν αὐτόν. ἔστι γὰρ ἐν τῷ Λευκτρικῷ
πεδίῳ τὰ σήματα τῶν τοῦ Σκεδάσου θυγατέρων,
ἃς Λευκτρίδας καλοῦσι διὰ τὸν τόπον· ἐκεῖ γὰρ
αὐταῖς ὑπὸ ξένων Σπαρτιατῶν βιασθείσαις συν-
4 έβη ταφῆναι. γενομένης δὲ χαλεπῆς οὕτω καὶ
παρανόμου πράξεως, ὁ μὲν πατήρ, ὡς οὐκ ἔτυχεν
ἐν Λακεδαίμονι δίκης, ἀρὰς κατὰ τῶν Σπαρτιατῶν ἀρασάμενος ἔσφαξεν ἑαυτὸν ἐπὶ τοῖς τάφοις
τῶν παρθένων, χρησμοὶ δὲ καὶ λόγια τοῖς Σπαρτιάταις ἀεὶ προὔφαινον εὐλαβεῖσθαι καὶ φυλάττεσθαι τὸ Λευκτρικὸν μήνιμα, μὴ πάνυ τῶν
πολλῶν συνιέντων, ἀλλ' ἀμφιγνοούντων τὸν τόπον, ἐπεὶ καὶ τῆς Λακωνικῆς πολίχνιον πρὸς τῇ
θαλάσσῃ Λεῦκτρον ὀνομάζεται, καὶ πρὸς Μεγάλῃ
πόλει τῆς Ἀρκαδίας τόπος ἐστὶν ὁμώνυμος. τὸ
μὲν οὖν πάθος τοῦτο πολὺ τῶν Λευκτρικῶν ἦν
παλαιότερον.

XXI. Ὁ δὲ Πελοπίδας ἐν τῷ στρατοπέδῳ
κατακοιμηθεὶς ἔδοξε τάς τε παῖδας ὁρᾶν περὶ
τὰ μνήματα θρηνούσας καὶ καταρωμένας τοῖς
Σπαρτιάταις, τόν τε Σκέδασον κελεύοντα ταῖς
κόραις σφαγιάσαι παρθένον ξανθήν, εἰ βούλοιτο
τῶν πολεμίων ἐπικρατῆσαι. δεινοῦ δὲ καὶ παρανόμου τοῦ προστάγματος αὐτῷ φανέντος ἐξ- 28
αναστὰς ἐκοινοῦτο τοῖς τε μάντεσι καὶ τοῖς ἄρ-
2 χουσιν. ὧν οἱ μὲν οὐκ εἴων παραμελεῖν οὐδ'
ἀπειθεῖν, τῶν μὲν παλαιῶν προφέροντες Μενοικέα
τὸν Κρέοντος καὶ Μακαρίαν τὴν Ἡρακλέους,
τῶν δ' ὕστερον Φερεκύδην τε τὸν σοφὸν ὑπὸ
Λακεδαιμονίων ἀναιρεθέντα καὶ τὴν δορὰν αὐτοῦ

Accordingly, it was decided to risk a battle, and at Leuctra they encamped over against the Lacedaemonians. Here Pelopidas had a dream which greatly disturbed him. Now, in the plain of Leuctra are the tombs of the daughters of Scedasus, who are called from the place Leuctridae, for they had been buried there, after having been ravished by Spartan strangers.[1] At the commission of such a grievous and lawless act, their father, since he could get no justice at Sparta, heaped curses upon the Spartans, and then slew himself upon the tombs of the maidens; and ever after, prophecies and oracles kept warning the Spartans to be on watchful guard against the Leuctrian wrath. Most of them, however, did not fully understand the matter, but were in doubt about the place, since in Laconia there is a little town near the sea which is called Leuctra, and near Megalopolis in Arcadia there is a place of the same name. This calamity, of course, occurred long before the battle of Leuctra.

XXI. After Pelopidas had lain down to sleep in the camp, he thought he saw these maidens weeping at their tombs, as they invoked curses upon the Spartans, and Scedasus bidding him sacrifice to his daughters a virgin with auburn hair, if he wished to win the victory over his enemies. The injunction seemed a lawless and dreadful one to him, but he rose up and made it known to the seers and the commanders. Some of these would not hear of the injunction being neglected or disobeyed, adducing as examples of such sacrifice among the ancients, Menoeceus, son of Creon, Macaria, daughter of Heracles; and, in later times, Pherecydes the wise man, who was put to death by the Lacedaemonians,

[1] The damsels, in shame, took their own lives. Cf. Pausanias, ix. 13, 3.

κατά τι λόγιον ὑπὸ τῶν βασιλέων φρουρουμένην,
Λεωνίδαν τε τῷ χρησμῷ τρόπον τινὰ προθυσά-
3 μενον ἑαυτὸν ὑπὲρ τῆς Ἑλλάδος, ἔτι δὲ τοὺς ὑπὸ
Θεμιστοκλέους σφαγιασθέντας ὠμηστῇ Διονύσῳ
πρὸ τῆς ἐν Σαλαμῖνι ναυμαχίας· ἐκείνοις γὰρ
ἐπιμαρτυρῆσαι τὰ κατορθώματα· τοῦτο δέ, ὡς
Ἀγησίλαον ἀπὸ τῶν αὐτῶν Ἀγαμέμνονι τόπων
ἐπὶ τοὺς αὐτοὺς στρατευόμενον πολεμίους ᾔτησε
μὲν ἡ θεὸς τὴν θυγατέρα σφάγιον καὶ ταύτην
εἶδε τὴν ὄψιν ἐν Αὐλίδι κοιμώμενος, ὁ δ᾽ οὐκ
ἔδωκεν, ἀλλ᾽ ἀπομαλθακωθεὶς κατέλυσε τὴν
4 στρατείαν ἄδοξον καὶ ἀτελῆ γενομένην. οἱ δὲ
τοὐναντίον ἀπηγόρευον, ὡς οὐδενὶ τῶν κρειττόνων
καὶ ὑπὲρ ἡμᾶς ἀρεστὴν οὖσαν οὕτω βάρβαρον
καὶ παράνομον θυσίαν· οὐ γὰρ τοὺς Τυφῶνας
ἐκείνους οὐδὲ τοὺς Γίγαντας ἄρχειν, ἀλλὰ τὸν
πάντων πατέρα θεῶν καὶ ἀνθρώπων· δαίμονας
δὲ χαίροντας ἀνθρώπων αἵματι καὶ φόνῳ πιστεύειν μὲν ἴσως ἐστὶν ἀβέλτερον, ὄντων δὲ τοιούτων ἀμελητέον ὡς ἀδυνάτων· ἀσθενείᾳ γὰρ καὶ
μοχθηρίᾳ ψυχῆς ἐμφύεσθαι καὶ παραμένειν τὰς
ἀτόπους καὶ χαλεπὰς ἐπιθυμίας.

XXII. Ἐν τοιούτοις οὖν διαλόγοις τῶν πρώτων
ὄντων, καὶ μάλιστα τοῦ Πελοπίδου διαποροῦντος,
ἵππων ἐξ ἀγέλης πῶλος ἀποφυγοῦσα καὶ φερομένη διὰ τῶν ὅπλων, ὡς ἦν θέουσα κατ᾽ αὐτοὺς
ἐκείνους, ἐπέστη· καὶ τοῖς μὲν ἄλλοις θέαν παρεῖχεν ἥ τε χρόα στίλβουσα τῆς χαίτης πυρσότατον

and whose skin was preserved by their kings, in accordance with some oracle; and Leonidas, who, in obedience to the oracle, sacrificed himself,[1] as it were, to save Greece; and, still further, the youths who were sacrificed by Themistocles to Dionysus Carnivorous before the sea fight at Salamis;[2] for the successes which followed these sacrifices proved them acceptable to the gods. Moreover, when Agesilaüs, who was setting out on an expedition from the same place as Agamemnon did, and against the same enemies, was asked by the goddess for his daughter in sacrifice, and had this vision as he lay asleep at Aulis, he was too tender-hearted to give her,[3] and thereby brought his expedition to an unsuccessful and inglorious ending. Others, on the contrary, argued against it, declaring that such a lawless and barbarous sacrifice was not acceptable to any one of the superior beings above us, for it was not the fabled typhons and giants who governed the world, but the father of all gods and men; even to believe in the existence of divine beings who take delight in the slaughter and blood of men was perhaps a folly, but if such beings existed, they must be disregarded, as having no power; for only weakness and depravity of soul could produce or harbour such unnatural and cruel desires.

XXII. While, then, the chief men were thus disputing, and while Pelopidas in particular was in perplexity, a filly broke away from the herd of horses and sped through the camp, and when she came to the very place of their conference, stood still. The rest only admired the colour of her glossy mane, which was fiery red, her high mettle, and the

---

[1] At Thermopylae. Cf. Herodotus, vii. 220.
[2] Cf. the *Themistocles*, xiii. 2 f.
[3] Cf. the *Agesilaüs*, vi. 4 ff.

ἥ τε γαυρότης καὶ τὸ σοβαρὸν καὶ τεθαρρηκὸς
2 τῆς φωνῆς, Θεόκριτος δὲ ὁ μάντις συμφρονήσας
ἀνεβόησε πρὸς τὸν Πελοπίδαν· "Ἥκει σοι τὸ
ἱερεῖον, ὦ δαιμόνιε, καὶ παρθένον ἄλλην μὴ περι-
μένωμεν, ἀλλὰ χρῶ δεξάμενος ἣν ὁ θεὸς δίδωσιν."
ἐκ τούτου λαβόντες τὴν ἵππον ἐπὶ τοὺς τάφους
ἦγον τῶν παρθένων, καὶ κατευξάμενοι καὶ κατα-
στέψαντες ἐνέτεμον αὐτοί τε χαίροντες καὶ λόγον
εἰς τὸ στρατόπεδον περὶ τῆς ὄψεως τοῦ Πελοπίδου καὶ τῆς θυσίας διδόντες.

XXIII. Ἐν δὲ τῇ μάχῃ τοῦ Ἐπαμεινώνδου
τὴν φάλαγγα λοξὴν ἐπὶ τὸ εὐώνυμον ἕλκοντος,
ὅπως τῶν ἄλλων Ἑλλήνων ἀπωτάτω γένηται
τὸ δεξιὸν τῶν Σπαρτιατῶν καὶ τὸν Κλεόμβροτον
ἐξώσῃ προσπεσὼν ἀθρόως κατὰ κέρας καὶ βιασάμενος, οἱ μὲν πολέμιοι καταμαθόντες τὸ γινόμενον
2 ἤρξαντο μετακινεῖν τῇ τάξει σφᾶς αὐτούς, καὶ
τὸ δεξιὸν ἀνέπτυσσον καὶ περιῆγον ὡς κυκλωσόμενοι καὶ περιβαλοῦντες ὑπὸ πλήθους τὸν
Ἐπαμεινώνδαν, ὁ δὲ Πελοπίδας ἐν τούτῳ προ-
εξέδραμε, καὶ συστρέψας τοὺς τριακοσίους δρόμῳ
φθάνει πρὶν ἀνατεῖναι τὸν Κλεόμβροτον τὸ κέρας
ἢ συναγαγεῖν πάλιν εἰς τὸ αὐτὸ καὶ συγκλεῖσαι
τὴν τάξιν, οὐ καθεστῶσιν, ἀλλὰ θορυβουμένοις
3 δι' ἀλλήλων τοῖς Λακεδαιμονίοις ἐπιβαλών. καίτοι πάντων ἄκροι τεχνῖται καὶ σοφισταὶ τῶν
πολεμικῶν ὄντες οἱ Σπαρτιᾶται πρὸς οὐδὲν
οὕτως ἐπαίδευον αὑτοὺς καὶ συνείθιζον, ὡς τὸ
μὴ πλανᾶσθαι μηδὲ ταράττεσθαι τάξεως διαλυ-

vehemence and boldness of her neighing ; but
Theocritus the seer, after taking thought, cried out
to Pelopidas : " Thy sacrificial victim is come, good
man ; so let us not wait for any other virgin, but do
thou accept and use the one which Heaven offers
thee." So they took the mare and led her to the
tombs of the maidens, upon which, after decking her
with garlands and consecrating her with prayers,
they sacrificed her, rejoicing themselves, and pub-
lishing through the camp an account of the vision of
Pelopidas and of the sacrifice.

XXIII. In the battle, while Epaminondas was
drawing his phalanx obliquely towards the left, in
order that the right wing of the Spartans might be
separated as far as possible from the rest of the
Greeks, and that he might thrust back Cleombrotus
by a fierce charge in column with all his men-at-
arms, the enemy understood what he was doing and
began to change their formation ; they were opening
up their right wing and making an encircling movement, in order to surround Epaminondas and envelop him with their numbers. But at this point
Pelopidas darted forth from his position, and with
his band of three hundred on the run, came up[1]
before Cleombrotus had either extended his wing or
brought it back again into its old position and closed
up his line of battle, so that the Lacedaemonians were
not standing in array, but moving confusedly about
among each other when his onset reached them. And
yet the Spartans, who were of all men past masters
in the art of war, trained and accustomed themselves
to nothing so much as not to straggle or get into

---

[1] There is only a hint of this strategy, and no mention
either of Epaminondas or Pelopidas, in Xenophon's account
of the battle (*Hell.* vi. 4, 9-15).

θείσης, ἀλλὰ χρώμενοι πᾶσι πάντες ἐπιστάταις
καὶ ζευγίταις, ὅποι ποτὲ καὶ συνίστησιν ὁ κίνδυνος, καταλαμβάνειν καὶ συναρμόττειν καὶ
4 μάχεσθαι παραπλησίως. τότε δὲ ἡ τοῦ Ἐπαμεινώνδου φάλαγξ ἐπιφερομένη μόνοις ἐκείνοις
καὶ παραλλάττουσα τοὺς ἄλλους, ὅ τε Πελοπίδας
μετὰ τάχους ἀπίστου καὶ τόλμης ἐν τοῖς ὅπλοις
γενόμενος, συνέχεον τά τε φρονήματα καὶ τὰς
ἐπιστήμας αὐτῶν οὕτως ὥστε φυγὴν καὶ φόνον
Σπαρτιατῶν ὅσον οὔπω πρότερον γενέσθαι. διὸ
τῷ Ἐπαμεινώνδᾳ βοιωταρχοῦντι μὴ βοιωταρχῶν,
καὶ πάσης ἡγουμένῳ τῆς δυνάμεως μικροῦ μέρους
ἄρχων, ἴσον ἠνέγκατο δόξης τῆς νίκης ἐκείνης καὶ
τοῦ κατορθώματος.

XXIV. Εἰς μέντοι Πελοπόννησον ἀμφότεροι
βοιωταρχοῦντες ἐνέβαλον καὶ τῶν ἐθνῶν τὰ
πλεῖστα προσήγοντο, Λακεδαιμονίων ἀποστή-
σαντες Ἦλιν, Ἄργος, Ἀρκαδίαν σύμπασαν,
αὐτῆς τῆς Λακωνικῆς τὰ πλεῖστα. καίτοι χειμῶνος μὲν ἦσαν αἱ περὶ τροπὰς ἀκμαί, μηνὸς δὲ
τοῦ τελευταίου φθίνοντος ὀλίγαι περιῆσαν ἡμέραι,
καὶ τὴν ἀρχὴν ἔδει παραλαμβάνειν ἑτέρους εὐθὺς
ἱσταμένου τοῦ πρώτου μηνός, ἢ θνήσκειν τοὺς μὴ
2 παραδιδόντας. οἱ δὲ ἄλλοι βοιώταρχαι καὶ τὸν
νόμον δεδιότες τοῦτον καὶ τὸν χειμῶνα φεύγοντες
ἀπάγειν ἔσπευδον ἐπ' οἴκου τὸ στράτευμα, Πελοπίδας δὲ πρῶτος Ἐπαμεινώνδᾳ γενόμενος σύμ-
ψηφος καὶ συμπαρορμήσας τοὺς πολίτας ἦγεν
ἐπὶ τὴν Σπάρτην καὶ διεβίβαζε τὸν Εὐρώταν.
καὶ πολλὰς μὲν ᾕρει πόλεις αὐτῶν, πᾶσαν δὲ τὴν
χώραν ἐπόρθει μέχρι θαλάττης, ἡγούμενος ἑπτὰ
μυριάδων Ἑλληνικῆς στρατιᾶς, ἧς ἔλαττον ἢ

confusion upon a change of formation, but to take anyone without exception as neighbour in rank or in file, and wheresoever danger actually threatened, to seize that point and form in close array and fight as well as ever. At this time, however, since the phalanx of Epaminondas bore down upon them alone and neglected the rest of their force, and since Pelopidas engaged them with incredible speed and boldness, their courage and skill were so confounded that there was a flight and slaughter of the Spartans such as had never before been seen. Therefore, although Epaminondas was boeotarch, Pelopidas, who was not boeotarch, and commanded only a small portion of the whole force, won as much glory for the success of that victory as he did.

XXIV. Both were boeotarchs, however, when they invaded Peloponnesus and won over most of its peoples, detaching from the Lacedaemonian confederacy Elis, Argos, all Arcadia, and most of Laconia itself.[1] Still, the winter solstice was at hand, and only a few days of the latter part of the last month of the year remained, and as soon as the first month of the new year began other officials must succeed them, or those who would not surrender their office must die. The other boeotarchs, both because they feared this law, and because they wished to avoid the hardships of winter, were anxious to lead the army back home; but Pelopidas was first to add his vote to that of Epaminondas, and after inciting his countrymen to join them, led the army against Sparta and across the Eurotas. He took many of the enemy's cities, and ravaged all their territory as far as the sea, leading an army of seventy thousand Greeks, of which the Thebans themselves were less than a

[1] In 370 B.C.

3 δωδέκατον ἦσαν αὐτοὶ Θηβαῖοι μέρος. ἀλλ' ἡ
δόξα τῶν ἀνδρῶν ἄνευ δόγματος κοινοῦ καὶ ψη-
φίσματος ἐποίει τοὺς συμμάχους ἕπεσθαι σιωπῇ
πάντας ἡγουμένοις ἐκείνοις. ὁ γὰρ πρῶτος, ὡς
ἔοικε, καὶ κυριώτατος νόμος τῷ σῴζεσθαι δεομένῳ
τὸν σῴζειν δυνάμενον ἄρχοντα κατὰ φύσιν ἀπο-
δίδωσι· κἂν ὥσπερ οἱ πλέοντες εὐδίας οὔσης ἢ
παρ' ἀκτὴν ὁρμοῦντες ἀσελγῶς προσενεχθῶσι
τοῖς κυβερνήταις καὶ θρασέως, ἅμα τῷ χειμῶνα
καὶ κίνδυνον καταλαμβάνειν πρὸς ἐκείνους ἀπο-
βλέπουσι καὶ τὰς ἐλπίδας ἐν ἐκείνοις ἔχουσι.
4 καὶ γὰρ Ἀργεῖοι καὶ Ἠλεῖοι καὶ Ἀρκάδες ἐν τοῖς
συνεδρίοις ἐρίζοντες καὶ διαφερόμενοι πρὸς τοὺς
Θηβαίους ὑπὲρ ἡγεμονίας, ἐπ' αὐτῶν τῶν ἀγώνων
καὶ παρὰ τὰ δεινὰ τοῖς ἐκείνων αὐθαιρέτως
πειθόμενοι στρατηγοῖς ἠκολούθουν.

5 Ἐν ἐκείνῃ τῇ στρατείᾳ πᾶσαν μὲν Ἀρκαδίαν
εἰς μίαν δύναμιν συνέστησαν, τὴν δὲ Μεσσηνίαν
χώραν νεμομένων Σπαρτιατῶν ἀποτεμόμενοι τοὺς
παλαιοὺς Μεσσηνίους ἐκάλουν καὶ κατῆγον
Ἰθώμην συνοικίσαντες, ἀπιόντες δὲ ἐπ' οἴκου
διὰ Κεγχρεῶν Ἀθηναίους ἐνίκων ἐπιχειροῦντας
ἀψιμαχεῖν περὶ τὰ στενὰ καὶ κωλύειν τὴν
πορείαν.

XXV. Ἐπὶ δὲ τούτοις οἱ μὲν ἄλλοι πάντες
ὑπερηγάπων τὴν ἀρετὴν καὶ τὴν τύχην ἐθαύμαζον, ὁ δὲ συγγενὴς καὶ πολιτικὸς φθόνος ἅμα τῇ
δόξῃ τῶν ἀνδρῶν συναυξόμενος οὐ καλὰς οὐδὲ
πρεπούσας ὑποδοχὰς παρεσκεύαζεν αὐτοῖς. θανάτου γὰρ ἀμφότεροι δίκας ἔφυγον ἐπανελθόντες,
ὅτι τοῦ νόμου κελεύοντος ἐν τῷ πρώτῳ μηνὶ
παραδοῦναι τὴν βοιωταρχίαν ἑτέροις, ὃν Βου-
κάτιον ὀνομάζουσι, τέτταρας ὅλους προσεπε-

398

twelfth part. But the reputation of the two men, without a general vote or decree, induced all the allies to follow their leadership without a murmur. For the first and paramount law, as it would seem, namely, that of nature, subjects him who desires to be saved to the command of the man who can save him; just as sailors, when the weather is fair or they are lying off shore at anchor, treat their captains with bold insolence, but as soon as a storm arises and danger threatens, look to them for guidance and place their hopes in them. And so Argives, Eleans, and Arcadians, who in their joint assemblies contended and strove with the Thebans for the supremacy, when battles were actually to be fought and perils to be faced, of their own will obeyed the Theban generals and followed them.

On this expedition they united all Arcadia into one power; rescued the country of Messenia from the hands of its Spartan masters and called back and restored the ancient Messenian inhabitants, with whom they settled Ithome; and on their way back homewards through Cenchreae, conquered the Athenians when they tried to hinder their passage by skirmishing with them in the passes.

XXV. In view of these achievements, all the rest of the Greeks were delighted with their valour and marvelled at their good fortune; but the envy of their own fellow-citizens, which was increasing with the men's fame, prepared them a reception that was not honourable or fitting. For both were tried for their lives when they came back, because they had not handed over to others their office of boeotarch, as the law commanded, in the first month of the new year (which they call Boukatios), but had added four

βάλοντο μῆνας, ἐν οἷς τὰ περὶ Μεσσήνην καὶ
Ἀρκαδίαν καὶ τὴν Λακωνικὴν διῴκησαν.

2   Εἰσήχθη μὲν οὖν πρότερος εἰς τὸ δικαστήριον
Πελοπίδας, διὸ καὶ μᾶλλον ἐκινδύνευσεν, ἀμφότεροι δὲ ἀπελύθησαν. τὸ δὲ συκοφάντημα καὶ
τὴν πεῖραν Ἐπαμεινώνδας ἤνεγκε πράως, μέγα
μέρος ἀνδρείας καὶ μεγαλοψυχίας τὴν ἐν τοῖς
πολιτικοῖς ἀνεξικακίαν ποιούμενος, Πελοπίδας
δὲ καὶ φύσει θυμοειδέστερος ὤν, καὶ παροξυνό-
μενος ὑπὸ τῶν φίλων ἀμύνασθαι τοὺς ἐχθρούς,
3   ἐπελάβετο τοιαύτης αἰτίας. Μενεκλείδας ὁ ῥή-
τωρ ἦν μὲν εἷς τῶν μετὰ Πελοπίδου καὶ Μέλωνος
εἰς τὴν Χάρωνος οἰκίαν συνελθόντων, ἐπεὶ δὲ τῶν
ἴσων οὐκ ἠξιοῦτο παρὰ τοῖς Θηβαίοις, δεινότατος
μὲν ὢν λέγειν, ἀκόλαστος δὲ καὶ κακοήθης τὸν
τρόπον, ἐχρῆτο τῇ φύσει πρὸς τὸ συκοφαντεῖν
καὶ διαβάλλειν τοὺς κρείττονας, οὐδὲ μετὰ δίκην
4   ἐκείνην παυσάμενος. Ἐπαμεινώνδαν μὲν οὖν
ἐξέκρουσε τῆς βοιωταρχίας καὶ κατεπολιτεύσατο
πολὺν χρόνον, Πελοπίδαν δὲ πρὸς μὲν τὸν δῆμον
οὐκ ἴσχυσε διαβαλεῖν, ἐπεχείρει δὲ συγκροῦσαι
τῷ Χάρωνι· καὶ κοινήν τινα τοῦ φθόνου παραμυθίαν ἔχοντος, ἂν ὧν αὐτοὶ μὴ δύνανται βελτίους
φανῆναι, τούτους ἀμῶς γέ πως ἑτέρων ἀποδείξωσι
κακίους, πολὺς ἦν πρὸς τὸν δῆμον αὔξων τὰ τοῦ
Χάρωνος ἔργα, καὶ τὰς στρατηγίας τὰς ἐκείνου
5   καὶ τὰς νίκας ἐγκωμιάζων. τῆς δὲ πρὸς Πλαταιὰς
ἱππομαχίας, ἣν πρὸ τῶν Λευκτρικῶν ἐνίκησαν
ἡγουμένου Χάρωνος, ἐπεχείρησεν ἀνάθημα τοιόνδε
ποιῆσαι. Ἀνδροκύδης ὁ Κυζικηνὸς ἐκλαβὼν

whole months to it, during which they conducted their campaign in Messenia, Arcadia, and Laconia.

Well, then, Pelopidas was first brought to trial, and therefore ran the greater risk, but both were acquitted. Epaminondas bore patiently with this attempt to calumniate him, considering that forbearance under political injury was a large part of fortitude and magnanimity ; but Pelopidas, who was naturally of a more fiery temper, and who was egged on by his friends to avenge himself upon his enemies, seized the following occasion. Menecleidas, the orator, was one of those who had gathered with Pelopidas and Melon at Charon's house, and since he did not receive as much honour among the Thebans as the others, being a most able speaker, but intemperate and malicious in his disposition, he gave his natural gifts employment in calumniating and slandering his superiors, and kept on doing so even after the trial. Accordingly, he succeeded in excluding Epaminondas from the office of boeotarch, and kept him out of political leadership for some time ; but he had not weight enough to bring Pelopidas into disfavour with the people, and therefore tried to bring him into collision with Charon. And since it is quite generally a consolation to the envious, in the case of those whom they themselves cannot surpass in men's estimation, to show these forth as somehow or other inferior to others, he was constantly magnifying the achievements of Charon, in his speeches to the people, and extolling his campaigns and victories. Moreover, for the victory which the Theban cavalry won at Plataea, before the battle of Leuctra, under the command of Charon, he attempted to make the following public dedication. Androcydes of Cyzicus had received a commission

παρὰ τῆς πόλεως πίνακα γράψαι μάχης ἑτέρας,
ἐπετέλει τὸ ἔργον ἐν Θήβαις· γενομένης δὲ τῆς
ἀποστάσεως καὶ τοῦ πολέμου συμπεσόντος, οὐ
πολὺ τοῦ τέλος ἔχειν ἐλλείποντα τὸν πίνακα
6 παρ' ἑαυτοῖς οἱ Θηβαῖοι κατέσχον. τοῦτον οὖν
ὁ Μενεκλείδας ἔπεισεν ἀναθέντας ἐπιγράψαι
τοὔνομα τοῦ Χάρωνος, ὡς ἀμαυρώσων τὴν Πελοπίδου καὶ Ἐπαμεινώνδου δόξαν. ἦν δὲ ἀβέλτερος
ἡ φιλοτιμία, παρὰ τοσούτους καὶ τηλικούτους
ἀγῶνας ἑνὸς ἔργου καὶ μιᾶς νίκης ἀγαπωμένης,
ἐν ᾗ Γεράνδαν τινὰ τῶν ἀσήμων Σπαρτιατῶν καὶ
τεσσαράκοντα μετ' αὐτοῦ πεσεῖν, ἄλλο δὲ οὐδὲν
7 μέγα πραχθῆναι λέγουσι. τοῦτο τὸ ψήφισμα
γράφεται Πελοπίδας παρανόμων, ἰσχυριζόμενος
ὅτι Θηβαίοις οὐ πάτριον ἦν ἰδίᾳ κατ' ἄνδρα
τιμᾶν, ἀλλὰ τῇ πατρίδι κοινῶς τὸ τῆς νίκης
ὄνομα σώζειν. καὶ τὸν μὲν Χάρωνα παρὰ πᾶσαν
τὴν δίκην ἐγκωμιάζων ἀφθόνως διετέλεσε, τὸν δὲ
Μενεκλείδαν βάσκανον καὶ πονηρὸν ἐξελέγχων,
καὶ τοὺς Θηβαίους ἐρωτῶν εἰ μηδὲν αὐτοῖς καλὸν
πέπρακται, ὥστε[1] Μενεκλείδαν ζημιῶσαι χρήμασιν, ἃ μὴ δυνάμενος ἐκτῖσαι διὰ πλῆθος,
ὕστερον ἐπεχείρησε κινῆσαι καὶ μεταστῆσαι τὴν
πολιτείαν. ταῦτα μὲν οὖν ἔχει τινὰ καὶ τοῦ βίου
ἀποθεώρησιν.

XXVI. Ἐπεὶ δὲ Ἀλεξάνδρου τοῦ Φερῶν τυράννου πολεμοῦντος μὲν ἐκ προδήλου πολλοῖς
Θετταλῶν, ἐπιβουλεύοντος δὲ πᾶσιν, ἐπρέσβευ-
σαν εἰς Θήβας αἱ πόλεις στρατηγὸν αἰτούμεναι
καὶ δύναμιν, ὁρῶν ὁ Πελοπίδας τὸν Ἐπαμεινών-

─────────────

[1] ὥστε Bryan's correction of the MSS. ὃ μὴ, which Sintenis
and Bekker retain, assuming a lacuna in the text.

from the city to make a picture of another battle, and was finishing the work at Thebes; but the city revolted from Sparta, and the war came on, before the picture was quite completed, and the Thebans now had it on their hands. This picture, then, Menecleidas persuaded them to dedicate with Charon's name inscribed thereon, hoping in this way to obscure the fame of Pelopidas and Epaminondas. But the ambitious scheme was a foolish one, when there were so many and such great conflicts, to bestow approval on one action and one victory, in which, we are told, a certain Gerandas, an obscure Spartan, and forty others were killed, but nothing else of importance was accomplished. This decree was attacked as unconstitutional by Pelopidas, who insisted that it was not a custom with the Thebans to honour any one man individually, but for the whole country to have the glory of a victory. And through the whole trial of the case he continued to heap generous praise upon Charon, while he showed Menecleidas to be a slanderous and worthless fellow, and asked the Thebans if they had done nothing noble themselves; the result was that Menecleidas was fined, and being unable to pay the fine because it was so heavy, he afterwards tried to effect a revolution in the government. This episode, then, has some bearing on the Life which I am writing.

XXVI. Now, since Alexander the tyrant of Pherae made open war on many of the Thessalians, and was plotting against them all, their cities sent ambassadors to Thebes asking for an armed force and a general. Pelopidas, therefore, seeing that Epami-

δαν τὰς ἐν Πελοποννήσῳ πράξεις διοικεῖν,[1] αὐτὸς
ἑαυτὸν ἐπέδωκε καὶ προσένειμε τοῖς Θεσσαλοῖς,
μήτε τὴν ἰδίαν ἐπιστήμην καὶ δύναμιν ἀργοῦσαν
περιορᾶν ὑπομένων, μήτε ὅπου πάρεστιν Ἐπαμεινώνδας ἑτέρου δεῖσθαι στρατηγοῦ νομίζων.
2 ὡς οὖν ἐστράτευσεν ἐπὶ Θεσσαλίαν μετὰ δυνάμεως, τήν τε Λάρισσαν εὐθὺς παρέλαβε, καὶ τὸν
Ἀλέξανδρον ἐλθόντα καὶ δεόμενον διαλλάττειν
ἐπειρᾶτο καὶ ποιεῖν ἐκ τυράννου πρᾶον ἄρχοντα
τοῖς Θεσσαλοῖς καὶ νόμιμον. ὡς δὲ ἦν ἀνήκεστος
καὶ θηριώδης καὶ πολλὴ μὲν ὠμότης αὐτοῦ,
πολλὴ δὲ ἀσέλγεια καὶ πλεονεξία κατηγορεῖτο,
τραχυνομένου τοῦ Πελοπίδου πρὸς αὐτὸν καὶ
χαλεπαίνοντος ἀποδρὰς ᾤχετο μετὰ τῶν δορυ-
3 φόρων. ὁ δὲ Πελοπίδας ἄδειάν τε πολλὴν ἀπὸ
τοῦ τυράννου τοῖς Θεσσαλοῖς ἀπολιπὼν καὶ πρὸς
ἀλλήλους ὁμόνοιαν, αὐτὸς εἰς Μακεδονίαν ἀπῆρε,
Πτολεμαίου μὲν Ἀλεξάνδρῳ τῷ βασιλεύοντι τῶν
Μακεδόνων πολεμοῦντος, ἀμφοτέρων δὲ μεταπεμ-
πομένων ἐκεῖνον ὡς διαλλακτὴν καὶ δικαστὴν καὶ
σύμμαχον καὶ βοηθὸν τοῦ δοκοῦντος ἀδικεῖσθαι
4 γενησόμενον. ἐλθὼν δὲ καὶ διαλύσας τὰς δια-
φορὰς καὶ καταγαγὼν τοὺς φεύγοντας, ὅμηρον
ἔλαβε τὸν ἀδελφὸν τοῦ βασιλέως Φίλιππον καὶ
τριάκοντα παῖδας ἄλλους τῶν ἐπιφανεστάτων, 29:
καὶ κατέστησεν εἰς Θήβας, ἐπιδειξάμενος τοῖς
Ἕλλησιν ὡς πόρρω διῆκε τὰ Θηβαίων πράγματα τῇ δόξῃ τῆς δυνάμεως καὶ τῇ πίστει τῆς
δικαιοσύνης.
5 Οὗτος ἦν Φίλιππος ὁ τοῖς Ἕλλησιν ὕστερον
πολεμήσας ὑπὲρ τῆς ἐλευθερίας, τότε δὲ παῖς ὢν

---

[1] διοικεῖν Bekker has διοικοῦντα, after Coraës.

nondas was busy with his work in Peloponnesus, offered and assigned himself to the Thessalians,[1] both because he could not suffer his own skill and ability to lie idle, and because he thought that wherever Epaminondas was there was no need of a second general. Accordingly, after marching into Thessaly with an armed force, he straightway took Larissa, and when Alexander came to him and begged for terms, he tried to make him, instead of a tyrant, one who would govern the Thessalians mildly and according to law. But since the man was incurably brutish and full of savageness, and since there was much denunciation of his licentiousness and greed, Pelopidas became harsh and severe with him, whereupon he ran away with his guards. Then Pelopidas, leaving the Thessalians in great security from the tyrant and in concord with one another, set out himself for Macedonia, where Ptolemy was at war with Alexander the king of the Macedonians. For both parties had invited him to come and be arbiter and judge between them, and ally and helper of the one that appeared to be wronged. After he had come, then, and had settled their differences and brought home the exiles, he received as hostages Philip, the king's brother, and thirty other sons of the most illustrious men, and brought them to live at Thebes, thus showing the Greeks what an advance the Theban state had made in the respect paid to its power and the trust placed in its justice.

This was the Philip who afterwards waged war to enslave the Greeks, but at this time he was a boy,

[1] In 369 B.C.

ἐν Θήβαις παρὰ Παμμένει δίαιταν εἶχεν. ἐκ δὲ
τούτου καὶ ζηλωτὴς γεγονέναι ἔδοξεν[1] Ἐπαμεινώνδου, τὸ περὶ τοὺς πολέμους καὶ τὰς στρατηγίας δραστήριον ἴσως κατανοήσας,[1] ὃ μικρὸν ἦν
τῆς τοῦ ἀνδρὸς ἀρετῆς μόριον, ἐγκρατείας δὲ καὶ
δικαιοσύνης καὶ μεγαλοψυχίας καὶ πραότητος,
οἷς ἦν ἀληθῶς μέγας ἐκεῖνος, οὐδὲν οὔτε φύσει
Φίλιππος οὔτε μιμήσει μετέσχε.

XXVII. Μετὰ δὲ ταῦτα πάλιν τῶν Θετταλῶν
αἰτιωμένων τὸν Φεραῖον Ἀλέξανδρον ὡς δια-
ταράττοντα τὰς πόλεις, ἀπεστάλη μετὰ Ἰσμηνίου
πρεσβεύων ὁ Πελοπίδας· καὶ παρῆν οὔτε οἴκοθεν
ἄγων δύναμιν οὔτε πόλεμον προσδοκήσας, αὐτοῖς
δὲ τοῖς Θετταλοῖς χρῆσθαι πρὸς τὸ κατεπεῖγον
2 τῶν πραγμάτων ἀναγκαζόμενος. ἐν τούτῳ δὲ
πάλιν τῶν κατὰ Μακεδονίαν ταραττομένων (ὁ
γὰρ Πτολεμαῖος ἀνῃρήκει τὸν βασιλέα καὶ τὴν
ἀρχὴν κατέσχεν, οἱ δὲ φίλοι τοῦ τεθνηκότος ἐκάλουν τὸν Πελοπίδαν), βουλόμενος μὲν ἐπιφανῆναι
τοῖς πράγμασιν, ἰδίους δὲ στρατιώτας οὐκ ἔχων,
μισθοφόρους τινὰς αὐτόθεν προσλαβόμενος μετὰ
3 τούτων εὐθὺς ἐβάδιζεν ἐπὶ τὸν Πτολεμαῖον. ὡς
δ᾽ ἐγγὺς ἀλλήλων ἐγένοντο, τοὺς μὲν μισθοφόρους
Πτολεμαῖος χρήμασι διαφθείρας ἔπεισεν ὡς αὑτὸν
μεταστῆναι, τοῦ δὲ Πελοπίδου τὴν δόξαν αὐτὴν
καὶ τοὔνομα δεδοικὼς ἀπήντησεν ὡς κρείσσονι,
καὶ δεξιωσάμενος καὶ δεηθεὶς ὡμολόγησε τὴν μὲν
ἀρχὴν τοῖς τοῦ τεθνηκότος ἀδελφοῖς διαφυλάξειν,
Θηβαίοις δὲ τὸν αὐτὸν ἐχθρὸν ἕξειν καὶ φίλον·
ὁμήρους δ᾽ ἐπὶ τούτοις τὸν υἱὸν Φιλόξενον ἔδωκε
4 καὶ πεντήκοντα τῶν ἑταίρων. τούτους μὲν οὖν

---

[1] ἔδοξεν . . . κατανοήσας Bekker has τισὶν ἔδοξεν . . . κατα-
νοήσασιν (to some . . . who observed), after Coraës.

and lived in Thebes with Pammenes. Hence he was believed to have become a zealous follower of Epaminondas, perhaps because he comprehended his efficiency in wars and campaigns, which was only a small part of the man's high excellence; but in restraint, justice, magnanimity, and gentleness, wherein Epaminondas was truly great, Philip had no share, either naturally or as a result of imitation.

XXVII. After this, when the Thessalians again brought complaint against Alexander of Pherae as a disturber of their cities, Pelopidas was sent thither on an embassy with Ismenias;[1] and since he brought no force from home with him, and did not expect war, he was compelled to employ the Thessalians themselves for the emergency. At this time, too, Macedonian affairs were in confusion again, for Ptolemy had killed the king and now held the reins of government, and the friends of the dead king were calling upon Pelopidas. Wishing, therefore, to appear upon the scene, but having no soldiers of his own, he enlisted some mercenaries on the spot, and with these marched at once against Ptolemy. When, however, they were near each other, Ptolemy corrupted the mercenaries and bribed them to come over to his side; but since he feared the very name and reputation of Pelopidas, he met him as his superior, and after welcoming him and supplicating his favour, agreed to be regent for the brothers of the dead king, and to make an alliance with the Thebans; moreover, to confirm this, he gave him his son Philoxenus and fifty of his companions as hostages.

[1] In 368 B.C.

ἀπέστειλεν εἰς Θήβας ὁ Πελοπίδας, αὐτὸς δὲ
βαρέως φέρων τὴν τῶν μισθοφόρων προδοσίαν,
καὶ πυνθανόμενος τὰ πλεῖστα τῶν χρημάτων
αὐτοῖς καὶ παῖδας καὶ γυναῖκας ἀποκεῖσθαι περὶ
Φάρσαλον, ὥστε τούτων κρατήσας ἱκανὴν δίκην
ὧν καθύβρισται λήψεσθαι, συναγαγὼν τῶν Θεσ-
5 σαλῶν τινας ἧκεν εἰς Φάρσαλον. ἀρτίως δ' αὐτοῦ
παρεληλυθότος Ἀλέξανδρος ὁ τύραννος ἐπεφαίνετο μετὰ τῆς δυνάμεως. καὶ νομίσαντες οἱ περὶ
τὸν Πελοπίδαν ἀπολογησόμενον ἥκειν ἐβάδιζον
αὐτοὶ πρὸς αὐτόν, ἐξώλη μὲν ὄντα καὶ μιαιφόνον
εἰδότες, διὰ δὲ τὰς Θήβας καὶ τὸ περὶ αὐτοὺς
ἀξίωμα καὶ δόξαν οὐδὲν ἂν παθεῖν προσδοκή-
6 σαντες. ὁ δέ, ὡς εἶδεν ἀνόπλους καὶ μόνους προσιόντας, ἐκείνους μὲν εὐθὺς συνέλαβε, τὴν δὲ
Φάρσαλον κατέσχε, φρίκην δὲ καὶ φόβον ἐνειρ-
γάσατο τοῖς ὑπηκόοις πᾶσιν ὥς γε μετὰ τὴν τηλικαύτην ἀδικίαν καὶ τόλμαν ἀφειδήσων ἁπάντων,
καὶ χρησόμενος οὕτω τοῖς παραπίπτουσιν ἀνθρώποις καὶ πράγμασιν ὡς τότε γε κομιδῇ τὸν ἑαυτοῦ
βίον ἀπεγνωκώς.

XXVIII. Οἱ μὲν οὖν Θηβαῖοι ταῦτα ἀκούσαντες ἔφερον βαρέως καὶ στρατιὰν ἐξέπεμπον
εὐθύς, δι' ὀργήν τινα πρὸς τὸν Ἐπαμεινώνδαν
ἑτέρους ἀποδείξαντες ἄρχοντας. τὸν δὲ Πελοπίδαν εἰς τὰς Φερὰς ἀπαγαγὼν ὁ τύραννος τὸ μὲν
πρῶτον εἴα τοὺς βουλομένους αὐτῷ διαλέγεσθαι,
νομίζων ἐλεεινὸν γεγονέναι καὶ ταπεινὸν ὑπὸ τῆς
2 συμφορᾶς· ἐπεὶ δὲ τοὺς μὲν Φεραίους ὁ Πελοπίδας ὀδυρομένους παρεκάλει θαρρεῖν, ὡς νῦν
μάλιστα δώσοντος τοῦ τυράννου δίκην, πρὸς δὲ
αὐτὸν ἐκεῖνον ἀποστείλας ἔλεγεν ὡς ἄτοπός ἐστι

These, then, Pelopidas sent off to Thebes; but he himself, being indignant at the treachery of his mercenaries, and learning that most of their goods, together with their wives and children, had been placed for safety at Pharsalus, so that by getting these into his power he would sufficiently punish them for their affront to him, he got together some of the Thessalians and came to Pharsalus. But just as he got there, Alexander the tyrant appeared before the city with his forces. Then Pelopidas and Ismenias, thinking that he was come to excuse himself for his conduct, went of their own accord to him, knowing, indeed, that he was an abandoned and blood-stained wretch, but expecting that because of Thebes and their own dignity and reputation they would suffer no harm. But the tyrant, when he saw them coming up unarmed and unattended, straightway seized them and took possession of Pharsalus. By this step he awoke in all his subjects a shuddering fear; they thought that after an act of such boldness and iniquity he would spare nobody, and in all his dealings with men and affairs would act as one who now utterly despaired of his own life.

XXVIII. The Thebans, then, on hearing of this, were indignant, and sent out an army at once, although, since Epaminondas had somehow incurred their displeasure, they appointed other commanders for it. As for Pelopidas, after the tyrant had brought him back to Pherae, at first he suffered all who desired it to converse with him, thinking that his calamity had made him a pitiful and contemptible object; but when Pelopidas exhorted the lamenting Pheraeans to be of good cheer, since now certainly the tyrant would meet with punishment, and when he sent a message to the tyrant himself, saying that

τοὺς μὲν ἀθλίους πολίτας καὶ μηδὲν ἀδικοῦντας
ὁσημέραι στρεβλῶν καὶ φονεύων, αὐτοῦ δὲ φειδό-
μενος, ὃν μάλιστα γινώσκει τιμωρησόμενον αὐτὸν
3 ἄνπερ διαφύγῃ, θαυμάσας τὸ φρόνημα καὶ τὴν
ἄδειαν αὐτοῦ, "Τί δέ," φησί, " σπεύδει Πελοπίδας ἀποθανεῖν;" κἀκεῖνος ἀκούσας, "Ὅπως,"
εἶπε, " σὺ τάχιον ἀπολῇ, μᾶλλον ἢ νῦν θεομισὴς
γενόμενος." ἐκ τούτου διεκώλυσεν ἐντυγχάνειν
αὐτῷ τοὺς ἐκτός.

Ἡ δὲ Θήβη, θυγάτηρ μὲν Ἰάσονος οὖσα, γυνὴ
δὲ Ἀλεξάνδρου, πυνθανομένη παρὰ τῶν φυλατ-
τόντων Πελοπίδαν τὸ θαρραλέον αὐτοῦ καὶ γενναῖον, ἐπεθύμησεν ἰδεῖν τὸν ἄνδρα καὶ προσειπεῖν.
4 ὡς δὲ ἦλθε πρὸς αὐτὸν καὶ ἅτε δὴ γυνὴ τὸ μὲν
μέγεθος τοῦ ἤθους οὐκ εὐθὺς ἐν τοσαύτῃ συμφορᾷ
κατεῖδε, κουρᾷ δὲ καὶ στολῇ καὶ διαίτῃ τεκμαιρο-
μένη λυπρὰ καὶ μὴ πρέποντα τῇ δόξῃ πάσχειν
αὐτὸν ἀπεδάκρυσε, τὸ μὲν πρῶτον ἀγνοῶν ὁ
Πελοπίδας τίς εἴη γυναικῶν, ἐθαύμαζεν, ὡς δὲ
ἔγνω, προσηγόρευσεν αὐτὴν πατρόθεν· ἦν γὰρ
τῷ Ἰάσονι συνήθης καὶ φίλος. εἰπούσης δὲ
ἐκείνης, "Ἐλεῶ σου τὴν γυναῖκα," "Καὶ γὰρ
ἐγώ σε," εἶπεν, "ὅτι ἄδετος οὖσα ὑπομένεις Ἀλέξ-
5 ανδρον." οὗτος ἔθιγέ πως ὁ λόγος τῆς γυναικός·
ἐβαρύνετο γὰρ τὴν ὠμότητα καὶ τὴν ὕβριν τοῦ
τυράννου, μετὰ τῆς ἄλλης ἀσελγείας καὶ τὸν
νεώτατον αὐτῆς τῶν ἀδελφῶν παιδικὰ πεποιημένου. διὸ καὶ συνεχῶς φοιτῶσα πρὸς τὸν
Πελοπίδαν καὶ παρρησιαζομένη περὶ ὧν ἔπασχεν
ὑπεπίμπλατο θυμοῦ καὶ φρονήματος καὶ δυσμενείας πρὸς τὸν Ἀλέξανδρον.

XXIX. Ἐπεὶ δὲ οἱ στρατηγοὶ τῶν Θηβαίων
εἰς τὴν Θετταλίαν ἐμβαλόντες ἔπραξαν οὐδέν,

it was absurd to torture and slay the wretched and innocent citizens day by day, while he spared him, a man most certain, as he knew, to take vengeance on him if he made his escape; then the tyrant, amazed at his high spirit and his fearlessness, said: "And why is Pelopidas in haste to die?" To which Pelopidas replied: "That thou mayest the sooner perish, by becoming more hateful to the gods than now." From that time the tyrant forbade those outside of his following to see the prisoner.

But Thebe, who was a daughter of Jason, and Alexander's wife, learned from the keepers of Pelopidas how courageous and noble the man was, and conceived a desire to see him and talk with him. But when she came to him, woman that she was, she could not at once recognize the greatness of his nature in such dire misfortune, but judging from his hair and garb and maintenance that he was suffering indignities which ill befitted a man of his reputation, she burst into tears. Pelopidas, not knowing at first what manner of woman she was, was amazed; but when he understood, he addressed her as daughter of Jason; for her father was a familiar friend of his. And when she said, "I pity thy wife," he replied, "And I thee, in that thou wearest no chains, and yet endurest Alexander." This speech deeply moved the woman, for she was oppressed by the savage insolence of the tyrant, who, in addition to his other debaucheries, had made her youngest brother his paramour. Therefore her continued visits to Pelopidas, in which she spoke freely of her sufferings, gradually filled her with wrath and fierce hatred towards Alexander.

XXIX. When the Theban generals had accomplished nothing by their invasion of Thessaly,

ἀλλὰ δι' ἀπειρίαν ἢ δυστυχίαν αἰσχρῶς ἀνεχώρησαν, ἐκείνων μὲν ἔκαστον ἡ πόλις μυρίαις
δραχμαῖς ἐζημίωσεν, Ἐπαμεινώνδαν δὲ μετὰ
2 δυνάμεως ἀπέστειλεν. εὐθὺς οὖν κίνησίς τις μεγάλη Θετταλῶν ἦν ἐπαιρομένων πρὸς τὴν δόξαν
τοῦ στρατηγοῦ, καὶ τὰ πράγματα τοῦ τυράννου
ῥοπῆς ἐδεῖτο μικρᾶς ἀπολωλέναι· τοσοῦτος ἐνε-
πεπτώκει φόβος τοῖς περὶ αὐτὸν ἡγεμόσι καὶ
φίλοις, τοσαύτη δὲ τοὺς ὑπηκόους ὁρμὴ πρὸς
ἀπόστασιν εἶχε καὶ χαρὰ τοῦ μέλλοντος, ὡς νῦν
3 ἐποψομένους δίκην διδόντα τὸν τύραννον. οὐ
μὴν ἀλλ' Ἐπαμεινώνδας τὴν αὑτοῦ δόξαν ἐν
ὑστέρῳ τῆς Πελοπίδου σωτηρίας τιθέμενος, καὶ
δεδοικὼς μὴ τῶν πραγμάτων ταραχθέντων ἀπο-
γνοὺς ἑαυτὸν Ἀλέξανδρος ὥσπερ θηρίον τράπηται
πρὸς ἐκεῖνον, ἐπηωρεῖτο τῷ πολέμῳ, καὶ κύκλῳ
περιιών, τῇ παρασκευῇ καὶ τῇ μελλήσει κατε-
σκεύαζε καὶ συνέστελλε τὸν τύραννον, ὡς μήτε
ἀνεῖναι τὸ αὔθαδες αὐτοῦ καὶ θρασυνόμενον μήτε
4 τὸ πικρὸν καὶ θυμοειδὲς ἐξερεθίσαι, πυνθανόμενος τὴν ὠμότητα καὶ τὴν ὀλιγωρίαν τῶν καλῶν
καὶ δικαίων, ὡς ζῶντας μὲν ἀνθρώπους κατώρυτ-
τεν, ἑτέροις δὲ δέρματα συῶν ἀγρίων καὶ ἄρκτων
περιτιθεὶς καὶ τοὺς θηρατικοὺς ἐπάγων κύνας καὶ
διέσπα καὶ κατηκόντιζε, παιδιᾷ ταύτῃ χρώμενος,
Μελιβοίᾳ δὲ καὶ Σκοτούσῃ, πόλεσιν ἐνσπόνδοις
καὶ φίλαις, ἐκκλησιαζούσαις περιστήσας ἅμα
τοὺς δορυφόρους ἡβηδὸν ἀπέσφαξε, τὴν δὲ λόγχην ᾗ Πολύφρονα τὸν θεῖον ἀπέκτεινε καθιερώσας

but owing to inexperience or ill fortune had retired disgracefully, the city fined each of them ten
thousand drachmas, and sent out Epaminondas
with an armed force.[1] At once, then, there was
a great stir among the Thessalians, who were filled
with high hopes in view of the reputation of this
general, and the cause of the tyrant was on the
very verge of destruction; so great was the fear
that fell upon his commanders and friends, and so
great the inclination of his subjects to revolt, and
their joy at what the future had in store, for they
felt that now they should behold the tyrant under
punishment. Epaminondas, however, less solicitous
for his own glory than for the safety of Pelopidas,
and fearing that if confusion reigned Alexander
would get desperate and turn like a wild beast upon
his prisoner, dallied with the war, and taking a
roundabout course, kept the tyrant in suspense by
his preparations and threatened movements, thus
neither encouraging his audacity and boldness, nor
rousing his malignity and passion. For he had
learned how savage he was, and how little regard he
had for right and justice, in that sometimes he
buried men alive, and sometimes dressed them in
the skins of wild boars or bears, and then set his
hunting dogs upon them and either tore them in
pieces or shot them down, making this his diversion;
and at Meliboea and Scotussa, allied and friendly
cities, when the people were in full assembly, he
surrounded them with his body-guards and slaugh-
tered them from the youth up; he also consecrated
the spear with which he had slain his uncle Poly-
phron, decked it with garlands, and sacrificed to it

---

[1] 367 B.C.

καὶ καταστέψας, ἔθυεν ὥσπερ θεῷ καὶ Τύχωνα
5 προσηγόρευε. τραγῳδὸν δέ ποτε θεώμενος Εὐριπίδου Τρῳάδας ὑποκρινόμενον ᾤχετο ἀπιὼν ἐκ
τοῦ θεάτρου, καὶ πέμψας πρὸς αὐτὸν ἐκέλευε
θαρρεῖν καὶ μηδὲν ἀγωνίζεσθαι διὰ τοῦτο χεῖρον,
οὐ γὰρ ἐκείνου καταφρονῶν ἀπελθεῖν, ἀλλ' αἰσχυνόμενος τοὺς πολίτας, εἰ μηδένα πώποτε τῶν
ὑπ' αὐτοῦ φονευομένων ἠλεηκώς, ἐπὶ τοῖς Ἑκάβης
καὶ Ἀνδρομάχης κακοῖς ὀφθήσεται δακρύων.
6 οὗτος μέντοι τὴν δόξαν αὐτὴν καὶ τοὔνομα καὶ
τὸ πρόσχημα τῆς Ἐπαμεινώνδου στρατηγίας
καταπλαγείς,

ἔπτηξ' ἀλέκτωρ δοῦλος ὡς κλίνας πτερόν,

καὶ τοὺς ἀπολογησομένους ταχὺ πρὸς αὐτὸν
ἔπεμπεν. ὁ δὲ συνθέσθαι μὲν εἰρήνην καὶ φιλίαν
πρὸς τοιοῦτον ἄνδρα Θηβαίοις οὐχ ὑπέμεινε,
σπεισάμενος δὲ τριακονθημέρους ἀνοχὰς τοῦ
πολέμου καὶ λαβὼν τὸν Πελοπίδαν καὶ τὸν
Ἰσμηνίαν ἀνεχώρησεν.

XXX. Οἱ δὲ Θηβαῖοι παρὰ τῶν Λακεδαιμονίων
καὶ τῶν Ἀθηναίων αἰσθόμενοι πρὸς τὸν μέγαν
βασιλέα πρέσβεις ἀναβαίνοντας ὑπὲρ συμμαχίας,
ἔπεμψαν καὶ αὐτοὶ Πελοπίδαν, ἄριστα βουλευ-
σάμενοι πρὸς τὴν δόξαν αὐτοῦ. πρῶτον μὲν
γὰρ ἀνέβαινε διὰ τῶν βασιλέως ἐπαρχιῶν ὀνο-
μαστὸς ὢν καὶ περιβόητος· οὐ γὰρ ἠρέμα διῖκτο
τῆς Ἀσίας οὐδ' ἐπὶ μικρὸν ἡ δόξα τῶν πρὸς
2 Λακεδαιμονίους ἀγώνων, ἀλλ', ὡς πρῶτος περὶ
τῆς ἐν Λεύκτροις μάχης ἐξέδραμε λόγος, ἀεί τινος
καινοῦ προστιθεμένου κατορθώματος αὐξανομένη

as to a god, giving it the name of Tycho.[1] Once
when he was seeing a tragedian act the "Trojan
Women" of Euripides, he left the theatre abruptly,
and sent a message to the actor bidding him be of
good courage and not put forth any less effort because of his departure, for it was not out of contempt
for his acting that he had gone away, but because he
was ashamed to have the citizens see him, who had
never taken pity on any man that he had murdered,
weeping over the sorrows of Hecuba and Andro-
mache. It was this tyrant, however, who, terrified
at the name and fame and distinction of the
generalship of Epaminondas,

"Crouched down, though warrior bird, like slave,
    with drooping wings," [2]

and speedily sent a deputation to him which should
explain his conduct. But Epaminondas could not
consent that the Thebans should make peace and
friendship with such a man ; he did, however, make
a thirty days' truce with him, and after receiving
Pelopidas and Ismenias, returned home.

XXX. Now, when the Thebans learned that ambassadors from Sparta and Athens were on their way
to the Great King to secure an alliance, they also
sent Pelopidas thither ; and this was a most excellent plan, in view of his reputation. For, in the
first place, he went up through the provinces of the
king as a man of name and note ; for the glory of
his conflicts with the Lacedaemonians had not made
its way slowly or to any slight extent through Asia,
but, when once the report of the battle at Leuctra
had sped abroad, it was ever increased by the addition

---

[1] That is, *Luck*.
[2] An iambic trimeter of unknown authorship ; cf. the
Alcibiades, iv. 3.

καὶ ἀναβαίνουσα πορρωτάτω κατέσχεν· ἔπειτα
τοῖς ἐπὶ θύραις σατράπαις καὶ στρατηγοῖς καὶ
ἡγεμόσιν ὀφθεὶς θαῦμα καὶ λόγον παρέσχεν, ὡς
οὗτος ἀνήρ ἐστιν ὁ γῆς καὶ θαλάττης ἐκβαλὼν
Λακεδαιμονίους καὶ συστείλας ὑπὸ Ταΰγετον καὶ
τὸν Εὐρώταν τὴν Σπάρτην τὴν ὀλίγον ἔμπροσθεν
βασιλεῖ τῷ μεγάλῳ καὶ Πέρσαις δι' Ἀγησιλάου
τὸν περὶ Σούσων καὶ Ἐκβατάνων ἐπαραμένην
3 πόλεμον. ταῦτ' οὖν ὁ Ἀρταξέρξης ἔχαιρε, καὶ
τὸν Πελοπίδαν ἐθαύμαζε ἐπὶ τῇ δόξῃ[1] καὶ μέγαν
ἐποίει ταῖς τιμαῖς, ὑπὸ τῶν μεγίστων εὐδαιμο-
νίζεσθαι καὶ θεραπεύεσθαι βουλόμενος δοκεῖν.
ἐπεὶ δὲ καὶ τὴν ὄψιν αὐτοῦ εἶδε καὶ τοὺς λόγους
κατενόησε, τῶν μὲν Ἀττικῶν βεβαιοτέρους, τῶν
4 δὲ Λακεδαιμονίων ἁπλουστέρους ὄντας, ἔτι μᾶλλον ἠγάπησε, καὶ πάθος βασιλικὸν παθὼν οὐκ
ἀπεκρύψατο τὴν πρὸς τὸν ἄνδρα τιμήν, οὐδ'
ἔλαθε τοὺς ἄλλους πρέσβεις πλεῖστον νέμων
ἐκείνῳ. καίτοι δοκεῖ μάλιστα τῶν Ἑλλήνων
Ἀνταλκίδαν τιμῆσαι τὸν Λακεδαιμόνιον, ὅτι τὸν
στέφανον, ὃν πίνων περιέκειτο, βάψας εἰς μύρον
5 ἀπέστειλε. Πελοπίδᾳ δὲ οὕτω μὲν οὐκ ἐνετρύ-
φησε, δῶρα δὲ λαμπρότατα καὶ μέγιστα τῶν
νομιζομένων ἐξέπεμψε καὶ τὰς ἀξιώσεις ἐπε-
κύρωσεν, αὐτονόμους μὲν εἶναι τοὺς Ἕλληνας,
οἰκεῖσθαι δὲ Μεσσήνην, Θηβαίους δὲ πατρικοὺς
φίλους νομίζεσθαι βασιλέως.

Ταύτας ἔχων τὰς ἀποκρίσεις, τῶν δὲ δώρων
οὐδὲν ὅ τι μὴ χάριτος ἦν σύμβολον καὶ φιλο-

---

[1] ἐπὶ τῇ δόξῃ Bekker, after Coraës : τῇ δόξῃ.

of some new success, and prevailed to the farthest
recesses of the interior; and, in the second place,
when the satraps and generals and commanders at
the King's court beheld him, they spoke of him with
wonder, saying that this was the man who had expelled the Lacedaemonians from land and sea, and
shut up between Taÿgetus and the Eurotas that
Sparta which, a little while before, through Agesilaüs,
had undertaken a war with the Great King and the
Persians for the possession of Susa and Ecbatana.
This pleased Artaxerxes, of course, and he admired
Pelopidas for his high reputation, and loaded him
with honours, being desirous to appear lauded and
courted by the greatest men. But when he saw him
face to face, and understood his proposals, which
were more trustworthy than those of the Athenians,
and simpler than those of the Lacedaemonians, he
was yet more delighted with him, and, with all the
assurance of a king, openly showed the esteem in
which he held him, and allowed the other ambassadors to see that he made most account of him. And
yet he is thought to have shown Antalcidas the
Lacedaemonian more honour than any other Greek,
in that he took the chaplet which he had worn at a
banquet, dipped it in perfume, and sent it to him.
To Pelopidas, indeed, he paid no such delicate com-
pliment, but he sent him the greatest and most
splendid of the customary gifts, and granted him his
demands, namely, that the Greeks should be independent, Messene[1] inhabited, and the Thebans
regarded as the king's hereditary friends.

   With these answers, but without accepting any
gifts except such as were mere tokens of kindness

   [1] Messene was the new capital of Messenia, founded on
the slopes of Mt. Ithome (cf. chapter xxiv. 5) by Epaminondas,
in 369 B.C.

417

φροσύνης δεξάμενος, ἀνέζευξεν· ὃ καὶ μάλιστα
6 τοὺς ἄλλους πρέσβεις διέβαλε. Τιμαγόραν γοῦν
Ἀθηναῖοι κρίναντες ἀπέκτειναν, εἰ μὲν ἐπὶ τῷ
πλήθει τῶν δωρεῶν, ὀρθῶς καὶ δικαίως· οὐ γὰρ
μόνον χρυσίον οὐδὲ ἀργύριον ἔλαβεν, ἀλλὰ καὶ
κλίνην πολυτελῆ καὶ στρῶτας θεράποντας, ὡς
τῶν Ἑλλήνων οὐκ ἐπισταμένων, ἔτι δὲ βοῦς
ὀγδοήκοντα καὶ βουκόλους, ὡς δὴ πρὸς ἀρρωστίαν
τινὰ γάλακτος βοείου δεόμενος, τέλος δὲ κατέβαινεν ἐπὶ θάλασσαν ἐν φορείῳ κομιζόμενος, καὶ
τέσσαρα τάλαντα τοῖς κομίζουσι μισθὸς ἐδόθη
παρὰ βασιλέως· ἀλλ' ἔοικεν οὐχ ἡ δωροδοκία
7 μάλιστα παροξῦναι τοὺς Ἀθηναίους. Ἐπικρά-
τους γοῦν ποτε τοῦ σακεσφόρου μήτε ἀρνουμένου
δῶρα δέξασθαι παρὰ βασιλέως, ψήφισμά τε
γράφειν φάσκοντος ἀντὶ τῶν ἐννέα ἀρχόντων
χειροτονεῖσθαι κατ' ἐνιαυτὸν ἐννέα πρέσβεις πρὸς
βασιλέα τῶν δημοτικῶν καὶ πενήτων, ὅπως λαμβάνοντες εὐπορῶσιν, ἐγέλασεν ὁ δῆμος· ἀλλ' ὅτι
Θηβαίοις ἐγεγόνει πάντα χαλεπῶς ἔφερον, οὐ
λογιζόμενοι τὴν Πελοπίδου δόξαν, ὅσων ἦν ῥη-
τορειῶν καὶ λόγων κρείττων παρ' ἀνθρώπῳ θερα-
πεύοντι τοὺς τῶν ὅπλων ἀεὶ κρατοῦντας.

XXXI. Ἡ μὲν οὖν πρεσβεία τῷ Πελοπίδᾳ
προσέθηκεν οὐ μικρὰν εὔνοιαν ἐπανελθόντι, διὰ
τὸν Μεσσήνης συνοικισμὸν καὶ τὴν τῶν ἄλλων
Ἑλλήνων αὐτονομίαν· Ἀλεξάνδρου δὲ τοῦ Φεραίου
πάλιν εἰς τὴν αὐτοῦ φύσιν ἀναδραμόντος καὶ
Θεσσαλῶν μὲν οὐκ ὀλίγας περικόπτοντος πόλεις,
Φθιώτας δὲ Ἀχαιοὺς ἅπαντας καὶ τὸ Μαγνή-

and goodwill, he set out for home; and this conduct
of his, more than anything else, was the undoing of
the other ambassadors. Timagoras, at any rate, was
condemned and executed by the Athenians, and it
this was because of the multitude of gifts which he
took, it was right and just; for he took not only gold
and silver, but also an expensive couch and slaves to
spread it, since, as he said, the Greeks did not know
how; and besides, eighty cows with their cow-herds,
since, as he said, he wanted cows' milk for some
ailment; and, finally, he was carried down to the sea
in a litter, and had a present of four talents from the
King with which to pay his carriers. But it was not
his taking of gifts, as it would seem, that most
exasperated the Athenians. At any rate, Epicrates,
his shield-bearer, once confessed that he had received
gifts from the King, and talked of proposing a decree
that instead of nine archons, nine ambassadors to the
King should be elected annually from the poor and
needy citizens, in order that they might take his
gifts and be wealthy men, whereat the people only
laughed. But they were incensed because the Thebans had things all their own way, not stopping to
consider that the fame of Pelopidas was more potent
than any number of rhetorical discourses with a man
who ever paid deference to those who were mighty
in arms.

XXXI. This embassy, then, added not a little to
the goodwill felt towards Pelopidas, on his return
home, because of the peopling of Messene and the
independence of the other Greeks. But Alexander
of Pherae had now resumed his old nature and was
destroying not a few Thessalian cities; he had also
put garrisons over the Achaeans of Phthiotis and the

τῶν ἔθνος ἔμφρουρον πεποιημένου, πυνθανόμεναι
Πελοπίδαν ἐπανήκειν αἱ πόλεις εὐθὺς ἐπρέσβευον
εἰς Θήβας αἰτούμεναι δύναμιν καὶ στρατηγὸν
2 ἐκεῖνον. ψηφισαμένων δὲ τῶν Θηβαίων προθύμως, καὶ ταχὺ πάντων ἑτοίμων γενομένων καὶ
τοῦ στρατηγοῦ περὶ ἔξοδον ὄντος, ὁ μὲν ἥλιος
ἐξέλιπε καὶ σκότος ἐν ἡμέρᾳ τὴν πόλιν ἔσχεν,
ὁ δὲ Πελοπίδας ὁρῶν πρὸς τὸ φάσμα συντε-
ταραγμένους ἅπαντας οὐκ ᾤετο δεῖν βιάζεσθαι
καταφόβους καὶ δυσέλπιδας ὄντας, οὐδὲ ἀποκιν-
3 δυνεύειν ἑπτακισχιλίοις πολίταις, ἀλλ' ἑαυτὸν
μόνον τοῖς Θεσσαλοῖς ἐπιδοὺς καὶ τριακοσίους
τῶν ἱππέων ἐθελοντὰς ἀναλαβὼν καὶ ξένους
ἐξώρμησεν, οὔτε τῶν μάντεων ἐώντων οὔτε τῶν
ἄλλων συμπροθυμουμένων πολιτῶν· μέγα γὰρ
ἐδόκει καὶ πρὸς ἄνδρα λαμπρὸν ἐξ οὐρανοῦ γεγονέναι σημεῖον. ὁ δὲ ἦν μὲν καὶ δι' ὀργὴν ὧν
καθύβριστο θερμότερος ἐπὶ τὸν Ἀλέξανδρον, ἤλπιζε δὲ καὶ τὴν οἰκίαν αὐτοῦ νοσοῦσαν ἤδη καὶ
διεφθαρμένην εὑρήσειν ἐξ ὧν διείλεκτο τῇ Θήβῃ.
4 μάλιστα δ' αὐτὸν καὶ παρεκάλει τὸ τῆς πράξεως
κάλλος, ἐπιθυμοῦντα καὶ φιλοτιμούμενον, ἐν οἷς
χρόνοις Λακεδαιμόνιοι Διονυσίῳ τῷ Σικελίας
τυράννῳ στρατηγοὺς καὶ ἁρμοστὰς ἔπεμπον,
Ἀθηναῖοι δὲ μισθοδότην Ἀλέξανδρον εἶχον καὶ
χαλκοῦν ἵστασαν ὡς εὐεργέτην, τότε τοῖς Ἕλλησιν ἐπιδεῖξαι Θηβαίους μόνους ὑπὲρ τῶν τυραν-
νουμένων στρατευομένους καὶ καταλύοντας ἐν
τοῖς Ἕλλησι τὰς παρανόμους καὶ βιαίους δυναστείας.

people of Magnesia. When, therefore, the cities
learned that Pelopidas was returned, they at once
sent ambassadors to Thebes requesting an armed
force and him for its commander. The Thebans
readily decreed what they desired, and soon everything was in readiness and the commander about to
set out, when the sun was eclipsed and the city was
covered with darkness in the day-time.[1] So Pelopidas, seeing that all were confounded at this
manifestation, did not think it meet to use compulsion with men who were apprehensive and fearful,
nor to run extreme hazard with seven thousand
citizens, but devoting himself alone to the Thessalians, and taking with him three hundred of the
cavalry who were foreigners and who volunteered for
the service, set out, although the seers forbade it,
and the rest of the citizens disapproved; for the
eclipse was thought to be a great sign from heaven,
and to regard a conspicuous man. But his wrath at
insults received made him very hot against Alexander, and, besides, his previous conversations with
Thebe[2] led him to hope that he should find the
tyrant's family already embroiled and disrupted.
More than anything else, however, the glory of the
achievement invited him on, for he was ardently
desirous, at a time when the Lacedaemonians were
sending generals and governors to aid Dionysius the
tyrant of Sicily, and the Athenians were taking
Alexander's pay and erecting a bronze statue of him
as their benefactor, to show the Greeks that the
Thebans alone were making expeditions for the relief
of those whom tyrants oppressed, and were over-
throwing in Greece those ruling houses which rested
on violence and were contrary to the laws.

[1] July 13, 364 B.C.　　[2] Cf. chapter xxviii. 3 ff.

XXXII. Ὡς οὖν εἰς Φάρσαλον ἐλθὼν ἤθροισε
τὴν δύναμιν, εὐθὺς ἐβάδιζεν ἐπὶ τὸν Ἀλέξανδρον.
ὁ δὲ Θηβαίους μὲν ὀλίγους περὶ τὸν Πελοπίδαν
ὁρῶν, αὐτὸς δὲ πλείους ἔχων ἢ διπλασίους ὁπλίτας τῶν Θεσσαλῶν ἀπήντα πρὸς τὸ Θετίδειον.
εἰπόντος δέ τινος τῷ Πελοπίδᾳ πολλοὺς ἔχοντα τὸν τύραννον ἐπέρχεσθαι, "Βέλτιον," ἔφη,
"πλείονας γὰρ νικήσομεν."

2   Ἀνατεινόντων δὲ πρὸς τὸ μέσον κατὰ τὰς
καλουμένας Κυνὸς κεφαλὰς λόφων περικλινῶν
καὶ ὑψηλῶν, ὥρμησαν ἀμφότεροι τούτους καταλαβεῖν τοῖς πεζοῖς. τοὺς δ᾽ ἱππεῖς ὁ Πελοπίδας
πολλοὺς κἀγαθοὺς ὄντας ἐφῆκε τοῖς ἱππεῦσι τῶν
πολεμίων. ὡς δὲ οὗτοι μὲν ἐκράτουν καὶ συνεξ-
έπεσον εἰς τὸ πεδίον τοῖς φεύγουσιν, ὁ δὲ Ἀλέξ-
3   ανδρος ἔφθη τοὺς λόφους καταλαβών, τοῖς ὁπλίταις τῶν Θεσσαλῶν ὕστερον ἐπερχομένοις καὶ
πρὸς ἰσχυρὰ καὶ μετέωρα χωρία βιαζομένοις
ἐμβαλὼν ἔκτεινε τοὺς πρώτους, οἱ δὲ ἄλλοι πληγὰς λαβόντες οὐδὲν ἔπρασσον. κατιδὼν οὖν ὁ
Πελοπίδας τοὺς μὲν ἱππεῖς ἀνεκαλεῖτο καὶ πρὸς
τὸ συνεστηκὸς τῶν πολεμίων ἐλαύνειν ἐκέλευεν,
αὐτὸς δὲ συνέμιξε δρόμῳ τοῖς περὶ τοὺς λόφους
4   μαχομένοις εὐθὺς τὴν ἀσπίδα λαβών. καὶ διὰ
τῶν ὄπισθεν ὠσάμενος εἰς τοὺς πρώτους τοσαύτην ἐνεποίησε ῥώμην καὶ προθυμίαν ἅπασιν ὥστε
καὶ τοῖς πολεμίοις ἑτέρους δοκεῖν γεγονότας καὶ
σώμασι καὶ ψυχαῖς ἐπέρχεσθαι. καὶ δύο μὲν ἢ
τρεῖς ἀπεκρούσαντο προσβολάς, ὁρῶντες δὲ καὶ
τούτους ἐπιβαίνοντας εὐρώστως καὶ τὴν ἵππον
ἀπὸ τῆς διώξεως ἀναστρέφουσαν εἶξαν, ἐπὶ σκέλος
5   ποιούμενοι τὴν ἀναχώρησιν. ὁ δὲ Πελοπίδας

XXXII. Accordingly, when he was come to Pharsalus, he assembled his forces and marched at once against Alexander. Alexander, also, seeing that there were only a few Thebans with Pelopidas, while his own men-at-arms were more than twice as many as the Thessalians, advanced as far as the temple of Thetis to meet him. When Pelopidas was told that the tyrant was coming up against him with a large force, "All the better," he said, "for there will be more for us to conquer."

At the place called Cynoscephalae, steep and lofty hills jut out into the midst of the plain, and both leaders set out to occupy these with their infantry. His horsemen, however, who were numerous and brave, Pelopidas sent against the horsemen of the enemy, and they prevailed over them and chased them out into the plain. But Alexander got possession of the hills first, and when the Thessalian men-at-arms came up later and tried to storm difficult and lofty places, he attacked and killed the foremost of them, and the rest were so harassed with missiles that they could accomplish nothing. Accordingly, when Pelopidas saw this, he called back his horsemen and ordered them to charge upon the enemy's infantry where it still held together, while he himself seized his shield at once and ran to join those who were fighting on the hills. Through the rear ranks he forced his way to the front, and filled all his men with such vigour and ardour that the enemy also thought them changed men, advancing to the attack with other bodies and spirits. Two or three of their onsets the enemy repulsed, but, seeing that these too were now attacking with vigour, and that the cavalry was coming back from its pursuit, they gave way and retreated step by step. Then Pelo-

ἀπὸ τῶν ἄκρων κατιδὼν ἅπαν τὸ στρατόπεδον
τῶν πολεμίων οὔπω μὲν εἰς φυγὴν τετραμμένον,
ἤδη δὲ θορύβου καὶ ταραχῆς ἀναπιμπλάμενον,
ἔστη καὶ περιέβλεψεν αὐτόν[1] ζητῶν τὸν Ἀλέξανδρον. ὡς δ' εἶδεν ἐπὶ τοῦ δεξιοῦ παραθαρρύ- 2
νοντα καὶ συντάττοντα τοὺς μισθοφόρους, οὐ
6 κατέσχε τῷ λογισμῷ τὴν ὀργήν, ἀλλὰ πρὸς τὴν
βλέψιν ἀναφλεχθεὶς καὶ τῷ θυμῷ παραδοὺς τὸ
σῶμα καὶ τὴν ἡγεμονίαν τῆς πράξεως, πολὺ πρὸ
τῶν ἄλλων ἐξαλόμενος ἐφέρετο βοῶν καὶ προκαλούμενος τὸν τύραννον. ἐκεῖνος μὲν οὖν οὐκ
ἐδέξατο τὴν ὁρμὴν οὐδὲ ὑπέμεινεν, ἀλλ' ἀναφυγὼν
πρὸς τοὺς δοφυφόρους ἐνέκρυψεν ἑαυτόν. τῶν
δὲ μισθοφόρων οἱ μὲν πρῶτοι συμβαλόντες εἰς
χεῖρας ἀνεκόπησαν ὑπὸ τοῦ Πελοπίδου, τινὲς δὲ
7 καὶ πληγέντες ἐτελεύτησαν, οἱ δὲ πολλοὶ τοῖς
δόρασι πόρρωθεν διὰ τῶν ὅπλων τύπτοντες αὐτὸν
κατετραυμάτιζον, ἕως οἱ Θεσσαλοὶ περιπαθή-
σαντες ἀπὸ τῶν λόφων δρόμῳ προσεβοήθησαν,
ἤδη πεπτωκότος, οἵ τε ἱππεῖς προσελάσαντες
ὅλην ἐτρέψαντο τὴν φάλαγγα καὶ διώξαντες ἐπὶ
πλεῖστον ἐνέπλησαν νεκρῶν τὴν χώραν, πλέον ἢ
τρισχιλίους καταβαλόντες.

XXXIII. Τὸ μὲν οὖν Θηβαίων τοὺς παρόντας
ἐπὶ τῇ τοῦ Πελοπίδου τελευτῇ βαρέως φέρειν,
πατέρα καὶ σωτῆρα καὶ διδάσκαλον τῶν μεγίστων
καὶ καλλίστων ἀγαθῶν ἀποκαλοῦντας ἐκεῖνον,
οὐ πάνυ θαυμαστὸν ἦν· οἱ δὲ Θεσσαλοὶ καὶ οἱ
σύμμαχοι πᾶσαν ἀνθρωπίνῃ πρέπουσαν ἀρετῇ
τιμὴν τοῖς ψηφίσμασιν ὑπερβαλόντες, ἔτι μᾶλ-

---

[1] περιέβλεψεν αὐτὸν Sintenis' correction of the MSS. περιέ-
στησεν αὐτόν ; Bekker, after Coraës and Amyot, corrects to
περιεσκόπησεν αὐτόν.

pidas, looking down from the heights and seeing that the whole army of the enemy, though not yet put to flight, was already becoming full of tumult and confusion, stood and looked about him in search of Alexander. And when he saw him on the right wing, marshalling and encouraging his mercenaries, he could not subject his anger to his judgement, but, inflamed at the sight, and surrendering himself and his conduct of the enterprise to his passion, he sprang out far in front of the rest and rushed with challenging cries upon the tyrant. He, however, did not receive nor await the onset, but fled back to his guards and hid himself among them. The foremost of the mercenaries, coming to close quarters with Pelopidas, were beaten back by him; some also were smitten and slain; but most of them fought at longer range, thrusting their spears through his armour and covering him with wounds, until the Thessalians, in distress for his safety, ran down from the hills, when he had already fallen, and the cavalry, charging up, routed the entire phalanx of the enemy, and, following on a great distance in pursuit, filled the country with their dead bodies, slaying more than three thousand of them.

XXXIII. Now, that the Thebans who were present at the death of Pelopidas should be disconsolate, calling him their father and saviour and teacher of the greatest and fairest blessings, was not so much to be wondered at; but the Thessalians and allies also, after exceeding in their decrees every honour that can fitly be paid to human excellence, showed

λον ἐπεδείξαντο τοῖς πάθεσι τὴν πρὸς τὸν ἄνδρα
2 χάριν. τοὺς μὲν γὰρ παραγεγονότας τῷ ἔργῳ
λέγουσι μήτε θώρακα θέσθαι μήτε ἵππον ἐκχαλι-
νῶσαι μήτε τραῦμα δήσασθαι πρότερον, ὡς
ἐπύθοντο τὴν ἐκείνου τελευτήν, ἀλλὰ μετὰ τῶν
ὅπλων θερμοὺς ἰόντας ἐπὶ τὸν νεκρὸν ὥσπερ
αἰσθανόμενον, τὰ τῶν πολεμίων κύκλῳ περὶ τὸ
σῶμα σωρεύειν λάφυρα, κεῖραι δὲ ἵππους, κεί-
3 ρασθαι δὲ καὶ αὐτούς, ἀπιόντας δὲ πολλοὺς ἐπὶ
σκηνὰς μήτε πῦρ ἀνάψαι μήτε δεῖπνον ἑλέσθαι,
σιγὴν δὲ καὶ κατήφειαν εἶναι τοῦ στρατοπέδου
παντός, ὥσπερ οὐ νενικηκότων ἐπιφανεστάτην
νίκην καὶ μεγίστην, ἀλλ' ἡττημένων ὑπὸ τοῦ
4 τυράννου καὶ καταδεδουλωμένων. ἐκ δὲ τῶν
πόλεων, ὡς ἀπηγγέλθη ταῦτα, παρῆσαν αἵ τε
ἀρχαὶ καὶ μετ' αὐτῶν ἔφηβοι καὶ παῖδες καὶ ἱερεῖς
πρὸς τὴν ὑποδοχὴν τοῦ σώματος, τρόπαια καὶ
στεφάνους καὶ πανοπλίας χρυσᾶς ἐπιφέροντες.
ὡς δὲ ἔμελλεν ἐκκομίζεσθαι τὸ σῶμα, προσελθόντες οἱ πρεσβύτατοι τῶν Θεσσαλῶν ᾐτοῦντο
τοὺς Θηβαίους δι' αὐτῶν θάψαι τὸν νεκρόν. εἷς
δὲ αὐτῶν ἔλεγεν· "Ἄνδρες σύμμαχοι, χάριν
αἰτοῦμεν παρ' ὑμῶν κόσμον ἡμῖν ἐπὶ ἀτυχίᾳ
5 τοσαύτῃ καὶ παραμυθίαν φέρουσαν. οὐ γὰρ
ζῶντα Θεσσαλοὶ Πελοπίδαν προπέμψουσιν, οὐδὲ
αἰσθανομένῳ τὰς ἀξίας τιμὰς ἀποδώσουσιν, ἀλλ'
ἐὰν ψαῦσαί τε τοῦ νεκροῦ τύχωμεν καὶ δι' αὐτῶν
κοσμῆσαι καὶ θάψαι τὸ σῶμα, δόξομεν ὑμῖν οὐκ
ἀπιστεῖν ὅτι μείζων ἡ συμφορὰ γέγονε Θετταλοῖς
ἢ Θηβαίοις· ὑμῖν μὲν γὰρ ἡγεμόνος ἀγαθοῦ
μόνον, ἡμῖν δὲ καὶ τούτου καὶ τῆς ἐλευθερίας
στέρεσθαι συμβέβηκε. πῶς γὰρ ἔτι τολμήσομεν

still more by their grief how grateful they were to him. For it is said that those who were in the action neither took off their breastplates nor unbridled their horses nor bound up their wounds, when they learned of his death, but, still heated and in full armour, came first to the body, and as if it still had life and sense, heaped round it the spoils of the enemy, sheared their horses' manes, and cut off their own hair; and when they had gone to their tents, many neither kindled a fire nor took supper, but silence and dejection reigned through all the camp, as if they had not won a great and most brilliant victory, but had been defeated by the tyrant and made his slaves. From the cities, too, when tidings of these things reached them, came the magistrates, accompanied by youths and boys and priests, to take up the body, and they brought trophies and wreaths and suits of golden armour. And when the body was to be carried forth for burial, the most reverend of the Thessalians came and begged the Thebans for the privilege of giving it burial themselves. And one of them said: "Friends and allies, we ask of you a favour which will be an honour to us in our great misfortune, and will give us consolation. We men of Thessaly can never again escort a living Pelopidas on his way, nor pay him worthy honours of which he can be sensible; but if we may be permitted to compose and adorn his body with our own hands and give it burial, you will believe, we are persuaded, that this calamity is a greater one for Thessaly than for Thebes. For you have lost only a good commander; but we both that and freedom. For how shall we

αἰτῆσαι στρατηγὸν ἄλλον παρ' ὑμῶν οὐκ ἀπο-
δόντες Πελοπίδαν;" ταῦτα μὲν οἱ Θηβαῖοι συνε-
χώρησαν.

XXXIV. Ἐκείνων δὲ τῶν ταφῶν οὐ δοκοῦσιν
ἕτεραι λαμπρότεραι γενέσθαι τοῖς τὸ λαμπρὸν
οὐκ ἐν ἐλέφαντι καὶ χρυσῷ καὶ πορφύραις εἶναι
νομίζουσιν, ὥσπερ Φίλιστος ὑμνῶν καὶ θαυμάζων
τὴν Διονυσίου ταφήν, οἷον τραγῳδίας μεγάλης τῆς
2 τυραννίδος ἐξόδιον θεατρικὸν γενομένην. Ἀλέξανδρος δὲ ὁ μέγας Ἡφαιστίωνος ἀποθανόντος οὐ
μόνον ἵππους ἔκειρε καὶ ἡμιόνους, ἀλλὰ καὶ τὰς
ἐπάλξεις ἀφεῖλε τῶν τειχῶν, ὡς ἂν δοκοῖεν αἱ
πόλεις πενθεῖν, ἀντὶ τῆς πρόσθεν μορφῆς κούρι-
μον σχῆμα καὶ ἄτιμον ἀναλαμβάνουσαι. ταῦτα
μὲν οὖν προστάγματα δεσποτῶν ὄντα, καὶ μετὰ
πολλῆς ἀνάγκης περαινόμενα καὶ μετὰ φθόνου
τῶν τυχόντων καὶ μίσους τῶν βιαζομένων, οὐδεμιᾶς χάριτος ἦν οὐδὲ τιμῆς, ὄγκου δὲ βαρβαρικοῦ
καὶ τρυφῆς καὶ ἀλαζονείας ἐπίδειξις, εἰς κενὰ καὶ
3 ἄζηλα τὴν περιουσίαν διατιθεμένων· ἀνὴρ δὲ
δημοτικὸς ἐπὶ ξένης τεθνηκώς, οὐ γυναικός, οὐ
παίδων, οὐ συγγενῶν παρόντων, οὐ δεομένου
τινός, οὐκ ἀναγκάζοντος, ὑπὸ δήμων τοσούτων
καὶ πόλεων ἁμιλλωμένων προπεμπόμενος καὶ
συνεκκομιζόμενος καὶ στεφανούμενος, εἰκότως
ἐδόκει τὸν τελειότατον ἀπέχειν εὐδαιμονισμόν.
4 οὐ γάρ, ὡς Αἴσωπος ἔφασκε, χαλεπώτατός ἐστιν
ὁ τῶν εὐτυχούντων θάνατος, ἀλλὰ μακαριώτατος,
εἰς ἀσφαλῆ χώραν τὰς εὐπραξίας κατατιθέμενος
τῶν ἀγαθῶν καὶ τύχην μεταβάλλεσθαι μὴ ἀπολείπων. διὸ βέλτιον ὁ Λάκων τὸν Ὀλυμπιονίκην
Διαγόραν, ἐπιδόντα μὲν υἱοὺς στεφανουμένους

have the courage to ask another general from you, when we have not returned Pelopidas?" This request the Thebans granted.

XXXIV. Those funeral rites were never surpassed in splendour, in the opinion of those who do not think splendour to consist in ivory, gold, and purple, like Philistus, who tells in wondering strains about the funeral of Dionysius, which formed the pompous conclusion of the great tragedy of his tyranny. Alexander the Great, too, when Hephaestion died, not only sheared the manes of his horses and mules, but actually took away the battlements of the city-walls, in order that the cities might seem to be in mourning, assuming a shorn and dishevelled appearance instead of their former beauty. These honours, however, were dictated by despots, were performed under strong compulsion, and were attended with envy of those who received them and hatred of those who enforced them; they were a manifestation of no gratitude or esteem whatever, but of barbaric pomp and luxury and vain-glory, on the part of men who lavished their superfluous wealth on vain and sorry practices. But that a man who was a commoner, dying in a strange country, in the absence of wife, children, and kinsmen, none asking and none compelling it, should be escorted and carried forth and crowned by so many peoples and cities eager to show him honour, rightly seemed to argue him supremely fortunate. For the death of men in the hour of their triumph is not, as Aesop used to say, most grievous, but most blessed, since it puts in safe keeping their enjoyment of their blessings and leaves no room for change of fortune. Therefore the Spartan's advice was better, who, when he greeted Diagoras, the Olympian victor, who had lived to see

Ὀλυμπίασιν, ἐπιδόντα δ᾽ υἱωνοὺς καὶ θυγατρι-
δοῦς, ἀσπασάμενος, "Κάτθανε," εἶπε, "Διαγόρα·
5 οὐκ εἰς τὸν Ὄλυμπον ἀναβήσῃ." τὰς δὲ Ὀλυμ-
πιακὰς καὶ Πυθικὰς νίκας οὐκ ἄν, οἶμαί, τις εἰς
τὸ αὐτὸ συνθεὶς ἁπάσας ἑνὶ τῶν Πελοπίδου
παραβαλεῖν ἀγώνων ἀξιώσειεν, οὓς πολλοὺς
ἀγωνισάμενος καὶ κατορθώσας, καὶ τοῦ βίου τὸ
πλεῖστον ἐν δόξῃ καὶ τιμῇ βιώσας, τέλος ἐν τῇ
τρισκαιδεκάτῃ βοιωταρχίᾳ, τυραννοκτονίᾳ μεμιγμένην ἀριστείαν ἀριστεύσας, ὑπὲρ τῆς τῶν Θεσσαλῶν ἐλευθερίας ἀπέθανεν.

XXXV. Ὁ δὲ θάνατος αὐτοῦ μεγάλα μὲν
ἐλύπησε τοὺς συμμάχους, μείζονα δὲ ὠφέλησε.
Θηβαῖοι γάρ, ὡς ἐπύθοντο τὴν τοῦ Πελοπίδου
τελευτήν, οὐδεμίαν ἀναβολὴν ποιησάμενοι τῆς
τιμωρίας κατὰ τάχος ἐστράτευσαν ὁπλίταις
ἑπτακισχιλίοις, ἱππεῦσι δ᾽ ἑπτακοσίοις, ἡγουμέ-
2 νου Μαλκίτου καὶ Διογείτονος. καταλαβόντες δὲ
συνεσταλμένον καὶ περικεκομμένον τῆς δυνάμεως
Ἀλέξανδρον ἠνάγκασαν Θεσσαλοῖς μὲν ἀποδοῦ-
ναι τὰς πόλεις ἃς εἶχεν αὐτῶν, Μάγνητας δὲ καὶ
Φθιώτας Ἀχαιοὺς ἀφεῖναι καὶ τὰς φρουρὰς
ἐξαγαγεῖν, ὀμόσαι δὲ αὐτὸν ἐφ᾽ οὓς ἂν ἡγῶνται Θηβαῖοι καὶ κελεύσωσιν ἀκολουθήσειν. Θηβαῖοι μὲν
οὖν τούτοις ἠρκέσθησαν· ἣν δὲ ὀλίγον ὕστερον τοῖς
θεοῖς ὑπὲρ Πελοπίδου δίκην ἔδωκε διηγήσομαι.

3 Θήβην τὴν συνοικοῦσαν αὐτῷ πρῶτον μέν, ὡς
εἴρηται, Πελοπίδας ἐδίδαξε μὴ φοβεῖσθαι τὴν
ἔξω λαμπρότητα καὶ παρασκευὴν τῆς τυραννίδος,
ἐντὸς τῶν ὅπλων καὶ τῶν φυλάκων οὖσαν· ἔπειτα
δὲ φοβουμένη τὴν ἀπιστίαν αὐτοῦ καὶ μισοῦσα
τὴν ὠμότητα, συνθεμένη μετὰ τῶν ἀδελφῶν,
τριῶν ὄντων, Τισιφόνου, Πυθολάου, Λυκόφρονος,

his sons crowned at Olympia, yes, and the sons of his sons and daughters, said; "Die now, Diagoras; thou canst not ascend to Olympus." But one would not deign, I think, to compare all the Olympian and Pythian victories put together with one of the struggles of Pelopidas; these were many, and he made them successfully, and after living most of his life in fame and honour, at last, while boeotarch for the thirteenth time, performing a deed of high valour which aimed at a tyrant's life, he died in defence of the freedom of Thessaly.

XXXV. The death of Pelopidas brought great grief to his allies, but even greater gain. For the Thebans, when they learned of it, delayed not their vengeance, but speedily made an expedition with seven thousand men-at-arms and seven hundred horsemen, under the command of Malcitas and Diogeiton. They found Alexander weakened and robbed of his forces, and compelled him to restore to the Thessalians the cities he had taken from them, to withdraw his garrisons and set free the Magnesians and the Achaeans of Phthiotis, and to take oath that he would follow the lead of the Thebans against any enemies according to their bidding. The Thebans, then, were satisfied with this; but the gods soon afterwards avenged Pelopidas, as I shall now relate.

To begin with, Thebe, the tyrant's wife, as I have said, had been taught by Pelopidas not to fear the outward splendour and array of Alexander, since these depended wholly on his armed guards; and now, in her dread of his faithlessness and her hatred of his cruelty, she conspired with her three brothers, Tisiphonus, Pytholaüs, and Lycophron, and made an

4 ἐπεχείρει τόνδε τὸν τρόπον. τὴν μὲν ἄλλην οἰκίαν
τοῦ τυράννου κατεῖχον αἱ φυλακαὶ τῶν παρανυ-
κτερευόντων, ὁ δὲ θάλαμος, ἐν ᾧ καθεύδειν εἰώθεσαν, ὑπερῷος ἦν, καὶ πρὸ αὐτοῦ φυλακὴν εἶχε
κύων δεδεμένος, πᾶσι φοβερὸς πλὴν αὐτοῖς ἐκείνοις καὶ ἑνὶ τῶν οἰκετῶν τῷ τρέφοντι. καθ᾽ ὃν
οὖν ἔμελλε καιρὸν ἐπιχειρεῖν ἡ Θήβη, τοὺς μὲν
ἀδελφοὺς ἀφ᾽ ἡμέρας εἶχε πλησίον ἐν οἴκῳ τινὶ
5 κεκρυμμένους, εἰσελθοῦσα δέ, ὥσπερ εἰώθει, μόνη
πρὸς τὸν Ἀλέξανδρον ἤδη καθεύδοντα καὶ μετὰ
μικρὸν πάλιν προελθοῦσα, τῷ μὲν οἰκέτῃ προσέ-
ταξεν ἀπάγειν ἔξω τὸν κύνα· βούλεσθαι γὰρ
ἀναπαύεσθαι μεθ᾽ ἡσυχίας ἐκεῖνον· αὐτὴ δὲ τὴν
κλίμακα φοβουμένη μὴ κτύπον παράσχῃ τῶν
νεανίσκων ἀναβαινόντων ἐρίοις κατεστόρεσεν·
6 εἶτα οὕτως ἀναγαγοῦσα τοὺς ἀδελφοὺς ξιφήρεις
καὶ στήσασα πρὸ τῶν θυρῶν εἰσῆλθεν αὐτή, καὶ
καθελοῦσα τὸ ξίφος ὑπὲρ τῆς κεφαλῆς κρεμάμε-
νον σημεῖον εἶναι τοῦ κατέχεσθαι τὸν ἄνδρα καὶ
καθεύδειν ἔδειξεν. ἐκπεπληγμένων δὲ τῶν νεανίσκων καὶ κατοκνούντων, κακίζουσα καὶ διομνυ-
μένη μετ᾽ ὀργῆς αὐτὴ τὸν Ἀλέξανδρον ἐξεγείρασα   2
μηνύσειν τὴν πρᾶξιν, αἰσχυνθέντας αὐτοὺς ἅμα καὶ
φοβηθέντας εἰσήγαγε καὶ περιέστησε τῇ κλίνῃ,
7 προσφέρουσα τὸν λύχνον. τῶν δὲ ὁ μὲν τοὺς πόδας
κατεῖχε πιέσας, ὁ δὲ τὴν κεφαλὴν λαβόμενος τῶν
τριχῶν ἀνέκλασεν, ὁ δὲ τρίτος τῷ ξίφει τύπτων
αὐτὸν διεχρήσατο, τῷ μὲν τάχει τῆς τελευτῆς
πρᾳότερον ἴσως ἢ προσῆκον ἦν ἀποθανόντα, τῷ
δὲ μόνον ἢ πρῶτον τυράννων ὑπὸ γυναικὸς ἰδίας
ἀπολέσθαι, καὶ τῇ μετὰ θάνατον αἰκίᾳ τοῦ σώματος ῥιφέντος καὶ πατηθέντος ὑπὸ τῶν Φεραίων,
ἄξια πεπονθέναι δόξαντα τῶν παρανομημάτων.

attempt upon his life, as follows. The rest of the tyrant's house was guarded by sentries at night, but the bed-chamber, where he and his wife were wont to sleep, was an upper room, and in front of it a chained dog kept guard, which would attack everyone except his master and mistress and the one servant who fed him. When, therefore, Thebe was about to make her attempt, she kept her brothers hidden all day in a room hard by, and at night, as she was wont, went in alone to Alexander. She found him already asleep, and after a little, coming out again, ordered the servant to take the dog outdoors, for his master wanted to sleep undisturbed; and to keep the stairs from creaking as the young men came up, she covered them with wool. Then, after bringing her brothers safely up, with their swords, and stationing them in front of the door, she went in herself, and taking down the sword that hung over her husband's head, showed it to them as a sign that he was fast asleep. Finding the young men terrified and reluctant, she upbraided them, and swore in a rage that she would wake Alexander herself and tell him of the plot, and so led them, ashamed and fearful too, inside, and placed them round the bed, to which she brought the lamp. Then one of them clutched the tyrant's feet and held them down, another dragged his head back by the hair, and the third ran him through with his sword. The swiftness of it made his death a milder one, perhaps, than was his due; but since he was the only, or the first, tyrant to die at the hands of his own wife, and since his body was outraged after death, being cast out and trodden under foot by the Pheraeans, he may be thought to have suffered what his lawless deeds deserved.

MARCELLUS

ΜΑΡΚΕΛΛΟΣ

I. Μάρκον δὲ Κλαύδιον τὸν πεντάκις ὑπατεύσαντα Ῥωμαίων Μάρκου μὲν υἱὸν γενέσθαι λέγουσι, κληθῆναι δὲ τῶν ἀπὸ τῆς οἰκίας πρῶτον Μάρκελλον, ὅπερ ἐστὶν Ἀρήϊον, ὥς φησι Ποσειδώνιος. ἦν γὰρ τῇ μὲν ἐμπειρίᾳ πολεμικός, τῷ δὲ σώματι ῥωμαλέος, τῇ δὲ χειρὶ πλήκτης, τῇ δὲ φύσει φιλοπόλεμος κἂν τούτῳ δὴ πολὺ τὸ γαῦρον 2 καὶ ἀγέρωχον ἐπιφαίνων ἐν τοῖς ἀγῶσι, τῷ δὲ ἄλλῳ τρόπῳ σώφρων, φιλάνθρωπος, Ἑλληνικῆς παιδείας καὶ λόγων ἄχρι τοῦ τιμᾶν καὶ θαυμάζειν τοὺς κατορθοῦντας ἐραστής, αὐτὸς δὲ ὑπ᾽ ἀσχολιῶν ἐφ᾽ ὅσον ἦν πρόθυμος ἀσκῆσαι καὶ μαθεῖν οὐκ ἐξικόμενος. εἰ γὰρ ἄλλοις τισὶν ἀνθρώποις ὁ θεός, ὥσπερ Ὅμηρος εἴρηκεν,

> ἐκ νεότητος ἔδωκε καὶ εἰς γῆρας τολυπεύειν
> ἀργαλέους πολέμους,

3 καὶ τοῖς τότε πρωτεύουσι Ῥωμαίων, οἳ νέοι μὲν ὄντες περὶ Σικελίαν Καρχηδονίοις, ἀκμάζοντες δὲ Γαλάταις ὑπὲρ αὐτῆς Ἰταλίας ἐπολέμουν, ἤδη δὲ γηρῶντες Ἀννίβᾳ πάλιν συνείχοντο καὶ Καρχηδονίοις, οὐκ ἔχοντες, ὥσπερ οἱ πολλοί, διὰ γῆρας ἀνάπαυσιν στρατειῶν, ἀλλ᾽ ἐπὶ στρατηγίας πολέμων καὶ ἡγεμονίας κατ᾽ εὐγένειαν καὶ ἀρετὴν ἀγόμενοι.

MARCELLUS

I. MARCU CLAUDIUS, who was five times consul of
the Romans, was a son of Marcus, as we are told,
and, according to Poseidonius, was the first of his
family to be called Marcellus, which means *Martial*.
For he was by experience a man of war, of a sturdy
body and a vigorous arm. He was naturally fond of
war, and in its conflicts displayed great impetuosity
and high temper; but otherwise he was modest,
humane, and so far a lover of Greek learning and
discipline as to honour and admire those who excelled
therein, although he himself was prevented by his
occupations from achieving a knowledge and pro-
ficiency here which corresponded to his desires. For
if ever there were men to whom Heaven, as Homer
says,[1]

" From youth and to old age appointed the accomplishment of laborious wars,"

they were the chief Romans of that time, who, in
their youth, waged war with the Carthaginians for
Sicily; in their prime, with the Gauls to save Italy
itself; and when they were now grown old, contended again with Hannibal and the Carthaginians,
and did not have, like most men, that respite from
service in the field which old age brings, but were
called by their high birth and valour to undertake
leaderships and commands in war.

[1] *Iliad*, xiv. 86 f.

II. Μάρκελλος δὲ πρὸς οὐδὲν μὲν ἦν μάχης
εἶδος ἀργὸς οὐδὲ ἀνάσκητος, αὐτὸς δ' ἑαυτοῦ
κράτιστος ἐν τῷ μονομαχεῖν γενόμενος οὐδεμίαν
πρόκλησιν ἔφυγε, πάντας δὲ τοὺς προκαλεσα-
μένους ἀπέκτεινεν. ἐν δὲ Σικελίᾳ τὸν ἀδελφὸν
Ὀτακίλιον κινδυνεύοντα διέσωσεν ὑπερασπίσας
2 καὶ ἀποκτείνας τοὺς ἐπιφερομένους. ἀνθ' ὧν
ὄντι μὲν ἔτι νέῳ στέφανοι καὶ γέρα παρὰ τῶν
στρατηγῶν ἦσαν, εὐδοκιμοῦντα δὲ μᾶλλον ἀγορα-
νόμον μὲν ἀπέδειξε τῆς ἐπιφανεστέρας τάξεως ὁ
δῆμος, οἱ δὲ ἱερεῖς αὔγουρα. τοῦτο δ' ἐστὶν ἱερω-
σύνης εἶδος, ᾧ μάλιστα τὴν ἀπ' οἰωνῶν μαντικὴν
ἐπιβλέπειν καὶ παραφυλάττειν νόμος δέδωκεν.

3   Ἠναγκάσθη δὲ ἀγορανομῶν δίκην ἀβούλητον
εἰσενεγκεῖν. ἦν γὰρ αὐτῷ παῖς ὁμώνυμος ἐν ὥρᾳ,
τὴν ὄψιν ἐκπρεπής, οὐχ ἧττον δὲ τῷ σωφρονεῖν
καὶ πεπαιδεῦσθαι περίβλεπτος ὑπὸ τῶν πολιτῶν·
τούτῳ Καπετωλῖνος ὁ τοῦ Μαρκέλλου συνάρχων,
ἀσελγὴς ἀνὴρ καὶ θρασύς, ἐρῶν λόγους προσή-
νεγκε. τοῦ δὲ παιδὸς τὸ μὲν πρῶτον αὐτοῦ καθ'
ἑαυτὸν ἀποτριψαμένου τὴν πεῖραν, ὡς δὲ αὖθις
ἐπεχείρησε κατειπόντος πρὸς τὸν πατέρα, βαρέως
ἐνεγκὼν ὁ Μάρκελλος προσήγγειλε τῇ βουλῇ τὸν
4 ἄνθρωπον. ὁ δὲ πολλὰς μὲν ἀποδράσεις καὶ   299
παραγραφὰς ἐμηχανᾶτο, τοὺς δημάρχους ἐπικα-
λούμενος, ἐκείνων δὲ μὴ προσδεχομένων τὴν
ἐπίκλησιν ἀρνήσει τὴν αἰτίαν ἔφευγε. καὶ μάρ-
τυρος οὐδενὸς τῶν λόγων γεγονότος ἔδοξε μετα-
πέμπεσθαι τὸν παῖδα τῇ βουλῇ. παραγενομένου
δ' ἰδόντες ἐρύθημα καὶ δάκρυον καὶ μεμιγμένον
ἀπαύστῳ[1] τῷ θυμουμένῳ τὸ αἰδούμενον, οὐδενὸς

---

[1] ἀπαύστῳ Bekker corrects to ἀπλάστῳ (*unfeigned*), after
Emperius.

II. Marcellus was efficient and practised in every kind of fighting, but in single combat he surpassed himself, never declining a challenge, and always killing his challengers. In Sicily he saved his brother Otacilius from peril of his life, covering him with his shield and killing those who were setting upon him. Wherefore, although he was still a youth, he received garlands and prizes from his commanders, and since he grew in repute, the people appointed him curule aedile,[1] and the priests, augur. This is a species of priesthood, to which the law particularly assigns the observation and study of prophetic signs from the flight of birds.

During his aedileship, he was compelled to bring a disagreeable impeachment into the senate. He had a son, named Marcus like himself, who was in the flower of his boyish beauty, and not less admired by his countrymen for his modesty and good training. To this boy Capitolinus, the colleague of Marcellus, a bold and licentious man, made overtures of love. The boy at first repelled the attempt by himself, but when it was made again, told his father. Marcellus, highly indignant, denounced the man in the senate. The culprit devised many exceptions and ways of escape, appealing to the tribunes of the people, and when these rejected his appeal, he sought to escape the charge by denying it. There had been no witness of his proposals, and therefore the senate decided to summon the boy before them. When he appeared, and they beheld his blushes, tears, and shame mingled

---

[1] Literally, *aedile of the more illustrious class, i.e.* patrician, in distinction from plebeian, aedile.

ἄλλου δεηθέντες τεκμηρίου κατεψηφίσαντο καὶ
χρήμασιν ἐζημίωσαν Καπετωλῖνον, ἐξ ὧν ὁ
Μάρκελλος ἀργυρᾶ λοιβεῖα ποιησάμενος τοῖς
θεοῖς καθιέρωσεν.

III. Ἐπεὶ δὲ τοῦ πρώτου τῶν Καρχηδονίων
πολέμων ἔτει δευτέρῳ καὶ εἰκοστῷ συναιρεθέντος
ἀρχαὶ πάλιν Γαλατικῶν ἀγώνων διεδέχοντο τὴν
Ῥώμην, οἱ δὲ τὴν ὑπαλπείαν νεμόμενοι τῆς
Ἰταλίας Ἴνσομβρες, Κελτικὸν ἔθνος, μεγάλοι καὶ
καθ᾽ ἑαυτοὺς ὄντες, δυνάμεις ἐκάλουν, καὶ μετεπέμποντο Γαλατῶν τοὺς μισθοῦ στρατευομένους,
2 οἳ Γαισάται καλοῦνται, θαυμαστὸν μὲν ἐδόκει καὶ
τύχης ἀγαθῆς γενέσθαι τὸ μὴ συρραγῆναι τὸν
Κελτικὸν εἰς τὸ αὐτὸ τῷ Λιβυκῷ πόλεμον, ἀλλ᾽
ὥσπερ ἐφεδρείαν εἰληφότας τοὺς Γαλάτας, ὀρθῶς
καὶ δικαίως ἀτρεμήσαντας μαχομένων ἐκείνων,
οὕτω τότε δὴ τοῖς νενικηκόσιν ἐπαποδύεσθαι καὶ
προκαλεῖσθαι σχολὴν ἄγοντας· οὐ μὴν ἀλλὰ
μέγαν ἥ τε χώρα παρεῖχε φόβον, διὰ τὴν γειτ-
νίασιν ὁμόρῳ καὶ προσοίκῳ πολέμῳ συνοισο-
μένοις, καὶ τὸ παλαιὸν ἀξίωμα τῶν Γαλατῶν,
οὓς μάλιστα Ῥωμαῖοι δεῖσαι δοκοῦσιν, ἅτε δὴ
3 καὶ τὴν πόλιν ὑπ᾽ αὐτῶν ἀποβαλόντες, ἐξ ἐκείνου
δὲ καὶ θέμενοι νόμον ἀτελεῖς εἶναι στρατείας τοὺς
ἱερέας, πλὴν εἰ μὴ Γαλατικὸς πάλιν ἐπέλθοι
πόλεμος. ἐδήλου δὲ καὶ τὸν φόβον αὐτῶν ἥ τε
παρασκευὴ (μυριάδες γὰρ ἐν ὅπλοις ἅμα τοσαῦ-
ται Ῥωμαίων οὔτε πρότερον οὔτε ὕστερον γενέσθαι λέγονται) καὶ τὰ περὶ τὰς θυσίας καινοτομού-

with quenchless indignation, they wanted no further proof, but condemned Capitolinus, and set a fine upon him. With this money Marcellus had silver libation-bowls made, and dedicated them to the gods.

III. After the first Punic war had come to an end in its twenty-second year, Rome was called upon to renew her struggles with the Gauls.[1] The Insubrians, a people of Celtic stock inhabiting that part of Italy which lies at the foot of the Alps, and strong even by themselves, called out their forces, and summoned to their aid the mercenary Gauls called Gaesatae. It seemed a marvellous piece of good fortune that the Gallic war did not break out while the Punic war was raging, but that the Gauls, like a third champion sitting by and awaiting his turn with the victor, remained strictly quiet while the other two nations were fighting, and then only stripped for combat when the victors were at liberty to receive their challenge. Nevertheless, the Romans were greatly alarmed by the proximity of their country to the enemy, with whom they would wage war so near their own boundaries and homes, as well as by the ancient renown of the Gauls, whom the Romans seem to have feared more than any other people. For Rome had once been taken by them,[2] and from that time on a Roman priest was legally exempt from military service only in case no Gallic war occurred again. Their alarm was also shown by their preparations for the war (neither before nor since that time, we are told, were there so many thousands of Romans in arms at once), and by the extraordinary sacrifices which they made to the gods. For though

[1] The First Punic War lasted from 265 B.C. till 241 B.C., and the Insubrians invaded Italy in 225 B.C.

[2] In 390 B.C. See the *Camillus*, xix.–xxiii.

4 μενα· βαρβαρικὸν μὲν γὰρ[1] οὐδὲν οὐδ' ἔκφυλον
ἐπιτηδεύοντες, ἀλλ' ὡς ἔνι μάλιστα ταῖς δόξαις
Ἑλληνικῶς διακείμενοι καὶ πρᾴως πρὸς τὰ θεῖα,
τότε τοῦ πολέμου συμπεσόντος ἠναγκάσθησαν
εἶξαι λογίοις τισὶν ἐκ τῶν Σιβυλλείων, καὶ δύο
μὲν Ἕλληνας, ἄνδρα καὶ γυναῖκα, δύο δὲ Γαλάτας ὁμοίως ἐν τῇ καλουμένῃ βοῶν ἀγορᾷ κατορύ-
ξαι ζῶντας, οἷς ἔτι καὶ νῦν ἐν τῷ Νοεμβρίῳ μηνὶ
δρῶσιν Ἕλλησι καὶ Γαλάταις ἀπορρήτους καὶ
ἀθεάτους ἱερουργίας.

IV. Οἱ μὲν οὖν πρῶτοι τῶν ἀγώνων νίκας τε
μεγάλας καὶ σφάλματα τοῖς Ῥωμαίοις ἐνέγκαντες
εἰς οὐδὲν ἐτελεύτησαν πέρας βέβαιον· Φλαμινίου
δὲ καὶ Φουρίου τῶν ὑπάτων μεγάλαις ἐκστρατευ-
σάντων δυνάμεσιν ἐπὶ τοὺς Ἴνσομβρας, ὤφθη μὲν
αἵματι ῥέων ὁ διὰ τῆς Πικηνίδος χώρας ποταμός,
ἐλέχθη δὲ τρεῖς σελήνας φανῆναι περὶ πόλιν
2 Ἀρίμινον, οἱ δὲ ἐπὶ ταῖς ὑπατικαῖς ψηφοφορίαις
παραφυλάττοντες οἰωνοὺς ἱερεῖς διεβεβαιοῦντο
μοχθηρὰς καὶ δυσόρνιθας αὐτοῖς γεγονέναι τὰς
τῶν ὑπάτων ἀναγορεύσεις. εὐθὺς οὖν ἔπεμψεν ἡ
σύγκλητος ἐπὶ τὸ στρατόπεδον γράμματα κα-
λοῦσα καὶ μεταπεμπομένη τοὺς ὑπάτους, ὅπως
ἐπανελθόντες ᾗ τάχιστα τὴν ἀρχὴν ἀπείπωνται
καὶ μηδὲν ὡς ὕπατοι φθάσωσι πρᾶξαι πρὸς τοὺς
3 πολεμίους. ταῦτα δεξάμενος τὰ γράμματα Φλα-
μίνιος οὐ πρότερον ἔλυσεν ἢ μάχῃ συνάψας τρέ-
ψασθαι τοὺς βαρβάρους καὶ τὴν χώραν αὐτῶν
ἐπιδραμεῖν. ὡς οὖν ἐπανῆλθε μετὰ πολλῶν λαφύρων, οὐκ ἀπήντησεν ὁ δῆμος, ἀλλ' ὅτι καλού-
μενος οὐκ εὐθὺς ὑπήκουσεν οὐδ' ἐπείσθη τοῖς
γράμμασιν, ἀλλ' ἐνύβρισε καὶ κατεφρόνησε,

[1] μὲν γὰρ Bekker, after Coraës : μέν,

they have no barbarous or unnatural practices, but cherish towards their deities those mild and reverent sentiments which especially characterize Greek thought, at the time when this war burst upon them they were constrained to obey certain oracular commands from the Sibylline books, and to bury alive two Greeks, a man and a woman, and likewise two Gauls, in the place called the "forum boarium," or cattle-market; and in memory of these victims, they still to this day, in the month of November, perform mysterious and secret ceremonies.

IV. The first conflicts of this war brought great victories and also great disasters to the Romans, and led to no sure and final conclusion; but at last Flaminius and Furius, the consuls, led forth large forces against the Insubrians. At the time of their departure, however, the river that flows through Picenum was seen to be running with blood, and it was reported that at Ariminum three moons had appeared in the heavens, and the priests who watched the flight of birds at the time of the consular elections insisted that when the consuls were proclaimed the omens were inauspicious and baleful for them. At once, therefore, the senate sent letters to the camp, summoning the consuls to return to the city with all speed and lay down their office, and forbidding them, while they were still consuls, to take any steps against the enemy. On receiving these letters, Flaminius would not open them before he had joined battle with the Barbarians, routed them, and overrun their country. Therefore, when he returned with much spoil, the people would not go out to meet him, but because he had not at once listened to his summons, and had disobeyed the letters, treating them with insolent contempt, they

μικροῦ μὲν ἐδέησεν ἀποψηφίσασθαι τὸν θρίαμβον
αὐτοῦ, θριαμβεύσαντα δὲ ἰδιώτην ἐποίησεν, ἀναγ-
κάσας ἐξομόσασθαι τὴν ὑπατείαν μετὰ τοῦ συν-
4 άρχοντος. οὕτω πάντα τὰ πράγματα Ῥωμαίοις
εἰς τὸν θεὸν ἀνήγετο, μαντειῶν δὲ καὶ πατρίων
ὑπεροψίαν οὐδ' ἐπὶ ταῖς μεγίσταις εὐπραξίαις
ἀπεδέχοντο, μεῖζον ἡγούμενοι πρὸς σωτηρίαν
πόλεως τὸ θαυμάζειν τὰ θεῖα τοὺς ἄρχοντας τοῦ
κρατεῖν τῶν πολεμίων.

V. Τιβέριος οὖν Σεμπρώνιος, ἀνὴρ δι' ἀνδρείαν
καὶ καλοκαγαθίαν οὐδενὸς ἧττον ἀγαπηθεὶς ὑπὸ
Ῥωμαίων, ἀπέδειξε μὲν ὑπατεύων διαδόχους Σκηπίωνα Νασικᾶν καὶ Γάιον Μάρκιον, ἤδη δὲ ἐχόντων αὐτῶν επαρχίας καὶ στρατεύματα, ἱερατικοῖς
ὑπομνήμασιν ἐντυχὼν εὗρεν ἠγνοημένον ὑφ' αὑτοῦ
2 τι τῶν πατρίων. ἦν δὲ τοιοῦτον· ὅταν ἄρχων
ἐπ' ὄρνισι καθεζόμενος ἔξω πόλεως οἶκον ἢ σκηνὴν μεμισθωμένος ὑπ' αἰτίας τινὸς ἀναγκασθῇ
μήπω γεγονότων σημείων βεβαίων ἐπανελθεῖν εἰς
πόλιν, ἀφεῖναι χρῆν τὸ προμεμισθωμένον οἴκημα
καὶ λαβεῖν ἕτερον, ἐξ οὗ ποιήσεται τὴν θέαν
αὖθις ἐξ ὑπαρχῆς. τοῦτο ἔλαθεν, ὡς ἔοικε, τὸν
Τιβέριον, καὶ δὶς τῷ αὐτῷ χρησάμενος ἀπέδειξε
τοὺς εἰρημένους ἄνδρας ὑπάτους. ὕστερον δὲ
γνοὺς τὴν ἁμαρτίαν ἀνήνεγκε πρὸς τὴν σύγκλητον.
3 ἡ δὲ οὐ κατεφρόνησε τοῦ κατὰ μικρὸν οὕτως
ἐλλείμματος, ἀλλ' ἔγραψε τοῖς ἀνδράσι· καὶ
ἐκεῖνοι τὰς ἐπαρχίας ἀπολιπόντες ἐπανῆλθον εἰς
Ῥώμην ταχὺ καὶ κατέθεντο τὴν ἀρχήν. ἀλλὰ
ταῦτα μὲν ὕστερον ἐπράχθη· περὶ δὲ τοὺς αὐτοὺς

came near refusing him his triumph, and after his
triumph, they compelled him to renounce the consulship with his colleague, and made him a private citizen.
To such a degree did the Romans make everything
depend upon the will of the gods, and so intolerant
were they of any neglect of omens and ancestral
rites, even when attended by the greatest successes,
considering it of more importance for the safety of
the city that their magistrates should reverence re-
ligion than that they should overcome their enemies.

V. For example, Tiberius Sempronius, a man most
highly esteemed by the Romans for his valour and
probity, proclaimed Scipio Nasica and Caius Marcius
his successors in the consulship, but when they had
already taken command in their provinces, he came
upon a book of religious observances wherein he
found a certain ancient prescript of which he had
been ignorant. It was this. Whenever a magistrate,
sitting in a hired house or tent outside the city to
take auspices from the flight of birds, is compelled
for any reason to return to the city before sure signs
have appeared, he must give up the house first hired
and take another, and from this he must take his
observations anew. Of this, it would seem, Tiberius
was not aware, and had twice used the same house
before proclaiming the men I have mentioned as
consuls. But afterwards, discovering his error, he
referred the matter to the senate. This body did
not make light of so trifling an omission, but wrote
to the consuls about it; and they, leaving their
provinces, came back to Rome with speed, and laid
down their offices. This, however, took place at a
later time.[1] But at about the time of which I am

---

[1] Tiberius Sempronius Gracchus, father of the two famous
tribunes, was consul for the second time in 163 B.C.

ἐκείνους χρόνους καὶ δύο ἱερεῖς ἐπιφανέστατοι τὰς
ἱερωσύνας ἀφῃρέθησαν, Κορνήλιος μὲν Κέθηγος
ὅτι τὰ σπλάγχνα τοῦ ἱερείου παρὰ τάξιν ἐπέδωκε,
4 Κούϊντος δὲ Σουλπίκιος ἐπὶ τῷ θύοντος αὐτοῦ
τὸν κορυφαῖον ἀπορρυῆναι τῆς κεφαλῆς πῖλον, ὃν
οἱ καλούμενοι Φλαμίνιοι φοροῦσι. Μινουκίου δὲ
δικτάτορος ἵππαρχον ἀποδείξαντος Γάϊον Φλαμίνιον, ἐπεὶ τρισμὸς ἠκούσθη μυὸς ὃν σόρικα
καλοῦσιν, ἀποψηφισάμενοι τούτους αὖθις ἑτέρους
κατέστησαν. καὶ τὴν ἐν οὕτω μικροῖς ἀκρίβειαν
φυλάττοντες οὐδεμίᾳ προσεμίγνυσαν δεισιδαι-
μονίᾳ, τῷ μηδὲν ἀλλάττειν μηδὲ παρεκβαίνειν
τῶν πατρίων.

VI. Ὡς δ᾽ οὖν ἐξωμόσαντο τὴν ἀρχὴν οἱ περὶ
τὸν Φλαμίνιον, διὰ τῶν καλουμένων μεσοβασι-
λέων ὕπατος ἀποδείκνυται Μάρκελλος. καὶ παραλαβὼν τὴν ἀρχὴν ἀποδείκνυσιν αὐτῷ συνάρχοντα
Γναῖον Κορνήλιον. ἐλέχθη μὲν οὖν ὡς πολλὰ
συμβατικὰ τῶν Γαλατῶν λεγόντων, καὶ τῆς
βουλῆς εἰρηναῖα βουλομένης, ὁ Μάρκελλος ἐξε-
2 τράχυνε τὸν δῆμον ἐπὶ τὸν πόλεμον· οὐ μὴν ἀλλὰ
καὶ γενομένης εἰρήνης ἀνακαινίσαι τὸν πόλεμον οἱ
Γαισάται δοκοῦσι, τὰς Ἄλπεις ὑπερβαλόντες καὶ
τοὺς Ἰνσόμβρους ἐπάραντες· τρισμύριοι γὰρ
ὄντες προσεγένοντο πολλαπλασίοις ἐκείνοις οὖσι,
καὶ μέγα φρονοῦντες εὐθὺς ἐπ᾽ Ἀκέρρας ὥρμησαν,
πόλιν ὑπὲρ ποταμοῦ Πάδου ἀνῳκισμένην. ἐκεῖθεν δὲ μυρίους τῶν Γαισατῶν ὁ βασιλεὺς Βριτό-

---

[1] Cf. the *Numa*, vii. 5.

[2] In 222 B.C. In republican times, an interrex was elected
when there was a vacancy in the supreme power, held office
for five days, and, if necessary, nominated his successor.
Any number of interreges might be successively ap-

speaking, two most illustrious priests were deposed
from their priesthoods, Cornelius Cethegus, because
he presented the entrails of his victim improperly,
and Quintus Sulpicius, because, while he was sacrificing, the peaked cap which the priests called flamens[1]
wear had fallen from his head. Moreover, because
the squeak of a shrew-mouse (they call it "sorex")
was heard just as Minucius the dictator appointed
Caius Flaminius his master of horse, the people
deposed these officials and put others in their places.
And although they were punctilious in such trifling
matters, they did not fall into any superstition, because they made no change or deviation in their
ancient rites.

VI. But to resume the story, after Flaminius and
his colleague had renounced their offices, Marcellus
was appointed consul[2] by the so-called "interreges."
He took the office, and appointed Gnaeus Cornelius
his colleague. Now it has been said that, although
the Gauls made many conciliatory proposals, and
although the senate was peaceably inclined, Marcellus
tried to provoke the people to continue the war.
However, it would seem that even after peace was
made the Gaesatae renewed the war; they crossed
the Alps and stirred up the Insubrians. They numbered thirty thousand themselves, and the Insubrians,
whom they joined, were much more numerous. With
high confidence, therefore, they marched at once to
Acerrae, a city situated to the north of the river Po.[3]
From thence Britomartus the king, taking with him

pointed, until the highest office was filled. Cf. the *Numa*,
ii. 6 f.

[3] According to Polybius (ii. 34), no peace was made,
although the Gauls offered to submit, and the consuls
marched into the territory of the Insubrians and laid siege
to Acerrae.

μαρτος ἀναλαβὼν τὴν περὶ Πάδον χώραν ἐπόρθει.

3 ταῦτα Μάρκελλος πυθόμενος τὸν μὲν συνάρχοντα πρὸς Ἀκέρραις ἀπέλιπε τὴν πεζὴν καὶ βαρεῖαν ὁμοῦ πᾶσαν ἔχοντα δύναμιν καὶ τῶν ἱππέων μέρος τρίτον, αὐτὸς δὲ τοὺς λοιποὺς ἱππεῖς ἀναλαβὼν καὶ τοὺς ἐλαφροτάτους τῶν ὁπλιτῶν περὶ ἑξακοσίους ἤλαυνεν, οὔτε ἡμέρας οὔτε νυκτὸς ἀνιεὶς τὸν δρόμον, ἕως ἐπέβαλε τοῖς μυρίοις Γαισάταις περὶ τὸ καλούμενον Κλαστίδιον, Γαλατικὴν κώμην οὐ πρὸ πολλοῦ Ῥωμαίοις ὑπήκοον

4 γεγενημένην. ἀναλαβεῖν δὲ καὶ διαναπαῦσαι τὸν στρατὸν οὐχ ὑπῆρξεν αὐτῷ· ταχὺ γὰρ αἴσθησιν τοῖς βαρβάροις ἀφικόμενος παρέσχε, καὶ κατεφρονήθη πεζῶν μὲν ὀλίγων παντάπασιν ὄντων σὺν αὐτῷ, τὸ δ' ἱππικὸν ἐν οὐδενὶ λόγῳ τῶν Κελτῶν τιθεμένων. κράτιστοι γὰρ ὄντες ἱππομαχεῖν καὶ μάλιστα τούτῳ διαφέρειν δοκοῦντες, τότε καὶ πλήθει πολὺ τὸν Μάρκελλον ὑπερέβαλλον. εὐθὺς οὖν ἐπ' αὐτὸν ὡς ἀναρπασόμενοι μετὰ βίας πολλῆς καὶ δεινῶν ἀπειλῶν ἐφέροντο, 30

5 τοῦ βασιλέως προϊππεύοντος. ὁ δὲ Μάρκελλος, ὡς μὴ φθαῖεν αὐτὸν ἐγκυκλωσάμενοι καὶ περιχυθέντες ὀλιγοστὸν ὄντα, τὰς ἴλας ἦγε πόρρω τῶν ἱππέων καὶ περιήλαυνε, λεπτὸν ἐκτείνων τὸ κέρας, ἄχρι οὗ μικρὸν ἀπέσχε τῶν πολεμίων. ἤδη δέ πως εἰς ἐμβολὴν ἐπιστρέφοντος αὐτοῦ συντυγχάνει τὸν ἵππον πτυρέντα τῇ γαυρότητι τῶν πολεμίων ἀποτραπέσθαι καὶ βίᾳ φέρειν ὀπίσω

6 τὸν Μάρκελλον. ὁ δὲ τοῦτο δείσας μὴ ταραχὴν ἐκ δεισιδαιμονίας τοῖς Ῥωμαίοις ἐνεργάσηται, ταχὺ περισπάσας ἐφ' ἡνίαν τῷ χαλινῷ καὶ περιστρέψας τὸν ἵππον ἐναντίον τοῖς πολεμίοις, τὸν ἥλιον αὐτὸς προσεκύνησεν, ὡς δὴ μὴ κατὰ τύχην,

ten thousand of the Gaesatae, ravaged the country about the Po. When Marcellus learned of this, he left his colleague at Acerrae with all the heavy-armed infantry and a third part of the cavalry, while he himself, taking with him the rest of the cavalry and the most lightly equipped men-at-arms to the number of six hundred, marched, without halting in his course day or night, until he came upon the ten thousand Gaesatae near the place called Clastidium, a Gallic village which not long before had become subject to the Romans. There was no time for him to give his army rest and refreshment, for the Barbarians quickly learned of his arrival, and held in contempt the infantry with him, which were few in number all told, and, being Gauls, made no account of his cavalry. For they were most excellent fighters on horseback, and were thought to be specially superior as such, and, besides, at this time they far outnumbered Marcellus. Immediately, therefore, they charged upon him with great violence and dreadful threats, thinking to overwhelm him, their king riding in front of them. But Marcellus, that they might not succeed in enclosing and surrounding him and his few followers, led his troops of cavalry forward and tried to outflank them, extending his wing into a thin line, until he was not far from the enemy. And now, just as he was turning to make a charge, his horse, frightened by the ferocious aspect of the enemy, wheeled about and bore Marcellus forcibly back. But he, fearing lest this should be taken as a bad omen by the Romans and lead to confusion among them, quickly reined his horse round to the left and made him face the enemy, while he himself made adoration to the sun, implying that it was not

PLUTARCH'S LIVES

ἀλλ' ἕνεκα τούτου τῇ περιαγωγῇ χρησάμενος·
οὕτω γὰρ ἔθος ἐστὶ Ῥωμαίοις προσκυνεῖν τοὺς
θεοὺς περιστρεφομένους. καὶ αὐτὸν ἤδη προσμι-
γνύντα τοῖς ἐναντίοις προσεύξασθαι τῷ φερετρίῳ
Διὶ τὰ κάλλιστα τῶν παρὰ τοῖς πολεμίοις ὅπλων
καθιερώσειν.

VII. Ἐν τούτῳ δὲ κατιδὼν ὁ τῶν Γαλατῶν
βασιλεὺς καὶ τεκμηράμενος ἀπὸ τῶν συμβόλων
ἄρχοντα τοῦτον εἶναι, πολὺ πρὸ τῶν ἄλλων
ἐξελάσας τὸν ἵππον ὑπηντίασεν, ἅμα τῇ φωνῇ
προκλητικὸν ἐπαλαλάζων καὶ τὸ δόρυ κραδαίνων,
ἀνὴρ μεγέθει τε σώματος ἔξοχος Γαλατῶν, καὶ
πανοπλίᾳ ἐν ἀργύρῳ καὶ χρυσῷ καὶ βαφαῖς καὶ
πᾶσι ποικίλμασιν, ὥσπερ ἀστραπή, διαφέρων
2 στιλβούσῃ. ὡς οὖν ἐπιβλέψαντι τὴν φάλαγγα
τῷ Μαρκέλλῳ ταῦτα τῶν ὅπλων ἔδοξε κάλλιστα
καὶ κατὰ τούτων ὑπέλαβε πεποιῆσθαι τῷ θεῷ
τὴν κατευχήν, ὥρμησεν ἐπὶ τὸν ἄνδρα, καὶ τῷ
δόρατι διακόψας τὸν θώρακα καὶ συνεπερείσας
τῇ ῥύμῃ τοῦ ἵππου ζῶντα μὲν αὐτὸν περιέτρεψε,
δευτέραν δὲ καὶ τρίτην πληγὴν ἐνεὶς εὐθὺς ἀπέ-
3 κτεινεν. ἀποπηδήσας δὲ τοῦ ἵππου, καὶ τῶν
ὅπλων τοῦ νεκροῦ ταῖς χερσὶν ἐφαψάμενος, πρὸς
τὸν οὐρανὸν εἶπεν· "Ὦ μεγάλα στρατηγῶν καὶ
ἡγεμόνων ἔργα καὶ πράξεις ἐπιβλέπων ἐν πολέμοις καὶ μάχαις φερέτριε Ζεῦ, μαρτύρομαί σε
Ῥωμαίων τρίτος ἄρχων ἄρχοντα καὶ βασιλέα
στρατηγὸς ἰδίᾳ χειρὶ τόνδε τὸν ἄνδρα κατεργασάμενος καὶ κτείνας σοι καθιεροῦν τὰ πρῶτα καὶ
κάλλιστα τῶν λαφύρων. σὺ δὲ δίδου τύχην ὁμοίαν
ἐπὶ τὰ λοιπὰ τοῦ πολέμου προτρεπομένοις."

4   Ἐκ τούτου συνέμισγον οἱ ἱππεῖς οὐ διακεκρι-

by chance, but for this purpose, that he had wheeled about; for it is the custom with the Romans to turn round in this way when they make adoration to the gods. And in the moment of closing with the enemy he is said to have vowed that he would consecrate to Jupiter Feretrius the most beautiful suit of armour among them.

VII. Meanwhile the king of the Gauls espied him, and judging from his insignia that he was the commander, rode far out in front of the rest and confronted him, shouting challenges and brandishing his spear. His stature exceeded that of the other Gauls, and he was conspicuous for a suit of armour which was set off with gold and silver and bright colours and all sorts of broideries; it gleamed like lightning. Accordingly, as Marcellus surveyed the ranks of the enemy, this seemed to him to be the most beautiful armour, and he concluded that it was this which he had vowed to the god. He therefore rushed upon the man, and by a thrust of his spear which pierced his adversary's breastplate, and by the impact of his horse in full career, threw him, still living, upon the ground, where, with a second and third blow, he promptly killed him. Then leaping from his horse and laying his hands upon the armour of the dead, he looked towards heaven and said: " O Jupiter Feretrius, who beholdest the great deeds and exploits of generals and commanders in wars and fightings, I call thee to witness that I have overpowered and slain this man with my own hand, being the third Roman ruler and general so to slay a ruler and king, and that I dedicate to thee the first and most beautiful of the spoils. Do thou therefore grant us a like fortune as we prosecute the rest of the war."

His prayer ended, the cavalry joined battle, fight-

451

μένοις τοῖς ἱππεῦσιν, ἀλλὰ καὶ πρὸς τοὺς πεζοὺς
ὁμοῦ προσφερομένους μαχόμενοι, καὶ νικῶσι νίκην
ἰδέᾳ τε καὶ τρόπῳ περιττὴν καὶ παράδοξον·
ἱππεῖς γὰρ ἱππεῖς καὶ πεζοὺς ἅμα τοσοῦτοι
τοσούτους οὔτε πρότερον οὔτε ὕστερον νικῆσαι
λέγονται. κτείνας δὲ τοὺς πλείστους καὶ κρατήσας ὅπλων καὶ χρημάτων ἐπανῆλθε πρὸς τὸν
συνάρχοντα μοχθηρῶς πολεμοῦντα Κελτοῖς περὶ
πόλιν μεγίστην καὶ πολυανθρωποτάτην τῶν Γα-
5 λατικῶν. Μεδιόλανον καλεῖται, καὶ μητρόπολιν
αὐτὴν οἱ τῇδε Κελτοὶ νομίζουσιν· ὅθεν ἐκθύμως
μαχόμενοι περὶ αὐτῆς ἀντεπολιόρκουν τὸν Κορνήλιον. ἐπελθόντος δὲ Μαρκέλλου, καὶ τῶν Γαισατῶν, ὡς ἐπύθοντο τὴν τοῦ βασιλέως ἧτταν καὶ
τελευτήν, ἀπελθόντων, τὸ μὲν Μεδιόλανον ἁλίσκεται, τὰς δὲ ἄλλας πόλεις αὐτοὶ παραδιδόασιν
οἱ Κελτοὶ καὶ τὰ καθ᾽ ἑαυτοὺς ἐπιτρέπουσι πάντα
Ῥωμαίοις. καὶ τούτοις μὲν ἦν εἰρήνη μετρίων
τυχοῦσι.

VIII. Ψηφισαμένης δὲ τῆς συγκλήτου μόνῳ
Μαρκέλλῳ θρίαμβον, εἰσήλαυνε τῇ μὲν ἄλλῃ λαμπρότητι καὶ πλούτῳ καὶ λαφύροις καὶ σώμασιν
ὑπερφυέσιν αἰχμαλώτων ἐν ὀλίγοις θαυμαστός,
ἥδιστον δὲ πάντων θέαμα καὶ καινότατον ἐπιδεικνύμενος αὐτὸν κομίζοντα τῷ θεῷ τὴν τοῦ βαρ-
2 βάρου πανοπλίαν. δρυὸς γὰρ εὐκτεάνου πρέμνον
ὄρθιον καὶ μέγα τεμὼν καὶ ἀσκήσας ὥσπερ
τρόπαιον ἀνεδήσατο καὶ κατήρτησεν ἐξ αὐτοῦ τὰ
λάφυρα, κόσμῳ διαθεὶς καὶ περιαρμόσας ἕκαστον.
προϊούσης δὲ τῆς πομπῆς ἀράμενος αὐτὸς ἐπέβη

ing, not with the enemy's horsemen alone, but also
with their footmen who attacked them at the same
time, and won a victory which, in its sort and kind,
was remarkable and strange. For never before or
since, as we are told, have so few horsemen conquered so many horsemen and footmen together.
After slaying the greater part of the enemy and
getting possession of their arms and baggage, Marcellus returned to his colleague, who was hard put
to it in his war with the Gauls near their largest and
most populous city.[1] Mediolanum was the city's
name, and the Gauls considered it their metropolis;
wherefore they fought eagerly in its defence, so that
Cornelius was less besieger than besieged. But when
Marcellus came up, and when the Gaesatae, on learning of the defeat and death of their king, withdrew,
Mediolanum was taken, the Gauls themselves surrendered the rest of their cities, and put themselves
entirely at the disposition of the Romans. They
obtained peace on equitable terms.

VIII. The senate decreed a triumph to Marcellus
alone, and his triumphal procession was seldom
equalled in its splendour and wealth and spoils and
captives of gigantic size; but besides this, the most
agreeable and the rarest spectacle of all was afforded
when Marcellus himself carried to the god the armour
of the barbarian king. He had cut the trunk of a
slender oak, straight and tall, and fashioned it into
the shape of a trophy; on this he bound and fastened
the spoils, arranging and adjusting each piece in due
order. When the procession began to move, he took
the trophy himself and mounted the chariot, and

---

[1] Acerrae had, in the meantime, been taken by the
Romans, who had then advanced and laid siege to Mediolanum (Milan). Cf. Polybius, ii. 34.

PLUTARCH'S LIVES

τοῦ τεθρίππου, καὶ τροπαιοφόρον ἄγαλμα τῶν
ἐκείνου κάλλιστον καὶ διαπρεπέστατον ἐπόμπευε
διὰ τῆς πόλεως. ὁ δὲ στρατὸς εἵπετο καλλίστοις
ὅπλοις κεκοσμημένος, ᾄδων ἅμα πεποιημένα μέλη
καὶ παιᾶνας ἐπινικίους εἰς τὸν θεὸν καὶ τὸν
3 στρατηγόν. οὕτω δὲ προβὰς καὶ παρελθὼν εἰς
τὸν νεὼν τοῦ φερετρίου Διός, ἀνέστησε καὶ καθιέ-
ρωσε, τρίτος καὶ τελευταῖος ἄχρι τοῦ καθ᾽ ἡμᾶς
αἰῶνος. πρῶτος μὲν γὰρ ἀνήνεγκε σκῦλα Ῥω-
μύλος ἀπὸ Ἄκρωνος τοῦ Καινινήτου, δεύτερος δὲ
Κόσσος Κορνήλιος ἀπὸ Τολουμνίου Τυρρηνοῦ,
μετὰ δὲ τούτους Μάρκελλος ἀπὸ Βριτομάρτου,
βασιλέως Γαλατῶν, μετὰ δὲ Μάρκελλον οὐδὲ εἷς.
4 καλεῖται δὲ ὁ μὲν θεὸς ᾧ πέμπεται φερέτριος
Ζεύς, ὡς μὲν ἔνιοί φασιν, ἀπὸ τοῦ φερετρευομένου
τροπαίου, κατὰ τὴν Ἑλληνίδα γλῶσσαν ἔτι
πολλὴν τότε συμμεμιγμένην τῇ Λατίνων, ὡς δὲ
ἕτεροι, Διός ἐστιν ἡ προσωνυμία κεραυνοβολοῦν-
τος. τὸ γὰρ τύπτειν φερῖρε οἱ Ῥωμαῖοι καλοῦσιν.
ἄλλοι δὲ παρὰ τὴν τοῦ πολεμίου πληγὴν γεγονέναι τοὔνομα λέγουσι· καὶ γὰρ νῦν ἐν ταῖς
μάχαις, ὅταν διώκωσι τοὺς πολεμίους, πυκνὸν τὸ
φέρι, τουτέστι παῖε, παρεγγυῶσιν ἀλλήλοις. τὰ
δὲ σκῦλα σπόλια μὲν κοινῶς, ἰδίως δὲ ὀπίμια
5 ταῦτα καλοῦσι. καίτοι φασὶν ἐν τοῖς ὑπομνήμασι
Νομᾶν Πομπίλιον καὶ πρώτων ὀπιμίων καὶ δευ-
τέρων καὶ τρίτων μνημονεύειν, τὰ μὲν πρῶτα
ληφθέντα τῷ φερετρίῳ Διὶ κελεύοντα καθιεροῦν,
τὰ δεύτερα δὲ τῷ Ἄρει, τὰ δὲ τρίτα τῷ Κυρίνῳ,
καὶ λαμβάνειν γέρας ἀσσάρια τριακόσια τὸν

454

thus a trophy-bearing figure more conspicuous and beautiful than any in his day passed in triumph through the city. The army followed, arrayed in most beautiful armour, singing odes composed for the occasion, together with paeans of victory in praise of the god and their general. Thus advancing and entering the temple of Jupiter Feretrius, he set up and consecrated his offering, being the third and last to do so, down to our time. The first was Romulus, who despoiled Acron the Caeninensian;[1] the second was Cornelius Cossus, who despoiled Tolumnius the Tuscan; and after them Marcellus, who despoiled Britomartus, king of the Gauls; but after Marcellus, no man. The god to whom the spoils were dedicated was called Jupiter Feretrius, as some say, because the trophy was carried on a "pheretron," or *car*; this is a Greek word, and many such were still mingled at that time with the Latin;[2] according to others, the epithet is given to Jupiter as wielder of the thunder-bolt, the Latin "ferire" meaning *to smite*. But others say the name is derived from the blow one gives an enemy, since even now in battles, when they are pursuing their enemies, they exhort one another with the word "feri," which means *smite*! Spoils in general they call "spolia," and these in particular, "opima." And yet they say that Numa Pompilius, in his commentaries, makes mention of three kinds of "opima," prescribing that when the first kind are taken, they shall be consecrated to Jupiter Feretrius, the second to Mars, and the third to Quirinus; also that the reward for the first shall be three hundred asses,[3] for the second

---

[1] Cf. the *Romulus*, xvi. 4–7.
[2] Cf. the *Romulus*, xv. 3; *Numa*, vii. 5.
[3] The Roman *as* corresponded nearly to the English penny.

πρῶτον, τὸν δὲ δεύτερον διακόσια, τὸν δὲ τρίτον
ἑκατόν. ὁ μέντοι πολὺς οὗτος ἐπικρατεῖ λόγος,
ὡς ἐκείνων μόνων ὀπιμίων ὄντων, ὅσα καὶ παρατάξεως οὔσης καὶ πρῶτα καὶ στρατηγοῦ στρατηγὸν ἀνελόντος. περὶ μὲν οὖν τούτων ἐπὶ τοσοῦτον.

6   Οἱ δὲ Ῥωμαῖοι τὴν νίκην ἐκείνην καὶ τοῦ
πολέμου τὴν κατάλυσιν οὕτως ὑπερηγάπησαν
ὥστε καὶ τῷ Πυθίῳ χρυσοῦν κρατῆρα ἀπὸ
λιτρῶν [1] . . . εἰς Δελφοὺς ἀποστεῖλαι χαριστή-
ριον, καὶ τῶν λαφύρων ταῖς τε συμμαχίσι μετα-
δοῦναι πόλεσι λαμπρῶς, καὶ πρὸς Ἱέρωνα πολλὰ
πέμψαι, τὸν Συρακουσίων βασιλέα, φίλον ὄντα
καὶ σύμμαχον.

IX. Ἀννίβου δὲ ἐμβαλόντος εἰς Ἰταλίαν ἐπ-
εμφθη μὲν ὁ Μάρκελλος ἐπὶ Σικελίαν στόλον
ἄγων· ἐπεὶ δὲ ἡ περὶ Κάννας ἀτυχία συνέπεσε
καὶ Ῥωμαίων οὐκ ὀλίγαι μυριάδες ἐν τῇ μάχῃ
διεφθάρησαν, ὀλίγοι δὲ σωθέντες εἰς Κανύσιον
συνεπεφεύγεσαν, ἦν δὲ προσδοκία τὸν Ἀννίβαν
εὐθὺς ἐπὶ τὴν Ῥώμην ἐλᾶν, ὅπερ ἦν κράτιστον
2 τῆς δυνάμεως ἀνῃρηκότα, πρῶτον μὲν ὁ Μάρκελλος ἀπὸ τῶν νεῶν ἔπεμψε τῇ πόλει φυλακὴν
πεντακοσίους καὶ χιλίους ἄνδρας, ἔπειτα δόγμα
τῆς βουλῆς δεξάμενος εἰς Κανύσιον παρῆλθε, καὶ
τοὺς ἐκεῖ συνειλεγμένους παραλαβὼν ἐξήγαγε
τῶν ἐρυμάτων ὡς οὐ προησόμενος τὴν χώραν.
Ῥωμαίοις δὲ τῶν ἡγεμονικῶν καὶ δυνατῶν ἀνδρῶν
οἱ μὲν ἐτεθνήκεσαν ἐν ταῖς μάχαις, Φαβίου δὲ
Μαξίμου τοῦ πλεῖστον ἔχοντος ἀξίωμα πίστεως
καὶ συνέσεως, τὸ λίαν ἀπηκριβωμένον ἐν τοῖς
ὑπὲρ τοῦ μὴ παθεῖν λογισμοῖς ὡς ἀργὸν ἐπὶ τὰς
3 πράξεις καὶ ἄτολμον ᾐτιῶντο· καὶ νομίζοντες

----
[1] ἀπὸ λιτρῶν Sintenis[1], Coraës and Bekker : ἀπὸ λύτρων.

two hundred, and for the third one hundred. However, the general and prevailing account is that only those spoils are "opima" which are taken first, in a pitched battle, where general slays general. So much, then, on this subject.

The Romans were so overjoyed at this victory and the ending of the war that they sent to the Pythian Apollo at Delphi a golden bowl [1] . . . as a thank-offering, gave a splendid share of the spoils to their allied cities, and sent many to Hiero, the king of Syracuse, who was their friend and ally.

IX. After Hannibal had invaded Italy,[2] Marcellus was sent to Sicily with a fleet. And when the disaster at Cannae came,[3] and many thousands of Romans had been slain in the battle, and only a few had saved themselves by flying to Canusium, and it was expected that Hannibal would march at once against Rome, now that he had destroyed the flower of her forces, in the first place, Marcellus sent fifteen hundred men from his ships to protect the city ; then, under orders from the senate, he went to Canusium, and taking the troops that had gathered there, led them out of the fortifications to show that he would not abandon the country. Most of the leaders and influential men among the Romans had fallen in battle ; and as for Fabius Maximus, who was held in the greatest esteem for his sagacity and trustworthiness, his excessive care in planning to avoid losses was censured as cowardly inactivity. The people thought they had

---

[1] The indication of its source or value which follows in the Greek, is uncertain.

[2] 218 B.C.   [3] 216 B.C.   Cf. the *Fabius Maximus*, xv. f.

ἀποχρῶντα τοῦτον ἔχειν πρὸς ἀσφάλειαν, οὐ
διαρκῆ δὲ πρὸς ἄμυναν στρατηγόν, ἐπὶ τὸν Μάρκελλον ἀφεώρων,[1] καὶ τὸ θαρραλέον αὐτοῦ καὶ
δραστήριον πρὸς τὴν ἐκείνου κεραννύντες καὶ
ἁρμόττοντες εὐλάβειαν καὶ πρόνοιαν, ποτὲ μὲν
ἀμφοτέρους ἅμα χειροτονοῦντες ὑπάτους, ποτὲ δὲ
ἐν μέρει, τὸν μὲν ὕπατον, τὸν δὲ ἀνθύπατον, ἐξ-
4 έπεμπον. ὁ δὲ Ποσειδώνιός φησι τὸν μὲν Φάβιον
θυρεὸν καλεῖσθαι, τὸν δὲ Μάρκελλον ξίφος. αὐτὸς
δὲ ὁ Ἀννίβας ἔλεγε τὸν μὲν Φάβιον ὡς παιδαγω- 30
γὸν φοβεῖσθαι, τὸν δὲ Μάρκελλον ὡς ἀνταγωνι-
στήν· ὑφ᾽ οὗ μὲν γὰρ κωλύεσθαι κακόν τι ποιεῖν,
ὑφ᾽ οὗ δὲ καὶ πάσχειν.

X. Πρῶτον μὲν οὖν ἀνέσεως πολλῆς καὶ θρασύ-
τητος ἐκ τοῦ κρατεῖν τὸν Ἀννίβαν τοῖς στρατιώταις ἐγγενομένης, τοὺς ἀποσκιδναμένους τοῦ
στρατοπέδου καὶ κατατρέχοντας τὴν χώραν
ἐπιτιθέμενος κατέκοπτε καὶ ὑπανήλισκε τῆς
δυνάμεως· ἔπειτα πρὸς Νέαν πόλιν καὶ Νῶλαν
βοηθήσας Νεαπολίτας μὲν ἐπέρρωσεν αὐτοὺς
καθ᾽ ἑαυτοὺς βεβαίους ὄντας Ῥωμαίοις, εἰς δὲ
Νῶλαν εἰσελθὼν στάσιν εὗρε, τῆς βουλῆς τὸν
δῆμον ἀννιβίζοντα μεταχειρίσασθαι καὶ καταρ-
2 τίσαι μὴ δυναμένης. ἦν γάρ τις ἀνὴρ εὐγενείᾳ
τε πρωτεύων ἐν τῇ πόλει καὶ κατ᾽ ἀνδρείαν ἐπι-
φανής, ὄνομα Βάνδιος· τοῦτον ἐν Κάνναις περι-
όπτως ἀγωνισάμενον καὶ πολλοὺς μὲν ἀνελόντα
τῶν Καρχηδονίων, τέλος δὲ αὐτὸν ἐν τοῖς νεκροῖς
εὑρεθέντα πολλῶν βελῶν κατάπλεων τὸ σῶμα,
θαυμάσας ὁ Ἀννίβας οὐ μόνον ἀφῆκεν ἄνευ

[1] ἀφεώρων Coraës and Bekker have κατέφευγον (took refuge),
after Stephanus.

in him a general who sufficed for the defensive, but was inadequate for the offensive, and therefore turned their eyes upon Marcellus; and mingling and uniting his boldness and activity with the caution and forethought of Fabius, they sometimes elected both to be consuls together, and sometimes made them, by turns, consul and proconsul, and sent them into the field. Poseidonius says that Fabius was called a shield, and Marcellus a sword.[1] And Hannibal himself used to say that he feared Fabius as a tutor, but Marcellus as an adversary; for by the one he was prevented from doing any harm, while by the other he was actually harmed.

X. To begin with, then, since Hannibal's victory had made his soldiers very bold and careless, Marcellus set upon them as they straggled from their camp and overran the country, cut them down, and thus slowly diminished their forces; secondly, he brought aid to Neapolis and Nola. In Neapolis he merely confirmed the minds of the citizens, who were of their own choice steadfast friends of Rome; but on entering Nola, he found a state of discord, the senate being unable to regulate and manage the people, which favoured Hannibal. For there was a man in the city of the highest birth and of illustrious valour, whose name was Bantius. This man had fought with conspicuous bravery at Cannae, and had slain many of the Carthaginians, and when he was at last found among the dead with his body full of missiles, Hannibal was struck with admiration of him, and not only let him go without a ransom, but

---

[1] Cf. the *Fabius Maximus*, xix. 3.

λύτρων, ἀλλὰ καὶ δῶρα προσέθηκε καὶ φίλον
3 ἐποιήσατο καὶ ξένον. ἀμειβόμενος οὖν τὴν χάριν
ὁ Βάνδιος εἷς ἦν τῶν ἀννιβιζόντων προθύμως, καὶ
τὸν δῆμον ἰσχύων ἐξῆγε πρὸς ἀπόστασιν. ὁ δὲ
Μάρκελλος ἀνελεῖν μὲν ἄνδρα λαμπρὸν οὕτω τὴν
τύχην καὶ κεκοινωνηκότα τῶν μεγίστων Ῥωμαίοις ἀγώνων οὐχ ὅσιον ἡγεῖτο, πρὸς δὲ τῷ
φύσει φιλανθρώπῳ καὶ πιθανὸς ὢν ὁμιλίᾳ προσά-
γεσθαι φιλότιμον ἦθος, ἀσπασαμένου ποτὲ τοῦ
Βανδίου αὐτὸν ἠρώτησεν ὅστις ἀνθρώπων εἴη,
πάλαι μὲν εὖ εἰδώς, ἀρχὴν δὲ καὶ πρόφασιν ἐν-
4 τεύξεως ζητῶν. ὡς γὰρ εἶπε, "Λεύκιος Βάνδιος,"
οἷον ἡσθεὶς καὶ θαυμάσας ὁ Μάρκελλος, "Ἡ γὰρ
ἐκεῖνος," ἔφη, "σὺ Βάνδιος, οὗ πλεῖστος ἐν Ῥώμῃ
λόγος τῶν ἐν Κάνναις ἀγωνισαμένων, ὡς μόνου
Παῦλον Αἰμίλιον τὸν ἄρχοντα μὴ προλιπόντος,
ἀλλὰ τὰ πλεῖστα τῶν ἐκείνῳ φερομένων βελῶν
5 ὑποστάντος τῷ σώματι καὶ ἀναδεξαμένου;" φήσαντος δὲ τοῦ Βανδίου καί τι καὶ παραφήναντος
αὐτῷ τῶν τραυμάτων, "Εἶτα," ἔφη, "τηλικαῦτα
γνωρίσματα φέρων τῆς πρὸς ἡμᾶς φιλίας οὐκ
εὐθὺς προσῄεις; ἢ κακοί σοι δοκοῦμεν ἀρετὴν
ἀμείβεσθαι φίλων οἷς ἐστι τιμὴ καὶ παρὰ τοῖς
πολεμίοις;" ταῦτα φιλοφρονηθεὶς καὶ δεξιωσάμενος ἵππον τε δωρεῖται πολεμιστὴν αὐτῷ
καὶ δραχμὰς ἀργυρίου πεντακοσίας.

XI. Ἐκ τούτου βεβαιότατος μὲν ἦν Μαρκέλλῳ
παραστάτης καὶ σύμμαχος, δεινότατος δὲ μη-
νυτὴς καὶ κατήγορος τῶν τἀναντία φρονούντων
ὁ Βάνδιος. ἦσαν δὲ πολλοί, καὶ διενοοῦντο τῶν
Ῥωμαίων ἐπεξιόντων τοῖς πολεμίοις αὐτοὶ διαρ-
2 πάσαι τὰς ἀποσκευάς. διὸ συντάξας ὁ Μάρ-

actually added gifts, and made him his friend and
guest. In return for this favour, then, Bantius was
one of those who eagerly favoured the cause of Hannibal, and was using his great influence to bring the
people to a revolt. Marcellus thought it wrong to
put to death a man so illustrious in his good fortune
who had taken part with the Romans in their greatest
conflicts, and, besides his natural kindliness, he had
an address that was likely to win over a character
whose ambition was for honour. One day, therefore,
when Bantius saluted him, he asked him who he
was, not that he had not known him for some time,
but seeking occasion and excuse for conversation
with him. For when he said, "I am Lucius Bantius," Marcellus, as if astonished and delighted, said :
"What! are you that Bantius who is more talked
of in Rome than any of those who fought at Cannae,
as the only man who did not abandon Paulus Aemilius the consul, but encountered and received in his
own body most of the missiles aimed at him?" And
when Bantius assented and showed him some of his
scars, "Why, then," said Marcellus, "when you bear
such marks of your friendship towards us, did you
not come to us at once? Can it be that you think
us loath to requite valour in friends who are honoured
even among our enemies?" These kindly greetings
he followed up by making him presents of a war
horse and five hundred drachmas in silver.

XI. After this Bantius was a most steadfast partisan
and ally of Marcellus, and a most formidable de-
nouncer and accuser of those who belonged to the
opposite party.[1] These were many, and they purposed, when the Romans went out against the
enemy, to plunder their baggage. Marcellus there-

[1] The story of Lucius Bantius is told by Livy also (xxiii.
15, 7—16, 1).

κελλος τὴν δύναμιν ἐντὸς παρὰ τὰς πύλας ἔστησε
τὰ σκευοφόρα, καὶ τοῖς Νωλανοῖς διὰ κηρύγ-
ματος ἀπεῖπε πρὸς τὰ τείχη προσπελάζειν. ἦν
οὖν ὅπλων ἐρημία καὶ τὸν Ἀννίβαν ἐπεσπάσατο
προσάγειν ἀτακτότερον, ὡς τῶν ἐν τῇ πόλει
ταραττομένων. Ἐν τούτῳ δὲ τὴν καθ' αὐτὸν
πύλην ἀναπετάσαι κελεύσας ὁ Μάρκελλος ἐξήλασεν, ἔχων μεθ' ἑαυτοῦ τῶν ἱπποτῶν τοὺς
λαμπροτάτους, καὶ προσπεσὼν κατὰ στόμα
3 συνείχετο τοῖς πολεμίοις. μετ' ὀλίγον δ' οἱ πεζοὶ
καθ' ἑτέραν πύλην ἐχώρουν μετὰ δρόμου καὶ
βοῆς· καὶ πρὸς τούτους αὖθις αὖ τοῦ Ἀννίβα
μερίζοντος τὴν δύναμιν ἡ τρίτη τῶν πυλῶν
ἀνεῴγνυτο, καὶ δι' αὐτῆς ἐξέθεον οἱ λοιποὶ καὶ
προσέκειντο πανταχόθεν ἐκπεπληγμένοις τῷ
ἀπροσδοκήτῳ καὶ κακῶς ἀμυνομένοις τοὺς ἐν
χερσὶν ἤδη διὰ τοὺς ὕστερον ἐπιφερομένους.
κἀνταῦθα πρῶτον οἱ σὺν Ἀννίβᾳ Ῥωμαίοις ἐνέ-
δωκαν, ὠθούμενοι φόνῳ πολλῷ καὶ τραύμασι
4 πρὸς τὸ στρατόπεδον. λέγονται γὰρ ὑπὲρ πεντα-
κισχιλίους ἀποθανεῖν, ἀποκτεῖναι δὲ Ῥωμαίων
οὐ πλείονας ἢ πεντακοσίους. ὁ δὲ Λίβιος οὕτω
μὲν οὐ διαβεβαιοῦται γενέσθαι μεγάλην ἧτταν
οὐδὲ πεσεῖν νεκροὺς τοσούτους τῶν πολεμίων,
κλέος δὲ μέγα Μαρκέλλῳ καὶ Ῥωμαίοις ἐκ κακῶν
θάρσος ἀπὸ τῆς μάχης ἐκείνης ὑπάρξαι θαυμαστόν, οὐχ ὡς πρὸς ἄμαχον οὐδὲ ἀήττητον,
ἀλλά τι καὶ παθεῖν δυνάμενον διαγωνιζομένοις
πολέμιον.

XII. Διὸ καὶ θατέρου τῶν ὑπάτων ἀποθανόντος

3(

fore drew up his forces inside the city, stationed his
baggage-trains near the gates, and issued an edict
forbidding the men of Nola to come near the city
walls. Consequently there were no armed men to
be seen, and Hannibal was thus induced to lead up
his forces in some disorder, supposing the city to be
in a tumult. But at this juncture Marcellus ordered
the gate where he stood to be thrown open, and
marched out, having with him the flower of his
horsemen, and charging directly down upon the
enemy joined battle with them. After a little his
footmen also, by another gate, advanced to the attack
on the run and with shouts. And still again, while
Hannibal was dividing his forces to meet these, the
third gate was thrown open, and through it the rest
rushed forth and fell upon their enemies on every
side. These were dismayed by the unexpected onset,
and made a poor defence against those with whom
they were already engaged because of those who
charged upon them later. Here for the first time
the soldiers of Hannibal gave way before the Romans,
being beaten back to their camp with much slaughter
and many wounds. For it is said that more than five
thousand of them were slain, while they killed not
more than five hundred of the Romans. Livy, however, will not affirm [1] that the victory was so great
nor that so many of the enemy were slain, but says
that this battle brought great renown to Marcellus,
and to the Romans a wonderful courage after their
disasters. They felt that they were contending, not
against a resistless and unconquerable foe, but against
one who was liable, like themselves, to defeat.

XII. For this reason, on the death of one of the

---

[1] *Vix equidem ausim adfirmare*, xxiii. 16, 15.

ἐκάλει Μάρκελλον ὁ δῆμος ἐπὶ τὴν διαδοχὴν
ἀπόντα, καὶ βίᾳ τῶν ἀρχόντων ὑπερέθετο τὴν
κατάστασιν ἕως ἐκεῖνος ἦλθεν ἀπὸ τοῦ στρατοπέδου. καὶ πάσαις μὲν ἀπεδείχθη ταῖς ψήφοις
ὕπατος, ἐπιβροντήσαντος δὲ τοῦ θεοῦ καὶ τῶν
ἱερέων οὐκ αἴσιον τιθεμένων τὸ σημεῖον, ἐμφανῶς
δὲ κωλύειν ὀκνούντων καὶ δεδιότων τὸν δῆμον,
2 αὐτὸς ἐξωμόσατο τὴν ἀρχήν. οὐ μέντοι τὴν
στρατείαν ἔφυγεν, ἀλλ᾿ ἀνθύπατος ἀναγορευθεὶς
καὶ πάλιν πρὸς Νῶλαν ἐπανελθὼν εἰς τὸ στρατόπεδον κακῶς ἐποίει τοὺς ᾑρημένους τὰ τοῦ
Φοίνικος. ὡς δὲ ὀξεῖαν ἐπ᾿ αὐτὸν θέμενος βοήθειαν ἐκεῖνος ἧκε, προκαλουμένῳ μὲν ἐκ παρατάξεως οὐκ ἠβουλήθη διαγωνίσασθαι, τρέψαντι
δὲ τὸ πλεῖστον ἐφ᾿ ἁρπαγὴν τοῦ στρατοῦ καὶ
μηκέτι προσδεχομένῳ μάχην ἐπεξῆλθε, διαδοὺς
δόρατα τῶν ναυμάχων μεγάλα τοῖς πεζοῖς, καὶ
διδάξας πόρρωθεν συντηροῦσι παίειν τοὺς Καρχηδονίους, ἀκοντιστὰς μὲν οὐκ ὄντας, αἰχμαῖς δὲ
3 χρωμένους ἐκ χειρὸς βραχείαις. διὸ καὶ δοκοῦσι
τότε δεῖξαι τὰ νῶτα Ῥωμαίοις ὅσοι συνέβαλον
καὶ φυγὴν ἀπροφάσιστον φυγεῖν, ἀποβαλόντες
ἐξ ἑαυτῶν νεκροὺς μὲν γενομένους πεντακισχιλί-
ους, αἰχμαλώτους δὲ ἑξακοσίους,[1] καὶ τῶν ἐλεφάντων τέσσαρας μὲν πεσόντας, δύο δὲ ζωοὺς
ἁλόντας. ὃ δ᾿ ἦν μέγιστον, ἡμέρᾳ τρίτῃ μετὰ
τὴν μάχην ἱππεῖς Ἰβήρων καὶ Νομάδων μιγάδες
αὐτομολοῦσιν ὑπὲρ τοὺς τριακοσίους, οὔπω πρότερον Ἀννίβᾳ τοῦτο παθόντος, ἀλλ᾿ ἐκ ποικίλων
καὶ πολυτρόπων συνηρμοσμένον ἐθνῶν βαρβαρι-

---

[1] αἰχμαλώτους δὲ ἑξακοσίους added to the text by Sintenis
and Bekker, after Livy, xxiii. 46, 4.

consuls,[1] the people called Marcellus home to succeed
him, and, in spite of the magistrates, postponed the
election until his return from the army. He was
made consul by a unanimous vote, but there was a
peal of thunder at the time, and since the augurs
considered the omen unpropitious, but hesitated to
make open opposition for fear of the people, he renounced the office of himself. He did not, however,
lay aside his military command, but having been
declared proconsul, he returned to his army at Nola
and proceeded to punish those who had espoused the
cause of the Carthaginian. And when Hannibal came
swiftly to their aid against him, and challenged him
to a pitched battle, Marcellus declined an engagement; but as soon as his adversary had set the greater
part of his army to plundering and was no longer
expecting a battle, he led his forces out against him.
He had distributed long spears used in naval combats
among his infantry, and taught them to watch their
opportunity and smite the Carthaginians at long
range; these were not javelineers, but used short
spears in hand to hand fighting. This seems to have
been the reason why at that time all the Carthaginians who were engaged turned their backs upon
the Romans and took to unhesitating flight, losing
five thousand of their number slain, and six hundred
prisoners; four of their elephants also were killed,
and two taken alive. But what was most important,
on the third day after the battle, more than three
hundred horsemen, composed of Spaniards and Numidians, deserted from them. Such a disaster had
not happened before this to Hannibal, but a barbarian
army made up of varied and dissimilar peoples had

---

[1] Lucius Postumius, who was utterly defeated and slain
by the Gauls in 215 B.C. Cf. Livy, xxiii. 24.

κὸν στράτευμα πλεῖστον χρόνον ἐν μιᾷ γνώμῃ
διαφυλάξαντος. οὗτοι μὲν οὖν πιστοὶ παρέμειναν
εἰς ἅπαν αὐτῷ τε τῷ Μαρκέλλῳ καὶ τοῖς μετ'
αὐτὸν στρατηγοῖς.

XIII. Ὁ δὲ Μάρκελλος ἀποδειχθεὶς ὕπατος
τὸ τρίτον εἰς Σικελίαν ἔπλευσεν. αἱ γὰρ Ἀννίβου περὶ τὸν πόλεμον εὐπραξίαι Καρχηδονίους
ἐπῆραν αὖθις ἀντιλαμβάνεσθαι τῆς νήσου, μάλιστα τεταραγμένων τῶν περὶ τὰς Συρακούσας
μετὰ τὴν Ἱερωνύμου τοῦ τυράννου τελευτήν.
διὸ καὶ Ῥωμαίων ἦν ἐκεῖ προαπεσταλμένη δύνα-
2 μις καὶ στρατηγὸς Ἄππιος. ταύτην παραλαμ-
βάνοντι τῷ Μαρκέλλῳ προσπίπτουσι Ῥωμαῖοι
πολλοὶ συμφορᾷ κεχρημένοι τοιαύτῃ. τῶν περὶ
Κάννας παραταξαμένων πρὸς Ἀννίβαν οἱ μὲν
ἔφυγον, οἱ δὲ ζῶντες ἥλωσαν, τοσοῦτον πλῆθος
ὡς δοκεῖν Ῥωμαίοις ὑπολελεῖφθαι μηδὲ τοὺς τὰ
3 τείχη διαφυλάξοντας. τοῖς δὲ ἄρα τοσοῦτο τοῦ
φρονήματος καὶ μεγαλοψυχίας περιῆν ὥστε τοὺς
μὲν αἰχμαλώτους ἐπὶ μικροῖς λύτροις ἀποδιδόντος
Ἀννίβου μὴ λαβεῖν, ἀλλ' ἀποψηφίσασθαι καὶ
περιιδεῖν τοὺς μὲν ἀναιρεθέντας, τοὺς δὲ πραθέν-
τας ἔξω τῆς Ἰταλίας, τῶν δὲ φυγῇ περιγενομένων
τὸ πλῆθος εἰς Σικελίαν ἀποστεῖλαι, διακελευσα-
μένους Ἰταλίας μὴ ἐπιβαίνειν ἕως πολεμοῦσι
4 πρὸς Ἀννίβαν. οὗτοι δὴ τῷ Μαρκέλλῳ παρα-
γενομένῳ προσπεσόντες ἀθρόοι, καὶ χαμαὶ καταβαλόντες αὑτούς, ᾔτουν τάξιν ἐπιτίμου στρατείας
μετὰ πολλῆς βοῆς καὶ δακρύων, ἐπαγγελλόμενοι
δείξειν δι' ἔργων ἀτυχίᾳ τινὶ μᾶλλον ἢ δι' ἀναν- 305

for a very long time been kept by him in perfect harmony. These deserters, then, remained entirely faithful both to Marcellus himself, and to the generals who succeeded him.[1]

XIII. And now Marcellus, having been appointed consul for the third time,[2] sailed to Sicily. For Hannibal's successes in the war had encouraged the Carthaginians to attempt anew the conquest of the island, especially now that Syracuse was in confusion after the death of the tyrant Hieronymus. For this reason the Romans also had previously sent a force thither under the command of Appius. As Marcellus took over this force, he was beset by many Romans who were involved in a calamity now to be described. Of those who had been drawn up against Hannibal at Cannae, some had fled, and others had been taken alive, and in such numbers that it was thought the Romans had not even men enough left to defend the walls of their city. And yet so much of their high spirit and haughtiness remained that, although Hannibal offered to restore his prisoners of war for a slight ransom, they voted not to receive them, but suffered some of them to be put to death and others to be sold out of Italy; and as for the multitude who had saved themselves by flight, they sent them to Sicily, ordering them not to set foot in Italy as long as the war against Hannibal lasted.[3] These were the men who, now that Marcellus was come, beset him in throngs, and throwing themselves on the ground before him, begged with many cries and tears for an assignment to honourable military service, promising to show by their actions that their

---

[1] Cf. Livy, xxiii. 46, 1–7.
[2] In 214 B.C. Fabius Maximus was his colleague.
[3] Cf. Livy, xxiii. 25, 7.

δρίαν αὐτῶν τὴν τροπὴν ἐκείνην γενομένην.
οἰκτείρας οὖν αὐτοὺς ὁ Μάρκελλος ἔγραψε πρὸς
τὴν σύγκλητον αἰτούμενος ἐκ τούτων ἀεὶ τῆς
5 στρατιᾶς τὸ ἐπιλεῖπον ἀναπληροῦν. λόγων δὲ
πολλῶν γενομένων ἐποιήσατο γνώμην ἡ βουλὴ
μηδὲν εἰς δημόσια πράγματα δεῖσθαι Ῥωμαίους
ἀνθρώπων ἀνάνδρων· εἰ δὲ βούλεται χρῆσθαι
Μάρκελλος αὐτοῖς ἴσως, μηδενὸς τῶν ἐπ' ἀνδρείᾳ
νομιζομένων στεφάνων καὶ γερῶν τυχεῖν ὑπ'
ἄρχοντος. τοῦτο τὸ δόγμα Μάρκελλον ἠνίασε,
καὶ μετὰ τὸν ἐν Σικελίᾳ πόλεμον ἐπανελθὼν
ἐμέμψατο τὴν βουλήν, ὡς ἀντὶ πολλῶν καὶ μεγάλων οὐ παρασχοῦσαν αὐτῷ τοσούτων δυστυχίαν
ἐπανορθώσασθαι πολιτῶν.

XIV. Τότε δ' ἐν Σικελίᾳ πρῶτον μὲν ἀδικηθεὶς
ὑπὸ Ἱπποκράτους Συρακουσίων στρατηγοῦ, ὃς
Καρχηδονίοις χαριζόμενος καὶ τυραννίδα κτώμενος αὑτῷ πολλοὺς διέφθειρε Ῥωμαίων πρὸς
Λεοντίνοις, εἷλε[1] τὴν τῶν Λεοντίνων πόλιν κατὰ
κράτος, καὶ Λεοντίνους μὲν οὐκ ἠδίκησε, τῶν δὲ
αὐτομόλων ὅσους ἔλαβε μαστιγώσας ἀπέκτεινε.
2 τοῦ δ' Ἱπποκράτους πρῶτον μὲν λόγον εἰς τὰς
Συρακούσας προπέμψαντος ὡς Λεοντίνους ἡβηδὸν
ἀποσφάττει Μάρκελλος, ἔπειτα δὲ τεταραγμένοις
ἐπιπεσόντος καὶ τὴν πόλιν καταλαβόντος, ἄρας
ὁ Μάρκελλος τῷ στρατῷ παντὶ πρὸς τὰς Συρακούσας ἐχώρει. καὶ καταστρατοπεδεύσας πλησίον εἰσέπεμψε μὲν πρέσβεις περὶ τῶν ἐν Λεοντίνοις διδάξοντας, ὡς δὲ οὐδὲν ἦν ὄφελος μὴ πειθο-
μένων Συρακουσίων (ἐκράτουν γὰρ οἱ περὶ τὸν
3 Ἱπποκράτην), προσβολὰς ἐποιεῖτο κατὰ γῆν ἅμα

---

[1] εἷλε with Reiske and Coraës : ... καὶ εἷλε, the lacuna to
be filled from Livy xxiv. 30, 1.

former defeat had been due to some great misfortune
rather than to cowardice. Marcellus, therefore,
taking pity on them, wrote to the senate asking
permission to fill up the deficiencies in his army
from time to time with these men. But after much
discussion the senate declared its opinion that the
Roman commonwealth had no need of men who
were cowards; if, however, as it appeared, Marcellus
wished to use them, they were to receive from their
commander none of the customary crowns or prizes
for valour. This decree vexed Marcellus, and when
he came back to Rome after the war in Sicily, he
upbraided the senate for not permitting him, in
return for his many great services, to redeem so
many citizens from misfortune.

XIV. But in Sicily, at the time of which I speak,
his first proceeding, after wrong had been done him by
Hippocrates, the commander of the Syracusans (who,
to gratify the Carthaginians and acquire the tyranny
for himself, had killed many Romans at Leontini),
was to take the city of Leontini by storm. He did
no harm, however, to its citizens, but all the deserters whom he took he ordered to be beaten with
rods and put to death. Hippocrates first sent a
report to Syracuse that Marcellus was putting all
the men of Leontini to the sword, and then, when
the city was in a tumult at the news, fell suddenly
upon it and made himself master of it. Upon this,
Marcellus set out with his whole army and came to
Syracuse. He encamped near by, and sent ambassadors into the city to tell the people what had
really happened at Leontini; but when this was of
no avail and the Syracusans would not listen to him,
the power being now in the hands of Hippocrates,
he proceeded to attack the city by land and sea,

469

καὶ κατὰ θάλατταν, Ἀππίου μὲν τὸν πεζὸν ἐπά-
γοντος στρατόν, αὐτὸς δὲ πεντήρεις ἔχων ἑξήκοντα
παντοδαπῶν ὅπλων καὶ βελῶν πλήρεις. ὑπὲρ δὲ
μεγάλου ζεύγματος νεῶν ὀκτὼ πρὸς ἀλλήλας συν-
δεδεμένων μηχανὴν ἄρας ἐπέπλει πρὸς τὸ τεῖχος,
τῷ πλήθει καὶ τῇ λαμπρότητι τῆς παρασκευῆς
καὶ τῇ δόξῃ τῇ περὶ αὐτὸν πεποιθώς· ἧς ἄρα
λόγος οὐδεὶς ἦν Ἀρχιμήδει καὶ τοῖς Ἀρχιμήδους
4 μηχανήμασιν. ὧν ὡς μὲν ἔργον ἄξιον σπουδῆς
οὐδὲν ὁ ἀνὴρ προὔθετο, γεωμετρίας δὲ παιζούσης
ἐγεγόνει πάρεργα τὰ πλεῖστα, πρότερον φιλοτι-
μηθέντος Ἱέρωνος τοῦ βασιλέως καὶ πείσαντος
Ἀρχιμήδη τρέψαι τι τῆς τέχνης ἀπὸ τῶν νοητῶν
ἐπὶ τὰ σωματικὰ καὶ τὸν λόγον ἁμῶς γέ πως δι'
αἰσθήσεως μίξαντα ταῖς χρείαις ἐμφανέστερον
καταστῆσαι τοῖς πολλοῖς.

5   Τὴν γὰρ ἀγαπωμένην ταύτην καὶ περιβόητον
ὀργανικὴν ἤρξαντο μὲν κινεῖν οἱ περὶ Εὔδοξον καὶ
Ἀρχύταν, ποικίλλοντες τῷ γλαφυρῷ γεωμετρίαν,
καὶ λογικῆς καὶ γραμμικῆς ἀποδείξεως οὐκ εὐπο-
ροῦντα προβλήματα δι' αἰσθητῶν καὶ ὀργανικῶν
παραδειγμάτων ὑπερείδοντες, ὡς τὸ περὶ δύο μέ-
σας ἀνὰ λόγον πρόβλημα καὶ στοιχεῖον ἐπὶ πολλὰ τῶν γραφομένων ἀναγκαῖον εἰς ὀργανικὰς
ἐξῆγον ἀμφότεροι κατασκευάς, μεσογράφους τινὰς
ἀπὸ καμπύλων γραμμῶν καὶ τμημάτων μεθαρμό-
6 ζοντες· ἐπεὶ δὲ Πλάτων ἠγανάκτησε καὶ διετεί-
νατο πρὸς αὐτοὺς ὡς ἀπολλύντας καὶ διαφθεί-
ροντας τὸ γεωμετρίας ἀγαθόν, ἀπὸ τῶν ἀσωμάτων

---

[1] See chapter xv. 3.   According to Polybius (viii. 6),
Marcellus had eight quinqueremes in pairs, and on each
pair, lashed together, a "sambuca" (or *harp*) had been

Appius leading up the land forces, and he himself
having a fleet of sixty quinqueremes filled with all
sorts of arms and missiles. Moreover, he had
erected an engine of artillery on a huge platform
supported by eight galleys fastened together,[1] and
with this sailed up to the city wall, confidently rely-
ing on the extent and splendour of his equipment
and his own great fame. But all this proved to be
of no account in the eyes of Archimedes and in
comparison with the engines of Archimedes. To
these he had by no means devoted himself as work
worthy of his serious effort, but most of them were
mere accessories of a geometry practised for amusement, since in bygone days Hiero the king had
eagerly desired and at last persuaded him to turn
his art somewhat from abstract notions to material
things, and by applying his philosophy somehow to
the needs which make themselves felt, to render
it more evident to the common mind.

For the art of mechanics, now so celebrated and
admired, was first originated by Eudoxus and
Archytas, who embellished geometry with its subt-
leties, and gave to problems incapable of proof by
word and diagram, a support derived from mechanical illustrations that were patent to the senses. For
instance, in solving the problem of finding two mean
proportional lines, a necessary requisite for many
geometrical figures, both mathematicians had recourse to mechanical arrangements, adapting to
their purposes certain intermediate portions of
curved lines and sections. But Plato was incensed
at this, and inveighed against them as corrupters
and destroyers of the pure excellence of geometry,

---

[1] constructed. This was a pent-house for raising armed men
on to the battlements of the besieged city.

καὶ νοητῶν ἀποδιδρασκούσης ἐπὶ τὰ αἰσθητά,
καὶ προσχρωμένης αὖθις αὖ σώμασι πολλῆς καὶ
φορτικῆς βαναυσουργίας δεομένοις, οὕτω διεκρίθη
γεωμετρίας ἐκπεσοῦσα μηχανική, καὶ περιορω-
μένη πολὺν χρόνον ὑπὸ φιλοσοφίας μία τῶν
στρατιωτίδων τεχνῶν ἐγεγόνει.

7   Καὶ μέντοι καὶ Ἀρχιμήδης, Ἱέρωνι τῷ βασιλεῖ
συγγενὴς ὢν καὶ φίλος, ἔγραψεν ὡς τῇ δοθείσῃ
δυνάμει τὸ δοθὲν βάρος κινῆσαι δυνατόν ἐστι· 30
καὶ νεανιευσάμενος, ὥς φασι, ῥώμῃ τῆς ἀποδείξεως εἶπεν ὡς, εἰ γῆν εἶχεν ἑτέραν, ἐκίνησεν ἂν
8   ταύτην μεταβὰς εἰς ἐκείνην. θαυμάσαντος δὲ τοῦ
Ἱέρωνος, καὶ δεηθέντος εἰς ἔργον ἐξαγαγεῖν τὸ
πρόβλημα καὶ δεῖξαί τι τῶν μεγάλων κινούμενον
ὑπὸ σμικρᾶς δυνάμεως, ὁλκάδα τριάρμενον τῶν
βασιλικῶν πόνῳ μεγάλῳ καὶ χειρὶ πολλῇ νεωλ-
κηθεῖσαν, ἐμβαλὼν ἀνθρώπους τε πολλοὺς καὶ
τὸν συνήθη φόρτον, αὐτὸς ἄπωθεν καθήμενος, οὐ
μετὰ σπουδῆς, ἀλλὰ ἠρέμα τῇ χειρὶ σείων ἀρχήν
τινα πολυσπάστου προσηγάγετο λείως καὶ ἀπταί-
9   στως καὶ ὥσπερ διὰ θαλάττης ἐπιθέουσαν. ἐκ-
πλαγεὶς οὖν ὁ βασιλεὺς καὶ συννοήσας τῆς τέχνης
τὴν δύναμιν, ἔπεισε τὸν Ἀρχιμήδην ὅπως αὐτῷ
τὰ μὲν ἀμυνομένῳ, τὰ δ' ἐπιχειροῦντι μηχανή-
ματα κατασκευάσῃ πρὸς πᾶσαν ἰδέαν πολιορκίας,
οἷς αὐτὸς μὲν οὐκ ἐχρήσατο, τοῦ βίου τὸ πλεῖστον
ἀπόλεμον καὶ πανηγυρικὸν βιώσας, τότε δ' ὑπῆρχε
τοῖς Συρακουσίοις εἰς δέον ἡ παρασκευὴ καὶ μετὰ
τῆς παρασκευῆς ὁ δημιουργός.

which thus turned her back upon the incorporeal things of abstract thought and descended to the things of sense, making use, moreover, of objects which required much mean and manual labour. For this reason mechanics was made entirely distinct from geometry, and being for a long time ignored by philosophers, came to be regarded as one of the military arts.

And yet even Archimedes, who was a kinsman and friend of King Hiero, wrote to him that with any given force it was possible to move any given weight ; and emboldened, as we are told, by the strength of his demonstration, he declared that, if there were another world, and he could go to it, he could move this. Hiero was astonished, and begged him to put his proposition into execution, and show him some great weight moved by a slight force. Archimedes therefore fixed upon a three-masted merchantman of the royal fleet, which had been dragged ashore by the great labours of many men, and after putting on board many passengers and the customary freight, he seated himself at a distance from her, and without any great effort, but quietly setting in motion with his hand a system of compound pulleys, drew her towards him smoothly and evenly, as though she were gliding through the water. Amazed at this, then, and comprehending the power of his art, the king persuaded Archimedes to prepare for him offensive and defensive engines to be used in every kind of siege warfare. These he had never used himself, because he spent the greater part of his life in freedom from war and amid the festal rites of peace ; but at the present time his apparatus stood the Syracusans in good stead, and, with the apparatus, its fabricator.[1]

[1] Cf. Polybius, viii. 5, 3–5 ; 9, 2 ; Livy, xxiv. 34.

XV. Ὡς οὖν προσέβαλον οἱ Ῥωμαῖοι διχόθεν,
ἔκπληξις ἦν τῶν Συρακουσίων καὶ σιγὴ διὰ δέος,
μηδὲν ἂν ἀνθέξειν πρὸς βίαν καὶ δύναμιν οἰομένων
τοσαύτην. σχάσαντος δὲ τὰς μηχανὰς τοῦ Ἀρχιμήδους ἅμα τοῖς μὲν πεζοῖς ἀπήντα τοξεύματά τε
παντοδαπὰ καὶ λίθων ὑπέρογκα μεγέθη, ῥοίζῳ
καὶ τάχει καταφερομένων ἀπίστῳ, καὶ μηδενὸς
ὅλως τὸ βρῖθος στέγοντος ἀθρόους ἀνατρεπόντων
τοὺς ὑποπίπτοντας καὶ τὰς τάξεις συγχεόντων,
2 ταῖς δὲ ναυσὶν ἀπὸ τῶν τειχῶν ἄφνω ὑπεραιωρού-
μεναι κεραῖαι τὰς μὲν ὑπὸ βρίθους στηρίζοντος
ἄνωθεν ὠθοῦσαι κατέδυον εἰς βυθόν, τὰς δὲ χερσὶ
σιδηραῖς ἢ στόμασιν εἰκασμένοις γεράνων ἀνα-
σπῶσαι πρῴραθεν ὀρθὰς ἐπὶ πρύμναν ἐβάπτιζον,
ἢ δι᾽ ἀντιτόνων ἔνδον ἐπιστρεφόμεναι καὶ περιαγό-
μεναι τοῖς ὑπὸ τὸ τεῖχος πεφυκόσι κρημνοῖς καὶ
σκοπέλοις προσήρασσον, ἅμα φθόρῳ πολλῷ τῶν
3 ἐπιβατῶν συντριβομένων. πολλάκις δὲ μετέωρος
ἐξαρθεῖσα ναῦς ἀπὸ τῆς θαλάσσης δεῦρο κἀκεῖσε
περιδινουμένη καὶ κρεμαμένη θέαμα φρικῶδες ἦν,
μέχρι οὗ τῶν ἀνδρῶν ἀπορριφέντων καὶ διασφεν-
δονηθέντων κενὴ προσπέσοι τοῖς τείχεσιν ἢ περιο-
λίσθοι τῆς λαβῆς ἀνείσης. ἦν δὲ ὁ Μάρκελλος
ἀπὸ τοῦ ζεύγματος ἐπῆγε μηχανήν, σαμβύκη μὲν
ἐκαλεῖτο δι᾽ ὁμοιότητά τινα σχήματος πρὸς τὸ
4 μουσικὸν ὄργανον, ἔτι δὲ ἄπωθεν αὐτῆς προσ-
φερομένης πρὸς τὸ τεῖχος ἐξήλατο λίθος δεκατά-

XV. When, therefore, the Romans assaulted them by sea and land, the Syracusans were stricken dumb with terror ; they thought that nothing could withstand so furious an onset by such forces. But Archimedes began to ply his engines, and shot against the land forces of the assailants all sorts of missiles and immense masses of stones, which came down with incredible din and speed ; nothing whatever could ward off their weight, but they knocked down in heaps those who stood in their way, and threw their ranks into confusion. At the same time huge beams were suddenly projected over the ships from the walls, which sank some of them with great weights plunging down from on high ; others were seized at the prow by iron claws, or beaks like the beaks of cranes, drawn straight up into the air, and then plunged stern foremost into the depths, or were turned round and round by means of enginery within the city, and dashed upon the steep cliffs that jutted out beneath the wall of the city, with great destruction of the fighting men on board, who perished in the wrecks. Frequently, too, a ship would be lifted out of the water into mid-air, whirled hither and thither as it hung there, a dreadful spectacle, until its crew had been thrown out and hurled in all directions, when it would fall empty upon the walls, or slip away from the clutch that had held it. As for the engine which Marcellus was bringing up on the bridge of ships, and which was called " sambuca " from some resemblance it had to the musical instrument of that name,[1] while it was still some distance off in its approach to the wall, a stone of ten talents' weight [2] was discharged at it, then a

[1] See chapter xiv. 3.
[2] A talent's weight was something over fifty pounds.

λαντος ὁλκήν, εἶτα ἕτερος ἐπὶ τούτῳ καὶ τρίτος,
ὧν οἱ μὲν αὐτῇ[1] ἐμπεσόντες μεγάλῳ κτύπῳ καὶ
κλύδωνι τῆς μηχανῆς τήν τε βάσιν συνηλόησαν
καὶ τὸ γόμφωμα διέσεισαν καὶ διέσπασαν τοῦ
ζεύγματος, ὥστε[2] τὸν Μάρκελλον ἀπορούμενον
αὐτόν τε ταῖς ναυσὶν ἀποπλεῖν κατὰ τάχος καὶ
τοῖς πεζοῖς ἀναχώρησιν παρεγγυῆσαι.

5   Βουλευομένοις δὲ ἔδοξεν αὐτοῖς ἔτι νυκτός, ἂν
δύνωνται, προσμῖξαι τοῖς τείχεσι· τοὺς γὰρ τό-
νους, οἷς χρῆσθαι τὸν Ἀρχιμήδην, ῥύμην ἔχοντας
ὑπερπετεῖς ποιήσεσθαι τὰς τῶν βελῶν ἀφέσεις,
ἐγγύθεν δὲ καὶ τελέως ἀπράκτους εἶναι διάστημα
τῆς πληγῆς οὐκ ἐχούσης. ὁ δ' ἦν, ὡς ἔοικεν, ἐπὶ
ταῦτα πάλαι παρεσκευασμένος ὀργάνων τε συμμέ-
τρους πρὸς πᾶν διάστημα κινήσεις καὶ βέλη
βραχέα, καὶ διὰ τὸ τεῖχος[3] οὐ μεγάλων, πολλῶν
δὲ καὶ συνεχῶν τρημάτων ὄντων,[3] οἱ σκορπίοι
βραχύτονοι μέν, ἐγγύθεν δὲ πλῆξαι παρεστήκεσαν
ἀόρατοι τοῖς πολεμίοις.

XVI. Ὡς οὖν προσέμιξαν οἰόμενοι λανθάνειν,
αὖθις αὖ βέλεσι πολλοῖς ἐντυγχάνοντες καὶ πληγαῖς, πετρῶν μὲν ἐκ κεφαλῆς ἐπ' αὐτοὺς φερομένων ὥσπερ πρὸς κάθετον, τοῦ δὲ τείχους τοξεύματα πανταχόθεν ἀναπέμποντος, ἀνεχώρουν ὀπί-
2   σω. κἀνταῦθα πάλιν αὐτῶν εἰς μῆκος ἐκτετα-
γμένων, βελῶν ἐκθεόντων καὶ καταλαμβανόντων
ἀπιόντας ἐγίνετο πολὺς μὲν αὐτῶν φθόρος, πολὺς
δὲ τῶν νεῶν συγκρουσμός, οὐδὲν ἀντιδρᾶσαι τοὺς
πολεμίους δυναμένων. τὰ γὰρ πλεῖστα τῶν ὁρ-

---

[1] αὐτῇ Bekker, after Coraës : αὐτῆς (of the engine itself).

[2] ὥστε before this word Sintenis[2] and Bekker assume a
lacuna in the text, comparing Polybius, viii. 7, fin.

[3] τὸ τεῖχος, ὄντων added to the text by Sintenis, who
compares Polybius viii. 7, 6.

second and a third; some of these, falling upon it with great din and surge of wave, crushed the foundation of the engine, shattered its frame-work, and dislodged it from the platform, so that Marcellus, in perplexity, ordered his ships to sail back as fast as they could, and his land forces to retire.

Then, in a council of war, it was decided to come up under the walls while it was still night, if they could; for the ropes which Archimedes used in his engines, since they imparted great impetus to the missiles cast, would, they thought, send them flying over their heads, but would be ineffective at close quarters, where there was no space for the cast. Archimedes, however, as it seemed, had long before prepared for such an emergency engines with a range adapted to any interval and missiles of short flight, and through many small and contiguous openings in the wall short-range engines called scorpions could be brought to bear on objects close at hand without being seen by the enemy.

XVI. When, therefore, the Romans came up under the walls, thinking themselves unnoticed, once more they encountered a great storm of missiles; huge stones came tumbling down upon them almost perpendicularly, and the wall shot out arrows at them from every point; they therefore retired. And here again, when they were some distance off, missiles darted forth and fell upon them as they were going away, and there was a great slaughter among them; many of their ships, too, were dashed together, and they could not retaliate in any way upon their foes. For Archimedes had built most of his engines close

γάνων ὑπὸ τὸ τεῖχος ἐσκευοποίητο τῷ Ἀρχιμήδει,
καὶ θεομαχοῦσιν ἐῴκεσαν οἱ Ῥωμαῖοι, μυρίων
αὐτοῖς κακῶν ἐξ ἀφανοῦς ἐπιχεομένων.

XVII. Οὐ μὴν ἀλλ' ὁ Μάρκελλος ἀπέφυγέ τε
καὶ τοὺς σὺν ἑαυτῷ σκώπτων τεχνίτας καὶ μη-
χανοποιοὺς ἔλεγεν· "Οὐ παυσόμεθα πρὸς τὸν
γεωμετρικὸν τοῦτον Βριάρεων πολεμοῦντες, ὃς
ταῖς μὲν ναυσὶν[1] ἡμῶν κυαθίζει ἐκ τῆς θαλάσσης,
τὴν δὲ σαμβύκην ῥαπίζων[1] μετ' αἰσχύνης ἐκβέ-
βληκε, τοὺς δὲ μυθικοὺς ἑκατόγχειρας ὑπεραίρει
2 τοσαῦτα βάλλων ἅμα βέλη καθ' ἡμῶν; " τῷ
γὰρ ὄντι πάντες οἱ λοιποὶ Συρακούσιοι σῶμα τῆς
Ἀρχιμήδους παρασκευῆς ἦσαν, ἡ δὲ κινοῦσα
πάντα καὶ στρέφουσα ψυχὴ μία, τῶν μὲν ἄλλων
ὅπλων ἀτρέμα κειμένων, μόνοις δὲ τοῖς ἐκείνου
τότε τῆς πόλεως χρωμένης καὶ πρὸς ἄμυναν καὶ
3 πρὸς ἀσφάλειαν. τέλος δὲ τοὺς Ῥωμαίους οὕτω
περιφόβους γεγονότας ὁρῶν ὁ Μάρκελλος ὥστ', εἰ
καλῴδιον ἢ ξύλον ὑπὲρ τοῦ τείχους μικρὸν ὀφθείη
προτεινόμενον, τοῦτο ἐκεῖνο, μηχανήν τινα κινεῖν
ἐπ' αὐτοὺς Ἀρχιμήδη βοῶντας ἀποτρέπεσθαι καὶ
φεύγειν, ἀπέσχετο μάχης ἁπάσης καὶ προσβολῆς,
τὸ λοιπὸν ἐπὶ τῷ χρόνῳ τὴν πολιορκίαν θέμενος.

Τηλικοῦτον μέντοι φρόνημα καὶ βάθος ψυχῆς
καὶ τοσοῦτον ἐκέκτητο θεωρημάτων πλοῦτον
Ἀρχιμήδης ὥστε, ἐφ' οἷς ὄνομα καὶ δόξαν οὐκ
ἀνθρωπίνης, ἀλλὰ δαιμονίου τινὸς ἔσχε συνέσεως,
4 μηθὲν ἐθελῆσαι σύγγραμμα περὶ τούτων ἀπολιπεῖν, ἀλλὰ τὴν περὶ τὰ μηχανικὰ πραγματείαν
καὶ πᾶσαν ὅλως τέχνην χρείας ἐφαπτομένην

---

[1] ταῖς μὲν ναυσὶν . . . ῥαπίζων an early anonymous correction
of the MSS. τὰς μὲν ναῦς ἡμῶν καθίζων πρὸς τὴν θάλασσαν
παίζων, adopted by Bekker. Cf. Polybius, viii. 8, 6.

behind the wall, and the Romans seemed to be fighting against the gods, now that countless mischiefs were poured out upon them from an invisible source.

XVII. However, Marcellus made his escape, and jesting with his own artificers and engineers, "Let us stop," said he, "fighting against this geometrical Briareus, who uses our ships like cups to ladle water from the sea, and has whipped and driven off in disgrace our sambuca, and with the many missiles which he shoots against us all at once, outdoes the hundred-handed monsters of mythology." For in reality all the rest of the Syracusans were but a body for the designs of Archimedes, and his the one soul moving and managing everything; for all other weapons lay idle, and his alone were then employed by the city both in offence and defence. At last the Romans became so fearful that, whenever they saw a bit of rope or a stick of timber projecting a little over the wall, "There it is," they cried, "Archimedes is training some engine upon us," and turned their backs and fled. Seeing this, Marcellus desisted from all fighting and assault, and thenceforth depended on a long siege.

And yet Archimedes possessed such a lofty spirit, so profound a soul, and such a wealth of scientific theory, that although his inventions had won for him a name and fame for superhuman sagacity, he would not consent to leave behind him any treatise on this subject, but regarding the work of an engineer and every art that ministers to the needs of life as ignoble and vulgar, he devoted his earnest

479

ἀγεννῆ καὶ βάναυσον ἡγησάμενος, εἰς ἐκεῖνα
καταθέσθαι μόνα τὴν αὑτοῦ φιλοτιμίαν οἷς τὸ
καλὸν καὶ περιττὸν ἀμιγὲς τοῦ ἀναγκαίου πρόσ-
εστιν, ἀσύγκριτα μὲν ὄντα τοῖς ἄλλοις, ἔριν δὲ
παρέχοντα πρὸς τὴν ὕλην τῇ ἀποδείξει, τῆς μὲν
τὸ μέγεθος καὶ τὸ κάλλος, τῆς δὲ τὴν ἀκρίβειαν
5 καὶ τὴν δύναμιν ὑπερφυῆ παρεχομένης· οὐ γὰρ
ἔστιν ἐν γεωμετρίᾳ χαλεπωτέρας καὶ βαρυτέρας
ὑποθέσεις ἐν ἁπλουστέροις λαβεῖν καὶ καθαρω-
τέροις στοιχείοις γραφομένας. καὶ τοῦθ᾽ οἱ μὲν
εὐφυΐᾳ τοῦ ἀνδρὸς προσάπτουσιν, οἱ δὲ ὑπερβολῇ
τινι πόνου νομίζουσιν ἀπόνως πεποιημένῳ καὶ
ῥᾳδίως ἕκαστον ἐοικὸς γεγονέναι. ζητῶν μὲν γὰρ
οὐκ ἄν τις εὕροι δι᾽ αὑτοῦ τὴν ἀπόδειξιν, ἅμα δὲ
τῇ μαθήσει παρίσταται δόξα τοῦ κἂν αὐτὸν
εὑρεῖν· οὕτω λείαν ὁδὸν ἄγει[1] καὶ ταχεῖαν ἐπὶ τὸ
6 δεικνύμενον. οὔκουν οὐδὲ ἀπιστῆσαι τοῖς περὶ
αὑτοῦ λεγομένοις ἐστίν, ὡς ὑπ᾽ οἰκείας δή τινος
καὶ συνοίκου θελγόμενος ἀεὶ σειρῆνος ἐλέληστο
καὶ σίτου[2] καὶ θεραπείας σώματος ἐξέλιπε, βίᾳ
δὲ πολλάκις ἑλκόμενος ἐπ᾽ ἄλειμμα καὶ λουτρόν,
ἐν ταῖς ἐσχάραις ἔγραφε σχήματα τῶν γεωμετρι-
κῶν, καὶ τοῦ σώματος ἀληλιμμένου διῆγε τῷ
δακτύλῳ γραμμάς, ὑπὸ ἡδονῆς μεγάλης κάτοχος
7 ὢν καὶ μουσόληπτος ἀληθῶς. πολλῶν δὲ καὶ
καλῶν εὑρετὴς γεγονὼς λέγεται τῶν φίλων δεηθῆναι καὶ τῶν συγγενῶν ὅπως αὐτοῦ μετὰ τὴν
τελευτὴν ἐπιστήσωσι τῷ τάφῳ τὸν περιλαμβάν-
οντα τὴν σφαῖραν ἐντὸς κύλινδρον, ἐπιγράψαντες
τὸν λόγον τῆς ὑπεροχῆς τοῦ περιέχοντος στερεοῦ
πρὸς τὸ περιεχόμενον.

[1] ἄγει Bekker, after Bryan : ἄγειν.
[2] καὶ σίτου Bekker has πότου καὶ σίτου (food and drink), a
suggestion of Coraës.

efforts only to those studies the subtlety and charm of which are not affected by the claims of necessity. These studies, he thought, are not to be compared with any others; in them the subject matter vies with the demonstration, the former supplying grandeur and beauty, the latter precision and surpassing power. For it is not possible to find in geometry more profound and difficult questions treated in simpler and purer terms. Some attribute this success to his natural endowments; others think it due to excessive labour that everything he did seemed to have been performed without labour and with ease. For no one could by his own efforts discover the proof, and yet as soon as he learns it from him, he thinks he might have discovered it himself; so smooth and rapid is the path by which he leads one to the desired conclusion. And therefore we may not disbelieve the stories told about him, how, under the lasting charm of some familiar and domestic Siren, he forgot even his food and neglected the care of his person; and how, when he was dragged by main force, as he often was, to the place for bathing and anointing his body, he would trace geometrical figures in the ashes, and draw lines with his finger in the oil with which his body was anointed, being possessed by a great delight, and in very truth a captive of the Muses. And although he made many excellent discoveries, he is said to have asked his kinsmen and friends to place over the grave where he should be buried a cylinder enclosing a sphere, with an inscription giving the proportion by which the containing solid exceeds the contained.[1]

---

[1] When Cicero was quaestor in Sicily (75 B.C.), he found this tomb, which had been neglected and forgotten by the Syracusans (*Tusc. Disp.* v. 64 ff.).

481

XVIII. Ἀρχιμήδης μὲν οὖν τοιοῦτος γενόμενος
ἀήττητον ἑαυτόν τε καὶ τὴν πόλιν, ὅσον ἐφ'
ἑαυτῷ, διεφύλαξε. τῆς δὲ πολιορκίας διὰ μέσου
Μάρκελλος εἷλε μὲν Μεγαρέας, πόλιν ἐν ταῖς
παλαιοτάταις τῶν Σικελιωτίδων, εἷλε δὲ τὸ Ἱπ-   30
ποκράτους πρὸς Ἀκρίλλαις στρατόπεδον, καὶ
κατέκτεινεν ὑπὲρ ὀκτακισχιλίους ἐπιπεσὼν χάρακα βαλλομένοις, ἐπέδραμε δὲ πολλὴν τῆς
Σικελίας καὶ πόλεις ἀπέστησε Καρχηδονίων καὶ
μάχας ἐνίκησε πάσας τοὺς ἀντιταχθῆναι τολμή-
2 σαντας. χρόνῳ δὲ προϊόντι Δάμιππόν τινα
Σπαρτιάτην ἐκ Συρακουσῶν λαβὼν ἐκπλέοντα
αἰχμάλωτον, ἀξιούντων ἐπὶ λύτροις τῶν Συρακουσίων κομίσασθαι τὸν ἄνδρα, πολλάκις ὑπὲρ
τούτου διαλεγόμενος καὶ συντιθέμενος πύργον
τινὰ κατεσκέψατο φυλαττόμενον μὲν ἀμελῶς,
ἄνδρας δὲ δυνάμενον δέξασθαι κρύφα, τοῦ τείχους
3 ἐπιβατοῦ παρ' αὐτὸν ὄντος. ὡς οὖν τό τε ὕψος
ἐκ τοῦ πολλάκις προσιέναι καὶ διαλέγεσθαι πρὸς
τὸν πύργον εἰκάσθη καλῶς καὶ κλίμακες παρε-
σκευάσθησαν, ἑορτὴν Ἀρτέμιδι τοὺς Συρακουσίους ἄγοντας καὶ πρὸς οἶνον ὡρμημένους καὶ παιδιὰν παραφυλάξας, ἔλαθεν οὐ μόνον τὸν πύργον
κατασχών, ἀλλὰ καὶ κύκλῳ τὸ τεῖχος παρεμ-
πλήσας ὅπλων πρὶν ἡμέραν γενέσθαι, καὶ τὰ
4 Ἑξάπυλα διακόψας. ἀρχομένων δὲ κινεῖσθαι
καὶ ταράττεσθαι τῶν Συρακουσίων πρὸς τὴν
αἴσθησιν, ἅμα πανταχόθεν ταῖς σάλπιγξι χρῆσθαι κελεύσας φυγὴν ἐποίησε πολλὴν καὶ φόβον,
ὡς οὐδενὸς μέρους ἀναλώτου μένοντος. ἔμενε δὲ

XVIII. Such, then, was Archimedes, and, so far as he himself was concerned, he maintained himself and his city unconquered. But during the progress of the siege Marcellus captured Megara, one of the most ancient cities of Sicily; he also captured the camp of Hippocrates at Acrillae and killed more than eight thousand men, having attacked them as they were throwing up entrenchments; furthermore, he overran a great part of Sicily, brought cities over from the Carthaginians, and was everywhere victorious over those who ventured to oppose him. Some time afterwards he made a prisoner of a certain Damippus, a Spartan who tried to sail away from Syracuse. The Syracusans sought to ransom this man back, and during the frequent meetings and conferences which he held with them about the matter, Marcellus noticed a certain tower that was carelessly guarded, into which men could be secretly introduced, since the wall near it was easy to surmount. When, therefore, in his frequent approaches to it for holding these conferences, the height of the tower had been carefully estimated, and ladders had been prepared, he seized his opportunity when the Syracusans were celebrating a festival in honour of Artemis and were given over to wine and sport, and before they knew of his attempt not only got possession of the tower, but also filled the wall round about with armed men, before the break of day, and cut his way through the Hexapyla. When the Syracusans perceived this and began to run about confusedly, he ordered the trumpets to sound on all sides at once and thus put them to flight in great terror, believing as they did that no part of the city remained uncaptured.[1] There remained, however,

[1] Cf. Polybius, viii. 37; Livy, xxv. 23 f.

τὸ καρτερώτατον καὶ κάλλιστον καὶ μέγιστον
(Ἀχραδινὴ καλεῖται) διὰ τὸ τετειχίσθαι πρὸς
τὴν ἔξω πόλιν, ἧς τὸ μὲν Νέαν, τὸ δὲ Τύχην
ὀνομάζουσι.

XIX. Καὶ τούτων ἐχομένων ἅμα φάει διὰ τῶν
Ἑξαπύλων ὁ Μάρκελλος κατῄει, μακαριζόμενος
ὑπὸ τῶν ὑφ' ἑαυτὸν ἡγεμόνων. αὐτὸς μέντοι
λέγεται κατιδὼν ἄνωθεν καὶ περισκεψάμενος τῆς
πόλεως τὸ μέγεθος καὶ τὸ κάλλος ἐπὶ πολὺ
δακρῦσαι τῷ μέλλοντι γίνεσθαι συμπαθήσας,
ἐννοήσας οἷον ἐξ οἵου σχῆμα καὶ μορφὴν ἀμείψει
μετὰ μικρὸν ὑπὸ τοῦ στρατοπέδου διαφορηθεῖσα.

2 τῶν γὰρ ἡγεμόνων οὐδεὶς μὲν ἦν ὁ τολμῶν ἐναν-
τιοῦσθαι τοῖς στρατιώταις αἰτουμένοις δι' ἁρ-
παγῆς ὠφεληθῆναι, πολλοὶ δὲ καὶ πυρπολεῖν καὶ
κατασκάπτειν ἐκέλευον. ἀλλὰ τοῦτον μὲν οὐδὲ
ὅλως προσήκατο τὸν λόγον ὁ Μάρκελλος, μάλα
δὲ ἄκων βιασθεὶς ἔδωκεν ἀπὸ χρημάτων καὶ
ἀνδραπόδων ὠφελεῖσθαι, τῶν δὲ ἐλευθέρων σωμάτων ἀπεῖπεν ἅψασθαι, καὶ διεκελεύσατο μήτε
ἀποκτεῖναί τινα μήτε αἰσχῦναι μήτε ἀνδραποδίσασθαι Συρακουσίων.

3 Οὐ μὴν ἀλλὰ καίπερ οὕτω μετριάσαι δόξας
οἰκτρὰ πάσχειν ἡγεῖτο τὴν πόλιν, καὶ τὸ συμ-
παθοῦν καὶ τὸ συναλγοῦν ὅμως ἐν τοσούτῳ μεγέθει χαρᾶς ἡ ψυχὴ διέφαινεν ὁρῶντος ἐν βραχεῖ
χρόνῳ πολλῆς καὶ λαμπρᾶς ἀφανισμὸν εὐδαιμονίας. λέγεται γὰρ οὐκ ἐλάττονα τοῦτον ἢ τὸν
ὕστερον ἀπὸ Καρχηδόνος διαφορηθέντα πλοῦτον
γενέσθαι· καὶ γὰρ τὴν ἄλλην πόλιν οὐ μετὰ

the strongest, most beautiful, and largest part (called Achradina), because it had been fortified on the side towards the outer city, one part of which they call Neapolis, and another Tyche.

XIX. When these parts also were in his possession, at break of day Marcellus went down into the city through the Hexapyla, congratulated by the officers under him. He himself, however, as he looked down from the heights and surveyed the great and beautiful city, is said to have wept much in commiseration of its impending fate, bearing in mind how greatly its form and appearance would change in a little while, after his army had sacked it. For among his officers there was not a man who had the courage to oppose the soldiers' demand for a harvest of plunder, nay, many of them actually urged that the city should be burned and razed to the ground. This proposal, however, Marcellus would not tolerate at all, but much against his will, and under compulsion, he permitted booty to be made of property and slaves, although he forbade his men to lay hands on the free citizens, and strictly ordered them neither to kill nor outrage nor enslave any Syracusan.

However, although he seems to have acted with such moderation, he thought that the city suffered a lamentable fate, and amidst the great rejoicing of his followers his spirit nevertheless evinced its sympathy and commiseration when he saw a great and glorious prosperity vanishing in a brief time. For it is said that no less wealth was carried away from Syracuse now than at a later time from Carthage ; for not long afterwards [1] the rest of the city

---

[1] In 212 B.C., the siege having lasted nearly three years. Cf. Livy, xxv. 24–31.

πολὺν χρόνον ἁλοῦσαν ἐκ προδοσίας ἐβιάσαντο
διαρπάσαι, πλὴν τῶν βασιλικῶν χρημάτων·
ταῦτα δὲ εἰς τὸ δημόσιον ἐξῃρέθη.

4 Μάλιστα δὲ τὸ Ἀρχιμήδους πάθος ἠνίασε
Μάρκελλον. ἔτυχε μὲν γὰρ αὐτός τι καθ' ἑαυτὸν
ἀνασκοπῶν ἐπὶ διαγράμματος· καὶ τῇ θεωρίᾳ
δεδωκὼς ἅμα τήν τε διάνοιαν καὶ τὴν πρόσοψιν
οὐ προῄσθετο τὴν καταδρομὴν τῶν Ῥωμαίων
οὐδὲ τὴν ἅλωσιν τῆς πόλεως, ἄφνω δὲ ἐπιστάντος
αὐτῷ στρατιώτου καὶ κελεύοντος ἀκολουθεῖν
πρὸς Μάρκελλον οὐκ ἐβούλετο πρὶν ἢ τελέσαι
τὸ πρόβλημα καὶ καταστῆσαι πρὸς τὴν ἀπό-
5 δειξιν. ὁ δὲ ὀργισθεὶς καὶ σπασάμενος τὸ ξίφος
ἀνεῖλεν αὐτόν. ἕτεροι μὲν οὖν λέγουσιν ἐπι-
στῆναι μὲν εὐθὺς ὡς ἀποκτενοῦντα ξιφήρη τὸν
Ῥωμαῖον, ἐκεῖνον δ' ἰδόντα δεῖσθαι καὶ ἀντι- 30
βολεῖν ἀναμεῖναι βραχὺν χρόνον, ὡς μὴ κατα-
λίπῃ τὸ ζητούμενον ἀτελὲς καὶ ἀθεώρητον, τὸν δὲ
6 οὐ φροντίσαντα διαχρήσασθαι. καὶ τρίτος ἐστὶ
λόγος, ὡς κομίζοντι πρὸς Μάρκελλον αὐτῷ τῶν
μαθηματικῶν ὀργάνων σκιόθηρα καὶ σφαίρας καὶ
γωνίας, αἷς ἐναρμόττει τὸ τοῦ ἡλίου μέγεθος πρὸς
τὴν ὄψιν, στρατιῶται περιτυχόντες καὶ χρυσίον
ἐν τῷ τεύχει δόξαντες φέρειν ἀπέκτειναν. ὅτι
μέντοι Μάρκελλος ἤλγησε καὶ τὸν αὐτόχειρα
τοῦ ἀνδρὸς ἀπεστράφη καθάπερ ἐναγῆ, τοὺς δὲ
οἰκείους ἀνευρὼν ἐτίμησεν, ὁμολογεῖται.

XX. Τῶν δὲ Ῥωμαίων τοῖς ἐκτὸς ἀνθρώποις
δεινῶν μὲν εἶναι πόλεμον μεταχειρίσασθαι καὶ
φοβερῶν εἰς χεῖρας ἐλθεῖν νομιζομένων, εὐγνω-

was betrayed and taken and subjected to pillage, excepting the royal treasure; this was converted into the public treasury.

But what most of all afflicted Marcellus was the death of Archimedes. For it chanced that he was by himself, working out some problem with the aid of a diagram, and having fixed his thoughts and his eyes as well upon the matter of his study, he was not aware of the incursion of the Romans or of the capture of the city. Suddenly a soldier came upon him and ordered him to go with him to Marcellus. This Archimedes refused to do until he had worked out his problem and established his demonstration, whereupon the soldier flew into a passion, drew his sword, and dispatched him. Others, however, say that the Roman came upon him with drawn sword threatening to kill him at once, and that Archimedes, when he saw him, earnestly besought him to wait a little while, that he might not leave the result that he was seeking incomplete and without demonstration; but the soldier paid no heed to him and made an end of him. There is also a third story, that as Archimedes was carrying to Marcellus some of his mathematical instruments, such as sun-dials and spheres and quadrants, by means of which he made the magnitude of the sun appreciable to the eye, some soldiers fell in with him, and thinking that he was carrying gold in the box, slew him. However, it is generally agreed that Marcellus was afflicted at his death, and turned away from his slayer as from a polluted person, and sought out the kindred of Archimedes and paid them honour.

XX. The Romans were considered by foreign peoples to be skilful in carrying on war and formidable fighters; but of gentleness and humanity

μοσύνης δὲ καὶ φιλανθρωπίας καὶ ὅλως πολιτικῆς
ἀρετῆς ὑποδείγματα μὴ δεδωκότων, πρῶτος δοκεῖ
τότε Μάρκελλος ὑποδεῖξαι τοῖς Ἕλλησι δικαιο-
2 τέρους Ῥωμαίους. οὕτω γὰρ ἐχρῆτο τοῖς συμ-
βάλλουσι καὶ τοσαῦτα καὶ πόλεις καὶ ἰδιώτας
εὐεργέτησεν ὥστε, εἴ τι περὶ Ἔνναν ἢ Μεγαρεῖς ἢ
Συρακουσίους ἔργον ἦν εἰργασμένον οὐκ ἐπιεικὲς
αὐτοῖς, τοῦτο τῶν πεπονθότων αἰτίᾳ μᾶλλον ἢ
τῶν πεποιηκότων δοκεῖν γεγονέναι. μνησθήσομαι
δὲ ἑνὸς ἀπὸ πολλῶν. πόλις ἐστὶ τῆς Σικελίας
Ἐγγύϊον οὐ μεγάλη, ἀρχαία δὲ πάνυ καὶ διὰ θεῶν
3 ἐπιφάνειαν ἔνδοξος, ἃς καλοῦσι ματέρας. ἵδρυμα
λέγεται Κρητῶν γενέσθαι τὸ ἱερόν· καὶ λόγχας
τινὰς ἐδείκνυσαν καὶ κράνη χαλκᾶ, τὰ μὲν ἔχοντα
Μηριόνου, τὰ δὲ Οὐλίξου, τουτέστιν Ὀδυσσέως,
ἐπιγραφάς, ἀνατεθεικότων ταῖς θεαῖς. ταύτην
προθυμότατα καρχηδονίζουσαν Νικίας, ἀνὴρ
πρῶτος τῶν πολιτῶν, ἔπειθε μεταθέσθαι πρὸς
Ῥωμαίους, ἀναφανδὸν ἐν ταῖς ἐκκλησίαις παρ-
ρησιαζόμενος καὶ κακῶς φρονοῦντας ἐξελέγχων
4 τοὺς ὑπεναντίους. οἱ δὲ φοβούμενοι τὴν δύναμιν
αὐτοῦ καὶ τὴν δόξαν ἐβουλεύσαντο συναρπάσαι
καὶ παραδοῦναι τοῖς Φοίνιξιν. αἰσθόμενος οὖν ὁ
Νικίας ἤδη καὶ παραφυλαττόμενον ἀδήλως ἑαυτόν,
ἐξέφερεν ἐν φανερῷ λόγους περὶ τῶν ματέρων
ἀνεπιτηδείους, καὶ πολλὰ πρὸς τὴν νομιζομένην
ἐπιφάνειαν καὶ δόξαν ὡς ἀπιστῶν καὶ καταφρονῶν ἔπραττεν, ἡδομένων τῶν ἐχθρῶν ὅτι τὴν
μεγίστην αἰτίαν αὐτὸς ἐφ᾽ ἑαυτὸν ὧν πείσεται
5 παρεῖχε. γεγονότων δὲ τῶν πρὸς τὴν σύλληψιν

and, in a word, of civil virtues, they had given no proofs, and at this time Marcellus seems to have been the first to show the Greeks that the Romans were the more observant of justice. For such was his treatment of those who had to do with him, and so many were the benefits which he conferred both upon cities and private persons, that, if the people of Enna or Megara or Syracuse met with any indignities, the blame for these was thought to belong to the sufferers rather than to the perpetrators. And I will mention one instance out of many. There is a city of Sicily called Engyium, not large, but very ancient, and famous for the appearance there of goddesses, who are called Mothers.[1] The temple is said to have been built by Cretans, and certain spears were shown there, and bronze helmets; some of these bore the name of Meriones, and others that of Ulysses (that is, Odysseus), who had consecrated them to the goddesses. This city, which most ardently favoured the Carthaginian cause, Nicias, its leading citizen, tried to induce to go over to the Romans, speaking openly and boldly in the assemblies and arguing the unwisdom of his opponents. But they, fearing his influence and authority, planned to arrest him and deliver him up to the Carthaginians. Nicias, accordingly, becoming aware at once of their design and of their secret watch upon him, gave utterance in public to unbecoming speeches about the Mothers, and did much to show that he rejected and despised the prevalent belief in their manifestations, his enemies meanwhile rejoicing that he was making himself most to blame for his coming fate. But just as they were ready to arrest

[1] Magna Mater, the Cretan Rhaea, often confounded with the Phrygian Cybele. Cf. Diodorus, iv. 79, 5-7.

ἑτοίμων ἦν μὲν ἐκκλησία τῶν πολιτῶν, ὁ δὲ
Νικίας μεταξύ τι λέγων καὶ συμβουλεύων πρὸς
τὸν δῆμον ἐξαίφνης ἀφῆκεν εἰς τὴν γῆν τὸ σῶμα,
καὶ μικρὸν διαλιπών, οἷον εἰκός, ἡσυχίας σὺν
ἐκπλήξει γενομένης, τὴν κεφαλὴν ἐπάρας καὶ
περιενεγκών, ὑποτρόμῳ φωνῇ καὶ βαρείᾳ, κατὰ
μικρὸν συντείνων καὶ παροξύνων τὸν ἦχον, ὡς
ἑώρα φρίκῃ καὶ σιωπῇ κατεχόμενον τὸ θέατρον,
ἀπορρίψας τὸ ἱμάτιον καὶ περιρρηξάμενος τὸν
χιτωνίσκον, ἡμίγυμνος ἀναπηδήσας ἔθεε πρὸς τὴν
ἔξοδον τοῦ θεάτρου, βοῶν ὑπὸ τῶν ματέρων ἐλαύ-
6 νεσθαι. μηδενὸς δὲ τολμῶντος ἅψασθαι μηδὲ
ἀπαντῆσαι διὰ δεισιδαιμονίαν, ἀλλ' ἐκτρεπο-
μένων, ἐπὶ τὰς πύλας ἐξέδραμεν, οὔτε φωνῆς
τινος οὔτε κινήσεως πρεπούσης δαιμονῶντι καὶ
παραφρονοῦντι φεισάμενος. ἡ δὲ γυνὴ συνειδυῖα
καὶ συντεχνάζουσα τῷ ἀνδρί, λαβοῦσα τὰ παιδία
πρῶτον μὲν ἱκέτις προσεκυλινδεῖτο τοῖς μεγάροις
τῶν θεῶν, ἔπειτα πλανώμενον ἐκεῖνον προσποιου-
μένη ζητεῖν κωλύοντος οὐδενὸς ἀσφαλῶς ἀπῆλθεν
7 ἐκ τῆς πόλεως. καὶ διεσώθησαν μὲν οὕτως εἰς
Συρακούσας πρὸς Μάρκελλον· ἐπεὶ δὲ πολλὰ
τοὺς Ἐγγυΐους ὑβρίσαντας καὶ πλημμελήσαντας
ἐλθὼν Μάρκελλος ἔδησε πάντας ὡς τιμωρησόμενος, ὁ δὲ Νικίας ἐδάκρυσε παρεστώς, τέλος δὲ
χειρῶν καὶ γονάτων ἁπτόμενος παρῃτεῖτο τοὺς
πολίτας, ἀπὸ τῶν ἐχθρῶν ἀρξάμενος, ἐπικλασθεὶς 31
ἀφῆκε πάντας καὶ τὴν πόλιν οὐδὲν ἠδίκησε, τῷ δὲ
Νικίᾳ χώραν τε πολλὴν καὶ δωρεὰς πολλὰς ἔδωκε.
ταῦτα μὲν οὖν Ποσειδώνιος ὁ φιλόσοφος ἱστόρησε.

XXI. Τὸν δὲ Μάρκελλον ἀνακαλουμένων τῶν
Ῥωμαίων ἐπὶ τὸν ἐγχώριον καὶ σύνοικον πόλεμον,
ἐπανερχόμενος τὰ πλεῖστα καὶ κάλλιστα τῶν ἐν

him, an assembly of the citizens was held, and here Nicias, right in the midst of some advice that he was giving to the people, suddenly threw himself upon the ground, and after a little while, amid the silence and consternation which naturally prevailed, lifted his head, turned it about, and spoke in a low and trembling voice, little by little raising and sharpening its tones. And when he saw the whole audience struck dumb with horror, he tore off his mantle, rent his tunic, and leaping up half naked, ran towards the exit from the theatre, crying out that he was pursued by the Mothers. No man venturing to lay hands upon him or even to come in his way, out of superstitious fear, but all avoiding him, he ran out to the gate of the city, freely using all the cries and gestures that would become a man possessed and crazed. His wife also, who was privy to his scheme, taking her children with her, first prostrated herself in supplication before the temples of the gods, and then, pretending to seek her wandering husband, no man hindering her, went safely forth out of the city. Thus they all escaped to Marcellus at Syracuse. But when Marcellus, after many transgressions and insults on the part of the men of Engyium, came and put them all in chains in order to punish them, then Nicias, standing by, burst into tears, and finally, clasping the hands and knees of Marcellus, begged the lives of his fellow citizens, beginning with his enemies. Marcellus relented, set them all free, and did their city no harm; he also bestowed upon Nicias ample lands and many gifts. At any rate, this story is told by Poseidonius the philosopher.

XXI. When Marcellus was recalled by the Romans to the war in their home territories, he carried back with him the greater part and the most beautiful of

Συρακούσαις ἐκίνησεν ἀναθημάτων, ὡς αὐτῷ τε
πρὸς τὸν θρίαμβον ὄψις εἴη καὶ τῇ πόλει κόσμος.
οὐδὲν γὰρ εἶχεν οὐδ' ἐγίνωσκε πρότερον τῶν
κομψῶν καὶ περιττῶν, οὐδὲ ἦν ἐν αὐτῇ τὸ χάριεν
2 τοῦτο καὶ γλαφυρὸν ἀγαπώμενον, ὅπλων δὲ βαρ-
βαρικῶν καὶ λαφύρων ἐναίμων ἀνάπλεως οὖσα
καὶ περιεστεφανωμένη θριάμβων ὑπομνήμασι καὶ
τροπαίοις οὐχ ἱλαρὸν οὐδ' ἄφοβον οὐδὲ δειλῶν
ἦν θέαμα καὶ τρυφώντων θεατῶν, ἀλλ' ὥσπερ
Ἐπαμεινώνδας τὸ Βοιώτιον πεδίον Ἄρεως ὀρχή-
στραν, Ξενοφῶν δὲ τὴν Ἔφεσον πολέμου ἐργα-
στήριον, οὕτως ἄν μοι δοκεῖ τις τότε τὴν Ῥώμην
κατὰ Πίνδαρον " βαθυπτολέμου τέμενος Ἄρεως "
3 προσειπεῖν. διὸ καὶ μᾶλλον εὐδοκίμησε παρὰ μὲν
τῷ δήμῳ Μάρκελλος ἡδονὴν ἐχούσαις καὶ χάριν
Ἑλληνικὴν καὶ πιθανότητα διαποικίλας ὄψεσι
τὴν πόλιν, παρὰ δὲ τοῖς πρεσβυτέροις Φάβιος
Μάξιμος. οὐδὲν γὰρ ἐκίνησε τοιοῦτον οὐδὲ μετή-
νεγκεν ἐκ τῆς Ταραντίνων πόλεως ἁλούσης, ἀλλὰ
τὰ μὲν ἄλλα χρήματα καὶ τὸν πλοῦτον ἐξεφό-
ρησε, τὰ δὲ ἀγάλματα μένειν εἴασεν, ἐπειπὼν τὸ
4 μνημονευόμενον· "' Ἀπολείπωμεν," γὰρ ἔφη, " τοὺς
θεοὺς τούτους τοῖς Ταραντίνοις κεχολωμένους."
Μάρκελλον δ' ᾐτιῶντο πρῶτον μὲν ὡς ἐπίφθονον
ποιοῦντα τὴν πόλιν, οὐ μόνον ἀνθρώπων, ἀλλὰ
καὶ θεῶν οἷον αἰχμαλώτων ἀγομένων ἐν αὐτῇ καὶ
πομπευομένων, ἔπειτα ὅτι τὸν δῆμον εἰθισμένον
5 πολεμεῖν ἢ γεωργεῖν, τρυφῆς δὲ καὶ ῥαθυμίας
ἄπειρον ὄντα καὶ κατὰ τὸν Εὐριπίδειον Ἡρακλέα,

Φαῦλον, ἄκομψον, τὰ μέγιστ' ἀγαθόν,[1]

---

[1] μέγιστ' ἀγαθόν with Coraës, as in the *Cimon*, iv. 4:
μέγιστά τε ἀγαθόν.

the dedicatory offerings in Syracuse, that they might grace his triumph and adorn his city. For before this time Rome neither had nor knew about such elegant and exquisite productions, nor was there any love there for such graceful and subtle art; but filled full of barbaric arms and bloody spoils, and crowned round about with memorials and trophies of triumphs, she was not a gladdening or a reassuring sight, nor one for unwarlike and luxurious spectators. Indeed, as Epaminondas called the Boeotian plain a "dancing floor of Ares," and as Xenophon [1] speaks of Ephesus as a "work-shop of war," so, it seems to me, one might at that time have called Rome, in the language of Pindar, "a precinct of much-warring Ares." [2] Therefore with the common people Marcellus won more favour because he adorned the city with objects that had Hellenic grace and charm and fidelity; but with the elder citizens Fabius Maximus was more popular. For he neither disturbed nor brought away anything of this sort from Tarentum, when that city was taken, but while he carried off the money and the other valuables, he suffered the statues to remain in their places, adding the well-known saying: "Let us leave these gods in their anger for the Tarentines." [3] And they blamed Marcellus, first, because he made the city odious, in that not only men, but even gods were led about in her triumphal processions like captives; and again, because, when the people was accustomed only to war or agriculture, and was inexperienced in luxury and ease, but, like the Heracles of Euripides, was

" Plain, unadorned, in a great crisis brave and true," [4]

[1] *Hell.* iii. 4, 17.   [2] *Pyth.* ii. 1 f.
[3] Cf. the *Fabius Maximus*, xxii. 5.
[4] A fragment of the lost *Licymnius* of Euripides (Nauck, *Trag. Græc. Frag.*[2] p. 507).

σχολῆς ἐνέπλησε καὶ λαλιᾶς περὶ τεχνῶν καὶ
τεχνιτῶν, ἀστεϊζόμενον καὶ διατρίβοντα πρὸς
τούτῳ πολὺ μέρος τῆς ἡμέρας. οὐ μὴν ἀλλὰ
τούτοις ἐσεμνύνετο καὶ πρὸς τοὺς Ἕλληνας, ὡς τὰ
καλὰ καὶ θαυμαστὰ τῆς Ἑλλάδος οὐκ ἐπισταμένους τιμᾶν καὶ θαυμάζειν Ῥωμαίους διδάξας.

XXII. Ἐνισταμένων δὲ τῶν ἐχθρῶν τῷ Μαρκέλλῳ πρὸς τὸν θρίαμβον, ἐπεὶ καὶ πράξεις τινὲς
ὑπολιπεῖς ἦσαν ἔτι περὶ Σικελίαν καὶ φθόνον
εἶχεν ὁ τρίτος θρίαμβος, συνεχώρησεν αὐτὸς[1]
τὸν μὲν ἐντελῆ καὶ μέγαν εἰς τὸ Ἀλβανὸν ὄρος
ἐξελάσαι, τὸν δὲ ἐλάττω καταγαγεῖν εἰς τὴν
πόλιν, ὃν εὔαν Ἕλληνες, ὄβαν δὲ Ῥωμαῖοι
2 καλοῦσι. πέμπει δὲ αὐτὸν οὐκ ἐπὶ τοῦ τεθρίππου βεβηκὼς οὐδὲ δάφνης ἔχων στέφανον οὐδὲ
περισαλπιζόμενος, ἀλλὰ πεζὸς ἐν βλαύταις, ὑπ'
αὐλητῶν μάλα πολλῶν, καὶ μυρρίνης στέφανον
ἐπικείμενος, ὡς ἀπόλεμος καὶ ἡδὺς ὀφθῆναι μᾶλλον ἢ καταπληκτικός. ὃ καὶ μέγιστον ἐμοὶ τεκμή-
ριόν ἐστι τοῦ τρόπῳ πράξεως, ἀλλὰ μὴ μεγέθει,
3 διωρίσθαι τοὺς θριάμβους τὸ παλαιόν. οἱ μὲν
γὰρ μετὰ μάχης καὶ φόνου τῶν πολεμίων ἐπι-
κρατήσαντες τὸν Ἀρήϊον ἐκεῖνον, ὡς ἔοικε, καὶ
φοβερὸν εἰσῆγον, ὥσπερ ἐν τοῖς καθαρμοῖς τῶν
στρατοπέδων εἰώθεσαν, δάφνῃ πολλῇ καταστέ-
ψαντες τὰ ὅπλα καὶ τοὺς ἄνδρας, τοῖς δὲ πολέμου
μὲν μὴ δεηθεῖσι στρατηγοῖς, ὁμιλίᾳ δὲ καὶ πειθοῖ
καὶ διὰ λόγου πάντα θεμένοις καλῶς, οἷον ἐπι-

---

[1] αὐτός Coraës and Bekker, following Stephanus, have
αὐτοῖς (*agreed with them*).

he made them idle and full of glib talk about arts and artists, so that they spent a great part of the day in such clever disputation. Notwithstanding such censure, Marcellus spoke of this with pride even to the Greeks, declaring that he had taught the ignorant Romans to admire and honour the wonderful and beautiful productions of Greece.

XXII. But when the enemies of Marcellus opposed his triumph, because something still remained to be done in Sicily and a third triumph would awaken jealousy, he consented of his own accord to conduct the complete and major triumph to the Alban mount, but to enter the city in the minor triumph; this is called "eua" by the Greeks, and "ova" by the Romans.[1] In conducting it the general does not mount upon a four-horse chariot, nor wear a wreath of laurel, nor have trumpets sounding about him; but he goes afoot with shoes on, accompanied by the sound of exceeding many flutes, and wearing a wreath of myrtle, so that his appearance is unwarlike and friendly rather than terrifying. And this is the strongest proof to my mind that in ancient times the two triumphs were distinguished, not by the magnitude, but by the manner, of the achievements which they celebrated. For those who won the mastery by fighting and slaying their enemies celebrated, as it would seem, that martial and terrible triumph, after wreathing their arms and their men with abundant laurel, just as they were wont to do when they purified their armies with lustral rites; while to those generals who had had no need of war, but had brought everything to a good issue by means of conference, persuasion, and argument, the law awarded

[1] Cf. the *Crassus*, xi. 8. The later Latin name was "ovatio."

παιανίσαι τὴν ἀπόλεμον ταύτην καὶ πανηγυρικὴν
4 ἀπεδίδου πομπὴν ὁ νόμος. καὶ γὰρ ὁ αὐλὸς
εἰρήνης μέρος καὶ τὸ μύρτον Ἀφροδίτης φυτόν, ἣ
μάλιστα θεῶν ἀπέχθεται βίᾳ καὶ πολέμοις. ὄβας
δ᾽ οὐ παρὰ τὸν εὐασμόν, ὡς οἱ πολλοὶ νομίζουσιν,
ὁ θρίαμβος οὗτος ὀνομάζεται (καὶ γὰρ ἐκεῖνον
ἐφευάζοντες καὶ ᾄδοντες παραπέμπουσιν), ἀλλ᾽ 3
ὑφ᾽ Ἑλλήνων εἰς τὸ σύνηθες αὐτοῖς παρῆκται
τοὔνομα, πεπεισμένων ἅμα καὶ Διονύσῳ τι τῆς
τιμῆς προσήκειν, ὃν Εὔιον καὶ Θρίαμβον ὀνομά-
ζομεν. οὐχ οὕτω δὲ ἔχει τὸ ἀληθές, ἀλλ᾽ ἐπὶ μὲν
τῷ μεγάλῳ θριάμβῳ βουθυτεῖν πάτριον ἦν τοῖς
στρατηγοῖς, ἐπὶ δὲ τούτῳ πρόβατον ἔθυον. ὄβα
δὲ τὰ πρόβατα Ῥωμαῖοι καλοῦσιν· ἐκ τούτου καὶ
5 τὸν θρίαμβον ὄβαν ὠνόμασαν. ἄξιον δὲ καὶ τὸν
Λακωνικὸν ἀποθεωρῆσαι νομοθέτην ὑπεναντίως
τῷ Ῥωμαϊκῷ τάξαντα τὰς θυσίας. θύει γὰρ ἐν
Σπάρτῃ τῶν ἀποστρατήγων ὁ μὲν δι᾽ ἀπάτης ἢ
πειθοῦς ὃ βούλεται διαπραξάμενος βοῦν, ὁ δὲ διὰ
μάχης ἀλεκτρυόνα. καίπερ γὰρ ὄντες πολεμικώ-
τατοι μείζονα καὶ μᾶλλον ἀνθρώπῳ πρέπουσαν
ἡγοῦντο τὴν διὰ λόγου καὶ συνέσεως πρᾶξιν ἢ
τὴν μετὰ βίας καὶ ἀνδρείας. ταῦτα μὲν οὖν ὅπως
ἔχει σκοπεῖν πάρεστι.

XXIII. Τοῦ δὲ Μαρκέλλου τὸ τέταρτον ὑπα-
τεύοντος οἱ ἐχθροὶ τοὺς Συρακουσίους ἀνέπεισαν
εἰς Ῥώμην ἀφικομένους κατηγορεῖν καὶ καταβοᾶν
πρὸς τὴν σύγκλητον ὡς δεινὰ καὶ παράσπονδα

the privilege of conducting, like a paean of thanks-giving, this unwarlike and festal procession. For the flute is an instrument of peace, and the myrtle is a plant of Aphrodite, who more than all the other gods abhors violence and wars. And this minor triumph is called "ova," not from the Greek "euas-mos," as most think (since they conduct the major triumph also with songs and cries of "eua!"), but the name has been wrested by the Greeks into con-formity with their speech, since they are persuaded that something of the honour has to do with Diony-sus also, whom they call Euius and Thriambus. This, however, is not the true explanation; but it was the custom for commanders, in celebrating the major triumph, to sacrifice an ox, whereas in the minor triumph they sacrificed a sheep. Now, the Roman name for sheep is "ova," and from this circumstance the lesser triumph is called ova.[1] And it is worth our while to notice that the Spartan lawgiver appointed his sacrifices in a manner opposite to that of the Romans. For in Sparta a returning general who had accomplished his plans by cunning decep-tion or persuasion, sacrificed an ox; he who had won by fighting, a cock. For although they were most warlike, they thought an exploit accomplished by means of argument and sagacity greater and more becoming to a man than one achieved by violence and valour. How the case really stands, I leave an open question.

XXIII. While Marcellus was serving as consul for the fourth time,[2] his enemies induced the Syracusans to come to Rome and accuse and denounce him before the senate for terrible wrongs which they

---

[1] It is hardly necessary to say that Plutarch's etymology, as often, is worthless. [2] In 210 B.C.

πεπονθότας. ἔτυχε μὲν οὖν ἐν Καπιτωλίῳ θυσίαν
τινὰ συντελῶν ὁ Μάρκελλος· ἔτι δὲ συγκαθεζο-
μένῃ τῇ γερουσίᾳ τῶν Συρακουσίων προσπεσόντων καὶ δεομένων λόγου τυχεῖν καὶ δίκης, ὁ μὲν
2 συνάρχων ἐξεῖργεν αὐτούς, ἀγανακτῶν ὑπὲρ τοῦ
Μαρκέλλου μὴ παρόντος, ὁ δὲ Μάρκελλος εὐθὺς
ἧκεν ἀκούσας. καὶ πρῶτον μὲν ἐπὶ τοῦ δίφρου
καθίσας ὡς ὕπατος ἐχρημάτιζεν, ἔπειτα, τῶν ἄλλων τέλος ἐχόντων, καταβὰς ἀπὸ τοῦ δίφρου καὶ
καταστὰς ὥσπερ ἰδιώτης εἰς τὸν τόπον ἐν ᾧ
λέγειν εἰώθασιν οἱ κρινόμενοι, τοῖς Συρακουσίοις
3 ἐλέγχειν αὐτὸν παρεῖχεν. οἱ δὲ δεινῶς μὲν συνε-
ταράχθησαν πρὸς τὸ ἀξίωμα καὶ τὸ πεποιθὸς τοῦ
ἀνδρός, καὶ τὸ ἐν τοῖς ὅπλοις ἀνυπόστατον ἔτι
μᾶλλον ἐν τῇ περιπορφύρῳ φοβερὸν ἡγοῦντο καὶ
δυσαντίβλεπτον. οὐ μὴν ἀλλὰ καὶ παραθαρρυ-
νόντων αὐτοὺς τῶν διαφερομένων πρὸς τὸν Μάρκελλον ἤρξαντο τῆς κατηγορίας καὶ διεξῆλθον
4 ὀλοφυρμῷ τινι μεμιγμένην δικαιολογίαν, ἧς ἦν
τὸ κεφάλαιον ὅτι σύμμαχοι καὶ φίλοι Ῥωμαίοις
ὄντες πεπόνθασιν ἃ πολλοῖς τῶν πολεμίων ἕτεροι
στρατηγοὶ μὴ παθεῖν ἐχαρίσαντο. πρὸς ταῦτα ὁ
Μάρκελλος ἔλεγεν ὡς ἀντὶ πολλῶν ὧν δεδράκασι
Ῥωμαίους κακῶς οὐδὲν πεπόνθασι, πλὴν ἃ πολέμῳ καὶ κατὰ κράτος ἁλόντας ἀνθρώπους κωλῦσαι
παθεῖν οὐ δυνατόν ἐστιν, οὕτω δὲ ἁλῶναι δι'
αὑτούς, πολλὰ προκαλουμένῳ πεισθῆναι μὴ ἐθε-
5 λήσαντας. οὐ γὰρ ὑπὸ τῶν τυράννων πολεμῆσαι
βιασθέντας, ἀλλὰ κἀκείνους ἐπὶ τῷ πολεμεῖν
ἑλέσθαι τυράννους.

had suffered contrary to the terms of surrender. It chanced, then, that Marcellus was performing a sacrifice on the Capitol, but, the senate being still in session, the Syracusans hurried before it and begged that they might have a hearing and justice. The colleague of Marcellus tried to have them expelled, angrily explaining that Marcellus was not present; but Marcellus, when he heard of it, came at once. And first, sitting as consul in his curule chair, he transacted the routine business; then, when this was all ended, coming down from his curule chair and taking his stand as a private citizen in the place where men under accusation usually plead their cause, he gave the Syracusans opportunity to press their charge. But they were terribly confounded by his dignity and confidence, and thought him yet more formidable and hard to confront in his robe of purple than he had been irresistible in arms. However, being encouraged by the rivals of Marcellus, they began their denunciation and rehearsed their demands for justice, which were mingled with much lamentation. The gist of their plea was that, although they were allies and friends of the Romans, they had suffered at the hands of Marcellus what other generals allowed many of their enemies to escape. To this Marcellus made answer that in return for many injuries which they had done to the Romans, they had suffered nothing except what men whose city has been taken by storm in war cannot possibly be prevented from suffering; and that their city had been so taken was their own fault, because they had refused to listen to his many exhortations and persuasions. For it was not by their tyrants that they had been forced into war, nay, they had elected those very tyrants for the purpose of going to war.

Λεχθέντων δὲ τῶν λόγων καὶ μεθισταμένοις,
ὥσπερ εἴωθεν, ἐκ τῆς βουλῆς τοῖς Συρακουσίοις
συνεξῆλθε Μάρκελλος, ἐπὶ τῷ συνάρχοντι ποιησάμενος τὴν σύγκλητον, καὶ πρὸ τῶν θυρῶν τοῦ
βουλευτηρίου διέτριβεν, οὔτε φόβῳ διὰ τὴν δίκην
οὔτε θυμῷ πρὸς τοὺς Συρακουσίους τοῦ συνήθους
μεταβαλὼν καταστήματος, ἀλλὰ πράως πάνυ
6 καὶ κοσμίως τὸ τῆς δίκης τέλος ἐκδεχόμενος. ἐπεὶ
δὲ διηνέχθησαν αἱ γνῶμαι καὶ νικῶν ἀπεδείχθη,
προσπίπτουσιν αὐτῷ οἱ Συρακούσιοι, μετὰ δακρύων δεόμενοι τὴν ὀργὴν εἰς αὐτοὺς ἀφεῖναι τοὺς
παρόντας, οἰκτεῖραι δὲ τὴν ἄλλην πόλιν μεμνη-
μένην ὧν ἔτυχεν ἀεὶ καὶ χάριν ἔχουσαν. ἐπικλασθεὶς οὖν ὁ Μάρκελλος τούτοις τε διηλλάγη, καὶ
τοῖς ἄλλοις Συρακουσίοις ἀεί τι πράττων ἀγαθὸν
7 διετέλει. καὶ τὴν ἐλευθερίαν ἣν ἀπέδωκεν αὐτοῖς,
καὶ τοὺς νόμους καὶ τῶν κτημάτων τὰ περιόντα
βέβαια παρέσχεν ἡ σύγκλητος. ἀνθ᾽ ὧν ἄλλας
τε τιμὰς ὑπερφυεῖς ἔσχε παρ᾽ αὐτοῖς, καὶ νόμον
ἔθεντο τοιοῦτον, ὁπόταν ἐπιβῇ Σικελίας Μάρκελλος ἢ τῶν ἐκγόνων τις αὐτοῦ, στεφανηφορεῖν
Συρακουσίους καὶ θύειν τοῖς θεοῖς.

XXIV. Τοὐντεῦθεν ἤδη τρέπεται πρὸς Ἀννίβαν. καὶ τῶν ἄλλων ὑπάτων καὶ ἡγεμόνων
σχεδὸν ἁπάντων μετὰ τὰ ἐν Κάνναις ἑνὶ στρατηγήματι τῷ φυγομαχεῖν χρωμένων ἐπὶ τὸν ἄνδρα,
παρατάττεσθαι δὲ καὶ συμπλέκεσθαι μηδενὸς
τολμῶντος, αὐτὸς ἐπὶ τὴν ἐναντίαν ὥρμησεν ὁδόν,
2 οἰόμενος τῷ δοκοῦντι καταλύειν Ἀννίβαν χρόνῳ
πρότερον ἐκτριβεῖσαν ὑπ᾽ ἐκείνου[1] λήσεσθαι τὴν
Ἰταλίαν, καὶ τὸν Φάβιον ἀεὶ τῆς ἀσφαλείας ἐχό-
μενον οὐ καλῶς ἔχειν[1] ἰᾶσθαι τὸ νόσημα τῆς

31

---

[1] ὑπ᾽ ἐκείνου, ἔχειν bracketed by Bekker.

When the speeches were ended, and the Syracusans, as the custom was, withdrew from the senate, Marcellus went forth with them, after giving to his colleague the presidency of the senate, and lingered before the doors of the senate-house, allowing no change in his accustomed demeanour either because he feared the sentence, or was angry with the Syracusans, but with complete gentleness and decorum awaiting the issue of the case. And when the votes had been cast, and he was proclaimed not guilty, the Syracusans fell at his feet, begging him with tears to remit his wrath against the embassy there present, and to take pity on the rest of the city, which always was mindful of favours conferred upon it and grateful for them. Marcellus, accordingly, relented, and was reconciled with the embassy, and to the rest of the Syracusans was ever afterwards constant in doing good. The freedom, also, which he had restored to them, as well as their laws and what was left of their possessions, the senate confirmed to them. Wherefore Marcellus received many surpassing honours from them, and particularly they made a law that whenever he or any one of his descendants should set foot in Sicily, the Syracusans should wear garlands and sacrifice to the gods.

XXIV. After this he moved at once against Hannibal. And although almost all the other consuls and commanders, after the disaster at Cannae, made the avoidance of all fighting their sole plan of campaign against this antagonist, and no one had the courage to engage in a pitched battle with him, Marcellus himself took the opposite course, thinking that before the time thought necessary for destroying Hannibal had elapsed, Italy would insensibly be worn out by him. He thought, too, that Fabius, by making safety his constant aim, was not taking the

πατρίδος, περιμένοντα τῇ Ῥώμῃ μαραινομένῃ
συναποσβῆναι τὸν πόλεμον, ὥσπερ ἰατρῶν τοὺς
ἀτόλμους καὶ δειλοὺς πρὸς τὰ βοηθήματα, τῆς
νόσου παρακμὴν τὴν τῆς δυνάμεως[1] ἐξανάλωσιν
3 ἡγουμένους. πρῶτον μὲν οὖν τὰς Σαυνιτικὰς
πόλεις μεγάλας ἀφεστώσας ἑλών, σῖτόν τε πολὺν
ἀποκείμενον ἐν αὐταῖς καὶ χρήματα καὶ τοὺς
φυλάσσοντας Ἀννίβου στρατιώτας τρισχιλίους
ὄντας ἔλαβεν· ἔπειτα τοῦ Ἀννίβου Φούλβιον
Γναῖον ἀνθύπατον ἐν Ἀπουλίᾳ κατακτείναντος
μὲν αὐτὸν σὺν ἕνδεκα χιλιάρχοις, κατακόψαντος
δὲ τῆς στρατιᾶς τὸ πλεῖστον, ἔπεμψεν εἰς Ῥώμην
γράμματα τοὺς πολίτας παρακαλῶν θαρρεῖν·
αὐτὸς γὰρ ἤδη βαδίζειν ὡς ἀφέλοιτο τὴν χαρὰν
4 Ἀννίβου. καὶ ταῦτα μὲν ὁ Λίβιός φησιν ἀνα-
γνωσθέντα τὰ γράμματα μὴ τῆς λύπης ἀφελεῖν,
ἀλλὰ τῷ φόβῳ προσθεῖναι, τῶν Ῥωμαίων μεῖζον
ἡγουμένων τοῦ γεγονότος τὸ κινδυνευόμενον ὅσῳ
Φουλβίου κρείττων ἦν Μάρκελλος· ὁ δέ, ὥσπερ
ἔγραψεν, εὐθὺς Ἀννίβαν διώκων εἰς τὴν Λευ-
κανίαν ἐνέβαλε, καὶ περὶ πόλιν Νομίστρωνα
καθήμενον ὑπὲρ λόφων ὀχυρῶν καταλαβὼν αὐτὸς
5 ἐν τῷ πεδίῳ κατεστρατοπέδευσε. τῇ δ' ὑστεραίᾳ
πρότερος εἰς μάχην παρατάξας τὸ στράτευμα
καταβάντος Ἀννίβου, συνέβαλε μάχην κρίσιν οὐ
λαβοῦσαν, ἰσχυρὰν δὲ καὶ μεγάλην γενομένην·
ἀπὸ γὰρ ὥρας τρίτης συμπεσόντες ἤδη σκότους
μόλις διελύθησαν. ἅμα δ' ἡμέρᾳ προαγαγὼν
αὖθις τὸ στράτευμα παρέταξε διὰ τῶν νεκρῶν

---

[1] τὴν τῆς δυνάμεως Bekker, after Coraës : τῆς δυνάμεως.

right course to heal the malady of the country, since
the extinction of the war for which he waited would
be coincident with the exhaustion of Rome, just as
physicians who are timid and afraid to apply reme-
dies, consider the consumption of the patient's
powers to be the abatement of the disease. First,
then, he took the large cities of the Samnites which
had revolted, and got possession of great quantities of
grain which had been stored in them, besides money,
and the three thousand soldiers of Hannibal who
were guarding them. Next, after Hannibal had
slain the proconsul Gnaeus Fulvius himself in Apulia,
together with eleven military tribunes, and had cut
to pieces the greater part of his army, Marcellus sent
letters to Rome bidding the citizens be of good
courage, for that he himself was already on the
march to rob Hannibal of his joy. Livy says [1] that
when these letters were read, they did not take
away the grief of the Romans, but added to their
fear; for they thought their present danger as much
greater than the past as Marcellus was superior to
Fulvius. But Marcellus, as he had written, at once
pursued Hannibal into Lucania, and came up with
him, and as he found him occupying a secure position
on heights about the city of Numistro, he himself
encamped in the plain. On the following day he
was first to array his forces when Hannibal came
down into the plain, and fought a battle with him
which, though indecisive, was desperate and long;
for their engagement began at the third hour, and
was with difficulty ended when it was already dark.
But at daybreak Marcellus led his army forth again,
put them in array among the dead bodies of the

[1] xxvii. 2.

καὶ προὐκαλεῖτο διαγωνίσασθαι περὶ τῆς νίκης
6 τὸν Ἀννίβαν. ἀναζεύξαντος δὲ ἐκείνου σκυλεύ-
σας τοὺς πολεμίους νεκροὺς καὶ θάψας τοὺς
φίλους ἐδίωκεν αὖθις· καὶ πολλὰς μὲν ὑφέντος
ἐνέδρας οὐδεμιᾷ περιπεσών, ἐν δὲ πᾶσι τοῖς ἀκροβολισμοῖς πλεῖον ἔχων ἐθαυμάζετο. διὸ καὶ τῶν
ἀρχαιρεσίων ἐπειγόντων ἔδοξε τῇ βουλῇ μᾶλλον
ἐκ Σικελίας τὸν ἕτερον ἀπάγειν ὕπατον ἢ Μάρκελλον Ἀννίβᾳ συνηρτημένον κινεῖν, ἐλθόντα δ'
ἐκέλευεν εἰπεῖν δικτάτορα Κόϊντον Φούλβιον.
7 Ὁ γὰρ δικτάτωρ οὐκ ἔστιν ὑπὸ τοῦ πλήθους
οὐδὲ τῆς βουλῆς αἱρετός, ἀλλὰ τῶν ὑπάτων τις ἢ
τῶν στρατηγῶν προελθὼν εἰς τὸν δῆμον ὃν αὐτῷ
δοκεῖ λέγει δικτάτορα. καὶ διὰ τοῦτο δικτάτωρ ὁ
ῥηθεὶς καλεῖται· τὸ γὰρ λέγειν δίκερε Ῥωμαῖοι
καλοῦσιν· ἔνιοι δὲ τὸν δικτάτορα τῷ μὴ προτι-
θέναι ψῆφον ἢ χειροτονίαν, ἀλλ' ἀφ' αὑτοῦ τὰ
δόξαντα προστάττειν καὶ λέγειν οὕτως ὠνομά-
σθαι· καὶ γὰρ τὰ διαγράμματα τῶν ἀρχόντων
Ἕλληνες μὲν διατάγματα, Ῥωμαῖοι δὲ ἔδικτα
προσαγορεύουσιν.

XXV. Ἐπεὶ δὲ ἐλθὼν ἀπὸ τῆς Σικελίας ὁ τοῦ
Μαρκέλλου συνάρχων ἕτερον ἐβούλετο λαβεῖν [1]
δικτάτορα, καὶ βιασθῆναι παρὰ γνώμην μὴ βουλόμενος ἐξέπλευσε νυκτὸς εἰς Σικελίαν, οὕτως ὁ μὲν
δῆμος ὠνόμασε δικτάτορα Κόϊντον Φούλβιον, ἡ
βουλὴ δ' ἔγραψε Μαρκέλλῳ κελεύουσα τοῦτον
εἰπεῖν. ὁ δὲ πεισθεὶς ἀνεῖπε καὶ συνεπεκύρωσε
τοῦ δήμου τὴν γνώμην, αὐτὸς δὲ πάλιν ἀνθύπατος

---

[1] λαβεῖν Bekker has λέγειν, after Coraës.

slain, and challenged Hannibal to fight it out with him for the victory. And when Hannibal withdrew his forces, Marcellus stripped the dead bodies of the enemy, buried those of his own men, and pursued him again. And though his adversary laid many ambushes for him, he escaped them all, and by getting the advantage of him in all the skirmishes, won admiration for himself. For this reason, too, when the consular elections drew near, the senate decided that it was better to recall the other consul from Sicily than to disturb Marcellus in his grappling with Hannibal, and when he was come, it bade him declare Quintus Fulvius dictator.

For a dictator cannot be chosen either by the people or by the senate, but one of the consuls or praetors comes before the assembled people and names as dictator the one whom he himself decides upon. And for this reason the one so named is called " dictator," from the Latin " dicere," to *name* or *declare*. Some, however, say that the dictator is so named because he puts no question to vote or show of hands, but ordains and declares of his own authority that which seems good to him ; for the orders of magistrates, which the Greeks call " diatagmata," the Romans call " edicta."

XXV. But the colleague of Marcellus, who had come back from Sicily, wished to appoint another man as dictator, and being unwilling to have his opinion overborne by force, sailed off by night to Sicily. Under these circumstances the people named Quintus Fulvius as dictator, and the senate wrote to Marcellus bidding him confirm the nomination. He consented, proclaimed Quintus Fulvius dictator, and so confirmed the will of the people ; he himself was

2 εἰς τοὐπιὸν ἀπεδείχθη. συνθέμενος δὲ πρὸς
Φάβιον Μάξιμον ὅπως ἐκεῖνος μὲν ἐπιχειρῇ Τα- 31
ραντίνοις, αὐτὸς δὲ συμπλεκόμενος καὶ περιέλκων
Ἀννίβαν ἐμποδὼν ᾖ τοῦ βοηθεῖν πρὸς ἐκεῖνον,
ἐπέβαλε περὶ Κανύσιον, καὶ πολλὰς ἀλλάσσοντι
στρατοπεδείας καὶ φυγομαχοῦντι πανταχόθεν
ἐπεφαίνετο, τέλος δ᾽ ἱδρυνθέντα προσκείμενος
3 ἐξανίστη τοῖς ἀκροβολισμοῖς. ὁρμήσαντος δὲ
μάχεσθαι δεξάμενος ὑπὸ νυκτὸς διελύθη· καὶ μεθ᾽
ἡμέραν αὖθις ἐν τοῖς ὅπλοις ἑωρᾶτο τὸν στρατὸν
ἔχων παρατεταγμένον, ὥστε τὸν Ἀννίβαν περι-
αλγῆ γενόμενον τοὺς Καρχηδονίους ἀθροῖσαι καὶ
δεηθῆναι τὴν μάχην ἐκείνην ὑπὲρ πασῶν ἀγωνίσασθαι τῶν ἔμπροσθεν. "Ὁρᾶτε γάρ," εἶπεν,
"ὡς οὐδὲ ἀναπνεῦσαι μετὰ νίκας τοσαύτας οὐδὲ
σχολὴν ἄγειν κρατοῦσιν ἡμῖν ἔστιν, εἰ μὴ τοῦτον
ὠσαίμεθα τὸν ἄνθρωπον."

4   Ἐκ τούτου συμβαλόντες ἐμάχοντο. καὶ δοκεῖ
παρὰ τὸ ἔργον ἀκαίρῳ στρατηγήματι χρώμενος
ὁ Μάρκελλος σφαλῆναι. τοῦ γὰρ δεξιοῦ πο-
νοῦντος ἐκέλευσεν ἓν τῶν ταγμάτων εἰς τοὔμ-
προσθεν προελθεῖν· ἡ δὲ μετακίνησις αὕτη ταρά-
ξασα τοὺς μαχομένους παρέδωκε τὸ νίκημα τοῖς
πολεμίοις, ἑπτακοσίων ἐπὶ δισχιλίοις Ῥωμαίων
5 πεσόντων. ἀναχωρήσας δὲ ὁ Μάρκελλος εἰς τὸν
χάρακα καὶ συναγαγὼν τὸν στρατόν, ὁρᾶν ἔφη
Ῥωμαίων ὅπλα πολλὰ καὶ σώματα, Ῥωμαῖον δὲ
μηδένα ὁρᾶν. αἰτουμένων δὲ συγγνώμην οὐκ ἔφη
διδόναι νενικημένοις, ἐὰν δὲ νικήσωσι, δώσειν·

appointed proconsul again for the ensuing year.[1]   He
then made an agreement with Fabius Maximus that,
while Fabius should make an attempt upon Tarentum, he himself, by diverting Hannibal and engaging
with him, should prevent him from coming to the
relief of that place.   He came up with Hannibal at
Canusium, and as his adversary often shifted his
camp and declined battle, he threatened him continually, and at last, by harassing him with his
skirmishers, drew him out of his entrenchments.
But though battle was offered and accepted, night
parted the combatants, and next day Marcellus appeared again with his army drawn up in battle array ;
so that Hannibal, in distress, called his Carthaginians
together and besought them to make their fighting
that day surpass all their previous struggles.   " For
you see," he said, " that we cannot even take breath
after all our victories, nor have respite though we
are in the mastery, unless we drive this man
away."

After this they joined battle and fought.   And it
would seem that Marcellus made an unseasonable
movement during the action, and so met with
disaster.   For when his right wing was hard pressed,
he ordered one of his legions to move up to the
front.   This change of position threw his army into
confusion and gave the victory to the enemy, who
slew twenty-seven hundred of the Romans.   Marcellus then withdrew to his camp, called his army
together, and told them that he saw before him
many Roman arms and Roman bodies, but not a
single Roman.   And when they asked for his pardon,
he refused to give it while they were vanquished,
but promised to do so if they should win a victory,

[1] 209 B.C.

αὔριον δὲ μαχεῖσθαι πάλιν, ὅπως οἱ πολῖται τὴν
6 νίκην πρότερον ἢ τὴν φυγὴν ἀκούσωσι. διαλεχθεὶς δὲ ταῦτα, προσέταξε ταῖς ἡττημέναις σπεί-
ραις ἀντὶ πυρῶν κριθὰς μετρῆσαι. δι᾽ ἃ πολλῶν
ἀπὸ τῆς μάχης ἐπικινδύνως καὶ πονήρως ἐχόντων
οὐδένα φασὶν ὃν οἱ Μαρκέλλου λόγοι τῶν τραυμάτων οὐχὶ μᾶλλον ἤλγυναν.

XXVI. Ἅμα δὲ ἡμέρᾳ προὔκειτο μὲν ὁ φοινι-
κοῦς χιτών, ὡς εἴωθε, μάχης ἐσομένης σύμβολον,
αἱ δὲ ἠτιμασμέναι σπεῖραι τὴν πρώτην αὐταὶ
δεηθεῖσαι τάξιν ἐλάμβανον, τὴν δὲ ἄλλην ἐξά-
γοντες οἱ χιλίαρχοι στρατιὰν παρενέβαλλον.
ἀκούσας δὲ ὁ Ἀννίβας, "Ὦ Ἡράκλεις," εἶπε,
"τί χρήσεταί τις ἀνθρώπῳ μήτε τὴν χείρονα
τύχην μήτε τὴν βελτίονα φέρειν εἰδότι ; μόνος
γὰρ οὗτος οὔτε νικῶν δίδωσιν ἀνάπαυσιν οὔτε
λαμβάνει νικώμενος, ἀλλ᾽ ἀεὶ μαχησόμεθα πρὸς
2 τοῦτον, ὡς ἔοικεν, ᾧ τοῦ τολμᾶν ἀεὶ καὶ τὸ
θαρρεῖν εὐτυχοῦντι καὶ σφαλλομένῳ τὸ αἰδεῖσθαι
πρόφασίς ἐστιν." ἐκ τούτου συνῄεσαν αἱ δυνά-
μεις· καὶ τῶν ἀνδρῶν ἴσα φερομένων ἐκέλευσεν
Ἀννίβας τὰ θηρία καταστήσαντας εἰς πρώτην
τάξιν ἐπάγειν τοῖς ὅπλοις τῶν Ῥωμαίων. ὠθισ-
μοῦ δὲ μεγάλου καὶ ταραχῆς εὐθὺς ἐν τοῖς πρώτοις γενομένης, εἷς τῶν χιλιάρχων ὄνομα Φλάβιος
ἀναρπάσας σημαίαν ὑπηντίαζε καὶ τῷ στύρακι
3 τὸν πρῶτον ἐλέφαντα τύπτων ἀπέστρεφεν. ὁ δὲ
ἐμβαλὼν εἰς τὸν ὀπίσω συνετάραξε καὶ τοῦτον
καὶ τοὺς ἐπιφερομένους. κατιδὼν δὲ τοῦτο Μάρκελλος ἐκέλευσε τοὺς ἱππεῖς ἐλαύνειν ἀνὰ κράτος

assuring them that on the morrow they should fight
again, in order that their countrymen might hear of
their victory sooner than of their flight. At the
close of his speech, moreover, he gave orders that
rations of barley instead of wheat should be given to
the cohorts that had been worsted. Therefore,
though many were in a wretched and dangerous
plight after the battle, there was not a man of
them, they say, to whom the words of Marcellus did
not give more pain than his wounds.[1]

XXVI. At daybreak the scarlet tunic, the usual
signal of impending battle, was displayed, the cohorts under disgrace begged and obtained for themselves the foremost position in the line, and the
tribunes led forth the rest of the army and put them
in array. On hearing of this Hannibal said : " O
Hercules ! what can be done with a man who knows
not how to bear either his worse or his better
fortune ? For he is the only man who neither gives
a respite when he is victorious, nor takes it when he
is vanquished, but we shall always be fighting with
him, as it seems, since both his courage in success
and his shame in defeat are made reasons for bold
undertaking ". Then the forces engaged ; and since
the men fought with equal success, Hannibal ordered
his elephants to be stationed in the van, and to be
driven against the ranks of the Romans. A great
press and much confusion at once arose among their
foremost lines, but one of the tribunes, Flavius by
name, snatched up a standard, confronted the
elephants, smote the leader with the iron spike of
the standard, and made him wheel about. The
beast dashed into the one behind him and threw
the whole onset into confusion. Observing this,
Marcellus ordered his cavalry to charge at full speed

[1] Cf. Livy, xxvii. 12 and 13.

πρὸς τὸ θορυβούμενον καὶ ποιεῖν ἔτι μᾶλλον
αὐτοῖς περιπετεῖς τοὺς πολεμίους. οὗτοί τε δὴ
λαμπρῶς ἐμβαλόντες ἀνέκοπτον ἄχρι τοῦ στρατοπέδου τοὺς Καρχηδονίους, καὶ τῶν θηρίων τὰ
κτεινόμενα καὶ πίπτοντα τὸν πλεῖστον αὐτῶν
4 φόνον ἀπειργάζετο. λέγονται γὰρ ὑπὲρ ὀκτακισχιλίους ἀποθανεῖν· Ῥωμαίων δὲ νεκροὶ μὲν
ἐγένοντο τρισχίλιοι, τραυματίαι δὲ ὀλίγου δεῖν
ἅπαντες. καὶ τοῦτο παρέσχεν Ἀννίβᾳ καθ᾽
ἡσυχίαν ἀναστάντι νυκτὸς ἆραι πορρωτάτω τοῦ
Μαρκέλλου. διώκειν γὰρ οὐκ ἦν δυνατὸς ὑπὸ
πλήθους τῶν τετρωμένων, ἀλλὰ κατὰ σχολὴν εἰς
Καμπανίαν ἀνέζευξε, καὶ τὸ θέρος ἐν Σινοέσσῃ
διῆγεν ἀναλαμβάνων τοὺς στρατιώτας.

XXVII. Ὁ δὲ Ἀννίβας ὡς ἀπέρρηξεν ἑαυτὸν
τοῦ Μαρκέλλου, χρώμενος ὥσπερ λελυμένῳ τῷ 314
στρατεύματι, πᾶσαν ἀδεῶς ἐν κύκλῳ περιϊὼν
ἔφλεγε τὴν Ἰταλίαν· καὶ κακῶς ἤκουσεν ἐν Ῥώμῃ
Μάρκελλος. οἱ δὲ ἐχθροὶ Πουβλίκιον Βίβλον,
ἕνα τῶν δημάρχων, ἀνέστησαν ἐπὶ τὴν κατηγορίαν αὐτοῦ, δεινὸν εἰπεῖν ἄνδρα καὶ βίαιον·
2 ὃς πολλάκις συναγαγὼν τὸν δῆμον ἔπειθεν ἄλλῳ
παραδοῦναι στρατηγῷ τὴν δύναμιν, " ἐπεὶ Μάρκελλος," ἔφη, "μικρὰ τῷ πολέμῳ προσγεγυμ-
νασμένος ὥσπερ ἐκ παλαίστρας ἐπὶ θερμὰ λουτρὰ
θεραπεύσων ἑαυτὸν τέτραπται." ταῦτα πυνθανόμενος ὁ Μάρκελλος ἐπὶ μὲν τοῦ στρατοπέδου
τοὺς πρεσβευτὰς ἀπέλιπεν, αὐτὸς δὲ πρὸς τὰς
διαβολὰς ἀπολογησόμενος εἰς Ῥώμην ἐπανῆλθεν.
3 ἐκ δὲ τῶν διαβολῶν ἐκείνων δίκην εὗρε παρεσκευα-
σμένην ἐφ᾽ αὑτόν. ἡμέρας οὖν ὁρισθείσης καὶ
τοῦ δήμου συνελθόντος εἰς τὸν Φλαμίνιον ἱππό-

upon the disordered mass and throw the enemy still
more into confusion. The horsemen made a brilliant
charge and cut the Carthaginians down as far as to
their camp, and the greatest slaughter among them
was caused by their killed and wounded elephants.[1]
For more than eight thousand are said to have been
slain ; and on the Roman side three thousand were
killed, and almost all were wounded. This gave
Hannibal opportunity to break camp quietly in the
night and move to a great distance from Marcellus.
For Marcellus was unable to pursue him, owing to
the multitude of his wounded, but withdrew by easy
marches into Campania, and spent the summer at
Sinuessa recuperating his soldiers.

XXVII. But Hannibal, now that he had torn himself away from Marcellus, made free use of his army,
and going fearlessly round about, wasted all Italy
with fire. Meantime, at Rome, Marcellus was in ill
repute, and his enemies incited Publicius Bibulus,
one of the tribunes of the people, a powerful speaker
and a man of violence, to bring a denunciation
against him. This man held frequent assemblies of
the people and tried to persuade them to put the
forces of Marcellus in charge of another general,
" since Marcellus," as he said, " after giving himself
a little exercise in the war, has withdrawn from it as
from a palaestra, and betaken himself to warm baths
for refreshment." On learning of this, Marcellus left
his legates in charge of his army, while he himself
went up to Rome to make answer to the accusations
against him. There he found an impeachment
prepared against him which was drawn from these
accusations. Accordingly, on a day set for the trial,
when the people had come together in the Flaminian

---

[1] Five were killed, according to Livy, xxvii. 14.

δρομον, ὁ μὲν Βίβλος ἀναβὰς κατηγόρησεν, ὁ δὲ
Μάρκελλος ἀπελογεῖτο, βραχέα μὲν καὶ ἁπλᾶ δι'
ἑαυτοῦ, πολλὴν δὲ καὶ λαμπρὰν οἱ δοκιμώτατοι
καὶ πρῶτοι τῶν πολιτῶν παρρησίαν ἦγον, παρακαλοῦντες μὴ χείρονας τοῦ πολεμίου κριτὰς
φανῆναι δειλίαν Μαρκέλλου καταψηφισαμένους,
ὃν μόνον φεύγει τῶν ἡγεμόνων ἐκεῖνος καὶ διατελεῖ
τούτῳ μὴ μάχεσθαι στρατηγῶν, ὡς τοῖς ἄλλοις
4 μάχεσθαι. ῥηθέντων δὲ τῶν λόγων τούτων τοσοῦτον ἡ τῆς δίκης ἐλπὶς ἐψεύσατο τὸν κατήγορον ὥστε μὴ μόνον ἀφεθῆναι τῶν αἰτιῶν τὸν
Μάρκελλον, ἀλλὰ καὶ τὸ πέμπτον ὕπατον ἀποδειχθῆναι.

XXVIII. Παραλαβὼν δὲ τὴν ἀρχὴν πρῶτον
μὲν ἐν Τυρρηνίᾳ μέγα κίνημα πρὸς ἀπόστασιν
ἔπαυσε καὶ κατεπράϋνεν ἐπελθὼν τὰς πόλεις·
ἔπειτα ναὸν ἐκ τῶν Σικελικῶν λαφύρων ᾠκοδομη-
μένον ὑπ' αὐτοῦ Δόξης καὶ Ἀρετῆς καθιερῶσαι
βουλόμενος, καὶ κωλυθεὶς ὑπὸ τῶν ἱερέων οὐκ
ἀξιούντων ἑνὶ ναῷ δύο θεοὺς περιέχεσθαι, πάλιν
ἤρξατο προσοικοδομεῖν ἕτερον, οὐ ῥᾳδίως φέρων
τὴν γεγενημένην ἀντίκρουσιν, ἀλλ' ὥσπερ οἰω-
2 νιζόμενος. καὶ γὰρ ἄλλα πολλὰ σημεῖα διετά-
ραττεν αὐτόν, ἱερῶν τινων κεραυνώσεις καὶ μύες
τὸν ἐν Διὸς χρυσὸν διαφαγόντες· ἐλέχθη δὲ καὶ
βοῦν ἀνθρώπου φωνὴν ἀφεῖναι καὶ παιδίον ἔχον
κεφαλὴν ἐλέφαντος γενέσθαι· καὶ περὶ τὰς ἐκ-
θύσεις καὶ ἀποτροπὰς δυσιεροῦντες οἱ μάντεις
κατεῖχον αὐτὸν ἐν Ῥώμῃ σπαργῶντα καὶ φλεγό-
μενον. οὐδεὶς γὰρ ἔρωτα τοσοῦτον ἠράσθη πράγματος οὐδενὸς ὅσον οὗτος ὁ ἀνὴρ τοῦ μάχῃ
3 κριθῆναι πρὸς Ἀννίβαν. τοῦτο καὶ νύκτωρ

circus, Bibulus rose up and denounced him. Then
Marcellus spoke briefly and simply in his own defence, and the leading and most reputable citizens,
with great boldness of speech and in glowing terms,
exhorted the people not to show themselves worse
judges than the enemy by convicting Marcellus of
cowardice, whom alone of their leaders Hannibal
avoided, and continually contrived not to fight with
him, that he might fight with the rest. When these
speeches were ended, the accuser was so far dis-
appointed in his hope of obtaining the verdict that
Marcellus was not only acquitted of the charges
against him, but actually appointed consul for the
fifth time.[1]

XXVIII. After assuming his office, he first quelled
a great agitation for revolt in Etruria, and visited
and pacified the cities there; next, he desired to
dedicate to Honour and Virtue a temple that he had
built out of his Sicilian spoils, but was prevented by
the priests, who would not consent that two deities
should occupy one temple; he therefore began to
build another temple adjoining the first, although
he resented the priests' opposition and regarded it
as ominous. And indeed many other portents disturbed him: sundry temples were struck by lightning, and in that of Jupiter, mice had gnawed the
gold; it was reported also that an ox had uttered
human speech, and that a boy had been born with
an elephant's head; moreover, in their expiatory
rites and sacrifices, the seers received bad omens,
and therefore detained him at Rome, though he was
all on fire and impatient to be gone.[2] For no man
ever had such a passion for any thing as he had for
fighting a decisive battle with Hannibal. This was

[1] For 208 B.C. Cf. Livy, xxvii. 20.
[2] Cf. Livy, xxvii. 11; 25.

ὄνειρον ἦν αὐτῷ καὶ μετὰ φίλων καὶ συναρχόντων
ἐν βούλευμα καὶ μία πρὸς θεοὺς φωνή, παρατατ-
τόμενον Ἀννίβαν λαβεῖν. ἥδιστα δ' ἄν μοι δοκεῖ
τείχους ἑνὸς ἤ τινος χάρακος ἀμφοτέροις τοῖς
στρατεύμασι περιτεθέντος διαγωνίσασθαι, καὶ εἰ
μὴ πολλῆς μὲν ἤδη μεστὸς ὑπῆρχε δόξης, πολλὴν
δὲ πεῖραν παρεσχήκει τοῦ παρ' ὀντινοῦν τῶν
στρατηγῶν ἐμβριθὴς γεγονέναι καὶ φρόνιμος,
εἶπον ἂν ὅτι μειρακιῶδες αὐτῷ προσπεπτώκει
καὶ φιλοτιμότερον πάθος ἢ κατὰ πρεσβύτην
τοσοῦτον. ὑπὲρ γὰρ ἑξήκοντα γεγονὼς ἔτη τὸ
πέμπτον ὑπάτευεν.

XXIX. Οὐ μὴν ἀλλὰ θυσιῶν καὶ καθαρμῶν
ὧν ὑπηγόρευον οἱ μάντεις γενομένων ἐξῆλθε μετὰ
τοῦ συνάρχοντος ἐπὶ τὸν πόλεμον, καὶ πολλὰ
μεταξὺ Βαντίας πόλεως καὶ Βενυσίας καθήμενον
ἠρέθιζε τὸν Ἀννίβαν. ὁ δὲ εἰς μάχην μὲν οὐ
κατέβαινεν, αἰσθόμενος δὲ πεμπομένην ὑπ' αὐτῶν
στρατιὰν ἐπὶ Λοκροὺς τοὺς Ἐπιζεφυρίους, κατὰ
τὸν περὶ Πετηλίαν λόφον ὑφεὶς ἐνέδρας πεντα-
2 κοσίους καὶ δισχιλίους ἀπέκτεινε. τοῦτο Μάρ- 315
κελλον ἐξέφερε τῷ θυμῷ πρὸς τὴν μάχην, καὶ
προσῆγεν ἄρας ἐγγυτέρω τὴν δύναμιν.

Ἦν δὲ μεταξὺ τῶν στρατοπέδων λόφος ἐπιεικῶς μὲν εὐερκής, ὕλης δὲ παντοδαπῆς ἀνάπλεως·
εἶχε δὲ καὶ σκοπὰς περικλινεῖς ἐπ' ἀμφότερα,
καὶ ναμάτων ὑπεφαίνοντο πηγαὶ καταρρεόντων.
ἐθαύμαζον οὖν οἱ Ῥωμαῖοι Ἀννίβαν ὅτι πρῶτος
ἑλὼν εὐφυᾶ τόπον οὕτως οὐ κατέσχεν, ἀλλ' ἀπέ-

his dream at night, his one subject for deliberation with friends and colleagues, his one appeal to the gods, namely, that he might find Hannibal drawn up to meet him. And I think he would have been most pleased to have the struggle decided with both armies enclosed by a single wall or rampart; and if he had not been full already of abundant honour, and if he had not given abundant proof that he could be compared with any general whomsoever in solidity of judgement, I should have said that he had fallen a victim to a youthful ambition that ill became such a great age as his. For he had passed his sixtieth year when he entered upon his fifth consulship.[1]

XXIX. However, after the ceremonies of sacrifice and purification which the seers prescribed had been performed, he set out with his colleague for the war, and gave much annoyance to Hannibal in his encampment between Bantia and Venusia. Hannibal would not give battle, but having been made aware that the Romans had sent some troops against Locri Epizephyrii, he set an ambush for them at the hill of Petelia, and slew twenty-five hundred of them. This filled Marcellus with mad desire for the battle, and breaking camp, he brought his forces nearer to the enemy.

Between the camps was a hill which could be made tolerably secure, and was full of all sorts of woody growth; it had also lookout-places that sloped in either direction, and streams of water showed themselves running down its sides. The Romans therefore wondered that Hannibal, who had come first to a place of natural advantages, had not occupied it, but left it in this way for his enemies.

[1] In 208 B.C.

3 λιπε τοῖς πολεμίοις. τῷ δὲ ἄρα καλὸν μὲν ἐν-
στρατοπεδεῦσαι τὸ χωρίον ἐφαίνετο, πολὺ δὲ
κρεῖττον ἐνεδρεῦσαι· καὶ πρὸς τοῦτο μᾶλλον
αὐτῷ χρῆσθαι βουλόμενος ἐνέπλησε τὴν ὕλην
καὶ τὰς κοιλάδας ἀκοντιστῶν τε πολλῶν καὶ
λογχοφόρων, πεπεισμένος ἐπάξεσθαι δι᾽ εὐφυΐαν
4 αὐτὰ τὰ χωρία τοὺς Ῥωμαίους. οὐδὲ ἀπεψεύσθη
τῆς ἐλπίδος· εὐθὺς γὰρ ἦν πολὺς ἐν τῷ στρατοπέδῳ τῶν Ῥωμαίων λόγος ὡς χρὴ τὸ χωρίον
καταλαμβάνειν, καὶ διεστρατήγουν ὅσα πλεονε-
κτήσουσι τοὺς πολεμίους, μάλιστα μὲν ἐκεῖ
στρατοπεδεύσαντες, εἰ δὲ μή, τειχίσαντες τὸν
λόφον. ἔδοξεν οὖν τῷ Μαρκέλλῳ μετ᾽ ὀλίγων
ἱπποτῶν ἐπελάσαντι κατασκέψασθαι. καὶ λαβὼν
τὸν μάντιν ἐθύετο· καὶ τοῦ πρώτου πεσόντος
ἱερείου δείκνυσιν αὐτῷ τὸ ἧπαρ οὐκ ἔχον κεφαλὴν
5 ὁ μάντις. ἐπιθυσαμένου δὲ τὸ δεύτερον ἥ τε
κεφαλὴ μέγεθος ὑπερφυὲς ἀνέσχε καὶ τἆλλα
φαιδρὰ θαυμαστῶς διεφάνη, καὶ λύσιν ἔχειν ὁ
τῶν πρώτων φόβος ἔδοξεν. οἱ δὲ μάντεις ταῦτα
μᾶλλον ἔφασαν δεδιέναι καὶ ταράττεσθαι· λαμ-
προτάτων γὰρ ἐπ᾽ αἰσχίστοις καὶ σκυθρωποτά-
τοις ἱεροῖς γενομένων ὕποπτον εἶναι τῆς μεταβολῆς τὴν ἀτοπίαν. ἀλλὰ γὰρ

Τὸ πεπρωμένον οὐ πῦρ, οὐ σιδαροῦν σχήσει
τεῖχος,

κατὰ Πίνδαρον, ἐξήει τόν τε συνάρχοντα Κρισπῖ-
νον παραλαβὼν καὶ τὸν υἱὸν χιλιαρχοῦντα καὶ
6 τοὺς σύμπαντας ἱππεῖς εἴκοσι καὶ διακοσίους. ὧν
Ῥωμαῖος οὐδεὶς ἦν, ἀλλ᾽ οἱ μὲν ἄλλοι Τυρρηνοί,
τεσσαράκοντα δὲ Φρεγελλανοί, πεῖραν ἀρετῆς καὶ

Now, to Hannibal the place did seem good for an encampment, but far better for an ambuscade, and to this use he preferred to put it. He therefore filled its woods and hollows with a large force of javelineers and spearmen, convinced that the place of itself would attract the Romans by reason of its natural advantages. Nor was he deceived in his expectations ; for straightway there was much talk in the Roman camp about the necessity of occupying the place, and they enumerated all the strategic advantages which they would gain over their enemies, particularly by encamping there, but if not that, by fortifying the hill. Marcellus accordingly decided to ride up to it with a few horsemen and inspect it. So he summoned his diviner and offered sacrifice, and when the first victim had been slain, the diviner showed him that the liver had no head. But on his sacrificing for the second time, the head of the liver was of extraordinary size and the other tokens appeared to be wonderfully propitious, and the fear which the first had inspired seemed to be dissipated. But the diviners declared that they were all the more afraid of these and troubled by them ; for when very propitious omens succeeded those which were most inauspicious and threatening, the strangeness of the change was ground for suspicion. But since, as Pindar says,[1]

> " Allotted fate not fire, not wall of iron, will check,"

Marcellus set out, taking with him his colleague Crispinus, his son, who was a military tribune, and two hundred and twenty horsemen all told. Of these, not one was a Roman, but they were all Etruscans, except forty men of Fregellae, who had

[1] Fragment 232 (Bergk).

517

πίστεως ἀεὶ τῷ Μαρκέλλῳ δεδωκότες. ὑλώδους
δὲ τοῦ λόφου καὶ συνηρεφοῦς ὄντος ἀνὴρ καθήμενος ἄνω σκοπὴν εἶχε τοῖς πολεμίοις, αὐτὸς
οὐ συνορώμενος, καθορῶν δὲ τῶν Ῥωμαίων τὸ
7 στρατόπεδον. καὶ τὰ γινόμενα τούτου φράσαντος
τοῖς λοχῶσι, προσελαύνοντα τὸν Μάρκελλον
ἐάσαντες ἐγγὺς προσελθεῖν ἐξαίφνης ἀνέστησαν,
καὶ περιχυθέντες ἅμα πανταχόθεν ἠκόντιζον,
ἔπαιον, ἐδίωκον τοὺς φεύγοντας, συνεπλέκοντο
τοῖς ὑφισταμένοις. οὗτοι δ᾽ ἦσαν οἱ τεσσαρά-
8 κοντα Φρεγελλανοί. καὶ τῶν Τυρρηνῶν εὐθὺς ἐν
ἀρχῇ διατρεσάντων αὐτοὶ συστραφέντες ἠμύνοντο
πρὸ τῶν ὑπάτων, ἄχρι οὗ Κρισπῖνος μὲν ἀκοντί-
σμασι δυσὶ βεβλημένος ἐπέστρεψεν εἰς φυγὴν
τὸν ἵππον, Μάρκελλον δέ τις λόγχῃ πλατείᾳ διὰ
τῶν πλευρῶν διήλασεν, ἣν λαγκίαν καλοῦσιν.
οὕτω δὲ καὶ τῶν Φρεγελλανῶν οἱ περιόντες ὀλίγοι
παντάπασιν αὐτὸν μὲν πεσόντα λείπουσι, τὸν δ᾽
υἱὸν ἁρπάσαντες τετρωμένον φεύγουσιν ἐπὶ τὸ
9 στρατόπεδον. ἐγένοντο δὲ νεκροὶ μὲν οὐ πολλῷ
τῶν τεσσαράκοντα πλείους, αἰχμάλωτοι δὲ τῶν
μὲν ῥαβδούχων πέντε, τῶν δὲ ἱππέων εἴκοσι δυεῖν
δέοντες. ἐτελεύτησε δὲ καὶ Κρισπῖνος ἐκ τῶν
τραυμάτων οὐ πολλὰς ἡμέρας ἐπιβιώσας. καὶ
πάθος τοῦτο Ῥωμαίοις συνέπεσε πρότερον οὐ
γεγονός, ἀμφοτέρους ἐξ ἑνὸς ἀγῶνος τοὺς ὑπάτους
ἀποθανεῖν.

XXX. Ἀννίβᾳ δὲ τῶν μὲν ἄλλων ἐλάχιστος
ἦν λόγος, Μάρκελλον δὲ πεπτωκέναι πυθόμενος
αὐτὸς ἐξέδραμεν ἐπὶ τὸν τόπον, καὶ τῷ νεκρῷ
παραστὰς καὶ πολὺν χρόνον τήν τε ῥώμην τοῦ
σώματος καταμαθὼν καὶ τὸ εἶδος, οὔτε φωνὴν

given Marcellus constant proof of their valour and
fidelity. Now, the crest of the hill was covered with
woods, and on its summit a man had been stationed
by the enemy to keep a lookout; he could not be
seen himself, but kept the Roman camp in full view.
This man, then, told those who lay in ambush what
was going on, and they, after permitting Marcellus
to ride close up to them, rose up on a sudden, and
encompassing him on all sides, hurled their javelins,
smote with their spears, pursued the fugitives, and
grappled with those who made resistance. These
were the forty men of Fregellae, who, though the
Etruscans at the very outset took to flight, banded
themselves together and fought in defence of the
consuls, until Crispinus, smitten with two javelins,
turned his horse and fled, and Marcellus was run
through the side with a broad spear (the Latin name
for which is "lancea"). Then the surviving men
of Fregellae, few all told, left him where he lay
dead, snatched up his son who was wounded, and
fled to their camp. Hardly more than forty were
slain, but five lictors were taken prisoners, and
eighteen horsemen.[1] Crispinus also died of his
wounds not many days after. Such a disaster as
this had never happened to the Romans before :
both their consuls were killed in a single action.

XXX. Hannibal made very little account of the
rest, but when he learned that Marcellus had fallen,
he ran out to the place himself, and after standing
by the dead body and surveying for a long time its
strength and mien, he uttered no boastful speech,

[1] Cf. Livy, xxvii. 26 and 27.

519

ἀφῆκεν ὑπερήφανον, οὔτε ἀπ' ὄψεως τὸ χαῖρον,
ὡς ἄν τις ἐργώδη πολέμιον καὶ βαρὺν ἀπεκτονώς,
2 ἐξέφηνεν, ἀλλ' ἐπιθαυμάσας τὸ παράλογον τῆς
τελευτῆς τὸν μὲν δακτύλιον ἀφείλετο, τὸ δὲ σῶμα   316
κοσμήσας πρέποντι κόσμῳ καὶ περιστείλας ἐντίμως ἔκαυσε· καὶ τὰ λείψανα συνθεὶς εἰς κάλπιν
ἀργυρᾶν, καὶ χρυσοῦν ἐμβαλὼν στέφανον, ἀπέστειλε πρὸς τὸν υἱόν. τῶν δὲ Νομάδων τινὲς περιτυχόντες τοῖς κομίζουσιν ὥρμησαν ἀφαιρεῖσθαι
τὸ τεῦχος, ἀντιλαμβανομένων δ' ἐκείνων ἐκβιαζό-
3 μενοι καὶ μαχόμενοι διέρριψαν τὰ ὀστᾶ. πυθόμενος δὲ Ἀννίβας, καὶ πρὸς τοὺς παρόντας εἰπών,
" Οὐδὲν ἄρα δυνατὸν γενέσθαι ἄκοντος θεοῦ,"
τοῖς μὲν Νομάσιν ἐπέθηκε δίκην, οὐκέτι δὲ κομιδῆς
ἢ συλλογῆς τῶν λειψάνων ἐφρόντισεν, ὡς δὴ κατὰ
θεόν τινα καὶ τῆς τελευτῆς καὶ τῆς ἀταφίας παρα-
4 λόγως οὕτω τῷ Μαρκέλλῳ γενομένης. ταῦτα μὲν
οὖν οἱ περὶ Κορνήλιον Νέπωτα καὶ Οὐαλέριον
Μάξιμον ἱστορήκασι· Λίβιος δὲ καὶ Καῖσαρ ὁ
Σεβαστὸς κομισθῆναι τὴν ὑδρίαν πρὸς τὸν υἱὸν
εἰρήκασι καὶ ταφῆναι λαμπρῶς.

Ἦν δὲ ἀνάθημα Μαρκέλλου δίχα τῶν ἐν Ῥώμῃ
γυμνάσιον μὲν ἐν Κατάνῃ τῆς Σικελίας, ἀνδριάντες
δὲ καὶ πίνακες τῶν ἐκ Συρακουσῶν ἔν τε Σαμο-
θράκῃ παρὰ τοῖς θεοῖς, οὓς Καβείρους ὠνόμαζον,
5 καὶ περὶ Λίνδον ἐν τῷ ἱερῷ τῆς Ἀθηνᾶς. ἐκεῖ δὲ
αὐτοῦ τῷ ἀνδριάντι τοῦτ' ἦν ἐπιγεγραμμένον, ὡς
Ποσειδώνιός φησι, τὸ ἐπίγραμμα·

Οὗτός τοι Ῥώμης ὁ μέγας, ξένε, πατρίδος ἀστήρ,
Μάρκελλος κλεινῶν Κλαύδιος ἐκ πατέρων,

---

[1] Of which he afterwards made fraudulent use (Livy,
xxvii. 28).

nor did he manifest his joy at the sight, as one
might have done who had slain a bitter and troublesome foe ; but after wondering at the unexpected-
ness of his end, he took off his signet-ring, indeed,[1]
but ordered the body to be honourably robed, suit-
ably adorned, and burned. Then he collected the
remains in a silver urn, placed a golden wreath upon
it, and sent it back to his son. But some of the
Numidians fell in with those who were carrying the
urn and attempted to take it away from them, and
when they resisted, fought with them, and in the
fierce struggle scattered the bones far and wide.
When Hannibal learned of this, he said to the bystanders : " You see that nothing can be done against
the will of God." Then he punished the Numidians,
but took no further care to collect and send back
the remains, feeling that it was at some divine
behest that Marcellus had died and been deprived
of burial in this strange manner. Such, then, is
the account given by Cornelius Nepos and Valerius
Maximus ; but Livy [2] and Augustus Caesar state
that the urn was brought to his son and buried with
splendid rites.

Besides the dedications which Marcellus made in
Rome, there was a gymnasium at Catana in Sicily,
and statues and paintings from the treasures of Syracuse both at Samothrace, in the temple of the gods
called Cabeiri, and at Lindus in the temple of Athena.
There, too, there was a statue of him, according to
Poseidonius, bearing this inscription :

" This, O stranger, was the great star of his country,
    Rome,—Claudius Marcellus of illustrious line,

[2] According to Livy, xxvii. 28, Hannibal buried Marcellus
on the hill where he was killed. Livy found many discordant
accounts of the death of Marcellus (xxvii. 27 *fin.*).

ἑπτάκι τὰν ὑπάταν ἀρχὰν ἐν Ἄρηϊ φυλάξας,
τὸν πολὺν ἀντιπάλοις ὃς κατέχευε φόνον.

τὴν γὰρ ἀνθύπατον ἀρχήν, ἢν δὶς ἦρξε, ταῖς πέντε
προσκατηρίθμησεν ὑπατείαις ὁ τὸ ἐπίγραμμα
6 ποιήσας. γένος δ' αὐτοῦ λαμπρὸν ἄχρι Μαρκέλλου τοῦ Καίσαρος ἀδελφιδοῦ διέτεινεν, ὃς Ὀκτα-
βίας ἦν τῆς Καίσαρος ἀδελφῆς υἱὸς ἐκ Γαΐου
Μαρκέλλου γεγονώς, ἀγορανομῶν δὲ Ῥωμαίων
ἐτελεύτησε νυμφίος, Καίσαρος θυγατρὶ χρόνον οὐ
πολὺν συνοικήσας. εἰς δὲ τιμὴν αὐτοῦ καὶ μνήμην
Ὀκταβία μὲν ἡ μήτηρ τὴν βιβλιοθήκην ἀνέθηκε,
Καῖσαρ δὲ θέατρον ἐπιγράψας Μαρκέλλου.

ΠΕΛΟΠΙΔΟΥ ΚΑΙ ΜΑΡΚΕΛΛΟΥ ΣΥΓΚΡΙΣΙΣ

I. Ὅσα μὲν οὖν ἔδοξεν ἡμῖν ἀναγραφῆς ἄξια
τῶν ἱστορημένων περὶ Μαρκέλλου καὶ Πελοπίδου,
ταῦτά ἐστι. τῶν δὲ κατὰ τὰς φύσεις καὶ τὰ ἤθη
κοινοτήτων ὥσπερ ἐφαμίλλων οὐσῶν (καὶ γὰρ
ἀνδρεῖοι καὶ φιλόπονοι καὶ θυμοειδεῖς καὶ μεγα-
λόφρονες ἀμφότεροι γεγόνασιν), ἐκεῖνο δόξειεν
ἂν διαφορὰν ἔχειν μόνον, ὅτι Μάρκελλος μὲν ἐν
πολλαῖς πόλεσιν ὑποχειρίοις γενομέναις σφαγὰς
ἐποίησεν, Ἐπαμεινώνδας δὲ καὶ Πελοπίδας οὐδένα πώποτε κρατήσαντες ἀπέκτειναν οὐδὲ πόλεις ἠνδραποδίσαντο. λέγονται δὲ Θηβαῖοι μηδὲ
Ὀρχομενίους ἂν οὕτω μεταχειρίσασθαι παρόντων
ἐκείνων.
2 Ἐν δὲ ταῖς πράξεσι θαυμαστὰ μὲν καὶ μεγάλα
τοῦ Μαρκέλλου τὰ πρὸς Κελτούς, ὠσαμένου

who seven times held the consular power in time of war, and poured much slaughter on his foes."

For the author of the inscription has added his two proconsulates to his five consulates. And his line maintained its splendour down to Marcellus the nephew of Augustus Caesar, who was a son of Caesar's sister Octavia by Caius Marcellus, and who died during his aedileship at Rome, having recently married a daughter of Caesar. In his honour and to his memory Octavia his mother dedicated the library, and Caesar the theatre, which bear his name.

COMPARISON OF PELOPIDAS AND MARCELLUS

I. This is what I have thought worthy of record in what historians say about Marcellus and Pelopidas. In their natures and dispositions they were almost exactly alike, since both were valiant, laborious, passionate, and magnanimous; and there would seem to have been this difference only between them, that Marcellus committed slaughter in many cities which he reduced, while Epaminondas and Pelopidas never put any one to death after their victories, nor did they sell cities into slavery. And we are told that, had they been present, the Thebans would not have treated the Orchomenians as they did.

As for their achievements, those of Marcellus against the Gauls were great and astonishing, since

τοσοῦτον πλῆθος ἱππέων ὁμοῦ καὶ πεζῶν ὀλίγοις
τοῖς περὶ αὐτὸν ἱππεῦσιν, ὃ ῥᾳδίως ὑφ' ἑτέρου
στρατηγοῦ γεγονὸς οὐχ ἱστόρηται, καὶ τὸν ἄρχοντα τῶν πολεμίων ἀνελόντος· ἐν ᾧ τρόπῳ
Πελοπίδας ἔπταισεν ὁρμήσας ἐπὶ ταὐτά, προαναι-
ρεθεὶς δὲ ὑπὸ τοῦ τυράννου καὶ παθὼν πρότερον
3 ἢ δράσας. οὐ μὴν ἀλλὰ τούτοις μὲν ἔστι παραβαλεῖν τὰ Λεῦκτρα καὶ Τεγύρας, ἐπιφανεστάτους
καὶ μεγίστους ἀγώνων, κρυφαίαν δὲ σὺν λόχῳ
κατωρθωμένην πρᾶξιν οὐκ ἔχομεν τοῦ Μαρκέλλου
παραβαλεῖν οἷς Πελοπίδας περὶ τὴν ἐκ φυγῆς
κάθοδον καὶ ἀναίρεσιν τῶν ἐν Θήβαις τυράννων
ἔπραξεν, ἀλλ' ἐκεῖνο πολὺ πάντων ἔοικε πρωτεύειν τῶν ὑπὸ σκότῳ καὶ δι' ἀπάτης γεγενημένων
4 τὸ ἔργον. Ἀννίβας φοβερὸς μὲν καὶ δεινὸς ἐνέκειτο Ῥωμαίοις,[1] ὥσπερ ἀμέλει Λακεδαιμόνιοι
τότε Θηβαίοις, ἐνδοῦναι δὲ τούτους μὲν Πελοπίδα
καὶ περὶ Τεγύρας καὶ περὶ Λεῦκτρα βέβαιόν ἐστιν,
Ἀννίβαν δὲ Μάρκελλος, ὡς μὲν οἱ περὶ Πολύβιον
λέγουσιν, οὐδὲ ἅπαξ ἐνίκησεν, ἀλλ' ἀήττητος ὁ
5 ἀνὴρ δοκεῖ διαγενέσθαι μέχρι Σκηπίωνος· ἡμεῖς
δὲ Λιβίῳ, Καίσαρι καὶ Νέπωτι καὶ τῶν Ἑλληνι-
κῶν τῷ βασιλεῖ Ἰόβᾳ πιστεύομεν, ἥττας τινὰς
καὶ τροπὰς ὑπὸ Μαρκέλλου τῶν σὺν Ἀννίβᾳ γενέ-
σθαι· μεγάλην δὲ αὗται ῥοπὴν οὐδεμίαν ἐποίησαν,
ἀλλ' ἔοικε ψευδόπτωμά τι γενέσθαι περὶ τὸν
6 Λίβυν ἐν ταῖς συμπλοκαῖς ἐκείναις. ὃ δὴ κατὰ
λόγον καὶ προσηκόντως ἐθαυμάσθη, μετὰ τοσαύτας τροπὰς στρατοπέδων καὶ φόνους στρατηγῶν
καὶ σύγχυσιν ὅλης ὁμοῦ τῆς Ῥωμαίων ἡγεμονίας

317

---

[1] ἐνέκειτο Ῥωμαίοις Coraës and Bekker, after an early
anonymous critic : ἐνέκειτο.

he routed such a multitude of horse and foot
with the few horsemen in his following (an action
not easily found recorded of any other general),
and slew the enemies' chieftain; whereas in this
regard Pelopidas failed, for he set out to do the
same thing, but suffered what he meant to inflict,
and was slain first by the tyrant. However, with
these exploits of Marcellus one may compare the
battles of Leuctra and Tegyra, greatest and most
illustrious of actions; and we have no exploit of
Marcellus accomplished by stealth and ambuscade
which we can compare with what Pelopidas did in
coming back from exile and slaying the tyrants in
Thebes, nay, that seems to rank far higher than
any other achievement of secrecy and cunning.
Hannibal, it is true, a most formidable enemy
for the Romans, but so, assuredly, were the Lacedaemonians in the time of Pelopidas for the Thebans,
and that they were defeated by Pelopidas at Tegyra
and Leuctra is an established fact; whereas Hannibal, according to Polybius,[1] was not even once defeated by Marcellus, but continued to be invincible
until Scipio came. However, I believe, with Livy,
Caesar, and Nepos, and, among Greek writers, with
King Juba, that sundry defeats and routs were inflicted by Marcellus upon the troops of Hannibal,
although these had no great influence upon the war;
indeed, the Carthaginian would seem to have practised some ruse in these engagements. But that
which reasonably and fittingly called for admiration
was the fact that the Romans, after the rout of so
many armies, the slaughter of so many generals, and
the utter confusion of the whole empire, still had

---

[1] Cf. xv. 11, 7, where Hannibal makes this claim, in a
speech to his men just before the battle of Zama (202 B.C.).

εἰς ἀντίπαλα τῷ θαρρεῖν καθισταμένων· ὁ γὰρ ἐκ
πολλοῦ τοῦ πάλαι περιδεοῦς καὶ καταπεπληγότος
αὖθις ἐμβαλὼν τῷ στρατεύματι ζῆλον καὶ φιλο-
7 νεικίαν πρὸς τοὺς πολεμίους, καὶ τοῦτο δὴ τὸ μὴ
ῥᾳδίως τῆς νίκης ὑφιέμενον, ἀλλὰ καὶ ἀμφισβη-
τοῦν τε καὶ φιλοτιμούμενον ἐπάρας καὶ θαρρύνας,
εἷς ἀνὴρ ἦν, Μάρκελλος· εἰθισμένους γὰρ ὑπὸ
τῶν συμφορῶν, εἰ φεύγοντες ἐκφύγοιεν Ἀννίβαν,
ἀγαπᾶν, ἐδίδαξεν αἰσχύνεσθαι σωζομένους μεθ'
ἥττης, αἰδεῖσθαι δὲ παρὰ μικρὸν ἐνδόντας, ἀλγεῖν
δὲ μὴ κρατήσαντας.

II. Ἐπεὶ τοίνυν Πελοπίδας μὲν οὐδεμίαν ἡττήθη
μάχην στρατηγῶν, Μάρκελλος δὲ πλείστας τῶν
καθ' αὑτὸν Ῥωμαίων ἐνίκησε, δόξειεν ἂν ἴσως τῷ
δυσνικήτῳ πρὸς τὸ ἀήττητον ὑπὸ πλήθους τῶν
κατωρθωμένων ἐπανισοῦσθαι. καὶ μὴν οὗτος μὲν
εἷλε Συρακούσας, ἐκεῖνος δὲ τῆς Λακεδαίμονος
ἀπέτυχεν. ἀλλ' οἶμαι μεῖζον εἶναι τοῦ καταλαβεῖν
Σικελίαν τὸ τῇ Σπάρτῃ προσελθεῖν καὶ διαβῆναι
2 πρῶτον ἀνθρώπων πολέμῳ τὸν Εὐρώταν, εἰ μὴ νὴ
Δία τοῦτο μὲν φήσει τις τὸ ἔργον Ἐπαμεινώνδᾳ
μᾶλλον ἢ Πελοπίδᾳ προσήκειν, ὥσπερ καὶ τὰ
Λεῦκτρα, τῶν δὲ Μαρκέλλῳ διαπεπραγμένων
ἀκοινώνητον εἶναι τὴν δόξαν. καὶ γὰρ Συρακούσας μόνος εἷλε, καὶ Κελτοὺς ἄνευ τοῦ συνάρχοντος
ἐτρέψατο, καὶ πρὸς Ἀννίβαν μηδενὸς συλλαμ-
βάνοντος, ἀλλὰ καὶ πάντων ἀποτρεπόντων, ἀντιταξάμενος καὶ μεταβαλὼν τὸ σχῆμα τοῦ πολέμου
πρῶτος ἡγεμὼν τοῦ τολμᾶν κατέστη.

III. Τὴν τοίνυν τελευτὴν ἐπαινῶ μὲν οὐδετέρου

the courage to face their foes. For there was one
man who filled his army again with ardour and ambition to contend with the enemy, instead of the
great fear and consternation which had long oppressed them, inspiring and encouraging them not
only to yield the victory reluctantly, but also to
dispute it with all eagerness, and this man was
Marcellus. For when their calamities had accustomed them to be satisfied whenever they escaped
Hannibal by flight, he taught them to be ashamed
to survive defeat, to be chagrined if they came
within a little of yielding, and to be distressed if
they did not win the day.

II. Since, then, Pelopidas was never defeated in
a battle where he was in command, and Marcellus
won more victories than any Roman of his day, it
would seem, perhaps, that the multitude of his successes made the difficulty of conquering the one
equal to the invincibility of the other. Marcellus,
it is true, took Syracuse, while Pelopidas failed to
take Sparta. But I think that to have reached Sparta,
and to have been the first of men to cross the Eurotas in war, was a greater achievement than the
conquest of Sicily; unless, indeed, it should be said
that this exploit belongs rather to Epaminondas than
to Pelopidas, as well as the victory at Leuctra, while
Marcellus shared with no one the glory of his achievements. For he took Syracuse all alone, and routed
the Gauls without his colleague, and when no one
would undertake the struggle against Hannibal, but
all declined it, he took the field against him, changed
the aspect of the war, and was the first leader to
show daring.

III. I cannot, indeed, applaud the death of either

τῶν ἀνδρῶν, ἀλλ' ἀνιῶμαι καὶ ἀγανακτῶ τῷ
παραλόγῳ τοῦ συμπτώματος· καὶ θαυμάζω μὲν
ἐν μάχαις τοσαύταις ὅσαις ἀπόκαμοι τις ἂν κατ-
αριθμῶν, μηδὲ τρωθέντα τὸν Ἀννίβαν, ἄγαμαι δὲ
καὶ τὸν ἐν τῇ Παιδείᾳ Χρυσάνταν, ὃς διῃρημένος
κοπίδα καὶ παίειν μέλλων πολέμιον, ὡς ὑπεσή-
μηνεν ἡ σάλπιγξ ἀνακλητικόν, ἀφεὶς τὸν ἄνδρα
2 μάλα πράως καὶ κοσμίως ἀνεχώρησεν. οὐ μὴν
ἀλλὰ τὸν Πελοπίδαν ποιεῖ συγγνωστὸν ἅμα τῷ
τῆς μάχης καιρῷ παράθερμον ὄντα καὶ πρὸς τὴν
ἄμυναν οὐκ ἀγεννῶς ἐκφέρων ὁ θυμός· ἄριστον
μὲν γὰρ νικῶντα σώζεσθαι τὸν στρατηγόν, " εἰ δὲ
θανεῖν, εἰς ἀρετὴν καταλύσαντα βίον," ὡς Εὐρι-
πίδης φησίν·[1] οὕτω γὰρ οὐ πάθος, ἀλλὰ πρᾶξις
3 γίνεται τοῦ τελευτῶντος ὁ θάνατος. πρὸς δὲ τῷ
θυμῷ τοῦ Πελοπίδου καὶ τὸ τέλος αὐτὸ τὸ τῆς
νίκης ἐν τῷ πεσεῖν τὸν τύραννον ὁρώμενον οὐ παντάπασιν ἀλόγως ἐπεσπάσατο τὴν ὁρμήν· χαλεπὸν
γὰρ ἑτέρας οὕτω καλὴν καὶ λαμπρὰν ἐχούσης
ὑπόθεσιν ἀριστείας ἐπιλαβέσθαι. Μάρκελλος δέ,
μήτε χρείας μεγάλης ἐπικειμένης, μήτε τοῦ παρὰ
τὰ δεινὰ πολλάκις ἐξιστάντος τὸν λογισμὸν ἐνθουσιασμοῦ παρεστῶτος, ὠσάμενος ἀπερισκέπτως
εἰς κίνδυνον οὐ στρατηγοῦ πτῶμα, προδρόμου δέ
4 τινος ἢ κατασκόπου πέπτωκεν, ὑπατείας πέντε
καὶ τρεῖς θριάμβους καὶ σκῦλα καὶ τροπαιοφορίας
ἀπὸ βασιλέων τοῖς προαποθνήσκουσι Καρχηδονίων Ἴβηρσι καὶ Νομάσιν ὑποβαλών. ὥστε
νεμεσῆσαι αὐτοὺς ἐκείνους ἑαυτοῖς τοῦ κατορθώ-

318

---

[1]
     Εἰ δὲ θανεῖν θέμις, ὧδε θανεῖν καλόν,
     εἰς ἀρετὴν καταλυσαμένους βίον

(Nauck, *Trag. Graec. Frag.*[2] p. 679). Cf. Plutarch, *Morals*,
p. 24 d.

of them, nay, I am distressed and indignant at their
unreasonableness in the final disaster. And I admire
Hannibal because, in battles so numerous that one
would weary of counting them, he was not even
wounded. I am delighted, too, with Chrysantes, in
the "Cyropaedeia,"[1] who, though his blade was lifted
on high and he was about to smite an enemy, when
the trumpet sounded a retreat, let his man go, and
retired with all gentleness and decorum. Pelopidas,
however, was somewhat excusable, because, excited
as he always was by an opportunity for battle, he
was now carried away by a generous anger to seek
revenge. For the best thing is that a general should
be victorious and keep his life, "but if he must die,"
he should "conclude his life with valour," as Euripides says; for then he does not suffer death, but
rather achieves it. And besides his anger, Pelopidas
saw that the consummation of his victory would be
the death of the tyrant, and this not altogether
unreasonably invited his effort; for it would have
been hard to find another deed of prowess with so
fair and glorious a promise. But Marcellus, when
no great need was pressing, and when he felt none
of that ardour which in times of peril unseats the
judgment, plunged heedlessly into danger, and died
the death, not of a general, but of a mere skirmisher
or scout, having cast his five consulates, his three
triumphs, and the spoils and trophies which he had
taken from kings, under the feet of Iberians and
Numidians who had sold their lives to the Carthaginians. And so it came to pass that these very
men were loath to accept their own success, when

---

[1] Xenophon, *Cyrop.* iv. 1, 3.

ματος, ἄνδρα Ῥωμαίων ἄριστον ἀρετῇ καὶ δυνάμει
μέγιστον καὶ δόξῃ λαμπρότατον ἐν τοῖς Φρεγελλανῶν προδιερευνηταῖς παραναλῶσθαι.

5 Χρὴ δὲ ταῦτα μὴ κατηγορίαν εἶναι τῶν ἀνδρῶν
νομίζειν, ἀλλ᾽ ὡς ἀγανάκτησίν τινα καὶ παρρησίαν
ὑπὲρ αὐτῶν ἐκείνων πρὸς αὐτοὺς καὶ τὴν ἀνδρείαν
αὐτῶν, εἰς ἣν τὰς ἄλλας κατανάλωσαν ἀρετὰς
ἀφειδήσαντες τοῦ βίου καὶ τῆς ψυχῆς, ὥσπερ
ἑαυτοῖς, οὐ ταῖς πατρίσι μᾶλλον καὶ φίλοις καὶ
συμμάχοις, ἀπολλυμένων.

6 Μετὰ δὲ τὸν θάνατον Πελοπίδας μὲν τοὺς συμμάχους ταφεὶς ἔσχεν, ὑπὲρ ὧν ἀπέθανε, Μάρκελλος δὲ τοὺς πολεμίους, ὑφ᾽ ὧν ἀπέθανε. ζηλωτὸν
μὲν οὖν ἐκεῖνο καὶ μακάριον, κρεῖττον δὲ καὶ
μεῖζον εὐνοίας χάριν ἀμειβομένης ἔχθρα λυποῦ-
σαν ἀρετὴν θαυμάζουσα. τὸ γὰρ καλὸν ἐνταῦθα
τὴν τιμὴν ἔχει μόνον, ἐκεῖ δὲ τὸ λυσιτελὲς καὶ
ἡ χρεία μᾶλλον ἀγαπᾶται τῆς ἀρετῆς.

a Roman who excelled all others in valour, and had the greatest influence and the most splendid fame, was uselessly sacrificed among the scouts of Fregellae.

This, however, must not be thought a denunciation of the men, but rather an indignant and outspoken protest in their own behalf against themselves and their valour, to which they uselessly sacrificed their other virtues, in that they were unsparing of their lives ; as if their death affected themselves alone, and not rather their countries, friends, and allies.

After his death, Pelopidas received burial from his allies, in whose behalf he fell ; Marcellus from his enemies, by whose hands he fell. An enviable and happy lot was the former, it is true ; but better and greater than the goodwill which makes grateful return for favours done, is the hatred which admires a valour that was harassing. For in this case it is worth alone which receives honour ; whereas in the other, personal interests and needs are more regarded than excellence.

A PARTIAL DICTIONARY OF
PROPER NAMES

A

Achillas, 317–325, one of the guardians of Ptolemy XII. (Dionysus), and commander of his troops when Caesar came to Egypt. According to *Bell. Alex.* iv., he was put to death by his sister Arsinoë.

Achradina, 485, the first extension on the mainland of the island city of Syracuse, stretching from the Great Harbour northwards to the sea.

Actium, 175, a promontory of Acarnania in northern Greece, at the entrance to the Ambraciot gulf.

Aesop, 429, a Greek writer of fables, who flourished in the first half of the sixth century B.C. Fables bearing his name were popular at Athens in the time of Aristophanes.

Afranius, 205, 211, 217, 229, 287, 291, Lucius A., a warm partisan of Pompey, and one of his legates in Spain during the war with Sertorius, as well as in Asia during the Mithridatic war. He was consul in 60 B.C. In 55 B.C. he was sent by Pompey with Petreius to hold Spain for him. He was killed after the battle of Thapsus (46 B.C.).

Amanus, 217, a range of mountains branching off from the Taurus in Cilicia, and extending eastwards to Syria and the Euphrates.

Amisus, 213, 223, a city of Pontus, in Asia Minor, on the southern shore of the Euxine Sea.

Amphipolis, 309, an important town in S.E. Macedonia, on the river Strymon, about three miles from the sea.

Androcydes of Cyzicus, 401, a celebrated painter, who flourished from 400 to 377 B.C. See Plutarch, *Morals*, p. 668 c.

Andros, 345, the most northerly island of the Cyclades group, S. E. of Euboea.

Antalcidas, 63, 73, 87, 417, an able Spartan politician, and commander of the Spartan fleet in 388 B.C. The famous peace between Persia and the Greeks, concluded in 387 B.C., was called after him.

Antigonus, 341, 343, the general of Alexander who was afterwards king of Asia, surnamed the One-eyed.

Antioch, 219, the capital of the Greek kings of Syria, on the river Orontes, founded by Seleucus in 300 B.C.

Antipater, 41, regent of Macedonia and Greece during Alexander's absence in the East, and also after Alexander's death, until 319 B.C.

Apollophanes of Cyzicus, 33, known only in this connection.

Appius, 467, 471, Appius Claudius Pulcher, military tribune at Cannae (216 B.C.), praetor in Sicily 215 B.C., and legate of Marcellus there in 214. He was consul in 212, and died in the following year.

Arbela, 211, a town in Babylonia, near which Alexander inflicted final defeat upon Dareius.

DICTIONARY OF PROPER NAMES

Archimedes, 471–477, the most famous of ancient mathematicians, lived 287–212 B.C.

Archytas, 471, a Greek of Tarentum, philosopher, mathematician, general and statesman, flourished about 400 B.C.

Ariminum, 273, 443, a city of Umbria, on the Adriatic, commanding the eastern coast of Italy and an entrance into Cisalpine Gaul.

Arsaces, 315, Arsaces XIV. (or Orontes I.), king of Parthia 55–38 B.C.

Arsis, 131, an error for Aesis, a river flowing between Umbria and Picenum, in N.E. Italy.

Asculum, 123 f., a city in the interior of Picenum, taken by Strabo during the Marsic war (89 B.C.) and burnt.

Athamania, 287, a district in northern Greece, between Thessaly and Epirus.

Aulis, 15, a town on the Boeotian side of the straits of Euripus, reputed to have been the rendezvous for the Greek chieftains under Agamemnon.

Auximum, 129, a city of Picenum, in N.E. Italy, just south of Ancona.

B

Bantia, 515, a small town in Apulia, about thirteen miles south-east of Venusia.

Beroea, 281, a town in Macedonia, west of the Thermaïc gulf (Bay of Saloniki).

Bibulus (1), 237–241, 259, Lucius Calpurnius B., aedile in 65, praetor in 62, and consul in 59 B.C., in each case a colleague of Julius Caesar. He was an aristocrat of moderate abilities. He died in 48 B.C.

Bibulus (2), 511, 513, Publicius B., not otherwise known.

Bosporus, 215, the territory on both sides of the strait between the Euxine Sea and the Maeotic Lake (Sea of Azov), and including the modern Crimea. The strait (p. 207) bears the same name.

Briareus, 479, a monster of mythology, having a hundred arms and fifty heads, called by men Aegaeon (*Iliad*, i. 403 f.).

Brundisium, 183 f., 279, 285, an important city on the eastern coast of Italy (Calabria), with a fine harbour. It was the natural point of departure from Italy to the East, and was the chief naval station of the Romans in the Adriatic.

Brutus, 129, 153, 155, Marcus Junius B., father of the conspirator, tribune of the people in 83, and, in 77 B.C., general under Lepidus.

C

Caenum, 213, the fortress mentioned without name in the preceding chapter. It was in Pontus, on the river Lycus, S.E. of Amisus.

Caepio, 239, Servilius C., a supporter of Caesar against his colleague Bibulus in 59 B.C. (Suetonius, *Div. Jul.* 21). Cf. the *Caesar*, xiv. 4.

Calauria, 175, a small island off the S.E. coast of Argolis in Peloponnesus. Its temple was the final refuge of Demosthenes.

Callicratidas, 343, the Spartan admiral who succeeded Lysander in 406 B.C., and lost his life in the battle of Arginusae. Cf. the *Lysander*, chapters v.–vii.

Callipides, 59, cf. the *Alcibiades*, xxxii. 2.

Callisthenes, 97, 381, of Olynthus, a philosopher and historian, who accompanied Alexander the Great on his expedition in the East until put to death by him in 328 B.C. Besides an account of Alexander's expedition, he wrote a history of Greece from 387 to 357 B.C.

Calvinus, 295, see Domitius (3).

Canusium, 457, 507, an ancient city of Apulia, about fifteen miles from the sea.

Capitolinus, 439, Caius Scantilius C., colleague of Marcellus in the aedileship about 226 B.C.

DICTIONARY OF PROPER NAMES

Carbo, 127–131, 137 f., Gnaeus Papirius C., a leader of the Marian party, consular colleague of Cinna in 85 and 84 B.C., put to death by Pompey in 82 B.C.

Carinas (or Carrinas), 129, Caius C., was defeated by Sulla in the following year (82 B.C.), captured and put to death.

Catana, 521, an ancient city on the eastern coast of Sicily, about midway between Syracuse and Tauromenium, directly at the foot of Mt. Aetna.

Catulus, 153, 157, 179, 181, 193, 197, Quintus Lutatius C., a leading aristocrat of the nobler sort, consul in 78 B.C., censor in 65, a supporter of Cicero against Catiline in 63, died in 60 B.C.

Caucasus Mountains, 209, the great mountain system lying between the Euxine and Caspian Seas.

Cenchreae, 399, the eastern harbour-town of Corinth.

Chabrias, 105, a successful Athenian general, prominent from 392 till his gallant death at the siege of Chios in 357 B.C.

Chaeroneia, 47, a small town at the entrance from Phocis into Boeotia, commanding an extensive plain on which many battles were fought in ancient times (cf. the *Marcellus*, xxi. 2). Here Philip of Macedon defeated the allied Greeks in 338 B.C. It was Plutarch's native city.

Chares, 345, a famous Athenian general, prominent from 367 to 334 B.C. He was able, but untrustworthy and rapacious.

Cinna, 123–127, Lucius Cornelius C., leader of the popular party and consul during the years of Sulla's absence in the East (87–84 B.C.).

Claros, 175, a place in Ionian Asia Minor, near Colophon, where there was a temple of Apollo, and an oracle of great antiquity.

Cleon, of Halicarnassus, 55, a rhetorician who flourished at the close of the fifth and the beginning of the fourth century B.C.

Cloelius, 129, an error for Coelius, Caius Coelius Caldus, tribune of the people in 107 B.C., consul in 94, a staunch supporter of the Marian party.

Cnidus, 47, a city at the S.W. extremity of Caria, in Asia Minor.

Colchis, 203, 207, a district of Western Asia, lying north of Armenia and east of the Euxine Sea.

Commagene, 231, a district of Syria, lying between Cilicia and the Euphrates.

Conon, 47, 63, a distinguished Athenian general. He escaped from Aegospotami in 405 B.C. (see the *Lysander*, xi. 5), and with aid from the Great King and Pharnabazus defeated the Spartan fleet off Cnidus in 394 B.C., and restored the Long Walls of Athens in 393 B.C.

Cornelius, 447, 453, Gnaeus Cornelius Scipio Calvus, consul with Marcellus in 222 B.C., afterwards (218 B.C.) legate of his brother Publius in Spain, where the two carried on war against the Carthaginians for eight years, and where both finally fell.

Coroneia, 41, 47, a town in N.W. Boeotia, the scene of many battles. Here reference is made to the victory of Agesilaüs over the Thebans and their allies in 394 B.C. (*Agesilaüs*, xviii.).

Cratippus, 311 f., of Mitylene, a Peripatetic philosopher highly regarded by Cicero, and by Cicero's son, whose teacher he was. Brutus attended his lectures at Athens (*Brutus*, xxiv. 1).

Crispinus, 517, 519, Titus Quinctius Pennus Capitolinus C., a trusted commander under Marcellus in Sicily, 214–212 B.C., and now (208) his colleague in the consulship. After the skirmish here described he was carried to Rome, where he died at the close of the year.

Culleo, 243, Quintus Terentius C., tribune of the people in 58 B.C., a friend of Cicero, whose banishment he tried to prevent, and whose recall he laboured to obtain.

Curio, 269 f., Caius Scribonius C.,

535

an able orator, but reckless and profligate. He was tribune of the people in 50 B.C., and sold his support to Caesar, who made him praetor in Sicily in 49. Thence he crossed into Africa to attack the Pompeians there, but was defeated and slain (Caesar, *Bell. Civ.*, ii. 23–44).

Cynoscephalae, 423, a range of hills in eastern Thessaly, so named from their supposed resemblance to the heads of dogs.

Cythera, 87, a large island directly south of Laconia in Peloponnesus.

Cyzicus, 401, a Greek city on the Propontis, in Mysia.

D

Damippus, 483, a Spartan at the court of Hieronymus, king of Syracuse. He tried to persuade the king not to abandon alliance with Rome. Marcellus gave him his liberty.

Deiotarus, 309, tetrarch of Galatia in Asia Minor, and an old man in 54 B.C. (cf. the *Crassus*, xvii. 1 f.). He was a faithful friend of the Romans in their Asiatic wars, and was rewarded by the senate, in 63 B.C., with the title of King. Caesar could never be brought to pardon him for siding with Pompey.

Demaratus the Corinthian, 39, a guest-friend of Philip of Macedon (cf. the *Alexander*, ix. 6 ; lvi.).

Didyma, 175, in the territory of Miletus, the site of a famous temple of Apollo.

Dionysius, 429, the Elder, tyrant of Syracuse from 405 to 367 B.C.

Dioscorides, 99, a pupil of Isocrates, author of a treatise on the Spartan polity, writing in the latter part of the fourth century B.C. (cf. the *Lycurgus*, xi. 4).

Domitius (1), 137, 141, Gnaeus Domitius Ahenobarbus, son-in-law of Cinna, and a partisan of Marius. When Sulla obtained the supreme power in 82 B.C.,

Domitius fled to Africa, where he died in 81 B.C.

Domitius (2), 251, 291, 295, 335, Lucius Domitius Ahenobarbus, consul in 54 B.C. He was a son-in-law of Cato, and one of the ablest supporters of the aristocratic party. He opposed both Pompey and Caesar until they quarrelled, then sided with Pompey. Caesar spared his life at Corfinium, in 49 B.C. (cf. the *Caesar*, xxxiv. 3 f.). He met his death at Pharsalus.

Domitius (3), 257, 295, Gnaeus Domitius Calvinus (wrongly called Lucius Calvinus, p. 295), consul in 53 B.C. He was a supporter of Bibulus against Caesar in 59 B.C., but after 49 B.C. an active supporter of Caesar. After Pharsalus he was Caesar's lieutenant in Asia.

Duris, 7, of Samos, a pupil of Theophrastus, historian and, for a time, tyrant of Samos, lived *circa* 350–280 B.C.

Dymé, 187, the most westerly of the twelve cities of Achaia in Peloponnesus. It had been destroyed by the Romans in 146 B.C.

Dyrrachium, 279, 309, a city on the coast of Illyricum, known in Greek history as Epidamnus. It was a free state, and sided with the Romans consistently.

E

Ecbatana, 39, 417, an ancient city of Media, the residence of the Great King during the summer months.

Eleusis, 69, 375, the sacred city of the Athenian mysteries, some twelve miles west of Athens.

Engyium, 489 f., a city in the interior of Sicily, the exact site of which is unknown.

Enna, 489, an ancient fortress-city nearly in the centre of Sicily.

Ephesus, 17, 23, 493, one of the twelve Ionian cities in Lydia of Asia Minor, near the mouth of the river Caÿstrus.

Ephorus, 381, of Cymé, pupil of

DICTIONARY OF PROPER NAMES

Isocrates, author of a highly rhetorical history of Greece from the "Dorian Invasion" down to 340 B.C., in which year he died.

Epidaurus, 175, a city on the east coast of Argolis in Peloponnesus, famous for its shrine and cult of Aesculapius.

Erasistratus, 41, otherwise unknown.

Eudoxus, 471, of Cnidus, a pupil of Archytas, most famous as a mathematician and astronomer, flourished about 360 B.C. He taught philosophy at Athens.

Eurypontidae, 329, one of the two royal families at Sparta ; the other was that of the Agidae.

F

Favonius, 275, 291, 309, 335, Marcus F., called the "Ape of Cato," aedile in 52 and praetor in 49 B.C. He joined Pompey in the East in spite of personal enmity to him, and accompanied him in his flight from Pharsalus.

Flaminius, 443, 447, Caius F., consul in 223 B.C., a violent opponent of senate and aristocrats. The Circus Flaminius and the Via Flaminia were constructed during his aedileship (220 B.C.). Cf. the *Marcellus*, xxvii. 3.

Fregellae, 517 f., 531, a city in S.E. Latium, on the river Liris. It was severely punished by Hannibal in 211 B.C. for its fidelity to Rome.

Fulvius (1), 503, Gnaeus Fulvius Flaccus, was praetor in 212 B.C., and received Apulia as his province, where, in 210 B.C., he was badly defeated (but not slain, as Plutarch says) by Hannibal. He had played the coward, and went into voluntary exile.

Fulvius (2), 505, Quintus Fulvius Flaccus, brother of Gnaeus, consul in 237, 224, 212, and 209 B.C. In 212 he captured Capua, which had gone over to Hannibal, and wreaked a dreadful vengeance upon the city.

G

Gabinius, 177, 183, 241, Aulus G., tribune of the people in 66, praetor in 61, consul with Piso in 58 B.C., the year during which Cicero was exiled. He was recalled from his province of Syria in 55, prosecuted for taking bribes, and exiled. He died in 48 B.C.

Geraestus, 15, a town and promontory at the south-western extremity of Euboea.

Gordyene, 209, a rather indefinite district of Asia, lying south of Armenia and west of the river Tigris.

H

Hecatombaeon, 79, the first month of the Attic year, comprising parts of our June and July.

Herennius, 159, Caius H., tribune of the people in 80 B.C. After the death of Sulla he joined Sertorius in Spain (76–72 B.C.).

Hermagoras, 225, of Tenedos, a distinguished rhetorician in the times of Pompey and Cicero. He was a mere formalist.

Hermione, 175, an ancient town at the south-eastern extremity of Argolis in Peloponnesus.

Hexapyla, 483, 485, probably a section of the wall fortifying Epipolae, the triangular plateau to the west of Syracuse.

Hiempsal, 145, king of Numidia after the Jugurthine war (111–106 B.C.), expelled from his throne by Gnaeus Domitius and restored to it by Pompey.

Hiero, 457, 471 f., Hiero II., king of Syracuse 270–216 B.C., for nearly half a century a faithful friend and ally of Rome.

Hieronymus (1), 37, of Rhodes, a disciple of Aristotle, flourishing about 300 B.C., frequently mentioned by Cicero.

Hieronymus (2), king of Syracuse 216–215 B.C., successor to Hiero II., whose policy of friendship with Rome he forsook for alliance with Carthage.

DICTIONARY OF PROPER NAMES

Himera, 139, a Greek city on the northern coast of Sicily.

Hippocrates, 469, 483, a Syracusan by birth, but educated at Carthage. He served under Hannibal in Spain and Italy. He persuaded Hieronymus, the young king of Syracuse, to abandon the Roman cause (216 B.C.).

Hydrieus the Carian, 37, otherwise unknown.

Hypsaeus, 263, Publius-Plautius H., tribune of the people in 54 B.C., and candidate for the consulship. He was accused of corrupt practices, tried, and convicted. Pompey, whom he had devotedly served, forsook him in the hour of need.

Hyrcania, 207 f., a district of Asia lying south of the Caspian (Hyrcanian) Sea.

I

Iarbas (or Hiarbas), 143, a king of Numidia, set on the throne by Gnaeus Domitius, instead of Hiempsal.

Iphicrates, 61, 343, a famous Athenian general, who increased the effectiveness of light-armed troops and defeated a Spartan division of heavy-armed men at Corinth in 392 B.C. He was prominent until about 348 B.C.

Isthmus, 175, the Isthmus of Corinth.

Ithome, 399, see Messene.

J

Jason, 411, tyrant of Pherae in Thessaly, and active in Greek affairs from 377 to 370, the year of his death. He was succeeded by Alexander of Pherae.

Juba, 315, 525, Juba II., king of Mauritania. He lived from 50 B.C. to about 20 A.D., was educated at Rome, and became a learned and voluminous writer. Among his works was a History of Rome.

L

Labienus, 293, Titus L., tribune of the people in 63 B.C., and devoted to Caesar's interests. He was an able and trusted legate of Caesar through most of the Gallic wars, but became jealous of his leader and deserted him for Pompey in 49 B.C. After Pharsalus he fled to Africa, and after the battle of Thapsus (46 B.C.) to Spain, where he was the immediate cause of the defeat of the Pompeians at Munda and was slain (45 B.C.).

Lacinium, 175, a promontory on the east coast of Bruttium, in Italy, some six miles south of Crotona.

Larissa, 43 f., 307, 405, an important town in N.E. Thessaly, on the river Peneius.

Lauron, 159, a small town in the S.E. part of Spain, south of Valentia, near the sea.

Lentulus (1), 273, 325, Lucius Cornelius L. Crus, consul in 49 B.C. with Claudius Marcellus, and a bitter opponent of Caesar (cf. the *Caesar*, xxx. 3). He joined Pompey in the East, fled with him from Pharsalus, and was put to death in Egypt.

Lentulus (2), 307, see Spinther.

Leontini, 469, a city of Sicily between Syracuse and Catana.

Lepidus, 151 ff., 197, 327, Marcus Aemilius L , father of the triumvir, praetor in Sicily in 81, consul in 78 B.C.

Leucas, 175, an island in the Ionian Sea, lying close to the coast of Acarnania.

Leuctra, 79, 391, and often, a village in Boeotia, south-west of Thebes, between Thespiae and Plataea, for ever memorable as the scene of the utter defeat of the Spartans by the Thebans in 371 B.C.

Lindus, 521, an ancient and important town on the east coast of the island of Rhodes.

Locri Epizephyrii, 515, a celebrated Greek city on the eastern coast of Bruttium, in Itaiy, said to have been founded in 760 B.C.

DICTIONARY OF PROPER NAMES

Luca (or Lucca), 249, a city of Liguria, N.E. of Pisa, a frontier-town of Caesar's province in good communication with Rome.

M

Macaria, 391, daughter of Heracles and Deïaneira. She slew herself in order to give the Athenians victory over Eurystheus.

Maeotic Sea, 207, the modern Sea of Azov.

Magnesia, 421, 431, a district on the eastern coast of Thessaly.

Mantinea, 85, 93 f., 99, 349, a powerful city in the eastern part of central Arcadia, in Peloponnesus.

Marcellinus, 249 f., Gnaeus Cornelius Lentulus M., consul in 56 B.C., a friend and advocate of Cicero, and persistently opposed to Pompey, who was driven by his hostility into alliance with Caesar.

Marcellus, 269 f., Caius Claudius M., consul in 50 B.C., a friend of Cicero and Pompey, and an uncompromising foe of Caesar. But after the outbreak of the civil war he remained quietly and timidly in Italy, and was finally pardoned by Caesar. He is not to be confounded with an uncle, Marcus Claudius Marcellus, consul in 51, or with a cousin, Caius Claudius Marcellus, consul in 49 B.C.

Marcius, 445, Caius M. Figulus, consul in 162 B.C., and again in 156 B.C.

Maximus, 521, Valerius M., compiler of a large collection of historical anecdotes, in the time of Augustus.

Megara, 483, 489, a Greek city on the eastern coast of Sicily, between Syracuse and Catana, It was colonized from Megara in Greece Proper.

Meliboea, 413, an ancient town on the sea-coast of Thessaly.

Memmius, 141, Caius M., after this, Pompey's quaestor in Spain, where he was killed in a battle with Sertorius (*Sertorius*, xxi.).

Mendes, 107 f., a prominent city in the north of Egypt.

Menecrates, 59, a Syracusan physician at the court of Philip of Macedon 359–336 B.C. According to Aelian (*Var. Hist.* xii. 51), it was from Philip that he got this answer.

Menoeceus, 391, son of Creon the mythical king of Thebes. He sacrificed himself in order to give his city victory over the seven Argive chieftains.

Meriones, 489, a Cretan hero of the Trojan war, the companion and friend of Idomeneus.

Messala, 257, Marcus Valerius M., secured his election to the consulship in 53 B.C. by bribery, but still had Cicero's support. In the civil war he sided actively with Caesar.

Messenia, Messene, 95, 99, 101, 331, 417 f., the south-western district in Peloponnesus, in earliest times conquered by the Spartans. Its stronghold, Ithome, was included in the capital city built by Epaminondas in 369 B.C. and named Messene. The names Messenia and Messene are sometimes interchanged.

Metellus (1), 121, (?) 187 f., Quintus Caecilius M. Creticus, consul in 69 B.C., and from 68 to 66 B.C. engaged in subduing Crete. On his return to Rome the partisans of Pompey prevented him from celebrating a triumph, for which he waited patiently outside of the city until 62 B.C.

Metellus (2), 277 f., 333, Lucius Caecilius M. Creticus, a nephew of the preceding Metellus, is little known apart from the incident here narrated.

Metellus (3), 133, 157 ff. 197, Quintus Metellus Pius, consul with Sulla in 80 B.C., and one of his most successful generals. After Sulla's death in 78 B.C., Metellus was sent as proconsul into Spain, to prosecute the war against Sertorius. He died about 63 B.C.

Minucius, 447, Marcus M. Rufus, consul in 221 B.C., and in 217 Master of Horse to the dictator

Fabius Maximus (*Fab. Max.* iv.–xiii.). It is not known in what year Minucius was dictator.

Mithras, 175, a Persian sun-deity, whose worship subsequently spread over the whole Roman Empire.

Mitylene, 225, 309 f., the chief city of the island of Lesbos.

Mucia, 225 f., Pompey's third wife (cf. the *Pompey*, ix.), and the mother by him of Gnaeus and Sextus Pompey.

Mutina, 155, an important city of Cisalpine Gaul, south of the Po, the modern Modena.

N

Nabataeans, 293, a people occupying the northern part of the Arabian peninsula, between the Euphrates and the Arabian Gulf.

Neapolis (1), an ancient city of Campania, the modern Naples.

Neapolis (2), a portion of what Plutarch calls the "outer city" of Syracuse, lying between Epipolae and Achradina.

Nepos, 521, 525, Cornelius N., a Roman biographer and historian, contemporary and friend of Cicero.

Nola, 459, 463 f., an important city of Campania, about twenty miles S.E. of Capua.

O

Oppius, 139, Caius O., an intimate friend of Caesar (cf. the *Caesar*, xvii.), author (probably) of Lives of Marius, Pompey, and Caesar.

Orchomenus, 47 f., 377, 381 f., 523, a city in northern Boeotia, near the Copaïc Lake.

Oricum, 285, a town on the coast of Epirus, north of Apollonia.

P

Paeonia, 221, a district in Thrace, north of Macedonia.

Paulus, 269, Lucius Aemilius P.,

consul in 50 B.C. with Claudius Marcellus. He had been a violent opponent of Caesar.

Pelusium, 317, a strong frontier-town on the eastern branch of the Nile.

Perpenna, 137, 159, 163 f., Marcus P. Vento, a leading partisan of Marius. On the death of Sulla (78 B.C.) he joined Lepidus in his attempt to win the supreme power, and, failing here, retired to Spain, where he served under Sertorius.

Petelia, 515, an ancient city of Bruttium, north of Crotona.

Petra, 221, the capital city of the Nabataeans, about half way between the Dead Sea and the Arabian Gulf.

Pharnabazus, 21, 29, 33 f., 47, 63, satrap of the Persian provinces about the Hellespont from 412 to 393 B.C.

Pharsalus, Pharsalia, 45, 293, 301, 335, 409, 423, a city and plain in southern Thessaly.

Pherae, 403, 407 f., 419, 433, a city in south-eastern Thessaly.

Pherecydes, 391, possibly Pherecydes of Syros is meant, a semi-mythical philosopher of the sixth century B.C., about whose death many fantastic tales were told.

Philippus, 119, 157, Lucius Marcius P., consul in 91 B.C., and a distinguished orator, a supporter of the popular party. He died before Pompey's return from Spain (71 B.C.).

Philistus, 429, the Syracusan, an eye-witness of the events of the Athenian siege of Syracuse (415–413 B.C.), which he described thirty years later in a history of Sicily.

Phlius, Phliasians, 67, a city in N.E. Peloponnesus, south of Sicyon.

Phthiotis, 419, 431, a district in S.E. Thessaly.

Picenum, 443, a district in N.E. Italy.

Piso (1), Caius Calpurnius P., consul in 67 B.C., a violent aristocrat, afterwards proconsul for the province of Gallia Narbonensis, which he plundered. He must have died before the outbreak of civil war.

Piso (2), Lucius Calpurnius P. Caesorinus, consul in 58 B.C., through Caesar's influence, recalled from his province of Macedonia in 55 because of extortions, consul again in 50 B.C. at Caesar's request, and after Caesar's death a supporter of Antony.

Plancus, 263, Titus Minutius P. Bursa, accused of fomenting the disorders following the death of Clodius (52 B.C.), found guilty and exiled. Pompey, whose ardent supporter he was, deserted him in the hour of need. Caesar restored him to civic rights soon after 49 B.C.

Plataea, 377, 401, an ancient and celebrated city in S.W. Boeotia, near the confines of Attica, where the Persians under Mardonius were defeated by the allied Greeks in 489 B.C.

Pollio, 305, Caius Asinius P., a famous orator, poet, and historian, 76 B.C.–4 A.D. He was an intimate friend of Caesar (cf. the *Caesar*, xxxii. 5), fought under him in Spain and Africa, and after Caesar's death supported Octavian. After 29 B.C. he devoted himself entirely to literature, and was a patron of Vergil and Horace. None of his works have come down to us.

Polybius, 381, of Megalopolis, in Arcadia, the Greek historian of the Punic Wars, born about 204 B.C., long resident in Rome, and an intimate friend of the younger Scipio, with whom he was present at the destruction of Carthage in 146 B.C.

Poseidonius, 225, 437, 459, 491, 521, of Apameia, in Syria, a Stoic philosopher, a pupil of Panaetius at Athens, contemporary with Cicero, who often speaks of him and occasionally corresponded with him.

Potheinus, 317, one of the guardians of the young Ptolemy. He plotted against Caesar when he came to Alexandreia, and was put to death by him (cf. the *Caesar*, xlviii. f.).

Ptolemy, 405 f., assassinated King Alexander II. of Macedon in 367 B.C., held the supreme power for three years, and was then himself assassinated by the young king, Perdiccas III.

Publius, 261, 311, Publius Licinius Crassus Dives, son of Marcus Crassus the triumvir. He was Caesar's legate in Gaul 58–55 B.C., followed his father to the East in 54, and was killed by the Parthians near Carrhae (cf. the *Crassus*, xxv.).

R

Roscius, 181, Lucius R. Otho. As one of the tribunes of the people in 67 B.C., he introduced the unpopular law which gave the knights special seats in the theatre.

Rullus, 149, Quintus Fabius Maximus R., five times consul, the last time in 295 B.C., when he was victorious over Gauls, Etruscans, Samnites and Umbrians in the great battle of Sentinum.

Rutilius, 213, Publius R. Rufus, consul in 105 B.C., unjustly exiled in 92 B.C., retired to Smyrna, where he wrote a history of his own times.

S

Samothrace, 175, 521, a large island in the northern Aegean Sea, some twenty miles off the coast of Thrace, celebrated for its mysteries (cf. the *Alexander*, ii. 1).

Sardis, 25, the capital city of the ancient kingdom of Lydia, and, later, the residence of the Persian satraps of Asia Minor.

Saturnalia, 205, a festival of Saturn, held at this time on the nineteenth of December. See the *Sulla*, xviii. 5.

Scipio (1), 149, 315, Publius Cornelius S. Africanus Major, the conqueror of Hannibal. His conquest of Spain occupied the years 210–202 B.C.

Scipio (2), Lucius Cornelius S. Asiaticus, belonged to the Marian party in the civil wars, and was consul in 83 B.C., the year when Sulla returned from the East. Cf. the *Sulla*, xxviii. 1–3. He was proscribed in 82, and fled to Massilia, where he died.

Scipio (3), 261, 279, 289, 295, 327, Publius Cornelius S. Nasica, adopted by Metellus Pius and therefore called Quintus Caecilius Metellus Pius S., or Metellus Scipio, was made Pompey's colleague in the consulship late in the year 52 B.C., and became a determined foe of Caesar. He was proconsul in Syria, joined Pompey in 48 B.C., commanded his centre at Pharsalus, fled to Africa, and killed himself after the battle of Thapsus (46 B.C.). Though a Scipio by birth, a Metellus by adoption, and a son-in-law of Pompey, he was rapacious and profligate.

Scipio (4), 445, Publius Cornelius Scipio Nasica Corculum, celebrated as jurist and orator, consul in 162 B.C. (when he abdicated on account of faulty auspices), and again in 155 B.C.

Scirophorion, 79, a month of the Attic year comprising portions of our May and June.

Scotussa, 293, 413, a town in central Thessaly, N.E. of Pharsalus.

Scythia, 221, a general term for the vast regions north of the Euxine Sea.

Seleucia, 317, probably the Seleucia in Syria on the river Orontes.

Sertorius, 155–167, 197, Quintus S., was born in a small Sabine village, began his military career in 105 B.C., was a consistent opponent of the aristocracy, retired to Spain in 82, where for ten years and until his death he was the last hope of the Marian party. See Plutarch's *Sertorius*.

Servilius, 151, Publius Servilius Vatia Isauricus, probably the consul of 79 B.C., who obtained a triumph over Cilicia in 74, and

died in 44 B.C. His son, of the same name, was consul with Caesar in 48 B.C., though a member of the aristocratic party.

Simonides, 3, of Ceos, the greatest lyric poet of Greece, 556–467 B.C.

Sinope, 223, an important Greek city on the southern coast of the Euxine Sea, west of Amisus.

Sinora (or Sinoria), a fortress-city on the frontier between Greater and Lesser Armenia.

Soli, 187, an important town on the coast of Cilicia, not to be confounded with the Soli on the island of Cyprus. See Xenophon *Anab.*, i. 2, 24.

Sophene, 203, a district of western Armenia.

Spartacus, 197, a Thracian gladiator, leader of the servile insurrection (73–71 B.C.). Cf. the *Crassus*, viii–xi.

Spinther, 245, 291, 307, Publius Cornelius Lentulus S., consul in 57 B.C., took part against Caesar in 49, was captured by him at Corfinium, but released. He then joined Pompey, and after Pharsalus fled with him to Egypt.

Strabo, 117, 123, Gnaeus Pompeius Sextus S., consul in 89 B.C., in which year he celebrated a triumph for his capture of Asculum. He tried to be neutral in the civil wars of Sulla and Marius. In 87 B.C. he was killed by lightning.

Sucro, 159, a river in S.E. Spain, between Valentia and Lauron.

Susa, 39, 417, an ancient city of Persia, residence of the Great King during the spring months.

Sybaris, 341, a famous Greek city of Italy, on the west shore of the gulf of Tarentum, founded in 720 B.C., noted for its wealth and luxury.

T

Tachos, 101–107, king of Egypt for a short time during the latter part of the reign of Artaxerxes II. of Persia (405–362 B.C.). Deserted by his subjects and mercenaries, he took refuge at the court of Artaxerxes III., where he died.

Taenarum, 175, a promontory at the southern extremity of Laconia, in Peloponnesus.

Tanagra, 377, a town in eastern Boeotia, between Thebes and Attica.

Tarentum, 493, 507, a Greek city in S.E. Italy. It surrendered to the Romans in 272 B.C., was betrayed into the hands of Hannibal in 212, and recovered by Fabius Maximus in 209.

Taurus, 185, a range of mountains in Asia Minor, running eastward from Lycia to Cilicia.

Taÿgetus, 417, a lofty mountain range between Laconia and Messenia, in Peloponnesus.

Tegea, 95, an ancient and powerful city in S.E. Arcadia, in Peloponnesus.

Tegyra, 77, 377 ff., 387, 525, a village in northern Boeotia, near Orchomenus.

Tempe, Vale of, 307, the gorge between Mounts Olympus and Ossa in N.E. Thessaly, through which the river Peneius makes its way to the sea.

Theodotus of Chios (or Samos), 317, 325, brought to Caesar the head and signet-ring of Pompey.

Theophanes, 213, 225, 247, 315, 319, of Mitylene in Lesbos, a learned Greek who made Pompey's acquaintance during the Mithridatic war, and became his intimate friend and adviser. He wrote a eulogistic history of Pompey's campaigns. After Pompey's death he was pardoned by Caesar, and upon his own death (after 44 B.C.) received divine honours from the Lesbians.

Theophrastus, 5, 103, the most famous pupil of Aristotle, and his successor as head of the Peripatetic school of philosophy at Athens. He was born at Eresos in Lesbos, and died at Athens in 287 B.C., at the age of eighty-five.

Theopompus, 27, 87, 91, of Chios, a fellow-pupil of Isocrates with Ephorus, wrote anti-Athenian histories of Greece from 411 to 394 B.C. and of Philip of Macedon from 360 to 336 B.C.

Thermodon, 209, a river of Pontus in Northern Asia Minor, emptying into the Euxine Sea.

Thesmophoria, 353, a festival in honour of Demeter as goddess of marriage, celebrated at Athens for three days in the middle of the month Pyanepsion (Oct.–Nov.).

Thespiae, 67 f., 97, 373 ff., an ancient city in S.W. Boeotia, north of Plataea.

Thetis, 423, a sea-nymph, wife of Peleus and mother of Achilles.

Thriasian plain, 69, 357, a part of the plain about Eleusis, in S.W. Attica.

Timagenes, 245, a Greek historian, of the time of Augustus, originally a captive slave. The bitterness of his judgments brought him into disfavour.

Timagoras, 419, an ambassador from Athens to the Persian court in 387 B.C. He spent four years there, and took part with Pelopidas rather than with his own colleague, Leon. He revealed state secrets for pay, and it was this which cost him his life.

Timotheus (1), 345, son of Conon the great Athenian admiral. He was made general in 378 B.C., and about 360 was at the height of his popularity and glory.

Timotheus (2), 39, of Miletus, a famous musician and poet, 446–357 B.C. His exuberant and florid style conquered its way to great popularity.

Tisaphernes, 21 f., 27, Persian satrap of lower Asia Minor from 414 B.C., and also, after the death of Cyrus the Younger in 401, of maritime Asia Minor, till his death in 359 B.C.

Tithraustes, 27. After succeeding Tisaphernes in his satrapy, Tithraustes tried in vain to induce Agesilaüs to return to Greece, and then stirred up a war in Greece against Sparta, in consequence of which Agesilaüs was recalled.

Trallians, 43, no tribe of this name is now known to have lived in

Thrace, nor are they mentioned in Herodotus (vii. 110).

Trebonius, 251, Caius T., tribune of the people in 55 B.C., and an instrument of the triumvirs. He was afterwards legate of Caesar in Gaul, and loaded with favours by him, but was one of the conspirators against his life.

Tullus, 275, Lucius Volcatius T., consul in 66 B.C., a moderate, who took no part in the civil war.

Tyche, 485, a portion of what Plutarch calls the "outer city" of Syracuse, lying between Epipolae and Achradina.

V

Valentia, 159, an important town in S.E. Spain, south of Saguntum.

Valerius, 147, Marcus V. Maximus, dictator in 494 B.C., defeated and triumphed over the Sabines.

Vatinius, 251, Publius V., had been tribune of the people in 59 B.C., and was a paid creature of Caesar. He was one of Caesar's legates in the civil war, and, after Pharsalus, was entrusted by him with high command in the East.

Venusia, 515, a prosperous city of Apulia, a stopping place for travellers on the Appian Way from Rome to Brundisium. It was the birthplace of the poet Horace.

Vibullius, 285, Lucius V. Rufus, a senator, captured by Caesar at Corfinium, at the outbreak of the war, and again in Spain, but pardoned both times.

PRINTED IN GREAT BRITAIN BY R. CLAY AND SONS, LTD.,
BRUNSWICK STREET, STAMFORD STREET, S.E. I, AND BUNGAY, SUFFOLK.